ra : how
ons of

formed A
$19.95
ocm60187958

The Southern Diaspora

The Southern

Diaspora

How the Great Migrations of Black and White Southerners Transformed America

James N. Gregory

The University of North Carolina Press

Chapel Hill

© 2005 The University of North Carolina Press
All rights reserved
Manufactured in the United States of America

Designed by April Leidig-Higgins
Set in Minion by Copperline Book Services, Inc.

This book was published with the assistance of the
Fred W. Morrison Fund for Southern Studies of the
University of North Carolina Press.

The paper in this book meets the guidelines for permanence and durability of the Committee on Production Guidelines for Book Longevity of the Council on
Library Resources.

Library of Congress Cataloging-in-Publication Data
Gregory, James N. (James Noble)
The southern diaspora: how the great migrations of
Black and White Southerners transformed America /
James N. Gregory.
p. cm.   Includes bibliographical references and index.
ISBN 0-8078-2983-8 (cloth: alk. paper)
ISBN 0-8078-5651-7 (pbk.: alk. paper)
    1. Migration, Internal—Southern States—
History—20th century.   2. Migration, Internal—
United States—History—20th century.   3. African
Americans—Migrations—History—20th century.
4. United States—Population—History—20th
century.   I. Title.
HB1971.A3G74 2006
304.8'0975—dc22   2005011753

cloth   09 08 07 06 05   5 4 3 2 1
paper   09 08 07 06 05   5 4 3 2 1

For Susan and Rachel
and for Larry

Contents

Illustrations, Figures, and Maps

Preface

On election night, 2 November 2004, the contest had come down to Ohio, the most embattled of the battleground states, where for weeks the Democrats and Republicans had traded charges of voter suppression and voter fraud and where even on election day federal judges were deciding critical procedural issues. Now the nation watched the vote tallies that gave President George W. Bush a narrow lead over Senator John Kerry and saw again and again television footage of Ohioans waiting in line to vote long after the polls were supposed to have closed. The cameras focused on two different parts of Ohio that seemed locked in a desperate battle for turnout: Cleveland in the north, where the Democrats had their strongest base among African Americans, and the Miami Valley in the southwestern corner of the state, where Republicans counted on white evangelical Protestants to vote for the incumbent president.

Most Americans went to sleep that night wondering if President Bush would hold on to his lead. I ended the night with an additional thought: "I'm going to have to rewrite the preface to my book." Although the television commentators had not known it, the battle for Ohio in 2004 was part of the legacy of the Southern Diaspora. Some of the Cleveland Democrats who stood in the voter lines for hours that day were veterans of the great migration of black southerners out of the South; more were the children and grandchildren of those migrants. Similarly, many of the Butler County and Hamilton County Republicans who stood in equally long lines were linked to the great migration of white southerners. Moreover, the electoral mobilizations of 2004 rested upon cultural and political institutions that had been shaped by these two great southern migrations, from churches to popular music to the urban and suburban racialized political regimes. Even though the Southern Diaspora had effectively ended a quarter of a century before, its effects were still showing up in Ohio and many other northern and western states on election night.

This book is about what may be the most momentous internal population movement of the twentieth century, the relocation of black and white Americans from the farms and towns of the South to the cities and suburbs of the North and the West. In the decades before the South became the Sun Belt, 20 million southerners left the region. In doing so, they changed America. They transformed American religion, spreading Baptist and Pentecostal churches and reinvigorating evangelical Protestantism, both black and white versions. They transformed American popular culture, especially music. The development of blues, jazz, gospel, R&B, and hillbilly and country music all depended on the southern migrants. The Southern Diaspora transformed American racial hierarchies, as black migrants in the great cities of the North and West developed institutions and political practices that enabled the modern civil rights movement. The Southern Diaspora also helped reshape American conservatism, contributing to new forms of white working-class and suburban politics. Indeed, most of the great political realignments of the second half of the twentieth century had something to do with the population movements out of the South. Finally, the Southern Diaspora transformed the nature of American regions, helping with the reconstructions that turned the South into an economic and political powerhouse and collapsing what had been huge cultural differences between that region and the rest of the United States. This book traces these and other ways that the great southern migrations rearranged twentieth-century America.

Migration is often best understood as a circulation rather than as a one-way relocation because, in many instances, migrants at some point circle back toward home. In writing this book, I too am circling back, returning to a subject that I thought I had left behind. My first book, *American Exodus: The Dust Bowl Migration and Okie Culture in California*, looked at one segment of the Southern Diaspora. I then moved on to other projects, but the issue of migration kept tugging at me. In 1998, *Labor History* published one of my articles ("Southernizing the American Working Class: Post-War Episodes of Regional and Class Transformation") and made it a forum exchange, inviting critiques by Thomas Sugrue, Grace Elizabeth Hale, and Alex Lichtenstein. Those comments inspired this book. Grace in particular suggested that it was time for someone to bring the subject of black migration and white migration together.

The challenge sparked something. I said to myself, "Maybe I should try." To the three critics who helped set this in motion, I offer the first of my thank-yous.

I have accumulated many other debts as this project moved from inspiration to publication. Grants from the Simpson Center for the Humanities and the Harry Bridges Center for Labor Studies, both at the University of Washington, have facilitated the work, and the Howard and Francis Keller Fund helped pay for the photographs. Joseph Wycoff assisted most ably with research and provided sage advice on both statistical and editorial issues. Trent Alexander, Ron Goeken, and the staff at the Minnesota Population Center did me a tremendous favor in agreeing to produce a special early version of the 1930 IPUMS sample so that I could meet a deadline.

Quintard Taylor joined the UW history department not long after I began this work and has been influential in its development. Stewart Tolnay joined the sociology department at roughly the same time, and this second happy coincidence meant that I have been able to consult with two of the most eminent scholars of black migration. Quintard's knowledge of western and urban black history, enthusiasm for the project, and criticism of several of the chapters have helped immensely. Stew's advice on statistical methods and his careful readings have been equally important. I tried a teaching experiment last year, giving a draft of the manuscript to graduate students in one of my seminars. I do not know what they thought of the experience, but it was crucial for the development of the book. The collective discussion and individual comments led me to rethink and rewrite several major issues. I especially thank Trevor Griffey, Robert Cruickshank, and Fred Brown.

Marc Rodriguez invited me to present part of this study at the Repositioning North American Migration History conference at the Princeton Davis Center, and Kathy Woodward and the Society of Scholars at the UW Humanities Center read another chapter. Thanks also to the following individuals for various kinds of advice and help: Donna Gabaccia, Richard Johnson, Richard Kirkendall, Walter Nugent, Nell Painter, and Nick Salvatore.

You would have to know my colleague Bill Rorabaugh to understand all of the ways that he helped this book. As the project unfolded, little gifts would appear in my mailbox: tiny slips of paper crammed with microscopic notations about ideas, facts, and useful citations. When I completed a draft of the manuscript, he read every word, sending back more ideas and more citations, saving me from dozens of errors.

Kimberley Phillips read the manuscript twice for the University of North Carolina Press, and her thorough and perceptive criticism helped me rethink several issues and reshape key parts of what you will read. I do not know how to thank Jim Grossman for all of his contributions. He not only gave me pages of critical advice regarding argument and content and more pages of line-edits, but he also offered me one of the maps that he created for his now classic book, *Land of Hope: Chicago, Black Southerners, and the Great Migration.*

Working with Chuck Grench and the staff at the University of North Carolina Press has been a pleasure. The Press has more than lived up to its reputation for excellence, efficiency, and courteous treatment of authors. Julie Bush copyedited the manuscript with an eagle eye and a sympathetic manner.

This volume is dedicated to Susan Glenn and Rachel Gregory, who have lived with this book from the beginning. Rachel's willingness to show interest in her father's work is a genuine gift. I also take inspiration from the way she forges a little bit of her identity from her own migration story. Born in Austin and raised in Berkeley and Seattle, she likes, at times, to think of herself as a Texan. Susan has shared not only this book but also a career and a marriage with me. I learn from her daily and cannot imagine how this book would have come together without her. Her editorial contributions are only part of it. She is also a master motivator. "Either finish it or throw it away," she advised more than once when things bogged down. We would laugh, and I would get back to work. We will now have to save that line for another project.

This book is also dedicated to Lawrence Levine. I have known Larry for nearly three decades, first as a teacher, later as a colleague, always as a friend. Much of what I have learned about writing history derives from that relationship, and the careful reader may pick out some of the ways that this volume is indebted to his pioneering works on African American and American-cultural history.

The Southern Diaspora

Introduction

It started on the very day that the freshman assemblyman arrived in Sacramento to join the California legislature in early January 1965. Still exhilarated from his upset victory, Willie Brown was confident that as the first African American from San Francisco elected to the legislature, he could make a difference. Eager to prove himself, he had almost immediately made a mistake. There was one critical rule in Sacramento, and it was simple: Don't mess with Big Daddy! Big Daddy was the 300-pound speaker of the Assembly, Jesse Unruh. The press called him a "political boss" and claimed he pulled more strings than the governor, Edmund G. "Pat" Brown. In fact, the governor and the speaker mostly worked together. Over the previous six years, they had passed a remarkable package of legislation that had given the state strong civil rights laws; redesigned education, transportation, and water systems; and financed ambitious urban and poverty programs. The governor took most of the credit, though Jesse Unruh, through his ruthless control of the legislature, had done much of the heavy lifting. He did not mind being notorious, although he disliked the Big Daddy label, which had come from Tennessee Williams's *Cat on a Hot Tin Roof.* What he disliked even more were legislators who did not know their place. He was not going to like Willie Brown.[1]

The Willie Brown–Jesse Unruh contest is one of the best-loved stories of recent California politics. A feud that turned ultimately into a succession story, it began that first day of the 1965 session when Brown refused to support Unruh's reelection to the speakership because Unruh had campaigned for Brown's primary election opponent. Unruh promptly retaliated, and over the next several years the Assembly understood that the very junior Brown and the very powerful Unruh were at war. Less obvious was the fact that a kind of mentorship had been going on almost from the start. Willie Brown was Jesse's star student. Long before Big Daddy quit the legislature, he had come to admire the younger man's ability to play the game of power. Unruh at one point in 1967 offered a compliment. "It's a good thing you're not white," said Jesse. "Why's that?" asked Willie. "Because if you were, you'd own the place."[2]

California journalists retell this story both because it unites two of the state's most flamboyant political personalities and because it confirms one of the central fables of late-twentieth-century America, the great transformation in racial opportunities that has taken place since the 1960s. Willie Brown did go on to "own the place." Elected Speaker of the California Assembly in 1981 with Unruh's help, he served longer (fifteen years) with more ingenuity than any predecessor, including Big Daddy. Without missing a beat, Brown then moved up the political ladder, winning election as San Francisco's mayor in 1996 and holding on to that office through thick and thin until term limits ended his reign in 2003. The fact that Brown managed to outdo his mentor has served to make the story of their relationship all the more interesting. In Willie and Jesse, California finds a comforting tale of racial progress, of the transformation from an old California where only whites like Jesse Unruh held power to a new California that gives power to Willie Brown.

But the Jesse Unruh–Willie Brown succession story has another dimension that few Californians realize and that in some ways complicates the neat dichotomies of old and new, white and black. Jesse Unruh was not part of old California, anymore than Willie Brown was. In fact, neither man was a Californian; neither had grown up there. And their backgrounds were curiously similar. Both were southerners; both were from Texas.

Unruh, whose parents named him after the train robber Jesse James, was the son of north Texas sharecroppers. Brown grew up in east Texas in circumstances that his biographer says may have been marginally more fortunate than Unruh's. Brown's family had a long history in the all-black town of Mineola and owned a nice home, even if money was short by the time he was born in 1934. Willie was raised by his grandmother, aunts, and uncles while his mother lived in Dallas, where she worked as a maid. His father, a waiter, left when Brown was four or five. Unruh was not born into poverty in 1922 but watched his family descend into it as his father lost his job as a bank clerk, then tried sharecropping, managing to eke out only the barest of livings through much of the 1930s. Both Texans benefited from family commitments to education, and each did well in school. After briefly trying college, Unruh in 1941, at age eighteen, decided to hitchhike to Los Angeles, thinking he would work in a defense plant. When the war broke out, he enlisted in the navy, spending the next three years in the lonely Aleutian

Former Texan Jesse Unruh (*left*) was Speaker of the California State Assembly when this photo was taken in 1966. With him is Robert Moretti (born in Detroit), who would become speaker in 1971, and fellow Texan Willie Brown, speaker from 1980 to 1995. (James D. Richardson Papers, Department of Special Collections and University Archives, The Library, California State University, Sacramento)

Islands, making plans for his future. Those plans were fixed on Los Angeles and a college education. When the navy let him go, he took his GI Bill and enrolled at the University of Southern California, finding there his love for politics. Even before he graduated in 1948, he was planning a way into politics.[3]

Willie Brown was entering the segregated high school in Mineola that year. When he graduated three years later, he briefly enrolled in one of the colleges that Texas set aside for African Americans, Prairie View A&M near Houston. But another idea had been brewing: he would go to Stanford. It was an impossible dream, of course. There was no money, and Brown's academic credentials would never pass muster at the elite school, but an uncle lived in San Francisco, and seventeen-year-old Willie Brown figured that was pretty close to Palo Alto. Stanford was on his mind in the summer of 1951 when he boarded the train heading west: "I came out with the intentions of going to Stanford and becoming a math professor."[4]

That these two Texans should cross paths in California in the mid-1960s was not particularly surprising. For more than half a century, Texans and other southerners had been leaving home by the hundreds of thousands, joining in a massive regional diaspora that had changed the face of race and politics and other dimensions of life in many corners of America. California felt the effects along with other western states, but the diaspora had also delivered its millions to the industrial states of the Midwest and Northeast. The numbers were enormous. By the end of the 1960s, so many black southerners and white southerners had left the region that it was as if the entire population of Alabama, Mississippi, Tennessee, and Arkansas had fled. Close to 11 million former southerners could be counted living outside the South in 1970. And that number is just a snapshot of population movements that over the course of the twentieth century involved millions more. In all, more than 28 million southerners—black and white—moved north or west during the twentieth century.[5]

Aretha Franklin and Merle Haggard should have crossed paths in the late 1960s. The two entertainers stood atop their respective branches of popular music, she the reigning queen of soul, he the king of country music. Like Brown and Unruh, they had more in common than they would have realized. Both were children of the Southern Diaspora. Franklin had grown up in Detroit after her family had moved there from Tennessee; Haggard in Bakersfield, California, after his parents relocated from Oklahoma. Their music continued the symmetry. Aretha recorded "Respect" in 1967, a song that instantly became a ringing anthem of black pride. Almost in answer, Merle Haggard wrote "Workin' Man Blues" and "Okie from Muskogee," anthems of the angry and conservative white working class. Seemingly politically opposite, the two musicians, both part of the diaspora, symbolized some of the sharpest polarizations in American politics and culture by the end of the 1960s.[6]

Billy Graham and C. L. Franklin should also have met. Fellow Baptists, fellow evangelists, fellow southerners who had built great religious enterprises in the North, they understood that they had much in common. As ministers of the gospel, they shared a mission. They would have prayed for their nation to heal its divisions and come together in a spiritual revival that would sweep away the hatreds of race. But even as their prayers might have joined, the meanings behind them would have been different. Graham, the most famous white Protestant leader of his day, a son of North Carolina who from his base in Minnesota had changed the face of evangelical Christianity, making it respectable where it had once seemed backward, preached a Christianity that was nine parts personal salvation. Franklin, a son of Mississippi (and father of Aretha), had been for many years one of the nation's most famous black evangelists. His sermons, recorded at New Bethel Church in Detroit, were known and loved throughout black America. But unlike Graham's, Franklin's preaching was not just about personal salvation; he also called for African Americans to stand together in the fight for rights and justice.[7]

Unlike these other pairs, Albert Murray and Willie Morris did know each other. Indeed, the black writer and the white writer had spent New Year's Day 1967 together in Murray's Harlem apartment, drinking bourbon, talking politics, and thinking about their parallel and nonparallel lives. Morris, the thirty-two-year-old editor of *Harper's* magazine, was just then completing a memoir, *North toward Home*, filled with critical memories of Mississippi and of the conflicts that rattled the faith of a liberal white southerner living in New York City. He wanted Murray to write something for the magazine about his own life's journey from rural Alabama to literary Harlem. Murray would eventually take the assignment and turn it into memoir whose syncopated rhythms and perambulating conversations had little in common with *North toward Home*. But the title, *South to a Very Old Place*, suggested something of the linked origins of the two books and the intertwined lives of their authors.[8]

This book is about Brown and Unruh, Franklin and Haggard, Graham and another Franklin, Murray and Morris, and the millions of other diaspora southerners and their impact on twentieth-century America. It is the first historical study of the Southern Diaspora in its entirety. Historians have until now fragmented the subject along lines of race and time period. The migration of African Americans out of the South has been studied extensively, especially in its early phase during and after World War I. Less has been written about the more massive sequence of migration that began during World War II, and a comprehensive treatment of the century-long story of black migration does not exist. Studies of white southerners on the move are more limited in number, and focus on discrete geographic segments of that migration. Those who have written about the movement of Appalachians and other southerners into northern cities pay little attention to the westward Dust Bowl migration to California.[9]

This book assembles and disassembles the various sequences of southern out-migration. African Americans and whites left the South for somewhat different reasons, moved in somewhat separate directions, and interacted on very different terms with the places they settled. In most respects, we need to think in terms of two Great Migrations out of the South. But they were also related. There were certain parallels along with huge differences in what black and white southerners experienced and accomplished in the North and West.

One of the strategies of this book involves the side-by-side comparison of the dual migrations. That stereoscopic view yields a host of new insights about each of the groups and their experiences. The chapters that follow will challenge many of the standard assumptions about the experiences of these former southerners. The image of white southerners struggling through decades of hard living in "hillbilly ghettos" like Chicago's Uptown crumbles as we widen the frame of reference. So do some of the stories that emphasize disappointments and failures among blacks. Comparison of the community building and political activities of the two groups is equally productive. The political accomplishments of African Americans become all the more impressive when set next to the endeavors of the much more numerous white migrants.

There is another reason for integrating these stories. In complicated ways, the fate of white and black southerners outside their home region was often intertwined. That was especially the case in the two decades following World War II when sociology and journalism created powerful arguments that linked the two populations of former southerners. Moreover, certain venues and projects drew upon southern culture in ways that sometimes pulled the two groups of expatriates into relationship. We see this in the postwar transformation of northern Protestantism and the separate but in some ways complementary influence of the evangelical churches that black migrants and white migrants built. Likewise, we see it in the transformation of American popular music — in the country music that the white migrants helped spread as well as the multiple genres that black migrants pioneered. And we see it in the reconstructions of northern politics — the new forms of urban politics and racial liberalism that black migrants forged and the new forms of white working-class conservatism that white migrants helped shape. Even when their lives were separate, the two groups of former southerners were never out of touch.

The book is not just about what the dual streams of former southerners experienced. More centrally, it examines what their comings and goings, their struggles and creations, have meant for the United States over the course of the twentieth century. The Southern Diaspora is one of the missing links in historical understandings of that recent century. As we will see, the great migrations of black and white southerners were instrumental in many of the key domestic transformations that the nation experienced, especially reorganizations of race, religion, and region. Some of the major stories of recent American history look very different when viewed through the lens of the Southern Diaspora.

One story that looks different concerns black struggles for civil rights. It is widely understood that migration to the North was important to the battle for rights and respect, but the geography of black politics has rarely been carefully examined. Here I pay close attention to the ways that African American migrants were able to use the unique political capacities of the great cities where they settled and how that political influence translated into policy changes that transformed racial relations first in the North and West and then also in the South.

The revival and spread of evangelical Protestantism (both black and white versions); the southernization of American popular music through the circulations of jazz, blues, and hillbilly and country music; new forms of black politics and racial liberalism; and new forms of white supremacist and conservative politics were also part of the diaspora effect. Indeed, key political realignments of various kinds pivoted on the two groups of southerners living outside their home region.

The reformulation of regions is another legacy of the dual diaspora. Classical economists see migration as an equilibrium mechanism that over time is supposed to balance labor surpluses and lead to a convergence of standards and wages. This book pursues an argument that bears a superficial resemblance to that theory but undermines its logic. Migration in this analysis contributed to a convergence of many regional forms, not just economic but also political and cultural. Southerners outside the South participated in a sequence of historical transformations that changed the regions where they settled and also changed the South, bringing the racial, religious, and political institutions of each into closer relation. But no equilibrium theory can explain this convergence. These changes prove to be the work of actual people, not abstract economic processes. Southern migrants of both races became agents of change who used the opportunities of geography to alter the cultural and political landscape of the nation and all its regions.

Region is a fluid geographical concept in the American context. States are the subnational spaces recognized in the Constitution and are equipped with clear boundaries and governmental institutions, while regions are spaces of uncertain integrity and confusing borders. That is true even of the South, long the most definite of American regions, thanks to the history of spatialized conflict over slavery and race. "If you look at the whole South long enough," writes sociologist John Shelton Reed, "it goes all indistinct around the edges. If you continue to stare, even the middle can seem to melt and flow away." So scholars fight endlessly about how to bound the South and describe its core meanings and structures. Those struggles have their uses, but not to this study. I will define the South loosely and even inconsistently, recognizing that definitions can change over time and depend upon perspective. Is Florida a Southern state? Some would say "yes" at the start of the twentieth century, "no" after decades of migration from New York and Cuba. Are Baltimore and Washington, D.C., southern cities? The argument here involves not only change over time but racial perspectives. What makes a space seem southern can differ for whites and blacks. For most purposes, I will follow the Census Bureau definition of sixteen states and the District of Columbia (Alabama, Arkansas, Delaware, Florida, Georgia, Kentucky, Louisiana, Maryland, Mississippi, North Carolina, Oklahoma, South Carolina, Tennessee, Texas, Virginia, and West Virginia). But at other points, I will reopen the issue of boundaries.[10]

Race is another concept that requires a note of clarification. White and black are never neat categories, even in a place like the South that did so much to inscribe them in law and where until late in the twentieth century low volumes of immigration minimized ethnic and religious diversity within the two dominant racial groups. Although there will be many generalized statements about white southerners and black southerners, more nuanced discussions at certain points will remind us that these are complicated population identities with mutable boundaries. In addition, it is important to note that not all southerners acknowledge either racial label and that southern-born Latinos and Native Americans also left the region during the diaspora period. Their experiences will be distinguished briefly at some points but unfortunately cannot be adequately examined in this study.

The book proceeds thematically rather than chronologically, the usual strategy for a work of history. Each chapter is an essay that addresses a set of particular questions using a stereoscopic method that moves back and forth between the two groups of southerners. Stereoscopes set two similar but different images next to each other, tricking eyes and brain into fusing the images in a way that makes them three-dimensional. Teasing out that third dimension is the goal of this book. Viewed in relation to each other, the black and white Southern Diasporas reveal the subject in entirely new ways.

Chapter 1 is an overview of the migration cycles and the changing economics and demography over the course of the twentieth century. It offers a new method for calculating migration volumes and shows the Southern Diaspora to have been numerically larger than previous scholars have understood. Chapter 2 surveys the public meanings surrounding the two exoduses and highlights the unique role that media institutions and social scientists played in shaping the expectations and interactions of southerners on the move. Chapter 3 answers questions about the economic experience of white and black southerners, dismantling the maladjustment paradigm that has been so prominent in previous scholarship while also showing the critical differences in the opportunity structure facing black and white southern migrants. Chapter 4 examines the communities that African Americans built in the major cities, resurrecting the label "Black Metropolis" and mapping the new and powerful cultural apparatus of those communities. Chapter 5 examines the very different community formations of white southerners who spread out through suburbs and rural areas as well as big cities and struggled with confusing issues of social identity. The whites, too, developed cultural institutions of historical import. Both diaspora country music and a white diaspora literary community would reshape understandings of region and race. Chapter 6 explores the diaspora's impact on American religion as both groups built Baptist and Pentecostal churches and helped revitalize and spread evangelical Protestantism, with important political as well as religious implications for America. Chapter 7 develops the issue of black political influence, demonstrating how important geography was to the initial phases of what ultimately became the civil rights movement. Chapter 8 brings the white migrants into the story of race, class, and regional transformations, exploring contributions to white working-class conservatism on the one hand and to new formulations of white liberalism on the other. Chapter 9 brings the diaspora to a close in the 1970s and 1980s and summarizes some of the major findings of the book.

A short invocation before we begin. This book in its largest sense is a call for new thinking about internal migration, one of the seriously underanalyzed issues of twentieth-century American historiography. While the scholarship of earlier centuries focuses imaginatively on the figure of the Moving American and treats the westward migration of Euro-Americans as a pivotal historical force, historians of the most recent century sideline the subject of internal migration. Migration is treated as an important matter for African American history, but other population movements rarely enter into the calculations of those writing the history of the American twentieth century.[11]

If historians have failed to adequately address the subject, social scientists have not done much better. Migration studies, once a cutting-edge enterprise for sociologists and economists, have been stuck for decades in dead-ends and stale formulations. Most of the work cannot get beyond the question of why migrations happen, the old push-pull conundrum. Huge debates rage between advocates of neoclassical economic theory and dependency theory, both of which contemplate migration as a response to differential economic development. A third formulation, migration systems theory, moves beyond economic conditions, treating migration as a social movement and specifying institutional and social-cultural factors that enable mass relocations, but it too concentrates solely on the causes of migrations while ignoring their effects. All of these perspectives see moving people as subject to history but not as its architects.[12]

An old theory, dating back to the late nineteenth and early twentieth centuries, holds some promise. It conceives of migration as a fundamental force of history. The social scientists who crafted it had in mind conquest migrations of the sort that rearranged European and Asian empires in millennia past or that transformed the Americas when Europeans came swarming across the Atlantic. But conquest may not be the only basis through which moving masses can redirect the flow of history. Infiltration can also be powerful. Certain peoples moving into certain places have managed to impart dramatic changes, achieving conquests of a sort without warfare and sometimes without major conflict. Can internal migrations have consequences of this sort? If so, how? Those are the questions animating this book.[13]

A Century of Migration

What is a diaspora? A mass migration? When do the ordinary relocations of people become extraordinary enough to earn a label? The answers are not precise. Mass migrations happen when the spatial moves of lots of people form a pattern that is recognized by participants or by hosts or others who have the capacity to publicize their observations. Mass migrations have as much to do with ways of noticing as with ways of moving. The term "diaspora" is of Greek origin and first was used to denote the colonizing migrations of the Hellenist world, then acquired a different meaning in association with the expulsion of Jews from ancient Israel. More recently, the meanings have shifted back toward the original. The term now describes historically consequential population dispersions of various descriptions, those inspired by opportunity as well as by oppression. I use the term "Southern Diaspora" to denote an era and a process of exceptionally heavy population movement out of the South, an era that covers the first three-quarters of the twentieth century.[1]

Is the term appropriate? A huge enterprise of diaspora studies now ranges across disciplines in order to puzzle the experiences, identities, and historical effects of mass migrations. The diasporic peoples in question usually have crossed national and often oceanic boundaries. Studies explore the diasporas of Africans, English, Dutch, Irish, and Spanish in the Atlantic world; Chinese, Filipinos, and others in the Pacific world; and the still more multidirectional dispersions of Jews, Palestinians, South Asians, and West Indians, to mention only a few of the peoples of interest. Does it make sense to associate the regional relocations of southern-born Americans with these stories of global relocations? I invoke the diaspora concept in part because it calls attention to global contexts and encourages us to think about the relationship between internal and transnational migration. It also emphasizes the importance and dynamism of this subject. A book about migration invites sleep. Diasporas have life and movement and power—exactly the qualities of moving southerners in twentieth-century America.[2]

Demography

The Southern Diaspora belongs to a particular era of American and world history—from the turn of the twentieth century through the 1970s. The dating is not exact. Some may prefer to designate the half century between 1915 and 1965, the period that saw the highest rates of southern out-migration. It can also be argued that the great migrations out of the South started much earlier. Indeed, for as long as there has been something called the American South, southerners in significant numbers have been leaving. The region itself expanded through migration as white southerners in the early 1800s carved out new states for cotton and slavery. Others moved to places that today are understood to be regionally separate from the South. Throughout the 1800s, white southerners flowed west, settling farmlands north of the Ohio River in Indiana and Illinois, pushing into Missouri, Kansas, Colorado, and New Mexico, joining the California gold rush and every subsequent rush that filled the Golden State. White out-migration grew especially heavy in the two decades after the Civil War, with many leaving for farming opportunities and others heading for the North's big cities—New York, Philadelphia, Boston, and Chicago—where the nation's commerce concentrated. New York at the end of the nineteenth century had almost 40,000 white former southerners, many of whom supported a lively network of southern heritage clubs and Confederate veterans' organizations. Altogether, census takers at the end of the century counted over 1 million southern-born whites living outside their birth region.[3]

They also counted more than 335,000 southern-born African Americans living in the North and West in 1900. African Americans had left the South in the nineteenth century for different reasons and in different directions. Before the Civil War, some had been taken west by slaveholders who dared move their bond people into California or Kansas. Some had escaped northward, typically to Ohio, upstate New York, Massachusetts, and Canada. And there was something of an exodus among the free black people of the South as conditions deteriorated after 1830, many of them settling in Pennsylvania, Ohio, Indiana, and Michigan. Emancipation brought freedom of travel and increased out-migration, much of it directed toward northern cities. New York and Philadelphia received thousands of freed people from Virginia and Maryland after the war, and these two cities along with Chicago would remain key destinations for African Americans leaving the South during the Gilded Age. Rural destinations were also important. Seeking farmland and social freedoms that had become hard to find in the South as Reconstruction came to an end, black southerners moved north into Indiana and west to Kansas in considerable numbers. Some of this was organized by "colonization" or "emigration" societies. Caught up in the "Kansas fever," tens of thousands of people left Mississippi, Louisiana, and Tennessee in the 1870s and 1880s.[4]

The twentieth century changed the volume and logic of both population movements. Southern out-migration picked up right from the start of the new century, with flows accelerating in the second decade thanks to the job opportunities of World War I. By 1920, southerners living outside their home region numbered more than 2.7 million and in 1930 more than 4 million. Another even larger surge during World War II raised the total to 7.5 million in 1950, 9.8 million in 1960, 10.8 million in 1970, and nearly 12 million in 1980. That was the peak. As the Sun Belt basked and northern cities rusted, the population of southern expatriates began to decline, dropping to 11.5 million in 1990 and less than 11 million in 2000 (figure 1.1).

There is a surprising amount of misinformation about even the basic demographics of the dual migrations—who moved, when, where, and in what numbers. An important new resource helps to clear up some of the confusion. The Integrated Public Use Microdata Series (IPUMS) that have been developed by historians at the University of Minnesota in cooperation with the Census Bureau are a gift to students of internal migration. Whereas the published census volumes are nearly useless for tracing the spatial rearrangements of Americans, the IPUMS samples make available a wealth of information about migrants.[5]

The size of the diaspora is the first revelation. Until recently, historians have looked at the decade-to-decade differences in the numbers of southerners living outside the region and treated those differences as the volume of out-migration. But that approach sees only the tip of an iceberg. To get a realistic idea of how many people left the South, we have to do more than count noses at the end of each decade. We also need some idea of how many earlier migrants died during the decade and how many had returned home—in other words, how many newcomers were needed just to keep the expatriate population stable. Figure 1.2 uses information about mortality and return migration to estimate the decade-by-decade volumes of migration from the South. I want to emphasize that these are estimates. The data on return migration are sketchy and for some intervals are just guesses. I have erred on the side of caution, employing low-end estimates. We can be confident that the actual numbers were higher.

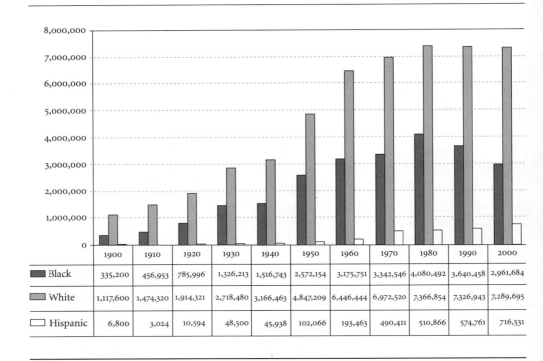

	1900	1910	1920	1930	1940	1950	1960	1970	1980	1990	2000
■ Black	335,200	456,953	785,996	1,326,213	1,516,743	2,572,154	3,175,751	3,342,546	4,080,492	3,640,458	2,961,684
■ White	1,117,600	1,474,320	1,914,321	2,718,480	3,166,463	4,847,209	6,446,444	6,972,520	7,366,854	7,326,943	7,289,695
☐ Hispanic	6,800	3,024	10,594	48,500	45,938	102,066	193,463	490,411	510,866	574,761	716,531

FIGURE 1.1. Southerners Living in Other Regions, 1900–2000

Source: Steven Ruggles, Matthew Sobek, Trent Alexander, Catherine A. Fitch, Ronald Goeken, Patricia Kelly Hall, Miriam King, and Chad Ronnander, *Integrated Public Use Microdata Series: Version 3.0* (machine-readable database) (Minneapolis, 2004).

Supporting data are found in tables A.2 and A.3 (all tables mentioned in this chapter can be found in appendix A). Methods are explained in appendix B.

The totals are much larger than have been reported for both the black southern migration and the white migration. Over the course of the twentieth century, close to 8 million black southerners, nearly 20 million white southerners, and more than 1 million southern-born Latinos participated in the diaspora, some leaving the South permanently, others temporarily. In figure 1.2, notice the way the century of migration divides into two distinct periods. The first phase starts with the initial decade of the century. Migration volumes grow in the second decade when at least 1.3 million southerners leave home, reach a peak in the 1920s with 2 million new migrants, then taper off in the 1930s. A much bigger second wave begins with World War II when more than 4 million southerners move north or west, grows even larger in the 1950s when at least 4.3

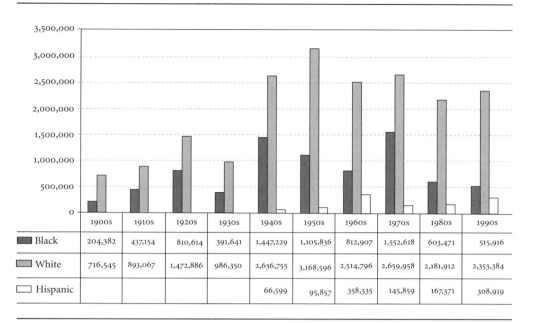

	1900s	1910s	1920s	1930s	1940s	1950s	1960s	1970s	1980s	1990s
▨ Black	204,382	437,154	810,614	391,641	1,447,229	1,105,836	812,907	1,552,618	603,471	515,916
▨ White	716,545	893,067	1,472,886	986,350	2,636,755	3,168,596	2,514,796	2,659,958	2,181,912	2,353,384
☐ Hispanic					66,599	95,857	358,335	145,859	167,371	308,919

FIGURE 1.2. Estimated Number of Southern-Born Leaving the South Each Decade

Source: Steven Ruggles, Matthew Sobek, Trent Alexander, Catherine A. Fitch, Ronald Goeken, Patricia Kelly Hall, Miriam King, and Chad Ronnander, *Integrated Public Use Microdata Series: Version 3.0* (machine-readable database) (Minneapolis, 2004).

million leave the South, remains near that level through the 1960s and 1970s, and then declines in the 1980s and 1990s.[6]

The chart also displays the relative size of black and white migrations, clearing up another issue. Nicholas Lemann writes that the African American diaspora was "one of the largest and most rapid internal movements of people in history—perhaps the greatest not caused by the immediate threat of execution or starvation." He is not alone in misreading the numbers. Several other historians also assert that black migrants outnumbered or nearly equaled their white southern counterparts. In fact, white out-migrants outnumbered blacks during every decade and usually by a very large margin. In the Great Migration era of the early twentieth century, when African Americans moved north for the first time in large numbers and established much-noticed communities in the major cities, less-noticed white southerners actually outnumbered them roughly two to one. The margins became larger after 1950 and still larger as the century drew to a close. Over the course of the twentieth century, more than 28 million southerners left their home region—28 percent were African Americans, 68 percent non-Hispanic whites, and 4 percent southern-born Latinos, Tejanos mostly, who had been joining the flow north and west since World War II (see also table A.1).[7]

Movers are one thing, permanent relocations another, and some of the confusion about the relative size of the two migrations has to do with the difference. The two migrations displayed different dynamics, especially in the frequency of return migration. African Americans left the South mostly for good, at least until the 1980s when return migration accelerated. Whites throughout the century were much more likely to sojourn in the North or West, often returning home after a period of months, years, or decades. Since 1940, census takers have asked respondents where they lived at some previous date, usually five years earlier. This interval leads to severe undercounts of mobility, since any two-way moves that have taken place within the five-year interval remain unrecorded and some people forget exactly where they lived five years back. Nevertheless, these data provide useful "minimal" estimates of return migration (see table A.2).[8]

The minimal estimates for whites are actually quite high. In most five-year intervals, the return rate has been 10 percent or higher, roughly 2 percent per year. We have clearer single-year data for 1949. In that year, 228,800 whites, 4.7 percent of all those who had been living in the North or West, returned to the South. This was an exceptional year of recession at the tail end of the World War II boom that had lured 2.6 million white southerners out of their home region. But if we had the same kind of single-year data for the rest of the postwar period, we would probably find that return migration rates often hit 3 or even 4 percent a year. There is another way to confirm the rapid turnover among white migrants. The question that identifies return migrants also identifies southerners who moved north or west during the five-year interval. Comparing those numbers, we can see that the ratio of returnees versus newcomers was consistently very high for whites. In the late 1950s, for every 100 white southerners migrating west or north, 54 headed home. In the late 1960s, the ratio increased to 78 returnees for each 100 new migrants, and by the end of the 1970s, it reached 98. Turnover was the key dynamic of the white diaspora. Fewer than half of the nearly 20 million whites who left the South actually left for good. That means that the white diaspora is best understood as a circulation, not as a one-way population transfer. It also means that veterans of the migration would be making an impact on the South as well as on the North and West (table A.2).[9]

Black southerners were much less interested in the revolving door. The rate of black return migration was only one-third the rate of white return migration

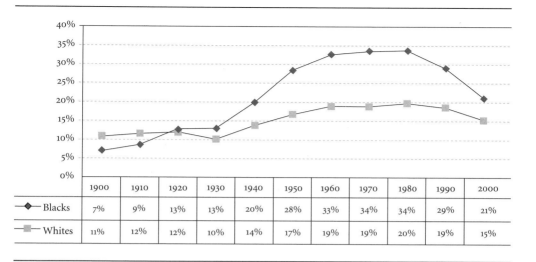

	1900	1910	1920	1930	1940	1950	1960	1970	1980	1990	2000
Blacks	7%	9%	13%	13%	20%	28%	33%	34%	34%	29%	21%
Whites	11%	12%	12%	10%	14%	17%	19%	19%	20%	19%	15%

FIGURE 1.3. Diaspora Southerners as Percentage of All Southern-Born Adults

Source: Steven Ruggles, Matthew Sobek, Trent Alexander, Catherine A. Fitch, Ronald Goeken, Patricia Kelly Hall, Miriam King, and Chad Ronnander, *Integrated Public Use Microdata Series: Version 3.0* (machine-readable database) (Minneapolis, 2004).

in most intervals. Still, some migrants did turn around. In 1949, 43,143 black southerners joined the 228,800 whites who decided to pack up and head back, representing 1.7 percent of all southern-born blacks then living in the North and West. These numbers are not tiny and should encourage us to think about the black diaspora also as a circulation, if on a much smaller scale than the white. And it probably had been that way from the start. During the first phase of the Great Migration in the 1910s and 1920s, return rates may have looked like those of the 1950s. For every ten African Americans leaving the South in the late 1950s, two former migrants were moving in the opposite direction (table A.2).[10]

What did these population movements mean for the demography of the South and other regions? The black exodus had by far the most important impact. African Americans were leaving the South at much higher rates than whites, despite the greater actual number of white out-migrants. They were also going to regions that previously had known little racial diversity. Their movements were going to dramatically change the nation's racial distributions. Figure 1.3 gives some idea of the demographic impact on the South. It graphs out-migrants as a percentage of all adults of each race born in that region. In 1970, one-third (34 percent) of all African American adults born in the South were living elsewhere, along with 19 percent of white southern-born adults.

The high rate of black out-migration virtually froze African American population growth in the South. A number of states experienced decade after decade of population decline, especially across the Deep South "black belt" where cotton had been king. In 1910, African Americans constituted more than half the population of South Carolina and Mississippi and more than 40 percent in Georgia, Alabama, and Louisiana. Sixty years later, African American population share in these states had dropped dramatically. Only in Mississippi (37 percent) did the African American representation remain above 30 percent. The disappearance of the "black belt" was one of the striking effects of the Southern Diaspora.[11]

The establishment of a substantial black presence outside the South was still more demographically significant. In 1900, just under 740,000 African Americans lived outside the South, only 8 percent of the nation's total black population. The diaspora (and a much smaller immigration from the West Indies) steadily changed those distributions. By 1970, more than 10.6 million African Americans lived outside the South, 47 percent of the nation's total. Somewhat more than a third of African Americans living in northern and western states at that date were former southerners, and most of the rest were children or grandchildren of migrants.[12]

The demographic effects of the white exodus were much less apparent. Some states, notably Oklahoma and Arkansas in the 1930s and 1940s and Kentucky and West Virginia in the 1950s and 1960s, experienced dramatic slowing of population growth or actual declines as a result of white out-migration, but in others, high birth rates easily compensated for losses. The fact that certain southern states experienced substantial in-migration, especially after 1940, also balanced the effects of the exodus. White population growth in the South as a whole slowed during the period of the diaspora but not as dramatically as among African Americans.[13]

Effects on areas outside the South varied dramatically. White southerners, black southerners, and Latino southerners moved to particular states in large numbers. The destinations only partly overlapped. Map 1.1 shows where former migrants were living in 1970 using standard census divisions. The largest number of black migrants lived in the Great Lakes states (Illinois, Indiana, Michigan, Ohio, and Wisconsin), which the Census Bureau calls the East North Central division. These states were also the key destination for white southerners. The Middle Atlantic states (New York, Pennsylvania, and New Jersey) were second as a destination for African Americans but much less popular with whites. New York City was the primary exception. Southerners of both races responded to the lure of the nation's commercial and cultural capital. The Pacific states made up the other important area of settlement for both groups.

Many went to California. In 1970, more than 1.6 million white and 571,000 black southerners lived in that state. California was also the chief destination for Tejanos and other southern-born Latinos, 213,000 of whom had settled there by 1970. Hispanic southerners had also moved in some numbers to Illinois, Michigan, Ohio, and Indiana.

Former southerners comprised a significant segment of the population in some of these states. In 1970, 12 percent of California residents were southern-born. This was proportionally similar to Ohio, where 1.4 million southerners of both races lived, and to Indiana, which was home to 617,000. In Illinois, where former southerners numbered close to a million, and Michigan, where there were more than 800,000, they constituted 9 percent of the population. New Mexico, Arizona, and Alaska had also been much affected by the diaspora, although mostly by the white and Latino contingents. In 1970, 18 percent of New Mexicans were southern-born, as were 13 percent of Arizonians and 17 percent of Alaskans, the latter because of the oil boom that had recently attracted thousands of Texans and Oklahomans. Table A.3 displays the number of southerners living in northern and western states as of 1970 and their percentage of that state's population. Unfortunately, we have no way of counting the children and grandchildren born in these states. They would certainly at least double the demographic impact.

History and Hydrology

More than 28 million southerners left their home region during the course of the twentieth century. Why? Read some of the books and articles on internal migration, and the answers will seem like lessons in hydrology. Those who write about migration are addicted to water metaphors. Moving people become migration flows that can surge or dry up, flood or be reduced to a trickle. Migrants move in waves, tides, streams, and rivers. Flows can be channeled, diverted, or pooled, and there is even backflow. Actual people disappear in this watery exercise, lost in migration streams and rivers moving gravitationally across graded terrains. These are not just convenient metaphors: much of the theory underlining migration studies involves hydrological thinking. For generations, social scientists have modeled migration as a gravitational process.[14]

Economists and demographers have until recently dominated the field of migration studies and have understood migration largely as a labor supply issue. People move because of an imbalance in economic opportunities, seeking higher wages, better farmland, more jobs, or some other economic advantage. Large-scale migrations occur in the context of regional imbalances and

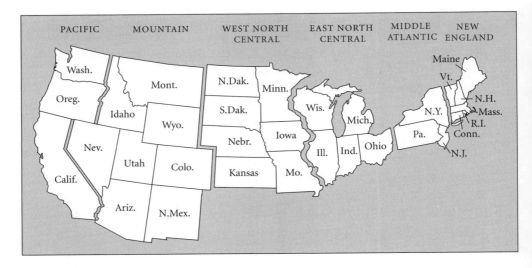

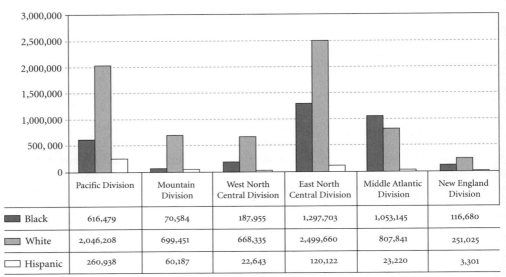

	Pacific Division	Mountain Division	West North Central Division	East North Central Division	Middle Atlantic Division	New England Division
■ Black	616,479	70,584	187,955	1,297,703	1,053,145	116,680
▨ White	2,046,208	699,451	668,335	2,499,660	807,841	251,025
☐ Hispanic	260,938	60,187	22,643	120,122	23,220	3,301

MAP 1.1. Where Former Southerners Lived in 1970

Source: Steven Ruggles, Matthew Sobek, Trent Alexander, Catherine A. Fitch, Ronald Goeken, Patricia Kelly Hall, Miriam King, and Chad Ronnander, *Integrated Public Use Microdata Series: Version 3.0* (machine-readable database) (Minneapolis, 2004).

will continue until there is more equilibrium of opportunities. In this view, the Southern Diaspora is easy to explain. The South by the early twentieth century was the most economically backward of America's regions, with little industry, small cities, and a huge farm population that would look for other opportunities as the decades progressed. Until the Sun Belt boom rebalanced opportunities, the South would shed population. Like individual droplets of labor, southerners white and black poured out of the region and into the more economically advanced centers of the North and West.[15]

Historians usually insist on complicating this formula. People have all sorts of reasons for moving, some having little or nothing to do with labor markets. And decisions are made in social contexts, influenced by families, networks, and communities and by information sources and legal institutions. Race also needs to be considered. The social and economic contexts were very different for black, white, and Latino southerners. Hydrology does not leave room for the dreams or fears that lead people to pack up and hit the road, nor the newspaper articles, friendships, or odd happenstances that help them choose a destination, nor the possibility that the North meant something different to an African American southerner from what it meant to the white neighbor. It takes more than economic gravity to explain the Southern Diaspora.[16]

Instead of a formula, I will spend the rest of this chapter sketching a history. The Southern Diaspora unfolded across an entire century of changing contexts, not as a single unchanging process but as a dynamic set of experiences that took different forms as conditions changed. But I want to begin with some observations about two overarching contexts, one involving labor markets and political economy, the other involving race.

Labor market analysis is the necessary starting point for understanding the diaspora; the economists are right on that point. But this is a context, not an explanation. It does not explain *why* people made individual decisions to move. The six or seven decades of escalating movement away from the South constituted a distinct era in American labor market formation, a time when both international relations and domestic political economy were structured in ways that encouraged southerners to look elsewhere for opportunity. In 1914, the United States, Europe, and to some extent the world as a whole entered a long phase of reduced international labor migrations. The disruptions of World War I followed by the collapsing economies of the 1930s, the greater destruction of World War II, and the sequences of decolonialization and the Cold War that followed brought to an end the process of European out-migration that had been for three centuries a driving force in American and global demography. The passage of American immigration restriction laws in 1920 and 1924 added to the effect and ensured that Asian as well as European immigration to America would effectively cease. Between 1925 and 1965, when the law was changed, the United States allowed in a mere 7.3 million immigrants, about the same number that had come in a single decade before World War I.[17]

Immigration restriction was one of the enabling conditions for increased internal migration. The rapid growth of labor-hungry American industries in northern settings was another. The United States had become the world's leading industrial economy by 1900, and each decade of the twentieth century until the 1960s would see that lead increase. Until World War II, the nation's manufacturing capacity was centralized in a handful of states: New York, Pennsylvania, Massachusetts, and New Jersey in the Northeast and Ohio, Illinois, Michigan, Indiana, and Wisconsin in the Great Lakes area. Those nine states supplied 76 percent of the nation's manufacturing jobs in 1920 and 57 percent of the nation's nonagricultural wealth. The sixteen states of the South meanwhile accounted for only 15 percent of manufacturing jobs and 16 percent of nonagricultural wealth while maintaining 31 percent of the nation's population. And while per capita incomes in the northern industrial belt exceeded national norms, in the South they fell way below. In ten southern states, per capita income was less than two-thirds of the national average. Residents of Alabama, Arkansas, and Mississippi earned less than half the national per capita average.[18]

There were, of course, many Souths—not all of them poor and backward and not all of them ready to contribute to the diaspora. Maryland, Delaware, and Florida were prosperous states with substantial urban centers that would attract, not lose, population throughout the twentieth century. Texas, at the other end of the South, would both lose and attract people as it rebalanced its economy of cotton, oil, and cattle. The rest of the region was also complex. It had its own industrial belt—a string of textile mill towns that followed the piedmont south from Virginia to Georgia—and a thriving steel center in Birmingham. It had cities, although they were small by northern standards. In 1920, only Baltimore, the least southern of the region's urban centers, ranked among major U.S. cities, with 733,000 residents. Washington, D.C., and New Orleans each had around 400,000 residents; Louisville and Atlanta claimed more than 200,000; and Birmingham, Richmond, Memphis, San Antonio, Dallas, and Houston broke 150,000.

Mostly the South was rural, and livelihoods remained tied to agriculture or extractive industries. Of the region's gainful workers, 46 percent were involved in farming in 1920, and a considerably larger portion of the population depended upon the farm economy. Cotton was of course the principal crop and the region's economic albatross. For a century, the South had committed itself to farming the fiber that clothed the world, and as late as the mid-1920s, the huge southern cotton belt was still expanding. Other crops filled in around the edges of the cotton zone, and extractive industries were important in particular areas: coal mining in the southern Appalachians, timber in the mountains and pine barrens, fishing and some shipbuilding in the Chesapeake and along the Gulf, oil in Oklahoma and Texas.[19]

It helps to group these rural Souths into two broad zones: an outer South and a lower South, one claiming a mixed economy of general farming and extractive industries, the other devoted to cotton. Not only did their economies move in separate cycles but also their demography was sharply different. The cotton belt, consisting of more than 600 counties stretching from the Carolinas to east Texas, was also the "black belt," home to the vast majority of southern African Americans. The outer South, in particular a band of states that curved from West Virginia through Kentucky, Tennessee, Arkansas, Oklahoma, and Texas, was largely white. The two major Southern Diasporas would separate along these racial/geographic lines. The black migration had its base in the cotton belt; most white migrants left the outer South.

Motivations also divided along the lines of race. As convenient as it is to explain both diasporas on the sole grounds of economic dislocation and opportunity, for African Americans there was much more to it. The differences in return migration tell the basic story. Many whites would yearn for home and look for chances to return. Among black southerners, the yearnings more often had a different trajectory. As long as Jim Crow ruled the South, that system of segregation, subordination, and terror created powerful incentives for leaving and staying away. "Persecution plays its part," sociologist Charles S. Johnson explained simply in 1923. Scholars since then have found the means to prove this, including plotting incidents of lynching against county-by-county migration rates. But the point is self-evident. Going north meant something different for black southerners than it did for white southerners. It meant, black migrants hoped, rights and freedoms and dignity that the South perpetually denied them.[20]

First Phase

Migration rates picked up from the start of the twentieth century, making that a convenient, if slightly problematic, marker for the first phase of the diaspora. The problem is that it violates a standard practice in the African American literature that fixes on World War I as the starting point for what has long been called the Great Migration. And the tradition has merit. The war not only accelerated but also changed the logic of out-migration in important ways, for whites as well as blacks. Where nineteenth- and early-twentieth-century migrants were (in the case of whites) often looking for farming opportunities and (in the case of blacks) following indefinite signals about the availability of jobs, the war initiated a period of labor recruiting by northern industrial concerns. Labor shortages, exacerbated by the shutting off of European immigration, forced key industries—notably railroads, steel, and coal—to look south. War production created in excess of 3 million new manufacturing jobs while immigration dropped from 1.2 million in 1914 to only 110,000 in 1918. The shortages dictated an urgent search for new domestic sources of workers. Newspapers helped spread the word that there were jobs with high wages in the northern cities. This marked the start of large-scale white southern entry into the northern industrial workforce. The change was even more significant for black southerners. As news spread that factories were finally opening their payrolls to African Americans, black southerners headed north in numbers that were much larger than ever before.[21]

There have been elaborate attempts to model the precise balance of push and pull factors underlying this early period of the diaspora, but the simple answer is that northern economic opportunities as opposed to southern distress best describes the dynamic of this first phase of white migration, and opportunities, both economic and social, underlay the first phase of black migration. The southern economy, although heavily agricultural, was not without opportunities. Through the early 1920s, farm prices held up and acreage was expanding in many areas of the South, although the boll weevil infestation that had begun at the turn of the century continued to damage cotton production in other areas. Farm populations in most southern states were just beginning to contract from the record levels achieved around 1910, but it was an orderly contraction, as young people chose to look for work in the towns and cities of the region rather than continue the agricultural ways of their parents. These were the prime candidates for out-migration in the war era and also in the decade that followed.[22]

Ada and George Wilson and Audie and Walter Moffitt were part of this first phase of the dual diasporas. In 1919, the Wilsons lived in a farming community named Promised Land, in the South Carolina piedmont midway between Charleston and Atlanta. The residents were all African Americans, mostly descendants of fifty families who had scraped together a few dollars, purchased small plots of cotton land, and given the community its wonderful name back in the 1870s. It was marginal land in the oldest part of the cotton belt and incapable of supporting the generations that followed. Even before the close of the nineteenth century, young people were leaving, some to sharecrop elsewhere, many to work for wages, and with each new decade the outflow increased. By World War I, Promised Land people were scattered throughout the nearby towns and cities of the lower South, working as railroad, pulp mill, and construction laborers, servants in homes, and porters in hotels. And there were others up north, in Philadelphia, New York, and Chicago.[23]

When the boll weevil reached Promised Land in 1919, Ada and George Wilson realized it was time to go. Most of their relatives had already left, many of them helped by Ada's sister Martha, who had been in Chicago since 1910. George went first, taking the local train to Atlanta and there connecting with the line that would carry him through northern Alabama to Memphis and due north to Chicago. The thousand-mile journey took more than a day, but once the train crossed into Kentucky, he could leave the crowded and uncomfortable Jim Crow car. In Chicago he stayed with Martha and her husband, Charlie, who helped him find a job. He worked hard, saved his money, rented an apartment, and then sent for Ada and their four children, supplying each with a ticket and a new pair of shoes. In the fall of 1920, the family boarded the train, heading, they must have hoped, for a new promised land.[24]

Audie and Walter Moffitt lived at the opposite end of the South and were also the Wilsons' opposite in many ways. White, educated, and town dwellers, they were newly married and living in western Arkansas as the 1920s began. Walter had been in the army during the war; Audie was a schoolteacher. They lived for a time in Little Rock and then in a couple of smaller Arkansas towns where Walter found various jobs, including work on a dairy farm. But he was looking for more. His father was the postmaster in the town where he grew up, and Walter and his brother both wanted to follow in those footsteps. This was going to be difficult in 1920s western Arkansas, which, like piedmont South Carolina, was on the leading edge of the rural depopulation process just beginning in the South.[25]

Some of Walter's friends had moved to Los Angeles and seemed to be doing well for themselves. One told him that the Goodrich Company was building a tire plant in the suburb of Belvedere Gardens and was looking for workers, offering wages that seemed extraordinary by Arkansas standards. Walter made an exploratory trip west, worked for several months, and then returned to Arkansas to convince his family that California was the place to be. A brand new Ford touring car helped.

In 1928, the Moffitts left Arkansas for good, making the 1,600-mile trip at high speed and in high spirits. They headed straight for Belvedere Gardens, managing to rent a furnished house on their first day in town. Both worked for Goodrich that first year in California, and then Walter got the chance he had been looking for: he passed the civil service exam and took a job delivering mail in Long Beach. A couple years later, his brother followed him to California and found a postal job in another town. "The Moffitts are all post office people," Audie said many years later, adding her son to a three-generation chain of postal employment that stretched from western Arkansas to southern California.

Two migration stories out of millions, the Wilsons and the Moffitts illustrate some of the dimensions of the first phase of the diaspora. Of different races and different classes and moving for different reasons in different directions, the Wilsons and Moffitts also had some things in common that linked a lot of migrants. They were in their prime working ages. They were ambitious, adventurous, and better educated than the community norms — standard characteristics of people who undertake serious relocations. Their decisions were based in part on test visits and networks of friends and relatives who had gone before, and they in turn helped others to make similar decisions. That means that over time, their former communities contributed a long sequence of out-migrants who tended to move in fairly consistent directions: a lot of Promised Land people to Chicago, a lot of western Arkansas folk to southern California.[26]

Not all of the migrants were married and already parents like the Wilsons and Moffitts. Young adults were the most likely candidates for such a move. Many were single, and many were female. Gender balance was one of the distinguishing features of this and other twentieth-century internal migrations. Males of both races outnumbered females by a small factor in the war-era migration, but in the 1920s, there were more African American women than African American men moving north, although this varied according to destination.[27]

The Wilson and Moffitt families also help us think about the occupational and social backgrounds of the migrants. One fits and the other does not fit the standard profile of the southern farm family heading north or west for a first encounter with factories and cities. Most of the whites and blacks who left the South in the first phase of the diaspora had been raised on farms, and a majority may have still been farmers, as the Wilsons were, when they packed their belongings. But people of other occupational experiences and social levels also moved and need to be continually factored into any calculations about how the twin migrations affected America.

White southerners of every sort were to be found among those moving, and farmers were, if anything, underrepresented in comparison to their presence in the southern population. The most likely to leave were young people with blue-collar skills. Some workers were simply following industrial pathways that led out of the South: oil workers to California; timber men to the forests of the Northwest; construction workers following the building booms that raged in cities from Detroit to Los Angeles. Others were responding to work and wage differentials that were increasingly publicized as the century progressed. The booming manufacturing economy in the industrial belt of the North and

Southern family arriving in Chicago during World War I. (Chicago Commission on Race Relations, *The Negro in Chicago* [Chicago, 1922])

key cities of the West created huge incentives for young southern workers to think about relocating.[28]

Also overrepresented in this first phase were southern whites with money, special ambitions, and education. They included salesmen who thought that Chicago, Detroit, or New York were the right markets for their skills and professionals who jumped at the chance to work for a big firm in a big city. They included merchants and businessmen with money to invest and looking for opportunities in settings livelier than the South. The West also attracted a substantial number of southerners with money to invest in land and new forms of agricultural production. Southern farmer-investors helped turn vast acreages in California and Arizona into cotton fields in the teens and twenties as the boll weevil cut into production farther east. Wofford B. Camp and James S. Townsend, a pair of South Carolinian cotton experts sent to California by the U.S. Department of Agriculture, introduced in 1917 a high-quality long-staple cotton that in time became the far West's most valuable crop.[29]

College students were another element in the white diaspora. The superior educational infrastructure of the North had long attracted southerners of ambition and privilege. As colleges expanded and the desire for a college education became more widespread in the 1920s, more young whites than ever before went north, some never to return. Wilbur Cash worried that the region was losing "its strength and brains."[30]

Writers and artists of various descriptions made the same trek, seeking in the publishing houses and magazines of New York and a few other cities opportunities difficult to find in the South — seeking, too, in some cases, escape from a social environment that the intelligentsia of this generation decried as small-town and small-minded. This intellectual out-migration would have its own momentum. Even as the first phase of migration was coming to a close, a young white North Carolinian who had left home to study theater at Harvard was finishing his first novel in a New York apartment. *Look Homeward, Angel* made Thomas Wolfe the literary phenomenon of 1929 and added more fuel to the notion that the South was no place for the intellectual.[31]

The composition of the black diaspora was also varied. The long-standing impression that the migrants were mostly sharecroppers with little urban experience and not much in the way of education or marketable work skills has been debated in recent years. Most scholars remain sure that farm families were the majority of migrants but agree that the Great Migration had many components.[32]

The black elite was one of those elements. If the white South was losing some of its "talented tenth," the black South was losing more. Carter G. Woodson long ago demonstrated that black professionals were leaving at very high rates, especially graduates of the Negro colleges who, unless they went into the ministry or teaching, had little chance of finding appropriate work in the South. Their numbers were small, but attorneys, social workers, writers, musicians, and other professionals along with merchants, preachers, and teachers were an important part of the Great Migration. When Asa Philip Randolph followed his thirst for education to New York in 1911, when William Dawson left Tennessee to study law in Chicago in 1915, when George Baker decided to move his ministry to Brooklyn and call himself Father Divine, and when Bessie Smith and Louis Armstrong took their music north in the 1920s, they too were part of the Southern Diaspora and part of why it became such a momentous force in the reorganization of American society.[33]

Depression Interlude

Migration patterns changed with the falling economy after 1929. The Depression kept most Americans close to home. As news spread about the crushing rates of unemployment in the major cities, rural people in particular had reason to stay put. In the difficult years of the early 1930s, people began to leave the cities in substantial numbers as journalists and politicians touted the benefits of going "back to the land." Unknown numbers of former southerners now returned, seeking help from relatives who had remained on the farms or in the small towns of the South. Incentives were strongest when the family owned land or at least a house and garden, which probably means that whites were more likely to return than blacks, although quite a few African Americans joined this return migration of the early 1930s. The best data come from Flint, Michigan, where a special household census was conducted in early 1934. The population of southern whites had decreased by 35.1 percent in the four years since 1930, while the number of southern-born blacks had fallen by 18.9 percent.[34]

Charles Denby headed home to Lowndes County, Alabama, in 1930 after losing his job in the foundry of a Detroit auto plant. He had been in the North six years, and although the work had never been steady, he had no desire to return to the cotton plantation where his parents were tenants and where he had spent the first seventeen years of life. "But I was laid off in 1929 and the little money I had saved was soon used up. . . . All winter I walked the streets." Finally leaving Detroit, he had trouble making the readjustment to rural Alabama, missing the excitement and sophistication of the big city and hating the rules of racial subordination in his old home town. "Don't think just because you've been up North you can forget you were raised here," a store keeper yelled after Denby forgot to say "Yes, sir." Denby was not sure he could survive in Alabama. "If you've been away they gave it to you even worse than if you stay. I told mother I'd rather be in prison in Detroit than to be free in the South. She cried and felt bad." Nevertheless, Denby stayed in the South for the next thirteen years, marrying, starting a family, waiting out the Depression. He would not see Detroit again until 1943.[35]

The South had its own economic problems. The Depression knocked the bottom out of agricultural prices, which in the case of cotton had already been depressed throughout the 1920s. Floods and drought devastated crops in some areas. And many farms were lost to foreclosure or tax default. When the New Deal administration attempted to raise commodity prices starting in 1933 through the Agricultural Adjustment Act program of crop reduction, more rural livelihoods were lost. Landowners took their poorest fields out of production and told sharecroppers and tenants to leave. By the mid-1930s, rural distress in some parts of the South was every bit as serious as the urban version.[36]

The most visible segment of the white southern exodus began under those circumstances. The western South states of Arkansas, Oklahoma, and Texas fell victim to some of the highest rates of farm failure and tenant displacement any-where as a result of the double effects of drought and depressed prices. The cities of those states suffered in kind, with escalating homelessness and little money for relief services. But not too far away there seemed to be opportunities. California, which had long been connected to the western South through earlier migration sequences, was recovering more rapidly from the economic crisis. Audie and Walter Moffitt and other pre-Depression migrants wrote their relatives back home, saying that there were jobs to be had in Los Angeles. The news from California's cotton region was also promising. Prices for the specialty strain of Acala cotton that California and Arizona monopolized had started to rise in 1934, and growers were expanding production. There was work picking and thinning, just the kind of work that many Oklahomans, Texans, and Arkansans knew well.[37]

What journalists called the Dust Bowl migration was first noticed in 1935 and then gained momentum through the remainder of the decade. By 1940, California had added more than 300,000 southerners to its already substantial population, almost all of them from Oklahoma, Arkansas, and Texas. Other western states—Arizona and New Mexico and to a lesser extent Oregon and Washington—were also recipients of this unique Depression-era population transfer. No other part of the South or of the United States lost population in such volumes during the stay-at-home 1930s. And only the far West gained people in large numbers. A rare combination of economic forces and social connections made this possible.[38]

The states to the east of the Mississippi River worked their way through the 1930s without large population losses, but southern out-migration did restart around mid-decade as the urban economies of the North recovered from the shutdowns of the early 1930s. There were particular dimensions to this late-1930s sequence that marked a change from the previous era. Both black and white migrants now tended to be more urban and better educated than the general southern populations. For African Americans in particular, much of this era's migration from the eastern South seems to have involved a circulation between cities.[39]

Information about this comes from the 1940 census, which asked where people had lived five years earlier, thereby identifying those who left the South in the last half of the decade. Only 23 percent of the African American recent migrants said they had lived on a farm in 1935, while a larger number identified one of the South's metropolitan areas as their former home, this at a time when more than half of the southern black population still lived on farms and still more in rural areas. Also revealing is the information the migrants provided about the extent of their schooling. They were considerably better educated than black southerners in general, 22 percent of adult out-migrants claiming a high school diploma compared to 6 percent of those remaining behind.[40]

None of this is terribly surprising given the conditions of the late 1930s. No job boom encouraged African Americans to come north. Unemployment rates among blacks in Chicago, New York, Philadelphia, and other major destinations remained at catastrophic levels through the end of the decade, with most families dependent on Works Progress Administration (WPA) jobs and other forms of emergency workfare. Newcomers often had trouble meeting eligibility requirements for WPA work or any other kind of relief, so it was mostly people with a clear plan, special skills, or strong social connections who undertook big relocations in that period.[41]

James Boggs had a plan when he and a friend hopped a freight train in 1937 heading north to join relatives in Detroit. He was eighteen, newly graduated from high school in Bessemer, Alabama, and figured that since his uncle had a job with an auto company, he would get one too. "I don't know why we thought we would," he said, looking back on his youthful naïveté. Detroit was hiring, but mostly only whites: "Weren't many blacks working in the auto industry at all." Boggs went on, "So what do you do? You get a job washing cars or like bums do now. Or somebody picks you up and you go out in the country somewhere and work in cabins, where people had their summer cabins." Then he got on with the WPA and spent the next two years building roads in and around Detroit. A WPA paycheck did not go far, especially after James decided to get married and raise a family. One room in a house that was shared with two other families was all he could afford. But he was also enrolled in a trade school, learning pattern making and other machine skills, and in 1940 the job expectation that had drawn him to Detroit finally came through. James Boggs got a job with Chrysler.[42]

Whites who headed north during the 1930s also tended to be more urban and educated than those who remained behind, although the differentials were less dramatic than among blacks. Whites as always had much better job prospects, and as northern industries recovered in the mid-1930s, migration networks that had been established earlier also revived. One connected the auto and tire cities of Michigan and Ohio with the lowland towns of Kentucky and Tennessee. Like James Boggs, Guy and Lillie Mae Tomlin were thinking about auto industry jobs when they left western Kentucky late in the decade. Many of the farm families from the area around Paducah had connections in Detroit, and they decided to follow the stream. They were much luckier than Boggs. Guy Tomlin got a job, not with one of the auto companies but with a supplier, the Commonwealth Brass Company, which hired him and in time trained him as a machinist. The young couple found an apartment, not the little room that the Boggs family squeezed into but a comfortable place in north central Detroit. A year later there was more luck: they had a daughter and named her Mary Jean. Two decades later she renamed herself Lily—Lily Tomlin.[43]

Second Phase

The selective migration streams of the 1930s stand in contrast to the general exodus of the 1940s, 1950s, and 1960s. World War II initiated the greatest spatial reorganization of Americans in the nation's history, and southerners were at the heart of the process. The ramping up of military production that began in 1939 created millions of jobs along the major industrial corridor stretching from New York to Chicago and on the coasts where shipbuilding facilities were concentrated. Over the next five years, millions of Americans moved to those areas to build the planes, tanks, rifles, and ships that the nation needed to fight the war. The mobilization of more than 16 million soldiers, sailors, and aviators shifted people in other directions, mostly to the West and South where, for political, strategic, and climatological reasons, training camps and military bases were located. Never before had so many Americans been in motion.

They kept moving after the war, across state lines and regional boundaries in all sorts of directions, achieving peacetime rates of mobility that exceeded anything previously known. Demographers calculated that in any given year during the 1950s and 1960s, 3–4 percent of all Americans undertook a long-distance move across state lines. The proliferation of cars and highways (not to mention moving vans) and what George Pearson called a culture of "perpetual transportation" made moving easier than ever before. But underlying it, too, were huge changes in the organization of the American economy, all of which powerfully affected the South and its peoples.[44]

World War II had marked a watershed in regional economic organization. As the federal government raced to build shipyards, aircraft plants, steel and aluminum facilities, and hundreds of military installations in the previously low-industrial regions, the future of both the West and the South started to become clear. The West was going to become a population magnet, attracting automobilized job seekers by the millions, tripling its population in the three decades after 1940. The South was going to urbanize—and do so at a stunning pace. The region's massive farm population, still almost as large in 1940 as at its 1910 peak, would leave the land, not only pouring into the cities and taking the jobs that the rapidly industrializing South could offer but also pouring out of the South, adding to the population movements of the West and North. As late as 1940, more than 14 million southerners lived on farms. By 1970, there were only 3 million, and ten years later, less than 1.5 million. The backward

Coming to work at River Rouge. Among the 96,000 employees at Henry Ford's Detroit plant by 1944 were 15,000 blacks and at least as many white southerners. (Walter P. Reuther Library, Wayne State University)

agricultural South was no more, and many of the South's formerly rural people were no longer southerners.[45]

The people who left the South in the second phase of the diaspora came from some new areas and backgrounds and moved in some directions that had not been standard in the preceding decades. Mississippi and Alabama replaced Georgia and the Carolinas as the prime zone of out-migration for African Americans. This core area of the cotton kingdom had prospered when other areas were failing. In the Delta lands along the Mississippi River south of Memphis, plantation owners were still draining and clearing land and recruiting sharecroppers as late as the 1920s, even after Promised Land people like the Wilsons had moved to Chicago. Some of the plantations shifted to centralized farm management in the 1930s, and the rest would do so by the 1950s, converting sharecroppers into farm laborers, employed when they were needed to thin and pick cotton. So when other opportunities beckoned, as they did with the onset of World War II, people left, their numbers escalating in the 1950s as mechanical cotton pickers destroyed what was left of the black rural economy.[46]

The main route out of the Deep South still led due north to Chicago, Detroit, and other Great Lakes cities, but World War II also opened a new migration geography for African Americans. Now black families from Texas, Louisiana, and Arkansas and some of their eastern South counterparts turned west, giving the Pacific Coast its first significant black population outside of Los Angeles. The family of nine-year-old Bobby Seale, future founder of the Black Panther Party, joined the nearly 100,000 African Americans who moved to the San Francisco Bay Area during the 1940s, an area that before the war had fewer than 20,000 black residents. Others moved to Seattle, Portland, and San Diego. Los Angeles saw its black population jump from 75,000 to 218,000. And there would be more to follow in the 1950s and 1960s. During the second Great Migration, African American southerners spread out into many more places than during the first, with big consequences for everyone. A people of the South at the turn of the century, a people of the South and the northern great cities in the interwar era, they would now have a significant presence in every region, in every major city and every major state.[47]

The South's Hispanic Americans had played little part in the earlier phase of the diaspora, but after 1940 that began to change. This was largely a Texas story. Ever since it was taken from Mexico, Texas had been the heartland for Latin Americans living in the United States. In 1920, 456,000 Texans claimed Hispanic names and Mexican ancestry, which was 36 percent of all Hispanics living in the United States and more than the Hispanic population of California, New Mexico, and Arizona combined. Most Tejanos were U.S.-born, but that earned little in the way of political rights or economic access. Facing a Jim Crow system of legal subordination and segregation not much different from what the state's African Americans dealt with, most Mexican Texans earned their livings either as sharecroppers or as itinerant agricultural workers who picked the vegetable crops in the Rio Grande valley and then moved through the Texas cotton belt.

They began to leave in some numbers in the late 1930s, usually moving westward looking for agricultural jobs. In 1940, 13 percent of Texas-born adult Latinos were living outside that state, mostly in California, New Mexico, and Arizona. Out-migration accelerated during and after World War II, the lure now industrial as well as agricultural employment. Figures 1.1 and 1.2 and tables A.1 and A.3 estimate those volumes, although it should be noted that census data on Latinos are less complete and accurate than for racial groups. The numbers were small compared to the other two diasporas, but 1950 found more than 102,000 southern-born Latinos living in other regions. By 1970, the number had jumped to 490,000. Migration by then had become almost as common for southern-born Latinos as for southern-born African Americans: 26 percent of all Texas-born adult Latinos lived outside that state, and the same ratio held for Latinos born in other southern states (notably Florida and Louisiana). Almost half of them had settled in California, which had replaced Texas as the center of Hispanic culture and population in the United States, but the rest had moved in new directions, including the Midwest. The industrial states of Michigan, Illinois, Indiana, and Ohio were home to 120,122 southern-born Latinos in 1970.[48]

The Tejano exodus was easily overlooked by contemporaries who usually failed to distinguish between Chicano migrants and newcomers from Mexico. Mexican immigration surged during World War II and continued to grow steadily in the decades that followed, attracting far more attention than did the internal relocations of U.S.-born Hispanics. But especially before the 1970s, the internal migrants were a significant part of the Hispanic remapping of the United States. As Latinos spread out into states that had before known little Hispanic settlement, some of that pioneering was done by Tejanos and other Chicanos. That was particularly the case in the Midwest. Provided that people were accurately specifying birthplaces on their census forms, it seems that in 1970, southern-born Latinos outnumbered foreign-born Latinos in Michigan, Indiana, and Ohio, accounting for 28 percent, 22 percent, and 27 percent of the adult Hispanic population of those three states. Elsewhere the representations were smaller. Southerners contributed little to the growing Hispanic presence in the Northeast, largely Caribbean in origin. And while Tejanos and other southerners most often moved west, so did everyone else. They accounted for just under 12 percent of the adults in California's fast-growing Latino population in 1970.[49]

The South's Indian peoples were also on the move, particularly those who lived in Oklahoma. Designated "Indian Territory" by Congress in the 1830s, Oklahoma spent the nineteenth century as a repository for the original southerners, the survivors of the Cherokee, Choctaw, Creek, Seminole, Chickasaw, Kiowa, Osage, and other tribes forcibly removed from southern and Great Plains lands. The Oklahoma reservations had in turn been lost when the federal government opened the territory to white settlement in 1889, but the state that was born there in 1907 remained home to more indigenous Americans than any other in the United States. During World War II, Indian Oklahomans began to follow their white and black neighbors to the job centers of California, while tribal groups in the eastern South saw some of their members head either west or north. Federal policies encouraging urban relocation and terminating some reservations gave further impetus to the migration in the 1950s and 1960s. By 1970, one out of five Native American adults had left the region. Among them was Lesa Roberts, a Choctaw whose migration story belonged in some symbolic ways to many of the South's native peoples.[50]

Lesa Phillip Roberts was born in Mississippi, part of the Choctaw group that had resisted relocation to Oklahoma in the early nineteenth century. In 1903, when Lesa was thirteen, her family joined several hundred other Mississippi Choctaw who belatedly accepted a federal offer of land in Oklahoma, small homesteads that were being parceled out to tribal members as the Dawes Commission dissolved the Oklahoma reservation. Over the next forty-one years, she raised six children and outlived four husbands while making a living farming, but the crisis and consolidations of the 1930s caused her children to leave home one by one, many going to California. She resisted yet another homeland removal, but at age sixty-three she had little choice. In 1944, she joined her eldest surviving son, then working in a shipyard in Richmond, California, completing what her grandson would later call a "Choctaw Odyssey" — an odyssey that was part of the Southern Diaspora.[51]

There were new developments too among white southerners. The mountainous counties of southern Appalachia that stretched from West Virginia to Alabama had been storing up population for decades thanks to the expansion of timber cutting and coal mining after the turn of the century. Those industries contracted sharply in the 1920s, and despite partial recoveries, the regional economy would no longer support its birth rate. In escalating numbers, young people left the upland counties looking for work in the lowland cities of the South and in the industrial centers of the North. Joining the mix of farm folk, blue-collar workers, and elite migrants from other sections of the South, Appalachians would bear a heavy burden of visibility in the decades to come.[52]

Jewish southerners contributed another segment of the second-phase exodus. In the 1950s and 1960s, as civil rights struggles dominated regional politics, new cohorts of southerners left the South for political reasons. Especially this was an option for young people, college-bound or recent graduates, both young African Americans and young whites of liberal ideals, including quite a few among the region's small Jewish population. The historian Helen Lefkowitz Horowitz recalls the steady exodus of younger generation Jews from Baton Rouge, where she grew up in the 1950s. When the college admission letters arrived, they packed their bags and left, most for good.[53]

The brain-drain effects of the first phase continued with some new dimensions in the second. Southern colleges and universities were beginning to improve, those serving blacks as well as those serving whites, with the infusions of talent and money that came under the GI Bill. But the college-bound of both races continued to leave in significant numbers. In 1970, 46,000 black southerners and 181,000 whites were attending college outside their home region. Those educated at southern colleges also exited in large numbers. In 1970, 38 percent of all southern-born African Americans who had previously been to college lived outside their home region, along with 20 percent of college-experienced white southerners.[54]

The military provided yet another pathway out of the South. Southern males, black and white, have joined the armed forces in disproportionate numbers throughout American history, serving prominently in every conflict from the War of 1812 to the wars against Iraq. Military service introduces people to new places and sometimes permanent relocations. World War I military service had that effect, particularly on black veterans, but the downsizing of the military establishment in the 1920s and 1930s made this a modest factor in the first phase of the diaspora. The second phase unfolded during an era when the United States continuously maintained massive armed forces, requiring the services of millions of young men. That meant that one cohort after another of southern recruits would be stationed in other parts of the country and that many would never return. In 1970, 41 percent of southern-born black veterans and 20 percent of southern-born white veterans lived outside their region of birth.[55]

Albert Murray's relocations reflect the geographic effects of two specialized occupations: the African American writer and the African American military officer. Born in Alabama in 1916, his father a laborer, the intellectually precocious Murray impressed neighbors and grammar school teachers enough to win admission to Tuskegee Institute, from which he graduated with a BA in literature in 1939. Ralph Ellison, two years ahead of him at Tuskegee, had followed the intellectual's North Star to New York before graduating. But not Murray. Invited to stay on and teach, he might have made a life career at Tuskegee had it not been for World War II and the U.S. Army Air Corps.

When the air corps decided to recruit and train African American pilots for a showcase all-black fighter squadron, Murray signed up and spent the last part of the war in the skies over Europe. Discharged, he returned to Alabama for a time but then, like a lot of other veterans, found that he wanted more than his old home and job could offer. Pursuing an interest in writing, he moved to Harlem with his wife and young daughter and earned an MA degree in literature at New York University. Reestablishing his friendship with Ralph Ellison, Murray thrilled to be part of the New York intellectual scene of the late 1940s and struggled to develop his literary talent. But earning a living came first, and in 1951 he rejoined the air force, taking up the rank of captain that he had held in 1945. The air force then sent him back home. Although he had a number of assignments over the next ten years, he spent most of the 1950s at Tuskegee teaching in the air force ROTC program. When he finally retired with the rank of major in 1962, he said his final good-bye not only to the military but also to Alabama and the South. New York and the writing career that he had long sought now called him with unmistakable clarity.[56]

Still, it was not the intellectuals or the veterans who comprised the great bulk of second-phase migrants. Even more than the first phase, the migration sequence of the 1940s, 1950s, and 1960s involved what is probably best described as a cross-section of the South, ranging across the region's many geographies and social categories, involving elites but reflecting also the preponderance of modestly educated people who had grown up in the once largely rural South but had started or were now starting their earning lives as blue-collar workers. This was preeminently a blue-collar migration prompted by regional disparities in wages, jobs, and labor supplies, a blue-collar migration aimed at the great job centers of the North and West during the prime decades of American industrial triumph.

Post-diaspora

The 1970s mark another turn, an end to the period of massive out-migration and the start of what might be labeled a post-diaspora period. Demographer C. Horace Hamilton caught a whiff of the change in the mid-1960s, announcing that "the traditional role of the South as a major supplier of the nation's population is changing, and the tide of migration from the South is slowing down." Census numbers at the end of that decade confirmed this, indeed showed that more Americans were moving to the South than away from it. The change caught nearly everyone by surprise. States that had been consistent net exporters of people now were attracting them. This was nothing new for Florida, Maryland, or Delaware, which regional analysts did not always consider part of the South anyway, but now Georgia, Texas, Virginia, North Carolina, South Carolina, Oklahoma, and Tennessee had joined them as net in-migration states. Altogether, 696,000 more people moved to the South between 1965 and 1970 than left it.[57]

The trend became crystal clear in the next decade when the South surpassed the West as a leading migration destination. People moving into the region outnumbered those leaving by 3.5 million during the 1970s, by 3 million in the 1980s, and by more than 2 million in the 1990s. Mostly they were coming from the same northern states that for half a century had been the prime destination for departing southerners. The Mid-Atlantic states suffered an actual population decline in the 1970s, as out-migrants exceeded in-migrants by almost 2 million. The East North Central states lost 1.3 million more people than they received through migration.[58]

The turnaround seemed more abrupt than in fact it was. The South had been attracting people in growing numbers since World War II, and throughout the second phase of the exodus something of an exchange had been going on between North and South. Mostly blue-collar southerners had been going north, and mostly white-collar northerners had been coming south. The fast-developing economy of the postwar South had been the key. The building of new industries, military facilities, educational institutions, transportation systems, and urban infrastructure had attracted the services of engineers, managers, professors, technicians, and others with high-end skills. Equally important, the region had been attracting capital. Fortune 500 companies had been opening offices and branch plants and sometimes moving whole operations to Florida, Georgia, North Carolina, Texas, and Virginia, which were the key growth nodes of the new South.[59]

The region's accelerating economic potential was tied to other changes that were helping to attract in-migrants. The conditions of life in the South had been altered thanks to air-conditioning, DDT, and huge federal expenditures on highways and airports. Florida had long competed with California for lifestyle migrants, both retirees and those in their productive years who had the option to think about sunshine and natural settings. Now other parts of the South would trade on the twentieth century's climatological reconstruction. The region that had once been considered the least healthy section of America —a land of boll weevils and pellagra, of enervating heat, deadly pests, and fevers—reemerged as the warm and attractive Sun Belt.

Racial reconstruction also played a role. The long struggle to break the South's system of racial apartheid had achieved some well-publicized results by the early 1970s, enough to undo the "benighted South" images that had been an obstacle for certain potential migrants. With voting rights and public access rights clarified by courts and Congress, with the threat of organized white-against-black violence much reduced, the South moved toward a reputation that was ambiguous enough so that most whites and many blacks could imagine living there. The fact that northern racial reconstruction had also reached a climax and that both white capital and white people were fleeing the major northern cities added to the Sun Belt reversal. The incentives and aversions that drove companies and the white middle class out into the suburbs encouraged some to move farther, finding in low-tax and nonunion southern spaces the ultimate refuge from northern big-city racial, fiscal, and union politics.[60]

The Sun Belt boom did not put a stop to southern out-migration. Even as larger numbers of northerners moved south, southern whites continued to leave the South in significant numbers, close to 2.7 million in the 1970s. That dropped to 2.2 million in the 1980s and 2.4 million in the 1990s. African Americans seem to have reacted more dramatically to the changing regional conditions. After continuing full-force through the mid-1970s, the number of black southerners leaving the region fell off sharply in the 1980s and 1990s. Fewer black southerners left their home region in the 1990s than in any decade since the Great Depression (figure 1.2).

Another feature of the new era was the accelerating rate of return migration by southerners who earlier had moved north or west and now found their way home. Returnees were an important component of the Sun Belt population surge, accounting for 20–25 percent of all persons moving to the South after 1970. In the last five years of the 1970s, 897,400 white expatriates and 210,800 black expatriates moved back to that region, joining about 3 million other Americans who sought opportunities in the reconstructed South. Some were coming home to retire. Others, younger, were making yet another opportunity-seeking move.[61]

The Sun Belt reversal brought the South's diasporic era to a close. In the past thirty years, the demographic presence of southerners outside their birth region has steadily diminished. Southern-born blacks, once a majority in northern and western African American communities, had become an aging remnant by the 1990s. So too the signs of a distinctive southern white presence or a distinctive Tejano presence in northern and western places have faded. As the twentieth century drew to a close, there were still more than 10 million southerners of various kinds living outside the region of their birth, but their presence was of more interest to historians than demographers. The great southern migrations belonged to the past.

This description of a century of migration tells us little about what the individual stories and group statistics mean or why they might be important. Economists and demographers can find meanings in the volumes alone, as they count people according to skill or resource levels and calculate impacts on labor markets or social service budgets. Students of American regionalism can see in these numbers an important symptom of the rearrangement of regional political economy over the course of the century, as the South rose from its position of disadvantage to one of considerable advantage, with population flows advertising the shift. But to move beyond these limited observations, we need to think not just about volumes but also about the social meanings attached to migration.

People move all the time, mostly without anyone saying they are part of a mass migration, still less a Great Migration or a regional diaspora. But southerners leaving home were noticed. They were talked about. They became a social phenomenon. The noticing and the talking as much as the act of re-location created the Southern Diaspora. Unnoticed, they were just families moving from one setting to another. Noticed, they became agents of change in the unfolding history of their century. We turn now to the subject of notic-ing, exploring when and how various migrating southerners came to public attention and the way that attention changed over the course of the century.

Migration Stories

America has long been guided by migration stories. The nation's popular literature has fixated on stories of ocean- and mountain-crossing migrants ever since Daniel Boone and the Pilgrims became national legends in the early nineteenth century. Those stories have always had the capacity to motivate as well as inform and amuse, helping to encourage risky relocations of various kinds and especially in westward directions over the course of the last two centuries. They have had much to do with how Americans shape personal and place identities. There is hardly a town in America that does not celebrate a tale of construction at the hands of adventurous pioneers, migrants who came from distant places with the goal of starting anew and building big and tall. The "Moving American," wrote cultural historian George W. Pierson in his 1973 book of that title, is part of "the great riddle of our national character." The terminology may be dated, but it would be hard to argue with the basic point that this nation has made much of such figures and stories.[1]

Southerners on the move in the twentieth century have attracted attention in part because of those traditions. But the imagery that came to surround both black southerners and white southerners was often ironically juxtaposed against the traditional Moving American story. Partly it was the different geography. Moving north to big cities was different from moving west to farm, dig gold, and build towns. Mostly it was a different century. Heroic migration stories had been the special concern of nineteenth-century cultural institutions, from novels to plays to Wild West shows. The twentieth century had different institutions and interests. The great migrations of the twentieth century were worked into stories that had more to do with difficulties than with triumphs, with dreams unmet rather than with dreams fulfilled, with tragedy and failure rather than with simple heroics. Southerners were moving across a cultural terrain that had decisively changed the mode of social analysis. These Moving Americans were going to be seen not as pioneers but as problems.

The evolution of cultural institutions affected how the two groups of southerners were seen. New and powerful media systems ensured that society could focus more attention upon the phenomenon of mass migration than ever before in American history and helped guide those stories into certain shapes. The diaspora first became an issue during the great age of newspapers, and the journalism of the early twentieth century gave the first phase of migration a particular constellation of attention and meanings. The advent of film, radio, photojournalism, and television shifted those attentions and meanings as the century progressed. So did the fact that many of these mass media were interacting with academic institutions. The second phase of the Southern Diaspora unfolded in an era infused with social science, when confidence in the diagnostic and therapeutic powers of sociology and psychology was at its height. The popularization of social scientific concepts and their appearance in journalism, literature, photography, film, and even music helped shape key understandings of the two migrations, which in turn became part of what southerners would deal with as they negotiated new lives away from home.

This chapter looks at the stories that have surrounded and infused the Southern Diaspora. Tracked by journalists, analyzed by sociologists, quantified by demographers, memorialized by novelists, lampooned by comics, and sung about by recording artists, the Southern Diaspora may have been the most heavily mediated mass migration in American history. The migrants would be making their way into new spaces, new relationships, and new identities in a very public process that was conditioned by an evolving set of narratives. The historians who in recent years have given us rich accounts of the Great Migration of African Americans and various sequences of white southern migration have relied heavily on this massive literature, which includes sociological studies as well as journalism, popular music, radio, television, film, and fiction. But mostly these materials have been treated as *artifacts of history*. Now we want to think about them also as *factors in history*. Because the migrants, the receiving communities, and policy makers were interacting with these media products, the stories themselves helped shape experiences and identities.[2]

The "Exodus" and the Age of Newspapers

The early stories about the Southern Diaspora were almost exclusively about African Americans on the move. Not until the end of the first migration period in the mid-1930s were white migrants noticed and profiled. Tejanos and Native American southern migrants would remain invisible to the media throughout the diaspora. The public never learned to see them as southerners, never learned to count them as part of the great migration cycles that were understood to be changing the face of America.

Newspapers drove the early noticing of black migrants. Articles about labor recruiters encouraging African Americans to head north for jobs in steel mills, coal mines, or packinghouses began to appear in the summer of 1916 and became an accelerating story the following year. As the nation geared for war, news-conscious Americans learned that something important was happening on the home front: tens of thousands of African Americans were heading north.

Just what the public learned about this movement out of the South depended upon the kind of newspaper read: northern or southern, white-owned or black. The early stages of the Southern Diaspora unfolded during decades when publishing was king, when newspapers and magazines exerted enormous force in public life. The revolution in publishing that had begun in the last decades of the nineteenth century had been consolidated in the first decades of the twentieth. Technological advances in printing, typesetting, and photoengraving and the "yellow journalism" pioneered by Joseph Pulitzer and William Hearst had transformed what and how Americans read. Mass circulation dailies and magazines now fought for readers using graphics and stories in new ways. Sensationalized writing and promotion, the ability to make news items into a riveting story and then to turn some stories into crusades, had become standard journalistic practice. That was part of how the Great Migration came to be Great. The mass movement of African Americans out of the South would have been noteworthy in any age, but in the newspaper-centered early twentieth century, this population relocation triggered a set of very big stories.[3]

Southern white newspapers were among the first to publicize the migration. Their accounts of labor recruiting and black departures built into a crisis story about potential labor shortages for southern agriculture. Headlines pumped anxiety. "Taking Away Our Labor," warned the *Montgomery Advertiser.* "Officers Look for 'Recruiters' Who Are Fooling the Negroes," headlined the *Jacksonville Times Union.* The departures prompted a bit of soul-searching in the more progressive newspapers, like the *Advertiser* and the *Galveston News*, which called for fairer treatment of African Americans, and the *Atlanta Constitution*, which demanded an end to lynching, but elsewhere the reforms most often stressed involved strengthening "anti-enticement laws" and arresting labor recruiters. The central story scheme of the white southern press reassured white readers that no fundamental problems existed. Articles and editorials suggested that migration was a mistake and that blacks were being tricked into leaving, would soon discover that northern opportunities were illusory and northern winters cold, and would eventually come home. "Negroes Were Badly Fooled and Deserted," ran a confirming headline in the *Jacksonville Times Union*; "Negroes Are Dying of Cold in North," reported the *Atlanta Constitution* during the winter of 1917, completing the message with the subhead "'We Want to Go Home,' Now the Cry of Hundreds Who Left South."[4]

Occasionally the term "exodus" would appear in the headlines of the white-owned newspapers, bleeding across the color line of southern journalism from black-owned weeklies, which used the exodus concept with purpose and effect. "The publication of a black newspaper in the South was a hazardous occupation," historian Henry Lewis Suggs has written. Several dozen weeklies served the black communities and rural hinterlands of the region at the outset of World War I. Most were small and precarious. Often one-man or one-woman operations with tiny circulations and little advertising, southern black newspapers rarely stayed in business more than a couple of years, sometimes only a couple of months, except in the largest cities. Financially strapped, they were also politically vulnerable, their copy open to scrutiny by whites, their editors aware that mobs or sheriffs could end their livelihoods at any time.[5]

Boldness was no hallmark of the southern African American press. Many editors joined the white dailies in denouncing the labor agents and calling on readers to stay put. The *Savannah Tribune* (circulation 1,400) and the *Norfolk Journal and Guide* (circulation 4,000) were two of the region's more stable black-run newspapers. Both cautioned against migration. The fact that the *Tribune*'s business manager was arrested after he helped a group of college students leave Savannah for summer jobs in Connecticut no doubt contributed to that paper's careful editorial policy. P. B. Young, publisher of the *Journal and Guide*, had other reasons. A firm believer in the Washingtonian strategy of self-help, he argued that "instead of running away from rural life because of its disadvantages the Negroes should stay and improve their opportunities." Other editors disagreed. Indeed, the *Raleigh Independent* engaged in a mock feud with the *Journal and Guide* over this issue, criticizing those "who would have the Negro erect a sort of Chinese wall around his southern home and allow no egress" and pointing out that "there are two ways by which we may improve our condition in this country. The one is segregation—voluntary segregation. The other is 'scatteration.'"[6]

But the debates did not detract from the two main themes of the southern African American press, one of them a biblical reference, the other a warning story directed at the white South. Their headlines were calling it an exodus, or "the Exodus," as early as the summer of 1916, conveying the power and importance of out-migration even as editors argued out their positions. The warning story followed by implication. African American editors all used migration as a argument for social change. Hoping to reach the white elite as well as black readers, they wrote endlessly on the subject, discussing the pros and cons of leaving, evaluating what it might mean for individuals and for the race, all the while using the issue to instruct whites about the need for change. Note the way that whites as well as blacks were being addressed in the page-long plea published in the *Atlanta Independent* under the headline "Don't Leave—Let's Stay Home": "This is our home and we do not want to leave—and we are not going to leave, unless we are driven by want and a lack of freedom from our native haunts, and we appeal to the white man who rules the country, who owns a greater part of its wealth, material and immaterial—not to drive us away but to open the doors of the shops, of the industries and the fields to our genius and push."[7]

Northern newspapers developed the story in different ways. The white-owned northern press was never as concerned about the migration as its southern counterpart and initially reported the news of black people arriving in numbers from the South in small articles and calm, dispassionate tones. The clipping files kept by the Tuskegee Institute include a substantial number of articles grouped under the index category "Northern white attitudes—sympathetic," pieces like the call for understanding toward "Our New Colored Citizens" published in the *Columbus State Journal* in August 1917.[8]

Sympathy varied by place and politics. Democratic newspapers worried as early as October 1916 that the migration was part of a "Plan to Colonize G.O.P. Voters in North." As the volume of migration increased in the summer of 1917, many more northern newspapers turned anxious and hostile. The terms "Negro Influx" and "Negro Problem" now dominated headlines, which became bigger and bolder. Articles raised various alarms. The migrants were a health menace; they were responsible for crime waves and vice problems; they would upset labor relations and the political balance of power; they would move into neighborhoods where they were not wanted and exacerbate racial tensions.[9] A sample of headlines suggests the tone:

"Negro Influx Is Burden to City" (*Philadelphia Public Ledger*)
"Negro Influx Proves Burden" (*New York Evening Sun*)
"Negro Problem Being Studied in Youngstown" (*Youngstown Telegram*)
"Race Problem in City Schools" (*New York Post*)

"North Does Not Welcome Influx of South's Negroes" (*Chicago Herald*)
"2,000 Negroes from South Are Sick Here" (*Philadelphia North American*)
"Ohio Defense Council to Study Negro Influx" (*Columbus Dispatch*)
"Negroes Flock in from South to Evade Draft" (*St. Louis Times*)
"Negro Influx On, Plan to Dam It" (*Newark News*)
"Negro Migration: Is It a Menace?" (*Philadelphia Record*)[10]

Negative newspaper portrayals of African Americans were not new in the northern white press. "The Negro Problem" had in fact been the story for decades. When African Americans appeared at all in white urban newspapers, they were represented as a social problem or, in the case of some black leaders, as working to ameliorate the problems of "their race." The war-era migration changed some important features of that story. Location was one. Before 1916, northern dailies tended to ignore the black population of their own cities (apart from sensationalized identifications of black suspects in crime accounts). The Negro Problem appeared in their pages largely as a southern story. Now that would change. Changing with it was an intensified interest in incidents suggesting racial conflict. This was an old pattern growing steadily stronger as the press fixated on race riots, the arming of black soldiers, and interracial crime and interracial sex. The Negro Problem would become local news and urgent news, moving from the back to the front pages, from dispassionate to passionate tones, from few stories to many. Chicago provides some data. In 1916 and 1917, the three main newspapers in that city published 96 editorials pertaining to racial matters, along with 108 letters and 1,338 news items, the vast majority of which focused on crime, vice, migration, interracial sex, and how blacks were affecting politics, housing, and education.[11]

The pumped-up Negro Problem story that major newspapers promoted during the war years played a role in the tensions that led to racial violence in several cities, including East St. Louis and Chicago. Those conflicts in turn cemented the key understanding that would long accompany white impressions of the black migration—that it was a problem for the North, a disaster for the cities affected.

When white bathers stoned and killed a black swimmer who had crossed an invisible line in Lake Michigan on a steamy Sunday afternoon in late July 1919, it set off four days of violence that took thirty-eight lives. It also set off a frenzy of newspaper coverage that in a sense completed the first round of white storytelling about the African American diaspora. If readers in places not directly affected by the Great Migration had not been paying attention, now they knew that Chicago and other major cities faced "problems" new to the North. A week of lurid front-page articles dominated newspapers across the country, building up the impression that Chicago faced an uprising by immense hordes of armed and violent blacks. The riots resulted in more black casualties than whites, but that would not have been understood by readers of most of the nation's daily newspapers. Press accounts were instead dominated by descriptions of blacks shooting and mobbing whites and especially by accounts of armed African Americans shooting at police officers and into white crowds.

The image of black men with guns acting with military-like coordination was especially alarming. "Flying Squadrons of Blacks in Automobiles Fire into Crowds of Whites," ran the headline that the *Los Angeles Times* added to an Associated Press report on day two of the week-long coverage. "Negroes Storm Armory in Effort to Obtain Arms and Ammunition," echoed the *New York Times*. Almost as alarming as the image of blacks with guns were the reports that enormous numbers of African Americans were involved in the fighting. The size of Chicago's black population seems to have been one of the points that the wire services strove to emphasize. Reports again and again referred to "thousands of blacks" fighting and rioting. On the third day of coverage, the Associated Press raised its estimates, claiming that "a hundred thousand negroes and an equal number of whites" were involved in the riots, an estimate that effectively counted among the rioters nearly every black Chicagoan who could walk. Hysterical, inflammatory, the mainstream press of the war era had rammed home a new life-changing reality: black people were now in the cities; the race problems of the South had moved north.[12]

The Promised Land Story

How much the hostile reporting of the white-owned press mattered to black southerners who were trying to build new lives in those places is not clear. Those accustomed to southern newspapers would have seen nothing new, and it may be that newcomers were little aware of the headlines and stories in the white-owned dailies. The leadership of the northern black communities were, on the other hand, very much aware, as were many established residents of those communities who saw in the newspapers clear indications of how relationships with white society were going to be transformed. But they were equally aware of another set of stories that whites were not reading, and that, even more than the mainstream press coverage, was helping to shape the black diaspora.

The innovations in publishing that revolutionized daily newspapers had also opened the way for new forms of media to serve specialized communities. News-papers had long served northern black communities as well as those in the South, and for the most part they had been the same sort of enterprise: small, precarious, often dependent on subsidies from one of the political parties. In the 1910s, several black publishers began to break out of that mold. Adopting some of the marketing and journalistic techniques of the mass circulation age, they built readerships that were much larger and newspapers that were much bigger and bolder than anything that had come before. The greatest of the northern publishers were Fred Moore of the *New York Age*, James Anderson of the *New York Amsterdam News*, Robert Vann of the *Pittsburgh Courier*, and Robert Abbott of the *Chicago Defender*.[13]

Abbott is credited with starting the revolution in black publishing. A Georgia native who had migrated to Chicago in 1897, Abbott launched the *Defender* in 1905 on a whim and a shoestring. Competing with four other black-run papers in Chicago and lacking the political ties that were typical of the others, he built circulation the way the Hearst and Scripps chains did: with colorful writing, eye-catching headlines, graphics and later photographs, and plenty of crime, sex, and human interest. Sometimes called "the William Randolph Hearst of Negro newspapers," Abbott's *Defender* looked so much like Hearst's *Evening American* that the Hearst Company sued and forced the *Defender* to modify its masthead.[14]

Abbott learned marketing from other hands. Until 1915, most of the *Defender*'s 16,000 circulation was in Chicago, but then Abbott decided to improvise on the techniques that magazine publishers had been using to build rural and small-town subscription lists. Using contests, promotions, and, most important, a sales staff that included Pullman porters and barnstorming entertainers, Abbott created a marketing and reporting network that followed the railroads. And Chicago railroads went everywhere, including the South. The newspaper claimed it was selling 65,000 copies each week by the end of 1916 and 125,000 two years later, two-thirds of them outside Chicago.[15]

Even more than the white urban dailies, the *Defender* and other black weeklies made the southern exodus their story. The *Defender* had always been big on causes and prior to 1916 had built a name for itself through angry coverage of lynching and other evils associated with the white South. The paper, however, said little about migration until the southern press took up the issue in the summer of 1916. But with Chicago industries now hiring black workers and migration fever building in the South, Abbott moved in. There was nothing subtle about his approach. Southerners passing around copies of the 2 September 1916 *Defender* were greeted with a large front-page photo showing hundreds of people crowding the train yard in Savannah, the headline above in big, bold letters proclaiming "THE EXODUS." A quarter-page cartoon on the back page of the same issue revisited the escape imagery of *Uncle Tom's Cabin*, picturing a planter with a gun and dogs chasing "Labor" across the ice toward the waiting

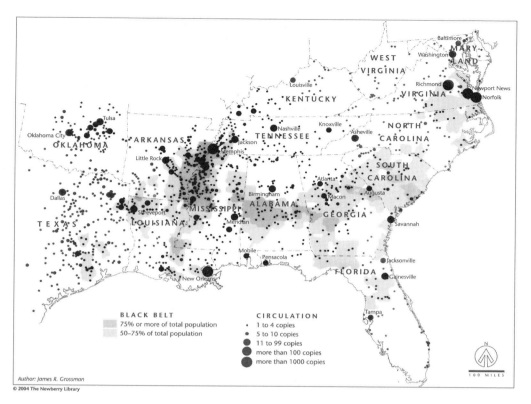

BLACK BELT
■ 75% or more of total population
□ 50–75% of total population

CIRCULATION
· 1 to 4 copies
• 5 to 10 copies
● 11 to 99 copies
⬤ more than 100 copies
⬤ more than 1000 copies

N

100 MILES

Author: James R. Grossman

© 2004 The Newberry Library

MAP 2.1. Southern Distribution of the *Chicago Defender*

Sold by Pullman porters and traveling musicians, the *Chicago Defender* circulated in most black communities of the South, as shown in this map.

Source: James R. Grossman, Ann Durking Keating, and Janice L. Reiff, eds., *The Encyclopedia of Chicago* (Chicago, 2004), 134.

car of "northern industries." A pair of shackles lay broken on the ground. Later, there would be caustic editorials ("Farewell, Dixie Land"), banner headline invitations ("Come Up North. Why Stay Down South."), and efforts to coordinate departures. Abbott would spend the early months of 1917 advertising his "Great Northern Drive," set for 15 May 1917 when thousands were expected to board trains headed north.[16]

The *Defender*'s crusade played on several themes, one of which was the concept of exodus and escape from the abusive South. But equally important were the stories the newspaper told about an inviting North. Another elegant drawing by the newspaper's talented cartoonist balanced the escape and invitation themes. Under the heading "THE AWAKENING," it shows a black man who has been sleeping on a giant bale of cotton beginning to wake up and look around.

The caption reads: "After fifty years of sound napping, depending on the white southerner and his 'cotton crop,' the members of the Race are migrating into northland, where every kind of labor is being thrown to them, where decent houses are obtainable for him to house his family and better schools to educate his children."[17]

The North as "Promised Land" was one of the oldest themes in black culture, but it had lost some of its power since the days of Frederick Douglass and Abraham Lincoln. Abbott and his fellow editors dressed up the story for the twentieth century. In the *Defender*'s pages, Chicago became the land of hope and deliverance, not from slavery but from abuse and poverty, not from Ole Massa but from Jim Crow. Chicago's promise was jobs, dignity, and, as historian James Grossman points out, excitement. The *Defender* "dazzled black southerners" with images of recreational opportunities, playgrounds, baseball games, and especially nightlife. Beyond that, the newspaper and its competitors were building portraits of something new in American experience: a space where African Americans controlled their own social life, a city within a city, a black metropolis.[18]

Starting at twelve full-size pages in mid-1916 and increasing its page count as circulation soared, the *Defender* had plenty of room to show off African American life in Chicago. Southerners hungry for information would have to wade past the crime and scandal stories that often dominated the front page, but almost as noticeable were the proud articles about black men joining the police force, successful businessmen, and new church buildings, all of which conveyed images of accomplishment on a new and impressive scale. The inside pages filled in the details of social life and recreational opportunity: a "Woman's Dept." packed with church news and "Clubs-Society" events and gossip; two sports pages that provided colorful coverage of Rube Foster's American Giants and other teams in the newly launched and northern-based Negro National League; a pair of theater pages that lauded African American vaudeville performers and musicians while advertising films and shows at half a dozen theaters that catered to black or mixed audiences. Whether the Washington Theater's large and lavish ads for the "positively adults only" show "The Evil Women Do" ("featuring the beautiful Elsie Jane Wilson") had anything to do with people coming to Chicago is doubtful. But it was one of many elements that helped convince southerners that something new and amazing was going on in the cities of the North.[19]

The *Defender* also updated another part of the Promised Land story, depicting the welcoming efforts of a modern and capable black community ready to guarantee the success and safety of the migrants just as abolitionists had done in an earlier story sequence. There would be help finding jobs through the Urban League, help from the churches, help from caring neighbors, and of course help from the *Defender*, whose advice columns and ads seemed like a road map to safety. "Your paper was all we had to go by so we are depending on you for farther advise," a would-be migrant wrote to the *Defender*, one of hundreds who corresponded.[20]

These promises affected northerners as well as southerners. With their "come north" invitations and information about services to be expected, the newspapers helped shape a process of community-building that would remake northern cities and northern politics in the years after World War I. The arrival of thousands of newcomers set in motion a frenzy of institution-building and institutional elaboration, both commercial- and social service–oriented, much of it presided over by African Americans previously established in northern settings. Stores, nightclubs, churches, employment services, and newspapers all flourished amidst the new demand generated by black population growth. This was not an unguided process. Through welcoming tones as well as through deliberate messages like the "Our Guests" editorial that the *Defender* aimed at old settlers, the newspaper mapped this community-building process just as it mapped the routes to Chicago. The *New York Amsterdam News* lectured black New Yorkers on how they should help build the Promised Land: "A heavy responsibility rests upon every colored leader, moral and civic, in these Northern states to take an especial interest in the newly arriving brethren." Enumerating the need for services, instruction, and help of various kinds, the editorial ended with an invocation that established the importance of the project at hand: "Let us press forward in the paths we should go. We are traveling toward the promised land."[21]

All of these newspaper stories—the "Don't Leave" and "Exodus" discourse in the southern newspapers, the "Negro Influx" and "Promised Land" agendas of the northern press—were in some sense collaborative. As varied as they were in tone, image, and purpose, newspaper representations converged around a key point: that history was being made as African Americans headed north. The mass movement of African Americans out of the South was going to be momentous in any case, but without the publicity or absent the particular quality of these media strategies, things would have been different. The stories helped shape the social atmosphere surrounding the migrants, creating incentives, resources, and challenges that would not have accompanied a less-publicized migration. And they greatly amplified the significance of the population movement. Together the various sets of newspapers turned the war-era black southern out-migration into a major media spectacle, an event that instantly gained historical import. The black newspapers of that era gave the event its first lofty names, "the exodus," "The Great Northern Drive," "the Second Emancipation." Within a generation, writers would call it "The Great Migration."[22]

Narrating the Black Metropolis

In American popular culture, African Americans were people of the plantation, linked not just to the South but also to cotton and soil. This was not wholly inaccurate. As late as the 1920s, close to half of African Americans did make their living on the land. But the locational references of popular media were extreme. Prior to the media changes of World War I, there were very few telling representations of African Americans living in cities, except as lone individuals. War-era "Negro Influx" stories in the white press and the Promised Land crusade in the *Defender* started the change. Americans contemplated for the first time the issue of large numbers of black people outside the South and inside the cities. The 1920s deepened that awareness. In new rounds of newspaper coverage and in several different popular media, stories about the black diaspora continued, altering somewhat the images of the migrants while fixating with special intensity on the phenomenon of the black urban community.[23]

Harlem was the center of much of this attention, followed by Chicago's South Side, soon to be called Bronzeville by that city's black press. Harlem was a name known only to New Yorkers prior to World War I. In the mid-1920s, it became famous worldwide as several different media fixed upon it as a subject of exotic curiosity. Here was something white Americans had never explored—a city within a city that belonged to African Americans—and many found it novel and fascinating. "I'd Like to Show You Harlem! This Prosperous City of 150,000 Negroes (Where Even the Cops Are Colored) Is One Bright Spot in Our Black Problem" read the headline for a 1921 article in the *Independent*, one of the first magazines to take up the subject. Many others would follow.[24]

Harlemania broke in several directions, some of it respectful, some not. Most white readers would be exposed only to a sensationalized Harlem that offered no real antidote to prevailing stereotypes of African Americans. Little of the literary production now celebrated as "Harlem Renaissance" made its way into the mass circulation publications. Only those whites who subscribed to liberal social policy magazines like the *Nation, New Republic, Survey,* or *World's Work* or black-edited periodicals like the *Crisis* (published by the National Association for the Advancement of Colored People [NAACP]) and *Opportunity* (published by the National Urban League) saw the serious side of Harlem or glimpsed the cultural resources that were coming together in the black metropolises.[25]

The Harlem that emerged from the *Saturday Evening Post*, the *Independent*, *Harper's*, and the other mass circulation magazines of the 1920s was a curiosity that could be read any number of ways. Coverage focused on the community's exotic stylings: its jazz clubs, strange religious life, excessive politics, and daring interracial opportunities. "His Excellency" Marcus Garvey, the "provisional president" of Africa, was one of the strongest images in this white readers' view of Harlem, which understood him as a poseur and charlatan, a would-be emperor capable of fooling the foolish.[26]

Black journalism took the same information but gave it a different meaning. African American writers were proud of the attention that the black metropolis was getting and were anxious to claim credit for at least some of its cultural forms. Harlem was wild and exotic but also wonderful. "Harlem is today the Negro metropolis and as such is everywhere known," James Weldon Johnson boasted first in a 1925 article and then in his 1930 book, *Black Manhattan*. "Throughout coloured America Harlem is the recognized Negro capital. Indeed, it is the Mecca for the sightseer, the pleasure-seeker, the curious, the adventurous, the enterprising, the ambitious, and the talented of the entire Negro world."[27]

Black Americans could also catch glimpses of their new geography in some other media. Harlem showed up in song titles and lyrics of some of the blues recordings that were marketed on Race Records in the urban North and rural South during the 1920s. And urban settings were preferred by the handful of companies that turned out films for the African American market. By the 1930s, the Harlem image was judged to be so popular with black audiences that filmmakers insinuated the reference into movies that had nothing to do with New York, most curiously in the horse operas *Harlem Rides the Range* and *Harlem on the Prairie*.[28]

Hollywood and Broadway, on the other hand, contributed little to Harlemania. The films and stage performances that white Americans watched during the 1920s kept African Americans mostly in the rural South. Despite occasional images of jazz clubs and maids and servants in urban locales, the major film studios and the musical stage created little room for African Americans outside of customary roles and customary settings: picking cotton, dancing and singing on the old plantation, serving white folks.[29]

But radio was another matter. This new entertainment medium, which began to reach into large numbers of homes in the mid-1920s, played an important role in updating the cognitive geography of race in America. If print journalism dominated the early story of black people leaving the South and of what they were doing in the northern big cities, radio handled the next phase. By the end of the 1920s, millions of Americans would be learning nightly lessons about the

Black Metropolis. Their teachers: a pair of white comedians pretending to be black southerners bumbling their way through Harlem.

Amos 'n' Andy initially found its way onto radio under a different name. In 1926, Chicago radio station WGN, owned by the powerful *Chicago Tribune*, began to broadcast a nightly ten-minute comedy serial called *Sam 'n' Henry* featuring a collection of characters speaking in what audiences recognized as "Negro dialect." The story line identified the two main characters as rural southerners who spent the first few episodes making their way from Alabama to Chicago and subsequent episodes clumsily adjusting to the unfamiliar city. The voices really belonged to a pair of veteran vaudevillians who had decided to rework some of the oldest schemes in American comedy and put them on the radio.[30]

One of them, Freeman Gosden, was a real southerner and a real migrant who had left his native Virginia about five years earlier. But he was a white southerner, not a black one. Blackface minstrel shows had been his specialty, and in that genre, his regional background and race gave him some advantages. White southerners could make special claims to "knowing" the ways of "colored folk," and Gosden made heavy use of this in later years when discussing the authenticity of his radio show. Minstrelsy was also a big part of the repertoire of Charles Correll, who grew up in Peoria, Illinois, in a family that claimed roots in the South. He had met Gosden in 1922 when they both worked for a touring company that staged variety shows in towns throughout the Midwest and central South. The two collaborated on various acts before finding their way to WGN and trying out their idea for a radio program.[31]

Sam and Henry were standard vaudeville figures. American comedy had long used the figure of the rural bumpkin in the city for laughs, and the black-face subgenre of comedy had made doubly powerful play with portrayals of slothful, slow-witted, "coon" figures confronting urban complexity. What was not standard was the format. Instead of once-only skits, *Sam 'n' Henry* was a nightly serial with enhanced narrative and descriptive capacities. Radio was expanding the powers of storytelling, combining the intimacy of aural performance with the frequency of the daily newspaper. One of the first teams to create what later would be called situation comedies, Gosden and Correll were introducing characters whose lives and surroundings would be explored on a daily basis by a faithful audience. It was a new departure in mass media and also a new departure in American racial relations, for this show about black southerners in Chicago was about to rename its characters, move them to Harlem, and become wildly popular. *Amos 'n' Andy* would see to it that Americans of all kinds would become familiar with the lives of fictional black southerners in the northern black metropolis.

Premiering in August 1929, the new show made radio history, generating

Posing in blackface for a *Chicago Daily News* feature in 1929, Freeman Gosden (a white migrant from Virginia, *left*) and Charles Correll were the voices behind *Amos 'n' Andy*, the most popular program on radio. The nightly radio skits helped change understandings of American racial geography while disseminating powerful images of black southerners in the big cities of the North. (Chicago Historical Society)

the biggest audiences that radio, to that point, had ever assembled. As many as 40 million people tuned in to the nightly fifteen-minute installments during the first two years of network management, and journalists pumped up the fad with reports that people everywhere were stopping what they were doing at 7:00 P.M. to listen to the broadcasts. Even restaurants and movie theaters felt compelled to offer *Amos 'n' Andy* intermissions so fans would not miss an episode. It was the most talked about entertainment phenomenon of 1929–31 and would remain a highly popular show for the next twenty years.[32]

There was nothing simple about the *Amos 'n' Andy* phenomenon. Historian Melvin Patrick Ely argues that the show was something of a Rorschach test, a comedic inkblot that attracted diverse audiences who found in it a thousand different meanings. Confirmation for the oldest and meanest stereotypes in the playbook of American racism competed with images that some listeners took in different directions. Ely thinks that the show coaxed some whites toward empathetic racial views, noting that some of the characters were capable, upstanding, and even wealthy. Blacks as well as whites tuned in, and the show became the subject of heated conflict within African American communities. The two major northern newspapers took opposite positions: the *Pittsburgh Courier* launched a nationwide campaign against the show for its demeaning depictions of blacks as incompetent, lazy, and ignorant, while the *Chicago Defender* lauded the show's wholesome themes and good-natured humor. The Chicago newspaper went so far as to feature Gosden and Correll at its annual community parade and picnic in 1931.[33]

Whatever the show's impact on the larger framework of racial understanding, *Amos 'n' Andy* had a substantial impact on the spatial and regional imagery surrounding African Americans, with important consequences for migrating southerners. The show's depiction of black urban life and its explicit use of southern migrants as the major characters drove home the story of the era's great demographic shift and perhaps helped whites become accustomed to these changes. Of all the new possibilities that came with taking comedy off the stage and spreading it out as a nightly serial, the capacity for sustained scene-setting may have been the most important. Over time, listeners assembled a picture of Harlem as a black city of considerable social complexity. Gosden and Correll presented a humorous and cleaned-up Harlem (carefully avoiding references to booze, jazz, vice, racial conflict, or other issues that might bother sponsors), and because they needed to keep plotting different stories, it was also a Harlem of some social range, with rich characters as well as poor, urbane voices interspersed among the fools.[34]

If the show strengthened the understanding that black people were now a presence in the big cities, it also tightened some particular images of the southerners who were building those black metropolises. The naive and eager Amos and the deeply ignorant, slothful Andy were marked unmistakably as southerners, with their exaggerated dialect and new-to-the-city bumblings a major comedic theme of the show. Gosden and Correll marked certain other characters as northerners with accents closer to standard English and roles that suggested various forms of urbanity, some positive, as in the case of Ruby Taylor and her father, the wealthy businessman, and others negative, as in various villains and con men. This opposition may have been too subtle for some listeners, especially whites primed to take the characteristics of the simpleton Andy as those of an entire race, but few would miss the fact that this was a show about migrants, about naive southerners out of their depth in the big city.

This regional imagery was certainly not new, and the show was just one of many cultural sites making southerners into rubes and stressing their awkward place in cities. But *Amos 'n' Andy* had a power all its own. Fans especially loved the hilarious, minstrel-derived malapropisms (most famously "I'se re-gusted") that Andy, Amos, and their friend Kingfish generated with nearly every sentence, many of which would make the watercooler rounds the next day. For actual southerners, especially those making new lives for themselves in the North, this was far from helpful. The southerner applying for a job gained nothing from the fact that his or her would-be employer spent most evenings laughing at the bumblings of radio-land southerners. As a result, the show may have exacerbated regional tensions within the black community. Whether or not whites caught the distinctions between the grammatically challenged main characters and the side figures like Ruby's father, a successful businessman who spoke in educated tones, many of the black listeners did. "Old settlers," as the northerners were apt to be known, found confirmation for class and regional stereotypes of "country folk" and "ignorant southern people" that already circulated in the cities. Newcomers had to think about these characterizations as well. Now that the simpleton Andy and the foolish Kingfish had pushed the bumpkin-coon image to new levels of visibility, a lot of people were going to be more conscious about self-presentation.

Amos 'n' Andy helped extend and refine the process of noticing that had accompanied the movements of African Americans out of the South since the onset of World War I. The newspapers, both black and white, that covered and commented on this first phase of the diaspora provided the initial publicity and set up some of its early meanings. The writers, again both black and white, who told the story of Harlem and jazz during the mid-1920s extended some of those meanings, depicting for those interested the development of one or more black metropolises as a signal effect of the southern out-migration. And then the enormously popular radio serial capped an era of writing with an audio drama that personalized the news that black people now lived in the northern cities, conveying images that confirmed the Black Metropolis story while opening wide the notion that southern black newcomers were singularly ill-equipped for the new life they had chosen. This later theme had been a small part of the noticing process up to that point. It would be a very large part of what was to follow.

Discovering the White Migrant

The Great Migration story that surrounded the experience of southern African Americans had no white equivalent. Although whites leaving the South outnumbered blacks throughout the period, there was little media attention to the white population movement until the 1930s. The contrast could not be stronger. While northern newspapers fixated on what the growing numbers of dark-skinned southerners would mean, lighter skinned southerners slipped largely unnoticed into the same cities.[35]

In daily life, the white migrants did sometimes attract attention. The white family from Tennessee moving into Chicago was hardly invisible, especially in a poor neighborhood where most of the whites spoke with eastern or southern European accents. The Texans and Oklahomans showing up in California were less remarkable, but old-time Californians did occasionally take note as the numbers increased in the late teens and twenties. However, until the mid-1930s, there was little media attention to amplify and shape the commentary and little reason for anyone to regard the migration of whites out of the South as a phenomenon of any consequence. Until then, the whites were just Moving Americans, little different in their eyes and most others' from any of the millions who left other places in the early decades of the century.[36]

The media discovery of white southern migration was the product of three somewhat separate cultural locations that all came together in the mid-1930s. One involved the policy nexus of the early Depression era as politicians, journalists, and welfare planners struggled to address problems of homelessness and transience. Another involved the literati—novelists and journalists—exercising a modernist interest in the exotic and the primitive. The third involved the new institutions of American comedy—comic strips, radio, and film—that were discovering that white southerners could be as much fun as black ones.

Americans had been writing and reading about white people on the move, especially moving west or moving to the city, since the early days of American publishing. By the turn of the century, reading publics understood rural-to-urban population movement to be one of the great transformations of their age and often understood it as an issue of moral and social complexity. But if Americans were accustomed to reading and thinking about white internal migration, it was rarely described as a crisis. In novels, journalism, and film, cities could be wicked or difficult places for farm folk, but moving white Americans were not thought to be harmful to the cities or other places they might settle. A xenophobic substream of journalism had argued just the opposite, hoping that wholesome rural newcomers would improve the cities, making them less foreign and Catholic. In many ways, the literature surrounding white internal migration had always been inversely related to debates over immigration from abroad. As long as foreign immigration occupied so much attention, it was hard to see much threat in internal movements. But when the restriction acts of the 1920s resolved the first issue, it became relatively easy for journalists, politicians, and other social analysts to shift focus.

That happened early in the Great Depression. As the economy collapsed and joblessness multiplied, welfare experts sounded the alarm about what was soon being called the "transient" problem. Cities prepared, as they had in past depressions, for expected influxes of unemployed men. Many states and municipalities had armed themselves in the Progressive Era with laws intended to discourage the transient unemployed, mostly vagrancy statutes and lengthy residency requirements for relief assistance. Others now rushed to pass or strengthen such measures. These restrictions were often effective. Mobility of all kinds, including among the jobless, dropped dramatically in the early 1930s. But press, politicians, planners, and social researchers had become fixated on the problem of indigent migration and would remain so all through the 1930s and into the next decade. The "transient" and the "migrant" became key representations of trouble and distress for the Depression era.[37]

As the issue of internal migration worked its way into public consciousness, it began to link up with an evolving set of images of white southerners that were largely the result of literary and journalistic influences. Historians George Tindall and Jack Temple Kirby have cataloged the literary construction of the "Benighted South" in the late 1920s and 1930s at the hands of writers who fastened on the region either because of its connection to reactionary and xenophobic political impulses or as a laboratory of American primitivism.[38]

The South became a target of accelerating cultural criticism in the aftermath of the celebrated "monkey trial" of John Scopes, the science teacher arrested for teaching evolution in Dayton, Tennessee. The 1925 trial attracted swarms of big-city journalists, among them master cynic Henry Louis Mencken. The Baltimore editor had for several years been enjoying himself at the expense of the South, the worst of those "forlorn backwaters" of the America he so dearly despised. Now the Scopes trial energized and broadened his campaign. Pushing the art of invective to new heights, Mencken delighted millions of readers and inspired hundreds of young journalists to follow his lead in picturing the South as the "bunghole of the United States, a cesspool of Baptists, a Miasma of Methodism, snake charmers, phony real-estate operators, and syphilitic evangelists."[39]

To the new journalistic gaze was soon added a stream of fictional production associated with what writer Ellen Glasgow disapprovingly called the "Southern Gothic School." T. S. Stribling, William Faulkner, and Erskine Caldwell were the leading contributors. In novels that began to appear in the late 1920s, the three southern writers turned what had long been a favorite and often best-selling topic (southern white plain folk) in a new direction, moving away from rural sentimentalism or even sympathetic realism into a naturalism that made their subjects seem pathetic, deeply ignorant, in some cases barely human. That is especially true of Erskine Caldwell, whose portraits of depraved southern white poverty became massive best-sellers in the 1930s. In *Tobacco Road*, published in 1931, Caldwell created a grotesque family of Georgia sharecroppers.

Jeeter Lester, his dim-witted wife, and their harelipped children are starving together on worn-out cotton land, the whole lot of them so incapacitated by ignorance that they fail to make even the most basic efforts to secure the food they need to survive.[40]

Tobacco Road not only was a best-selling novel and one of the most popular stage plays of the era but also became a mass culture phenomenon, so much discussed that the title and the name Jeeter Lester remained part of the American social vocabulary for decades. In concert with other novels appearing in the early 1930s and supported by social research reports and journalism about the plight of the southern sharecropper, the book helped focus public attention on the South as a troubled region and on poor southern whites as a troubled social group. While most of those who produced the reports, articles, novels, and photographs were motivated by the desire to help the victims of southern poverty, their efforts also resulted in the circulation of distorted and demeaning images of those they sought to help. Among middle-class readers in the North and West, the grotesqueries of the southern gothic novel were apt to be taken literally. "The nation has become Tobacco Road conscious," a sociologist who studied the South worried in 1938. Everywhere, she reported, "a relatively new and almost universal caricature of the great body of poor southern rural and industrial folk as 'poor whites'" had taken hold.[41]

Other media venues were also contributing imagery and vocabulary that helped frame understandings of the white South and became part of the discovery of the southern white migrant. Americans had been reading about the Appalachian region since the late nineteenth century and loved the notion that the mountains were home to a curious population of people out of step in one way or another with modern America. Gilded Age writers seeking local color, missionaries and educators looking for schools to build, and early folklorists looking for ancestry and tradition had discovered, or as historian Henry Shapiro puts it, "invented," Appalachia. Popular books and mass circulation magazines pictured a region lost in time and described the "mountaineers" as "our contemporary ancestors" or, in a related reference that looked back to Scotland, as America's "highlanders." Early films also used the region, often focusing on moonshine wars and clan feuds (most famously the Hatfield-McCoy feud), subjects that pulp magazines also loved to celebrate.[42]

In the 1920s, Appalachian fascination shifted into a new gear, becoming a subject of humor as well as folkloric curiosity, signified by the proliferation of the term "hillbilly." The image of mountaineer now became entangled with that of the fool and moved into several genres of comedic performance. Hollywood and vaudeville had introduced a few hillbilly characters and hillbilly skits before World War I but warmed to the subject in a much bigger way in

The most popular show on television in the early 1960s, *The Beverly Hillbillies* continued the tradition of hillbilly representations in literature, music, comics, and film that had influenced southern white identities since the 1920s. (Author's collection)

the late 1920s. In 1926, the same year that WGN brought radio to bear on the comedic image of two rural southern black men, the movie *Rainbow Riley* set up a filmland subgenre that used hillbillies or other rural simpletons either as targets for the laughter of the sophisticate or as foils to deflate urban and highbrow pretensions. Hillbilly characters would populate many of the film and radio comedies of the 1930s and 1940s (most memorably in the Ma and Pa Kettle films and Red Skelton and the Arkansas Traveler on network radio). Hillbillies would then move effortlessly into television (*The Real McCoys*, *The Red Skelton Show*, *The Andy Griffith Show*, *The Beverly Hillbillies*, *Petticoat Junction*, *Hee Haw*, *Green Acres*, *Gomer Pyle U.S.M.C.*).[43]

    The recording industry may have been even more influential in promoting the hillbilly figure. Okeh Records, based in New York, began to record fiddle music in the early 1920s after discovering that there was a market for what was initially called old-time tunes, especially in the South. In 1925, four musicians from Virginia traveled to New York City to record for Okeh and left the studio with a new name. They became the "Hill Billies," the moniker chosen by marketing executive Ralph Peer who soon made them not only famous but also the archetype for an emerging genre of commercial music. Imitators appropriated the concept and embellished on the music and the act. By the end of the decade, there were so many hillbilly string bands that the term "hillbilly music" had become the unofficial label for the whole subset of commercial music that decades later would rename itself "country music."[44]

Cartoonists were not far behind. Hollywood began to feature various hillbilly cartoon figures in 1935, one year after *Snuffy Smith* and *Li'l Abner* comic strips appeared in many of the nation's newspapers. By then, nearly everyone was in on the joke. And the timing was perhaps more than fortuitous. Xenophobic humor was by the early 1930s running into trouble. Just as the figures of the hypochondriac Jew and drunken Irishman were (temporarily) exiting the comedic stage, the dim-witted hillbilly was taking their place. Suddenly hillbillies were everywhere in popular culture, and Americans were laughing.[45]

All of these images of primitive white southerners began to connect with public policy concerns surrounding interstate migrants in the mid-1930s. It happened nearly simultaneously in two different settings. California had been beset by severe migration anxieties since 1933, and the fear of indigent newcomers had been a critical issue in the 1934 election season. In the summer of 1935, a pair of much-noticed articles called attention to what seemed to be a concentrated migration of poor families from the southern plains states of Oklahoma, Arkansas, and Texas. A piece by agricultural economist Paul Taylor in *Survey Graphic*, the admired social issues magazine, first flagged the migration and raised the intriguing image of "refugees" fleeing dust storms and drought conditions of the Great Plains. A month later, *Collier's*, with a circulation of 2 million, featured a long article, "California, Here We Come," complete with the photographic images of overloaded jalopies and tent encampments. These articles triggered the first public awareness of what journalists were soon calling the "Dust Bowl migration," a label that wrongly construed the origins of most of the newcomers. However, a less friendly label was soon circulating. "Okie" would become the West Coast equivalent of "hillbilly," a term of derision applied not just to Oklahomans but to all sorts of newcomers from the South and also the Great Plains—basically to anyone who spoke with what Californians described as a "twang."[46]

Just a few months earlier, in February 1935, Louis Adamic had published an article in the *Nation* that seems to have provided the first public notice of southern white migration to the North. In "The Hill-Billies Come to Detroit," he wrote about the estimated 15,000–30,000 southerners ("impoverished whites, 'white trash' or little better, from the rural regions") competing for jobs in the auto industry and getting them, he sneered, by undercutting wages and standards. One way for a man to get a job in Detroit, he wrote, is to affect a southern accent. "Another good way . . . is to look and act stupid."[47]

These discovery articles and the torrent of others that followed meant that the social terrain would soon be changing for white southerners outside their home region. Invisibility would be replaced by a highly problematic visibility. Soon anyone revealing a southern accent was apt to be labeled "hillbilly," "Okie," "ridge runner," or "white trash." And these associations would last far longer than the 1930s, shaping the social environment for white southern migrants for decades to come. All through the middle of the twentieth century, as the second phase of migration built up the numbers of white southerners in the far West and Midwest, the labels "hillbilly" and "Okie" would shadow them, sustained not just by social practice but by new rounds of media production and circulation.

Sociologizing the Diaspora

The second phase of the Southern Diaspora began with World War II and continued into the 1970s. It would be by far the larger of the two sequences of migration. More than 4 million southerners would move north and west during the 1940s, followed by more millions in the 1950s and 1960s. This would bring the total of former southerners living outside their home region to more than 10 million by 1970 and would dramatically increase the impact of the diaspora.

Much was different about this migration era, including the role of the various media surrounding, scrutinizing, and depicting the new surge of southern newcomers. The issues and images would change in several ways. The enormous attention paid to African American migrants in the first decades of the twentieth century would be scaled back, put in different context, and paired with depictions of white southern migrants. Where media representations of the teens and twenties had been sharply racialized, those of the middle century tended in comparison to de-emphasize race. They also de-emphasized sensation. There would be no replay of the alarmist invasion stories that accompanied the first phases of the Great Migration. In fact, the whole tone of media representation would be different, becoming more clinical, more sociological.

The second phase of the Southern Diaspora was going to experience the new power of the sociological perspective.

If American social science enjoyed a golden age, it was the middle third of the twentieth century, three decades beginning in the 1930s when sociologists, economists, psychologists, and others spoke with more authority and their voices reached farther than in any other period before or since. Government sponsorship and the eager attentions of other media, especially journalism and literature, helped social researchers move their ideas out of academic circles and into policy and popular consideration. The new reach had something to do as well with the sophistication and applicability of some of the theories being developed. Confidence in the scientific grounding of sociology and related disciplines soared as scholars formalized methodologies, shed some of their links to social work and social reform, and developed penetrating theories that seemed capable of answering key questions about the individual, the group, and society.[48]

The issue of migration, especially rural-to-urban migration, was close to the heart of this expanding social science enterprise. Between 1930 and 1970, few subjects were more studied by the corps of sociologists, demographers, labor economists, and social psychologists who devoted their professional lives to understanding American society. Some sense of the size of this undertaking can be gleaned from the bibliographic guide to *Rural-Urban Migration Research in the United States* compiled by Daniel O. Price and Melanie M. Sikes. It includes 1,232 books and articles, but the editors stress that the list is far from exhaustive and mostly contains research from 1950 to 1972. Many of these studies focused on white or black southerners whose migration and resettlement was often taken to be the purest form as well as the most visible example of rural-to-urban relocation.[49]

Urban "adjustment" was the main issue of interest behind this research. Scholars had by the 1930s worked out a theory that would have important implications for the two primary subject groups. Adjustment was an old concept. It was long understood that rural people faced challenges and changes in the big cities, but the dimensions of that transition were mostly unspecified. Sociologists at the University of Chicago developed an integrated theory of what happened when rural people came to the city, a theory that emphasized trauma and stress and also emphasized the relationship between internal migration and cross-border migration. In their hands, migration from farm to city became an "uprooting," a disruptive, disorganizing experience much more complicated for everyone involved than previously envisioned, similar to what people experience in moving to a new country. Long associated with images of pioneers, internal migration was now going to be linked to immigration. Interstate migrants, thanks to the sociologists, were about to become immigrants, immigrants within their own country.[50]

William I. Thomas and Florian Znaniecki had introduced the basic elements of the theory in their influential study *The Polish Peasant in Europe and America* (1918), which combined the issues of immigration and rural-urban adjustment and argued that urban adjustment was an attenuated process involving distinct stages. Rural migrants experienced a long phase of "social disorganization" followed by an equally complicated stage of "social reorganization" as they struggled with new social rules and influences of the modern city. Robert Park and Ernest Burgess added to the theory over the next two decades, Park filling in some of the psychological dimensions that accompanied the disorganization and reorganization stages, Burgess focusing on urban ecology and mapping spatially the stages of adjustment. Park's concept of the "marginal man" added an important theoretical wrinkle and a still more telling publicity effect, crystallizing the theory in a form that journalists as well as scholars could disseminate. Developed initially in a 1928 essay, "Human Migration and the Marginal Man," the marginal man was the individual caught between two milieus or cultures, psychologically transformed in the process. In that first essay, Park restricted the concept to some fairly unique circumstances, but in short order the term was in play, applied to all sorts of situations involving migration or personal transitions. By the late 1930s, marginal men were showing up everywhere in journalism and fiction.[51]

By then, the Chicago migration paradigm was in full dress, and scholars were busy recording the uprootings and adjustment problems of various peoples, many of them immigrant groups, but they were also applying the formula to rural Americans on the move, especially the two groups of southerners. A flurry of work on black migrants told the new story, notably T. J. Woofter's *Negro Problems in Cities* (1928), Louise Venable Kennedy's *The Negro Peasant Turns Cityward* (1930), Clyde Vernon Kiser's *Sea Island to City* (1932), and E. Franklin Frazier's *The Negro Family in Chicago* (1932).

The discovery of the "hillbilly" migration in the mid-1930s opened up another subject for study. By 1937, there were at least three WPA-funded studies underway focused on southern white adjustment in different cities of the Midwest. Grace Leybourne's article "Urban Adjustments of Migrants from the Southern Appalachian Plateaus" (1937) was the first to make it into print and a good example of the uprooting paradigm in application. Leybourne used survey research to gauge the assimilation potential of migrants who had settled in Cincinnati, proceeding from the assumption that Appalachians came from "areas far removed in culture and habits of life, if not in distance, from the city." Leybourne first cataloged the social habits associated with that "highly unsuitable background to city life" and then used the survey data to evaluate job and residential placement and school usage and to see whether the newcomers joined unions, clubs, and churches at the same rate as other whites. Any variations were taken as evidence of "adjustment difficulties." Her conclusion stressed that the migrants were making progress but faced continued obstacles, partly having to do with the prejudices of older residents, partly "springing from habits of life belonging to isolated Highlands."[52]

This was just the beginning. Urban adjustment research kicked into a new gear after World War II as new sociology departments and research institutes joined the game. In addition to the University of Chicago, which continued to turn out urban ecological and ethnographic studies all through the 1950s and 1960s, the Universities of Michigan, Minnesota, and Kentucky become major research nodes. The first two specialized in survey research that often compared the adjustment experiences of black and white southerners, while the University of Kentucky sociologists conducted longitudinal studies of Appalachian migration streams.

This vast sociological enterprise has proved to be a wonderful resource for the historians who study the Southern Diaspora and other aspects of twentieth-century social history. But it is important to understand that the academics were not merely studying the migrants; their theories and observations were also affecting the people they studied. The key concepts of the urban-adjustment school circulated widely, moving beyond academia into journalism, literature, and performance media where they helped shape new images of the two groups of southerners and thus new challenges and sometimes opportunities for the migrants.

The sociological influence is apparent in the way the major newspapers and popular magazines covered the huge migration sequences of World War II, reflected both in a new tone that was often restrained and diagnostic and in different images of the migrants, whose need for various kinds of assistance was now emphasized. Perhaps the most striking change in the pattern of wartime coverage was the new way of handling race. Instead of large numbers of articles about black migration, the major news organizations mostly offered reports that were biracial in focus. Even as black migration volumes soared high above those of the previous war era, the inflammatory Negro Invasion headlines were less common. Much of the press now used a more race-neutral terminology centered on the term "defense migrant." "Great Defense Migration," "Whither the Migrants?" and "Rolling Tide of War Migrants" are typical of the titles that war-era readers encountered in mass circulation magazines.[53]

Those headlines introduced articles that generally discussed both white and black migrants while suggesting a basic symmetry in their backgrounds and experiences. Even those articles that explored the dangers of massive migration often did so in ways that took some of the emphasis off African Americans. *Life* magazine ran a prescient lead article in the summer of 1942 warning about conditions in boomtown Detroit a full year before the devastating race riot of 1943. Headlined "Detroit Is Dynamite," the article described the city as teeming with newcomers and "seething with racial, religious, political, and economic unrest." But *Life* did not focus just on African Americans. Instead, it folded blacks into a larger picture of unadjusted newcomers, first mentioning "the 260,000 Polish Catholics," then "the 200,000 Southern whites who have migrated to Detroit with their barbecue stands and tent shouting evangelists." Only then is there a reference to "150,000 Negroes." The same sense of symmetry is apparent in the magazine's eight pages of photographs, which depict blacks crowding into one kind of inadequate housing, whites into another, and warn of Communist influence among the former, Ku Klux Klan activity among the latter.[54]

Newspaper coverage patterns did not always closely follow these magazine trends. One can certainly find alarmist Negro Invasion stories that were similar to those of the World War I era. On the West Coast, in shipbuilding centers like Portland, Oregon, and Richmond and Oakland, California, where before the attack on Pearl Harbor African Americans had been present only in very small numbers, wartime migrants faced newspaper-orchestrated campaigns of alarm and hostility. But in most major cities, the leading newspapers were more restrained in their treatment of the migration issue and apt to draw parallels between southern white and southern black newcomers. We can see this in the coverage of the riot that broke out in Detroit in the summer of 1943. The worst outbreak of racial violence since the 1919 Chicago conflagration, the incident offers an opportunity to examine the changes in newspaper strategies between the two migration eras.[55]

The differences are striking, even though the events had much in common. Another hot day at the beach led to the Detroit violence, which started when crowds of young men of both races began to mix it up near the Belle Isle bridge that led to the city's beaches. Rumors spread the rioting in two directions: into Paradise Valley, the black neighborhood, where whites were targeted, and onto Woodward Avenue, where mobs of young whites attacked African Americans. When the police moved in force into Paradise Valley, the violence escalated. Federal troops finally suppressed the fighting at the end of the second day, but by then nine whites and twenty-five blacks lay dead.[56]

Detroit newspapers exploded in hysterical coverage, but newspapers away from that city handled this story very differently from the way they had responded to the 1919 Chicago riot. The Chicago tragedy had been described in

Detroit erupted in racial violence on 21 June 1943. Newspapers across the country carried photos like this, often showing whites attacking blacks on Woodward Avenue not far from the offices of the *Detroit News* and the *Detroit Free Press*. Influenced by sociological theory, journalism of the 1940s changed some of the images and understandings of the two migrations, de-emphasizing racial difference and focusing in both cases on the issue of urban maladjustment. (© Corbis)

lurid and gory detail in urban dailies across the country. For almost a week, banner headlines had screamed out the death toll while subheads and text fixated on images of rampaging blacks with guns. In 1943, most newspapers reported the Detroit riot without banner headlines and moved the story off the front page on the second day. The focus, format, and tone were very different. The image of black mobs was now much reduced, as were inflammatory descriptions of violence. The center of the story for those newspapers that carried either Associated Press or United Press International wire reports was the arrival of federal troops and the president's command that they suppress the rioting. Readers had to move well into the article (and, in the *Los Angeles Times*, jump to the second page) to begin to get a description of the fighting.[57]

The changing format of newspapers, especially the use of large-format photographs, also helped change the racial implications of the coverage. With few exceptions, the photos showed white mobs and white violence against blacks, even while accompanying articles usually tried to balance descriptions of black and white violence. In 1919, violence by blacks had been the major story. In 1943 coverage, blacks seem more often to be the victims of violence by whites.[58]

Notable too about the newspaper coverage of the Detroit riot was how quickly the focus shifted to diagnosing causes and how much of that diagnosis rested on popular extractions from sociological and psychological theory. In its first-day editorial, the *New York Times* blamed housing shortages, congested public facilities, and the absence of recreational opportunities for the 1943 outbreak. Twenty-four years earlier, the editors had blamed Bolsheviks. The *Los Angeles Times* had raved about "colored fanatics" and primitive lawlessness back in 1919. In 1943, the conservative newspaper worried about the role of Communists but also made room for extensive social diagnostics, offering up psychological terms like "war hysteria," "safety valve," and "inferiority complex" as it explored the causes and solutions to racial unrest.[59]

Migration itself loomed large in many of the explanations for the wartime violence as newspapers evoked images of pressure cookers or volatile mixtures to suggest that uncontrolled population movements were dangerous. And with some frequency, southern whites were brought into the equation. A number of newspapers aired the charge that southern whites, raised to believe in white supremacy and stirred up by the Ku Klux Klan, had caused the riot. Walter White, president of the NAACP, and R. J. Thomas, president of the United Auto Workers union, were among those calling for investigations into the Klan and other hate groups that "played upon the prejudices of the large southern white population which has moved into Detroit war jobs."[60]

Blaming both groups of southerners for the riot was another formula. The deeply conservative *Chicago Tribune* spent most of its energy blaming the Roosevelt administration for poor planning and for sending mixed messages to blacks about job and housing integration. And it indulged in a full search for agitators, airing charges that Japanese agents were at work in Detroit's black community as well as the counterclaim about Klan agitation among white southerners. The newspaper seemed to find value in that kind of symmetry. The key diagnostic article published on the second day of coverage ended with the assessment of a Detroit police official who blamed "the 'economic situation' as well as the influx of southern whites and Negroes as underlying causes of the riots."[61]

Maladjusted Migrants

The converging stories of white and black southerners formed part of the social environment of the second phase of the Southern Diaspora, generating images and expectations that would influence policy makers and that migrants would have to deal with on a personal level. Not just during World War II but over the next three decades, depictions of the two groups of migrants would often be linked, sometimes in ways that were not apparent on the surface but instead through the mutual concept of urban maladjustment. Both whites and blacks would be understood to be facing serious social, psychological, and economic challenges in the cities where they settled. Both would be pictured as needing professional social services to meet the challenges of uprooting and adjustment. And both at times would be seen as dangerous, so damaged by the combination of rural backwardness and urban challenge that they posed a threat to the communities where they settled. Developed in hundreds of formal sociological studies, this paradigm leaked into the literature, the journalism, the entertainment sectors, and the many realms of public policy, setting up a lasting and challenging framework of expectations about the two groups of southerners, a framework of low expectations.

There were varieties and differences in the maladjustment construction of the two groups. The popular figure of the white southerner tended to be tightly drawn and one-dimensional, while the black southerner became increasingly complicated in the second-phase era, especially as media focused more and more on issues of civil rights in the 1950s and 1960s. The figure of the white migrant carried very strong images of uprooting and the psychological burdens of urban adjustment. Many of the most popular representations pictured southern white families as innocents lost in the city. *The Dollmaker* by Harriette Arnow (1954) was the most widely read novel about the southern white migration to the North. It tells the story of Gertie and Clovis Nevels and their three children who leave their tiny farm in the Kentucky hills to seek a better livelihood in wartime Detroit. Clovis finds work in a defense plant and the family can make a living in the big city but cannot make the psychological and social adjustments that it requires. Gertie, whose interior perspectives center the novel and whose woodcarving skill gives the book its title and metaphorical subdrama, is a "marginal woman" caught hopelessly in the transition between two worlds. She tries to accommodate the impersonal, pecuniary values of the city, only to pay a terrible price, losing first her art and then her dearest child. In the end, she gathers the surviving members of the family, and they return to the Kentucky hollow they never should have left.[62]

A best-seller in 1954 and celebrated again when it was reissued in 1972, this sentimental but elegant novel helped extend and personalize the issues that sociologists had been working with. Here the adjustment issues are rendered as personal tragedy: the city strips not only culture but also dignity and even life from these proud but unprepared people. An unbridgeable distance separates farm and city or at least hill country and big city, and those who try to cross it will suffer and often fail.[63]

Similar images of whites cut off from home and unable to make the transition circulated in other media, including television and popular music. In the early 1960s, *The Beverly Hillbillies* became the most popular show on television, its central gag the rube-in-the-city formula. Stepping straight out of *Li'l Abner*, the Clampetts trade in their hillbilly hollow for a mansion in Beverly Hills after an oil company finds a gusher on their property. Hilariously out of place amidst the glitzy materialism of Beverly Hills, the naive Clampetts are not the biggest fools in this sitcom. Their naïveté instead exposes the shallowness and venality of those purported to be modern and urban. But the last laugh is not really theirs. Television audiences were still delighting in the image of the ignorant hillbilly lost in the modern city.[64]

Another medium was building even more persuasive images of maladjusted white migrants. Here is a verse from one of the best-selling songs of the early 1960s, "Detroit City," which Bobby Bare made into a crossover hit in 1963, played on both country and rock and roll stations:

Home folks think I'm big in Detroit City,
From the letters that I write they think I'm fine;
By day I make the cars and by night I make the bars,
If only they could read between the lines.[65]

The song is about homesickness, its narrator a migrant from the South who is lost in Detroit and dreaming, like Gertie Nevels, of "home." It is one of an endless number of country songs that worked with that theme. No reference is more central to country music than "home," and no song-induced emotion is more powerful than the nostalgic yearnings that are meant to attach to someplace left behind. Since the first recording of "Home, Sweet Home" in 1927, the medium has gone through generation after generation of songs that evoke homesickness and associate those feelings with green mountain homes and other rural, generally southern places.[66]

The wanderer is another of the genre's key references and part of its home-centered discursive play. Although the great varieties of country music wanderers (notably cowboys, hoboes, trainmen, truck drivers, and prisoners) are sometimes happy and fulfilled on the road, more often they are lost souls trying to sing their way back home. Cities are generally figured as anti-home in this country music cosmology. With their "bright lights" signifying false values and their honky-tonks breaking up families, they are places of alienation and distress. In Bill Anderson's "City Lights," another chart-topping favorite of the early 1960s, the city lures the lonely and only makes them more lost:

> The bright array of city lights as far as I can see,
> The Great White Way shines through the night for lonely guys like me.[67]

These song images line up so well with the sociological and journalistic constructions of white southerners that they have often been taken to be a form of proof for the southern white maladjustment thesis. Ethnographers listened to the lyrics and watched emotion-choked audiences in hillbilly taverns or country music concerts and built those descriptions into their arguments that southern whites longed for home and had a hard time making it in the cities of the North. But this notion that the music somehow conveys the unmediated values and longings of the migrants is probably wrong and may even reverse the actual relationships between music, sociological theory, and the southern white migrants.[68]

Why sociology and country music lyrics supported each other so closely is an issue that deserves more attention than is possible here. But one thing is clear: country music has never been a folk product of southern whites that operates in isolation from ideological influences derived from other parts of society. It has been a thoroughly commercialized medium since the late 1920s, heavily influenced by New York–based record companies and radio networks and by Hollywood films. As early as 1927, industry executives were designing hit songs, choosing themes, and hiring songwriters and musicians according to their calculations of what audiences would buy. This does not mean that country music had no relationship to core audiences and their values, but it does mean that we cannot treat country songs as transparent expressions of group values. The homesickness and adjustment issues expressed in "Detroit City" and countless other songs may indeed have spoken to the deep concerns of rural whites in transition, but they also helped inspire those concerns. Whether songwriters got their ideas from watching homesick people or because they had learned to think of southern whites as out-of-place in the city from reading journalism and popular literature, the fact is that here was another powerful instrument cementing into place the dominant representation of the white southerner in the North, helping to convince many Americans, including some of the migrants themselves, that big cities posed special adjustment problems for southern whites.[69]

The Dangerous Migrant

There was no shortage of similar representations of disoriented black migrants. The naive and needy black southerner appeared often in the fiction, journalism, and comedy that surrounded the second phase of the African American diaspora. The nation's most famous southern fools, Amos and Andy, carried their radio antics all the way through the 1940s and jumped to television in the early 1950s. And some of the most important novels of those two decades featured migrant characters, including Richard Wright's *Native Son* (1940), William Attaway's *Blood on the Forge* (1941), Ann Petry's *The Street* (1946), Ralph Ellison's *Invisible Man* (1947), Dorothy West's *The Living Is Easy* (1948), and James Baldwin's *Go Tell It on the Mountain* (1953). But in these works and in other venues, the figure of the black migrant does not congeal as tightly as that of the southern white migrant. Ellison's *Invisible Man*, to take one example, depends very much on migration sociology (for example, marginal man theory), but this southerner in Harlem is not simply lost in the metropolis and yearning for home. There is no home, not in the South and not in the North. And his torment derives not just from the transition from rural setting to urban; it is all about race.[70]

These novels also suggest how the media figure of the black migrant often veered from innocence into violence. The text that established this trend was a work of fictionalized sociology by Richard Wright. His novel *Native Son* was a breakthrough on many fronts. The first massive best-seller by an African American author, it was chosen by the Book of the Month Club and then was the subject of a six-page photo spread in *Look* magazine, circulation 2 million. A long-running play and a mediocre movie added to the impact. But the real test of the book's influence was the way its characterizations and issues echoed through public discourse. Bigger Thomas, like Gatsby, Babbitt, and Tom Joad, became one of those references that millions of people who had not read the book understood, part of the social vocabulary of large numbers of Americans.

Bigger Thomas was another marginal man. Richard Wright was trying to write a novel that used the insights of the University of Chicago sociologists whom he had come to know quite well, particularly Horace Cayton Jr., protégé of Robert Park. But unlike Gertie Nevels, Bigger is not simply an innocent destroyed by the city. He is also a destroyer, a murderer, a nightmare. Bigger is the epitome of what social scientists called the damaged Negro. The story reveals that he has grown up in Mississippi and learned there lessons of race and mechanisms of survival that distort personality and deprive blacks of the avenues of self-realization that American culture promises. Moving to Chicago,

Bigger's damaged self is twisted further by an unfamiliar urban environment that tortures him with dangerous temptations and then lures him into murder. Fear and confusion make this migrant a monster as well as a victim, as he accidentally murders a white woman and then casually strangles a black one. The self-awareness that comes to him during his trial for murder and while awaiting execution is the awareness that Wright dared white Americans to contemplate: that the only freedom for such victims came through rage, through violence, through murder. Wright wanted white America to worry about these native sons.[71]

White migrants could also be pictured as damaged and dangerous. The theory of social pathology that grounded representations of the damaged Negro had as much to do initially with the marginality of rural-urban migration as it did with race. A flurry of reportage that broke out in 1957 provides an example of the damaged white story. It started when the Chicago Commission on Human Relations decided to find out whether southern whites in the city were depending upon welfare and contributing to social problems in ways comparable to African Americans. The report, typical of many such assessments, said yes. The *Chicago Tribune* then picked up the scent and ran a high-profile series of eight articles that described the "Southern hillbilly migrants" in terms that readers would readily connect with African Americans. The "hillbillies" were described as a degenerate population "with the lowest standard of living and moral code (if any) . . . and the most savage tactics when drunk, which is most of the time." National publicity followed, with stories in *Time*, *Look*, and *Harper's*, the latter under the headline "The Hillbillies Invade Chicago." That article's subhead gave away the racial slippage: "The city's toughest integration problem has nothing to do with Negroes. . . . It involves a small army of white Protestant, Early American migrants from the South—who are usually proud, poor, primitive, and fast with a knife." The message was clear and intentional: these people are "worse than the colored."[72]

This 1957 series was unusually mean-spirited, which probably had much to do with the renewed focus on the bigotry of whites in the South in the wake of the Brown decision, the Montgomery boycott, and the rising tide of white resistance to the civil rights movement. Albert Votaw, author of the *Harper's* article, clearly tried to disrupt racial prejudices, stressing at one point that "these country cousins confound all notions of racial, religious, and cultural purity" and later that "this immigrant is hated because he proves our prejudices wrong." In its reuse of the Negro Invasion theme and its appropriation of images of violence, dangerous sexuality, and urban blight that came directly from the literature of white fear of urban blacks, this article was more overt than most.[73]

The more common representation of the dangerous white migrant turned on the reputation for racism. As seen in the coverage surrounding the 1943 Detroit riot, southern white migrants were readily suspected of fomenting hatred and violence against African Americans. That association grew stronger as civil rights struggles attracted more and more attention. Throughout the postwar period, southern whites at home and southern whites up North were pictured as the worst of bigots and the foremost enemy of civil rights. Racial liberals kept up a drumbeat of charges about the white migrant's impact on race relations. Both in California, where Okies became the chief suspect behind every flare-up of the Ku Klux Klan, and in the Midwest, where hillbillies were blamed for everything from the Black Legion of the late 1930s to the backlash campaigns of the 1960s, the white migrants provided a large and useful target. The white migrant as bigot became one of the defining stories of the wartime and postwar news media and as such served as something of an equivalent or mirror opposite to the threatening figure of Bigger Thomas or, later, the Black Militant.[74]

The equivalence goes only so far. The dangerous southern white never loomed as large in media productions or the public consciousness as did the dangerous black. Nor did many of the other images and stories line up. Whereas mid-twentieth-century cultural production was saturated in discussions of African American "problems" and "pathologies," the white southern migrant was too minor a figure to warrant similar concern.

Moreover, the two figures veered apart on the issue of "southernness." Southern origins had always been a secondary marker for black migrants. When white Americans think of "southerners," they generally mean white southerners. As Horace Mann Bond once put it, "The white is the Southerner, the Negro—well, a Negro." But as the postwar era progressed, media attentions to southern origins and their valuations slid farther apart. The figure of the black migrant faded from view while the white migrant, especially the Appalachian white, gained clarity. It is a subtle point but useful in thinking about how these media constructions affected lives and identities. The civil rights era transformed media representations of regions, especially for African Americans. As journalists covered the campaigns for basic rights in the South, the image of the ignorant and ill-equipped black southerner gave way to something much more positive. The reversal became very clear in 1964. Twenty-four years after Bigger Thomas appeared in print, thirteen years after Ralph Ellison's rural southerners were committing incest (a trope also for southern white imagery), the nation met their updated version in the person of Fannie Lou Hamer, the former sharecropper who led the Mississippi Freedom Democratic Party delegation in the televised fight for recognition at the Democratic Party convention. Gone was the notion of rural pathology. This televised sharecropper was a symbol of resistance, hope, and determination.[75]

Noticing and Naming

The two southern migrations were framed by the evolving media institutions and evolving social consciousness of twentieth-century America. In the early phases, only one migration was of interest. African Americans moved north under intense public scrutiny, accompanied by newspaper coverage that heightened the significance of their move and affected social interactions. The community-building strategies and political and cultural initiatives that we will explore in future chapters gained impetus from this cycle of media stories. Meanwhile, their white migrant counterparts remained all but invisible. Although vastly outnumbering black migrants, white southerners were simply another set of Moving Americans finding their way anonymously in the thriving northern and western economies of the early part of the century.

The second period—mid-1930s through the 1960s—was dramatically different for whites, who now had to account for themselves amidst hillbilly and Okie imagery that was new and demeaning. Moreover, the institutions of culture now drew the two sets of migrants together in certain ways. In an age much given to sociological instincts and obsessed with the notion that rural and urban were psychological and social opposites, the press and other media pictured both sets of southerners as people who would play out a tense drama of maladjustment in the big cities. It was a unique story that belonged to a unique time. In no other era did the issue of internal migration and the notions of the "migrant" and "maladjustment" loom so large. In no other period were black and white moving southerners so likely to be linked.

The new round of stories would, as we will see in the chapters ahead, set up some similar personal challenges for African American and white southerners as they grappled with the image of maladjustment in workplaces and some other settings. But mostly the media paradigms carried different implications for the two diaspora populations. African American communities would gain some political opportunities as the Negro Invasion story broadened into the Defense Migration story and as the publicity about troublesome southern whites moderated, at least slightly, the hysteria about black newcomers. For diaspora whites, the new stories were more uniformly difficult. The haunting figures of the hillbilly and the Okie would have much to do with the complicated patterns of community formation and identity transformations that we will be examining.

The media systems of the mid-twentieth century taught Americans, including many of the southerners themselves, to see the participants in the diaspora in particular ways. Seen as backward, both black and white southerners were set up to be underachievers who would be lucky to make it in their new homes. Seen as needy, it was easier to understand their relocations in terms of burdens rather than contributions. Seen as outsiders, they appeared to be marked by cultural differences and social problem complexes. Most important was the sheer volume of all that "seeing." Constantly a public issue, the two groups of southerners would experience challenges that set them apart from other inter-state movers. Seen as "migrants," they were never allowed to be merely Moving Americans.

Success and Failure

"In the beginning we were all in one room, the children and my wife and me; and Cincinnati is a hot, sticky city in the summer." So begins a typical narrative of one family's attempt to make it in the North. Cincinnati was just the first stop. "I kept hearing that we'd have a better chance to find work in Chicago. Well, I heard right and I heard wrong. . . . It's true there are plenty of temporary jobs here, but none that I can keep and hold onto. I get up at four in the morning and I go and try to find something. . . . It's not good. The factories take people who've got friends and relatives, and now it's slow for the factories anyway; they're laying off, a lot of them, not hiring." The story moves on in the same familiar key, detailing a struggle to find and keep jobs, describing help received from churches and charities, miserable lodgings in broken-down buildings ("the halls are as bad as can be—pitch-black, and holes in the stairs. My boy tripped and fell and his arm was broken"), children growing up on the streets as parents lose control, the father spending too much time and money at the local bar—a rough beginning for what was supposed to be a new life.

This narrative is an example of the urban maladjustment story that is the most common representation of the Southern Diaspora. It could have come from any of a hundred books and articles that have been written about southern migrants over the course of the twentieth century. It could be about a black family or a white one. It could refer to almost any time period from 1916 to the early 1970s and any city of the North or West. It could be a work of fiction, like William Attaway's *Blood on the Forge* or Harriette Arnow's *The Dollmaker*, or a work of journalism, sociology, anthropology, or history. It happens to be a case study from psychiatrist Robert Coles's *The South Goes North* (1972), a volume of oral narratives by black and white migrants, this one belonging to a white family who moved north from Kentucky in the 1960s.[1]

No image is more familiar than that of the migrant family, white or black, facing the kinds of difficulties that this father describes. Southerners of both races have been seen as disadvantaged newcomers and chronic underachievers in the economies of the metropolitan North and West. But is that true? Now that we have explored the development of such imagery in the media institutions of the mid-twentieth century, it is time to reconsider these most basic understandings of the diaspora. Much of the imagery associated with the two groups of migrants turns out to be misleading. The notions that southerners were ill-equipped for the transitions ahead, that they faced huge challenges because of their social and cultural background, and that they would struggle with high rates of poverty and disappointment for years to come are in various ways incorrect.

This chapter examines issues of opportunity and accomplishment and breaks decisively with the urban maladjustment paradigm that has long structured understandings of the two southern migrations. It does so using some new tools. Until recently, it was difficult to obtain reliable data on the economic experiences of migrants. Much of what has been written about the black diaspora has relied on published census reports that cannot distinguish between southern migrants and northern-born African Americans. Those concerned with white southern experience have been even more hampered by data problems. Forced to rely on small samples and ethnographies of certain highly visible and mostly poor communities, scholars have seriously misinterpreted key features of the white migrant experience. The IPUMS census samples provide a way around these problems, allowing us to distinguish the southern-born and examine experiences in different locales and settings over the course of the twentieth century. Tables will be found in Appendix A. Appendix B has information on the source and its reliability. The chapter will first discuss white migrant economic experiences, then look at the experiences of black migrants.[2]

Beyond the Joads

The idea that white southern migrants suffered high rates of poverty and difficulty is so ingrained that it needs to be confronted head-on. In recent years, new rounds of journalism, sociology, and history have portrayed the whites as disadvantaged, sometimes arguing that along with black southerners they have been the chief victims of structured patterns of poverty in the urban North. That portrait is inaccurate. Only in exceptional cases have southern whites found

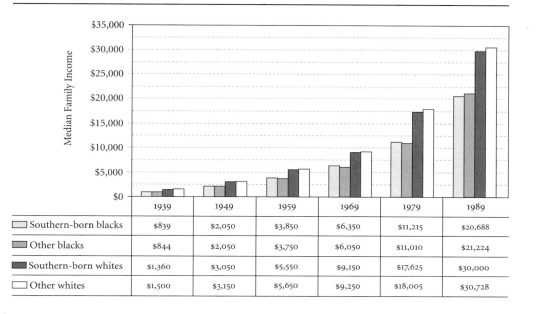

	1939	1949	1959	1969	1979	1989
Southern-born blacks	$839	$2,050	$3,850	$6,350	$11,215	$20,688
Other blacks	$844	$2,050	$3,750	$6,050	$11,010	$21,224
Southern-born whites	$1,360	$3,050	$5,550	$9,150	$17,625	$30,000
Other whites	$1,500	$3,150	$5,650	$9,250	$18,005	$30,728

FIGURE 3.1. Comparing Family Incomes of Southerners Living in North and West, 1939–1989

Source: Steven Ruggles, Matthew Sobek, Trent Alexander, Catherine A. Fitch, Ronald Goeken, Patricia Kelly Hall, Miriam King, and Chad Ronnander, *Integrated Public Use Microdata Series: Version 3.0* (machine-readable database) (Minneapolis, 2004).

themselves in lasting economic difficulty. The data are quite clear: throughout the twentieth century, white migrants from the South have mostly done well in the economies of the North and West.[3]

Census takers have collected information on family incomes since 1940, asking respondents about the previous year's earnings. Figure 3.1 and table A.4 compare median family incomes across half a century. In the aggregate, southern whites achieved incomes that are close to those of other white families in the areas where they settled. The median income for southern-born white families living in the North and West in 1939 was $1,360, which was 91 percent of the $1,500 median income of other white families. In subsequent decades, the income difference became even smaller. Only 2 or 3 percentage points separate southern-white and other-white medians in 1949, 1959, 1969, 1979, and 1989. Note also that the incomes of southern-white families were far above those earned by southern-born and northern-born African Americans.[4]

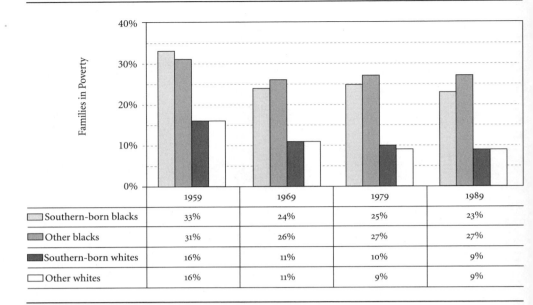

	1959	1969	1979	1989
Southern-born blacks	33%	24%	25%	23%
Other blacks	31%	26%	27%	27%
Southern-born whites	16%	11%	10%	9%
Other whites	16%	11%	9%	9%

FIGURE 3.2. Poverty Rates of Southerners and Nonsoutherners Living in North and West, 1959–1989

Source: Steven Ruggles, Matthew Sobek, Trent Alexander, Catherine A. Fitch, Ronald Goeken, Patricia Kelly Hall, Miriam King, and Chad Ronnander, *Integrated Public Use Microdata Series: Version 3.0* (machine-readable database) (Minneapolis, 2004).

The federal government began designating a "poverty line" in the 1960s, setting income thresholds deemed adequate for a very modest standard of living. Figure 3.2 traces poverty rates from 1959 to 1989, showing again that southern-born whites closely paralleled the broader population of whites in the North and West. Only 16 percent of southern whites fell into the poverty category in 1959, exactly the same as other whites. By 1969, all but 11 percent of white migrants earned more than poverty incomes, again in line with the rest of the white population. In comparison, 24 percent of southern black migrant families reported poverty-level incomes that year.

How could the journalists and sociologists have been so wrong in their assessments of southern white experiences? Largely it was a matter of geographic confusion. Those who studied the white migration mostly focused on some particular locations where indeed there was evidence of economic difficulty. One of the much noticed geographies of poverty was the San Joaquin Valley of California, the setting for John Steinbeck's *The Grapes of Wrath* (1939). In 1940, a majority of southern white males living in that part of California earned their livings as farm workers or other unskilled laborers, and median family income was only 55 percent of what other white families earned. By 1950, both the job profile and income levels were improving, but large aggregations of poverty remained. With 38 percent of southern whites living below what today's statisticians would define as the poverty line, the association between "Okies" and hard living in that region would remain strong. This would be true as well in some other parts of the rural West. Cotton-growing areas in Arizona had also attracted large numbers of white southerners, as had other crop regions in northern California, eastern Washington, and southern Colorado. Timber had also been something of a migration magnet, attracting workers from the pine forests of Arkansas and Louisiana to the lumber towns of northern California, Oregon, and Washington. And often in these areas, opportunities proved limited. If they lacked specialized skills or capital to buy land, newcomers in some parts of the rural West might spend years or decades in or near poverty.[5]

In the Midwest, scholars focused their attention on the older neighborhoods in the big cities, where again they found pockets of poverty. Uptown in Chicago, Lower Price Hill in Cincinnati, part of the Cass Corridor in Detroit, and a dozen other big city neighborhoods became known as "hillbilly ghettos," decaying urban enclaves where southern whites appeared to congregate amidst crime, poverty, and high rates of welfare dependency. But the observers had the geography wrong. Most white southerners were not settling in inner cities, and the poor people living in them were not typical of the white migration.[6]

Scholars should have been combing the suburbs instead of dense urban neighborhoods. As early as the 1930s, there were indications that southern whites in Detroit and Los Angeles were avoiding inner-city and low-rent neighborhoods and looking for housing on the urban fringe. Later, as the postwar housing boom created massive new suburbs, southern whites were even more inclined to spread out, proving to be among the most eager suburbanites of that suburban age. Table A.6 provides a clearer sense of those settlement patterns for the Great Lakes region and the Pacific states, showing why it is wrong to concentrate on so-called hillbilly ghettos. In 1960 in Ohio, Indiana, Illinois, Michigan, and Wisconsin, only 13 percent of southern-born whites lived in multifamily housing in one of the region's core cities, the kind of setting that was standard for southern-born blacks. Another 24 percent of the whites lived in a city but in single-family houses or duplexes. Meanwhile, 35 percent lived in the suburbs, and 29 percent lived in small-town and rural areas.[7]

By 1970, the suburbanization trend had become stronger. A mere 9 percent of southern white families now lived in dense urban settings, while 47 percent lived in the suburbs. In California and the other Pacific Coast states, the suburban settlement rate was even higher: 50 percent of southern whites in 1960 lived in a West Coast suburb; 56 percent in 1970. Clearly the notion that the white migrants were prisoners of the city, doomed to experience the difficult urban transitions associated with earlier immigrant groups, was wrong. Many did their adjusting while spending little or no time in the actual city, let alone poor neighborhoods like Uptown and Lower Price Hill. The 1970 IPUMS identifies recent migrants, southerners who had moved north within the previous five years. Of those, 50 percent had found residence in the suburbs, and only 12 percent lived in multifamily urban housing. Places like Uptown were seeing only the most unfortunate of the newcomers. Most of the migrants had more attractive options (table A.6).

Blue-Collar Odyssey

Options may also be the operative word when considering the experiences of southern whites in the labor markets of the regions where they settled. Unlike the starving Joads or the unfortunate Kentuckians who led off this chapter, most southern white migrants seemed to negotiate the challenges of finding work and building secure livelihoods in reasonably short order. As already noted, median family incomes of white migrants were close to the norm for all whites from 1939 on. Tables A.7, A.8, A.9, and A.10 provide a closer look at job and income profiles during the first and second phases of the diaspora.

The census of 1920 caught the first-phase migrants as they were getting established and shows why at that stage no one thought of the southern white migration as a social problem. The occupational distributions of former migrants closely track the distributions of other whites. Notable in that 1920 profile were the large number of white-collar and skilled jobs and the small number of unskilled laboring positions held by white migrants. Among southern-born males, 25 percent had found white-collar jobs and 20 percent worked as foremen, craftsmen, or other skilled positions; only 22 percent held unskilled laboring or service jobs. No wonder the migration remained invisible. Most white southern newcomers in that first phase of the diaspora were anything but poor and disadvantaged (table A.7).

The 1950 census captured the changes that came with the second phase. The war-era exodus drew large numbers of southerners of modest means and backgrounds, and the profile in table A.8 shows the effects. Now the migrant group claimed fewer white-collar jobs compared to the rest of the white population (28 percent versus 35 percent among males; 50 percent versus 60 percent among employed females). But they compensated with large numbers of skilled and semiskilled blue-collar jobs: 23 percent of southern-born males held craftsmen

Henry Ford's massive Willow Run B-24 bomber plant at Ypsilanti, Michigan, hired thousands of southern migrants during World War II, mostly whites. Ford had taken the lead in hiring black workers in the 1910s and 1920s but changed course in the early 1940s after black workers joined the United Auto Workers union. (Walter P. Reuther Library, Wayne State University)

and foremen positions; another 25 percent were semiskilled factory operatives and transportation workers. Even at this early point in the second phase, with its vast numbers of supposedly unprepared rural-origin migrants, only 19 percent of males worked as unskilled laborers or in service jobs. With a median family income of $3,050, southern whites were within $100 of the median for other American-born white families, despite their reduced representation among professional, sales, and clerical workers (table A.4). Overwhelmingly blue-collar, southern whites had mostly found the kind of jobs that provided a solid and secure income.[8]

By 1970, the second wave had crested, and many of the white southerners who had moved north or west were in their prime earning years, helped by the superheated Vietnam-era economy. White-collar employment had increased since 1950, but compared to other segments of the white population, former southerners were still concentrated in blue-collar jobs, largely toward the high end. In the Great Lakes states, 25 percent of southern-born white males held white-collar jobs while 59 percent did skilled or semiskilled blue-collar work, compared with 37 percent and 44 percent for other U.S.-born white males (table A.10). Female employment patterns were skewed in similar directions. Southern-born white women entered the labor force at much the same rates as other white women and like them mostly found jobs as clerical or sales workers. But the southerners were somewhat underrepresented in the pink-collar/white-collar sector and somewhat overrepresented in factory and waitress jobs. Still, there was little difference in earning power. Despite the disposition toward blue-collar work, southern-born women and southern-born men earned incomes comparable to other whites. That is why overall family income for the southerners was very close to white norms. The median family income of $9,450 earned by southern whites in the Great Lakes states was just $200 less than the median for other U.S.-born whites in the region. More important, it was almost twice as large in inflation-adjusted dollars as the median of 1950.

Did it matter what part of the South the migrants had come from? Were Appalachians, who in the second phase received so much attention, also doing well? Table A.11 shows that there were some variations in income and occupation patterns based on state origins, with migrants from West Virginia, Kentucky, and Tennessee claiming median incomes that were somewhat lower and poverty rates that were somewhat higher than other white southerners. White migrants from those states who were living in the Great Lakes region earned a median income of $9,050 in 1969 (compared with $10,050 for other southerners) and counted 12 percent of their number below the poverty line (compared to 9 percent of families headed by other southern-born whites). This modest difference apparently grows larger if we focus on migrants from the upland counties of those states. J. Trent Alexander has distinguished county origins in the 1940 and 1980 IPUMS and reports that people from Appalachian counties contended with measurably higher rates of poverty in their first five years in the North than did other southern newcomers.[9]

For the most part, then, these data turn around the usual story of the southern white migration. Apart from some high-profile episodes, this was no tragedy. Southern whites in the aggregate did quite well. None of the migrants' supposed disadvantages seem to have mattered very much. Low skill levels, low educational attainments, rural backgrounds, southern accents, complicated family commitments — none of these factors hurt economic prospects the way the adjustment theorists predicted.

We can demonstrate that by focusing on the economic performance of those southerners who would appear to be the most disadvantaged: those with eight or fewer years of schooling, a selection that includes many of those raised on farms. These poorly educated migrants consistently fell behind others in occupational standing and income measures, but taken on their own terms, most did quite well (table A.12). In the Great Lakes states, the median personal income in 1969 for southern-born white males in their prime working years (age twenty-five to fifty-four) who had never gone past the eighth grade was $8,050. This was about 20 percent less than the median income of other U.S.-born whites in that age group who had been to high school or college. Family incomes lagged by a similar factor, which seems modest in relation to the way educational disadvantages have worked in other times and places. The bottom line is that even these grammar school–educated white migrants were for the most part earning stable and respectable incomes. What is more, 66 percent of the poorly educated segment were homeowners.

Productive Stereotypes

How did southern whites negotiate these outcomes? Why wasn't education and regional background more of an issue? The simple answer is that they were white. The mid-twentieth-century industrial economy was very kind to white families, or at least those headed by a working-age male. White migrants from other regions also did well (table A.12). Men who had migrated to the Great Lakes states from the northern plains states of Nebraska, Kansas, Iowa, Minnesota, and the Dakotas earned higher average incomes than their southern white counterparts. I have added the sons of Italian and eastern European immigrants for a further comparison. There was little that was special about the economic accomplishments of the white people who left the South.

The key to most of these examples was an economy still hungry for blue-collar workers and a political-social system that in the postwar era pushed up the wages of many of the lower skilled job categories, especially those reserved for white males. The "long New Deal," roughly the 1930s through the 1960s, was the golden age for unionization and blue-collar wages. At no other point in American history were the opportunities so great for a white male of modest education and modest work skills. Entry jobs were plentiful, and income differentials had never been lower. The impoverished factory workers of the turn of the century had become the lower-middle-income factory workers of midcentury.[10]

That is the main story to tell about the economic experiences of second-phase white southern migrants: they were part of a lucky generation experiencing the last and greatest expansion of blue-collar opportunities. Deindustrialization was beginning to affect some settings even as this second phase of the southern exodus hit the North, but not the settings that mattered to the white migrants. They got into the factories and into trades and better service jobs before the doors closed. They were among the last to do so.[11]

Still, there are some particular features of the southern white experience that need to be illuminated. In fact, they were not "just whites" (who is?). Media stories had made the second-phase migrants visible and controversial, helping ensure that opportunities fell into certain patterns. Southern whites were now perceived to be a social group. There were opportunities as well as obstacles in that formulation.

Most migrants were keenly aware of the stories and stereotypes that pictured them as a different sort of white American. They heard the references to "dumb Okies" and "ignorant hillbillies" and knew that southerners were looked down upon by many. They knew too that it affected job opportunities and potential social interactions. Years later, some recalled instances of prejudice and discrimination, remembering landlords who refused to rent to them or employers who sent them away without a job. And there is no question that such things happened. Sociologist Lewis Killian spoke with managers of fourteen Chicago factories in 1947 for a study of southern whites living on that city's Near West Side and heard all sorts of derogatory comments. Most managers described the southerners as lazy, unreliable, and ignorant. Many said that "hillbillies" would not stick with a job but were always taking off to drive back to the old homestead for a visit. Another set of comments pictured southern whites as too independent and stubborn to be good workers, with some managers adding that they were also disruptive and quick to fight with fellow workers.[12] These images, all derived from the voluminous 1930s and 1940s literature on hillbillies and Okies, hurt employment chances. But how much? Killian, noting that his study was made during a period of low unemployment, found that southern whites were finding jobs despite the stereotypes and that even the employers who held strongly negative opinions hired them, although they preferred other white workers. Elmer Akers had studied employment patterns ten years earlier in Detroit when labor markets were less favorable, but his assessment was similar. Despite all sorts of derogatory comments about southerners and preference for "Michigan fellows," the newcomers were getting jobs, although sometimes the route into the preferred auto industry was complicated.[13]

Other studies add to the impression that stereotypes were a modest rather than powerful barrier to job access. Some employers learned to discount southern white labor, finding that newcomers could be hired at lower wages than resident workers. Geographer John Thompson looked at employment in the Ohio cities of Hamilton and Middletown in the early 1950s and, like Killian and Akers, found that southern whites were readily hired in lower-wage factories where employers learned to think of them as cheap and plentiful workers. The dual labor market, however, was porous and temporary. With some experience, the southerners could move into the higher-wage factories. In addition, one of the derogatory stereotypes at times worked in favor of the white migrant. The idea that southerners were tied together in a vast kinship system came to be attractive to certain employers who decided that this provided access to a reliable pool of reserve workers. "By exploiting kinship," historian Chad Berry explains, "some companies stabilized personnel and kept waves of cheap labor coming."[14]

Another set of stereotypes may have had a still more productive effect on opportunities. Union leaders in many industries harbored the impression that southern whites were hard to organize and potentially hostile to unions. The stereotype, which would be true in some cases, false in others, derived from the ever-popular stories of fiercely independent mountaineers fighting over moonshine and psychologically ill-equipped for any form of cooperation. A federal official in California blithely let that stereotype extend to newcomers from Oklahoma (a state that had had a strong Socialist Party) as he explained why they would never be good union material. "These are men who got a shotgun and guarded a stalk of cotton that was hanging over the fence so that the farmer on the other side of the fence wouldn't pick it. . . . They are the greatest individuals on earth."[15]

The anti-union image became a factor in shaping job opportunities, mostly, it seems, to the benefit of the southerners. It is hard to find examples of migrants blocked from working because of the union worries, although it may have happened in the rare situations where unions exercised job control, such as in the printing, brewing, and sometimes the construction trades. In the late 1930s, the Building Trades Council in Kern County, California, issued a warning about the Okies pouring into that area and may have tried for a time to keep the newcomers from doing construction work. If so, it does not seem to have worked. Construction became a favored option for a significant number of southerners, some of whom had been formally trained, others just handy with tools. By 1940, white southerners were making an impact in the California construction trades and, ten years later, in 1950, controlled about 10 percent of the state's construction jobs. By 1970, the total was up to 14 percent with 61,000 former migrants earning their living in California's building industry. Similar patterns were evident in the Great Lakes region. Almost 70,000 white southerners were working construction in Ohio, Indiana, Illinois, Michigan, and Wisconsin in 1970, where they were roughly 10 percent of all workers (table A.13).[16]

Instead of hurting job prospects, the anti-union stereotype had a beneficial effect in many settings, at least in terms of job access. Eager to undercut unions, some employers gave preference to the allegedly anti-union migrants. Managers interviewed in several studies freely acknowledged the strategy. In southern Ohio, firms like Procter and Gamble, Armco Steel, and National Cash Register eagerly recruited Kentuckians, hoping to avoid the collective bargaining that was becoming standard in that area. An Armco official told an investigator in the early 1950s that it was these recruiting practices that had kept his firm competitive.[17]

Something similar was going on in the auto industry. Henry Ford liked to hire farm boys, thinking they were good with their hands and would stay away from unions. Southern whites (and southern blacks) owed their initial enclave at Ford Motor Company to that particular prejudice. And while job access for blacks at that company was highly variable, southern whites seem to have had steady access to jobs at Ford and many other auto firms, and most noticeably as union campaigns picked up in the late 1930s. Leaders of the United Auto Workers union accused both Ford and GM of stocking up on southerners in the face of their organizing drives, and quite a few now-retired auto workers are sure that the stereotype got them their first jobs. Max Green thinks the notion was still in play long after the union had won its organizational battles. The young Georgian arrived in Detroit in 1948 and had no trouble landing jobs first with the Dodge Company, then with Chrysler. "They liked us hillbillies because most of us would work . . . and didn't give them a lot of trouble compared to the native Detroit people."[18]

The stereotype that pictured southern whites as ferocious racists had less predictable consequences. In those firms that did open their doors to African Americans, the desire to avoid racial tensions might have led to discrimination against southern whites, and there are a few stories to that effect. But there are more stories of companies hiring southern whites in order to avoid dealing with blacks. Killian found a couple of Chicago firms that tried to avoid pressure from the Fair Employment Practices Commission (FEPC) by building a hiring network of southern whites. Any open job was instantly advertised in the "grapevine" so that it would be filled before a black worker could apply.[19]

These examples of stereotypes helping rather than hurting employment chances begin to reveal some of the fortuitous conditions that southern whites encountered in the job markets of northern and western metropolitan zones. They benefited not only from labor market conditions that were, with the exception of the 1930s, very positive for almost all white males but also from the particular patterns of class and racial reconfiguration underway in the regions where they settled. Two titanic struggles rippled across the metropolitan labor markets of the North and West during the era of the Southern Diaspora, one determining the role of unions, the other the place of African Americans. Southern whites benefited from both struggles. Hired sometimes as part of a strategy to block unions, they gained a double advantage when the unions won their struggles and raised wages in those industries. Hired in preference to black workers, whose skills and background were often remarkably similar, southern whites profited along with other whites from the deep structures of racism in the labor markets of those regions.[20]

Employment Niches

These prejudices/preferences were among the factors helping southern whites build employment networks in some of the key industries and highest-paying blue-collar job sectors in the regions where they settled. Employment assistance is a central feature of any mass migration. The sharing of information among relatives, friends, and neighbors and the building up of access to jobs in particular firms or industries are a big part of what encourages people to move and helps them choose destinations. Some ethnic groups have been heavily dependent on network hiring to overcome difficulties they face in an open labor market. That was not generally the case for southern whites. Because they were white, because they spoke English, and because, with the exception of the 1930s, they had chosen full employment decades in which to be moving and looking for work, white southerners on the whole had less need to depend upon kin and friendship networks than many of the earlier groups that had entered the industrial economy. Still, the easiest way to get almost any kind of blue-collar work is through personal connections, and over the decades these spread out in a somewhat distinctive pattern.[21]

Key spaces and key industries became opportunity zones for southern whites. Out west, as already mentioned, agricultural work of certain kinds, the timber industry, and construction became enclaves of southern white employment, in each case because many southerners were familiar with the work. Oil drilling and refining was another one. With workers circulating between Oklahoma and Texas oil fields and the rigs and refineries near Los Angeles and in the San Joaquin Valley, the oil industry became something of an Okie enterprise. In 1970, 19 percent of all oil workers in California claimed southern births, and some of the rest had parents from the South (table A.13).[22]

Other employment niches had nothing to do with familiar skills. Instead, they developed over time through some combination of employer preferences and group self-recruiting. It is hard to say why the aircraft industry became an important source of jobs for white southerners. On the West Coast, it may have had something to do with racial preferencing during World War II. Aircraft manufacturers and the most powerful union in the industry, the International Association of Machinists, conspired to keep African Americans out of the Los Angeles and Seattle aircraft plants despite labor shortages and orders from the FEPC. White workers from the South faced no such obstacles, and the networks they established during the 1940s seem to have lasted through the Cold War. In 1970, more than 40,000 southern whites were working in the West Coast aerospace plants. In California, they controlled 11 percent of jobs in that critical industry (table A.13).[23]

The southernization of the tire plants in Ohio and Indiana started much earlier. In 1920, more than 14,000 southern whites claimed jobs in the Akron-centered industry that made the tires for the new automobile age. Employment would peak near 23,000 jobs in 1960, by which time southern-born whites were close to 20 percent of that industry's workforce. If we could identify the northern-born sons and daughters of the migrants, the southern share of that industry's workforce might approach 40 percent (tables A.13, A.14).[24]

White Southerners were also well placed within the two premier industries of the Great Lakes region. They started showing up in automobile plants in the teens and by 1920 claimed about 12,000 jobs in that fast-growing industry. Over the next generation, the enclave grew. In 1950, there were almost 75,000 southern white auto workers. The number climbed to 86,000 in 1960 and 101,000 in 1970. This made them one of the largest recognizable subgroups in the industry, controlling 10 percent of all jobs in both the male and female sectors of the workforce. If we could count their northern-born offspring, southern whites would have outnumbered the 157,000 African Americans in the midwestern auto plants. As it was, the white migrants were more numerous than the first- and second-generation eastern Europeans, whose ethnicity is often evoked when the general public imagines the auto industry. The auto industry in turn was a major source of the jobs that white southerners counted on, particularly in Michigan, where one in four employed southern white males worked in auto assembly or auto parts (table A.14).

Steel was an even more important source of jobs, employing just over 100,000 male and female white southerners in the Great Lakes states in 1970 and another 35,000 in Pennsylvania and California (and untold numbers of their children). The Pittsburgh mills saw their share of southern whites, but the strongholds were the furnaces of south Chicago, Gary, Indiana, and Youngstown, Ohio, and even more the fabrication plants that were spread throughout Ohio. One in seven workers in Ohio's steel industry was a white of southern birth in 1970 (table A.14).[25]

These key industries offered not just jobs but secure and high-paying jobs, thanks to the accomplishments of CIO unions during the long New Deal. There was something very lucky about the way the white diaspora interacted with the history of unionization and labor relations in the North. Building initial enclaves during an era when management hoped they would undercut unions, southern whites gained additional advantages after the CIO organized these industries in the 1930s and 1940s and drove up wages. Defying expectations, some southern whites participated eagerly in the labor movement. Others did not but benefited anyway when the plants unionized. Either way, the timing was perfect. Jobs in these industries became steadily more lucrative through the decades. The median income earned in 1939 by a southern-born white male auto worker was $1,400. Ten years later, that median income had risen to $3,150, and twenty years after that to $9,050. Inflation took some of the increase, but even so the wage had almost tripled in constant dollars in those three decades. That was quite a boost. It elevated workers in this and many other industries far above poverty. By the 1950s, many southern white blue-collar workers were buying homes. By the 1960s, wages like that were sending kids to college. Workers in these industries had been lucky. They were now part of what contemporaries liked to call the lower-middle class (table A.14).

This was the basic secret. If the economic story of the southern white diaspora can be synthesized, it would center on families of modest education who through one means or another—a productive prejudice, a friendship network, dogged persistence, or a lucky break—found jobs in the unionized sectors of the blue-collar economy in the industries that saw major improvements in wages, benefits, and job security systems during the postwar era, not just auto, steel, and rubber but dozens of industries where unions became strong in the northern and western metropolitan zones. This does not cover everyone. It leaves out the many southern migrants who joined the white-collar and professional class and also the smaller segment of troubled families who struggled with poverty. But the easiest way to understand the main trend of the white diaspora is to recognize it as a working-class success story, a blue-collar odyssey that delivered on many of the hopes for a good job and an improved standard of living that had led people to leave their homes.

Wages of Blackness

This portrait of southern whites moving through a welcoming mid-twentieth-century economy suggests what African American migrants might also have experienced had opportunities not been so heavily racialized. Black and white southern migrants shared most of the important skill determinants of occupational positioning: similar if not identical educational and rural backgrounds and similar times of entry into the metropolitan labor force. But none of that mattered as much as skin color. We can almost put a dollar figure on that skin-color effect. Figure 3.3 tracks individual incomes for working-age male and female wage earners of southern birth living in the metropolitan areas of the Great Lakes states from 1939 to 1969.

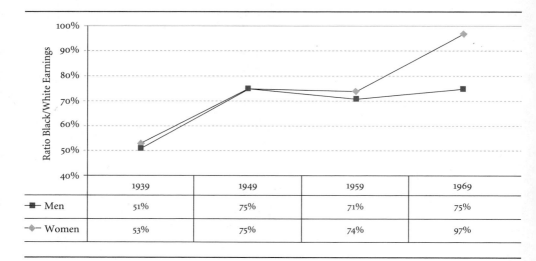

	1939	1949	1959	1969
—■— Men	51%	75%	71%	75%
—◆— Women	53%	75%	74%	97%

FIGURE 3.3. Income of Working-Age (25–54) Black Southerners as Percentage of Income of White Southerners in Metropolitan Areas of Great Lakes States, 1939–1969

Source: Steven Ruggles, Matthew Sobek, Trent Alexander, Catherine A. Fitch, Ronald Goeken, Patricia Kelly Hall, Miriam King, and Chad Ronnander, *Integrated Public Use Microdata Series: Version 3.0* (machine-readable database) (Minneapolis, 2004).

In 1939, the wage gap was monstrous. Black southern migrants aged twenty-five to fifty-four earned roughly half of what white southern migrants earned, and the proportion held for women as well as men. In the following decades, the gap narrowed, and from 1949 to 1969 the skin-color effect fluctuated around the 75 percent level, varying with educational levels and by sex. Table A.5 provides more detail, controlling for education. For black males, the wage gap worsened as educational levels increased. Those with only grammar school experience earned roughly 80 percent of what white migrants with similar educations took home from 1959 on. The disparity widened for those who had been to high school and still further for those who had spent any time in college. College experience earned a black male migrant on average only 63 percent of his white counterpart's income in 1949; 60 percent in 1959; and 66 percent in 1969. There was a similar income differential between black and white migrant women at lower educational levels until the 1960s (again close to 75 percent in most years). By 1969, the wage gap for females had closed dramatically. While poorly educated black southerners still lagged behind poorly educated white southerners, black women with college experience now earned more than their white migrant counterparts. Overall, the two groups of southern-born women earned comparable average incomes in 1969.[26]

But income data cannot really measure the differences. Black southerners encountered all sorts of restrictions that affected their ability to earn incomes and that changed the value of those dollars they did earn. If the white migrants moved into a world with many options, their black counterparts encountered restrictions at every turn: restrictions on where they could live, where they could work, where they could spend their money, and where their children could go to school. Nothing was the same. Where whites dispersed through an open job market, blacks were channeled into particular racialized sectors. Where light-skinned southerners enjoyed numerous housing options and over time spread out in the suburbs, dark-skinned southerners were required to find housing in the high-density portions of the cities, where jobs were fewer, prices higher, and home-ownership less likely. An income that turned a family of white southerners into home-owners often left black migrants still renting an apartment. Nothing was the same.[27]

Opportunities and restrictions, however, were never constant; the rules of race changed significantly over the course of the diaspora, and it is helpful to briefly sketch the patterns. Prior to World War I, African Americans in the North had dealt with a labor market that was almost as restrictive as what they faced in the South. Employment was largely limited to service jobs, with most earning their living as maids, servants, waiters, porters, barbers, laundresses, elevator operators, and the like. Laboring and factory jobs were more precarious, subject to the battles that unions and employers waged throughout the metropolitan North. Hired during strikes or by anti-union employers, African Americans could lose these jobs when white workers organized against them. They could also lose their lives.[28]

World War I modified this pattern. The need for wartime labor and the interruption of European immigration encouraged certain employers to hire African Americans, who now broke into the industrial working class in significant numbers. This was a momentous breakthrough, key to many changes in northern black community formations. It was also a conditional breakthrough, mostly at the lowest ranks involving unskilled labor and largely in firms that did not face powerful unions. Railroads, steel mills, and packinghouses were the industries that most aggressively recruited southern blacks during the war, while among the automakers only Henry Ford followed suit. Some parts of the construction industry also now made room for African Americans, but mostly in those hauling and digging jobs that whites did not want. Breakthrough it was, but a limited one. In 1920, 70 percent of southern-born African American males worked either as unskilled laborers or at service jobs, ranks that occupied just 22 percent of southern white males, and 78 percent of employed black female migrants worked as maids or other service jobs, compared to 27 percent of their white counterparts (table A.7).[29]

And even these jobs, especially the industrial ones, were precarious. What would happen when whites wanted that work or when unions got strong enough to demand it? That happened during the Great Depression. As unemployment mounted, black workers were usually the first to be fired. Driven out of the factories and off the construction sites, they also lost many of the service jobs that had been the traditional stronghold of the northern black economy. By 1932, unemployment in the black communities of the North was double what it was among whites, and that ratio would remain in place until the end of the decade. If it had not been clear before, the Depression showed that the rules of race in the North meant that African Americans participated in the labor market as a reserve force, eligible to fill in the lower ranks only as far as the supply of white workers and the power of hostile unions allowed.[30]

The rules of race changed again for the second phase of the diaspora. Even as mass migration resumed in the early years of World War II, some of the factors governing the labor market had been rearranged, largely because of political steps that will be examined later. The CIO unions that organized the major industrial establishments in the 1930s and 1940s were learning the dangers of racial exclusivity and now would change their tune. Governmental bodies, both federal and many urban regimes, were also playing a new role, providing a growing number of public sector jobs and developing the legal and rhetorical framework that would support African American claims to a more open labor market.[31]

The results would show up slowly, but the southerners who came north as part of the second phase enjoyed more work options than their predecessors. The black economy would now include more numerous and more secure industrial jobs and a growing white-collar sector. In 1920, professional, managerial, clerical, and sales jobs had accounted for less than 7 percent of black employment in northern and western metropolitan areas. By 1950, white-collar work accounted for 15 percent of jobs held by blacks, rising to 20 percent in 1960 and 33 percent in 1970. In that year, 22 percent of African American men and 46 percent of African American women held office or sales jobs.[32]

The white-collar sector was also positioned differently. Before World War II, a tiny number of professionals, business owners, and clerical and sales workers had mostly served the African American community. It was highly unusual for a black man or woman to find an office job in a firm that catered to whites. Moreover, especially in the 1930s, a significant portion of white-collar work

In 1940 when this picture was taken, blacks were excluded from most clerical, sales, and white-collar jobs. Firms that served the black community, such as this Chicago-based insurance company, provided a handful of opportunities for well-educated migrants to use their skills. (Library of Congress, Prints and Photographs Division, FSA-OWI Collection)

had been tied to the ghetto's major internal industry: gambling. The policy rackets generated many of the best jobs in the black communities of Chicago, New York, Detroit, and other major cities, and the profits from gambling also supported legitimate enterprises, including insurance companies, newspapers, baseball teams, and many of the ghetto's retail stores that doubled as "policy stations" where gamblers could register their bets.[33]

White-collar workers broke out of the ghetto in the 1940s, 50s, and 60s, making slow but measurable inroads into the office sector of the dominant economy. Government work was the most important new avenue. The New Deal buildup of government services had opened one door. Changes in urban politics had opened another. High school– and college-educated African Americans would begin to find jobs as welfare workers, teachers, postal employees, and clerical and research staff with government agencies, both local and federal. Job ceilings and discriminatory hiring patterns would remain a problem, but public sector openings would grow throughout the postwar era, and, at a more halting pace, private sector white-collar opportunities would follow.[34]

If the job spectrum facing migrants of the second phase included a component of white-collar positions, it included a much larger complement of blue-collar industrial jobs. Hiring barriers began to crack and break during World War II as a result of labor shortages combined with new political pressures, including the Roosevelt administration's FEPC, the CIO's declarations against discrimination, and the growing muscle of the black communities. The effects were uneven, barely noticeable in some entire industries and in many firms. Even in steel and autos, which were becoming the backbone of the African American economy in the Midwest and where CIO unions made their strongest commitments to reducing discrimination, progress was erratic. African American job access varied from firm to firm and department to department. One auto plant might be integrated, another segmented (with blacks in the paint shops and doing janitorial work), and a third virtually all white.[35]

But compared to the interwar period, the jobs were becoming better and more secure. In 1920, just 24 percent of southern-born black males had held semiskilled or skilled positions in industry. By 1950, that had improved to 39 percent and twenty years later reached 47 percent. For women, too, the job options were improving steadily. Domestic service had accounted for 62 percent of the jobs held by southern-born African American women in 1920, falling to 39 percent in 1950 and 14 percent in 1970. Women's new jobs had come in several areas: semiskilled factory work (25 percent in 1950; 21 percent in 1970); nondomestic service (21 percent, then 27 percent); and clerical/sales (7 percent, then 23 percent) (see tables A.7, A.8, A.9).

If all this was an improvement from the labor market conditions of the earlier era, it did not change the fundamental fact that African Americans still faced restrictions. The race rules had changed but had not disappeared. Compare the 1970 job profiles of southern blacks with those of southern whites in table A.9. The whites had much greater presence in white-collar positions and were less dependent on the least attractive service and unskilled jobs. The median job for a black southern-born man in 1970 was semiskilled factory operative; for his white counterpart, it was a skilled worker or foreman. Among black females from the South, 66 percent worked in factories or service jobs, while 57 percent of white women worked in offices or stores. African Americans had made much progress, but a substantial job opportunity gap remained.[36]

Ghettos

Housing markets followed related patterns over the course of the diaspora, improving for African Americans during the postwar era but never offering black newcomers the freedoms or prices available to the whites. Spatial segregation had been an inconsistent aspect of northern racial rules prior to World War I. African Americans had lived in various areas of most cities, usually in small concentrations in the poorer districts, but also scattered about, their presence not a source of great distress to white neighbors. The big population increases of the World War I era brought new restrictions. Whites now organized in ways that forced blacks to concentrate in particular neighborhoods. The 5,000 African Americans in Detroit in 1910 had lived in semiscattered concentrations amidst Jews and other recent immigrants. But the 35,000 newcomers who joined them during the next decade flowed mostly into the city's oldest and most disreputable slum area. Low rents and willing landlords started the process, but white resistance soon made "Black Bottom" into a district of high density and high rents and virtually the only area where black people might safely live.[37]

Various tools were used to confine African American housing options. Real estate brokers and neighborhood associations organized the market, using housing covenants and zoning ordinances to back up the informal system of racial exclusion. Violence was the key. In Detroit and every other city where the new ghettos took shape, whites used terror to keep African Americans in the black belt. Dynamite greeted many of the families who dared buy property in a white neighborhood. Hundreds of houses were damaged or destroyed by bombs or fire in the 1920s in cities across the North. Mob action was equally common, the most famous example taking place in Detroit in 1925. Dr. Ossian Sweet, a Florida-born gynecologist, bought a house three miles west of the black belt. He knew what this meant and was prepared for the mob of angry whites that gathered the night he took possession. Joined by his wife, brother, and several friends and armed with rifles and shotguns, the defenders fired into the crowd that assaulted the home, killing one man and wounding another. The police then dispersed the crowd and arrested Dr. Sweet and his companions. His acquittal in the subsequent murder trial was hailed as a victory by the NAACP, which hired Clarence Darrow to argue the case of self-defense. But it did little to stop the housing mobs and midnight bombers.[38]

Residential containment doubled the effects of discrimination in the job markets, making it difficult for black people to commute to many jobs and raising costs, especially the cost of housing, far above what white people faced. Studies conducted in New York in the 1920s found that Harlem rents were more than 20 percent higher than what whites would have paid for comparable accommodations. Other costs cannot be measured. The ghettos of the interwar era were the most overcrowded and underserviced sections of their cities.[39]

The second phase of the diaspora experienced housing opportunities that were somewhat different. The expansion of governmental capacity that occurred under the New Deal had huge implications for the spatial and racial design of cities. Government had almost never built or financed housing before the 1930s. Now it would do both. Public housing projects, initiated in a small way in the 1930s and expanded during and after the war, were one part of the new equation. Federal home loan mortgage guarantees, also a New Deal invention, would be still more important, fueling the home-building, home-buying revolution that turned America into a nation of home-owners (from 40 percent of families in 1940 to 65 percent in 1974) and opening the door to the suburbanization and "white-flight" spatial patterns of the postwar metropolis.[40]

Whites benefited more than blacks from government interventions in the housing market, but there were new opportunities also for African Americans. Cities in the postwar era gave ground more readily than they had in earlier decades. Quite literally, the spatial gains for blacks were larger and easier. As with the job ceilings, housing markets went through an adjustment, not a revolution. Segregation in the big northern metropolises remained just as much the rule in 1960 as it had in 1930, but it was a different kind of segregation. The first ghettos had taken shape in the oldest and most dilapidated neighborhoods of most cities. And as they expanded in the teens and twenties, whites had forced that growth to follow what might be called pathways of blight. Militantly defending nearby middle-class and working-class districts, urban regimes channeled ghetto expansion into undesirable spaces. The first ghettos offered little neighborhood variety. Even African Americans with solid jobs and good incomes jammed together into overcrowded, mixed-use blocks. "In many Negro communities," wrote journalist Roi Ottley in 1942, "there is no such thing as a *strictly residential* area."[41]

The second ghetto expanded in a different fashion, usually facing less resistance than the first had. Whites were losing some of the weapons they had used before and also some of the will to fight black residential expansion. In 1948, the Supreme Court ruled that deed provisions and racially restrictive housing covenants would no longer be enforced by the courts. Also in many cities, elected officials were now taking notice of black voters and the changing judiciary. That meant that neighborhood segregationists could not count on city hall to the same extent as before. Similarly, the mainstream press no longer justified housing terror, as had often been the case in the 1920s. Most important, white home-owners now had a safety valve: they could flee. The suburban building boom offered an alternative to resistance. There was no shortage of white violence, but it was less sustained and less effective than before. The second ghetto thus often expanded into the kind of single-family neighborhoods that had been militantly defended in the prewar period. This allowed for residential class separations within the black community. As families with higher incomes and steady jobs moved into the newly acquired neighborhoods, the older ghetto spaces continued to house the black poor.[42]

The two eras of the African American diaspora were thus marked by considerable change within the framework of racial disadvantage. Opportunities improved over time, and making a living for the most part became easier. There were gains in standards of living that are sometimes overlooked when we concentrate only on the disparities between white and black. The lives of most black families in the northern cities improved dramatically after the 1930s, helped by these changes in the job and housing markets. Adjusted for inflation, the spending power of the average family headed by a southern-born male or female increased by 33 percent in the 1940s, another 54 percent in the 1950s, and then 31 percent in the 1960s (table A.4). Housing improved markedly, showing up in census reports in the form of much higher rates of indoor plumbing and lower ratios of persons per room. In 1940, 44 percent of housing units occupied by African Americans living outside the South had been missing some or all plumbing facilities. In 1970, only 4 percent lacked full facilities. In 1940, 28 percent of households were overcrowded, with more than one person per room. In 1970, 15 percent were overcrowded. Home-ownership rates rose as well, from 16 percent of metropolitan African American households in 1940 to 36 percent in 1970 (still not much more than half the home-ownership rate of whites). These changes were accompanied by significant improvements in health standards, educational opportunities, and other measures of well-being. In short, two stories need to be told simultaneously about the black opportunity structure over the course of the diaspora, one recording progress and accomplishments, another clarifying continuing inequalities based on race.[43]

A Southern Success Story

How did the southern-born fare within these evolving patterns of racialized opportunity? For several generations, it was axiomatic that one source of difficulty for the northern African American communities was the continuing migration from the South. It was understood that southerners, because of their rural ways and less-adequate education, were both a social and an economic burden on the existing communities. From W. E. B. Du Bois writing about Philadelphia's black community in 1898 through the Moynihan report and a dozen other major studies of the ghetto produced in the 1960s, scholars assumed that it was the migrants who were having the most difficulty in the northern urban economy and that some of the black community's issues of poverty and "social disorganization" could be blamed on them. "Much of what looks like 'racial poverty,'" wrote Edward Banfield in *The Unheavenly City*, his 1970 report on the urban crisis, "is really 'rural Southern' poverty."[44]

Then in the 1970s, several studies turned up something interesting. By most measures, southern-born African Americans were doing better, not worse, than their northern-born counterparts. Using the then newly released 1970 census public user sample, demographer Larry Long found that contrary to expectations, southern-born African Americans living in the major northern cities were less likely to depend on welfare assistance or to suffer below-poverty-line incomes and enjoyed slightly higher median incomes despite inferior education and lower representations in white-collar jobs. Other reports indicated that southerners were less likely to be involved with the courts and prisons, had lower rates of juvenile delinquency, and were less likely to have been arrested in the 1960s riots. Larry Long summed up his findings: "Black migrants to the North become more economically successful and less likely to engage in criminal behavior than blacks born in the North."[45]

Historians have largely ignored these reports, either missing them altogether or neglecting to think about their implications. Nicholas Lemann admits that he overlooked these studies. His much-read 1991 book, *The Promised Land*, pushes an old argument about sharecropper pathology that flies in the face of the statistical evidence. Lemann wants to find a major source of ghetto problems in the culture of southern sharecroppers. Jacqueline Jones does not share Lemann's fascination with the culture of poverty formulations, but her 1992 book, *The Dispossessed*, also has migrant southerners contributing disproportionately to the black underclass of the North. Most historical studies of the first phase of the Great Migration have also ignored Long's findings, albeit with more justification. He examined the data only from 1970 and argued that the superior economic performance of southerners was related to recent changes in the self-selection patterns of those moving north.[46]

Here we consider the issue of relative performance throughout the course of the diaspora, building on recent work by Stewart Tolnay, Thomas Maloney, and J. Trent Alexander, who have been using IPUMS to reassess the economic position of black southern migrants. The profile over time is more ambiguous than Larry Long's stark declaration from 1970 data that southerners were more successful than northerners, but it is clear that in the aggregate, they did much better than scholars have assumed over the years.[47]

Historians have argued that "old settlers" and northern-born African Americans had advantages in the first-phase diaspora economy. That seems to have been true up to point, but the distinctions were modest and do not support the implication that old settlers and newcomers occupied different economic classes. Tables A.15 and A.16 display home-ownership rates and occupational distributions of northern-born, southern-born, and foreign-born black men and women living in the metropolitan areas of the North and West as reported in the 1920 census. Northerners were more likely to own homes and claimed disproportionate shares of the black community's best occupations—merchants, salespeople, doctors, lawyers, teachers, preachers, clerical workers, skilled craftsmen, foremen—although in neither case was the disparity very large. While 22 percent of northern/western-born male household heads owned or were buying their homes in 1920, they were joined by 17 percent of the southern-born. Where 18 percent of nonsouthern males claimed elite occupations, among southerners it was 15 percent.[48]

There were differences, too, in the way non-elite jobs were distributed in

1920. Northern-born males were more likely than southerners to hold jobs in the commercial service sector, especially positions in hotels and as railroad porters; 23 percent of the former worked in such positions compared with 19 percent of the southerners. Southerners, on the other hand, were overrepresented in the mass production industries that had recently begun to hire blacks (steel, meatpacking, various manufacturing plants) and also in the unskilled casual labor force. In the 1920 census, 50 percent of southern males were listed as unskilled laborers compared with 38 percent of men born in other regions. Certainly in terms of status and probably also in income, old settler males enjoyed labor market advantages as of 1920 (table A.16).

Northern-born black women did as well. Less likely to be in the labor force, they claimed most of the clerical, sales, and professional jobs and had disproportionate access to such service jobs as elevator operators, ushers, and custodial work. Southern-born women were heavily concentrated in private domestic service, finding 63 percent of their work opportunities in private households compared to 54 percent for northern-born women. Southern women did dominate one entrepreneurial niche: they kept most of the boarders, trading on hometown connections to fill beds and bring in rent money (table A.16).[49]

While the distinctions are significant, they need to be kept in perspective. There is no evidence of a two-tiered opportunity structure or a migration-based class system in the northern black communities. Tables A.15 and A.16 show that southerners, not northerners, claimed 57 percent of the best jobs and owned 63 percent of the homes in 1920. Even while the northerners had proportional advantages, the number of southerners was so overwhelming that they dominated almost all sectors of the black economy. It is true that some of the most successful southerners were "old settlers" who had come north years or perhaps decades before the big surge of migration, but there are also plenty of examples of newcomers moving quite rapidly into some of the best positions that the northern economy afforded black Americans.

Entries in the 1927 *Who's Who in Colored America* confirm the picture of former southerners sharing high-status jobs in northern communities. The volume profiles illustrious African American men and women, mostly doctors, educators, businessmen, and journalists, some of whom paid fees to the publisher. Roughly half of the entries belong to men and women living in the South, half in northern or western places. For the northern and western group, birthplace information was provided in 420 entries, 61 percent of them listing southern birthplaces, 33 percent northern or western birthplaces, and 6 percent foreign birthplaces. These data confirm an important point. More than most scholars have realized, southerners in these first Great Migration years came from a spectrum of backgrounds and brought with them a spectrum of skills. Although the vast majority of newcomers struggled with the least desirable jobs, others were moving into the top and middle ranks of the northern black economy.[50]

The advantages that northerners had earlier enjoyed still remained in 1940 (tables A.15, A.17). Northern-born African Americans again claimed a disproportionate number of the best jobs: professional, sales, skilled blue-collar, and especially the clerical sector. In addition, northerners continued to own more than their share of businesses and more than their share of homes. But these occupational differences did not result in large income disparities. Figure 3.4 compares average earnings separately for men, women, and families. In 1939, southern-born migrants of both sexes earned less than blacks born in other regions. However, the family incomes of the two populations were not far apart. The average income of a family headed by a southerner was 95 percent of the income of those headed by nonsoutherners. This is largely because southerners were more likely to maintain two-earner families. Southern marriages remained more stable, and southern-born women were more likely to be in the labor force than were northerners or westerners of the same age.[51]

If the prewar era conformed to expectations that old settlers would do better in the search for jobs and income than would southern migrants, the postwar era did not. Figure 3.4 shows that southern-born family incomes and also individual male incomes had caught up by 1949 and through the following two decades would equal or surpass those of the northern-born. The timing is ironic. The central decades of the twentieth century were the high-water mark for arguments that stressed the difficulties of urban adjustment and the disabilities associated with the "southern peasantry." Sociologists, journalists, black community leaders, and doubtless many employers assumed that rural southern blacks were less likely than northerners to possess not just education and formal work skills but also the ambition, work habits, familial structures, and social attitudes that would make for occupational achievement. Evidently, they were very wrong.

Actually, the converging earning patterns are a surprise on many levels. They would not be predicted on the basis of job distributions, since northerners continued to have greater access to high-status jobs in the white-collar and skilled labor categories in 1949 (table A.18). The earnings convergence would certainly not be predicted on the basis of educational distributions, since northerners continued to enjoy a major educational advantage, claiming on average three years more schooling than comparably aged southerners. But education counted for little in the African American economy. In fact, the IPUMS income data expose a tragic idiosyncrasy in the racialized labor markets of the midcentury North. Despite generations of talk about the value of education, in 1949

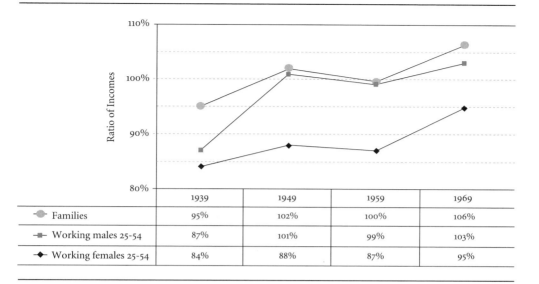

	1939	1949	1959	1969
Families	95%	102%	100%	106%
Working males 25-54	87%	101%	99%	103%
Working females 25-54	84%	88%	87%	95%

FIGURE 3.4. Income of Southern-Born Blacks as Percentage of Income of Other Blacks Living in North and West, 1939–1969

Source: Steven Ruggles, Matthew Sobek, Trent Alexander, Catherine A. Fitch, Ronald Goeken, Patricia Kelly Hall, Miriam King, and Chad Ronnander, *Integrated Public Use Microdata Series: Version 3.0* (machine-readable database) (Minneapolis, 2004).

(and as late as 1959) a grammar school drop-out African American migrant could earn almost the same income as a high school graduate. Table A.21, which compares earnings for working-age men and women of different educational levels, shows that high school diplomas had little monetary value in the job markets open to African Americans, which did not include the skilled apprenticeship programs, sales jobs, and foremen positions that whites with high school degrees might access. In 1949, southern-born black male high school graduates earned on average $2,568, which was just $293 more than the average earnings of his grammar school–educated counterparts. Northern-born high school graduates earned even less. But in the white economy, the high school degree paid handsomely. A southern-born white male with a high school diploma earned on average $764 more than a similarly aged migrant who had left school before the ninth grade. Two years of schooling or twelve, it did not seem to greatly change the earning power of African Americans in the factory and service sectors where they struggled for jobs.[52]

Undereducated black southerners took advantage of this distorted labor market. Indeed, if we control for educational background, we see just how competitive they were. The typical southern-born working-age male with a grammar school education earned on average 9–10 percent more than a comparably educated northern-born man in 1949, 1959, and 1969, and those with more education also generally earned more than their counterparts (table A.21). Why? Larry Long and the others who puzzled the data from 1970 assumed it was a fairly new development and hypothesized that southern migrants had certain motivational advantages in the postwar era. While second- and third-generation northerners absorbed northern standard-of-living expectations that too often led to discouragement, southerners had more reasonable expectations, were less familiar with welfare as a resource, and, like most immigrants, had been self-selected for ambition and commitment to work. The fact that by the 1960s, most migrants were coming not from rural areas but from previous urban experiences also figures in Long's hypothesis.[53]

But if southern "success" was not a new pattern, then both the new migration pattern and discouragement theses lose some of their force. Rural people had been a big part of the migration stream all the way through the 1940s; welfare was not much of a resource; and the northern black communities of 1950 cannot be described as zones of discouragement. Moreover, the supporting data that might show southerners to be more motivated workers is not there. Larry Long found in 1970 that higher percentages of working-age northern-born black males were out of the labor force compared to southern-born black males. But not in 1950. Labor force rates were similar for males, slightly higher for southern-born females.

Instead of focusing on the morale of northerners, it makes sense to think about the southerners and apply some of the insights yielded by the investigation of southern whites in the economy. There too we saw that educational disadvantage did not matter in the golden age of blue-collar job creation. Second, for all the talk of discrimination against southerners, there was compensating beneficial discrimination by employers who expected to take advantage of the southern reputation for "labor conservatism." Finally, and probably most important, the migrants were self-selected for ambition and apt to be inspired throughout their working lives by evidence and self-mythology of their own success.

All of these descriptions seem to apply as much to black southern migrants as to whites. It may be true that the northern political economy began to breed discouragement among young northern-born African Americans as the decades passed (labor force participation rates among northern-born men declined in 1960 and 1970). But the more interesting and long-lasting story is the drive and determination and the resulting "success" of the southerners within the confines of racialized opportunity structures that could easily have been discouraging for everyone.[54]

Southern Expectations

If southerners of both races often exceeded the expectations of the experts who predicted only difficulty, they also tended to do better than southerners who stayed behind. The assessment that led so many to leave home—that there were better jobs and higher incomes to be had outside the South—more often than not proved true.

We can get a rough sense of the economic advantages of migration by comparing average earnings of migrants and nonmigrants of comparable age and education. Tables A.22 and A.23 do this for 1949 and 1969, using two different views of the southern opportunity structure, one involving the whole nonmigrant population of the region, the other just the metropolitan areas where most of the region's economic growth was concentrated. If we take the former as a measure of the kind of income that a nonmigrant might have expected, the advantages to leaving the South seem overwhelmingly clear; if we use the latter, making the assumption that those who shared the ambitions of the outmigrants would have headed for a southern city, the differentials shrink but still seem substantial, especially in the case of African Americans.

In 1949, a black male aged thirty-five to forty-nine who had moved north earned on average 36 percent more than his counterpart in a southern metropolis, not counting cost of living differences. Education affected this migration premium. College-educated migrants earned 18 percent more than did the stay-at-homes with the same education, while migrants who finished their education in grammar school or high school gained a 35 or 37 percent earnings advantage by leaving the South (table A.22). Twenty years later, the South was catching up economically, but migration was still paying hefty premiums for black males. In 1969, a grammar school–educated southerner who had moved north earned 44 percent more than his counterpart living in a southern metropolitan area, 24 percent more if he was college-educated (table A.23).[55]

Black females enjoyed an even larger wage advantage in the North, unless they were well educated. Migrant working women with grammar school backgrounds earned 51 percent more than their counterparts in southern cities in 1949 and 62 percent more in 1969. But the differential shrank with high school experience and disappeared for those who had attended college. In 1949, well-educated black women living in a southern city averaged higher incomes than their counterparts who had moved to a northern city. In 1969, the outmigrants enjoyed a slight advantage of 5 percent (tables A.22, A.23).

If black migrants realized fairly consistent economic advantages all the way through the diaspora period, the patterns for white migrants were more ambiguous, or perhaps only harder to measure. The metropolitan comparison method is less appropriate for evaluating what whites gained or lost through migration. Average incomes in the southern cities were skewed upward by the presence of established elites who were not typical candidates for migration. Still, it is obvious that there was some advantage, at least for those with modest educational backgrounds. In 1969, grammar school–educated white males who had migrated north or west earned 20 percent more than their counterparts in the southern cities, 30 percent more than comparably educated whites in all settings of the South (table A.23).

Another source confirms the basic idea that migration paid off economically for the average southerner but disagrees about how much. In *Opportunity and Change*, sociologists David Featherman and Robert Hauser used a pair of large sample surveys of working-age men taken in 1962 and 1973 to look at various dimensions of male economic performance. Controlling for more background factors than are possible with the IPUMS data, they came up with estimates of the earnings value of migration that reverse the impression that African Americans found greater relative advantage than whites. They report that a black male migrant living in the North in 1961 earned only 10 percent more ($400) than he would have had he stayed in the South, while a white migrant earned a premium of $1,600, or 25 percent. By 1972, regional earnings differentials had fallen for both groups of migrants, blacks now earning just $300 and whites $400 more than their stay-at-home counterparts.[56]

Many former migrants would have wondered about Featherman and Hauser's findings, convinced that migration had paid off in more than a few hundred dollars a year. Those veterans of the Southern Diaspora who have volunteered to speak about their experiences have mostly been sure that migration was key to a successful life story, blacks no less than whites. They say this in the hundreds of oral histories and interviews that have been collected over the last thirty years as the diaspora has become a subject of interest to journalists and historians. There is hardly a university that does not claim an oral history project featuring the life stories of African Americans who remade their lives through migration. On a smaller scale, the stories of white migrants have also been published or preserved. These collections cannot be taken to be representative. The men and women interviewed are often chosen precisely because of their accomplishments, but the way they tell their stories is intriguing. It is striking how proud the two groups of former southerners tend to be. The standard response is almost triumphant. We struggled, we worked hard, and we made it, most seem to say.[57]

Recounting a life that was never easy, starting in a sharecropper's cabin in Woodland, Mississippi, and followed by sixty years of hard work in Chicago where she took jobs as a domestic and ran a family business while her husband labored in a steel mill, Maggie Comer is one of the best known of these storytellers, thanks to the oral history that her son, eminent psychiatrist James P. Comer, published in 1988 under the title *Maggie's American Dream*. Maggie Comer's story, like so many others, is filled with a sense of accomplishment, especially in the knowledge that the couple's dedication made it possible for all five of their children to earn college degrees. She concludes her narrative with a simple benediction. "I'm so proud and so thankful. I think back from where I came, I think of all the things that could have happened . . . and I get a chill. Sometimes I just pace the floor and say, 'Thank you, Jesus.' "[58]

Similar reflections show up in the only known survey of former migrants. In the 1980s, sociologist E. Marvin Goodwin distributed a questionnaire to 700 elderly black Chicagoans who had left the South at various ages, mostly between 1930 and 1960. Not a random sample, it consisted of relatives and acquaintances of undergraduate volunteers at a local university, what Goodwill calls an "availability sampling." There is no way to tell how representative the group might be. Occupational and educational levels were somewhat high but not greatly out of line with generational norms: 69 percent of the respondents finished their working lives as blue-collar (including service) workers. Respondents answered various questions bearing on their feelings of accomplishment, and Goodwin concluded that most felt a high "level of satisfaction with themselves and their communities."[59]

Clearly, there is a strong basis for overturning the old stories and the even older expectations about southerners and their economic difficulties. There is a nice irony to the fact that the people who were expected to do so poorly in fact did fairly well, at least within the confines of their racially separate labor markets. Thought to be lacking in ambition, most rural southerners of both races turned out to be quite ambitious. Thought to be burdened by family systems, social habits, and education that would hinder their work lives, the migrants showed that little of that mattered. Indeed, a century or more of stereotypes crumble in these data. The slow-moving ignorant hillbilly and the slow-moving ignorant sharecropper dissolve into the proud former Mississippians, Alabamans, and other black southerners in Goodwin's sample and in the oral histories in Timuel D. Black Jr.'s *The Bridges of Memory*; into the proud former Appalachians whose stories fill Carl Feather's *Mountain People in a Flat Land* and Chad Berry's *Southern Migrants: Northern Exiles*; and into the proud former Oklahomans, Texans, and Arkansans speaking in Dona L. Irvin's *The Unsung Heart of Black America* and in the online *Dust Bowl Migration Digital Archive*.[60]

We might easily turn the myth all the way around, as some of the migrants themselves do, claiming that their heritage made them uniquely ambitious, turning their accomplishments into something triumphant and extraordinary. And some journalists are beginning to see the poetry in that reverse mythology. An *Ebony* article about Matel Dawson Jr., who spent fifty-six years in a Detroit auto plant, saved his money, and has now given more than $700,000 to colleges and churches, and a book about the Yokum family, who worked their way from Arkansas rags to California riches, both point the way. But reversing the story to this extent is a mistake. Mostly, the Southern Diaspora did not yield extraordinary success stories. Instead, they are modest, mundane, and almost normal. They reflect well on the character of the migrants but say little about heritage or culture. The success of these two groups of southerners was very clearly keyed to opportunities that were beyond individual control, opportunities that were lifting most families in the regions where they settled along racialized tracks and, not incidentally, were also improving dramatically for those who stayed behind.[61]

The Black Metropolis

The remainder of the book examines the impact of the Southern Diaspora on American society, exploring ways that southerners changed their new surroundings and transformed institutions of political and cultural significance. It is an axiom of African American historiography that the Great Migration was a turning point in the long struggle for rights and respect. The chapters ahead will specify the new resources and institutions that became available as a result of migration and how the important transformations worked. Southern white migrants are rarely counted as a historical force, despite their huge numbers. The chapters ahead will change that impression.

To understand how the African American exodus changed history, we must start with the observation that the migrants were moving into some of the most important places in America, the half dozen or so largest cities. And they were doing so precisely as those cities enjoyed their era of greatest political and cultural authority. New York, Chicago, Detroit, Los Angeles, Philadelphia, Cleveland, Washington, D.C. — these cities, all but one outside the South, were the chief money centers, media centers, and political centers for early- and mid-twentieth-century America, the place to be for anyone looking for access to those forms of power. Black southerners found ways to influence some of the institutions hosted by these dominant cities and through them gained leverage that eventually, over the course of decades, would be used to shift the nation's systems of racial relations and also regional relations. Key to that evolving influence was a distinct community formation that came together in big northern cities during the second quarter of the twentieth century. Contemporaries called it the "Black Metropolis."

Until recently, it has been difficult for historians to recognize the capacities of the Black Metropolis. The term itself largely disappeared from public discourse by the 1960s, replaced by the concept of the ghetto, a label that evokes images of distressed neighborhoods locked in poverty and lacking in resources and infrastructure. There were good reasons for this terminological shift. Activists and scholars needed to drive home the facts of racial containment and racial inequality in northern spaces. But the ghettoization model was incomplete. Concentrating on what was missing in the way of opportunities, resources, institutions, and political power, it underplayed what was present. Recent historians have found a new balance, substituting what Richard Thomas calls a "community building process" approach for the ghettoization scheme. Without neglecting the context of racism, the new studies manage to suggest some of the pride and energy that went into the development of the major urban black communities.[1]

I am going a step further and urging reconsideration of the concept of Black Metropolis. It has utility for a couple of reasons. First, it calls attention to the particular setting of the principal black communities—in the major metropolitan areas of the nation. The great cities in their age of maximum greatness yielded black communities that were different from those in other settings. Second, the term Black Metropolis resurrects a celebratory terminology that African American journalists used for several decades before the sociological perspective undercut it.

Ironically, the most famous use of the term occurs in the book that started to erase its meaning. *Black Metropolis: A Study of Negro Life in a Northern City*, published in 1945 by St. Clair Drake and Horace R. Cayton, is a classic work of sociology that echoes more profoundly through the literature of black urban history than perhaps any other book of the twentieth century. A 767-page study of Chicago's South Side, the community dubbed "Bronzeville" by the local black press, the book develops an extraordinarily rich portrait of what the authors hailed as "the second largest Negro city in the world," with a population exceeding 300,000. Richard Wright wrote the book's introduction and called it a "landmark of research and scientific achievement," and historians and social scientists ever since have relied upon its blend of riveting ethnographic observation, detailed institutional and historical data (the product of a 100-person research team financed by the WPA), and probing analysis of the social system of this city within a city.[2]

Drake and Cayton's biggest analytical achievement was their close attention to the "color line." Focusing tightly on the dynamics of racial containment, they drove home the message that tense segregation was the central theme of African American experience in the North just as it was in the South. Their second concern was class. Drake had been a student of Yale sociologist Lloyd Warner, who pioneered studies of social stratification. *Black Metropolis* takes a close look at social divisions within the black community, sifting residents into an unorthodox class structure consisting of a tiny upper class, a small middle class, and a huge lower class, all subdivided into "respectables" and "shadies" in recognition of the large role that gambling, prostitution, hustling, and other illegal or semilegal activities played in the community. Because of these two main concerns, the book in many ways distances itself from its title, emphasizing not the integrity and prospects of a Black Metropolis but the limitations of community tightly compressed within walls of racial subordination. The authors assess Bronzeville's resources and mostly find them wanting: the business sector is too small, the religious sector too large, the newspapers too sensational, the politicians too corrupt, the "shadies" too powerful, the middle class too irresponsible, the lower class too large and demoralized. Detached and clinical, imbued with the social disorganization theory that dominated Drake and Cayton's academic disciplines, *Black Metropolis* introduces the ghetto story that would guide the next half century.

African American journalists of the 1920s, 30s, and 40s looked at Bronzeville and Harlem and Detroit's "Paradise Valley" (also named by a black newspaper) and usually saw something different. In 1943, just months before *Black Metropolis* appeared, journalist Roi Ottley published *"New World A-Coming": Inside Black America*, a book about Harlem, which the author described as "the Negro capital . . . the nerve center of advancing Black America . . . a vibrant, bristling black metropolis." A New York–born columnist for the *Amsterdam Star News* and *Pittsburgh Courier,* the thirty-seven-year-old Roi Ottley had written a book that would initially sell far more copies than the sociological study, reportedly 50,000 copies before the year was out. Heavily promoted by the black press, *"New World A-Coming"* echoed the tone of a thousand articles and editorials that had appeared in northern black newspapers in the years since the Great Migration. Ottley described Harlem in terms that left no doubt about his sense that this was a powerful and hopeful space. A "place of curious extremes," it had enormous problems, but more important it had enormous prospects. Where Drake and Cayton dwelt on the "world of the lower class," Ottley focused on Harlem's activists and elites. The community's vitality stood front and center, as it had in James Weldon Johnson's *Black Manhattan* (1930). In this "cultural and intellectual hub of the Negro world," Ottley found creativity in many of the institutions that Drake and Cayton discounted: in the churches and new unorthodox religious movements; in the community's newspapers and periodicals, some of them with nationwide circulation; in what he called the "colored café society" of artists, writers, composers, musicians, and actors who gathered in the bars and cafés and at parties hosted by wealthy sponsors; and most of all in the vibrant political life of black Manhattan. Harlem was a cauldron of newly created political organizations and ideologies, a frenzy of activism aimed at lifting the barriers of segregation and poverty. "Day-to-day living seems to be an endless vigil of picket lines, strikes, boycotts, mammoth mass meetings, as well as a series of colorful parades, jazzy picnics," he wrote, finding in all that activism, not the confusion and disorder that Cayton and Drake disparaged, but the great hope for his race, a means to deliverance and freedom.[3]

Ottley's 1943 song of celebration lacks the critical distance that historians today require. It passes quickly over urban problems, devoting just one of its twenty-two chapters to poverty and other symptoms of "slum shock." There is no detailed discussion of social structure and only the barest account of the large and important infrastructure of gambling, hustling, prostitution, and criminality. It is not an analytical work, offering no sustained explanation of how the Black Metropolis functioned or why it developed its capacities. Yet *"New World A-Coming"* is a perceptive book that in its own breezy way sets us up to understand how the Southern Diaspora and the rise of the Black Metropolis were changing America. His chapters wander across a cityscape of institutions, describing the power of the black press, the ideas and influence of a growing black intelligentsia, the chaos and creativity of urban churches, new forms of entertainment and celebrity, and new forms of politics. It is a tour worth following.[4]

New scholarship also guides the way. Adam Green's study of 1940s black Chicago and Susanne Smith's exploration of Detroit in the Motown era show the new forms of cultural influence that those African American communities generated in the decades after Ottley's book appeared. Both historians map the infrastructures of cultural production and make impressive arguments about the way that publishing, music, and political enterprises reinforced each other and generated new expressions of black identity and community in the postwar decades. I think we can backdate those arguments to the interwar era and see that, beginning in the 1920s, African Americans settling in the major cites were developing an infrastructure, a cultural apparatus, of historic import. Ghettos for those who lived in them, these impoverished and imprisoned spaces would nonetheless be responsible for the production of an evolving complex of cultural forms that would facilitate the transformation of American racial systems.[5]

Boomtown Dynamics

The Black Metropolis was a product of several circumstances, including tightly targeted migration patterns that built up African American population in a select number of great cities. Eight metropolitan areas (New York–Newark, Philadelphia-Camden, Chicago-Gary, Detroit, Cleveland, St. Louis, Los Angeles–Long Beach, San Francisco–Oakland) had become home to 1,003,000 black southerners by 1940, which was two out of every three southern-born African Americans living outside the South. The second phase continued the pattern. In 1970, those same cities housed 2,154,000 black southerners (and still more of their children and grandchildren), again more than two-thirds of the entire migrant population (table A.24). Other cities—including Boston, Buffalo, Pittsburgh, Cincinnati, Indianapolis, Columbus, Milwaukee, Kansas City, Portland, and Seattle—also attracted black southerners in numbers that became significant over time, and in addition there was a certain amount of migration to the towns and rural areas of the North and West. Nevertheless, the concentration of the main force of the African American diaspora into a handful of the largest and most politically and culturally significant cities was a fact of great consequence. It would be the enabling condition for much of what black southerners would accomplish in the North and West.[6]

Important too was a particular pattern of community-building, an ethos of growth and welcome that would facilitate the absorption of southern newcomers and help the emerging Black Metropolises develop new political and cultural institutions. Each of the major cities had African American communities that predated the Great Migration, and these "old settlers" had reason to wonder about the costs and benefits of massive black population growth. "The northern Negro . . . faces a peculiar dilemma," W. E. B. Du Bois explained in 1923. "He knows that his southern brother will and must migrate just as he himself migrated either in this generation or the last. He feels more or less acutely his own duty to help the newcomers. . . . But, on the other hand, the black northerner knows what this migration costs."[7]

Some old settlers acted on their anxieties in ways that might have hindered migration or divided communities. Black Philadelphia, led by a proud mulatto elite who looked back on almost a century of influence in the nation's third-largest city, probably displayed greater tensions than any other northern black community. By 1912, when Richard R. Wright Jr. (the cleric, not the novelist) completed his doctoral dissertation, "The Negro in Pennsylvania," the city already claimed a black population in excess of 85,000 and a community apparatus that, while spatially dispersed, was the envy of African Americans in other cities. A network of strong churches anchored the community and provided the backbone for a complex of institutions that included two hospitals, a private secondary school and several technical schools, a set of segregated public elementary schools that hired only black teachers, various fraternal and women's organizations, insurance clubs, building and loan associations, and a variety of social service organizations, including the Armstrong Association, the city's forerunner to and later affiliate of the National Urban League. Moreover, the community enjoyed some political influence and remembered enjoying more. In 1899, three African Americans had served on the city council.[8]

Although many of the "Old Philadelphians," as the elite liked to be known, were themselves southern-born, the Great Migration posed a complicated challenge for older settlers. Between 1916 and 1919, the community absorbed at least 40,000 newcomers and then another 85,000 during the 1920s, bringing the total African American population of Philadelphia to 219,599 at the time of the 1930 census, 11 percent of the total population. Pouring into and overflowing the three separated zones where African Americans had previously established themselves, the newcomers raised housing prices, exacerbated densities and slum conditions, and turned what had been in some cases mixed-race neighborhoods into fully segregated neighborhoods. Old settlers who could afford to do so fled along with the whites, sometimes making costly and physically dangerous moves into contiguous all-white neighborhoods, only to see the newcomers follow them when whites abandoned these areas. Analyzing the effects of the migration in a 1921 study, Sadie T. Mossell, daughter of an Old Philadelphia family, recorded widespread anxiety among "Negroes of culture, education and some financial means" who resented the "generally uneducated and untrained" newcomers and blamed them for upsetting what the old settlers remembered as equitable relations with the whites. The Old Philadelphians, she claimed, "had always enjoyed the same social and educational facilities as the whites and courteous treatment from them."[9]

But how did these issues play out? Not in ways that left significant social divisions. There were some conflicts early in the Great Migration period, including one for control of "Mother" Bethel Church, the 100-year-old founding symbol of the African Methodist Episcopal denomination. In 1920, after hundreds of newcomers had joined the congregation and changed aspects of worship, the old settlers rose up, fired the pastor, and cemented their own control over the historic church. But incidents of this nature mostly occurred in the first few years of rapid population growth. Not even in Philadelphia did the divisions last. The "greenhorn" and "FOB" (fresh off the boat) syndromes or the home-country regionalism that sometimes hindered community-building within immigrant populations were not major obstacles in the fast-growing northern black communities. Instead, what stands out is the comparatively rapid process of social integration.[10]

Only a few northern black communities (notably Pittsburgh and Cincinnati) were organized in ways where elites could exert the kind of influence shown in Philadelphia. Old settlers in other locales were in some cases so numerically overwhelmed that, whatever their private worries and resentments, there was little chance of acting on them. In other cases, community leaders were firmly committed to the migration in principle and practice. That was true in the two northern cities that, along with Philadelphia, had the largest African American communities prior to World War I.[11]

The social dynamics of migration and settlement in New York was nothing like Philadelphia. Black New York had a complex demography that kept tensions between old settlers and newcomers from the South from becoming significant. The city absorbed larger numbers of African American newcomers during the Great Migration than any other city, its black population more than tripling from 91,000 in 1910 to 327,000 in 1930. But they were not all southerners. The islands of the Caribbean also contributed to the growth of New York's black population, especially the British islands of Jamaica, Trinidad, and Barbados. One in six black New Yorkers in 1930 was foreign-born. Substantial numbers of northern-born blacks were also moving to New York, which had become the universal magnet for African Americans. A spatial opportunity added another unique dimension to the New York story. Beginning around 1905, African Americans were able to capitalize on a soft housing market in a recently constructed uptown neighborhood designed for middle-class whites, and over the next two decades much of the existing black population joined tens of thousands of the newcomers in making Harlem their new home. Another new settlement area opened up in the Bedford-Stuyvesant neighborhood of Brooklyn. Black New York, to put it simply, was in motion. Old settlers, newcomers from the South, newcomers from the North, and newcomers from the Caribbean spent the Great Migration decades building an immense black community that would in fact be new to all.[12]

In this context, the most highly charged interactions were not between southerners and northerners but between West Indians and U.S.-born African Americans. Indeed, rivalries and disagreements between islanders and old settlers helped to ease the situation of southern newcomers who at moments found themselves courted by both groups. It was the West Indians who were most resented by long-term New Yorkers and who most upset existing frameworks of status and authority. Capturing more than their share of entrepreneurial and professional positions in the African American community, they also upset many of the political equations of black New York behind the extraordinary initiatives of Marcus Garvey. Old settlers reacted with what sociologist Ira De A. Reid described as "intra-group" prejudices, resenting West Indians as "overbearing," "clannish," "hot-tempered," and "troublemakers." All of this was probably good for the southern newcomers. While Garvey's United Negro Improvement Association challenged them to turn away from the "mulatto race traitors" and join a movement based on blackness, churches and political organizations dominated by old settlers urged them to join in the name of "Negro Americans." In any case, no one was singling out the southerners for serious resentment. A community of many factions and exuberant politics, black New York was too dynamic and too divided to manifest even the limited parochialism of the Old Philadelphians.[13]

Black Chicago in the early part of the century was a still different story. Although it lacked the triangulating demography, Chicago's black community was led by men who were deeply committed to the Great Migration and had little time for anxieties of the sort that Sadie Mossell described. The challenges, if anything, were even greater than in the mid-Atlantic cities, for Chicago's 1910 African American population of 44,000 would increase fivefold to 234,000 by 1930 and would struggle for space in a context more violent than New York or Philadelphia. In 1910, most black Chicagoans lived in a thin corridor of neighborhoods that extended south from downtown, although only one portion of the corridor was densely African American. The war-era migration more than filled in this narrow strip, creating a thirty-five-block-long black belt that whites in adjoining neighborhoods were determined to contain. Amidst unending violence, which between 1917 and 1921 included a massive race riot and at least fifty-eight house bombings, the black belt broke key boundaries as its northern portion pushed east toward Lake Michigan, doubling in physical size in the 1920s. That expansion, however, only modestly relieved the congestion and housing turmoil. If they chose to focus on the way that newcomers seemed to make Chicago a more segregated, tense, and complicated social environment, Chicago's old settlers could easily have found reasons to resent and turn against the southerners who poured into the city. But that does not seem to have been the spirit. Chester Wilkins, a veteran Pullman porter, recalled much later that the old settlers had their concerns. "They didn't seem to open-arm welcome" the newcomers, he explained, "but they seemed to welcome them."[14]

The reason had something to do with the pattern of leadership in Chicago, a pattern that would be echoed in many other communities. Before the turn of the century, black Chicago had taken its cues from a set of leaders who might very well have worried about the costs of massive population growth. Some of these doctors, businessmen, ministers, newspaper editors, and other professionals moved in a racially integrated middle-class social circle that involved white clients and patrons and was tied closely to the Republican Party. But in the decade leading up to World War I, that old elite had been shouldered aside by a "new middle class" of businessmen and ministers whose interests were entirely within the African American community and who, as a result, were in a position to worry less than their predecessors about relations with whites and white patronage.

These entrepreneurs, many of them from the South, had everything to gain from community growth, and they created institutions that facilitated migration and welcomed the newcomers. Jesse Binga, Oscar DePriest, Lacey Kirk Williams, and Robert Abbott were among those who set the tone for black Chicago's response to the Great Migration. Binga, a Detroit-born businessman who made his first fortune in real estate and then turned to insurance and banking; DePriest, an Alabama native (raised in Kansas) who worked his way into the city's Republican political machine, becoming first an alderman, then the first black congressman to win election anywhere in the country during the twentieth century; Williams, a Texan who turned Olivet Baptist into a social service agency to help southern newcomers and one of the largest congregations anywhere in the country; Abbott, a Georgian who published the most successful black newspaper of the era and helped inspire and guide the Great Migration—the four stand as symbols of a Chicago leadership that applauded and facilitated population growth.[15]

Chicago modeled the ethos of growth and welcome that most other black communities would follow. Whatever the tensions of the first few years, they subsided rather quickly as black communities across the North and then later in the West became accustomed to a regime of population expansion and community-building. That would also be the case during the second-phase migrations. As black populations in the northern and now also western cites doubled, tripled, and quadrupled in the 1940s and 1950s, there were once again challenges and disruptions that could easily have flared into factional hostilities between newcomers and old-timers. But instead, there were few serious manifestations of old settler antagonism. Once again, these communities mostly welcomed the thousands of southerners.[16]

These dynamics enabled northern black communities to take maximum advantage of the skills and talents of the newcomers. Since there were few social barriers, migrants moved readily into all sorts of roles and positions, including community leadership roles. Indeed, southerners had some clear advantages. The brain-drain segment of the Great Migration included men and women with money and entrepreneurial skills and others with educational credentials and specialized occupational training, among them significant numbers of attorneys, writers, teachers, social workers, and ministers whose occupations encouraged the exercise of community leadership. The northern cities were going to absorb their talents, and they in turn would continually transform the capacities of the Black Metropolises. The examples are many. Arthur Mitchell, William Dawson, Herbert Chauncey, Clayborne George, Charles W. White, and Eugene Washington Rhodes head a long list of southern-educated attorneys who quickly entered into leadership positions in northern and western cities during the first phase of the diaspora. Politically active southern-educated doctors included Charles Garvin, Frank S. Hargrave, and Ossian Sweet. Teachers, social workers, and writers numbered Eugene K. Jones, Ella Baker, John Dancy, Whitney Young Jr., James Farmer, James Weldon Johnson, Walter White, A. Philip Randolph, Ted Poston, and John Sengstacke among their ranks. Another occupational stream of this southern leadership invasion flowed through the churches as preachers, either following their flocks or responding to the calls of established congregations, moved straight into positions of prominence and influence. Archibald Carey, George Baker, Lacey Kirk Williams, Joseph H. Jackson, Leon Howard Sullivan, and William Jacob Walls would be prominent on that list.[17]

No city was immune to this southern leadership infusion, not even Philadelphia, whose entries in the 1927 *Who's Who in Colored America* contained more southerners than northerners. By then, the Old Philadelphians were acknowledging the talents of migrants like the South Carolinian E. Washington Rhodes, editor of the community's newspaper, the *Philadelphia Tribune*; Maj. Richard R. Wright Sr., a Georgian and founder of the community's chief financial institution, Citizens and Southern Bank; and the North Carolinian Marshall Shephard, who led one of the city's largest congregations and in 1934 would become the first black Pennsylvanian elected to the state legislature. The point is simple. These communities, in ways that the *Chicago Defender* had first signaled back in 1916, were building social frameworks that readily included newcomers at all levels.[18]

Did the Black Metropolises become southernized in the process? Historian Kimberley Phillips has stressed the ways that black Cleveland was turned into "AlabamaNorth" by the thousands of newcomers who established institutions and social practices similar to what they had known in the South. Cleveland had features that distinguished it from Philadelphia, New York, and Chicago. Before World War I, its African American population was very small, only 8,448 as of 1910. That tiny community was overwhelmed by newcomers, 26,000 of them during the war era, another 37,000 in the 1920s, giving black Cleveland the dynamics of a migrant boomtown. Black Detroit grew at an even faster pace. Its old settlers all but disappeared in the sea of southerners as the city's African American population swelled from 5,741 in 1910 to 120,066 in 1930.

The wonder is that old settlers had any role to play in the face of this explosive growth.[19]

These boomtown communities took on looks and sounds and institutions that had been marked as southern. The proliferation of Baptist, Pentecostal, and Holiness churches spoke to that process. The business infrastructure bore other signs: barbecue stands and grocery stores emphasizing southern food ways; insurance companies and funeral clubs based in Atlanta, Durham, and other southern cities and employing business practices familiar to southerners. In addition, southerners had introduced styles of music, dance, socializing, and worship that over time became standard features of Cleveland and Detroit community life. But it was not just these cities. The tone and look of every northern black community changed as southerners took over old institutions and built new ones. It was true even in New York. Roi Ottley remembered feeling "embarrassed" as a child in Harlem because he did not have a southern accent like most of his friends. Born in the city, his father an immigrant from the Caribbean who had built a successful New York real estate business, Ottley had moved into a Harlem that was much more culturally complicated than one of the fully southernized Black Metropolises. But there too the diaspora had not just expanded the black community; it had transformed it.[20]

The vectors of change ran in more than one direction. Southerners changed too, in many cases eagerly adopting forms that were labeled northern. Social elites in each of the black communities put considerable effort into "educating" the poorer migrants, instructing those who would listen about standards of deportment, especially involving clothes and proper behavior on streetcars and other public places. These efforts by teachers, ministers, social workers, and editors were often couched in a language of northern chauvinism. "We are not in the Southland," the *Defender* and other newspapers would remind readers. The notoriety of *Amos 'n' Andy* added to the pressures. Making fun of newcomers for acting "country" or speaking in southern accents remained part of the culture of the northern black community all through the diaspora. The result was a lasting discursive connection between the North and respectability, the South and backwardness.[21]

At some moments, these status patterns could look like regional divisions. In the 1920s, a "northernized" middle class, most of whose members were in fact southern-born, was readily distinguished from a more overtly southern working class. But in later decades, even these jumbled distinctions mostly disappeared. By the mid-1940s, the markings and vectors of cultural exchange were all mixed up. Forms of music, religion, food ways, speech, and much social practice that a previous generation had marked as southern were now part of the fabric of life in northern black communities, even while those communities sustained the idea that northern ways were superior and that most southerners needed to learn sophistication. We can argue over the proper weightings. Was Cleveland really AlabamaNorth? Was black Detroit really "Detroit Memphis," as one of its largest social clubs liked to claim? Were other Black Metropolises fully southernized? What is clear is that the northern cities were absorbing southerners in ways that minimized tensions and stresses. This had implications for individual adjustment and also would contribute to the development of institutions that would affect the future not only of African Americans in those cities but of Americans everywhere.[22]

New Cultural Apparatus

The institutions that counted most involved politics, the subject of chapter 7. Here we want to think about cultural institutions that were associated with or antecedent to the political reorganizations of the diaspora. Because of where they settled and how their new communities functioned, African Americans developed media institutions and other cultural enterprises that had not been sustainable or perhaps even imaginable in the South. These new enterprises depended in some measure on the external resources and interactions available in the key northern cities and, just as critically, on the internal resources of the emerging Black Metropolis. The concentrated consumer power of tens and hundreds of thousands of wage-earning families—even in the marginal job categories reserved for blacks—constituted an enormous new resource. So did the entrepreneurial energies of the men and women who thought of ways to attract and use those consumer dollars. As Adam Green has recently argued, the long-held notion that the black business and professional classes were inept or irrelevant is off the mark. The evolving cultural apparatus of the Black Metropolis depended upon entrepreneurship in the linked worlds of business, politics, and culture. It also depended upon forms of community and class relations that were more fluid than scholars have often assumed. As we will see when we look at the contrasting community and class relationships among the white migrants, what is striking about the Black Metropolis was the extent to which elite and working-class African Americans participated in common enterprises.[23]

Reorganized institutions of communications keyed the new black cultural apparatus. African Americans gained a national press as a result of the diaspora, newspapers and magazines that for the first time reached very large numbers of black readers across many communities. There had been publications that had tried to do this earlier, but none had ever managed a circulation to match its ambition. Now a set of weekly newspapers and monthly maga-

Selling the *Chicago Defender*, 1942. Newspapers were at the center of the new cultural apparatus that southern migrants built in the great cities of the North. (Library of Congress, Prints and Photographs Division, FSA-OWI Collection)

zines and a Chicago-based news agency would find ways to reach hundreds of thousands of readers while fixing themselves into the fabric of African American life. Roi Ottley, from the vantage point of 1943, described the press as the most influential force in black America, more important even than churches. A journalist, he may have exaggerated the last point, but not when he declared that "they have an influence in American life far beyond the imagination of most white people."[24]

Communications theorists will recognize that in describing an influence "far beyond the imagination of most white people," Ottley was alluding to the changing dimensions of the black public sphere. Understanding the production and circulation of various forms of public discourse and the relationship between communications and the formation of identities and/or political action has been one of the important theoretical projects of recent years, and scholars of African American experience have begun to use these terms and tools in productive ways. Instead of taking group consciousness and political activism for granted, the concept of a black public sphere or spheres invites us to investigate the changing modes, sites, content, and capacity of public expression. Catherine Squires argues that those dimensions changed dramatically as African Americans built new kinds of communities and institutions in the northern metropolises of the early twentieth century. The Black Metropolis enabled the emergence of a unique black "counterpublic" with mature institutions of formal communication that were secure enough to publicly "argue against dominant conceptions of the group" and do so using group-specific codes and styles of discourse. This was different from what she calls the "enclave" black public sphere of the nineteenth century that was largely hidden from whites except for carefully crafted productions by black leaders trying to appeal across the color line. Her terminology may be too emphatic. Late-nineteenth-century black publics did manage to circulate periodicals of various descriptions and used networks of religious organizations, women's clubs, men's fraternal and business organizations, and the Republican Party to support national systems of communication and political action and could be bolder and less hidden than the term "enclave" implies. Nevertheless, there was much that was different about the institutions, the content, and the capacities of the black public sphere that emerged in the context of the Great Migration.[25]

The development of national mass circulation publications had been pioneered by the *Chicago Defender*, the first of the northern weeklies to sell widely in the South. By 1920, Robert Abbott's *Defender* claimed a circulation of 230,000. That number declined in the early 1920s when the paper doubled its price to ten cents and as competitors followed its lead, but circulation remained above 150,000 throughout the decade. Most of the readers were outside of Chicago and received one of four special editions that the *Defender* published. With more than 2,000 sales agents, the *Defender* went almost everywhere that African Americans lived. And it represented a news vehicle as new in style as in range. This was no four- or eight-page sheet. A staff of seventy-five turned out a thick newspaper filled with the kinds of special sections that white newspapers offered: a sports section, an entertainment section, a foreign news section, "Police Court Doings," cartoons and comics, a "Woman's Dept.," a "Health Department," a "Children's Dept.," and a "Clubs-Society" section. News from black communities around the country constituted another section, covering at least five pages.[26]

The *Defender* helped make Chicago one of the media capitals of black America. The city also hosted several other black-owned weeklies, which mostly concentrated on local circulation but were successful enough to deepen the pool of talented journalists looking for opportunities in Chicago. The leading competitors during the 1920s and 1930s were the *Whip* and the *Bee*. More important to the development of a national system of black-owned media was the Associated Negro Press (ANP), which Claude Barnett founded in 1919. The *Defender* had its own national network of correspondents. Barnett's plan was to build something similar that other black-owned newspapers could access. Subscribing newspapers received twice-weekly packets of news items and articles that had been gathered either by ANP staff correspondents or provided by the other newspapers in the pool. It all came out of Chicago, where Barnett's operation became more sophisticated with each passing year. By the early 1940s, ANP dispatches were appearing in 112 weekly newspapers, and the press service had correspondents in Europe and Africa as well as throughout the United States. That decade also witnessed a second generation of media creation that would secure Chicago's leadership for decades to come. In 1942, John H. Johnson, a young employee of the Supreme Life Insurance Company who had come north nine years earlier from Arkansas, decided to try publishing a magazine modeled after the *Reader's Digest*. His *Negro Digest* was almost immediately successful in part because of the way he used the existing black press for marketing opportunities. In 1945, he was ready with another idea, a *Life* magazine for black Americans called *Ebony*, that quickly became the single most popular and important communication vehicle of black America. Selling 400,000 copies a month by 1949 and read by hundreds of thousands more in barber and beauty shops across the country, *Ebony* ensured that the Johnson Publishing Company and Chicago would remain the center of African American magazine publishing all through the second half of the twentieth century.[27]

Harlem could also claim media leadership. Black New York sustained several newspapers, including the venerable *New York Age* (founded in 1885) and the newer *Amsterdam News* (1909), which, like the *Defender*, had circulation networks reaching into the South. More important, Harlem served as headquarters for a variety of national organizations that published periodicals distributed throughout the nation. Started by Marcus Garvey in 1921, the *Negro World* was the weekly voice of the United Negro Improvement Association (UNIA) and a major vehicle for spreading Garvey's ideas and movement. The UNIA claimed that circulation neared 200,000 at some points in the early 1920s, probably a large exaggeration, but it is clear that the *Negro World* was showing up in black communities across the country and bringing with it not only political ideas that challenged African Americans to think in new ways about their future but also news that was very urban-centered, largely about Harlem. The *Messenger*, a monthly edited by A. Philip Randolph and Chandler Owen, was initially linked to the Socialist Party. Although its circulation never exceeded 20,000, it too became an important element in the evolving African American media system, especially after 1925 when Randolph agreed to lead the effort to organize a union of Pullman porters. The *Messenger* went everywhere that the trains went. Another of the New York–based periodicals was *Opportunity*, published by the National Urban League. Launched in 1923 and edited initially by Charles S. Johnson, *Opportunity* became a principal vehicle of the Harlem Renaissance, publishing fiction and poetry as well as social analysis, much of it focused on urban black life, a lot of it New York–centered.[28]

The most important of the New York–based monthlies was the *Crisis*, edited by W. E. B. Du Bois and owned by the NAACP. An opponent of Garveyism, just as he had earlier been an opponent of Booker T. Washington's voluntary segregation, Du Bois made the *Crisis* into a crusading publication whose reach and impact probably had no parallel among African Americans. Circulation had been modest in the first years of publication, which began in 1910 but soared during the war and Great Migration as the NAACP launched protests against lynching in the South, hate riots in St. Louis, and revivals of *The Birth of a Nation* in northern cities. With hundreds of new NAACP chapters springing up in the South and thousands of new members joining northern chapters, circulation briefly reached 100,000 during 1919, then receded in the 1920s as most of the southern chapters were suppressed or folded. Even at its low point in 1934, when Du Bois resigned and the NAACP had to decide whether it could afford to publish the monthly, the *Crisis* remained influential. The politicized segment of African American communities paid attention to the *Crisis*, as did the editors and writers of the black-owned weeklies. Far beyond what its circulation might suggest, this monthly made itself felt, becoming part of the central nervous system of African American public life in the diaspora decades.[29]

Two other cities belong in this discussion of the developing communication networks of black America. The black community of Pittsburgh, while not large, was one of the wealthiest in the nation during the 1920s thanks to jobs in the steel industry. However underpaid they were by white standards and despite hiring practices that kept African Americans in the most menial and dangerous work, steel industry employment (like auto employment in Detroit) paid higher wages than were common in other cities. Robert Vann used those wages to build a powerful newspaper. A North Carolinian, Vann had come to Pittsburgh in 1903 after having won a scholarship to attend Western University. In 1910, equipped with a law degree and an interest in writing, he helped launch the *Pittsburgh Courier*, which struggled at first but prospered amidst the surge of newcomers that began with World War I. In the mid-1920s, Vann decided to take on the *Defender* and aggressively expand circulation outside of Pittsburgh. Within a decade, his publication surpassed the *Defender* in circulation, thanks to first-class writers like George Schuyler and to Vann's editorial and managerial skills. By 1947, the paper employed more than 300 people in the main office and twelve branch offices and published fourteen separate editions with a sworn circulation of 277,000.[30]

Baltimore and nearby Washington, D.C., would also qualify together as a key media center. The ANP and the major newspapers maintained correspondents in the nation's capital to follow the political news and also to report on the many African American organizations that were headquartered there.

Howard University was another focus of attention. The federally funded school was the most important of the Negro colleges and the setting for many projects and initiatives of national significance, particularly during the New Deal era. E. Franklin Frazier, Ralph Bunche, Abram Harris Jr., Alain Locke, William Hastie, and many other leading black academics found employment there. In addition, the Baltimore-Washington area was home to one of the newspapers that was building national circulation, the *Afro-American*.[31]

This raises an important issue since Baltimore and Washington, D.C., are southern cities, at least under the definition that the Census Bureau has long used. We could argue otherwise, and many would agree that Maryland is better described as a border state than a southern state, but it is more useful to acknowledge the complication and use this opportunity to clarify some conceptual issues. If the development of large urban communities was critical to the development of new forms of African American cultural expression, what about the southern cities where black populations were growing at rates almost comparable to the North? Was urbanization the main source of change instead of regional relocation? Emphatic answers to these questions would be a mistake. Black Metropolises of a sort were taking shape in Atlanta, New Orleans, Birmingham, Richmond, Memphis, Norfolk, and Houston as well as in Baltimore and Washington, and these communities would soon have a strengthened, if still vulnerable, black press and also some of the other institutions we will be exploring. But if we lump all of the cities together, we misunderstand the relationship between these places. Certain communities led; others followed. The leaders were mostly in the North where African American incomes were highest, where political and cultural freedom of expression was easiest, where useful interactions with whites were possible, and where the "promised land" story attracted talent and inspired innovation. Baltimore-Washington was the exception that illustrates the rule.[32]

One learns a lot about the geographic recentering of black America from the pages of the *Baltimore Afro-American*, which, even as it made itself into a premier media institution, readily acknowledged the leadership of New York and Chicago. Founded in 1892 and purchased soon after that by John H. Murphy, the *Afro-American* achieved an early stability that eluded most turn-of-the-century black-owned newspapers, especially in the South. Well-managed and supported by more advertising than was typical for the black press, Murphy's paper was also quietly outspoken in defense of black Americans and their rights, evincing an editorial integrity that impressed even critics and won loyal readers. The setting helped. Baltimore had a comparatively wealthy black community and a political system that provided African Americans with greater access to political rights than most southern cites.[33]

Despite its favorable setting, the media revolution was slow in coming to the *Afro-American*. In 1917, while the *Defender* claimed a circulation of 125,000, the Baltimore paper sold less than 6,000. While the *Defender* was pioneering feature-rich journalism, with huge headlines, large photos, and graphics, the *Afro-American* remained an eight-page weekly with a gray layout, dull writing, tiny headlines, and few photos. None of the sensationalism, boldness, or range of Abbott's Chicago paper is evident in Murphy's Baltimore paper. A few articles and editorials about federal policy or national events affecting black Americans and a complement of news and notices from Baltimore and nearby counties of Maryland suggest a lingering localism that contrasted sharply with the Chicago paper.

However, by 1925, the *Afro-American* was a new paper. It had started to change even before John H. Murphy's death in 1922, but the new format and tone owed much to Carl Murphy, who took over from his father and moved aggressively to build circulation and give the newspaper an updated look. By 1925, it had a confirmed circulation of close to 50,000 and had become the leading black newspaper in Washington, D.C., as well as in Baltimore. Later there would be more editions and extensive circulation up and down the eastern seaboard. In 1947, the company was distributing close to 200,000 copies.[34]

The 1925 editions of the *Afro-American* testify to the rapid reorganization of black cultural institutions and public discourse in the early phase of the diaspora. Gone was the localism of just a few years before. The Baltimore paper carried news of black communities across the nation and especially from the northern cities. Items from New York filled at least half a page under the heading "The World's Metropolis." Black Chicago, Cleveland, Philadelphia, and Los Angeles also were covered, as were southern cities. Much of this news was identified as coming from the Chicago-based ANP. It was not all good news. The *Afro-American* made sure that its readers saw scary headlines about "Chicago Church Bombing" and read that "Race Troubles Finally Reach Pacific Coast." But the newspaper's editors knew that important things were happening in the northern metropolises that should be models for the South. Political accomplishments were closely monitored. The appointment of black police officers, rare in the South, had special resonance. "Officers Make Bid for Glory," ran the headline for a story about three black Chicago officers, one a detective, credited with apprehending a gang of robbers. A large photograph of the three accompanied the piece.[35]

The changing cultural apparatus of black America showed up in other sections of the *Afro-American*. In 1917, the newspaper had devoted little space to entertainment, saving its eight pages for church and civic news. In 1925, almost half of its 20–28 pages were devoted to sports, entertainment, humor, and gossip, and in those sections an evolving new framework of celebrity could be seen. Where before, publicity was reserved for educators, churchmen, and other civic leaders, now musicians, vaudevillians, chorus girls, college football teams, and baseball stars claimed the headlines and especially the photographs. Those had been rare in the 1917 paper, just an occasional single column headshot of a Baltimore- or Washington-area political leader, usually accompanying a story meant to demonstrate a milestone in Negro progress. In its 1925 editions, the *Afro-American* published many photos and made them large and exciting. The pretext was often similar, another racial milestone, but the subjects and geography were different. Entertainers were the favorite subject, their fame, travels, glamour, and purported acceptance by white audiences all providing the milestones. "In Far Away Sunny Italy," read the upper caption of a photo showing six beautiful young women arranged in provocative poses. The lower caption identified them as "former members of Brown Skin Vamps . . . now in Milan, after an extensive engagement at Moulin Rouge, Paris."[36]

New Intelligentsia

Even as the Black Metropolises of the interwar era were fostering new media, they were also sponsoring a new intelligentsia of writers, editors, artists, and social scientists whose ideas and energies would play an important role in the twentieth-century political struggles of African Americans. The two developments were related. The new intelligentsia found its voice partly through black-run media and partly through relationships with white-run media institutions based in the northern cities.[37]

Historians use the term "Harlem Renaissance" in connection with the florescence of African American art and literature after World War I. It makes sense because Harlem was the initial center, the celebrated meeting ground, for the first cohort of writers, poets, artists, and editors to attract media attention. Their names are now famous: Claude McKay, Langston Hughes, Arna Bontemps, James Weldon Johnson, Aaron Douglass, Jessie Fauset, Countee Cullen, Zora Neale Hurston, Nella Larsen, Jean Toomer, Sterling Brown, Wallace Thorman, Richmond Barthé, Alain Locke, Charles S. Johnson, and W. E. B. Du Bois. But this was a renaissance, if that is the right term, that reached well beyond those men and women, well beyond Harlem, and well beyond the 1920s. Harlem was not entirely unique even in the 1920s. Blacks in Chicago, Cleveland, and even Los Angeles proclaimed their own renaissance before the decade was over. And the 1930s and 1940s added new dimensions to these intellectual formations. Richard Wright, Ralph Ellison, William Attaway, Chester Himes, Jacob Lawrence, Gwendolyn Brooks, Katherine Dunham, Charles

White, Frank Marshall Davis, Margaret Walker, and Gordon Parks were among the celebrated novelists and artists to emerge in that era, many of them beneficiaries of the federal arts patronage that the New Deal brought to key cities. Expanding too was the corps of African American social scientists, most famously St. Clair Drake, Horace R. Cayton, Charles S. Johnson, E. Franklin Frazier, Ira De A. Reid, and Ralph Bunche. Altogether the three decades following World War I constitute an era when African American intellectuals gained a new kind of presence and new kinds of voices and contributed greatly to setting the stage for new understandings of what African Americans were and could be in American society.[38]

A complicated geography of places and institutions underlay these developments. Northern cities were critical. New York and to a lesser extent other cities provided the publishing outlets, graduate schools, and mixed-race intellectual contacts that inspired and nourished this awakening. Relationships with certain whites and with key white-owned institutions were important, as were the population density and relative political freedom of black communities and the vigorous attention of the activist black press, all of which was hard to duplicate outside of the northern metropolises.

Recent studies of the Harlem intellectual scene help illuminate some of the dynamics, describing the New York literary world of the 1920s as an interracial meeting ground of enormous vitality and freedom where the project of modernism opened relationships and accesses of various kinds for black writers and artists. As literary critic George Hutchinson sees it, the setting provided two kinds of creative densities: "a freer atmosphere for the black artist both because of the concentration, dynamism, and diversity of racial consciousness in Harlem *and* because of the greater freedom and variety of *inter*racial and *inter*ethnic relations, which only intensified the experimental development of new forms of 'racial expression.'" Whether the interracial contacts (and the often overbearing patronage of white benefactors and publishers) also limited the possibilities for certain kinds of artistic production and racial identification is another matter of continuing interest, but there is no doubt that the breakthrough generation of black artists, writers, and sociologists owed its formation to the unique circumstances of the intellectual zones of New York, Chicago, and a handful of other great cities.[39]

This intellectual formation was not entirely a northern story. Indeed, like all other examples of the rearrangements of black cultural enterprises, this one needed both the northern metropolises and key southern settings as well as patterns of population circulation between them. In this case, the circulation involved the Negro college system of the South, which, all through the diaspora period, provided the chief higher educational institutions for African

Americans, educating not just southerners but also many young northerners who, either because of obstacles elsewhere or family loyalties, attended one of the southern institutions. Students moved in both directions, some coming south, others going north, especially to take graduate courses, largely unavailable in the Negro colleges. Graduates, as previously noted, disproportionately moved north in search of jobs. The circulations also involved faculty, whose movements were still more complicated. Many of the leading writers and artists of the Harlem Renaissance and other northern intellectual networks taught for a time in the southern Negro college system. W. E. B. Du Bois, Charles S. Johnson, E. Franklin Frazier, James Weldon Johnson, Zora Neale Hurston, Arna Bontemps, Horace R. Cayton, and Sterling Brown were just some of the prominent intellectuals who moved back and forth between the southern colleges and the northern literary zones, typically using college teaching as a backup when writing or editing assignments in the North failed to pay the bills.[40]

The work lives of the two most widely respected black sociologists of the middle twentieth century are instructive. Charles S. Johnson was born in Virginia and educated in that state's black school system. For graduate school, he headed north to work with Robert Park at the University of Chicago in 1917. Johnson not only studied with Park but also worked under him in the Chicago Urban League office as research director and then as principal author of the *The Negro in Chicago*, the pioneering report by the Chicago Commission on Race Relations. Those assignments led him to New York, where between 1923 and 1928 he edited *Opportunity*, the National Urban League's new monthly magazine and one of the key outlets for the writers and poets associated with the Harlem Renaissance. New York and Chicago were the places to be for black editors and journalists but not necessarily for sociologists. In 1927, Johnson accepted a position at Fisk University in Nashville and spent the next thirty years conducting studies and writing books about the conditions of rural life for blacks in the South. In 1947, he became the first African American to serve as president of that historically black college.[41]

E. Franklin Frazier's career involved a more complicated set of circulations between southern colleges and northern cities. Raised in Maryland, he graduated from Howard University in 1916, then taught for several years at Tuskegee Institute and other southern schools. The chance to do graduate work in sociology drew him north to Clark University in Massachusetts in 1919, where he earned an MA, followed by further study in New York and Denmark. In 1922, he accepted a job as sociology professor at Morehouse College in Atlanta. The next five years clarified the limitations that black intellectuals encountered in much of the South, where they might earn a living but faced a different kind of scrutiny than in the northern cities. When Frazier published "The Pathology of Race Prejudice" in *Forum* magazine in 1927, influential whites in Atlanta denounced him and others threatened violence. He was forced to resign his post and leave that southern city. He headed for Chicago to resume his graduate studies in the department that Robert Park had made into the center for race relations studies. Two years later, while writing the dissertation that would set up his first two books, *The Negro Family in Chicago* (1932) and *The Negro Family in the United States* (1939), he accepted a job under Charles Johnson at Fisk, later moving to Howard where he became head of the sociology program and which remained his principal base for the remainder of his illustrious career. In 1948, Frazier was elected president of the American Sociological Association, becoming the first African American ever to head a national professional society.[42]

Historian John Hope Franklin followed a similar geography. Younger than the others, he was born in 1915 in Oklahoma in the tiny black community of Rentiesville. His father, an attorney, and his mother, a schoolteacher, moved the family to Tulsa in time for John Hope to attend high school. At age sixteen he began his undergraduate education at Fisk University since Oklahoma offered nothing equivalent for African Americans. Graduating in 1935, his heart set on a Ph.D. in history, Franklin looked north, as did virtually all black southerners with graduate school aspirations. He entered Harvard that year and spent the remainder of the 1930s in graduate studies, including a stint in Berlin. But when it came time to look for a teaching job, he, like the others, had to look south. His first job was at St. Augustine's College in North Carolina, followed by a post at North Carolina College for Negroes at Greensboro, and a third at Howard. In 1956, having authored three books — one of them, *From Slavery to Freedom*, destined to become perhaps the most influential African American history text of all time — Franklin was offered and accepted a position in the North, at Brooklyn College.[43]

This specialized geography, so complicated for the individuals involved, probably increased the cultural importance of the new black intelligentsia. Like the *Chicago Defender* circulating its northern stories and southern critiques in the barbershops of Mississippi and Alabama, intellectuals like Johnson, Frazier, and Franklin brought the perspectives and examples of the Black Metropolis with them when they took up posts in the South. The Negro colleges would become staging grounds for all sorts of projects that would transform the South over the coming decades. Much of the black southern New Deal would depend on northern-trained educators and scholars based at those institutions. Some of the political boldness that showed up in black southern communities in the 1940s and the civil rights era would also emanate from those same institutions.

There would be many sources of change, but one of the vectors that would broaden the "New World" that Ottley saw coming ran between the northern Black Metropolises and the offices of educators like Charles Johnson, Arna Bontemps, Franklin Frazier, and W. E. B. Du Bois, whose occupations moved them back and forth, North and then South.[44]

Jazz Cities

Few white Americans noticed the reorganization of the black press or paid much attention to the new African American intelligentsia of the 1920s and 1930s. The writers of the Harlem Renaissance, so well known today, had few white readers, and some of those who did pay attention saw the work through condescending eyes. The developments examined so far were felt mostly within the black public sphere. African Americans read the black press, and in doing so many learned to value the contributions of the black literati. Newspapers reported important speeches and reviewed books. Women's clubs and church groups, in the South as well as the North, read novels and poems and debated their meanings. Whether this engagement extended deep into the black working class is not clear, and Langston Hughes's famous quip that "the ordinary Negro hadn't heard of the Harlem Renaissance. And if they had, it hadn't raised their wages any" is worth considering. In any case, only African American publics were involved; most of this was lost on white America.[45]

It was in the realm of entertainment that the Black Metropolises offered access to new forms of external visibility, the sort of visibility that had some potential to influence racial relations. Music is the big story, the great twenti-eth-century channel to fame, fortune, and cultural influence, the first substantial venue where whites were willing to acknowledge a pattern of black creativity and authority. Ragtime, Dixieland jazz, blues, gospel, bebop and free jazz, rhythm and blues, rock and roll, soul, funk, and hip-hop — the list of musical genres pioneered by black artists and audiences extends from one end of the century to the other. And since music is never just music, this most social of art forms became a conduit for other forms of cultural influence: in fashion, language, social styles, and values that whites learned from black performers. No other enterprise can compare to the way that popular music has Afro-Americanized aspects of broader American culture.[46]

The Black Metropolises and the circulation of the Southern Diaspora were key to all that. Complicated debates surround the precise origins of blues and jazz and the exact mechanisms that turned them into the wellsprings of twentieth-century American (and world) popular music, but the basics are clear: southern musical styles needed to come north to achieve commercial takeoff.

The Black Metropolises became for musicians what they were for writers, settings that supported both innovation and recognition.[47]

The Mississippi River served as the chief highway of the jazz/blues revolution. Black musicians had been traveling its length either by boat or train in the late nineteenth century, some following the minstrel show circuit, others the red light districts from New Orleans to Memphis, St. Louis, and on to Chicago. Scott Joplin pushed ragtime up the river in the late 1890s, performing and publishing his rags in St. Louis and Sedalia, Missouri, Chicago, and then New York, where after the turn of the century the syncopated beat found its way into countless Tin Pan Alley compositions and vaudeville shows, raising the tempo of American popular music.[48]

Dixieland jazz followed during World War I. The sound had circulated in New Orleans and other cities for years before a white bandleader, Tom Brown, took it to Chicago and New York in 1916 and made it the new popular sensation. A little controversy helped. After Chicago's musicians union objected to the nonunion band and their low-class "jazz" music, Brown came up with a new name, "Brown's Dixieland Jass Band," and watched the crowds multiply. The band was invited to make a record by the Victor Talking Machine Company, one of the New York record companies that, along with the vaudeville companies and the songwriting teams known as Tin Pan Alley, dominated commercial music production. "Dixieland Jazz Band One-Step," released in early 1917, would over the course of the next decade sell more than a million copies. Victor made another important record that year. William C. Handy, a classically trained African American bandleader who had taken an interest in the musical structure of blues songs that he had heard during several years in rural Mississippi, had begun to write, publish, and perform his own compositions. Moving to Harlem in 1915, he convinced Victor to record "St. Louis Blues," which the company gave to the Jewish vaudevillian Sophie Tucker to sing. Like the up-tempo jazz record, the blues solo was a huge hit. Victor's future was set. The Jazz Age had been launched.[49]

It would be several years before African American artists were making records and almost two decades before bands led by Louis Armstrong, Duke Ellington, and Count Basie began to share the exposure and opportunities that white musicians like Tom Brown and Paul Whiteman, "The King of Jazz," enjoyed. But even in its early years of rampant expropriation, the jazz revolution paid dividends in the Black Metropolises, where, in the words of pianist Willie (the Lion) Smith, cabarets were "sprouting up like dandelions in the spring." It was not just cabarets. In very short order, these communities hosted elaborate entertainment infrastructures and had become centers for an important regional and racial cultural exchange.[50]

Black New York had well-established links to the entertainment industries headquartered in that city. African American comedians, minstrel groups, musicians, and songwriters had been finding their way to the city for more than half a century, looking for opportunities in the vaudeville and theatrical venues that catered to the city's population or in the traveling shows that New York producers sent round the country. Actors like Charles Gilpin and the comedy team Bert Williams and George Walker, bandleaders like Ford Dabney and James Reese Europe, and songwriters like Will Marion Cook and J. Rosamond Johnson and his brother James Weldon Johnson were pillars of turn-of-the-century black New York and numerous enough to create a small black-owned entertainment sector. A pair of west-side hotels, the Marshall and the Maceo, provided the main venues for a club and theater scene that drew the cream of the black community and sometimes white actors, musicians, and other entertainers looking for interesting material.[51]

By the 1920s, the scene had moved to Harlem, and there was nothing small about it. The community claimed three full-size and several small theater companies, with fares alternating between drama and more often musical revue. Nightclubs, dozens of them, employed hundreds of dancers, comedians, and musicians. The most lavish, the Cotton Club, catered to whites-only audiences; a few drew mixed crowds; and the smaller and cheaper venues rarely saw a white face. Prohibition, prostitution, and gambling added to the atmosphere of Harlem's entertainment zone, attracting certain whites even as these illegal activities increased the stigmatic associations. Jazz music, Harlem, African Americans, booze, and vice — the images all flowed together in a mix that some found enticing and profitable, others repellent.[52]

In any case, the entertainment complex was a major part of black New York. The 1930 census counted 1,177 professional actors and showmen along with 1,844 professional musicians among the city's black inhabitants. Likely an undercount, given the peripatetic and part-time nature of those professions, entertainers nevertheless far outnumbered other professional occupations and comprised roughly 2 percent of the African American workforce in New York. More stunning is the fact that New York City was home to almost as many black entertainers as was the entire southern region of the United States. Only 882 actors and showmen and 3,827 professional musicians and music teachers had been counted in the sixteen southern states and the District of Columbia that year.[53]

Harlem was the most important, but other northern cities also developed black entertainment zones. Chicago's South Side, with more than 1,000 actors, dancers, and musicians, had more professional entertainers than the combined states of Louisiana, Mississippi, and Tennessee, where the blues and jazz were

Part of black Chicago's large entertainment zone, this cabaret catered to well-heeled audiences, mostly whites on this evening in 1941. More than 1,000 musicians, actors, and dancers worked in Bronzeville's entertainment sector. (Library of Congress, Prints and Photographs Division, FSA-OWI Collection)

said to have originated. Bronzeville claimed a theater and club scene almost as energetic and disreputable as Harlem and, in terms of musical development, probably more important. Many of the jazz bands of lasting reputation (King Oliver, Louis Armstrong, Jelly Roll Morton) made Chicago their home base, as did even more of the blues singers. The record companies that began to mine this talent in the mid-1920s set up studios in Chicago and used the *Chicago Defender* as the primary advertising vehicle for their "race records." From the 1920s through the 1950s, if the blues and its progeny had a principal base, it was, as Robert Johnson would have said, "Sweet Home Chicago."[54]

Other cities were also involved. St. Louis and Kansas City had more clubs and musicians than New Orleans and Memphis. Detroit, Philadelphia, and Cleveland each had thriving jazz quarters. Even the West Coast cities—Los Angeles with a 1930 black population of 38,000, the Bay Area with 7,000, Seattle with only 3,300 African Americans—had become entertainment centers. In recent years, a curious competition has emerged as local historians make competing claims about which city had the most dynamic music scene or hosted various jazz innovations. But behind that parochial boosterism lies a critical observation. Collectively, these northern and western black communities were centers for a set of interactions that were remaking American music and other institutions of popular culture.[55]

The interactions were multiple and bi-directional. The Black Metropolises drew the musically talented and musically curious from all over and from various ethnicities. One of the interchanges was between black and white musicians, some of them Jewish. The whites came to the blues and jazz clubs in Harlem, on Chicago's South Side, and on Central Avenue in Los Angeles to listen and learn, taking many of the sounds they heard and turning them into numbers that big crowds of young whites danced to in the ballrooms and clubs across town. There was flattery in this theft—and much more. The white jazz bands paved the way for mainstream white audiences to begin to appreciate new forms of music and the black artists who produced it. By the 1930s, some African American bandleaders would be working the big ballrooms and appearing on the popular radio shows. The swing era would also see the first high-visibility integrated bands, most notably the Benny Goodman Orchestra. White musicians got by far the better end of the bargain, but these interactions were changing not only the sounds but also the sociology of American music.[56]

Another interaction was regional. The northern city entertainment zones were the principal hubs of an occupational migration system that both drew musicians out of the South and moved them back through it again. Like the attorneys, writers, and artists who knew they had to move north to practice their professions, musicians were drawn to Chicago, New York, Los Angeles, and other cities by the chance to make a career and hopefully a living. The record companies, booking agents, and important clubs were almost all in those cities, and so was the excitement of hearing, learning, and perhaps creating the hottest new music.

Southern cities had a role to play in this musical system. Atlanta, Birmingham, New Orleans, Houston, Dallas, and Memphis each had numerous and important jazz clubs and blues cellars. In the mid-1920s, after race records had proved their market, the invention of portable electric recording machines made it possible for the record companies to send teams to these and other southern cities looking for new talent. But the southern recording tours, which ended in 1931 when the Depression gutted the record industry, did not alter the fundamental geography of musical opportunity. The southern cities served as unofficial farm teams for the Black Metropolises (just as they would in the system of Negro baseball that was developing contemporaneously). Southern musicians got started on Atlanta's Decatur Street or Memphis's Beale Street, and the best of them then headed for New York, Chicago, Kansas City, or Los Angeles, hoping for a chance in the majors. Alphabetically, we can list a hundred names of blues and jazz greats, from Perry Anderson to Muddy Waters, and all will tell the same story: grew up in the South, honed their skills in the bordellos or clubs of a southern city, and went on to fame, if rarely fortune, in one of the music capitals of the North or West.[57]

But this was no one-way migration. The life of the musician was a life on the move: the successful ones on scheduled road tours, the less successful often moving on, looking for a new gig or a new band. These circulations had all sorts of implications, not only for musical development but also for other aspects of black cultural life. Musicians were part of the human circulatory stream of black America, carrying information and styles of music, dress, and deportment from city to town to city, from North to South to West, wherever audiences of African Americans could be found.[58]

This musicians' circuit gave the South some of its most striking images of the wealth and glory that a few had found in the North. When Bessie Smith, the first great musical celebrity of the era, returned to the South as the "Empress of Blues" on her various tours of the mid-1920s, she was doing more than singing. Southern audiences may have remembered her from her years on the southern vaudeville circuit, but it was her move to Philadelphia in 1922 that opened the door to fame and wealth. When Columbia Records, the biggest of the record companies and the last to set up a race records division, decided to take the plunge, its talent scout, black pianist and songwriter Clarence Williams, invited the tall blues shouter to make a record. "Downhearted Blues" sold more than 700,000 copies, and Columbia had an "Empress" to promote.[59]

For black America, it was something new. Even as Columbia was cheating her out of royalties, the company was working with the black press to turn her into an icon. Bessie Smith was soon known not only for her voice but also for her wealth and glamour. She was a new kind of figure, a black female celebrity, a woman of fame and fortune whose image as well as music spoke to millions.[60]

Smith exemplifies several dimensions of the cultural power that followed from the Great Migration and the buildup of the Black Metropolises. These settings not only were creating new celebrities and changing the forms of cultural production but also were altering basic patterns of social structure, including gender. The industry that created the "Empress of Blues" was playing a role in that. As records and northern clubs became the most important venues for the blues, female blues singers replaced men as the most celebrated interpreters of the music. Ma Rainey, Ida Cox, Mamie Smith, Clara Smith, Sippie Wallace, and Ethel Waters were some of the female blues stars who shared the limelight with Bessie Smith during the 1920s at a time when neither records nor performances by males enjoyed the same kind of demand. This was a development with implications beyond the music world. The elevation of women to celebrity status and the extraordinary imagery associated with their blues material and performance styles—images of female power, earthy wisdom, and raw sexuality—reverberated widely. There were many ways that the Great Migration changed gender relations, and the musically engineered shift in female iconography—from club women to blues women, from Ida B. Wells to Bessie Smith—was one of them.[61]

The beachhead in American popular culture established in the 1920s would be expanded in the decades that followed as African American musicians developed new musical forms that achieved commercial takeoff in the great metropolises. Big band swing in the 1930s and 1940s brought a new kind of legitimacy and bigger audiences of whites. Duke Ellington, Count Basie, and Louis Armstrong gained recognition and respect that went beyond the patterns of the 1920s. Sophisticated whites now acknowledged musical genius instead of primitive talent. On the opera stage, Marian Anderson and Paul Robeson gained a related level of credibility with their voices, as they shuttled between European and New York theaters and opera houses. The fusions of gospel music offered a third musical front. Refined and promoted by Thomas Dorsey and Sallie Martin, the gospel blues sounds and professional gospel soloists and choirs took root first in the black churches of Chicago, then spread nationwide in the 1930s. In the next decade, those sounds would cross over into pop music behind the soulful styles of Mahalia Jackson, Sam Cooke, and others.

Each of these steps added to the musical legacy of the Southern Diaspora and to the evolving cultural credibility of African American artists. The issue of cultural recognition is tricky. The role of the black entertainer has been the subject of much debate. Did the increasing presence and visibility of African American musicians, singers, actors, and sports figures signify a breakthrough in the scheme of racial containment or a minor adjustment? Was there power in these roles or just another form of exploitation? Did whites learn to respect the genius of black artists or merely biologize accomplishments with revised discourses on the "natural" abilities of the African race? Answers have shifted back and forth over the decades. African American journalists in the 1930s and 1940s usually assumed that there was cultural empowerment in the kind of fame that key musicians and entertainers had managed to claim, even while political activists and social scientists cautioned otherwise. Gunnar Myrdal warned in 1944 against the double-sided accomplishments of black musicians: "The Negro is often praised for his artistic talents—frequently in a rather derogatory way, for the implication is that this is the only domain where he is capable of noteworthy achievements."[62]

The *Chicago Defender* and John H. Johnson's magazines were more optimistic. The *Defender* devoted at least a page of each issue during the 1940s to music news, with headlines that left no doubt that musicians were winning important battles for "the Race." "Negroes Predominate Annual Esquire's All-Star Band Poll," the weekly announced as it reported the results of *Esquire* magazine's 1944 survey. Johnson's *Ebony* would also take celebrity at face value. One of the secrets to its mass-market success proved to be its big photo spreads and gossipy articles about Lena Horne, Louis Armstrong, and other heroes of the bandstand.[63]

Negro Digest took the time to consider the question more carefully. In one of its initial issues in 1943, the magazine reprinted an article, "The Negro in Show Business," that had recently appeared in *Billboard*, adding this introductory blurb:

"Billboard survey shows tremendous gains by race despite many obstacles." The article, by a white writer, Paul Denis, was carefully balanced. It detailed the many areas where black entertainers were forced into demeaning roles or excluded altogether, pointing especially to the practices of the radio industry. "Radio still has a rule that a Negro cannot be represented in any drama except in the role of a servant or as an ignorant or comical person. Also, the role of the American Negro in the war effort cannot be mentioned in a sponsored program." But in other venues, there had been "terrific progress." "The biggest break . . . has been the recognition of Negroes as first-rate jazz musicians," which the writer thought was having important symbolic effects. "The Cotton Club version of slaphappy Negroes has started to give way to the Café Society version of Negroes as serious, formal-dress concert-style creative musicians and singers."[64]

This "biggest break" may not seem very big out of its own context, and Myrdal was right about the way many whites viewed black musical accomplishments, but the influence of this enterprise and of the other institutions that were developing in the Black Metropolis did not depend upon universal acknowledgment. It depended mostly on what African Americans, not whites, thought about these developments. The Black Metropolis was creating celebrities that most contemporary white Americans never heard of. It was creating intellectuals whose ideas would be acknowledged by learned whites only much later. It was creating music that would one day be viewed as classical but in the 1940s could still be dismissed in some quarters as primitive. But you would not understand that from reading the major black-owned newspapers. The black press hailed these accomplishments and celebrities with a vigor that permitted no doubt about their significance. In the parallel universe of black America, it was self-evident that these accomplishments meant new cultural influence. And that belief proved to be self-fulfilling. The sense of progress and the sense of increasing acceptance of black art and black celebrities were critical to the morale and momentum and activism that enabled African Americans to push through the great political as well as cultural breakthroughs of the middle twentieth century. Cultural credibility may have been slower in coming than many African Americans understood, but their confidence was one of the forces that ensured that it would, in time, happen.

A League of Their Own

Roi Ottley thought he knew exactly when the big breakthrough in cultural recognition had come. "The night of June 25, 1935, was a memorable one for Black America," he wrote seven years later. It "marked a dramatic highlight in the race's march along the glory road." On that night in homes across America, families had stayed by the radio waiting to learn the outcome of a much ballyhooed fight between a young boxer from Detroit named Joe Louis and his much larger and more experienced opponent, the Italian Primo Carnera. Not since Jack Johnson's last title defense in 1915 had a black boxer been allowed to fight in the top ranks of the heavyweight division. Louis was not fighting for the crown that June night, but when he knocked out Carnera in the sixth round, it might as well have been the title fight. "Pandemonium broke loose" in Harlem, Ottley reported. "Tens of thousands marched through the streets, slapping backs, shaking hands, and congratulating each other." The celebration had several meanings. It was a victory over Italy, then engaged in the cruel conquest of Ethiopia, the last independent black African nation. It was a victory over the color line, over the system of sports segregation that prevented black athletes from competing against whites. Mostly it was a victory for racial pride and morale, a triumph, Ottley explained, that was "credited not only to him, but to the whole race."[65]

Sports became the other major arena where African Americans in the second quarter of the twentieth century established beachheads of credibility, earning acknowledgments of talent from substantial numbers of whites while adding to the resources of race pride. And as with the other institutions we have examined, the new geography of black America was key. The Black Metropolises of the North led the development of professional sports capacity for the same basic reasons that they nourished the other formations of this era: they provided a richer consumer base than existed anywhere in the South, a cohort of enterprising business leaders with money to invest, more freedom of action and interactions with useful white agents and industries, and proximity to the major black-owned newspapers. The African American press played "electrician," to borrow a concept from historian Henry Lewis Suggs, "turning on the lights" for black commercial sports just as it had done for African American entertainers. And the juice flowed both ways. Sports helped build the new black press, just as it built massive circulations for white-owned dailies during the interwar decades. This was the golden age of spectator sports and also sports journalism. Americans in later decades would spend more money and perhaps more time watching sporting events, but this was the era for reading about them. Nothing took a back seat to sports journalism, which featured some of the best writing to appear in the newspapers of that era and was thought to be responsible for much of the male readership. Sports were front page in both the black press and the white urban dailies.[66]

The most important sport by far was baseball, an enterprise that had clear racial and regional coordinates. Professional baseball had once been selectively integrated, but by the turn of the century the major leagues and the official minor leagues enforced a rigid ban on black players. African Americans answered with teams and leagues of their own. Until the 1920s, these were haphazardly organized. Teams came and went, leagues existed more in theory than practice, and the few organizations that actually paid real salaries made most of their money barnstorming from town to town staging exhibition games against local talent. Andrew (Rube) Foster is credited with putting Negro baseball on a different footing. The Texas-born ballplayer had come north in 1902 and had earned fame and a modest living pitching for teams based in New York, Philadelphia, and Chicago. In the next decade, he switched to management. As player-manager and co-owner, he turned the Chicago American Giants into the most successful and financially healthy club in African American baseball. A close relationship with the *Chicago Defender* was one of his secrets. Robert Abbott's newspaper lavished attention on the Texan and his team.[67]

In 1920, Foster called a meeting of owners of the most successful clubs and proposed that they form the Negro National League to be operated on principles similar to those of the whites-only major leagues. The teams that started official competition the next year were based mostly in the midwestern cities (Chicago, Kansas City, Detroit, Indianapolis, Cincinnati, Columbus, and St. Louis). A rival Eastern Colored League came together two years later under Nat C. Strong, a white booking agent and owner of the Brooklyn Royal Giants. The Eastern Colored League had teams in Brooklyn, Harlem, Atlantic City, Darby (outside Philadelphia), and Baltimore. Neither league achieved the stability that Foster had hoped for, and both fell victim to the Great Depression, but during their years of operation in the 1920s, black athletics gained a visibility that could not be undone. The leagues, with their (mostly) regular schedule of competition, turned black professional baseball from a novelty into a sustained sport that fans could follow from week to week with the help of the supportive black press. The major newspapers now built up the fan base while creating a set of sports celebrities whose names would become famous throughout black America—none more important than the king of Negro baseball, Rube Foster, who, thanks to the *Defender*, was becoming a living legend.[68]

The Negro leagues were reorganized starting in 1933 under the guidance of W. A. (Gus) Greenlee, a Pittsburgh tavern owner and numbers racketeer who worked with the *Pittsburgh Courier* the way Foster (who had died in 1930) had worked with the *Defender*. By 1937, there was a Negro National League in the East Coast cities and a Negro American League in the Midwest and South. These organizations would prove more stable than their predecessors in part because many were owned by policy kings, men like Greenlee who needed a legitimate cover for their gambling operations and had money to invest and sometimes lose. The next ten years would be remembered as the great years of Negro baseball, with big crowds, fairly stable finances, and star players like Satchel Paige, Josh Gibson, Oscar Charleston, Judy Johnson, and Cool Papa Bell, all of whom played at one point for Greenlee's Pittsburgh Crawfords and had the *Courier* following their every move.[69]

The geography of black baseball mirrored that of most other new cultural enterprises. The major teams, with a few exceptions, were in the North. The South provided the talent. The Negro Southern League had been formed in the 1920s, but it had none of the financial resources of the two dominant leagues and was generally regarded as a minor league. The exceptions were Baltimore, Birmingham, and Memphis, which hosted major teams fairly consistently from the mid-1920s until the leagues collapsed in the 1950s. The regional distribution had something to do with the greater wealth of northern black communities, but that was not the only factor. These baseball clubs depended upon barnstorming for a significant part of their income, even after the establishment of genuine league play. And barnstorming in the North was more productive in two senses than was barnstorming in the South: financially and in terms of publicity. In the North, there was a market for interracial competition, which in many southern states was illegal. Whites in the small cities and towns of the North (and also out west in California) paid to see the black teams play the hometown favorites, either a minor league or semiprofessional club.[70]

Even more exciting were exhibition games between a black team and a barnstorming group of white major leaguers. These competitions became a big part of the lore of black baseball. African American fans loved to read about Satchel Paige shutting down Dizzy Dean's All-Stars in the summer of 1934 when the African American team won four of six exhibition games against the white team. Sportswriters like Wendell Smith and Chester L. Washington of the *Courier*, Sam Lacy and Art Carter of the *Afro-American*, and Frank "Fay" Young of the *Defender* mined these contests (and also the winter league competitions in Cuba and Mexico) for evidence that Paige would triumph in the big leagues, that Josh Gibson might equal the slugging power of the great Babe Ruth, that Cool Papa Bell might be the fastest man on the base paths, that the 1938 Homestead Grays, "the New Gas House Gang," might be as good as the St. Louis Cardinals.[71]

Those speculations became part of the political work of baseball. The Negro leagues held enormous symbolic power for black Americans. Denied the right to compete in the athletic systems of a sports-obsessed society, African Americans could take pride in this shadow system that had grown strong enough to invite these kinds of speculations and comparisons. The fact that some white sportswriters also began to pay attention to the Negro leagues and their stars was added confirmation. Long before Jackie Robinson finally got his chance in

1947 with the Dodgers, "Josh the Basher" and "Old Satch" had found their way into the sports columns of major newspapers and sometimes onto the pages of major periodicals. By the early 1940s, quite a few white readers shared in the game of speculation that sold so many issues of the *Courier*: How good were these guys?[72]

One event each year crystallized black baseball's contribution to the power and pride of African Americans. The East-West Negro League All-Star game was first held on 10 September 1933, just months after the major leagues staged their initial All-Star game and in the same venue, Comiskey Park, home of the Chicago White Sox. Gus Greenlee conceived the event, and the *Courier* spent a month promoting the contest, telling its readers across the country that major league managers and owners would be watching the showcase of talent and quoting Pittsburgh Pirates president William Benswanger as saying that some of the black stars were "worthy of the highest in baseball." The contest drew a crowd of 8,000 that first year despite bad weather. The second year, 25,000 attended, including, said the *Courier*, "countless celebrities" and "nearly 5,000 white fans."[73]

By then, other newspapers had joined in promoting the East-West classic, which would soon become not only the centerpiece of the baseball season but also a showpiece for black society. With attendance soaring above 40,000 in the 1940s, it became an annual testament to the consumer power of the Black Metropolis as well as to the baseball prowess of black stars. Held most years in Comiskey Park, the game attracted a who's who of African American celebrities and an impressive lineup of white Chicago politicians and sports aficionados. The black press covered it from every angle, and the three major papers (the *Defender*, the *Courier*, and the *Afro-American*) also printed the ballots that fans used to vote for the All-Stars. For black Americans of the 1930s and 1940s, the East-West All-Star game stood for more than baseball; it signified achievement and recognition and expectation. The attendance numbers were themselves a source of mounting pride. "Sunday, July 27 was a banner day in Negro sports history," Fay Young informed *Defender* readers in 1941. "Fifty thousand fans watched the 'dream game' at Comiskey Park, Chicago. It was the largest crowd to ever attend a sport event in Negro history."[74]

This and other "banner days" owed a lot to Joe Louis. His breakthrough had set the standard for baseball and many other endeavors. His 1935 victory over Primo Carnera had been followed by a string of momentous contests that over the next three years electrified the boxing world. A huge win over former title-holder Max Baer was followed by a surprising loss to the German Max Schmeling, an outcome that thrilled Adolph Hitler and quite a few American racists. Louis then tore up the rest of the competition and in 1937 earned a title shot against the reigning champion, Jimmy Braddock. When Louis floored the Irishman in the eighth round, he had the crown and the distinction of being the youngest heavyweight champion in history. But the real climax was still to come. In June 1938, he stepped back in the ring with Max Schmeling with not only his reputation but the symbolism of New Deal America versus Nazi Germany on the line. Louis by then had become America's hope, America's champion, supported by most newspapers and public leaders, including Franklin Roosevelt, who had invited the champ to the White House and told him, "Joe, we need muscles like yours to beat Germany." It is estimated that 70 million Americans listened to what radio announcer Clem McCarthy called "the greatest fight of our generation." It was also one of the shortest. It took Louis only 124 seconds to put Schmeling on the canvas and to erase all doubts about his greatness.[75]

The significance of all this for black Americans can hardly be overstated. Louis had given African Americans a taste of something new. Not only did he triumph in the ring, he also triumphed in the public eye, becoming the first African American to achieve mass media celebrity status. He was one of the first African Americans to break into the front pages of the daily newspapers. At a time when black political leaders were rarely acknowledged, when black entertainers were just beginning to gain publicity, Louis broke the race barrier of mainstream journalism. Sportswriter Damon Runyon marveled at the coverage. "It is our guess that more has been written about Louis in the past two years than about any living man over a similar period of time, with the exception of Lindbergh." Of course Jack Johnson had also been on the front pages, but that had been a different sort of coverage. The white press had turned him into a threat and a monster. More recently the mainstream media had made room for Father Divine but had turned his religious movement into an object of curiosity and ridicule. And not everything written about Louis was laudatory. Biographer Christopher Mead has sifted through the newspaper coverage, finding plenty of jungle references, ignorant darky imagery, and obsessive fascination with skin color.

Sportswriters during the 1930s had an inane passion for alliterative nicknames, and Louis's race inspired their most imaginative work. Besides the well-known nicknames "Brown Bomber" and "Dark Destroyer," various writers also called Louis "the Sepia slugger," "the mahogany maimer," "the dark dynamiter," "the dusky David from Detroit," "the sable cyclone," "the tawny tiger-cat," "the saffron sphinx," "the dusky downer," "Mike Jacob's pet pickaninny," "the shufflin' shadow," "the saffron sandman," "the heavy-fisted Harlemite," "the coffee-colored kayo king," "the murder man of those maroon mitts," "the tan-skinned terror," "the chocolate chopper," "the mocha mauler," and "the tan Tarzan of thump."

But the mainstream media also responded to Louis in ways that allowed him to become a positive symbol and ultimately a hero to whites as well as to blacks.[76]

Joe Louis's journey to the boxing greatness was, like Louis Armstrong's journey to jazz greatness, a product of southern migration and northern Black Metropolises. Born in a sharecropper's cabin in Alabama in 1914, Joe Louis Barrow was the seventh of eight children born to Lillie and Munroe Barrow. The parents split up when he was young, Lillie remarried, and in 1926 the family moved to Detroit where Joe's stepfather found a job on the Ford assembly line. Failing at school, Joe Barrow as a teenager worked odd jobs and hung out with a street gang. But it was not in the streets that he discovered his talent for boxing. That sport, even more than baseball, followed distinct institutional pathways. The place to learn boxing was in a youth recreational program of a sort African Americans would find only in big cities like Detroit. Had he stayed in rural Alabama or even moved to Birmingham, the world might never have heard of Joe Louis. It was at Brewster Recreation Center, not far from where he lived, that Joe first put on gloves. He evidently changed his name at about the same time, dropping Barrow so that his mother would not learn of his hobby and make him quit—not a big problem, it turned out.

In late 1932, Louis moved into Golden Gloves competition, taking advantage of a citywide amateur system that had already sent at least one competitor to the Olympics. His success in the amateur ranks brought him to the attention of John Roxborough, an attorney who ran Detroit's numbers operation and who, like a lot of gambling operators, was also involved in professional boxing. Roxborough had the funds and connections to launch Louis's career. He took Louis to Chicago and turned him over to Jack Blackburn for training. Blackburn had been a professional fighter and, briefly, Jack Johnson's sparring partner. Now he trained others, mostly white boys, and had handled two world champions in the lighter divisions.[77]

Louis was in good hands, the kind of hands that could be found only in the institutional nexus of the Black Metropolis. In Roxborough and his partner Julian Black, who took over management, and in Blackburn, who would be his trainer, he had found men who would teach him the finer points of the sport and also negotiate the tricky connections to get him past the color line that since 1915 had kept black boxers out of contention in most divisions, especially the all-important heavyweight division. Unlike baseball, boxing's segregation was haphazard and effective mostly at the top. In the North, black and white fighters competed regularly, but only the latter had access to the big purses and

Boxing great Joe Louis with John Roxborough, the attorney/policy king/business-
man who, with his partner Julian Black, managed the fighter's career. Twelve years
old when his family moved to Detroit from rural Alabama, Louis broke boxing's
color line using the institutional resources of the Black Metropolis. (Walter P.
Reuther Library, Wayne State University)

title contention. It would take skill and connections — and some luck — to get
Louis into the big time, and in 1934 and 1935, as Louis pounded his way through
the heavyweight competition, these came together. Roxborough and Black
persuaded a New York boxing syndicate to tamper with the color line. The
20th Century Sporting Club was a new company looking for a marquee fight
that would help it break the Madison Square Garden monopoly. Moreover, the
syndicate included Damon Runyon and the sports editors of the Hearst chain's
two New York newspapers as secret partners. Not only was Louis going to get
his fight, but with Runyan and his Hearst partners on board, he was going to
be the beneficiary of the largest sports publicity apparatus in America.[78]

Richard Wright refused to believe in the Black Metropolis, at least in the sense
of a hopeful and powerful space. Late in 1951, he contacted John H. Johnson of
Ebony magazine and offered an article. Wright had recently revisited Chicago
after a dozen years in New York and Paris and wanted to share his homecom-

ing impressions with the half-million readers of what was now the premier media outlet for black America. When Johnson read the piece, he was dismayed. Wright had taken another look at the city of *Native Son* and decided that not much had changed, or not enough had changed. Appearing as the lead article in the December issue, "The Shame of Chicago" begins with Wright complaining about Chicago's basic "ugliness" and weighing that against the beauty of Paris and New York. He then revisits the South Side, and for a moment he is impressed. Many of the worst neighborhoods have been upgraded, and the miserable kitchenettes are mostly gone, he finds, and there is a vigorous commercial zone and signs of wealth. "I was surprised to find a tremendous increase in material prosperity, flourishing business establishments and new hotels." He even concedes at one point that "the Black Belt had grown rich." But then he shifts gears and focuses on the limitations, on the fact that Bronzeville is still mostly a slum, that segregation has not been broken, that African Americans are still residentially contained and occupationally limited. And he concludes with the pessimistic tone that marked *Native Son*, declaring that Chicago's South Side still breeds "helplessness" and "hopelessness."[79]

Johnson had published Wright's article but was not about to let him have the last word. The publisher and the writer had much in common; both had left the South as teenagers and finished their growing up in Chicago. Chicago had also supplied the connections and stimulations that had unlocked their respective careers. But the nation's most celebrated African American author and its most important African American publisher disagreed vehemently in their perspectives on the Black Metropolis, and Johnson wanted *Ebony*'s readers to know it. The issue's editorial page featured a long rebuttal under the heading "Return of the Native Son," which criticized Wright for clinging to the images of the past. "The Editors of *Ebony* were faced with a puzzling dilemma," it began. "We were confronted with the strange situation of offering a hearty amen to everything that Wright says and yet feeling that his report was distorted and one-sided." Wright was "wearing blinders" when it came to the "better side of Negro life in Chicago." The editorial then went on to develop a different balance. "It is true that some of the worst slums in America are found on the South Side but right next to these slums are encouraging signs that point to a new era for Chicago. In the Hyde Park area, once the home of Chicago's richest millionaires, there are now many Negro families living next door to whites" who are "not 'evacuating' the neighborhood, as they have so often in the past. . . . Chicago has its sins in the slums built by racial hate," the editorial continued. "But Chicago has its virtues, too. . . . Negroes have better jobs, enjoy more luxuries, wield more political power in Chicago than in any other U.S. city." The editorial then ends with an invocation that captures some of the differences in perspectives: "Let us occasionally mix pride and self-esteem with discontent and belligerence."[80]

Johnson was not finished. The following year, he asked a pair of eminent black journalists to debate "New York vs. Chicago: Which Is Better for Negroes?" Ted Poston, an award-winning reporter for the *New York Post* and one of the first African Americans to hold such a position at a major daily, wrote the case for New York. Roi Ottley argued for Chicago, convinced nine years after the publication of *"New World A-Coming"* that "Chicago's South Side has displaced Harlem as the hub of advancing Black America." The real point of the exercise was not the competition but another chance to refute Richard Wright and show the accomplishments of both Black Metropolises.[81]

Poston began with a count of New York gains in employment, education, and politics and a reminder that "not even the most rabid Chicagophile has seriously challenged the supremacy of New York as an intellectual and artistic center. It is sufficient to note that Richard Wright observed Bigger Thomas in Chicago, but came to New York to write about him." Poston's key point, however, had less to do with accomplishments than with the progress of race relations. He maintained that New York was more tolerant and that the "Negro New Yorker is less penned in than his Chicago counterpart." In contrast to Chicago, where violence greeted blacks who tried to find homes outside the ghetto, New Yorkers had been steadily leaving Harlem without, he claimed, "one act of violence, without one case of arson or vandalism, without one near-riot or terrorist attack."[82]

Ottley refuted none of this, building his case for Chicago not on the issue of prospects for integration but through his portrait of new opportunities and power within black Chicago. He emphasized expanding home-ownership, the huge business cohort (5,000 black-owned businesses, he claimed), Bronzeville's publishing empires, its advancing unionized working class, its growing white-collar sector, its voting power, and its physical expansion. "Chicago's Negro population has been expanding steadily. The white population has ceased to grow within Chicago. Actually, the whites are moving to the suburbs out of the voting districts of the city. It is with this in mind that some people are predicting that it will not be too many years before Chicago will have a Negro mayor —a development unthinkable within any foreseeable time in New York!"[83]

These *Ebony* exchanges in 1951 and 1952 highlight the conflicting meanings and dimensions of the Black Metropolis. These men were seeing and describing different things. The Black Metropolis was first of all an actual community, but it could also be seen both as a symbol of power and progress and as an institutional complex and cultural formation. Wright saw black Chicago the way most whites did, as a slum, and the way a generation of black activists would, as a ghetto imprisoned behind walls of structured racial inequality. By all objective measures, he was right. It is only within the relativist framework of Johnson, Poston, and Ottley, who measured progress not against white society but against the greater limitations of other places and other times, that the celebratory concept of a Black Metropolis made sense. Ottley sensed the third dimension: that these unattractive places turned out to be empowering places. Ghettos for those who lived in them, these spaces nevertheless held the key to new forms of influence and new expressions of identity that would help in the struggle for change. Ottley glimpsed the potential and named it. The Black Metropolis was the future in embryo: a New World A-Coming.

# Uptown and Beyond

Mary Jean (Lily) Tomlin had lived in Detroit all of her life. Aretha Franklin, three years younger, had done most of her growing up there. In the mid-1950s, these two daughters of the Southern Diaspora were still some years away from fame and fortune. Tomlin, whose family had migrated from Kentucky in 1938, a year before her birth, had spent most of her youth in north central Detroit in a neighborhood that in the 1950s was making a rapid transition from white to black. Her father was a metal worker at the Cleveland Brass Company, earning a solid living but not enough to lure the family into home-ownership. They lived in an apartment in a neighborhood that was something of a crossroads in the social history of Detroit. On one side was 12th Street, Detroit's Jewish commercial district. A few blocks to the north were nice homes where wealthy families lived; a few blocks to the east was Woodward Avenue, once the dividing line between white and black Detroit. That line had started to crumble when Mary Jean was in elementary school, and by the early 1950s, most of the whites, including her family, were leaving.[1]

The Tomlins settled in the nearby suburb of Highland Park just about the time that Aretha Franklin enrolled in Mary Jean's old school, Hutchins Junior High. Aretha had been living one mile to the east in very different circumstances. Her father had brought his family north in the early 1940s from Memphis, where he had pastored a Baptist church. First serving a church in Buffalo, in 1946 Rev. C. L. Franklin accepted the call to lead Detroit's New Bethel Baptist Church. The congregation was large but far from wealthy, mostly factory workers and maids, many of them recent migrants. They loved Franklin, whose beautiful sermons soon attracted even more worshipers. By the mid-1950s, New Bethel claimed one of the largest African American congregations in Detroit, and Franklin was famous. Touring the country part of each year, preaching in churches and rented halls and charging several thousand dollars per appearance, C. L. Franklin's sermons and "million dollar voice" made him one of the most admired black ministers in America.[2]

Aretha grew up in the vortex of the Black Metropolis, surrounded by the people and the institutions that were giving African Americans a new sense of place and mission. It was in no way a typical childhood. She lived in a large house in the best neighborhood in black Detroit, surrounded by the community's most prominent members. Editors and political leaders dropped by to talk with her father. Wealthy businessman Charles Diggs Sr. lived on the same block, and his son and future congressman Charles Diggs Jr. was a family friend. Famous ministers were guests in the home and preached in her father's church, among them Adam Clayton Powell Jr. and Martin Luther King Jr. Aretha paid most attention to the entertainers. "Politics were way over my head," she says of her youth, "while music hit me right at home." Literally. The great names of the gospel music world passed through her front door. Mahalia Jackson, Clara Ward, Dinah Washington, Sam Cooke, and Lou Rawls were all friends of C. L. Franklin. James Cleveland was choir director in his church. Aretha's gospel roots were set early.[3]

For Lily Tomlin, there was no white southern metropolis to grow up in. Despite the fact that southern whites were almost as numerous in Detroit as southern blacks, and despite patterns of prejudice that labeled both groups as outsiders, the two populations developed sharply different community formations. This chapter examines the identity struggles and community-building of the white diaspora and corrects some of the inadequate understandings in the sociological and historical literature, where the focus on "hillbilly ghettos" encourages the notion that southern white migrants built well-defined communities similar to those forged by black migrants or by some immigrant groups. The reality was more complicated. For the whites, there would be nothing equivalent to the kind of solidarity, the dense institutional matrix, and the resulting cultural and political influence that came together in black Detroit and other Black Metropolises. Where black southerners of necessity resided together in physically connected communities, white southerners would separate geographically, dispersing across a thousand settings, some in the big cities, many in the suburbs, others in small cities and rural areas. The whites would also separate by class, displaying little of the cross-class civic consciousness that was key to the empowerment of the Black Metropolis. And their fragmented community formations would have much to do with the cultural and political legacy of the white diaspora. Not as a coherent social group with a shared identity, but with different and sometimes contradictory politics and identities, southern whites would contribute ideas, institutions, and energies that would affect the places they settled and also the region they had left behind.

Social Challenges

It was easy to assume that black southerners and white southerners occupied similar positions in 1950s Detroit when Lily Tomlin and Aretha Franklin were teenagers. Their numbers were similar. At the start of the decade, the census had counted 199,000 southern-born whites and 221,000 southern-born blacks within a metropolitan population of 3 million. Other Detroiters saw both groups as outsiders and equivalent in many ways. In a 1952 survey, a large sample of Detroit residents were asked to identify a particular group of people who were "undesirable and not good to have in the city." Negroes and "southerners or hillbillies" were two of the favorite choices, trailing only criminals and gangsters on the undesirable list.[4]

The need to respond to prejudice and hostility would dominate the social strategies of both populations of migrating southerners, but the challenges were in fact very different. For black newcomers, racism was inescapable and life-shaping. It affected where they could live and what kinds of jobs they might hold, and it helped structure both a physical community and a powerful sense of racial solidarity. White southerners faced attitudes that operated at a different level. Prejudice could make a deep impression but usually did not set limits on where southern whites might live or work and did not enforce strong patterns of social separation. Relations with nonsoutherners were more often strained than hostile. "You had a constant be on your toes, have your guard up," former Kentuckian Jim Hammitte recalled of his early years in Detroit in the 1940s. As soon as he would open his mouth, his "southern language" would earn a comment, "some northern person [would] grab it and poke fun at you immediately."[5]

There was much confusion in such exchanges, symptomatic of the complicated identity issues among the white migrants. For one thing, white southerners were not accustomed to thinking of themselves as "ethnic others"; they were, after all, white and as fully American as anyone. Many did not even think of themselves as southerners. That regional identity was not much used in large sections of Oklahoma, Texas, Kentucky, and West Virginia, each of which contributed heavily to the white diaspora. Moreover, the stereotypes haunting the migrants—the key figures being the hillbilly and the Okie—did not seem to apply to all southerners. Both overlapped so strongly with the idea of "poor white trash" that it was easy to assume that these were not regional but class stereotypes directed only at those migrants who violated behavioral norms. Hillbillies were those people "over there," not respectable southerners "like us." And there was further geographic confusion. Did the label "Okie" envision anyone other than Oklahomans? Did "hillbilly" refer only to people from the mountains? Should flatland southerners feel implicated? Who should?[6]

All of this made the social situation complicated and unique, not really comparable to the challenges that groups marked by different national origins (who are prepared to be seen as Polish or Mexican, and so on) have experienced. Neither were the responses. People reacted to the tension surrounding their regional origins in various ways depending upon context and personality, some defensively, others by ignoring the problem or convincing themselves that the hillbilly and Okie comments did not apply to them.[7]

One way to handle the stereotypes about southerners was to stop acting southern. More readily than most ethnic identities, southern regional markings were easy to shed. A change of accent and regional grammatical expressions was usually enough to achieve social invisibility, to become just another white person. Some of the migrants and even more of their children chose this course. Sociologist Lewis Killian interviewed a young woman in the late 1940s who had successfully dropped her southern accent and spoke northern, at least most of the time. "When I went to Columbus, Ohio, from North Carolina, they called me more names than I ever heard of—hillbilly, stumpjumper, and all that stuff. Right then I decided to get rid of my accent. The only time I talk like a southerner now is when I get schnapps under my belt!"[8]

The strategy was especially common among the middle class and the socially ambitious. A 1976 study of the linguistic habits of former Oklahomans living in California's San Joaquin Valley suggests both the ease of language shifting and the class-linked pattern. Bruce Berryhill found that those with an incentive to do so learned to speak "Californian." These adjustments were easiest at young ages, but Oklahomans of middle-class status who had arrived in California as adults also changed accents. On the other hand, working-class former Oklahomans retained more of their native speaking style, leading Berryhill to suggest that "Oklahoma speech" had become a social dialect of the white working-class in that part of California. The latter was a special effect of the southern San Joaquin Valley, where southerners were so numerous that over time they dominated the white working class, but the insight about middle-class incentives to change accents and other markings applies broadly.[9]

There are examples too of former southerners who took the invisibility strategy even further, lying about backgrounds in order to avoid what they regarded as the stigma of their birth. One Oklahoman who came to California as a child in the 1930s let her own children grow up believing that she was a Californian by birth. A man of the same generation spent most of his life living in what he later called his "Okie closet," afraid to reveal his background. Beverly Barrett later resented her parents' efforts to hide their Oklahoma origins. "My dad joined the Masons, went from being a Southern Baptist to a Presbyterian, and just generally worked to cut himself off from his past. . . . Us kids were sent to speech class to get rid of our accents, forbidden to listen to Okie music, given music lessons and encouraged to date the sons of local doctors and attorneys."[10]

Efforts to achieve social invisibility were most common among the middle class and are noteworthy not only because of their psychological dimension but also because of their effect on community formation. Class separation became one of the salient features of southern white migrant experience. Unlike black communities where elites and working class were bound together into a single physical and political community, middle-class white migrants typically wanted nothing to do with laboring-class migrants. Lewis Killian spent two years studying southern whites in Chicago in the late 1940s and noted the pattern of class alienation. Migrants with white-collar jobs sometimes joined nonsoutherners in very harsh assessments of their fellow southerners. The manager of a department store who had been transferred to Chicago from the South told Killian: "The southern people that live around here are what you'd call white trash in the South. . . . People call 'em 'hillbillies' up here." A wholesale produce salesman claimed that "there's a big difference between a 'hillbilly' and a 'southerner.' I'm a southerner, but I'm not a hillbilly. You know what the hillbillies are—they're the lowest class of white people." Other middle-class southerners expressed sympathy for their fellow migrants while keeping an emotional distance. "People do call the southern whites living around here 'hillbillies,'" explained the Texas-born wife of a Chicago businessman. "I suppose they apply it to the working class people. I don't think they'd call us that unless they were angry with us—and then not to our faces. They wouldn't dare!" She continued in what Killian called a "paternalistic" vein: "I object to hearing foreigners call our people, many of them fine people, 'poor white trash' or 'hillbillies.' They're working people, to be sure. Some of them are quite poor and don't have much education. But they are charming people."[11]

Whether responding defensively or sympathetically, wealthy and middle-class migrants mostly kept carefully away from their working-class counterparts. Living scattered in neighborhoods where there were no concentrations of southerners, those of the white-collar class were typically very careful about behaviors and associations that might invite the hillbilly stereotype. Killian was in a good position to understand these class dynamics. The University of Chicago sociology graduate student was himself from Georgia.[12]

Some elite southerners stressed their regional background rather than hid from it. Killian did not mention them, but there were two small chapters of the United Daughters of the Confederacy in Chicago in the late 1940s, their members very proud of their southern heritage and very careful about their social standing. Other cities also had UDC chapters, and in New York, occupying a stately brownstone, was the Southern Society, a men's organization that had been founded in 1886 "to promote friendly relations among Southern men resident or sojourning in New York City, and to cherish and perpetuate the memories and traditions of the Southern people."[13]

These southern heritage organizations had lost most of their membership by the late 1940s and even more of their public visibility. In the early part of the century, before southern white migration had become an issue, the New York Southern Society had been much in the public eye. With hundreds of members — including some of the wealthiest and most powerful men in the city — the Southern Society had, among other feats, helped Woodrow Wilson secure the 1912 Democratic Party presidential nomination. The Daughters of the Confederacy was a larger organization and had also been very active and visible. Founded in 1894, its principal theater of operations was the South, but the Daughters had chapters in most of the northern and western states. The 1932 annual report lists 121 chapters in twenty nonsouthern states. Missouri, a border state with its own Confederate history, had the largest contingent of 46 chapters and 1,851 members, but California was not far behind with 32 chapters and 1,420 members, followed by New York (426 members), Ohio (303), Colorado (188), Pennsylvania (171), Illinois (150), Washington (130), and Massachusetts (111).[14]

UDC units devoted themselves initially to raising funds and caring for aging veterans of the Confederate army, but as the veterans died off, the organization concentrated on historical projects. Like their sisters back home, the expatriate Daughters worked at public education, sponsoring gatherings to celebrate the birthdays of Robert E. Lee and Jefferson Davis, offering prizes to stimulate writing and teaching about the Old South, and lobbying schools and libraries to make sure that they told the right kind of stories about the boys in gray. They tried to be very visible, looking for public venues, especially parades, where they might display their southern pride and teach about the valiant Confederacy. The Ohio division was proud to report in 1932 that "we took part in the Army Day parade at Columbus, Ohio, with auto decorated in Confederate colors and flags. This was the first time that the Daughters of the Confederacy have been invited to take part in this annual celebration and the first time a Confederate flag has ever been waved on the streets of Ohio's capital city."[15]

That kind of visibility started to wane in the late 1930s, just about the time that newspaper pages began to fill with stories about the hillbilly and Okie migrants. Membership also fell off. Between 1932 and 1943, California membership dropped from 1,420 to 957, despite a huge increase in the number of southern-born whites in that state. The New York membership fell from 426 to 221; Ohio from 303 to 196; Illinois from 150 to 69. The timing is curious. These were years when the expatriate population was growing and also years when UDC units in the South were enjoying a revival, thanks to Margaret Mitchell, David O. Selznick, and *Gone with the Wind*. Staging *GWTW* showings, readings, and dress-up parties, the southern units enjoyed a renewed burst of confidence and energy, but not the units outside the South. It looks like they were doing less public work and were having trouble recruiting new members. Or maybe they were reluctant to try.[16]

It is a curious pattern, evidence of the complicated class dimensions of the white diaspora. Elite white expatriates had become increasingly nervous as the migration of poor southern whites became a public issue. Whatever pride they may have felt in their origins, many after the mid-1930s were cautious about how they expressed it. The New York Southern Society lowered its profile. It maintained its elegant club quarters and exclusive membership and very occasionally would attract attention when a controversial Jim Crow southern politician came to New York to give a speech. It finally closed its doors in 1973. Daughters of the Confederacy chapters also survived, some working on commemorative projects, like the decades-long effort to convince legislatures in the far West to designate thousands of miles of public roadways as the Jefferson Davis Memorial Highway. But the Daughters also worked on their image as aristocratic southern ladies and distanced themselves from the working-class migrants whose presence had complicated their lives. Lily Tomlin's mother, a Kentuckian, may not have wanted to celebrate the Confederacy, but if she did, she and most other southern-born women living in Detroit would not have felt welcome in Detroit's UDC chapter. The chapter reported in 1940 that its forty-nine members held their annual Jefferson Davis Memorial at the Grosse Pointe Yacht Club, one of the most exclusive and expensive venues in that city.[17]

Hillbilly Ghettos and Southernized Valleys

Working-class southern white migrants were less likely to undertake the dramatic personal revisions that white-collar migrants often used to avoid unpleasant stigmas. Some in fact responded to the social challenges of resettlement in the way that sociologists expected, by seeking the company of fellow migrants and creating socially separate communities. Ethnographers had no trouble finding examples, either in the North, where communities of this sort came to be called "hillbilly neighborhoods," or in California, where the favorite term was "Little Oklahomas." Most big cities had one or more areas that would be known through the postwar decades for their concentrations of southern whites. Chicago had several, including a Near West Side neighborhood sometimes designated Tennessee Valley and Uptown, well north of the Loop. In Detroit, part of the Cass Corridor became the major hillbilly zone. Cincinnati had both Lower Price Hill and the Over-the-Rhine neighborhood. Cleveland offered its "West Virginia Ghetto" on the near west side. In Los Angeles, Bell Gardens was said to be where the Okies lived, while the suburb of San Pablo across the bay from San Francisco had the same reputation. In addition, there were two broader geographies that brought southern whites together in densities that promoted group cohesion, both valleys: one in the West (the San Joaquin Valley of California) and one in the North (the Miami Valley of Ohio).

Chicago's Uptown became the most famous example of a metropolitan southern white neighborhood, a favorite site for social workers, sociologists, and journalists. Located six miles north of the downtown, not far from the lake, Uptown had been a prosperous middle-class neighborhood of tony apartments in the 1920s. But parts of the area began to decline in the 1930s and at an accelerating rate after the war as speculators divided large apartments into smaller units. Southerners and other low-income whites began to move into the aging buildings in the late 1940s, and by the early 1960s the area had acquired a firm reputation as Chicago's "hillbilly ghetto." The title was never accurate. Uptown actually had many populations. Its northern and lakefront sections remained upscale and nonsouthern throughout the postwar period. In the deteriorating zone, many of the poorest residents, elderly inhabitants of a string of skid-row hotels, also had little to do with the southern migration. Even on the streets near the rundown business district, southerners shared the low-rent apartments with Native Americans, Latinos, and other whites, probably never claiming a majority. Nevertheless, whites from West Virginia, Tennessee, Kentucky, Alabama, and other southern states did constitute a critical mass in this poor Chicago neighborhood, giving it not only a reputation but also a social atmosphere that was markedly different from other parts of the city.[18]

Uptown and its counterparts served only a particular portion of the migrant population, and then for the most part briefly. Residents were almost exclusively working-class, and many were newcomers who lived there a short time, taking advantage of social connections and cheap rents to get themselves established, then moving on, typically to the suburbs if they felt that Chicago was to become their new home, otherwise back to where they had come from. A port-of-entry for the newest and poorest of the newcomers, the neighborhood cycled many thousands through its apartment houses.[19]

For some migrants, Uptown and the other hillbilly enclaves were also valued as communities. Some chose to live there because they wanted the company of fellow southerners and because of the southern-oriented institutions and services located there. This infrastructure was limited, certainly nothing like the range of institutions that immigrant or African American neighborhoods usually supported. The absence of a southern white middle class was telling. Killian carefully noted the weak institutional apparatus in the hillbilly neighborhood on Chicago's Near West Side that had preceded Uptown as the city's best-known southern white area until it disintegrated as African Americans and Puerto Ricans moved in during the 1950s. Unlike immigrant communities, he found only what he called a "truncated special service structure" and noted that nonsoutherners owned many of the establishments that catered to the migrants. Nevertheless, the hillbilly neighborhoods did offer a number of venues for community interaction: barbecue stands and other eateries that catered to southern tastes; hillbilly taverns, so named because they featured country music, cheap beer, and a hard-knuckle reputation as "fighting and dancing clubs"; and various Baptist and Pentecostal churches.[20]

In the 1960s, the apparatus of community became more complex as governmental and nonprofit agencies responded to the publicity surrounding the hillbilly migration and began to treat these neighborhoods as if they constituted ethnic communities, designating their populations "Appalachians" and providing cultural as well as social services. In 1963, the Chicago Southern Center opened its doors in Uptown. A community center that helped residents find jobs, assisted with their health needs, and provided poverty services, it also hosted square dances and educational activities designed to promote a positive sense of Appalachian identity. Sponsored by the Council of the Southern Mountains, which from its base at Berea College in Kentucky had been for fifty years the champion of Appalachian heritage, the Chicago Southern Center and similar agencies in Cincinnati, Detroit, Dayton, and Columbus reflected the energies of social workers who were devoted to the idea that diaspora southern whites constituted a culturally distinct population. Director Raleigh Campbell, a Kentuckian himself, later explained that the Southern Center was intended as a place "where people could develop an identity. It was a place where they could hold on to parts of their culture which were positive and learn the skills to make it in a new culture."[21]

The hillbilly ghettos were unattractive spaces catering mostly to the poorest elements in the white diaspora, but in the two southernized valleys, more inclusive patterns of community-building developed. The San Joaquin Valley in California and the Miami Valley in Ohio recorded the heaviest densities of southern white population, thanks to massive and ongoing migration sequences. Over time, these areas became home to so many white southerners that, almost without trying, the newcomers found themselves rubbing shoulders, becoming neighbors, reproducing southern cultural practices, and developing distinctive communities.[22]

The San Joaquin Valley, the setting for John Steinbeck's *The Grapes of Wrath*, saw huge and continued waves of migration from the western South, initially because of the prospect of work in the cotton fields, fruit orchards, and oil fields that anchored the valley economy. But in time, the newcomers worked their way into positions of influence in the economy and politics. When journalist Oliver Carlson drove through the area in 1952, white southerners comprised close to one-third of the white population and dominated many of the smaller cotton and oil towns in the southern portion of the valley. These towns seemed to have been lifted out of a different part of America. "The Texas twang and the Arkansas drawl pervade discussions at the cotton gin, the filling stations, the bars and the market," Carlson observed. Even Bakersfield, the medium-sized trading and agricultural finance center for the southern valley, showed signs of southernization. It was not just the accents. Religious and commercial institutions also told the story. Instead of the Methodist, Presbyterian, Episcopalian, and Lutheran churches that usually graced California towns, the valley was dotted with Baptist and Pentecostal churches. The jukeboxes in cafés and bars carried another clue: stacks of records from *Billboard*'s "country and western" charts. So did the menus: barbecue, chicken-fried steak, and biscuits and gravy were favorites. And then there were the even more obvious signs, like the one outside the P&J Café in Arvin, which called itself "The Home of the Oakies."[23]

The Miami Valley was not the same kind of valley as the San Joaquin, not in the twentieth century anyway. Industry dominated this west Ohio valley, which extends from Cincinnati north and includes the cities of Hamilton, Middletown, and Dayton. With Kentucky just across the Ohio River from Cincinnati, this area has always known migration from that and nearby southern states. As the nearest and most easily accessed of the industrial zones offering jobs during the diaspora period, the Miami Valley gained proportionately more southern white newcomers than any other extended area in the North. Here, migrants from Kentucky and Tennessee established themselves in numbers and concentrations similar to Oklahomans, Arkansans, and Texans in the San Joaquin Valley. And the social dynamics appear to be similar. Southern whites established enduring neighborhoods inside the cities and dominated some of the suburbs around them, including Norwood outside of Cincinnati and New Lebanon near Dayton.[24]

The industrial city of Hamilton, forty miles north of Cincinnati, might well be considered the Miami Valley's equivalent of Bakersfield. Both medium-sized cities became more and more southernized as the effects of concentrated migration and economic mobility allowed southern white community-building to reshape an entire city. Home to a large paper company and several other firms that had deliberately recruited Kentuckians from the 1920s on, Hamilton's population of southern whites increased decade by decade, most coming from Kentucky, followed by West Virginia and Tennessee. By the 1950s, white southerners dominated the working class and were also showing up more and more in white-collar sectors, where some were taking a professional interest in ethno-community development. Entrepreneurial Kentuckians in Hamilton were setting up stores and services to cater to their fellow migrants, including cafés and taverns that flagged southern tastes. Here too were the religious enterprises that helped structure Okie communities in the San Joaquin Valley. Butler County, encompassing the two small cities of Hamilton and Middletown, Ohio, had as many evangelical churches in 1971 as did Detroit or Chicago.[25]

But these areas—the two valleys and the various hillbilly ghettos—have loomed too large in scholarly and popular understandings of the southern white diaspora. Most southern whites never lived in any of these southernized spaces. The majority in fact chose to live in places that were not identified as southern white communities. What most wanted was not social separation but a good home in a nice white neighborhood, even if there were only a few families of their background nearby.

Lily Tomlin's parents could have looked for an apartment in Detroit's Cass Corridor, near the Third Avenue hillbilly taverns and barbeque stands that earned that street the nicknames "Tennessee Valley" and "Little Kentucky." Instead, they found an apartment in the ethnically mixed Twelfth Street neighborhood two miles to the north. Living next to other southerners was not something they cared about one way or another, Lily remembers. A 1959 survey of 140 employed southern white male household heads living in Chicago found most expressing the same view. Only 10 percent said they preferred to live in a neighborhood where many of their neighbors would share their regional background. That was actually less than the 12 percent who said they wanted absolutely no southern neighbors. The vast majority were split between those who said they did not care one way or another and those who preferred a neighborhood composed of both southern and nonsouthern whites.[26]

This survey was a fairly accurate portrait of not just preferences but actual residential outcomes by the end of the 1960s. One of the IPUMS samples from the 1970 census provides information on the neighborhoods (census tracts) where former southerners lived. The samples for each neighborhood are too small to say anything definitive, but the data line up closely with the Chicago survey and are worth reporting. First, they show a broad pattern of residential dispersion. White southerners resided in 68 percent of the 3,112 neighborhoods belonging to the cities and suburbs of the six major metropolitan areas of the Great Lakes region (Chicago, Detroit, Cleveland, Milwaukee, Indianapolis, and Cincinnati). Second, there were some but not many neighborhoods where southern white densities exceeded 30 percent. If the samples are correct, less than 10 percent of former migrants lived in such areas. Some 35 percent lived in neighborhoods where former southerners were very scarce and a slightly larger number (36 percent) in a neighborhood where other southerners resided in numbers that exceeded population norms without suggesting neighborhood domination, where 10 to 20 percent of households shared that background. Blue-collar neighborhoods of single-family homes either inside the city or on its suburban outskirts, all-white but ethnically mixed, these, not the hillbilly enclaves, were the modal spaces for southern white residence by 1970. In Detroit, they went by names like Taylor, Hazel Park, Madison Heights, Lincoln Park, Plymouth, and Warren. In Cleveland: Brunswick, Lakewood, Brook Park, Berea, Parma, and Middleburgh Heights. In Los Angeles: South Gate, Bell Gardens, Inglewood, Hawthorne, and North Long Beach.[27]

Not Quite Home

Residential dispersion meant that for most white migrants, the resettlement experience would be an exercise in integration. They settled in communities where they were strangers, where their accents and backgrounds attracted attention, and where to various degrees they felt out of place. In many of those communities, the differences were not just regional. In white working-class neighborhoods in the industrial North, their neighbors were often second-generation immigrants of various European ancestries. The accents, the customs, the religious institutions (mostly Catholic)—all of it seemed new and challenging.

Moving north from Kentucky in 1942 to work in the defense plants, Jim Hammitte's family initially lived in a succession of central city neighborhoods, sometimes in apartments but in public housing when they could get it. Some of their neighbors were southerners, but most were northerners, usually of immigrant stock, and Hammitte describes relations as uneasy: "I never felt comfortable for a lot of years." In 1950, after almost eight years in the city, the family bought a house in the suburbs, exchanging urban social complexity for a suburban version. The new neighborhood was "practically all northern," says Hammitte, elaborating, "I'm talking about Germans, Polish, you name

Warren, Michigan, 1956. This Detroit suburb and similar suburbs across the North and West were favored residential choices for white southern migrants. (Walter P. Reuther Library, Wayne State University)

it. But we seemed to dig in there and the southern aspect of it seemed to melt away."[28]

"We seemed to dig in there." Hammitte's words speak for the generation of whites who moved north or west in the second phase of the diaspora, the mid-1930s through the 1960s, the period when volumes were greatest and Okies and hillbillies were in the public eye. Those efforts at integration followed no single formula. Some "dug in" quickly, others slowly. Some were more willing than others to let their southernness "melt away." The particulars of the situation and the personalities involved made each experience slightly different, but the basic sense of tension was very common. More than is normal with interstate white migrants, southern whites often felt uneasy about their social circumstances and struggled to feel at home in their new homes, and many would remain for years self-conscious about their regional background.

That may have been one of the reasons for the high rates of return migration. As discussed earlier, whites had much higher return rates than their black counterparts. That is how Jim Hammitte's story ends. The Hammittes learned to like Detroit but never quite enough. When Jim's auto parts company (he had worked his way up to a supervisor position in the plant) announced that it was leaving high-wage Detroit for low-wage Alabama in 1972, the Hammittes seized the opportunity. They still had friends and family in the southeastern Kentucky county that they had left thirty years earlier and had been thinking about returning. "We felt we wanted to come back South, anyhow at retirement."[29]

The Tomlins each made their own peace with Detroit. Guy worked hard and spent much of his leisure time in bars and betting parlors, where he enjoyed the camaraderie of men of similar tastes, some but not all of southern background. Mother Lillie Mae saw to the kids and wanted very much for the family to achieve something. Better educated than her husband, she attended PTA meetings, encouraged Lily and her brother to broaden their intellectual and social horizons, and worried about her husband's drinking. Lily remembers that her mother was always "very lady-like and well spoken" and careful not to appear in any way like an uneducated hillbilly. On the other hand, she was not cutting herself off from fellow southerners. Quite a few of the friends she socialized with were from Kentucky, and Lillie Mae was a member of Detroit's largest southern-based Baptist church. Moreover, she kept up the old home connections, hauling the kids back to Kentucky to visit cousins during the summers. When Guy died in the early 1970s, Lillie Mae moved back to Paducah.

Mary Jean (Lily) and her younger brother, Richard, had long since gone their own ways. A self-described "free spirit," Lily does not remember being much aware of the issues of social identity that challenged not just her elders but many of her peers. She may have been making choices that reduced her contacts with other southern whites in her age group. She attended the city's premier academic high school, Cass Technical, which straddled all sorts of social lines in the mid-1950s. She joined the popular crowd, became a cheerleader ("the best white cheerleader Detroit ever had," she says with a laugh), and was a member of a trend-setting sorority ("I was one of the cool kids"). Most of her friends came from families wealthier than her own and not southern. She does not recall thinking her background mattered. But it did to some. It comes as a surprise to her that one of her high school friends would much later describe Tomlin's family as "borderline hillbillies." The term, she thought, applied only to low-class disreputable sorts, not solid, working-class families like her own. "I have a feeling I just didn't compute what was going on. Survival instinct, I guess."[30]

Scholars have long sought the right language to clarify the social transformations associated with the white diaspora. One argument is that southern whites developed an ethnic group relationship. It dates back to 1938 when University of Michigan sociologist Erdman Beynon observed that "there appears to be an emergent group consciousness among the southern white laborers" derived, he thought, from the fact that northerners treated them like a "homogeneous group." Four years later, economist Stuart Jamieson offered a similar suggestion about Oklahomans, Arkansans, and Texans living in California's valleys who were taking on the "appearance of a distinct 'ethnic group'" in response to the label "Okie." Lewis Killian followed up in 1949 with a more detailed analysis of the social-psychological factors encouraging white southerners in Chicago to forge an ethnic relation. He emphasized context, holding that external prejudice was one of the keys. He noted that the proliferating stereotypes of white southerners as hillbillies produced a defensive response among working-class southerners, who developed "heightened group consciousness" and "resentment of the out-group." He found that many southerners had begun to call themselves hillbillies, even while resenting the term and even while pointing out that it made no sense since few southerners in Chicago hailed from the upland Ozarks or Appalachia. They also developed a "counter stereotype," stories that emphasized that southern whites were superior to northerners, whom they sometimes labeled "Chicago alley rats." In the most powerful version of the counterfable, southerners described themselves as the only genuine Americans in a city of "foreigners." "You'll find that ninety per cent of the people in Chicago are either dagoes, polacks or niggers," claimed one respondent. "If you took the hillbillies out of Chicago, there wouldn't be nothing left but niggers and foreigners."[31]

These early studies all emphasized contextual factors while paying little attention to the possibility that white southerners shared a cultural heritage that might encourage group identity. Culture was much more on the mind of the generation of sociologists and historians who revisited the issues of ethnicity in the 1970s and 1980s, often arguing that an Appalachian heritage or southern white heritage provided the symbolic materials for a sense of ethnicity that existed before migration. In a collection of studies mostly focused on Cincinnati and other Miami Valley locations, Phillip Obermiller, William Philliber, Clyde McCoy, John D. Photiadis, Bruce Tucker, and others embraced the argument that the migrants from the southern mountains shared an ethnic group relation either in all contexts or because of the challenges of urban resettlement.[32]

I have argued elsewhere that the ethnic concept needs to be handled carefully. It is appropriate to say that Okies and Appalachians developed ethnic relationships in some times and some places, but in other contexts the concept of ethnicity implies too much group consciousness and too much group interaction. Overused, the ethnic concept causes us to overlook the Tomlins and the Hammittes, working-class migrants who wanted to "dig in" and "melt away," and miss the middle-class migrants who wanted nothing to do with anything that evoked the hillbilly image and who may have been energetically changing accents. In short, it keeps us from thinking about the varieties of identities and the dispersed and fragmented residential patterns. It also keeps us from noticing some of the enterprises that particular groups of diaspora southerners were building.[33]

Professional Southerners

Migrations make history not merely through the movement of bodies but because of the consumer and political choices that the newcomers exercise and because of new forms of enterprise that commercial, cultural, and political activists introduce. The black diaspora became in the circumstances of the big cities a prolific engine of cultural change, enabling the production of media, entertainments, religion, and politics that would over time change the conditions of life for black Americans, indeed for all Americans. Although there would be no equivalent to the Black Metropolis, diasporic white southerners would also shape a set of enterprises that would have history-making effects, contributing to changes in the politics of race, religion, and region.

We begin with recreational and intellectual enterprises that had much to do with changing patterns of visibility and identity among southern whites, both those in diaspora and those at home. These endeavors depended upon the specialized skills of white migrants who have been overlooked in earlier studies of the diaspora: writers, entertainers, and sports figures who left the South in a talent transfer that was similar in some respects to the exodus of African Americans in those fields. For whites as well as blacks, the South in the first half of the century had nothing like the cultural resources of the North. The region's colleges were mostly second-rate. It had very few publishing houses other than those dedicated to religious materials. Major league sports came no farther south than St. Louis, Cincinnati, and Washington, D.C. Music, theater, film — the centers for each of these media were located outside the South. That meant that aspiring white actors, musicians, writers, and ballplayers would be prime candidates for migration, drawn by the geography of opportunity that was also pulling professional African Americans out of the South. Indeed, they found their way into the same institutions — music, publishing, and sports — that African Americans turned to advantage.

This talent transfer had important implications for all white southerners, because these professional-class migrants sometimes also became "professional southerners" who found in northern and western locales opportunities to speak for and about the South. Historians of the South have thought little about this, but quite a few of the celebrity white southerners who were taken to be representatives of or experts on the South actually lived and worked outside the region. Some of the men and women producing key images and understandings that helped change the way white southerners thought of themselves and the way the rest of America viewed white southerners were members of the diaspora.

An important point before beginning: these projects did not cohere in the same way that African American diaspora institutions did. We cannot look at the different endeavors and say that they all advanced the pride and power of white southerners. On the contrary, they reflected the fragmented class and community formations and contrasting politics and identities that white migrants developed in their new homes.

When Lily Tomlin was young, she lived across the street from Cobb Field, one of Detroit's recreational parks. She played there all of the time, even pitching for the Police Athletic League baseball team. The name Cobb means nothing to her now, and may or may not have mattered to her parents and other southerners living in the neighborhood in the 1940s. But that park was also part of the Southern Diaspora, a disconnected part that scholars have so far failed to consider. It was named after Ty Cobb, the most famous Detroit Tiger of all time and (sorry Lily) the most famous of the city's white southerners.[34]

Major league baseball encouraged its own southern diaspora of white athletes and turned quite a number of them into professional southerners—celebrities who in various ways seemed to represent the white South. In 1900, almost all of the major leaguers hailed from the northeastern and midwestern states where the teams were located. But the number of southerners playing for big league teams increased steadily through the first half of the century. By the 1940s, white southerners accounted for roughly one-third of all the players on those rosters. Moreover, on a per capita basis, the South in general and Alabama, North Carolina, and Oklahoma in particular were sending far more than their share of players to the big time. There were other baseball producers, especially California, Missouri, Illinois, and Pennsylvania, but the white South was very much in the game and, in the opinion of some, ruled the game. Wendell Smith and some of the other black sportswriters blamed the large number of boys "from Dixie" for baseball's refusal to accept black players. In a 1938 *Pittsburgh Courier* article, he angrily described the typical major leaguer as a bigot who "comes from Mississippi, Georgia, Texas or any other place you can think of below the Mason-Dixon Line."[35]

This baseball cohort did not belong to the southern white expatriate community in the way that the Negro league teams belonged to the Black Metropolis. Major league teams were in no way dependent upon the white migrants as a fan base, and the well-paid stars had no particular reason to attend closely to their fellow expatriates, although there are a few stories of players hanging out in hillbilly bars.

They did, however, belong to the white South. Just as baseball had enormous symbolic power for African Americans, it had a role to play in the formulations of southern white images and identities. The careers of big-league stars were followed closely in home state newspapers. Tris Speaker, star outfielder first for the Boston Red Sox, then for the Cleveland Indians, was big news in his birth state of Texas. That state also kept up on the colorful career of Rogers Hornsby, perennial National League batting champion. Georgians tracked the successes of their state hero, Ty Cobb. Although he spent his entire twenty-one-year career in Detroit, Cobb was regarded as a state treasure by Georgians, who gloried in his accomplishments and loved the fact that newspapers everywhere called him the "Georgia peach." The connection was so important that when the American League tried to punish Cobb for one of his violent outbursts, the Georgia congressional delegation intervened, threatening to investigate whether major league contracts violated the Sherman Anti-trust Act.[36]

It was not just home folks who knew about players' regional origins. Colorful nicknames based on ethnic or regional stereotypes were one of the conventions of baseball and of the sports journalism that made it so important in American life. Newsmen or teammates slapped a nickname on all of the leading players and reached frequently into the bag of standard images when working on the southerners. "Throughout the 20th century," historian John DiMeglio writes, "the lineups of major league clubs have been dotted with such nicknames as 'Dixie,' 'Reb,' 'Tex,' and 'Catfish.'"[37]

And with the nicknames came images and stories that jumped off the sports pages, adding to the ways that southerners and nonsoutherners constructed understandings of the white South. In their quest for spice and color, baseball's scribes loved to depict southern players as fresh from the farm. "Shoeless" Joe Jackson, South Carolina's most famous contribution to the sport, was never allowed to outgrow the story of how he arrived in Philadelphia, barefoot and bewildered by the big city. Luke Appling, the great White Sox shortstop from Georgia, was one of a number of southerners whose statements to reporters would appear in the next day's newspaper in dialect, especially if they could catch him using an "I reckon" or "shucks." Enos "Country" Slaughter, the Cardinal's star outfielder, was fairly well educated, his high school degree equivalent to the educational credentials of most sportswriters, but his baseball persona was that of a tough-as-nails scrapper who understood only baseball and tobacco farming. Projections of a journalism that stocked baseball teams the way Hollywood stocked its melodramas, southern white players were expected to appear in certain roles. Baseball made them celebrities but gave them little control over their public image.[38]

Dizzy Dean would have disagreed. Baseball's greatest celebrity of the late 1930s, the man who replaced Babe Ruth as the most entertaining and beloved figure in the game, Dean thought he was very much in control of the publicity apparatus that made him famous. The wisecracking, fireball-throwing pitcher for the St. Louis Cardinals certainly knew how to work the press. His bombastic "I am the greatest" speeches and frequent practical jokes made such good copy that reporters followed him everywhere. But the press in turn worked him into a particular type of star who fit very well within the current images of southerners. Ol' Diz became baseball's hillbilly, a real-life Li'l Abner whose humorous antics were linked to his Ozark upbringing.[39]

Dizzy Dean's story began the way every great sports legend did—at a typewriter. It was J. Roy Stockton, sportswriter for the *St. Louis Post-Dispatch*, who gave him his persona, developing a set of stories that jumped from sports page to sports page in the fall of 1934 as Dean led the Cardinals to an unexpected World Series victory. Stockton then followed up with a set of larger-than-life profiles for the *Saturday Evening Post*, the nation's premier feature magazine that each week landed in nearly 3 million homes. The key elements in the profile involved Dean's irrepressible sense of humor, gargantuan ego, and childlike naïveté, attributable to his humble regional origins. He was born "with a golden wisecrack in his mouth, ants in his pants, and an abiding faith in humanity, of which he knew he was the most important part," wrote Stockton in his opening paragraph for the *Saturday Evening Post*. That paragraph also noted confusion over Dean's birthplace: was it Lucas, Arkansas? Bond, Mississippi? Holdenville, Oklahoma? Dizzy had told various stories, and Stockton used the confusion to set up the tension that dominated the Dean persona. Was he very ignorant or very clever? How naive was this former "cotton picker" who barely finished the fourth grade and who claimed he "didn't have an entire pair of shoes until he joined the Army"? Stockton's profiles played it both ways, allowing Dean to be both the foolish man-child and the clever showman who knew how to tease writers and work his audience.[40]

The synthesis worked. Dean pitched only two more winning years with the Cardinals, followed by three sore-armed seasons with the Chicago Cubs. But defeat and retirement did little to dampen his popularity. In the 1940s, he moved his baseball hillbilly act into the announcing booth, becoming the radio voice of the Cardinals and later a very popular television announcer. On the air he turned malapropisms into an art form, delighting audiences who waited for him to announce that a player had "throwed" the ball or "slud" into base. "Musial stands confidentially at the plate," he declared in one of his finer moments. And he liked to end the broadcast with the reminder, "Don't fail to miss tomorrow's game." Second only to *Amos 'n' Andy* in his ability to fracture language, he used the skill to stay in the public eye. When a group of Missouri schoolteachers complained that he was corrupting the speech of the state's children, the *New York Times* gave Diz a chance to explain: "My mother died when I was three years old and me and Paul had to go out and pick cotton to get dough to keep the fire up. I guess we didn't get much education. And I reckon that's why when now I come up with an ain't once in a while, I have the Missouri teachers all stirred up. They don't like it because I say that Marty Marion or Vern Stephens slud into second base. What do they want me to say— slidded?"[41]

Baseball's ready stereotypes meant that its southern white celebrities operated in ways that mostly confirmed stock images. But in those confirmations, it is possible that something significant was going on. Dizzy Dean was staging the figure of the hillbilly in a particular way, using celebrity to make it not only laughable but also somewhat attractive. The Missouri teachers were right to be worried. A celebrity like Dean could turn some of the meanings of symbols associated with the white South. Operating on one of the big stages of early-twentieth-century popular culture, these southern expatriates were in a position to play with if not overcome some of the meanings associated with their origins. Dean made it easier to be from Arkansas (or Oklahoma or Mississippi, the other two states he claimed as birthplaces). He made it easier to speak "southern" and to handle comments about hillbillies. Not for everyone. But for those who wanted to try, he showed how to turn the hillbilly into something appealing and fun.

Diaspora white players would also have an important part to play when baseball became a prime staging ground for the rearrangement of racial opportunities in the late 1940s. As the major league teams contemplated ending the ban on black players in response to intense pressure from African Americans and from public officials in states like New York that had passed Fair Employment Practices laws, team owners fell back on the much-publicized excuse that their southern white players would not tolerate it, a story owners had been telling the black press for decades. Thus, when Branch Rickey's Brooklyn Dodgers finally broke ranks and played Jackie Robinson in 1947, one of the key media angles involved the threat of resistance by the white boys from Dixie. Black and white sportswriters jumped on two major examples in the 1947 season: Ben Chapman, the Alabama-born manager of the Philadelphia Athletics who told his players to "ride" Robinson when the teams met at Ebbets Field for their first series of the season, and the threatened but unconsummated boycott that Country Slaughter and fellow southerner Terry Moore tried to organize among the St. Louis Cardinals. Equally revealing was the counterstory that the press told about Robinson's own teammates Pee Wee Reese and Eddie Stanky, two southerners who were said to have overcome their own misgivings and led their teammates in welcoming Robinson. Nonsouthern whites had also been involved in all of these incidents, but the white southerner provided journalists with a convenient symbol of bigotry and/or redemption. Baseball's integration story would be told, as would America's integration story, as a battle between black and white southerners.[42]

Hillbilly Music

If the professional southerners of major league baseball worked in an enterprise that owed little to the millions of southern white migrants living in the North and West, another entertainment enterprise had a much firmer grounding among the expatriate population. The history of country music and the white diaspora are so entwined that it is hard to imagine one without the other. The diaspora was critical to the development and expanding popularity of the commercial music form, and the music in turn played a role in shaping the social identities and social relations of southern white migrants and southern whites at home. Called "hillbilly music" until the 1950s, the musical genre was one of the primary vehicles for circulating the term "hillbilly" and making it into a label that challenged white southerners living in the North. And there would be further identity challenges. At various stages, hillbilly/country music would help constitute the profile of the white southern migrant even as the migrants were helping to constitute the music.

Hillbilly music began to congeal as a defined commercial form in the mid-1920s in the wake of the commercial success of blues and jazz. Finding that they could make money selling race records, entrepreneurs looked for other untapped markets and discovered a demand for what was initially described as "old-time" or "old-fashioned" music. Radio helped with the discovery. As stations sprang up in the early 1920s, most opened their microphones to whatever local talent lay close at hand. From professionals to amateurs, from operatic tenors to barbershop quartets, early radio in all parts of the country offered a haphazard selection of music. WSB in Atlanta, the South's first station, was said to have used "anybody who could sing, whistle, play a musical instrument, or even breathe heavily." Fiddlers and string bands were part of the mix, as were singers who performed old-time favorites, songs that had been commercially produced in the late nineteenth century. The popular response to these forms encouraged some stations to schedule a weekly "Fiddler's Hour" or "Barn Dance" show of old-time music. Whether the idea originated at Atlanta's

WSB, Fort Worth's WBAP, or Chicago's WLS is subject to continuing debate, but by mid-1924, not long after the Sears Roebuck–owned Chicago station began broadcasting what became its *National Barn Dance*, a new (but allegedly old) musical genre had begun to take shape.[43]

Record companies, mostly the same ones that had recently begun to market race records, moved to take advantage. Okeh, the pioneer in race music, captured the first commercially important hillbilly recording almost by accident in 1923. Company agent Ralph Peer had come south to Atlanta with two assistants and recording equipment intending to hold sessions with some of that city's blues singers. At the suggestion of the furniture store owner who wholesaled Okeh records in the Southeast, Peer also agreed to record Fiddlin' John Carson, the champion of fiddlers' competitions in the Atlanta area. The resulting record, distributed just in Georgia, sold well and encouraged Okeh and then its competitors to explore the market further. Over the next couple of years, many of the companies established recording series that went into their catalogs under such labels as "old-time music," "old familiar tunes," "hill country tunes," or "songs from Dixie."[44]

As the last two labels suggest, there was an early association with the South. Record companies focused on the region, assuming it to be the place where both artists and audiences for old-time music would be most plentiful. Once the label "hillbilly music" caught on, the regional association became stronger. Ralph Peer apparently came up with the designation in 1925. Four young men from Virginia—Al Hopkins, his brother Joe, Tony Alderman, and John Rector—had driven to New York and presented themselves at Okeh studios hoping for a chance to record. Peer liked the sound of the string band, recorded six songs, and then asked them what they wanted to be called. Al said something like, "We're nothing but a bunch of hillbillies from North Carolina and Virginia. Call us anything." Peer jumped at the image and promptly dubbed the group the "Hill Billies." Folklorist Archie Green marks this a pivotal intervention in the construction of the hillbilly label for the emerging musical genre and in the related proliferation of hillbilly figures throughout popular media. Other bands were encouraged to adopt hillbilly imagery in names (the Skillet Lickers, the Possum Hunters, the Fruit Jar Drinkers, and the Georgia Pot Lickers were early examples), in costumes (overalls, bandannas, and floppy hats became the uniform of the hillbilly band), and in performance styles (a large dose of aw-shucks comedy was part of almost every act). Driven by the New York–based recording company executives who assumed that they were dealing with a novelty form that would need comedic elements in order to attract a market and also by the fact that vaudeville and medicine shows offered the best venues for paid employment, ambitious musicians readily adopted the hillbilly act. By the end of the 1920s, musicians across the South and outside the South were calling themselves hillbillies and dressing the part.[45]

These early moves would give the medium some unique and lasting dimensions. Never fully breaking the link to comedy, the genre would throughout the twentieth century depend on costumes and performance styles that were fanciful as opposed to realistic, historical rather than contemporary, rural as opposed to urban, self-deprecating rather than this-is-art serious. The styles would change. The hillbilly would in time give way to the cowboy as the key folkloric reference, but country music would continue to distinguish itself from other popular media through its theatricality and its comedic-historical play. Right up to the present, it signs itself as anti-contemporary and semi-serious. Although it is not the case today, for many decades these characteristics required consumers to engage the product on a somewhat different level than most pop music, which based its appeal on a promise of up-to-dateness, or classical music, which claimed status as a sophisticated historical art. Country music, in contrast, struggled with low levels of cultural credibility. As critic Dorothy Horstman notes, "Country music is unique. Like jazz, it is an important American art form. Unlike jazz, it was not taken seriously . . . until very recently." Instead, through much of its history, country music courted ridicule and needed audiences who either enjoyed the joke, missed the joke, or did not care.[46]

Hillbilly music would find its chief market, most of its performers, and most of its symbolic references in the South, as would its descendant, country music. More than any other major segment of commercial popular culture, country music has remained a strikingly regional product. "The bulk of the major performers still come, overwhelmingly, from the South," historian Bill Malone explains, "and they exhibit their southernness through their dialects, speech patterns, and lifestyles and through the values and themes of the music that they perform." Indeed, Richard Peterson and Russell Davis have found that fully 75 percent of all "country music notables" in the fifty years between 1925 and 1975 were born in the South, which they label "the fertile crescent of country music."[47]

Those linkages in turn have made country music a powerful force for the construction of southern white identities. Much like the way that the blues, R&B, soul, and hip-hop have served as expressive vehicles for African Americans, hillbilly and country music have spoken for white southerners and spoken to them, modeling behaviors and understandings that have helped in the refashioning of southern white culture and identities. And there is another parallel. A diaspora story lurks deep in the heart of country music.

She was born a coal miner's daughter in a one-room cabin in Butcher Hollow, Kentucky, in 1935, and if anyone represents the idealized image of country music as a product of the white working-class South, it is Loretta Lynn, the straight-talking, unpretentious queen of Nashville whose life (married at thirteen, four kids by eighteen) and lyrics ("Don't Come Home A-Drinkin' with Lovin' on Your Mind") have made her since the 1960s an industry icon. But Loretta Lynn could also serve as a symbol of the white diaspora and of the complicated geography of country music. For while it is true that the South is the fertile crescent, it is also true that country music, like jazz, depended very much on the circulations of southerners outside the home region.[48]

Loretta Lynn's country music career began not in Kentucky or Tennessee but 2,000 miles away in a logging town hard up against the Canadian border near Bellingham in Washington State. Butcher Hollow had been her first home, but by the time she reached Nashville, she had spent almost half her life on the West Coast. Named after the actress Loretta Young, she was born the second of eight children to Melvin and Clara Webb, each part Cherokee, both natives of the coal and lumber town tucked deep in the hills of Johnson County in eastern Kentucky. Her father worked in the mines when Loretta was young and earned a modest but decent living until black lung cost him his job in the late 1940s.

By then, his eldest daughter had left home. Loretta had married Doolittle Lynn, an army veteran who had returned to Johnson County after the war. She was not quite fourteen years old. The Lynn family, like the Webb family, had deep roots in eastern Kentucky, but the Lynns were also old hands at migration. During the Depression, when the local mine had closed, Doolittle's father had heard that there were mining jobs in Washington State and had taken the family west. They stayed a number of years and then, in a move that defied the general trend, returned to Kentucky just after the start of World War II. Having done part of his growing up there, Doolittle wanted to return to Washington, and not long after the marriage he set off to find a job and a new home. Loretta followed in the autumn of 1949. It was her first train ride. She was thrilled and scared and very pregnant.

For the next twelve years, the Lynns lived in rural northern Washington, Doolittle earning a living in a variety of jobs including farm work, logging, and as an auto mechanic, Loretta caring for the four children born to the couple in those years. They had made a wise move and had few regrets. "We were making it in Washington," she later explained, and they proudly owned their own house. Besides, there was not much back home. A few years after they left, the mining company closed the Butcher Hollow operation, and many of their friends and relatives had headed north or west. Wabash, Indiana, was a favorite destination. That is where Loretta's parents settled in the mid-1950s.[49]

Washington State is a long way from Nashville, but in 1960 it was the right place to launch one particular country music career. Loretta had done little

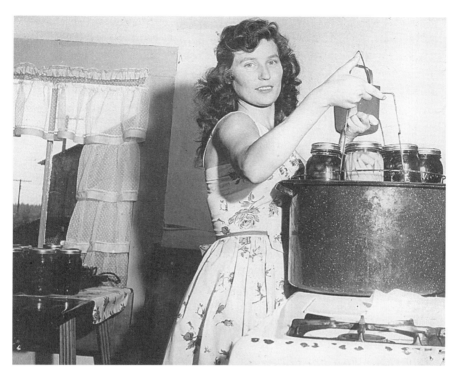

Loretta Lynn's country music career began not in Kentucky but in northern Washington State. Winner of seventeen blue ribbons for canning at the Northwest Washington State Fair, she posed for this 1958 newspaper photo. That was also the year she joined a band and began singing in local clubs. (*Bellingham Herald*)

with music in her Kentucky years or her first ten years out west. Doolittle had bought her a cheap guitar, and during spare moments she taught herself to play and enjoyed singing Kitty Wells songs and other material that she heard on the radio. Country music was not the most popular music in Washington State, but it had a solid fan base in the port cities and timber towns where white southerners had been settling in significant numbers. Loretta says that it was her husband who pushed her to perform in public, convincing her to audition with a group called the Westerneers that had a local radio show. They liked her, and she began performing regularly at dances and in taverns in the towns of northern Washington. A few months later, she formed her own group, Loretta's Trail Blazers, which allowed her to perform songs she was now writing.

Then came the two big breaks that launched her on the road to Nashville. The first was winning a televised amateur competition hosted by up-and-coming West Coast country music star Buck Owens. The second was finding a patron, a wealthy lumberman who heard her sing and thought it might be fun to get into the record business. He sent her to Los Angeles, which in 1960 still remained as important to country music recording as Nashville. She made her first record, "Honky Tonk Girl"; spent months promoting it on the West Coast while her husband mailed out copies to 3,500 radio stations around the country; and watched in amazement as the song broke into the country music charts.

This did not make her a star; that would happen later in Nashville, where she soon headed and where she found and made more lucky breaks. And in Nashville some years later she would write a song and call herself "a coal miner's daughter," knowing how powerfully that origin story would resonate in the world of country music. Yet in many ways, the persona she built around Butcher Hollow was less interesting than the real story of a life and a career that had been formed many miles from Kentucky in one of the corners of America that had been touched and changed by the Southern Diaspora.[50]

Loretta was not the first diaspora southerner to play a role in country music. Indeed, from the very beginning the geography of the music industry made this most regionally defined form of popular culture more complicated than it seemed. The South supplied much of the talent, symbolism, and audience, but some of the must important venues for performing, recording, marketing, and also innovating lay outside the South. Nashville, now famous as the capital city of country music, became so late in the development of that industry. In its formative decades, when the genre was called hillbilly music, the centers were New York, Chicago, and Los Angeles.

New York, for all its urbanity, was a key node of this most anti-urban form. The recording companies were based there, and that was also the place to get noticed if one wanted to break into the major vaudeville circuits. Several New York radio stations, including WABC and WHN, hired hillbilly acts. There was hardly an important hillbilly performer in the 1920s, 30s, and 40s who did not spend time in New York.

Radio station WLS made Chicago almost as important. Long before Nashville's competing program, the *Grand Ole Opry*, reached beyond a local market, the WLS *National Barn Dance* was the most prestigious and widely heard variety program of hillbilly music. At 50,000 watts, the WLS signal covered much of the Midwest and upper South and was backed by the reputation and publicity system of its owner, Sears Roebuck. In 1933, the NBC blue network picked up the show. All through the 1930s and 1940s, the *National Barn Dance* could be heard Saturday nights on stations coast to coast.

Los Angeles in the mid-1930s became the third magnet for hillbilly talent after Hollywood discovered the alchemy of guitars, horses, six-guns, and big hats. The era of the singing cowboy added the hillbilly genre to Los Angeles's burgeoning music world, and in the 1940s, no place was more important to the production of what the industry was starting to call hillbilly and western music.[51]

This geography fostered an important set of opportunities for white southerners living in those areas: career opportunities for musicians, different kinds of opportunities for those migrants who loved the familiar sounds and would help build its nonsouthern fan base. From an early date, musically inclined former southerners found openings in the new entertainment medium. Record companies, vaudeville promoters, and radio station managers looking for hillbilly musicians valued the southern pedigree, thinking that audiences wanted the genuine article. In California in the late 1920s, the Crockett family, formerly of West Virginia, parlayed their talents into one of that state's most successful hillbilly acts, performing first on radio in Fresno, then developing a radio and vaudeville act based in Los Angeles. They were the first of a long line of expatriate southerners who would find their way to entertainment careers and sometimes stardom in the Golden State. In their footsteps would come Elton Britt, Stuart Hamblen, Patsy Montana, Gene Autry, Rose Maddox, Woody Guthrie, Tex Ritter, Spade Cooley, Bob Wills, Jimmie Wakely, Merle Travis, Tennessee Ernie Ford, Buck Owens, Merle Haggard, Glen Campbell, and many more. Some were professional musicians before they headed west; others gained their first opportunities in California, where southerners were so closely identified with hillbilly and western music that nonsouthern performers sometimes pretended to have southern backgrounds, "Tex" Williams (actually from Illinois) being one of the more famous examples.[52]

Southern backgrounds had similar value for performers in the Midwest and Northeast. When Chicago's wLS *National Barn Dance* needed a hillbilly singer in 1926, the music director asked around, and someone mentioned Bradley Kincaid, a student at a local college who was from Kentucky and supposedly knew some old folksongs. Kincaid, who had gone to Chicago to become a social worker, instead became one of the premier hillbilly singers of the late 1920s and 1930s. Vernon Dalhart found that a Texas birthplace worked just as well. The first genuine hillbilly recording star, whose million-selling recording of "The Prisoner's Song" and "The Wreck of the Old 97" convinced New York executives that there was real money to be made in the genre, Dalhart made an imperfect hillbilly. Born Marion Slaughter in Texas, he had trained as an opera singer at the Dallas Conservatory of Music and after graduating moved to New York to pursue a successful career in light opera and popular music. Between 1916 and 1924, he made several hundred records for different companies, all in popular singing styles. But in 1924, sensing that his light opera career was fad-ing, Dalhart approached Victor Records about making a hillbilly record. His Texas origins providing, as they would for many other former southerners, all the credentials Victor needed, Dalhart chose a well-known ballad about a 1903 train wreck and a flip-side sad song about a lonely convict. The resulting record not only established Dalhart as the first real star of the new format but also changed the format, introducing the solo singer, where earlier acts had been mostly fiddlers and string bands. Paving the way for Jimmie Rodgers, Gene Autry, and all the other guitar strummers, Dalhart was only the first of the expatriate southerners to introduce pivotal innovations.[53]

Country music historians typically stress the music's close connection to the culture of the rural and working-class white South, and while acknowledging the importance of New York record companies and other commercial structures, they are happiest telling the story of Jimmie Rodgers, the Carter family, Roy Acuff, and other great musicians who reshaped the sounds and styles of country music while remaining in the South. But the industrial geography of commercial music gave special advantages to those performers, like Dalhart and Kincaid, who made their careers outside of the South, just as it did for diaspora blues musicians like Bessie Smith and Louis Armstrong. And while it would be a mistake to claim that most of the innovations occurred outside the South, it is true that some of the most important changes originated on what we might call the "frontier of country music," the northern and western cities where the genre fought for recognition and expanded audiences.[54]

The popularization of cowboy songs is a key example. In the 1930s, hillbilly music began a symbolic and musical turn of great significance as cowboy songs and western names and paraphernalia first joined and then gradually replaced the figure of the hillbilly. By the 1940s, nearly all performers wore cowboy gear, and even in the Southeast, where loyalty to hillbilly personas and green mountain homes remained strongest, they had to share musical space with songs about lonely cowboys and wide-open plains.[55]

The man most responsible for that shift was Gene Autry, and the places most responsible were Chicago and Los Angeles. Cowboy songs had been part of the early eclectic mix of old-time music but a minor part until Autry. Born in Texas in 1907, Autry grew up in Oklahoma, where his father had a business that included horse-trading, although there is no indication that young Orvon Gene Autry took any interest. He did like to sing, having learned the guitar from his mother, and he caught the entertainment bug as a teenager when the owner of a traveling medicine show invited him to spend a summer touring, singing, doing blackface comedy, and selling "Fields' Pain Annihilator." He finished high school and worked a couple of years as a telegraph operator but wanted to be a singer, more interested in pop styles than anything else.

In 1928, he caught a train to New York to look up a friend of the family who was a successful musician on Broadway and radio. Autry managed to get a record company audition and some advice: "Forget that Jolson stuff" and go back home and "learn to sing some yodel songs" of the sort that Jimmie Rodgers had recently made popular. Autry took heed and over the next two years established himself as a hillbilly singer, modeling both his sound and style on that of the "Singing Brakeman." His first hit record came in 1931 ("That Silver-Haired Daddy of Mine") and yielded a much-prized job offer on Chicago's WLS, the premier outlet for hillbilly music. It came with more advice. "I wanted to be a dreamy-eyed singer of love songs like Rudy Vallee," Autry later explained, but record producer Art Satherley and WLS staffer Ann Williams convinced him to become "Oklahoma's Singing Cowboy." Over the next three years, he and WLS popularized, as it had not been before, the sounds and styles of the cowboy song, helped along by the Sears Roebuck catalog, which heavily promoted the Gene Autry Round-up Guitar for $9.95.[56]

Hollywood came calling in 1934. Westerns had long been one of the most popular genres in filmdom, and a few of them had made room for a cowboy song or two, but when Autry's small singing part lit up the screen of *In Old Santa Fe*, Republic Studio's Nat Levine sensed the possibility for something new. Soon Autry was starring in westerns that were half action, half musical, and he was not alone. The "horse opera" became one of the box office goldmines of the late 1930s and lasted all the way through the 1940s before jumping to television in the early 1950s. Autry's success set off what historian Douglas Green describes as a "stampeding herd" of singing cowboys who found time on radio stations in every market and headed in large numbers to Los Angeles, hoping for a chance on the silver screen. Hollywood obliged many. Enormous numbers of singing cowboy westerns turned some into movie stars, including Dick Foran, Tex Ritter, Roy Rogers, Fred Scott, Ray Whitely, and Rex Allen, while scores of other hillbilly and cowboy performers were offered the chance to perform a song or two on-screen.[57]

The western turn had been inspired by the search for new audiences and had been made possible by the cross-pollination of media, both of which happened most readily in the media capitals of the North and West. Searching for ways to break out of the margins of the music world, record companies and music entrepreneurs paid disproportionate attention to nonsouthern places and audiences in the 1930s and 1940s. One can see that on the pages of *Billboard* magazine, the eyes and ears of the music industry. Radio station managers, booking agents, and other professionals who subscribed and tried to follow new developments in what the magazine in the 1940s called "American folk music" found coverage focused mostly on Los Angeles, Chicago, New York, and Ohio, where WLW broadcast *Midwestern Hayride* out of Cincinnati. The magazine also paid attention to Nashville's *Grand Ole Opry*, but no more than to these nonsouthern venues. Meanwhile, other southern centers were largely ignored.[58]

The industry did not initially pay much attention to southern white audiences in those diaspora cities. Unlike the marketing of race records and the consumer base of blues singers and African American jazz bands that depended on the growing populations of southerners in the Black Metropolises, southern white migrants were not the early target. Promoters of hillbilly music through the 1930s aimed at audiences of farm families in the regions outside the South. Popular radio programs like the WLS *National Barn Dance*, WLW's *Midwestern Hayride*, and WHO's *Iowa Barn Dance Frolic* (Des Moines) were designed to appeal to rural midwesterners, folks in the corn belt, not the émigrés from the cotton belt. Former southerners were buying records and listening to the hillbilly broadcasts, but until the late 1930s surge of media attention about Dust Bowl migrants heading for California and hillbillies in the northern cities, there was no reason for the music industry to realize that this group might be large enough or cohesive enough to be of market interest. That started to change when the first hillbilly taverns opened in Chicago, Detroit, and other midwestern cities in the late 1930s. It changed even more during World War II.

The war convinced the industry that hillbilly and cowboy music had urban as well as rural appeal and that relocated southerners were the core of that new market. *Billboard* magazine seemed to discover the migrant southerner in 1943 in Los Angeles. In several articles and notes, the magazine exalted the city's burgeoning music scene and the dozens of venues where orchestras performed nightly before dance-crazed crowds of war workers. *Billboard* noted that some of the most popular clubs featured "hillbilly jazz" and "western" dance music, now known as western swing. "Coast Orks Go 'Billy,'" ran one headline, gaining some of its punch from the double abbreviation ("ork" for orchestra, "billy" for hillbilly). The subhead offered further word play: "Khaki and Overalled Oakies Make Metropolitan Maestri Feed 'Em Down Home Tunes." The translation followed, explaining that servicemen and war workers from the South were packing Los Angeles ballrooms and clubs and demanding their kind of music, to the point that even jazz bandleaders like Louis Armstrong felt the need to play "ditties with a Texas-Oklahoma flavor to please the dancing Oakies." Armstrong said that he did not mind, explaining that "those cats in slacks (war workers) and all the servicemen don't want to hear anything else." In Detroit, too, the war brought new attention to white southerners and their musical tastes. Late in 1943, radio station WWJ announced that it would begin broadcasting the *Grand Ole Opry*.[59]

Southern white migrants were by no means the only ones dancing, but once they caught the eye of promoters, the industry made some important moves. Performers and club owners began to cater closely to the target audience, not just playing their music but also recognizing them in significant ways. On radio and on stage, performers now spoke directly to and about the southern migrants, joking about the strange ways of California (or Chicago or Detroit) and feeding home state pride with stories of life back home in Oklahoma, Texas, Tennessee, or Kentucky. In the North, where the label "hillbilly music" established a presumed proprietorial relationship between the migrants and the medium, club owners made it tighter by giving their taverns names like the "Southern Inn" and "Hillbilly Hangout."[60]

In California, the whole musical genre underwent an informal name shift. Musicians, promoters, and much of the general public now called it "Okie music." A spate of songs about Okies ("Oakie Boogie," "Dear Okie," "Oklahoma Blues") added to the relationship, as did the stage names that certain performers adopted. Bands performing in the Golden State in the war years seemed always to have a "Tex" at the microphone or an "Okie Paul" playing guitar. One of the state's most popular bands, led by Spade Cooley, who claimed the title "King of Western Swing," managed a trifecta of migrant-pleasing stage names. The band's three singers were "Arkie" Shibley, "Smokey Okie" Rogers, and "Tex" Williams.[61]

It is impossible to say what portion of the expanding urban market for hillbilly records, radio, and live performances was actually attributable to southern migrants; it was probably less than observers assumed. The music was picking up nonsouthern fans from the massive circulation of cowboy songs in western films and also because of the circulation of GIs through the South during the war era. Many a young northerner learned to like the music while stationed in the South or because he heard it overseas on Armed Forces Radio. A core audience, an audience with special reasons for liking and promoting hillbilly/country music, the southerners of the diaspora were just one of the factors in its spreading appeal, but their role did give them a very strong emotional stake in this important cultural enterprise.

Diaspora Intellectuals

Separate from and indeed largely out of touch with the southern white working-class formation was another cultural enterprise that involved literary instead of musical production. Scholars have failed to recognize the existence of a white migrant intelligentsia, even though it had much in common with the diaspora African American intelligentsia. In fact, the exodus of white writers, artists, and academics was numerically larger than that of black southerners. What is more, the two intellectual formations had somewhat complementary effects. Both white and black writers promoted highly critical views of the South from which they had fled.[62]

All through the decades of the diaspora, an out-migration of white writers and academic intellectuals paralleled the outflow of black intellectuals. The urgency was less, but some of the incentives were similar. Seeking the publishing resources of New York and other key cities or the educational resources of the major northern universities, the white intellectuals were also sometimes drawn to what they perceived to be the greater freedom or cosmopolitan stimulation of the North. The talent transfer was substantial. Among the many white southerners who built their careers elsewhere were novelists Erskine Caldwell, Thomas Wolfe, Evelyn Scott, Katherine Anne Porter, Carson McCullers, Harriette Arnow, William Styron, Earl Hamner, and Robert Penn Warren; dramatists Stark Young, John Mason Brown, Lillian Hellman, and Tennessee Williams; humorists Will Rogers and Irwin S. Cobb; sports journalists Grantland Rice, Curt Smith, Mel Allen, and Red Barber; essayists and journalists James Agee, Thomas Sancton, Thomas Mitchell, Truman Capote, Willie Morris, Tom Wolfe, Robert Sherrill, Larry L. King, Tom Wicker, David Brinkley, and Bill Moyers; and social scientists and historians William C. Dodd, David Herbert Donald, V. O. Key, C. Wright Mills, David Potter, and C. Vann Woodward.[63]

It is something of a struggle to associate these men and women with the millions of less illustrious white southerners who made new homes in the North and West, despite the fact that many of the intellectuals were highly self-conscious about their own migration. A number of them considered themselves expatriates and constructed their art and careers around it. Thomas Wolfe set the pattern, establishing the trope of the southern writer in emotional exile with his acclaimed 1929 novel *Look Homeward, Angel* and his subsequent autobiographical excursions, *Of Time and the River* (1935), *The Web and the Rock* (1939), and *You Can't Go Home Again* (1940). Wolfe's self-portrait of the artist who must leave in body but not fully in spirit, who finds no more refuge in salons of New York and Paris than in the claustrophobic and small-minded southern town of his youth, became the touchstone for multiple generations of white southern writers. Those who stayed as much as those who left (and especially those like Tennessee Williams who came and went) wrestled with the issue of the southern intellectual expatriate.[64]

The expatriates comprised a literary and social community of considerable influence, especially in the construction of ideas about their home region. Literary historians mark what is usually called the Southern Renaissance without contemplating the fact that many of its participants wrote from exile. More particularly, southern literary liberalism—the several generations of critical writings about the South and its class and racial systems—owed much to the expatriates, white and black. There were stay-at-homes who were equally important, and it would be a mistake to claim that the multisided enterprise of southern letters was dominated by the expatriates. But it is worth thinking about the many ways that the actual expatriates and the idea of the southern writer as expatriate influenced the construction of ideas about the South and agendas for changing the South. From Erskine Caldwell, James Agee, Lillian Hellman, Thomas Sancton, and Carson McCullers in the 1930s and 1940s through Tennessee Williams, Robert Penn Warren, William Styron, Willie Morris, and C. Vann Woodward in the postwar decades, the expatriates were responsible for some of the most trenchant and searing critiques of southern life and institutions, critiques that played an important role in changing that region.[65]

The practice of leaving the South to write about the South had a long and self-reinforcing history, dating back at least to Angelina Grimke and other abolitionist southerners. In the late nineteenth century, George Washington Cable and Walter Hines Page continued the tradition, both moving north in the 1880s after suffering the taunts and threats of neighbors who did not take kindly to their critical views. Cable in Massachusetts and Page in New York helped build colonies of southern writers in the northeastern intellectual and publishing centers. Page in particular had a huge impact on southern letters and southern criticism. Editor of a string of important periodicals (*Atlantic, Forum, World's Work*), he also founded the book publisher Doubleday, Page and Company, which became a major source of books about the South. Booker T. Washington's *Up from Slavery* (1901), Ray Stannard Baker's *Following the Color Line* (1908), Thomas Dixon's *Leopard's Spots* (1902) and *The Clansman* (1905), and the novels of Ellen Glasgow all came from that publishing house, which, says historian John Milton Cooper, "published most of the widely read books on southern and racial topics between 1900 and World War I."[66]

The 1920s added to the logic of literary exile. H. L. Mencken's crusade of regional damnation and his dominant voice in the world of letters convinced young southerners by the thousands that their homeland was "the Sahara of the Bozart," a wasteland for anyone of intelligence and ambition. Some stayed home and proved him wrong, but others fled at the first opportunity. Evelyn Scott sailed for Brazil and later New York and Europe. Erskine Caldwell tried journalism for a while at the *Atlanta Journal* but then decided that a cabin in Maine was the proper place to write about the folkways and poor people of the South. For both, it was a matter of perspective. "I had lived all my life in the

South, and I wanted to be where I would find a new and different perspective," Caldwell later explained. "I intended to write about Southern life as I knew it, and it seemed to me that I could best view it from a distance."[67]

There were practical reasons for heading north. The major magazines, book publishers, theaters, films—most of the literary apparatus of the nation—were to be found in New York, Boston, Chicago, Los Angeles, and a few other cities. Even sportswriters like Tennessean Grantland Rice knew he had to move to New York to practice his art at the highest level. The New York and Chicago newspapers with their syndication systems dominated the production of sports news all through the first half of the century. And for those who were not yet at the highest level, there were other considerations: contacts, communities of writers, and publishing-related work that could pay the bills when writing did not.[68]

While there was no Harlem to structure a formal sense of community among southern white intellectuals in the North, several considerations helped foster networks and some sense of common purpose. One was subject matter. Although migrant intellectuals did not always write about the South, many felt compelled to even after initially contemplating other subjects. Lillian Hellman, who can be counted as a Jewish southern expatriate, wrote her first play, *The Children's Hour* (1934), without apparent reference to the New Orleans and Mississippi world of her youth, but she then turned toward home in her next effort, *Little Foxes* (1939). Publishers and peer pressure helped. Erskine Caldwell spent his first years up north cranking out stories about Maine as well as Georgia, but it was the southern themes that drew the most interest from publishers and reviewers. Like the advice Gene Autry had received from a different New York–based media, Caldwell and the others were encouraged to become "professional southerners."[69]

The romantic notion of exile also drew the expatriates together. After Thomas Wolfe's books had time to do their work, the idea of the wandering southern writer became so much the cliché that thousands of young southerners went off to college or to look for opportunities up north equipped with the notion that "I can't go home again." Carson McCullers left her hometown of Columbus, Georgia, to study at Columbia University in the mid-1930s, then tried living in North Carolina as she was writing *The Heart Is a Lonely Hunter* (1940). Finding it too parochial for her bohemian sense of self, she fled back to New York, vowing never again to live in the land of her birth, planning only to return periodically to renew her "sense of horror." Robert Penn Warren claimed no such feelings of alienation. In and out of the South in his younger years, he left his natal region for good in 1942 and spent much of the next forty-seven years styling himself as a wanderer far from home. He called himself a DP (displaced person) in a 1950 letter to Frank Owsley in which he congratulated the historian on moving to the University of Alabama, "your home country." "I wish I could get back in mine more often. . . . I've been a DP a long time, but I don't get entirely used to it."[70]

The southern white intellectual faced particular challenges in the North, especially after the 1930s and the escalation of regional stereotypes. The issues of accent and background played out in complicated ways at these social strata, creating some urgency in the establishment of both intellectual and political credentials. How to sound smart when your accent was associated with ignorance was one challenge. How to deal with the close political scrutiny in the largely liberal literary circles was another. Sociologist Lewis Killian confronted these issues at two stages of his academic career, first as a graduate student in Chicago in the late 1940s, then twenty years later when he left Florida State University for the University of Massachusetts at Amherst. In both settings, his Georgia accent invited questions about his racial and political views and also, of course, about the southern migrant disease: homesickness. He tells of the reception for new faculty at the University of Massachusetts. In the greeting line to meet the president, Killian and his wife followed two couples of European origin. "All of them, with their pronounced Middle European accents, preceded us through the receiving line and were greeted cordially but with no unusual comments. We, too, were given a warm welcome; but the president added, 'My, you must feel a long way from home!' "[71]

These irritants helped bring expatriate intellectuals together, if only, say several, to grouse about the hypocrisy and crudeness of some of the pretentious northerners. The public scrutiny in some cases also charged the political commitments of these writers, most of whom identified themselves as liberals. We can find conservative voices and indeed some institutions that encouraged them. The New York Southern Society and the United Daughters of the Confederacy nourished a community of Confederate writers in the late nineteenth century and tried to continue the project of southern adulation in the twentieth. But the authority systems of the publishing industry favored those who would write critically about their home region. This was especially the case in the middle third of the twentieth century. It was hard enough to be a conservative in many of these literary settings during the 1930s and 1940s, harder still to be a southern conservative. That near uniformity of purpose is part of what gave the expatriate writers importance as a cultural enterprise. Not only were they involved in producing new ideas about the South, they were also developing certain kinds of ideas.[72]

In some ways, the white migrant intelligentsia complemented the African American intelligentsia that the black diaspora had helped establish. Much of the literary output of the white expatriates added to the critiques of the Jim Crow South that black writers and political leaders produced. In the 1930s and early 1940s, few of the white writers focused on race, but the gothic novels of Caldwell and the suffocating South critiques of Wolfe, Hellman, Scott, and others tore at the legitimacy of the old regime. A few of the whites in the 1940s and more in the 1950s and 1960s addressed racial themes and sought relationships with their intellectual counterparts in the African American diaspora.

Thomas Sancton was doing that at the *New Republic* in the early 1940s. The New Orleans–raised journalist had come to New York to work for the Associated Press and soon after decided he had to write about his troubled home region. After winning a coveted Nieman Fellowship for a year's study at Harvard, he moved into the job of managing editor at the *New Republic*, where fellow expatriate Stark Young wrote drama criticism and served on the liberal weekly's editorial board. Sancton soon began to write regularly about the South and especially about the region's great problem: Jim Crow. Returning from an investigative tour at the end of 1942, he began a series of articles called "Trouble in Dixie" in which he blasted the bigoted politicians and newspaper editors who stirred up race hatred. He also wrote articles defending the Negro Press and explaining the war-era black protests. "In a sense, it is 1776 for the Negro," he wrote in 1943 in an article titled "What the Negro Wants." The war, he was sure, would prove the great turning point in the long struggle for equal rights.[73]

Sancton was one of the voices articulating a new form of southern white liberalism in the 1940s. The New York exile joined stay-at-home activists like Lillian Smith, Will Alexander, Frank Porter Graham, and Virginia Durr, who were prepared to support a movement for genuine racial equality and to drop all of the old "leave us alone, we can reform ourselves" waffles that old-guard liberals like Ralph McGill and Virginia Dabney employed. In the *New Republic*, Sancton endorsed Carey McWilliams's call for a "National Fair Racial Practices Act paralleling the Wagner Act, with an enforcement arm like the National Labor Relations Board." In another 1943 essay for the short-lived *Negro Quarterly*, co-edited by a young Ralph Ellison, Sancton offered an analysis of southern white liberalism, criticizing the "liberalism of yielding," of those who would not squarely commit to "full and unconditional equality of citizenship."[74]

It was not only the intellectual and publishing establishment of New York that encouraged white expatriates to critique their home region. The black press had an interest as well, as Sancton's *Negro Quarterly* publication indicates. John H. Johnson's *Negro Digest* picked up two more of his articles and made much of Sancton's regional background, describing him as "a young southerner who has lived in the Northeast for the past three years . . . [writing] a book on the need for more open-minded attitudes in the South."[75]

That a white southerner would join the call for racial justice was understood to be highly significant, not only because he was assumed to have special insights into the regional mores but also because he offered hope that other southern white minds might be changed. That was the role that columnist Harold Preece played for the *Chicago Defender* in 1944. His column, "The Living South," appeared in every issue of the African American weekly, usually with an identifying reference ("my folks, the Southern poor whites") that clarified his race and regional origin. Like Sancton, he blazed away at southern bigots like Congressman John Rankin and Senator Theodore Bilbo of Mississippi. When the reactionary Texas congressman Martin Dies complained of one of his attacks and called him a "Negro writer" and Communist, Preece got off one of his best lines: "Fact is, I'm as white as my wife's bed sheets, hanging out on the line a few yards from where I'm typing this. I'm whiter than Martin who's red-headed and freckle-faced." He went on to clarify: "Now, nobody can insult me by calling me a Negro, by identifying me with the people who are joining with my people to plow all the Martin Dies and all the Cotton Ed Smiths under the cotton rows. Without bragging, but as a simple statement of fact, I've taken my stand with my Negro fellow-southerners." Preece also wrote hopefully of the "new white men" in the South who realize that they are "in the second class with Negroes." Noting that his class of white southerners has discovered the pain of bigotry ("they don't like to be called Hillbillies"), he promised his African American audience that they were now learning not to use racially derogatory terms.[76]

The privileged literary position of the white southern expatriate speaking on racial matters encouraged an interesting shift in self-identification on the part of one long-time racial liberal. In the 1930s, when she won first the Pulitzer and then the Nobel Prize for literature, few of her readers knew Pearl Buck as a southerner. The author of *The Good Earth* (1931) and several dozen other books on China emphasized the fact that she had grown up in that country as a daughter of American missionaries. But the woman who has been called "the most influential Westerner to write about China since . . . Marco Polo" was in fact born in Hillsboro, West Virginia, and though she was taken to China as an infant, she could, when it made sense to do so, call herself a southerner. Her parents were third-generation Virginians and missionaries sponsored by the Southern Presbyterian denomination, and when Pearl reached maturity she had spent four years attaining a bachelor's degree at Randolph-Macon Woman's College in Lynchburg, Virginia.[77]

It started to make sense to claim that identity and become a professional southerner in the 1940s. Pearl Buck had returned to the United States in 1934 and almost immediately had joined the NAACP and made clear her commitment to racial justice for African Americans and Asian Americans. That commitment accelerated in the 1940s, and as it did, so did her interest in proclaiming her own southern roots. In 1949, she wrote a book based on deep conversations with her friend Eslanda Robeson, wife of Paul Robeson. It was called *American Argument* and explored the moral and political thought of both women, focusing on issues of race, womanhood, family, and also Communism — the last, the only real arena of argument. The introduction established the symmetry that made the book work: "Both Eslanda and I came from the South. Both of us know we do not want to live there or bring up our children there, and for the same reason. It is too tiresome to have to remember what color we are. . . . So we live where we can feel free, most of the time."[78]

Robert Penn Warren had much more credibility among whites in the region of his birth than did Pearl Buck. The former Vanderbilt "Agrarian" and Pulitzer Prize–winning novelist and poet walked a cautious political line through the 1940s, earning the respect of the northern literary establishment with books like *All the King's Men* (1946) that were also widely read and loved in the South. He kept that balance in part by finding ways to avoid commenting on his home region's racial horrors. But like many who faced the complications of being a professional southerner in the North, his political balance in time shifted, helped by a new marriage to "Yankee" writer Eleanor Clark, whose politics ran well to the left of his own. By 1954, when the Supreme Court issued its historic *Brown v. Board of Education* ruling, Robert Penn Warren was ready to use his authority as one of the preeminent men of southern letters in a new way, taking a position — a moderate but still instructive one for the many white southerners who looked up to him — on segregation and racial justice.[79]

Late in 1955, *Life* magazine asked him to write something about what the court ruling would mean for the South. He agreed and made two trips, wandering through Tennessee, Mississippi, and nearby states, observing and interviewing, before settling down to write "Divided South Searches Its Soul," which carried the subhead "Noted Southerner Records the Inner Turmoil over Integration" when published in the 9 July 1956 issue. A long and complicated article (for that magazine), Warren registered the divisions and turmoil of his home region both in the voices of those he interviewed and in his introspective conclusion. He finished the piece by interviewing himself, recording both his anxieties and his new commitment. Integration must come, he said, but "it will take time" and "mutual education." He held out hope that whites as well as blacks would benefit: "If the South is really able to face up to itself and its situation, it may achieve identity, moral identity." But stronger than any tone of optimism is the sense that a necessary but tragic crisis lay ahead. The most poignant passage of the entire article is one in which he registers his relief at the end of his research tour as he heads back to Connecticut, to his home in exile: "Out of Memphis, I lean back in my seat on the plane and watch the darkness slide by. I know what a Southerner feels, going out of the South, the relief, the expanding vistas."[80]

Although he would remain a cautious advocate for change in the South, in the late 1950s and early 1960s Warren helped anchor a literary circle that brought together many of the men and women whose novels, articles, poems, and historical studies were remaking key images and understandings of the South—and significantly the group included black as well as white expatriates. Biographer Joseph Blotner describes Warren's home in Fairfield, Connecticut, midway between Yale and New York, as a center of much visiting and memorable parties. Among the frequent guests: William Styron, Katherine Anne Porter, Cleanth Brooks, Allen Tate, C. Vann Woodward, and Ralph Ellison. Ellison later described the "famous black-tie parties." "Fanny and I were often among their week-end guests. Marked by good food, fine drinks, and live music for dancing, these were pleasurable occasions of a truly rare order. We were introduced to an array of people—writers, artists, curators, publishers, academics—whom otherwise we might not have encountered." Ellison and Warren had become close friends when both spent several months at the American Academy in Rome. It was there, remembered Ellison, "that any bars to our friendship that might have been imposed by Southern manners and history went down the drain and left the well-known Fugitive poet and the fledgling writer and grandson of Freedmen marvelously free to enjoy themselves as human beings."[81]

That influential literary circle was still operating in 1963 when Willie Morris stepped off a Greyhound bus in Manhattan, his head full of "you can't go home again" Wolfe quotations. The twenty-nine-year-old Mississippi-born journalist would guide the southern-born literary community into its next phase, presiding over a final burst of expatriate journalism that helped define the terms for a new generation of white southern liberals and helped advance the project of racial reconstruction in the South.

Morris, born in 1935, had grown up in Faulkner country, Yazoo, Mississippi, and he left it for the University of Texas at Austin a precocious seventeen years later. That is where he discovered writing and his critical view of the South, all amidst a little knot of young journalists who wrote for the *Daily Texan* and the muckraking monthly, the *Texas Observer*. After editing first one, then the other, he left Texas in the early 1960s, tried graduate school at Stanford, and then followed his muse to New York, determined to know the sights and sounds and stimulations of literary Manhattan that Thomas Wolfe had memorialized a generation earlier. He landed a job on the editorial staff of *Harper's* and quickly began to make his mark, turning the venerable monthly into a crusading journal that published some of the most memorable journalism of the 1960s, especially on the dual subjects of race and the South.

In doing so, he relied upon and expanded the network of white and black expatriate writers living in the Northeast. Even before he was appointed executive editor of the magazine in 1966 and editor-in-chief in 1967, he had managed to commission articles by William Styron, C. Vann Woodward, Ralph Ellison, Whitney Young, Arna Bontemps, Louis Lomax, Douglas Kiker, Tom Wicker, Louis Lusky, and Larry L. King. Later there would be others, including Albert Murray and Willie Morris's old college classmate Bill Moyers. After Moyers resigned as press secretary to President Johnson, the *Harper's* editor helped him make the transition to journalism—New York–based diaspora journalism. In *North toward Home*, the best-selling autobiography that he published in 1967, Morris explained how he found emotional refuge as well as professional talent in literary New York's "burgeoning and implacable Southern expatriate community" comprised of "exiles . . . alienated from home yet forever drawn back to it, seeking some form of personal liberty elsewhere yet obsessed with the texture and the complexity of the place from which they had departed."[82]

Third Dimension

The white professional southerners of the literary world, like the professional southerners of country music and major league baseball, helped rework the symbols of race and region, creating both celebrity models and new agendas and ideas that circulated widely, especially among white southerners. All through the middle third of the twentieth century, key debates about southern white identity and southern white politics drew upon the work of these men and women, which is why it is so significant that much of this cultural production took place outside the South. The geography of America's cultural industries had lured many of the South's cultural workers north and given these expatriates privileged access to key media. Not alone, but with considerable authority, diaspora intellectuals and diaspora entertainers helped the white South negotiate the transitions from the age of underdevelopment to the age of the Sun Belt, from the age of Jim Crow to the age of racial reconstruction.

In thinking about that geography and influence, it is tempting to again use the concept of empowering places, as we did when contemplating the cultural authority of the Black Metropolis. Expatriate white intellectuals and entertainers, like their black counterparts, found themselves in locations that provided resources and avenues of influence not readily available in the mid-twentieth-century South. But the spatial and community dynamics were in fact quite different. Where black southern expatriates built a new cultural apparatus based on the consumer power and civic consciousness of the urban black public, white professional southerners found discrete niches in already established literary and entertainment industries, some of which depended not at all on the support of fellow migrants. And the ideas and agendas generated by the cohort of white diaspora cultural workers did not cohere in the way that the cultural production of the Black Metropolis did. Country music imagery, baseball's professional southerners, and the literary southerners moved in various directions, some producing hillbilly iconography, others modifying or refuting those figures; some supporting white supremacy, others challenging it; some emphasizing the proud heritage of the traditional white South, others calling for a reconstructed biracial South.

This variety makes it difficult to summarize the cultural implications of the white diaspora. Indeed, the task is impossible if we think of white southerners as an ethnic population with a group imperative similar to African Americans. Much of the cultural production generated by white expatriates had little to do with the white diaspora population, and some of it served the interests of black southerners as readily as that of white southerners.

This opens up one of the key insights of this book. The reason to write about the Southern Diaspora as a whole rather than separate the black and white migrations is that in some ways they interacted, creating the "third dimension" in the stereoscopic strategy of this volume. Nowhere was this clearer than in the realm of cultural production, particularly in the efforts of the two diaspora intelligentsias. Black and white expatriate literati would interact socially to some extent, and, more important, they would produce critiques of the old South and visions of a new South that were often complementary. Other enterprises generated imagery that worked at cross-purposes. The hillbilly/country music of the whites and the blues/jazz of the blacks interacted musically but conveyed images and messages that spoke separately about two different Souths. Baseball's two groups of diaspora stars were often pictured as still more antagonistic. From the era of Rube Foster and Ty Cobb to the near-confrontation featuring Jackie Robinson and "Country" Slaughter, baseball's southern celebrities (and some in the music and literary worlds) seemed to tell a story of implacable racial opposition. But in those oppositions—no less than in the collaborate energies of some of the artists, writers, and academics—the two diasporas were never out of touch. The cultural production of one almost always referenced the other. Together, the various diaspora cultural enterprises generated models, images, and ideas that contributed to important reformulations of racial identities and southern identities over the course of the twentieth century.

Exile

Willie Morris was one of the white intellectuals most keen to transcend racial boundaries and build a South and a southern literature not of whites and blacks but of unmarked southerners. He counted Albert Murray and Ralph Ellison as two of his closest friends and credited them with helping him see the South and his relationship to it in a new way. "For a long time in my life, I had been ashamed of my Mississippi origins," wrote Morris in *North toward Home*. The two veterans of the African American diaspora helped him realize that "shame was too simple and debilitating an emotion, too easy and predictable—like bitterness." They helped him commit to "*understand* one's origins" instead of condemn and escape from them.

There is something contrived and revealing about the way that Morris talks about his relationship to Murray and Ellison. He brings them into the central drama of his autobiography, which is all about the quest for perspective, healing, and the "home" that he cannot find in the South and does not come easily in New York. He eventually finds a sense of peace in the New York "cave," largely because of its network of white and black southern literary expatriates and especially because of the presence of the two former Tuskegeeans, Ellison and Murray. The symbolism is suspiciously attractive—white and black southerners finding fellowship outside the land of their birth—and replays the relationship that Pearl Buck and Eslanda Robeson publicized almost two decades earlier. Here is Morris's key memory: "At Al Murray's apartment in Harlem, on New Year's Day 1967, the Murrays, the Ellisons, and the Morrises congregated for an unusual feast: bourbon, collard greens, black-eyed peas, ham-hocks, and cornbread—a kind of ritual for all of us. Where else in the East but in Harlem could a Southern white boy greet the New Year with the good-luck food he had had as a child, and feel at home as he seldom had thought he could in the Cave?"[83]

That Willie Morris wanted to find his "home" in Harlem speaks powerfully to the complicated role of the white literary expatriate and the fragmented identities and communities of the larger white diaspora. Unlike Ellison, Murray, and black expatriate intellectuals, the white literati had no community of their own, or at least no connection to the larger body of diaspora southern whites. Even though many of them became "professional southerners" and in that role contributed significantly to the critical discourse that would help reshape the South, few of the white intellectuals took note of the massive southern white migrant population of which they were an element. It is curious, even somewhat amazing, that expatriate writers could explore so many dimensions of the South and its peoples and yet not write about the millions of ordinary white southerners who moved north and west. Why did Erskine Caldwell and James Agee leave it to John Steinbeck and Dorothy Lange to follow the moving southerners of the 1930s? Why did former Mississippian Willie Morris and former Georgian William Emerson (editor of the *Saturday Evening Post*) leave it to other editors to publish the 1960s articles about Uptown and other "hillbilly ghettos"?[84]

Of the dozens of sociologists who studied migrant adjustment issues in the North and West, only Lewis Killian came to the subject as a white former southerner. Harriette Arnow is the only other white expatriate intellectual who found the issue of migration worthy of her typewriter. Born in western Kentucky, she published her first novel (*Mountain Path*) before moving to Detroit in 1944 so her husband could accept a job at the *Detroit News*. That first year they lived in a Detroit public housing project surrounded by fellow migrants from Kentucky and Tennessee, and even as she worked on another novel (*Hunters Horn*), the idea for *The Dollmaker* must have been taking shape. The book was named runner-up for the National Book Award in 1954 and settled into a long-lasting reputation as the defining hillbilly migration novel.[85]

It is remarkable that *The Dollmaker* is almost the only novel on that subject. While black diaspora intellectuals made mass migration and northern adjustment a central theme of their writing, turning the migration narrative, says literary critic Farah Jasmine Griffin, into "one of the twentieth century's dominant forms of African-American cultural production," the white literary expatriates (with these two exceptions) ignored all but their own adjustment issues while keeping their eyes firmly on the South. The difference is striking and signifies the contrasting emotional geography and community structures of the two migrations. The African American literati wrote as participants in and observers of the most momentous historical process of their time, the Great Migration and the building of the Black Metropolis. They wrote, even the most alienated of them, like Richard Wright, as members of that community. The whites, by contrast, saw themselves as cut off from every sort of community. They wrote as loners, wanderers, "DPs," "exiles," and "expatriates," feeling apart from community, apart from history, apart from home.[86]

Gospel Highways

Sunday mornings in the late 1940s would find Aretha Franklin and Lily (Mary Jean) Tomlin doing something remarkably similar. On this one day each week, the routines of the two daughters of the Southern Diaspora seemed almost identical. Aretha would accompany her father to New Bethel Baptist Church on Hastings Street in the black commercial zone in the heart of Paradise Valley. Lily would accompany her mother to Temple Baptist Church, a mile west and north of New Bethel on Woodward and Amsterdam and, like New Bethel, a church dominated by southerners. Across Detroit and across the North and West, many black and white southerners spent Sunday mornings worshiping in churches that were distinctly southern. One set of Baptist churches for the whites, another set for the blacks, these institutions were critical to the way that many framed their new lives. They were also one of the keys to how the two Southern Diasporas would change America.[1]

Historians of the American twentieth century are just beginning to think productively about religion. Apart from the dedicated specialists, the historical profession has routinely sidelined this rich and complicated subject, passing off references to religious institutions and belief systems quickly, paying close attention only when faith becomes forcefully politicized as it did during the fundamentalist struggles of the 1920s and in the culture wars of the late twentieth century. That is a mistake. Religion matters. The churches that relocated southerners built would affect the entire landscape of faith and also the landscape of politics in the places they settled. And they would do so in ways that make religion something of a synecdoche for the larger story of the Southern Diaspora, an example that captures the mix of convergence and divergence, collaboration and opposition in the experiences of the two groups of former southerners.[2]

From one perspective, church-building by the two groups of former southerners was collaborative, contributing to a major reorganization in American religious patterns. Religious historians locate two great trends in American religious practice in the second half of the twentieth century. One involves a dramatically expanded pluralism of faith and form. The other involves the resurgence of evangelicalism, the fervent, born-again Protestantism that had seemed to be disappearing earlier in the century. Both of these developments were partially an outgrowth of the Southern Diaspora. Over time, the two groups of migrant southerners helped change the balance of religious forces in the regions where they settled, especially in the great cities of the North. Once overwhelmingly Catholic, metropolitan areas like Detroit, Chicago, Cleveland, Philadelphia, and most others except New York and Boston became, as the century progressed, increasingly Protestant—and new kinds of Protestant. Black southerners in the central cities and white southerners in the surrounding suburbs spread Baptist and Pentecostal churches while making born-again Christianity the most dynamic force in the religious mix of those areas. Some religious scholars have called this the "southernization of American religion."[3]

From another perspective, the religious energies of white and black southerners were not collaborative. Their faiths were similar, but their churches operated quite differently in the secular world. Black church-building contributed in various ways to the push for African American empowerment. Indeed, nothing was more critical to the development of urban African American civic life and political influence and the consequent reorganization of race and rights. The road walked by Adam Clayton Powell Jr. and Martin Luther King Jr. passed through the churches that black southerners would build in the North. White migrant church-building typically had nearly opposite implications. Most of these institutions would promote various forms of social conservatism and would help, at some moments, to move the civic culture of white suburbs and working-class neighborhoods to the right. The road to Jerry Falwell and the Moral Majority also passed through diaspora churches. In their secular effects, these parallel bodies of southern-origin churches were not parallel at all.

Had Lily Tomlin and Aretha Franklin been old enough to wonder about such things, they would have been in a good position to observe the similarities and differences in the two religious enterprises. New Bethel Baptist and Temple Baptist had two of the largest congregations in Detroit by the late 1940s, with official memberships numbering in the thousands and uncounted others tuning in to their radio ministries. Outsiders would have said they both served up "shoutin' religion," loud and emotional by the standards of most northern

Protestants. They both adhered to the central tenets of the Baptist faith: salvation through individual revelation, adult baptism, and full congregational autonomy. Both were part of the evangelical movement that was bringing new voices and new vigor to Detroit's religious mix.

But observers would have had no trouble recognizing huge differences in what went on in the two churches. Aretha's father, C. L. Franklin, led a congregation of former southerners and some northerners who joined easily in a service featuring powerful music and cadenced, "whooping" sermons. New Bethel's gospel choirs and its frequent guest performers were already legendary by the late 1940s and would become more so when Franklin put together his road show with Clara Ward in the mid-1950s. Music filled New Bethel and filled its pews, attracting overflow crowds who swayed with the irresistible rhythms. They moved too with the words of Reverend Franklin, described by Jesse Jackson as "the most imitated soul preacher in history." Franklin would start with a passage from the Bible, often an Old Testament verse about the challenges faced by the early Israelites. As he explicated the text and turned it into a lesson, his voice would establish a poetic rhythm, one that would build in intensity, then fall back, build again to a higher level, then retreat. Finally he would break into a chant, singing his words in rhythmic waves, "whooping" as it is called, building toward a powerful crescendo. His audience, carried along by every phrase, moved with him as he spoke, urging him on with "Amens" and "Hallelujahs," letting the spirit grow until, by the end, most were standing, swaying, praying, screaming.[4]

Not long after coming to Detroit in 1946, the Mississippi-born Franklin had arranged to broadcast his weekly sermon on a local radio station. The broadcasts became very popular and helped expand the congregation. In 1953, a local record store owner asked to record some of them and secured a marketing deal with Chicago-based Chess Records. Franklin's records were soon selling in black communities throughout the country. They were also being played on radio, especially Nashville's WLAC-AM, a powerful radio station whose signal reached listeners in several states. "Did not our ears perk up for years before we had a television or an elected official in America, if we could just hear WLAC, Nashville, Tennessee . . . on a Sunday night?" recalls Jesse Jackson, then a teenager growing up in Greenville, South Carolina. "Sunday night, New Bethel, Hastings Street, was the common frame of reference for the black church." Ultimately seventy sermons were recorded and became the basis for launching the C. L. Franklin Gospel Caravan, which toured the South and the major cities of the North. At each stop, Franklin would repeat one of his recorded sermons. It was what audiences wanted, he later recalled. "They want to hear what they have been hearing" on the radio.[5]

A mile away, Lily, her brother, and mother listened to another famous

Rev. C. L. Franklin turned New Bethel Baptist Church into one of the largest and most politically active black churches in Detroit. Father of Aretha Franklin, C. L. grew up in rural Mississippi and held his first important pastorate in Memphis. The family moved to Detroit in 1946. (Walter P. Reuther Library, Wayne State University)

preacher, also known for the power and energy of his sermons. J. Frank Norris had made Temple Baptist into the largest and most controversial church in Detroit, claiming close to 10,000 members by the late 1940s. As at New Bethel, most of the congregation was from the South, as was the pastor. Norris was from Texas and actually still lived there. In fact, he commuted to Detroit from Fort Worth, where he pastored another megachurch of 15,000. A sojourner who treated the northern city as a mission, not a home, Norris worked that theme into his ministry in ways that Franklin would not. Where the black minister spoke positively of the North, the white minister reminded his congregants that they were "people of the Southland" and urged them to be wary of the ways of the "Northland."[6]

There were other differences wrapped in apparent similarities. Both men had mastered the art of radio ministry, Norris's sermons going out each Sunday on station WJR, at 50,000 watts Detroit's most powerful station. Norris's broadcasts lacked the lyrical qualities of Franklin's sermons but employed other devices, including anger and sarcasm. Where Franklin coaxed, Norris thundered. Where Franklin wrapped his audience in a rush of words, Norris

Rev. J. Frank Norris turned Detroit's Temple Baptist Church into a bastion of right-wing fundamentalism. Norris (*right*) joins Michigan governor Luren Dickinson, a prohibitionist, at a 1940 campaign rally. Norris commuted between his churches in Detroit and Ft. Worth from 1935 to 1950. (Walter P. Reuther Library, Wayne State University)

slapped and beat and pounded out a message. One was described as having a "million-dollar voice," the other as a "militant, swashbuckling, hell-busting, hammer-and-tongs Texas preacher."[7]

Their divergent messages were what most separated the two Baptist ministers. Although both men preached mostly about the Bible, the word of God, rebirth in Jesus' name, and the Christian duty to lead a moral life and spread the gospel, those invocations were packaged with sharply differing social and political concerns. Franklin was known as a race leader in Detroit, and while his sermons were rarely politically explicit, he was eager to help further the cause of racial equality. His greatest contributions would come in the 1960s when he became one of the leaders of the Detroit civil rights struggles that changed the face of the city. Active too on the national level, he was with Martin Luther King in Washington in 1963, served on the board of the Southern Christian Leadership Conference, joined the Poor People's Campaign, and, by the end of the 1960s, was known to assist the Republic of New Africa and other militant groups.

That kind of activism was not his way in the late 1940s and early 1950s, but even then New Bethel was a civil rights church. Franklin urged his congregation to be involved in the affairs of the community, city, and nation. His church cooperated with the West Side Progressive Civic League and the NAACP, and when Congressman (and Reverend) Adam Clayton Powell Jr. came to Detroit in 1954 to speak on "the Detroit Negro's progress" and community integration campaigns, he did so at New Bethel.[8]

Moreover, Franklin worked the issues of segregation and racial injustice into his sermons, often invoking comparisons with the Israelites' sufferings at the hands of the Babylonians. In "The Prophet and the Valley of Dry Bones; from Bones to Destiny" (one of his most famous 1950s sermon records), he describes Babylon as "a valley of disenfranchisement, a valley of hopelessness, a valley of dry bones," much as America was "to the Negro . . . a valley of slave huts, a valley of slavery and oppression, a valley of sorrow." God planned deliverance for the Israelites, Franklin preached, but required much of them, required them to maintain their faith and to work at making miracles. God instructed Ezekiel to go out and preach to those dry bones. Ezekiel resisted and doubted but finally did what he was told, and as he did, the bones came together and life returned. " 'Hear my words,' " God had said. "And that is my solution tonight," echoed Franklin, "that's my answer to every problem that we have: that is to hear God's words."[9]

The call to faith was Franklin's core message in this sermon and most others, but the surrounding references called also for black Americans to work for deliverance from their Babylon. Jesse Jackson remembers well the "Valley of Dry Bones" sermon. Franklin repeated it at the younger man's ordination service in 1968. "I still try to preach to the bones in the valley," says Jackson, "the despised, the damned, the disinherited, the disrespected."[10]

C. L. Franklin would not have been considered a crusading minister in his early years, but crusader is exactly the label that fellow Baptist J. Frank Norris cultivated. For thirty years Norris had been one of most famous (and infamous) leaders of the Protestant fundamentalist movement. Born in Alabama in

1877, raised in Texas, and educated at Baylor and Southern Baptist Theological Seminary, he entered the ministry in 1905 and soon was a rising star in Texas Baptist circles. When tensions between modernizers and theological conservatives sharpened into denomination-ripping combat following the launch of the World Christian Fundamentals Association in 1919, Norris emerged as the key voice of the fundamentalist forces in the southern states. In the 1920s he added prohibition, anti-evolution, and anti-Catholicism to his list of causes and watched his national reputation grow in 1928 as he took up the challenge of turning Democrats in Texas and other southern states against Alfred E. Smith, the Catholic New Yorker who had won the party nomination for president. "Are we ready to permit a man to occupy the highest office, the chief magistracy over this Government, who owes his first alliance to a foreign power . . . ?" he asked in a much-circulated pamphlet entitled *The Conspiracy of Rum and Romanism to Rule This Government*.[11]

The fundamentalist movement struggled for public legitimacy in the 1930s, hurt by publicity that followed the Scopes "monkey trial." In books and film and in the journalism that poured out of northern-based media outlets, fundamentalists were mocked, pictured as dupes and charlatans or as small-minded bigots intent on turning back the clock of American progress. Norris, who liked to call himself the "Texas Cyclone," was undeterred. From his base at First Baptist of Fort Worth, he published the *Fundamentalist*, a weekly that was distributed through sympathetic churches across the country. He took to the road, preaching revivals and building a network of affiliated churches. He saw the North as a particular challenge. That was why he listened in 1934 when a delegation from Detroit's Temple Baptist Church asked him to become their head pastor. Detroit would become his northern base, his beachhead for a direct assault on the citadels of atheism, Communism, Catholicism, and Protestant modernism. He was also thinking about Detroit demographics. He told readers of the *Fundamentalist* in 1934 that there were "200,000 southerners in Detroit" looking for a church.[12]

By 1934, he had also recalibrated his targets. Christian modernism was always his chief concern. Not a sermon would he deliver that did not offer some choice jabs at the "modern infidels" who are "stealing the crown of our Lord." "I have ten thousand times more respect for any Catholic who is faithful to Roman Catholicism that I have for Modernism," he told the Temple Baptist congregation in one of his early sermons, explaining that Catholics at least "believe in God and in Christ and in immortality, and these modern infidels don't believe in anything!" Indeed, his anti-Catholicism and nativism would take a backseat to anti-Communism once he reached Detroit, a city with a huge Catholic population and a powerful Catholic archdiocese. Norris would remain adamantly opposed to Catholicism throughout his life and worried about its potential to interfere with "American" institutions, but in the 1930s and 1940s, he worried much more about the dangers of radicalism. Anti-Communism, anti-modernism, and "hellfire and brimstone" soul-saving preaching would be the cornerstones of his ministry at Temple Baptist.[13]

Baptists on the Move

As with race and political systems, religion before the diaspora was sharply regionalized. Catholics numerically dominated the major cities of the North, with Jews comprising a small but visible minority in some of them. Protestants maintained a significant presence in cities, especially among the middle and upper classes, while ruling the smaller cities and the hinterland. Northern Protestantism was noted for its diversity: Lutherans, Methodists, Baptists, Presbyterians, Congregationalists, Episcopalians, and many smaller faiths shared northern spaces. Lutherans were strongest in the Midwest, Congregationalists and Presbyterians in the Northeast, and Methodists and Baptists were sprinkled everywhere. The far West had still greater diversity. A little bit of everything and a sizable number of "unchurched" citizens was the western religious formula. The South had the simplest scheme. This was Baptist country, that one faith far outdistancing all others. Methodists and Presbyterians were in second and third place, but in most southern states, well over half of white churchgoers were Baptists, as were about three-quarters of African American worshipers. Indeed, nowhere else on the planet was quite like the American South. Denominational leaders liked to call it the "Baptist center of gravity in the world."[14]

The diaspora was largely a migration of Baptists, millions of Baptists, into zones where other faiths were dominant. There were Baptist churches in the North, but they belonged to a different denomination, at least on the white side of the Baptist enterprise. The sectional crisis of the mid-nineteenth century had divided most of the Protestant denominations. In the 1840s and 1850s, southern Baptists, southern Methodists, and southern Presbyterians had split off and started their own denominations. White southerners leaving home thus faced a problem (and black southerners also to some extent): they were moving into places where the churches were different from what they had known. The newcomers either had to convert to something new or form their own churches. They did both, on the one hand adding to the ranks of all kinds of Protestant churches, on the other hand creating huge new Baptist enterprises in the North and West.[15]

Finding a church represented a fundamental step in the settling-in process for many migrants. Some did it quickly, regarding Sunday worship as no less essential than food and shelter. Others let years, sometimes decades, pass before returning to the ways of organized religion. Women typically led the way, choosing a church and enrolling their children in Sunday school with or without the participation of husbands. That was the story in the Tomlin household. Mother Lillie Mae, her son, and daughter spent their Sundays at Temple Baptist. Guy Tomlin had other things to do. The pattern was similar among black migrants, although not in a family like the Franklins. Women filled the churches, but the preachers and deacons were mostly male.

Joining a church seems to have been easier for black southerners than for their white counterparts—another indication of the different social dynamics of the two diasporas. African American newcomers poured into churches in the cities where they settled, contributing to an early and ongoing explosion of religious activity in the Black Metropolises. Older churches filled and overfilled, while new churches sprang up by the dozen. It all happened very quickly compared to other relocating populations, including southern whites. In Detroit's diaspora black community, a researcher charged with conducting a religious census in 1926 found the task almost too difficult: "There has been such a rapid development of churches in Detroit within the last ten years that it is impossible to give the exact number." But another survey counted more than 100 churches and estimated membership at almost 45,000, roughly half the city's rapidly growing black population. A 1926 Harlem survey found 140 churches. One in Cleveland four years later counted 132. A Chicago survey in 1928 located 275, and a follow-up ten years later raised the total to 475 with an estimated membership of close to 200,000, again roughly half the population.[16]

That was just the first phase of the diaspora. Church expansion in the 1940s and 1950s kept pace with the new armies of migrants. Indeed, throughout the decades of mass migration, experts worried that there were too many churches for the health and well-being of the Black Metropolises. Certainly there was no shortage. Any newcomer with half an interest in religion had every opportunity to find a compatible institution.[17]

It was different for white migrants. Dispersion and social awkwardness made it harder for many to find a new religious home. Some joined the Northern Baptist churches or tried out another Protestant denomination. But this was often difficult, especially for the large numbers of working-class and rural-origin migrants. In some settings, the major Protestant denominations served largely middle-class congregations. The existing churches could be socially intimidating. They could also be religiously challenging. The Northern and

Southern Baptist denominations were moving apart theologically as the twentieth century progressed. As a result of the struggles over fundamentalism, the Northern Baptist Convention (NBC) (today called American Baptists) became increasingly identified with theological modernism and political liberalism. The denomination contributed heavily to the Federal Council of Churches, the ecumenical movement that devoted some of its energies to social reform. Individual churches set their own course, and Northern Baptist preachers spanned a spectrum that included rock-ribbed fundamentalists, but the denominational leadership and most of its ministers by the 1930s joined Northern Methodists on the liberal side of American Protestantism.[18]

The Southern Baptist Convention (SBC) followed a different trajectory. Largely unaffected by the fundamentalist struggles of the early part of the century because orthodoxy was so standard that it did not need to be rigorously debated, most Southern Baptists were used to what they called "old-style religion," which in the North would have been identified as fundamentalist. The Bible was truth, its passages taken literally, not metaphorically. Services centered on the struggle for faith, on the tortures that awaited the unredeemed, and on the glories of a personal relationship with the Lord. Emotion flowed freely on Sundays back home. A good preacher raised his voice and stirred his flock. Style as much as doctrine made some of the migrants feel that Northern Baptist churches were not for them. Ruth and Wofford Clark liked the First Baptist Church in Los Angeles, at least at first. It was much grander than the church they had attended in Oklahoma City. But after a couple of months they stopped attending. There were just too many things about the big church that seemed unfamiliar and wrong. "It was just different . . . just something you didn't know."[19]

Black migrants faced some of the same challenges when they tried out the existing churches. Again there was a denominational issue. Prior to the Great Migration, the largest number of black churches in the North were affiliated with two Methodist denominations: the African Methodist Episcopal Church (AME) and the African Methodist Episcopal Zion Church (AMEZ). Only small numbers of Baptist churches predated the twentieth-century exodus, and black southerners, like their white counterparts, sometimes found these northern institutions cold and formal.[20]

Yet these issues weighed less heavily on African American newcomers because of the very different settlement and community dynamics explored previously. Where established white churches usually did little to ease the way for southern newcomers, most of the established black churches eagerly sought new members. And newcomers often enjoyed some leverage in the black churches. Because of their numbers relative to the "old settlers," they could often coax changes. "Shouting" was one of the divisive issues of the early diaspora period, as newcomers broke the decorum of AME and established Baptist churches with loud "Amens," "Hallelujahs," and other enthusiastic contributions. Initially, congregations resisted these southernisms, but over time there were compromises. When St. Clair Drake and Horace Cayton studied Chicago's black churches in the late 1930s, they reported that "shouting" was nearly universal, that a certain amount of "emotional display" was standard even in the most socially pretentious establishments.[21]

Building new churches was also easier in the black communities. The concentration of African Americans meant that migrants of like minds could readily locate one another. Baptists were particularly well equipped for the enterprise of church-building. Members of a denomination that vests total autonomy in the congregation, Baptists were famously self-starting, able to create new churches, writes historian Milton Sernett, by "spontaneous combustion." If there were not the right kind of churches where they were going, lay Baptists would organize them. If experienced preachers were not available, someone else might feel the call. In its organizational dynamics, the Baptist tradition was ideal for people on the move.[22]

New Bethel was a product of those dynamics. In 1910, Detroit's black community claimed just one Baptist congregation. By 1931, that original church, Second Baptist, had been joined by sixty-eight other Baptist congregations. Some had originated at Second Baptist, either as intentional missionary projects or as breakaway groups who left the mother church over some conflict. But most of the newer Baptist organizations had sprouted anew. Many of the newcomers felt lost in a huge church like Second Baptist, which claimed 4,000 members in 1926, and, yearning for the fellowship of the small rural church they had known back home, had formed prayer groups with friends and relatives. Those fellowships, meeting first in an apartment, sometimes evolved into churches, especially if a preacher from back home agreed to come north.[23]

New Bethel began in 1932 as a prayer group of former Mississippians who initially met in Eliza Butler's home. Word spread, others wanted to join, and soon there was enough interest to begin looking for a pastor and a storefront meeting place. The congregation grew by fits and starts in the 1930s as several pastors came and went. Struggling with finances and internal disagreements, the church suffered a serious split in 1940 and another one in 1946, an event that precipitated the decision to call C. L. Franklin to the pastorate. Turmoil was fairly standard among the newer churches, many of which failed within a few years. New Bethel was a success story. By the time Franklin arrived, it had a congregation of several hundred members and a sanctuary on Hastings Street in the heart of Paradise Valley. The building was a converted bowling alley. The congregation was poor, mostly maids and factory workers, and mostly migrants from Mississippi, Alabama, and Louisiana, but they had built a church from scratch and were determined to see it thrive. C. L. Franklin took care of that. Within two years, he would add a thousand members.[24]

White Baptists built new churches too but at a much slower pace. This was partly because the SBC refused until the 1940s to sanction church-building in Northern Baptist territory. The churches established before the 1940s either remained independent or affiliated with one of the smaller Baptist denominations, like the Missionary Baptist Association. These splinter denominations usually offered the strictest versions of fundamentalist practice, too strict for many of the migrants.[25]

Some Northern Baptist churches were also taken over by southerners. That was what happened at Temple Baptist. The church dated back to 1892 and had long been one of Detroit's premier Baptist institutions. In the 1920s, the membership, following the leadership of Pastor Albert Johnson, took the fundamentalist side in the struggle that wracked the NBC. The church's theological conservatism and its location, not far from the central Detroit neighborhoods where many working-class southern whites were finding housing, probably attracted some southerners in those years, although historian Douglas James Curlew, who interviewed dozens of Temple Baptist veterans in the early 1990s, thinks that there were not many. That would soon change. Almost immediately after Norris replaced Johnson in 1934, the congregation began what Curlew describes as a total transformation. Norris's appointment had been controversial, and some of the more moderate members of the congregation left immediately. Norris's "dictatorial" style, his reconstruction of the Sunday school, and his decision to abolish all clubs and activities other than the visiting committees that went into the community knocking on doors and "winning souls" cost the church much of its old membership.[26]

No matter. The Texan "rebuilt the congregation with new people." He southernized the church from top to bottom. One of his first moves was to end the affiliation with the Northern Baptist Convention. Temple would become part of the World Fundamental Baptist Missionary Fellowship, a small body that Norris had launched some years before. Norris also brought a number of protégés north to assist him his Detroit mission, including the Kentucky-born G. Beauchamp Vick, who would serve as general superintendent of the church during the Norris years and then as pastor after Norris was forced out in 1950.[27]

The new team targeted southern whites both in the neighborhoods nearby and throughout the city, people who heard Norris on the radio Sunday nights and responded to his high-voltage, hellfire-and-brimstone styles or whose names ended up on one of the cards that the visiting committees used to identify new prospects. That may have been how the Tomlins came to worship at

Temple Baptist. By the time they arrived in Detroit in 1938, Norris had added thousands of new members and was building a massive new facility that could seat the 3,000–4,000 who attended services each Sunday. At least 75 percent and perhaps as many as 90 percent of the members were from the South, veterans estimate. The church's visiting committees had become expert at locating newcomers from Kentucky and Tennessee and were sending from 50 to 100 volunteers into the neighborhoods each Monday and Thursday evening to talk with them. Mrs. Tomlin must have answered the door.[28]

But Temple Baptist was unusual, especially for the 1930s. Churches dominated by southern whites were few in number before World War II, and those that did develop were mostly small, poor, and relatively inconspicuous. The growth period for white Baptists coincided with the second phase of the diaspora and may have had something to do with increases in wealth and security in that era. It also had much to do with policy changes in the SBC. Reluctant to "invade" Northern Baptist territory during the first phase of the diaspora, the SBC changed course in the 1940s and agreed to sanction church formation in the western and northern states.[29]

With denominational support, Southern Baptist preachers now followed the highways out of the South to "recapture their lost flocks." An SBC newsletter in California put out the call for missionaries in 1942: "It has been estimated that there are between seventy-five and a hundred thousand Southern Baptists living in the State. . . . They [are] as sheep scattered abroad not having a shepherd." The call was answered. By 1952, the denomination claimed more than 400 churches in California. Hundreds more had been started in other western states and in the northern settings where white migrants had congregated. And the Southern Baptist project was only beginning. Church-building would accelerate all through the second phase of the white diaspora. In 1971, the Southern Baptist denomination claimed 1.6 million adherents in states outside its home region, and twenty years later there would be 7,300 churches and 2.8 million members outside the South. By then they had almost caught up to the estimated 3 million African American Baptists living in northern and western regions.[30]

Diaspora Innovations

The expanding Baptist enterprises were not the only manifestations of the religious energies set loose by the Southern Diaspora. Religious movements of all kinds gained members from the southerners who settled in their communities. Black southerners added numbers to churches belonging to white-dominated denominations (Methodist, Congregationalist, Episcopal, and also

Catholic) as well as to AME and AMEZ churches. White southerners also filtered into every sort of church. A 1963 church membership survey in San Francisco and neighboring counties indicates that in addition to their dominance in Southern Baptist churches, southern migrants accounted for 8 percent of white Methodists in the sample, 10 percent of the Episcopalians, 14 percent of the American Baptists, 14 percent of the Disciples of Christ, 16 percent of Seventh-Day Adventists, and 29 percent of the membership in the Churches of Christ. There may have been special factors at work in the San Francisco area that encouraged this spreading out into different Protestant faiths, but the key point would be valid anywhere. The diaspora was adding a lot of worshipers to many different kinds of churches.[31]

The diaspora also promoted some of the most important religious innovations in twentieth-century America. Southerners moving north and west would help launch entirely new religious movements and in doing so would help rewrite the rules of religiosity. The Black Metropolises led the sequence of religious innovation. The 1920s witnessed an explosion of new and controversial religious movements in Harlem, South Side Chicago, Detroit, and other northern black communities. Among the new forms were Holiness, Apostolic, and Pentecostal churches, all sometimes called "sanctified" churches; African Orthodox churches, first organized in 1921 by Garveyites who broke away from the Episcopal Church; and Spiritualist churches, which combined communication with the dead with Christian elements. New too were Black Hebrew organizations and Islamic movements, including the Nation of Islam, which was founded in Detroit in the 1930s. And there were organizations that defied even these categories, dozens of one-of-a-kind religions that won adherents through dynamic leadership or attractive promises. The most famous of these was Father Divine's New York–based Kingdom and Peace Mission, which in the 1920s and 1930s gained tens of thousands of members who accepted Father Divine as the "only living God."[32]

Contemporary observers derided these "cults" and "storefront churches," and much of subsequent scholarship has interpreted them as abnormal, symptomatic of urban distress. But historians Clarence Taylor and Milton Sernett consider religious diversification and innovation one of the by-products of the African American diaspora. The Black Metropolises transformed African American religion by creating needs that could not readily be met by existing religious organizations and by providing the wealth and freedom that encouraged others to try. The combination of relocated southerners looking for new religious homes, their money—more than had ever before been accumulated by African Americans—and the entrepreneurial talents set loose and encouraged by the migration turned these communities into unique zones of religious competition.[33]

Pentecostalism was the most important of the new faiths. The dramatic spread of Pentecostal churches and charismatic practice within non-Pentecostal churches is one of the important legacies of the diaspora, both black and white wings. As much a creation of the diaspora as of the South itself, the Pentecostal movement would stir up religious energies, challenge basic notions of what was legitimate religious practice, and provide a conduit for a variety of significant social and cultural changes.[34]

Pentecostalism emerged as a distinct doctrine during the first decade of the twentieth century within churches that had been part of the Holiness revival of the late nineteenth century. Holiness groups believed that salvation was a two-stage process involving not just conversion but a later experience of "sanctification." Pentecostals argued there was also a third stage, the baptism of the Holy Spirit, which was manifested through speaking in tongues (glossolalia). They also emphasized miracles of faith, developing one of their most effective points of appeal through the practice of faith healing. Ridiculed in the popular media as "Holy Rollers," the Pentecostal groups would spend much of the twentieth century dealing with a reputation as lowbrow religious extremists.

The movement had initially developed in the South and among southerners who had left that region. Southerners in Los Angeles played a key early role. That city was the site of the famous Asuza street revival that many Pentecostals see as the cradle of their faith. Beginning in 1906 and lasting two years, the revival, led by William Seymour, a black preacher from Texas, attracted thousands of religious seekers, both black and white, who came to experience spirit baptism. The movement then spread, particularly in the South where evangelists built followings among rural blacks and whites. What was to become the most important black denomination, the Church of God in Christ, had been founded a few years earlier in Mississippi by Charles Harrison Mason, a Holiness preacher. Mason made his way to Azusa Street in 1907, was "filled with the Glory of the Lord," and committed the Church of God in Christ to the new way. For several years, the denomination was the major source of new Pentecostal preachers, ordaining whites as well as blacks in a faith that initially crossed the color line. But the fellowship did not last. Whites began to form separate organizations, including the Assemblies of God, which remains today the most important white-led Pentecostal denomination.[35]

The ongoing southern exodus proved a huge opportunity for these infant religious movements. Although only a tiny segment of the southern population of either race belonged to these faiths, in the diasporic communities the

Elder Lucy Smith (here in 1941) led All Nations Pentecostal Church, Chicago's largest Pentecostal assembly. The dynamic faith healer migrated from Georgia in 1910. (Library of Congress, Prints and Photographs Division, FSA-OWI Collection)

"saints" would reap a whirlwind of souls. That early growth shows up in a religious survey conducted in black Chicago in 1938. Out of 475 churches, 107 were Holiness or Pentecostal (215 were Baptist), encompassing an estimated 6,000 or 7,000 members. Most were modest storefront operations, but a handful of large congregations played a prominent role in the community, one of them led by Elder Lucy Smith, a sensational faith healer whose miracles and high-powered radio preaching made her famous throughout Chicago.

Smith's All Nations Pentecostal Church combined many of the elements that Pentecostals would use to great effect in the diasporic communities. She was theatrical, staging her preaching in ways that others criticized as unworthy of a religious service. She used radio: the sanctified groups were not alone in seizing the airways, but they created some of the most sensational radio ministries. She used music in new and powerful ways. Pentecostals brought every sort of musical instrument and up-tempo singing into their churches, again crossing boundaries that others thought profane. Gospel music, with its reintegration of blues sounds and sacred texts, found one of its early bases in churches like Elder Lucy Smith's. And of course, she was a she. Women rarely were accepted as preachers in the Baptist and Methodist denominations. But some of the most effective Pentecostal evangelists were women, including Bishop Ida Robinson of the Mt. Sinai Holy Church of America, based in Philadelphia, and Mother Rosa Horne, who led one of the largest churches in Harlem.[36]

White Pentecostals spread more selectively. In the 1920s and 1930s, the movement capitalized on the westward migration to California but had only a modest presence in the northern communities where white southerners settled. Los Angeles, the birthplace of the movement, had continued to nourish it, especially after the arrival of Aimee Semple McPherson, destined to become the most successful early evangelist of Pentecostalism and the inspiration for Elder Lucy and other females who followed. A Canadian who had married a Pentecostal preacher and then discovered her skill as an evangelist, the widowed McPherson arrived in the City of Angels in 1918 and very quickly established a reputation for brilliant theatrics and miracles of faith. By 1923, she had collected a following large enough to fill her brand-new 4,300-seat Angelus Temple, one of the largest church buildings anywhere. Soon she also had a radio station, KFSG, that broadcast her sermons and stirring programs of music and religious guidance to thousands across the L.A. basin. Initially affiliated with the Assemblies of God, she later formed her own denomination, the International Church of the Foursquare Gospel. By the end of the 1920s, there were several hundred affiliated churches, mostly in California.[37]

Pentecostalism also followed the white diaspora into northern states but gained less ground in the decades before World War II. Takeoff came in the 1940s and 1950s during the healing revivals that swept through most of the nation's major metropolitan areas. Thousands flocked to see evangelists Oral Roberts, William Branham, Jack Coe, and A. A. Allen perform miraculous cures, and tens of thousands more listened to the syndicated radio ministries that now blanketed the country. The movement grew in a second big spurt starting in the late 1960s as television replaced radio, and Rex Humbard, Oral Roberts, and later Pat Robertson, Jimmy Swaggart, and Jim and Tammy Faye Bakker created television ministries that appealed well beyond the bounds of the diaspora population. Many of the evangelists now looked beyond denominations, preaching Holy Ghost baptism and miracles of faith in terms that won converts in non-Pentecostal denominations. Since the 1970s, these "charismatic" practices (tongues speaking and faith healing) have diffused widely, and scholars speak of two related phenomena, the denominationally explicit Pentecostal movement and the transdenominational charismatic movement. Nowadays there are charismatic believers and even whole charismatic congregations within the mainline Protestant denominations and also among Catholics. No one knows how to count the believers, but there are many. The charismatic project has been the fastest growing religious phenomenon of recent decades.[38]

Civic Structures

Church-building had implications beyond the realm of religion. Churches for the two groups of migrants were gateway institutions that led to other commitments and helped frame both individual lives and whole communities. Often the most important social commitment beyond the family, church life, for those who joined, would provide distinctive social, cultural, and political orientations. For the cities and suburbs where the southern-origin churches proliferated, they could also provide distinctive orientations, powerful enough to affect the dynamics of community and power. The black churches would foster civic activism on a broad and continuous basis, facilitating political education and political action and helping African Americans intrude powerfully into the affairs of the city. In contrast, the white diaspora churches would be a less consistent source of community activism and at times would encourage social separation and political disengagement. In other instances, southern white preachers like Frank Norris would promote political activism, usually of a very conservative kind.

Our thinking about the civic role of churches in cities of the African American diaspora is complicated by some dramatic shifts in the scholarly literature. Much of the scholarship from the 1930s through the 1960s was critical of African American religious institutions. The sociological perspective that fostered popular paradigms of southern maladjustment in the cities yielded related images of black (and also southern white) churches. In the writings of social scientists like Horace Cayton Jr., St. Clair Drake, Gunnar Myrdal, and E. Franklin Frazier and in the journalism of both the left-wing and the mass-market periodicals, black religious practice was understood to be "excessive" and symptomatic of social distress. Black communities had too many churches, where the worship was too emotional and distracted too much from the real needs of the population.

Black Metropolis, the masterful 1945 Chicago study by Drake and Cayton, is a prime example of such scholarship. The authors wrote critically about the nearly 500 churches of "Bronzeville," airing complaints that some were "rackets" run by unscrupulous preachers and that there were too many churches draining too much of the community's financial resources. Like almost every other report of the period, they worried about "emotional" religion and unorthodox "cults" — the "Black Gods of the Metropolis" — implying that they flourished as a result of poverty, backwardness, and the stresses of urban adjustment. Drake and Cayton spent little energy exploring the civic contributions of Chicago's black churches beyond noting that they preached against the life of sin and the streets and offered an avenue of "respectability" in competition with the "shady" world of gambling, drinking, sex, and hustling that claimed a large segment of Bronzeville's population. Most tellingly, they argued that the churches were losing their central role in the community, that residents were drifting away while secular institutions—unions, political parties, newspapers, and advancement organizations—assumed leadership. They do not say so in so many words, but there is an implication that the religious system of Black Metropolis is anachronistic and an obstacle to the progress they hoped to see.[39]

The civil rights era created obvious reasons to rethink this perspective. The inspired political leadership of preachers like Adam Clayton Powell Jr., Martin Luther King Jr., C. L. Franklin, and Jesse Jackson and the critical role of churches in the civil rights campaigns encouraged scholars to reexamine the place of religion in black history and to give it a much more positive valence. The re-examination has mostly centered on the South, but recent books have given us some new ways to think about the place of churches in the developing community life and politics of the Black Metropolises.[40]

The diaspora, in its early stages, increased the size and importance of certain key black churches. As the first phase of migrants hit the cities during World War I, some of the already established churches played a critical role in welcoming and helping them. In each city, a few congregations moved aggressively to serve and recruit the newcomers, creating in the process the first African American megachurches, institutions that loomed larger in the scheme of their cities than ever before. As Evelyn Brooks Higginbotham explains, these churches were sometimes following the lead of white advocates of the social gospel who had been calling for urban "institutional churches" to minister to poor populations along the lines of settlement houses. But unlike the white institutional churches, the successful black churches, while responding through social service, also turned up the spiritual temperature, winning new members and inspiring older ones with high-voltage preaching and other revivalist techniques that had not been part of northern religious tradition. It was a synthesis that Milton Sernett argues was new to African American religion and to American Protestantism, a balanced fusion of the evangelical and the social gospel, of "praise and protest."[41]

Olivet Baptist in Chicago exemplified the new black megachurch. The oldest black Baptist church in the city, dating back to 1850, it had been led since 1902 by Elijah John Fisher, a former Georgian who by 1915 had turned it into the leading black church in the city with a membership approaching 4,000. His successor, Lacey Kirk Williams, took over just as the World War I influx was hitting Chicago and turned it into something much bigger. A newcomer himself from Texas, Williams moved boldly into the process of helping the migrants, adding to Olivet's already extensive list of agencies and functions. By 1920, Olivet had forty-two departments, committees, and auxiliaries led by more than 500 volunteer officers and a professional staff of twenty-four. Olivet committees met the trains and helped newcomers find housing; they operated a placement agency that could deliver jobs in the stockyards and with some other prime employers; and they provided a nursery, kindergarten, and a variety of clubs and recreational programs for young people as well as adults. Educational programs—Sunday school for the younger generation, vocational and refinement classes for adults—kept more volunteers busy. The church also now claimed 9,000 members, making it one of the largest religious assemblies of any kind in the country. Williams also made sure that African Americans elsewhere learned about the Olivet model. A rising star in the National Baptist Convention, he publicized Olivet as a showpiece institution. Even before Williams became president of the National Baptist Convention in 1924, Olivet was famous throughout black America—famous for its grandeur, size, and central role in Black Chicago, standing as a beacon of accomplishment and a model for emulation.[42]

Leading churches played a large role in defining community standards and providing political leadership in the early decades of the diaspora. This varied from city to city, depending upon the strength of other black community institutions. Less pronounced in Harlem and Chicago where strong newspapers, well-developed political machines, and other secular forces vied for community leadership, church influence was very evident in Philadelphia, where leading clerics constituted for a time a quasi-community government, operating first through a ministerial association and then creating in 1919 the Colored Protective Association to speak for black Philadelphia. Likewise in Detroit, a handful of churches—Second Baptist, Bethel AME, and St. Matthews Episcopal—took a leadership role, providing a large share of the community associational and political structure as that fast-growing black community negotiated the late teens and early twenties.[43]

Whether leading from in front or leading from behind, the churches provided much of the impetus behind the distinctive community-building ideology of the period. They were a principal source of the atmosphere of welcome that greeted migrants, of the call to service that old settlers answered, and of the "we are building the promised land" story that newspapers trumpeted. Not alone but in concert with newspapers, women's clubs, and some other community institutions, the leading churches promoted notions of civic responsibility that helped communities minimize the chaos of the first Great Migration and ease the transitions for both old and new residents. In the tightly squeezed, violence-surrounded, governmentally neglected, service-deprived, impoverished new ghettos of the North, these civic ideals counted for a lot. They were the difference between collective demoralization and community pride. They were the source of the claim that something wonderful was being constructed in those spaces, that Black Metropolises were emerging.

The civic ideals coming out of the leading churches were gendered in particular ways. Women filled most of the pews, raised most of the money, staffed most of the committees, and did most of whatever projects a church undertook. Engines of female activism, the churches of the early black diaspora also promoted a social ideology focused on standards of female respectability. That is the argument that historian Victoria Wolcott makes in a recent study of African American women in 1920s Detroit. Focusing in part on the women of Second Baptist Church, the largest and oldest black Baptist organization in the city, she shows that Second Baptist committees of volunteers honeycombed the community and backed up the secular service organizations, including the brand-new Urban League and NAACP and the network of women's clubs that had a longer Detroit history. These church committees were run by women, staffed by women, helped mostly women and children, and operated within a political discourse of uplift and respectability that was largely centered on the figure of the female newcomer, the black woman upon whose character would rest the future of the community and the race.[44]

There were limits to what the big churches and their civic ideals could accomplish. It would be wrong to imply that the free-flowing black communities of the early diaspora period conformed to these or any other singular vision. Most observers found it easier to notice the organized vice than the organized morality of these zones, and gamblers and prostitutes were not the only groups not listening to the church committees. That said, churches played a critical role in those defining early years. They provided the foundation for almost all community projects, from newspapers that needed their advertising and hoped preachers would promote readership, to causes and organizations like the NAACP, the Urban League, the Republican Party, the Colored YMCA, and even the United Negro Improvement Association. All turned to the churches for meeting space, for endorsements, for the critical support of respected preachers, and to borrow the energies and organizing talents of the women who filled the pews. Gayraud Wilmore describes the tight relationship between the NAACP in the teens and twenties and the major churches. "It used to be a truism in many communities that the 'black church is the NAACP on its knees.'" This statement can be broadened. Much of the civic consciousness of the developing diaspora communities rested on those same knees.[45]

The 1930s initiated transformations in social organization and leadership that would reduce the stature and undercut some of the political importance of leading churches like Second Baptist and Olivet Baptist. Competition with the newer religious groups—new Baptist congregations, Pentecostal churches, and various smaller sects—was part of the change. The Depression was the other factor. It was impossible for the big churches to maintain their social service activities in the face of massive unemployment, and with the advent of the New Deal, government agencies would take over many of these functions. Political struggles also impinged on church authority. As new radical groups vied for influence, as black communities negotiated a turn from Republican to Democratic loyalties and from dependence on corporate benevolence to alliances with organized labor, many of the preachers and churches that exercised community leadership in the 1920s retreated into quieter forms of community service. I will return to these political changes later. The point for now is that the 1930s meant both greater religious diversity and a reduced role for churches in the political systems of the Black Metropolises. Historian Robert Gregg describes it as a shift from the church as community to the church as communion. In the 1930s, the big churches lost the ability to coordinate the Black Metropolises.[46]

Churches now pulled in different directions, offering variation in the spiritual messages and also in their social and political orientations. Many of the new churches, especially of the sanctified tendencies, were rigidly separatist and "otherworldly," urging believers to save souls, not societies, and to avoid commitments outside the faith. Other churches were intensely political, supporting radical or nationalist movements that vied for influence in African American communities. The Garvey movement lived on through the 1930s in part through the congregations of African Orthodox churches. Father Divine's Peace Missions earned headlines in the 1930s as a religious movement allied with the Left. The cult, which at its peak may have counted 50,000 followers in New York and the other cities of the North and West, practiced a religion that was as much political as spiritual. Living together in the dormitory-style missions; sharing wages or working in stores, restaurants, farms, and other businesses owned by the missions; flaunting their militant integrationism and attracting enough white members to make it real, Divine's followers found common cause for a time with the Communist Party. Members took to the streets on behalf of the "Scottsboro Boys" and the International League against War and Fascism and took to the voting booths in support of left-wing causes like the All People's Party, a New York party formed in 1936 to combat racism and gain a fair share of services for Harlem.[47]

Left-wing politics divided church groups during the 1930s, especially as the agenda shifted toward unionization. When Socialist labor pioneer A. Philip Randolph set out to organize a union of Pullman porters, the Brotherhood of Sleeping Car Porters, in 1925, he ran into a buzz saw of church opposition, especially in Chicago where George Pullman's company was seen as an important community patron. The leading black ministers, including Lacey Kirk Williams of Olivet Baptist and Archibald James Carey of Quinn Chapel, the largest AME church, attacked the union and pointed out that organized labor had always been foe, not friend, of the black community. When the drive for a porters union resumed in 1933, the churches were no longer a solid opposition. Some ministers (in Chicago, Junius Austin of Pilgrim Baptist and Harold Kingsley of Church of the Good Shepherd) now supported the union and other left-wing causes. Others had fallen quiet, keeping their heads down as the fight over unions intensified. Similar divisions developed in Detroit as activists challenged black workers to rethink their loyalty to Henry Ford and join the new auto workers union. Churches took different sides. Bethel AME and some others cooperated with the union, but most Detroit churches, including Second Baptist, retained their ties to Ford and other automakers all through the decade, backing away from anti-unionism only in the 1940s.[48]

If the 1930s had complicated the religious landscape and the political engagements of churches, religious institutions still remained key to the civic culture of those black communities. Drake and Cayton recognized this even as they underplayed the observation. As varied as they were, churches almost all accepted what the authors described as a dual responsibility, committed to serving as "race institutions" as well as religious institutions. Preachers of all denominations denounced the system of racial subordination that had been a constant in African American experience. Pentecostal leaders might instruct their followers that deliverance would come through faith, not politics, but most others urged their members to be active in the struggle for change. Even those preachers whom the Left denounced as misleaders or conservatives taught the value of civic activism, even if they disagreed over definitions and vehicles. They also taught the value of the vote. In his 1935 study of Chicago politics, political scientist Harold Gosnell calculated that at least half of all voting African Americans in that city were church members. Churches at all points remained centers of political education, places where new generations of young people and new cohorts of migrants heard discussions of current issues and learned the spirit of civic responsibility.[49]

The post–World War II era provided a new context for church-community relations as an invigorated urban civil rights movement emerged. Dedicated to extending Fair Employment Practices legislation and breaking down commercial and housing segregation, the movement was based in several different institutions, including the newspapers, the NAACP, CIO unions, the urban Democratic Party, and the churches. The NAACP, which had faced left-wing competition in the 1930s, now came into its own, building a mass membership in each of the communities of the North and West (and also moving into the South). Churches played a critical role in the expansion of the NAACP and in the campaigns to desegregate the cities. Key ministers and deacons served in the leadership committees of NAACP chapters and other civil rights organizations. Some churches provided space and facilities for rallies and meetings, while many more publicized campaigns and raised funds.[50]

The political role of churches was also enhanced by a maturing relationship between black ministers and white ministers in the liberal Protestant denominations. The Christian-to-Christian connection had long been useful to black communities. The older black churches in the northern cities often had relationships dating back to the mid-nineteenth century with white "sister" institutions. The relationship was mostly based on charity, but clever ministers could use them not just for financial assistance but also to secure allies in issues affecting the whole community. On a national basis, the Federal Council of Churches had also been useful. Founded in 1908, this ecumenical organization of what would later be called the mainstream denominations had welcomed the major Afro-Methodist and Afro-Baptist denominations. It also had channeled resources in modest amounts into projects like the Colored YMCAs and had maintained since 1921 a Department of Race Relations headed by the energetic African American activist and scholar Dr. George Haynes.[51]

Those modest beginnings blossomed into a much more important resource after World War II. Coaxed into action by black ministers, in 1946 the Federal Council endorsed a strong statement against segregation and called on member churches to work against racial discrimination in society as well as in their own churches. After the Federal Council reconstituted itself as the National Council of Churches in 1950, the new and better-funded organization would provide support for civil rights activism both on a national level and through metropolitan church councils. Coalitions of black and white ministers and black and white churchwomen operated in many cities and sometimes secured major breakthroughs. When Washington State passed a fair employment law in 1949, some of the credit went to the Christian Friends for Racial Equality, an all female biracial organization that had been lobbying effectively against segregation in Seattle for five years.[52]

New Bethel participated in the postwar activism of black Detroit. When Franklin arrived in 1946, the congregation was, as he put it, "conservative." The church had concerned itself in its early years strictly with religious matters, leaving politics to other venues. Franklin led the congregation toward greater involvement in civic affairs. As a young minister first in Mississippi, then in Memphis, he had been very cautious about introducing anything other than spiritual matters. "The white people had taught the preacher that politics had no place in the church," he recalled years later. But a few of the Memphis ministers were cautiously promoting civil rights in the early 1940s, and Franklin had joined them. He did more in Detroit. He joined the NAACP and encouraged New Bethel members to do likewise. He quietly supported unions, and several of his deacons were active in the United Auto Workers union. He invited Adam Clayton Powell and later Martin Luther King to visit and preach. He told members they needed to register to vote and be politically active, and he allowed certain candidates to address the congregation during election seasons. In the mid-1950s, he formalized this program by creating a New Bethel political action committee to handle voter registration and political education and to make voter recommendations. He recalled later that all this was standard in the churches of the northern cities. "In Buffalo, or Detroit, or Chicago, or Los Angeles, the minister is involved," Franklin explained. "He helps his congregation in terms of presenting before them different candidates, and recommending. He leaves them free, of course, to choose; but he recommends certain people. . . . And the minister is interested in what the Board of Education is doing, if the classrooms are too crowded, things like that. He's involved in the total structure."[53]

Not every black church functioned this way in the 1950s, but many did. To a far greater extent than in most white communities of the twentieth century, churches were key animating forces in the black diaspora communities. Pulling in different directions, offering a spectrum of different faiths and institutional profiles, they imposed a rigorous competition and pluralism on the Black Metropolis, so much so that many observers felt they absorbed energies and resources that could better be used elsewhere. But many, if not all, of these same institutions promoted values, orientations, and actions that would be critical to the development of those communities and to their political capacity. Agents of political socialization, economic uplift, racial pride, and community pride, the churches throughout the diaspora period were framing institutions that contributed directly and indirectly to a civic culture that would yield important historical changes.

Faithful Kingdoms

Church-building by white migrants also had important community and political implications. Again, the concept of gateway institution is useful. The choice of where to go to church or whether to go to church set the terms for other aspects of the migrant's social adjustment. Joining a church could be an important part of the settling-in process, signaling a willingness to build a new life in a new place. And the direction of that new life had something to do with the kind of church chosen. For white migrants, the choice of a Southern Baptist or Pentecostal church had a tendency to reinforce southern identities, while participation in a mainline denomination usually promoted forms of integration with nonsoutherners.[54]

More than most black churches, the churches that southern whites built tended toward an all-embracing evangelicalism that sometimes worked against secular involvements. Especially this was so in the 1920s and 1930s when most of the church-building was carried out by pioneering Pentecostals and fervent Baptist fundamentalists. It was a time when both movements practiced intense sectarianism, insisting on perfection in their institutions and fighting over how it was defined. Temple Baptist, with its high-profile politics, was far from typical. Most of the churches southerners built or joined during this early era were small in size and small in public voice, their members more interested in being alone to practice their faith than in the kind of battles that J. Frank Norris chose to wage.[55]

Rev. James Wilson spent the summer of 1942 visiting churches in California's Central Valley for research for a dissertation on the religious institutions associated with the Okie migration. The Baptist, Assemblies of God, and other evangelical churches he observed were mostly small in size, modest in resources, and, he noted, usually disengaged from the affairs of the community or broader society. Pentecostals in particular, but also many of the Baptists, emphasized the goal of a "separated life," stressing not just high moral standards but also urging members to turn away from nonbelievers and the enticements of secular society. "Worldliness is anything that doesn't pertain to the Christian life," explained Rev. H. C. Lafferty, pastor of the Pentecostal Assembly of God in the little town of Live Oaks. And he went on to enumerate recreational activities that were off-limits: "playin' cards, goin' to shows, or dancin'." Politics was also a distraction, as another Pentecostal minister made clear: "I just preach a clean Gospel and hit sin where I find it. I don't mess up with politics and things like that."[56]

Like most African American churches, these faith communities promoted a tight sense of internal solidarity. Church members helped each other in all sorts of ways, sharing information about jobs and housing opportunities and assisting during emergencies. They also reinforced southern identities, appealing to home state pride while building on feelings of alienation. Some of this was implicit, just an easy and natural way that preachers might increase the sense of solidarity. It also grew quite naturally out of the cultural critique that was the great lesson of the evangelicals. The evidence of an America that had lost its way and of a world heading toward apocalyptic resolution seemed palpable in the North and West where great cities teemed with vice, crime, and corruption, where the great purveyors of sin and secularism were headquartered.[57]

The dedicated otherworldliness of many of the early institutions limited their impact on the communities around them. Historian Becky Nicolaides found this to be the case in her study of the Los Angeles suburb of South Gate. A white working-class suburb that had been created in the 1920s near newly built automobile and tire plants, South Gate's population included southerners, perhaps 20–25 percent of the population, who were the prime but not sole constituents of more than a dozen small Baptist and Pentecostal churches. Four mainline institutions—a Presbyterian, a Methodist, a Catholic, and a Lutheran church—dominated the social life of the young suburb through recreational programs that included everything from picnics to Boy Scout troops, sports leagues to drama clubs. They also dominated politics, with members playing active roles in the chamber of commerce and the city council. In contrast, the evangelical congregations remained as of the 1930s separate and disengaged: "Church life became a force that distanced Evangelical—mostly working class—from the local seats of power, leaving leadership to those of other persuasions."[58]

Still, some evangelicals defied the trend and managed to be both a visible and forceful presence in political life. The "fighting fundamentalists," as historian Joel Carpenter calls them, were distinguished from other evangelicals, especially the Pentecostals, by their determination to wage a public struggle for their faith. J. Frank Norris was part of this small but "contentious lot" who styled themselves as holy warriors and used pulpit, radio, and a militarized vocabulary (*The Sword of the Lord* was a principal publication) to battle the forces of a corrupt and irreligious world. Baptists and Presbyterians mostly, some had pulled out of the main northern denominations after failing to dislodge the modernizers in the 1920s. Other had stayed put, continuing guerrilla warfare within the mainline denominations while building networks of Bible institutes, fundamentalist publications, and seminaries that would play an important role in the revival of fundamentalism in the postwar era. Some were extreme reactionaries. Gerald B. Winrod, a Kansas Baptist preacher and leader of an organization called Defenders of the Christian Faith, and Gerald K. Smith, a minister in the Church of Christ and for a time Huey Long's right-hand man, would gravitate so far into anti-Semitism and Far Right politics that contemporaries were justified in calling them fascists. But most politically active fundamentalists voiced a conservatism that fell within conventional boundaries. Some, like Norris, attacked Roosevelt, New Deal Democrats, and CIO unions as part of a package of oppositions that explicitly favored the Republican Party. Others stayed away from partisanship and concentrated on denouncing radicalism and policies and institutions that spread sinfulness

(Hollywood, universities, the liquor interest). And of course much of their fire was directed at the "machine," Norris's term for the modernists who controlled the mainline denominations.[59]

The fundamentalist movement did not begin as a diaspora enterprise. Most the combatants of the 1920s and 1930s had been in place for many years and were carrying on the struggle that had begun in the seminaries and big cities of the North before the First World War. But southerners moving north and west brought fresh resources to the battle in the form of new members for fundamentalist congregations and much of the leadership. Many of the most important leaders of northern fundamentalism had, like Norris, been raised, been educated, and begun their ministries in the South.

William Bell Riley, widely considered the dean of American fundamentalism, was raised in Kentucky. He belonged to an earlier era of migration, having come north before the turn of the century to serve as pastor of the First Baptist Church of Minneapolis. From that base he helped shape the cause of conservative Protestantism. His book, the *Menace of Modernism* (1917), and leadership in founding the World Christian Fundamental Association in 1919 were decisive early contributions to the movement. He spent the 1930s and early 1940s preaching an increasingly pessimistic gospel larded with conspiracies of Communists and Jews, but at his death in 1947 he left behind a legacy of Bible institutes and churches in the upper plains states that would guide the next generation of fundamentalists.[60]

John Roach Straton pastored New York's Calvary Baptist Church through the 1920s and used that post to battle booze, dance halls, short skirts, modern literature, prizefights, Al Smith, and the Catholic "takeover" of the Democratic Party. Straton was a southerner by upbringing. Born in Illinois, he grew up in Georgia where his father was a Baptist preacher, was educated in Southern Baptist institutions, and held most of his early pastorates in the South, moving to New York in 1918. Famous, as was Norris, for his theatrics both in church and in various publicity-generating civic crusades, Straton became such a figure in 1920s New York that one columnist called him the "Protestant Pope." Sinclair Lewis studied his flamboyant style and is said to have partly modeled Elmer Gantry after Straton.[61]

J. C. Massee, who directed the Tremont Temple Baptist Church in Boston during the 1920s and followed that with an influential career as a traveling evangelist during the 1930s, was another southerner instrumental in the fundamentalist movement, as was J. Gresham Machen, leader of the Presbyterian fundamentalists, who founded Westminster Theological Seminary in Philadelphia in 1929 and then led ultraconservatives out of the northern Presbyterian denomination in 1935, creating what would become the Orthodox Presbyterian Church. Other influential southerners included Curtis Lee Laws, who in 1920 coined the term "fundamentalist" and who edited until 1936 the New York–based *Watchman-Examiner*, principal voice for the fundamentalist movement within the Northern Baptist denomination; Dallas Billington, who by the late 1940s had turned Akron Baptist Temple into the "largest church in the world" with 21,000 members; Carl McIntire, who from his base in Collingswood, New Jersey, led breakaway Presbyterians and the extreme right of the fundamentalist movement all through the postwar era; and, as already mentioned, G. Beauchamp Vick, who would follow Norris as pastor of Temple Baptist and also lead the Baptist Bible Fellowship, the strictly fundamentalist denomination that grew out of Norris's efforts.[62]

California's most important "fighting fundamentalist" was Robert Shuler, "Fighting Bob," as he liked to be known. Shuler created in Los Angeles a political movement of the Protestant Right that was a model for what Norris hoped to achieve in Detroit. Born in Virginia and ordained in the Southern Methodist denomination (which would reunite with Northern Methodism in 1939), Shuler may have crossed paths with Norris in Texas where both found early prominence as fiery fundamentalists, one within the Baptist fold, the other within the Methodist. In 1920, Shuler moved to Los Angeles to Trinity Methodist, a downtown church that was one of the southern denomination's outposts in California. Northern Methodists were much stronger, but the Methodist Episcopal South had maintained a small number of churches in the far West since the 1850s. Trinity was one of the oldest, and before Shuler arrived it claimed a respectable reputation and congregation of 900, including some of the city's most prominent families.[63]

Shuler shook things up, turning Trinity into a center of controversy while adding huge numbers of new members, many but not all newcomers from the South. Fundamentalism and righteous conservatism, he decided, needed a champion in Los Angeles, a city that in the early 1920s was beginning to acquire its reputation for eccentricity and hedonism. "Fighting Bob" threw himself into the battle, using his pulpit, an attentive press, and later his own magazine and radio station to denounce religious modernism and a host of other evils. Like Norris, Shuler's fundamentalism went way beyond biblical literalism. A holy war needed to be waged in public life as well as in the sanctuaries of faith, and the enemies were many. Jazz, films, bootleggers, prostitutes, corrupt politicians, Al Smith, Catholics, Jews, and Communists were all on the list, as were Pentecostal "charlatans" like fellow Los Angeleno Aimee Semple McPherson. Nativism played a big role in his crusades of the 1920s, as they had for Norris, and "Fighting Bob" outdid the "Texas Cyclone" in his enthusiasm for the Ku Klux Klan.[64]

He was also more willing to work directly with the machinery of electoral politics and government. Norris, as a Baptist, believed that religion and the state should not be entangled, and while critics might say that he violated that premise, in his view his public crusades were all about keeping the forces of godlessness from using the state for evil purposes. Shuler, a Methodist, had fewer qualms. By the late 1920s, his radio station was a major force in electoral politics, capable of mobilizing a sizable vote. In 1929, his candidate, John C. Porter, a political unknown and former Klansman, was elected mayor of Los Angeles. For the next four years, as the nation drifted deeper and deeper into depression, Shuler and his mayor would do their best to clean up Los Angeles. The regime poured resources into enforcing prohibition, fired scores of city employees and replaced them with conservative Protestants, insulted the president of France (when Porter refused to join in a toast), and beefed up the police "Red Squad," the latter helping the city achieve its early 1930s reputation as the "national capital of police 'Cossackism.'"[65]

In 1932, the Southern Methodist minister took his own swing at public office, running for U.S. Senate as the candidate of the Prohibition Party. He gained 560,088 votes and came in just behind the Republican candidate in the three-party race. That was Shuler's high-water mark, but not the end of his influence. Like Norris, Shuler's fundamentalism became deeply entwined with anti-Communism in the New Deal era, and while the Methodist pastor was less of a stuntman than his Baptist counterpart, he stayed in the public eye. In 1942 he ran for Congress as a Republican against incumbent Jerry Voorhis and managed to wound the left-wing Democrat with charges that he consorted with Communists. Four years later, with Shuler's help, young Richard Nixon would repeat the charges, beat Voorhis, and head off to Washington. Retiring from his pastorate in 1953, Shuler drifted further to the right. His magazine, the *Methodist Challenge*, became identified with the extremist fringe of American fundamentalism and American politics. Anti-Communist, anti-Catholic, anti-Semitic, and opposed to civil rights and integration, "Fighting Bob" remained also a committed southerner. "I am not only a southerner," he wrote in 1958 in the context of the civil rights battles, "I love her social and political ideology."[66]

White-Flight Gospel

Shuler may have remained a proud southerner throughout his long career, but not all of his fellow white migrants were proud of him. Right-wing fundamentalists like Norris and Shuler were highly visible but also highly controversial. They represented just one strand of a complicated evangelical movement that had many voices, most of them not as strident and extreme. But a calmer sort of conservatism can be associated with the white gospel diaspora. In the postwar era when Southern Baptists began to build hundreds and then thousands of churches, and as Assemblies of God and other Pentecostal organizations accelerated their growth, southern-origin evangelicalism would become a growing influence in white communities throughout the North and West, helping to shape some of the values and politics circulating in those settings. Particularly this was so in the suburbs that were rapidly spreading out from metropolitan cores. White southerners were often the most eager suburbanites and eager suburban church-builders. Evangelical churches would be well represented in the new suburbs, indeed sometimes in a position to significantly influence the quality of civic culture.

Evangelical Protestantism reinvented itself in the World War II era. Images of extremism, ruralism, conflict, and otherworldliness were superseded by a new bid for respectability. The changes were partly engineered through some new organizations. One was the National Association of Evangelicals that came together in 1942, determined to create a broad coalition of born-again Christians and get beyond the debates and defeats that had plagued the previous decades. The name helped. The NAE would drop references to fundamentalism and reclaim the historically potent "evangelical" label. So did the policy of inclusiveness. The new organization included Holiness and Pentecostal groups, members of mainline denominations as well as the recognizably conservative organizations. This kind of ecumenism had its critics. Many of the most committed fundamentalists stayed outside the NAE, some of them joining instead the American Council of Christian Churches led by the uncompromising Carl McIntire. But a new and much broader and much more appealing umbrella organization had been created.[67]

Another new organization was Youth for Christ, a cooperative venture that set out in the early 1940s to find ways to reach young people and succeeded in reinventing the techniques of revivalist preaching. Youth for Christ preachers adopted up-to-date styles, taking their sharp suits, smooth demeanor, and with-it lingo straight from popular culture. They also put some swing into their rallies, updating white church music with modern instrumentation and rhythms and flourishes borrowed from big band swing. The results were electric. Beginning in 1943, Youth for Christ rallies drew unprecedented crowds in city after city, winning souls and capturing headlines. A 1945 Memorial Day rally at Chicago's Soldier Field attracted a crowd of 70,000 who spent the day enjoying a 300-piece band; a 5,000-member choir; marching units that included a contingent of 400 nurses, famous athletes, and war heroes who testified to their faith; and several of the Youth for Christ movement's best young preachers. The wire services and newsmagazines picked up the story. William Randolph Hearst ordered his chain of newspapers to cover future rallies and, as one minister put it, "puff YFC." "Not since the Scopes trial," writes Joel Carpenter, "had evangelical Christianity received such coverage, and this time most of it was friendly."[68]

Part of the reason these rallies attracted media coverage was that Americans everywhere were thinking about religion in new ways. The 1940s and 1950s would witness a great revival in religious activity that touched every faith and every community. Catholics, Jews, liberal Protestants, and conservative Protestants would all participate in an era of heightened spirituality and energetic expansion that seemed to fit the mood of a generation that had lived through a world war and now faced a dangerous and lingering Cold War. All faiths benefited, but the new era promised special advantages to evangelicals whose commitments seemed to line up well with the political configurations and public moods of the day. The power of faith, a commitment to conventional standards of morality, and clear-minded opposition to Communism and other radicalisms — these were no longer controversial holdings, as long as they were moderately expressed. But moderation was the key. The evangelicals needed leaders who could set a tone very different from either the wildly otherworldly Pentecostals or the fighting fundamentalists. They would find it in a new group of revivalist preachers, many of whom, like Oral Roberts, came from the South or, like Jack Shuler (son of "Fighting Bob"), were children of the diaspora.

First among this new cohort was another commuting southerner. Billy Graham grew up near Charlotte, North Carolina, the son of a prosperous farmer. At age sixteen, he knew he was destined for the ministry. After attending Bible college in Florida, he found an opportunity to study further at Wheaton College, the fundamentalist school located near Chicago that liked to call itself the "Harvard of the Bible Belt." He arrived in 1940, spent three years at his studies, and then began to preach in nearby Illinois towns. That brought him to the attention of the Youth for Christ organization, and in 1945 he hit the circuit, quickly gaining a reputation as one of the most successful of the young evangelists. Two events then catapulted him to a higher level. In 1947, William Bell Riley, the old father figure of American fundamentalism, asked Graham to come quickly to Minneapolis. Riley was dying and announced that he was turning over his Northwestern Bible School to the twenty-nine-year-old evangelist. It was a gesture of great significance, the older leader designating his successor. Graham ran the school for only a few years, much preferring the role of itinerant evangelist to the responsibilities of administration, but even after he resigned, he kept his office and headquarters in Minneapolis. His home, on the other hand, was in the hills of North Carolina, or at least that is where his wife and growing family lived. The evangelist lived on the road. In the decades that followed, he would be gone most of each year, finding his way back to North Carolina during the brief interludes in his busy worldwide crusade.[69]

The second elevating event was the revival Graham led in Los Angeles in the fall of 1949. He had been scheduling citywide revivals for some time, moving his now substantial road show from city to city at the behest of cooperating associations of churches that would turn out members for week-long or two-week-long revivals. The results were good but not spectacular until Los Angeles. That meeting broke through the sound barrier of midcentury evangelism. Graham secured a high-profile celebrity conversion when Texas-born country music star Stuart Hamblen announced on his own daily radio show that he had been saved. That brought out the crowds and more media attention, and soon more celebrities and hundreds of ordinary Los Angelenos were finding their way to Jesus. The press was all over it. Newspaper headlines and magazine stories heralded the miracle revival underway in Los Angeles. By the time the marathon ended after eight weeks, sponsors could claim an attendance of more than 300,000, salvations numbering in the thousands, and publicity of a sort that had not been available since Billy Sunday wowed the crowds in the first decades of the century. The new Billy was in *Life* magazine, his attractive image centering a big photo spread under the headline "A New Evangelist Arises."[70]

Graham would go on to create an evangelical enterprise more influential than any that preceded him. Working as expertly with business and governmental leaders as he did with huge audiences, he would become a confidant and spiritual adviser to nearly all the presidents of the next half century, starting with Dwight D. Eisenhower, who, after meeting with the evangelist, became the first president ever baptized in the White House. For evangelicals, Graham was indeed a miracle worker. He blew through all of the constraints that had formerly hindered the evangelical project. He charmed his way into the editorial boardrooms and oval offices using the same balance that worked so well with revival tent and later television audiences. He managed to jettison the lowbrow image that had plagued revivalists while keeping their populist sensibility and adding gestures of humility that seemed utterly genuine. He dropped the anger and belligerence of the old fundamentalists but not the vehemence and certitude. He held his arms open to a much wider group of believers, including modernists, and was denounced as a result by the old sectarians. But he never backed away from the core evangelical commitments to biblical inerrancy and salvation through Jesus. And he balanced in the same way the political messages of his faith, preaching anti-Communism but without the excesses of a Norris or Shuler, siding mostly with Republicans without alienating Democrats, urging moral reform without triggering the defenses of Hollywood and other advocates of an open culture.[71]

Graham symbolized the expanding public voice of evangelicals in the postwar era, a voice that registered at the local level every bit as much as it did in the White House. It would no longer be just the exceptional firebrand like Norris speaking out on public issues. Evangelical churches would become active participants in civic life and mostly in ways that coincided with moral and political conservatism. I do not want to overstate this. There are examples of white ministers whose belief in Christian rebirth led them to embrace social reform and even political radicalism. Liberal evangelicals have indeed contested the political reputation of the movement all through the twentieth century, just as they do today behind the example of former president Jimmy Carter. But the main tendency of the movement as it competed with modernist mainstream Protestantism in the postwar era was to emphasize social and political conservatism in a range of stances that either echoed Billy Graham or moved further to the right. Identification with traditionalism, opposition to radicalism, and opposition to most of the postwar apparatus of social change was an important part of the appeal of evangelicalism, part of the reason these churches expanded more rapidly than liberal Protestantism.[72]

Race figured into the patterns of growth and the patterns of white evangelical politics. The postwar metropolis with its portentous struggles over race and space offered key opportunities for the white evangelicals to expand their civic authority as well as membership. As African Americans broke down barriers in the central cities and moved into formerly all-white neighborhoods, churches of various kinds became important players in the tense confrontations, both because people were looking for guidance from clerical leaders and because churches are neighborhood institutions. As the great epic of housing wars and racial relocation unfolded in the 1950s and 1960s, black churches served as staging grounds for African American assaults on neighborhood segregation, and white churches served as staging grounds for white responses. Some mainstream white Protestant churches and some Catholic institutions aided the cause of integration, at times paying for their idealism as white members fled to the suburbs and as angry conservatives criticized liberal ministers and withdrew their memberships. Evangelical churches positioned themselves very differently, sometimes actively, sometimes passively taking advantage of white resistance to racial integration.

J. Frank Norris had always been as clear about race and segregation as about Communism, Catholicism, and modernism. Whites and blacks could not be equal—"Well, God did not make them that way." Segregation was God's plan. Integration was Lenin's plan—a Communist scheme to create a "mongrel race." And those who advocated it, like the NAACP and the National Council of Churches, were part of the Communist conspiracy. Norris's outspoken racism led to accusations that Temple Baptist helped foster hate strikes and race riots in the 1940s, although the charge was never proven. Still, there is no denying that segregation and white supremacy were part of the conservative value scheme that Norris promoted at the church.[73]

It continued under his successor, G. Beauchamp Vick. The Kentucky-born Vick had been general superintendent since 1936, in charge of the church on a day-to-day basis while Norris commuted to Detroit every two weeks for a highly publicized sermon. In 1950, Vick replaced the aging and ill Texan after a nasty falling-out between the two men. Norris was to live only two more years. Under Vick's leadership, Temple Baptist continued to thrive and remained a citadel of right-wing fundamentalism. Less flamboyant, less confrontational, Vick concentrated more on soul-saving than his headline-grabbing predecessor did. But the church's political and religious stances remained much the same. He would have nothing to do with the NAE, launching instead the Baptist Bible Fellowship, an independent denomination that a few years later would train and ordain a bright young Virginian named Jerry Falwell. Anti-Communist and anti-Catholic, Vick denounced Pentecostals and Youth for Christ, and although he was initially impressed by Billy Graham, after the mid-1950s he had few kind words for the young evangelist.[74]

Segregation remained a firm commitment for Vick. "God warned repeatedly in the Old Testament against Israel's mixture with other races," he wrote in 1949, "and we believe that it is not only unwise but unchristian to thus cause confusion by mixtures of the races." He never changed that view. African Americans were not allowed to join Temple Baptist during the twenty-five years of Vick's pastorship, nor, for that matter, under the first two pastors who succeeded him. It was not until 1986—and then only because of threatened demonstrations by civil rights groups—that Temple Baptist changed its whites-only membership policy.[75]

The church also played a role in the fight-and-flight neighborhood struggles that transformed postwar Detroit. In 1954, Vick moved the church from its location in fast-transitioning central Detroit to a huge new facility several miles to the west on Grand River Avenue. Capable of seating 5,000, the costly new church was a symbol of the huge congregation's size and financial strength. But within a few years, the new neighborhood was experiencing integration pressures. Located in the Wyoming Corridor, in the heart of a string of "defended neighborhoods" and near Livernois Avenue that had become the new line of segregation for west-side Detroit, Temple Baptist became a center of white resistance. Members used church facilities to hold neighborhood association meetings. Plans were developed to foil "blockbusters" and to convince white home-owners to stand by the neighborhood. Resistance worked for a time, but in the early 1960s the line began to crumble. As white home-owners fled to the suburbs, the church found itself stranded, serving a commuting population of members who drove into the city for services and church activities. In 1965, Vick began planning another relocation, and three years later Temple was no longer in Detroit. He had moved it just outside the city limits into the all-white township of Redford.[76]

Temple's strict and long-lasting segregationist policies were not standard among the evangelicals, at least not by the 1980s. By the late 1960s, most Southern Baptist and the Assemblies of God congregations outside the South were getting rid of the official whites-only membership barriers, although few became in any meaningful way racially integrated. Nor were evangelicals typically in the thick of the urban housing wars. Despite the example of Temple Baptist and a few others, Catholic parishes were much more important sites of white resistance in Detroit and most other big cities. Evangelical institutions typically ducked the challenge of neighborhood transformation. Most were small and new and opted for flight at the first signs of neighborhood change. They "have sold out completely and gone suburban," a Detroit Catholic priest complained in 1960, noting the difference between the Catholic commitment to staying in the city and the response of many non-Catholic institutions. Historian John T. McGreevy examines that Catholic commitment in detail, exploring the internal struggle between Catholic liberals like Detroit's Archbishop John Dearden who supported integration and those priests and lay Catholics who mobilized to fight it. With both sides committed to staying in the cities, Catholic communities and Catholic clergy were at the center of the integration struggles. As Dearden explained in 1967 after years of trying to foster understanding and accommodation, the "Negro-white confrontation in American cities is in great part a Negro-Catholic confrontation."[77]

It was in the suburbs more than the cities that the evangelical churches made their major contributions to racial politics and postwar civic culture. While Catholics wrestled with the urban transformations, joined in some cases by liberal Protestant congregations, evangelicals led the race to the suburbs and enjoyed as a result an institutional head-start in those newly important spaces, at least the ones geared to the white working class. That head-start shows up in the naming patterns of suburban Baptist churches. In older communities throughout the North and West, the high-status name "First Baptist Church" belongs almost always to a congregation affiliated with the American (Northern) Baptist denomination. But this is not necessarily so in the white-flight suburbs. In northern California, to take one example, the bedroom communities surrounding Oakland and Berkeley show who won the race. The First Baptist Churches of San Leandro, Pleasanton, Fremont, Newark, Rodeo, and Concord all belong to the Southern Baptists.[78]

Where the big cities had been dominated architecturally and in every other sense by Catholic cathedrals and stately sanctuaries of venerable mainstream Protestant congregations, in the stucco suburbs the Assemblies of God, Southern Baptist, and independent Baptist and Full Gospel churches would make their presence felt. It would be wrong to say that they were dominant during the era of white-flight (although that is sometimes the case now), but they were in a position to be much more influential than ever before. That was partly because of the speed with which they established themselves in the suburbs and partly because of the configurations of religion, race, and politics.[79]

In her study of South Gate, Becky Nicolaides follows the community's religious organizations through the postwar era. The evangelical churches multiplied after the war as the blue-collar suburb filled in, and where in the 1920s and 1930s these churches had been socially isolated, now they participated in civic affairs, gaining community influence first in the context of the anti-Communist and family-and-religion campaigns of the early 1950s, then in the context of the civil rights campaigns of the early 1960s. South Gate lay right across a busy boulevard from Watts, which in the 1940s had turned from a white neighborhood into an African American community. A militant white backlash movement formed in 1963–64, intent on defending the racial barrier. Secular institutions—the local newspaper, city council, and chamber of commerce—took the lead. But active support did come from certain fundamentalist ministers (as well as from the deeply conservative Cardinal Francis McIntyre, who presided over southern California's Catholic archdiocese). Equally important was the quiet and coded support that segregationists found in most evangelical institutions. Even if the subject never turned to race, preachers helped the backlash movement by denouncing radicals, by railing against vice and crime, and by continuing the now generations-long critique of modernists who preferred to meddle in the affairs of the world instead of spreading "The Word." Indeed, since the mainline denominations and many individual ministers were now actively supporting civil rights efforts, the evangelicals often let their silence do the talking. Years later, Rev. Don Argue, president of the NAE, would characterize it in these terms: "White evangelicals were, for the most part, absent during the civil-rights struggle."[80]

Whether on the front lines of the backlash campaigns or in the suburban background, whether loud or "absent," the evangelical churches that white southerners had built played an important role in the spatial and racial politics of the 1960s, offering a conservative alternative to the civil rights liberalism that many other churches now supported. And they would play a bigger role in politics in the decades to come. Having established themselves in the white-flight suburbs, they would benefit from the growth patterns of those spaces and from the fact that the suburbs would be vying with cities as centers of political gravity. We will explore those developments in chapter 8.

Southern Effects

The Southern Diaspora turns out to have been a critical factor in the twentieth-century history of American religion. The gospel highways coming out of the South carried change throughout the land, into cities and into suburbs across the North and across the West, indeed also across national borders. Southern-origin evangelical movements today operate on every continent. The SBC supports more than 5,000 missionaries in 116 different countries, making that denomination by itself one of the most important proselytizing agents in modern Christianity. Pentecostal and charismatic foreign missionaries have been potentially even more effective, especially in Latin America where in recent decades they have broken open the monopoly of faith that Catholicism established centuries ago. The movement out of the South seems to have been only the beginning of the evangelical expansion. These faiths have now spring-boarded beyond American borders and constitute one of the most controversial forces in the global projection of American cultural influence.[81]

The expanding force of evangelicalism has depended on many people, not just diaspora southerners. Evangelicalism never belonged exclusively to the South, and all of the evangelical denominations and other movement bodies have in recent decades reached well beyond the base of southerners and former southerners. By the mid-1980s, denominational officials in the Assemblies of God and the SBC were sure that the majority of members in California and presumably other states were no longer of southern background. Moreover, the most dramatic additions to the evangelical cause in the last quarter century have come in institutions that profess no particular links to the South, in churches that are in some cases nondenominational, in others that are independent Baptist or independent Pentecostal congregations, and in still others that remain affiliated with denominations that have not in the past been considered evangelical.[82]

Some might then question whether this dynamic religious force should be seen as a product of the South and its diaspora. But if we think about how movements develop momentum, the answer is clear. Evangelicalism fueled itself into aggressive growth in the second half of the twentieth century based on momentum that began with the diaspora. It may be somewhat analogous to the contribution that the Irish diaspora made to American Catholicism in the nineteenth century. The Irish were not the founding force behind the American church, yet they came in such numbers and with such strength of commitment and leadership resources that they were able to take over and transform American Catholicism, creating an enormously powerful institution that would remain in some ways Irish even as it grew beyond that ethnic group. The analogy is not perfect. Southern identity is not the same as Irish nationalism, and the centralized Catholic Church operates in very different ways than the loosely coordinated evangelical movement. Still, it seems appropriate to note the parallel effects of the Irish and southern diaporas, both of them providing key demographic and cultural underpinnings for expansive religious projects.

And there were other diaspora effects no less important than the evangelical movement. The most profound change in American religious life during the course of the twentieth century has been not the elevation of evangelicals but an escalating pluralism of faith, the multiplying of religious options, and the rebalancing of religious influences in civic life. Black southerners played a key role, breaking open Catholic domination of the major cities and introducing new religious organizations that added diversity of worship while also challenging the civic priorities of the white-dominated religious institutions —challenging them to take up the issue of racial injustice. White southerners added further complexity to northern and western religious life, building churches that helped dethrone and reorient mainstream Protestant denominations, battling for influence in the suburbs and smaller cities, and adding a contradictory challenge on the issue of race. Together, the two segments of the Southern Diaspora roiled the waters and raised the temperature of religious life throughout the regions where they settled. Indeed, the gospel highways leading out of the South carried something that was not particularly southern: religious division, religious debate, religious diversity.

Leveraging Civil Rights

That the Southern Diaspora helped African Americans in their historic struggle for civil rights is widely understood. But how it did so has not been carefully explained. Indeed, since the 1960s scholars have written about black political development in ways that undervalue the role of the northern Black Metropolises. Partly it is because the southern civil rights struggles of the 1950s and 1960s loom so large that there is a tendency to treat everything that came before as prologue. Partly it is because few of the historians and political scientists who have written on the subject have cared enough about political geography. The result is an oddly inconsistent narrative that always includes the point that the black diaspora brought with it voting rights and increased political visibility but fails to follow up in any consistent manner.[1]

This chapter does so, making the point that the Black Metropolises provided the base for a sequence of extremely important political developments that were not just prelude but precondition to the southern civil rights breakthroughs of the 1960s. There was a particular regional dynamic behind the twentieth-century drive for rights and equality, an almost Archimedean logic: African Americans had to leave the South in order to gain the leverage needed to lift it and the rest of the nation out of Jim Crow segregation.[2]

The issue of black political capacity is a conceptual minefield. Is it a story of power or powerlessness, of extraordinary gains achieved against overwhelming odds, or one that ends every time in tokenism, marginality, and failure to get at the roots or racism and inequality? What constitutes black politics and political capacity? When complicated interracial coalitions argue for equal rights laws and presidents and courts enact them at least in part because of international embarrassment and the desire to facilitate foreign policy, should we see that as an example of African American political accomplishment? What about when white people flee to the suburbs? Or when politicians scramble to find ways to mitigate racial tensions? Can these be considered expressions of African American influence? Until recently, most scholars said no. From Ralph Bunche though James Wilson and Ira Katznelson to Manning Marable, writers have typically defined black politics in narrow terms that dictate pessimistic conclusions about the accomplishments of black political activism.[3]

Interpretations of African American political action in the northern cities are further complicated because of the tendency to see the past through the lens of the ongoing "urban crisis." Ever since Martin Luther King's ill-fated 1966 campaign to break school and housing segregation in Chicago, northern civil rights struggles have generally been considered a failure. The conventional approach stresses the contrast between the measurable breakthroughs against Jim Crow in the South and the violent and clouded events in the North where, after 1965, riots and troubled war on poverty programs seemed to bring little that was beneficial to the ghettos. The fact that since the late 1970s, black central city populations have experienced escalating job loss and poverty, drug wars, and other social problems and that many school systems have given up on integration has exacerbated the problem of historical interpretation. The urgent need to understand the current dimensions of racial inequality and current patterns of black political difficulty has fed a tendency to read the same conditions back into the past.[4]

But the past needs to be taken on its own terms. For much of the "long civil rights era," it was in the northern cities more than the South that the resources for political change were being developed, and in those spaces African Americans recorded a pattern of impressive accomplishments. Taking into account the obstacles faced, diaspora African Americans were remarkably effective both in the accumulation of influence and in engineering beneficial public policy. That brings up one last issue. Narratives of the civil rights era have become important currency in contemporary politics, used now with increasing force by conservatives as arguments against current efforts to redress racial inequality. I want to make it clear that what follows has no such intent. I will emphasize the accomplishments of a generation of southern-origin African American activists, not to celebrate the completion of a struggle, but to illuminate its architecture at a pivotal juncture and to show one of the great legacies of the Southern Diaspora.[5]

Tools of Black Politics

African Americans developed political capacities in the North that were not available in the South. The right to vote is obvious. As Thomas Brooks once put it, migration out of the South was a move "almost literally, from no voting to voting." But that by itself explains little. Voting does not automatically translate into influence, especially for social groups that are outnumbered and socially isolated. It was not the vote itself that would prove important; it was the way it was used and the context in which it was used. One of the most important forms of power that African Americans would develop in the North was the ability to marshal votes in contexts of competitive politics. Because the spaces they occupied offered a number of balance of power opportunities, northern black voting became highly productive at certain junctures.[6]

Voting was only one of the tools that became available in the North. The ability to build productive alliances was another. Here, too, context was key. The diaspora was fortuitously aimed at a select set of cities that were uniquely situated as centers of American cultural and political influence and that had resources available nowhere else. Over time, black communities developed political relationships in those cities that gave them access to various forms of influence. Evolving ties to the urban intelligentsia, to Socialists and Communists, to Jewish communities, and to organized labor and through these groups to the northern Democratic Party would provide openings in turn for influencing government practice and policy at various levels.

Protest was the third new tool that the North offered. The ability to raise voices and move into the streets, to be visible, demanding, militant, and at times violent, was another political device that belonged to the big cities. Pioneered by organized labor, street tactics had become part of northern urban political culture by the time of the Great Migration and proved an essential weapon in the arsenal of black political practice. The threat of disruption would at various junctures compensate for the limitations of the other levers—strategic voting and alliance-building—forcing some of the allies to take black needs and demands more seriously than they otherwise intended.[7]

Sectionalism was the fourth weapon in the arsenal of northern black politics. One of the keys to building alliances and gaining white support at critical junctures was the notion that the white South was primarily to blame for racial injustice and that the South should be the chief focus for both rhetorical and legislative struggles. This was a position that the NAACP adopted when it made lynching its high-profile issue in the 1920s, but it went back much further, woven into the history of the Republican Party, a sectional solidarity that white northerners and black northerners had shared since the Civil War. All the way up to the mid-1960s, this eyes-on-the-South agreement served in complicated ways to help African Americans build influence and leverage.

None of this would have mattered in the same way had it not been that these cities themselves were unique instruments of public authority. Timing was critical. African Americans were developing political influence in New York, Chicago, Detroit, Cleveland, Philadelphia, Pittsburgh, St. Louis, Los Angeles, and San Francisco when those cities were at the apex of their own political influence. An age of metropolitan optimism, when soaring skyscrapers advertised the economic strength, population growth, and cultural vitality of the great cities, this was also the half century when city needs had first call on the nation's resources and city-originated policy often became the law of the land. The "long New Deal," from 1932 to 1968, brought to power presidents and congresses more responsive to big city needs than any in previous history. Money for social services and infrastructure developments flowed into those cities while legislation and reform agendas first pioneered in those places flowed out. If Archimedes had been looking for the ideal point of leverage to begin to exert political force on America's racial order, he could not have done better than these cities at this point in the nation's history.[8]

Another context variable also needs further attention. Earlier chapters have described the migration of educated southerners and the building of a black intelligentsia and other leadership elements in northern and western cities. It now needs to be emphasized that black leadership systems were moving northward even faster than the general population. Harlem and Chicago had begun to replace Atlanta-Tuskegee as the capitals of black America even before the Great Migration got officially underway. By the end of the 1920s, the shift was profound, with the *Chicago Defender* serving as a national newspaper and the *Crisis, Opportunity,* the *Messenger,* and the Garveyite *Negro World* coming out of New York; with the NAACP, the National Urban League, the UNIA, and the Brotherhood of Sleeping Car Porters all based in Harlem; with Chicago hosting more black-owned banks and insurance companies than Atlanta. And with an unprecedented literary and entertainment "renaissance" underway in both cities, the attentions and ambitions of black America were fixed on the North as never before.

The numerically small brain-drain migration was politically anything but small. The college graduates, business owners, preachers, and especially the lawyers who moved north added to the political resources of the Black Metropolises, enriching the leadership pool, contributing to the rising levels of debate and activism in those communities. Drawn into politics both by ambition and by community dynamics and often underemployment, these elites gave the northern communities a depth of political talent unmatched not only in the South but also in most white communities, where the ambitious had multiple occupational outlets. In his pioneering 1935 study, *Negro Politicians: The Rise of Negro Politics in Chicago*, Harold Gosnell noted the unique leadership resources that African Americans brought to politics: "In comparison with other ethnic groups the Negroes may lack wealth and social prestige, but in politics they make up for these deficiencies by utilizing to the full their own community life." Doctors, lawyers, social workers, postal workers, business owners, real estate brokers, college students, women's clubs, fraternal organizations, and above all the churches could all be counted on to take an interest in the affairs of the community and the affairs of the race. Huge obstacles stood in the way of political effectiveness and often discouraged mobilization, but the wealth of potential leadership was a major resource and key diasporic effect.[9]

Balances of Power

African American political capacity emerged in the interstices of the changing metropolitan polity. Chicago first showed the political potential of the black diaspora. "By 1920, Negroes had more political power in Chicago than anywhere else in the country," reports historian Allan Spear. A fortuitous balance of power opening provided the breakthrough in 1915. Republican machine boss and mayoral candidate William Hale Thompson needed the votes of the fast-growing black community, and he was prepared to deal. Instead of the crumbs that Republicans normally dispensed to black communities, Thompson's regime paid off in the kind of patronage that white ethnic groups expected: alderman and legislative seats, black ward bosses, various midlevel administration appointments, positions as policemen and teachers, and, most spectacularly in 1928, a congressional seat. When Oscar DePriest, the ever astute and not always machine-loyal Republican, won election to the House of Representatives, black Americans everywhere cheered. The first African American in Congress since the last of the southern Reconstruction seats fell to Jim Crow in 1901, DePriest was the first African American to ever win election from the North. Alabama-born and self-schooled in the art of Chicago politics, he was a fitting symbol of the political changes that migration would bring.[10]

What was remarkable about Chicago's community and ultimately about the African American communities in other cities was the level of electoral activity given the poverty and recent arrival of most of the population. Many minority groups have moved slowly into politics, finding the disincentives more compelling than the incentives. The important fact about African Americans in the diaspora period is how quickly they developed political capacity and how consistently they practiced it and made it grow. The contrasting experience of many of the European immigrant groups who had moved into the same cities before the turn of the century is instructive. A full generation passed before Italian and Polish voters muscled their way to recognition in the mostly Irish-dominated political systems of the big cities. The precocious electoral behavior of migrating African Americans also stands out in comparison to Asian Americans and Mexican Americans. In western cities like Seattle, tiny African American communities would be much more politically aggressive than larger populations of Chinese and Japanese Americans.[11]

There were obvious reasons for this strong attraction to politics. In one sense it can be considered an African American tradition, dating back to abolitionism and the rise of the Republican Party. Voting was one of the new freedoms of the North, and at impressive rates newcomers signed up to do it. A young couple from Mississippi, the Edwardses, told interviewers that one of the first things they did after arriving in Chicago in 1922 was talk with Republican Party workers. Mrs. Edwards explained that she was very anxious to vote "because her parents had never had the chance."[12]

How many other migrants joined the Edwardses in taking up the ballot depended on the particular city. Some cities offered strong incentives; others did not. Participation rates in Chicago were legendary. According to one set of calculations, blacks registered to vote at higher rates than whites throughout the 1920s. In 1930, 77 percent of eligible adults in the city's black Second Ward were registered, compared to 68 percent of white voters citywide. The Thompson machine had made the Second Ward one of its cornerstones, building up what political scientists call a black submachine under Oscar DePriest, who channeled patronage jobs, funds, and favors into the ward and marshaled a disciplined vote and high turnout on election days. That the level of patronage and scale of material rewards was meager in comparison to what white ward bosses could expect only underscores the ease with which black Chicagoans joined the political process and in turn the leadership capacities of the small army of lawyers, insurance salesmen, and hustlers who were the precinct organizers of the machine. The community may indeed have been shortchanged, as critics frequently charged, but something very important was happening nonetheless. Black Chicago was establishing a political practice and political visibility that would pay off down the road in coin more important than patronage.[13]

No other community came close to the Chicago level of mobilization in the 1920s, but Cleveland and Pittsburgh also showed the political potential of the Great Migration. Cleveland's story is in some ways the most remarkable because its African American population was overwhelmingly new, having surged from less than 10,000 in 1910 to nearly 70,000 by the mid-1920s. A group of astute newcomers saw the potential in these numbers and built a political operation that for a time offered the community a glimpse of power. Claybourne George and Charles White were examples of the leadership payoff of the diaspora. Southerners, graduates of Howard and Fisk, they were among the hundreds of attorneys seeking opportunities in the Black Metropolises in the 1920s. Drawn into political activism in part because it was intimately connected with the practice of their profession, they first helped rebuild Cleveland's NAACP chapter and then saw an opportunity to intervene in electoral politics. Pulling away from the regular Republican organization, they created an independent Republican political club that played the two major parties against each other and gained some impressive leverage. In 1927, George and another independent, E. J. Gregg, won election to the city council, along with a third African American, GOP regular Thomas Fleming. Continuing to work the balance of power possibilities within a city council that was divided between Democrats and Republicans, the so-called Black Triumvirate over the next half-dozen years managed to leverage both the parties and city hall, gaining patronage positions and some key benefits for the African American community.[14]

Pittsburgh witnessed another display of early political prowess, but in other cities, effective mobilization would come much later. External incentives were important. In cities where neither party cared about the black vote or where the political system offered no organized competition, it was hard to make electoral politics matter. Gerrymandering and systems of at-large voting would be a continual menace. The redrawing of wards and other election districts in order to dilute black voting strength typically had the double effect of discouraging electoral participation and marginalizing it when it was tried.

Philadelphia and Detroit showed little of the political potential of Chicago during the 1920s. Philadelphia's black Republican organization dated back to the Civil War and once, at the turn of the century, had played an important role in city politics, earning in return up to three seats for the African Americans on the city council. But as the Republican machine became more powerful and the Democratic opposition shriveled, the black community lost much of its leverage. All through the 1920s, turnouts remained modest as an aging leadership went through the motions of delivering the black vote to the GOP.[15]

Detroit's black community was even more marginalized. The tens of thousands of newcomers who joined what had been a tiny pre–World War I population found themselves in a city with a reformed political structure that discouraged both party voting and ethnic blocs. With nonpartisan races and an at-large system for electing council members, black voters were doomed to irrelevancy in city politics until their numbers changed them from a small minority to a large one and until new issues created the possibilities for an electoral partnership, all of which would start to happen at the end of the 1930s. But even in the period of minimal incentives, Detroit's African American new-comers were starting to vote. Loyalty to the GOP in presidential years, loyalty to Henry Ford when the black community's chief employer sent his minions to guide the vote in important state and local races, and occasional direct appeals by candidates in close races brought African Americans to the polls in numbers sufficient to impress analysts with the possibilities of this community.[16]

These cases point to the equation that would be critical to the development of black electoral influence. It was not the votes themselves that mattered but the context in which they were deployed. African Americans in Chicago and Cleveland were among the first to find themselves in a position of electoral leverage, where the main urban political parties were evenly balanced and one or both realized that they needed black voters in order to win. Balance of power opportunities would emerge at different times in different cities, the product of forces beyond the control of resident African Americans. But it was their good fortune to have moved in force into these cities at a time when competitive politics was generally on the increase. Many of the political machines that had monopolized municipal politics would run into trouble over the course of this half century, some destined to collapse, others rebuilding themselves with new constituents. Cities like Detroit and Cleveland with reformed political systems would experience their own eras of party or coalitional competition that provided openings for African American bloc leverage. And at the state and federal levels, electoral competition brought further opportunities. From the mid-1930s through the mid-1960s, northern black voters would find themselves again and again in privileged electoral positions, where their votes not only counted but were in enough demand to gain important advantages, at some points history-making advantages.[17]

Bloc voting helped in this game of numbers and became one of the keys to African American leverage. As ethnic communities go, blacks were probably no more disciplined than others and in some situations probably less, but it was the perception of whites that African Americans voted not only in bloc but in an easily manipulated bloc. "The Negro vote is notoriously venal," columnist Dorothy Thompson wrote in the thick of the 1936 presidential race. "Ignorant and illiterate, the vast mass of Negroes are like the lower strata of the early industrial immigrants, and like them are 'bossed' and 'delivered' in blocs by venal leaders, white and black." The stereotype of blacks as ignorant voters, easily bossed and bought, had been used to great effect in the turn-of-the-century disfranchisement campaigns that destroyed black political rights in the South, and those stereotypes remained very much in circulation through the middle

Harlem voters waiting in line to cast their ballots in the 1936 election. African American votes had mattered in some cities since World War I. Now they began to matter in presidential politics. (© Corbis)

decades of the century, reinforced by stories concerning the Chicago machine and the Memphis machine of boss Ed Crump. Ironically, it was a stereotype that offered certain compensating advantages. In the game of electoral strategy, a disciplined bloc vote can loom large. It is predictable, accessible, and, for the party that neglects it, can hurt twice, not just in lost votes but in votes that shift to the opponent. The editors of the *Chicago Defender* had all this in mind when they warned Democrats on the eve of the 1944 party convention to pay attention to black voters. The editorial carried the title "Up for Sale: The Negro Vote."[18]

For those who knew politics in Harlem, the notion that African Americans moved in any sort of well-organized bloc must have seemed ludicrous. African Americans in New York contended with political structures and with an internal demography that made political unity difficult. The party system was one factor. A weak Republican Party, a long-dominant Democratic machine headquartered at Tammany Hall, and an electorally important Socialist movement gave African Americans in New York incentives to diversify. As a result, Harlem early on developed multifactional political patterns. A black Republican organization that gained little in the way of patronage or independence from the white organization could count on most of the votes in presidential races and often statewide until the 1930s, but in local politics, many of those same votes went to Democrats.[19]

Tammany had been reaching out for black votes since the turn of the century and had built an organization, United Colored Democracy, that could compete with the Republican Party, making this the first black community in the country to swing in two-party competition. Democratic mayors and governors from 1917 on campaigned in Harlem and learned to respect the black vote, while Tammany dispensed the kind of patronage that outside of Chicago black voters had rarely seen. Ferdinand Q. Morton, the southern-born head of United Colored Democracy, chaired the Municipal Civil Service Commission and used that position to reward other black Democrats with jobs. By 1930, the city's payroll numbered 2,627 African Americans, most of them in janitorial and other low-level positions but also including policemen, teachers, and a small number of high-profile positions such as assistant district attorneys and assistant corporation counsels. There would be no black congressional seat for Harlem until 1944, but the black community did control a pair of seats in the state legislature and two on the board of aldermen. In 1930, two new judgeships were also created for the community.[20]

Harlem was also home to significant numbers of energetic radicals, including a group of black Socialists gathered around the *Messenger* magazine, published by A. Philip Randolph and Chandler Owen, and another led by Cyril Briggs and the Communist-linked African Blood Brotherhood. These leftists, although not large in numbers, added another layer of militancy and criticism to a community already becoming accustomed to sharp political debate. With their journals, their soap-boxing, and their failed efforts to persuade Harlemites to vote for third-party candidates, they raised the noise level in the 1920s while also pioneering one of the critical relationships of the next era. This was the group that would build the first links to organized labor, opening channels that would become extremely important in the 1930s and 1940s. Here too were some of the new leaders that African Americans across the country would look to in the decades to come.[21]

Much larger was the movement that Marcus Garvey built. In its brief florescence (roughly the 1920s), the Universal Negro Improvement Association changed decisively the terms of twentieth-century African American politics, introducing a language of blackness that finished off lingering forms of color pretension among northern black political elites and clearly establishing that masses of African Americans might rally behind bold tactics and forthright expressions of race pride. In New York, where the movement was centered, it had another important effect, adding powerfully to the political fragmentation. Supported most vigorously by West Indians, the association attracted the unrelenting enmity of other Harlem political groups, especially the Socialists and NAACP militants, but including also the two major black newspapers, the *New York Age* and the *Amsterdam News*. Even as the UNIA faded, political factionalism based on the West Indian versus native-born dichotomy continued, helping to sustain the multivocal and often highly charged climate of African American politics in New York.[22]

Electoral politics in the decade and a half after World War I accomplished relatively little. The handful of elected and appointed black officials gained in the exchange of votes with party organizations were not in a position to accomplish much, and some of what they did gain was of questionable value. Some scholars have dismissed interwar black electoral efforts as "clientage politics" and have argued that urban African Americans were shortchanged and misled. It is charged, for example, that the major beneficiaries of Chicago's black machine were the gambling and vice lords who gained protection for their rackets. But in time, strategic voting in the northern cities would yield important benefits, becoming one of the tools that brought African Americans into the New Deal coalition.[23]

Alliances

Another key political instrument was the capacity to build new political relationships with groups outside the black community. The North offered opportunities for alliances that could not be built as long as African Americans lived more or less exclusively in the South. The most productive of these would be the relationships with the northern Democratic Party and organized labor that began to form in the 1930s, but these in turn were based on a complex set of new ties that had emerged in the northern cities, involving Jewish and Protestant liberals, Communists, Socialists, segments of the New York intelligentsia, and segments of the northern philanthropic establishment.

One of the difficulties implicit in the study of black politics is that throughout American history, so much of it is a story of alliances with whites, and often alliances that can be criticized as unequal and potentially unproductive. From the Republican Party alliance of the mid-nineteenth century through the "accommodationist" politics of the Booker T. Washington era and the "integrationist" alignments of the mid-twentieth century, it has not always been easy to sort out where black initiative ends and white patronage or social control picks up. Fierce debates have raged both contemporary to these arrangements and in subsequent scholarship over what is accomplished and who benefits. And many are the voices, again both past and present, yearning for a story of black political development that is more self-sufficient, that has more to do with pride and power and less with "clientage" and complicated alliances. As understandable as that is, the impulse in some ways has shortchanged black political history, leaving Americans insufficiently impressed with the political skills of this singular minority. Alliance-building may seem from one vantage point a strategy based on weakness, but the American political system makes it a necessary route to influence for social minorities in most contexts.[24]

Prior to World War I, the most important set of alliances ran through Booker T. Washington's Tuskegee office. The Washington system had three principal components. First was the national Republican Party, which through spotty patronage appointments maintained a small and largely ineffectual party base in the South consisting of some whites and the small number of blacks who could still exercise the franchise. Second were northern Protestant denominations that had established and maintained schools for African Americans in the South. These religious bodies, especially Congregationalists, Northern Methodists, Northern Presbyterians, and Northern Baptists, played a large and very direct role in the system of African American education, particularly the colleges. Religious philanthropy was supplemented by the third element, moneys from some of the major foundations of the North. Washington was personally responsible for this relationship, winning the support of the Carnegie Endowment, the Rockefeller Foundation, the Phelps-Stokes Fund, and George Peabody (a white expatriate southern businessman), among other major donors.[25]

The Great Migration enabled a new set of alliances that would be based in the northern cities. And some of them would involve a different set of social principles than the heavily paternalistic relationships of the Booker T. Washington era. White philanthropy and whites exercising the impulse to teach and control would play a role in some of the alliances that now emerged, but others were based on mutual need and mutual benefit. Now that African Americans were a growing part of the nation's biggest cities, they were in a position to deal in new ways with new groups of whites.

The NAACP and the National Urban League were concrete expressions of the alliance-building potential of the northern cities. Founded in New York in the decade before World War I, both brought together white Protestant and Jewish liberals with activist elements of the various black communities. Both organizations were heavily dependent upon funds supplied by wealthy whites and, especially in the early years, before the 1930s, responded more to white leadership than black. But if all this seemed at moments to be reminiscent of the subservience and supplication that the Washingtonians endured, it was really not at all the same. These northern-based biracial organizations secured much more than money and condescension from their white members and benefactors.

The Urban League's purpose was to provide and coordinate welfare services in the city neighborhoods where blacks were settling. It was dominated in its early years by social workers, academics, religious groups, and some key philanthropists, most importantly Julius Rosenwald, the Jewish benefactor and Sears Roebuck millionaire who also bankrolled Colored YMCAs, gave money to the NAACP, and played a directing role in all of these organizations. The Urban League's role in black communities has been much debated. In the first-phase years, branches in the big cities provided information services to newcomers and acted as an employment service funneling migrants into jobs with cooperating employers. Since many of those firms were hiring African Americans to undercut white unions and since many of the League's benefactors, like Henry Ford, were notoriously anti-union, the organization later endured much criticism. But looked at another way, the Urban League was building up relationships that would over time prove very valuable for African Americans. During the New Deal era, branches helped negotiate jobs and relief payments with the new federal agencies, trading on social work connections that now became essential to the urban black economy. The organization's expertise was also important as black communities negotiated the new framework of understanding with organized labor, and finally, at the level of national politics, National Urban League contacts played an important role in building a base for black issues within the Roosevelt administration.[26]

The NAACP was a still more important example of the politically productive relationships that could be built in the northern cities. Founded in 1909 by a group of white Socialists and progressives who joined with the black remnants of the Niagara movement started a few years earlier by W. E. B. Du Bois and William Monroe Trotter, the organization undertook to fight for civil rights and against segregation using pressure group tactics that depended largely on lawyers and high-level political connections ("litigation, legislation and education"). Supported largely by wealthy white New Yorkers and New York institutions, including the left-wing Garland Fund for Public Service, it depended upon and helped to elaborate a network of liberal whites, many of them Jewish, with skills, money, and connections and a willingness to use them in the cause of civil rights for African Americans.[27]

At the national level, the NAACP was a biracial organization; at the local level, mostly African Americans were involved. In both guises, the NAACP proved critical to the apparatus of racial liberalism that was taking shape in the North. Its black members, by far the majority, maintained the chapters and used them

Some of the delegates to the 1919 convention of the NAACP held in Cleveland. The biracial organization was an example of the new political alliances that became possible in the Black Metropolises of the North. (Emma and Lloyd Lewis Family Papers [LLF neg. 14B], Special Collections, The University Library, University of Illinois at Chicago)

for a variety of purposes within the black communities, the most important being ongoing political education, surveillance of local injustice, and mobilizing responses, usually in the form of publicity and lobbying, sometimes through lawsuits. The local battles of NAACP chapters have often been overlooked because their accomplishments prior to World War II are not easily summarized. Activist chapters in the 1920s, like those in Cleveland, Pittsburgh, and Detroit, kept up a steady resistance to the forces of segregation in those communities, pressing for open access to major stores and public facilities and contesting discrimination in the schools and police misconduct. Some of the protests and lawsuits succeeded, but the victories usually were small.[28]

But the importance of the NAACP local chapters went way beyond these outcomes. This organization guided the political development of many northern and western black communities in the second and third decades of the twentieth century, linking up churches and newspapers and establishing or continuing a tradition of civil rights activism in each of the communities where chapters met. Emerging at an early moment in the development of the Black Metropolises, the NAACP chapters both reflected and shaped the distinctive civic culture of those communities. The habit of protest should not be taken for granted; the NAACP nurtured it all the way through the early diaspora decades. Also important were the fluid class lines of the local organizations, in particular their ability to draw a significant portion of the black middle class into civil rights activity. The NAACP chapters were contributing powerfully to the political education of urban northern African Americans.

The role of whites in the organization was complicated. The smaller branches were lucky to have a handful of prominent whites to list on a letterhead and to call upon for financial support and legal assistance. The bigger chapters were sometimes saddled with a largely white leadership, which, as historian Christopher Reed shows in the case of Chicago, could lead to chapter inactivity, since in most cases the whites saw themselves as allies more than participants. When Harold Ickes, a prominent Chicago attorney, agreed to serve as chapter president in 1922, he made it clear that he had no time for day-to-day affairs. For the next three years, he treated the job as largely honorific, in theory leaving things in the hands of the paid branch secretaries, both African American, in practice stifling chapter activism through a combination of inattention and ill-timed intervention.[29]

Things were no less awkward in the New York national office, where whites dominated the executive board and where big donors like Julius Rosenwald sometimes exercised great influence. Initially, W. E. B. Du Bois was the only African American on the board. As editor of the *Crisis*, he operated largely independently of the rest of the organization. The balance of blacks and whites in the national organization began to shift after 1920, when Florida-born James Weldon Johnson became general secretary, and still more under his successor, the very light-skinned former Georgian Walter White, who served from 1931 to 1954. Still, the NAACP's biracialism was always a challenge, and some have argued that it impeded the development of race-conscious mass political mobilization.[30]

But there was an upside to these complicated biracial relationships. The whites were doing work in arenas that were not always visible. Doors were opening and contacts were being made that would pay off in expanding patterns of access and assistance in the years to come. The whites, like Ickes, who were drawn into the NAACP (and Urban League) in the teens and twenties brought the cause of racial justice to the attention of wider communities of whites within the complex that we call urban liberalism. The channels led in a variety of directions: into the Jewish community, where the NAACP found money, some of its lawyers, access to certain media, and intellectual and political support for the fight against racism; into the networks of liberal Protestantism, where institutions like the Federal Council of Churches, the Fellowship of Reconciliation, the magazine *Christian Century*, and Union Theological Seminary would contribute instrumentally to the long cause of civil rights; into the philanthropic system, where new sources like the Garland Fund would be tapped; into the academic and literary world, where support for the idea of racial equality and opposition to bigotry would become evolving truths; and eventually into the urban Democratic Party, where white liberals like Harold Ickes, Robert F. Wagner, and Al Smith were building a coalition that would in time reach out to black voters.[31]

The geography of all of these new relationships is important. They were based in the North, although often the political focus was the South. That was very much true of the NAACP, which did not succeed in establishing many active southern chapters until the late 1930s. Essentially a northern-based organization, it nevertheless focused most of its national campaigns on the southern systems of racism, notably lynching, southern voting rights, and school segregation. This equation—a northern base with a southern focus—would become typical too for some of the important alliances that emerged in the Depression decade, including those involving the Democratic Party and, to some extent, organized labor.

The changed relationship with organized labor had its own genesis that traces in part to black and white radicals operating in three initial geographies: in the coal fields, where biracial unionism had proved a successful formula for the United Mine Workers; in Chicago, where the failure to build an effective biracial union had led to disaster in the 1919 stockyards strike; and in New York, where A. Philip Randolph was determined to build a showcase all-black union among the nation's sleeping car porters and where the Communist Party had its strongest base.[32]

The role of the Communists deserves special attention, not only because it was critical to the process that moved organized labor away from white supremacy but also because the Communist Party approached African Americans in a manner that was unprecedented for a white-dominated organization: not as reluctant ally but as suitor. The courtship began in the 1920s when the new party, guided by Soviet revolutionary theory, concluded that black nationalism (à la Garvey) should be nurtured into revolutionary fervor. The relationship deepened in 1931, the year that the party turned the trial of the "Scottsboro Boys" into an international scandal and nominated James R. Ford for vice president of the United States. The arrest of nine young African Americans on dubious rape charges in Scottsboro, Alabama, their quick trial before an all-white jury, their death sentences, and then the years of appeals handled by party lawyers brought Jim Crow justice into the light of public attention in a way that the NAACP with its anti-lynching campaigns had never managed. The Communist Party's publicity apparatus made Scottsboro into the black equivalent of the 1926 Scopes trial, with sustained media coverage that served to inform and mobilize northern and liberal public opinion. It was a breakthrough. Jim Crow justice was at last on trial. It was one of the steps that cleared the way for the northern Democratic Party to begin its racial realignment.[33]

When the Communist Party announced that James R. Ford, an African American, would be the party's vice presidential candidate in the 1932 elections, that too was a breakthrough, a pioneering gesture of respect that blacks of many political persuasions acknowledged as a milestone. But the significance lay in the follow-up. The party now embarked on a campaign to publicize and extend its commitment to racial equality. Insisting on full social integration inside the party, the Communists promoted inclusion and respect in other contexts as well. Of critical importance was the Communist Party's role in the new unions that took shape in the mid-1930s under the umbrella of the CIO. Wherever the Communists were strong, the principle of racial inclusion was emphasized, and efforts were made to overcome the old image of unions as anti-black.[34]

The Communists contributed in other ways to the changing political chemistry of the Black Metropolis. In significant numbers, the black intelligentsia drew close to the Communist Party in the 1930s. Reworking Marxist ideas about class, revolution, nationalism, and internationalism, African American leftist intellectuals engineered critical shifts in cultural production. From Richard Wright, Ralph Ellison, Langston Hughes, and others would come ghetto-centered, black-worker-centered, and black-rage narratives that added to the evolving culture of black protest. From W. E. B. Du Bois and C. L. R. James (a Trotskyite) would come explorations of nationalism/internationalism that would help shift the discourse of black identity.[35]

Black party members contributed to important changes in political practice as well as in political ideas, promoting street tactics and a total-commitment model of political activism that helped raise the temperature in the Black Metropolises and forced other organizations to emulate and compete. NAACP chapters, Urban League branches, Socialist cadres, newspaper publishers, even churches and social organizations had to respond in some manner to the energy level and ideas of the African American Communists. Many of these groups swung to the left, embracing militant tactics, mass-based organization, and the idea of a labor alliance as the 1930s progressed.

Street tactics also gave the Black Metropolises a new and threatening aspect that would affect negotiations with white elites. Street militancy showed up first in the "Don't Spend Your Money Where You Can't Work" boycotts that began in Chicago in the late 1920s and soon spread to other cities. Led in some cities by Socialists, in others by Communists and NAACP chapters, and in Cleveland by a group calling itself the Future Outlook League, the demonstrations yielded some jobs and a lot of political experience as the activists who led them moved on to organize other protests under the Worker Alliance (fighting for WPA jobs) and the National Negro Congress (launched in 1936 to compete with the NAACP). The proving moment for the new politics of the street came in the summer of 1935 when rioting erupted in Harlem after rumors spread that a black resident had been shot by a white policeman. For the first time in modern history, African Americans were using mass violence proactively instead of defensively, in the face of grievances rather than guns, targeting the property of white-owned businesses perceived to be exploiting the community. And the tactic clearly worked, as had to some extent the earlier eviction demonstrations and Don't Shop boycotts. As the La Guardia administration began to pump jobs and WPA projects into Harlem, it was not just the Communists who realized that a new age was dawning and that force and militancy would now have their place in black political practice.[36]

The changed relationship with organized labor would be one of the key building blocks in the Archimedean system that was being assembled in the Black Metropolises. It evolved during the 1930s, partly because of the efforts of black and white radicals, but in a more basic sense it was dictated by the demographic logic of the Great Migration. Organized labor was forced to change more or less in the same way that some of the big city political bosses were forced to change. Migration, and what Joe Trotter calls "proletarianization," had placed African Americans in a position of critical leverage in the politics of labor relations, particularly for the mass production industries that had become the core of the American economy. Clustered in or near the big cities of the North, some employing African Americans, others with the potential to do so, the electrical, steel, auto, rubber, chemical, and meatpacking companies had all in one way or another turned labor's commitment to white supremacy into a key anti-union advantage. Labor strategists knew that the color line had to go. Most of the union leaders who set out to organize the basic industries in the 1930s understood that if the CIO was to have a chance, African Americans had to be part of the campaign. Realism spoke louder than the idealism of the Left.[37]

Still, the relationship did not come together smoothly or easily. In 1935, with the backing of the United Mine Workers and the two garment workers unions, all of which had experience with interracial unionism, the Committee on Industrial Organizing (later the Congress of Industrial Organizations) began to fund organizing drives in the major industries. The newly formed CIO unions adopted constitutions that eliminated the infamous whites-only clauses that were typical of the older AFL unions. At the 1937 convention that proclaimed CIO independence from the parent body, delegates voted additional constitutional language establishing that the unions would be open to all. They also passed resolutions designed to signal that this body supported the NAACP's call for federal laws against lynching and for abolishing the poll tax. These pronouncements and some high-level consultation were enough to win endorsements from the national-level NAACP and Urban League officials, but at the local level, things took more time.[38]

The new relationship first solidified in Pittsburgh and Chicago, where the new Steel Workers Organizing Committee adopted the biracial tactics of its parent union, the United Mine Workers, and aggressively recruited black workers, long a significant presence in the mills. With a still higher percentage of black workers in the Chicago meatpacking industry, the Packinghouse Workers Organizing Committee followed a similar strategy. Black leadership groups in the two cities responded, and both the *Pittsburgh Courier* and *Chicago Defender* heralded the new unions and urged black workers to join. There was early cooperation as well in New York, where Socialist-dominated garment workers unions and the Communist-dominated Transport Workers Union took steps to reach out to blacks and where Harlem leftists had long worked to educate the community on the value of the labor alliance.[39]

But in Philadelphia, Cleveland, Detroit, and elsewhere, alliances took longer to build. African Americans in Detroit needed more than platitudes from the United Auto Workers union that was trying to organize the auto industry. For twenty-five years, Henry Ford had been a source of jobs and a community benefactor when other employers and white workers had said no to African American workers. When the UAW moved to organize Ford plants in 1937, the black community helped defeat the effort. The UAW leadership then got serious and used its influence to remove (slowly) the hiring barriers that kept African Americans out of most plants and in the least desirable units of those which did hire them. The union also hired black organizers in significant numbers and began to support the Detroit black community in some of its political initiatives, signaling the start of an alliance in local politics that would continue for decades. And in 1941, when the union next tested Ford, black workers and much of the community responded, helping the UAW bring the Lord of Dearborn to heel.[40]

New Deal Realignments

A new relationship with the two major political parties was the critical piece of the puzzle. Midway through the 1930s, the northern Democratic Party, both at state and local levels—and, most important, within the Roosevelt administration—began to pay attention to black communities and black voters. Over the next several decades, that relationship would mature, helped along by continued Republican Party competition for black votes. And out of those delicately evolving political alignments would come access to the kinds of power that could change the dimensions of America's racial order, not just for African Americans in the North but also in the South. In some ways it is more accurate to describe all this as a new relationship to the American state. Governmental systems changed radically in the 1930s as the federal government took on broad new functions and, in doing so, altered the way that other governmental systems, especially cities, operated. Changed too were the operating rules of politics, affecting not just parties but also interest groups and individuals. The new state encouraged different forms of political behavior. In this context, the political importance of the Great Migration became especially clear.[41]

The Black Metropolises of the North now began to show their political potential. The key was gaining access to the Roosevelt administration and the new forms of power emanating from Washington, D.C., power that included vastly augmented programs of social provisioning (jobs, welfare and subsidy payments, housing and infrastructure projects) and equally vast new possibilities for the redesign and regulation of economic and social opportunity. African Americans in the South played a distinctly secondary role in the search for access, hindered not just by the inability to vote but also by breaks in the Republican chain of patronage. The southern African American leadership had historically enjoyed a certain level of access to Republican presidents. Booker T. Washington's Tuskegee machine was founded upon that leverage, and his successor, Robert Moton, had also been able to depend upon modest patronage of various kinds during the 1920s. With the election of a Democratic president in 1932, Moton's political operation essentially shut down. Neither he nor the other customary leaders of the black South, mostly educators and ministers backed by important congregations, had the right kind of contacts in Washington. Nor were they very adept at dealing with the local agents of the new state as the first New Deal programs of relief assistance, public works projects, Agricultural Adjustment, and National Recovery Act Blue-Eagle price and wage programs reached the South after the spring of 1933. White elites took charge of virtually all of these programs, typically using them in ways that aggravated black unemployment and economic distress, especially in the cotton belt where crop reduction subsidies pushed many sharecroppers off the land. In time, southern black communities would become more adept at pulling resources from the New Deal, especially after 1935 when the WPA and the National Youth Administration reached the region. But it would take some adjustments in leadership in those communities and some higher level adjustments in Washington, D.C., to make that happen, and both of those had a lot to do with the urban North.[42]

As Robert Moton retreated into his office, Walter White, Ben Davis, Robert Weaver, Ralph Bunche, and others were finding ways to get inside the New Deal. Their tools were the alliances and the techniques of lobbying that had been acquired in the North, especially in New York where the NAACP and its new leader, Walter White, had developed a healthy set of connections with leading Democrats. It has been said that the New Deal was invented in New York, tried out first in the gubernatorial regimes of Al Smith and Franklin Roosevelt. We might add that the African American relationship with the New Deal began in the same setting. There, African Americans first began giving their votes to Democrats, and there, Democratic politicians first began opening their doors to black leaders. When New Yorkers flooded into Washington in 1933 to make a new federal government, some of those open-door habits went with them.

Walter White's most famous open-door claim concerned Eleanor Roosevelt, who after 1934 began corresponding with the NAACP chief and evidently conveyed some of his concerns to the president. Another was Robert Wagner, the senior senator from the Empire State and right from the start of the New Deal one of the most influential men in Washington. Not only would he carry bills like the ill-fated Wagner-Costigan anti-lynching law and fight in Congress for beneficial legislation, but his influence within the cabinet and even within the judiciary could be profound. The former judge had protégés everywhere. So did the former congressman-turned-mayor of New York, Fiorello La Guardia, a Republican. La Guardia remained a huge force in Washington all through the Roosevelt years. Despite his New York duties, he seemed to be constantly in the nation's capital, advising the president and cabinet, cajoling Congress, leading the U.S. Conference of Mayors, his hand in everything having to do with policy toward cities and much of what concerned black Americans.[43]

A Chicago connection was equally important. Harold Ickes was Roosevelt's secretary of the interior and in charge of the big public works projects of the early New Deal. The Chicagoan may not have done much as head of an NAACP branch in the 1920s, but in his new post he was invaluable, helping to funnel civil rights supporters into positions of midlevel influence throughout the administration. The so-called Black Cabinet of race advisers that was in place by 1935 owed much to his sponsorship as well as to the lobbying efforts of other allies that had been acquired in the formative period of northern political development.[44]

It is not clear at what point the counting of black votes began to influence the New Dealers. Du Bois and White had tried to get some mileage out of the

1932 election, pointing to the fact that in New York and Pittsburgh, African Americans had given the majority of their votes to FDR; the two called it a historic shift. Two years later, after the bi-year congressional elections, administration analysts may have had more reason to take notice. Democrats won a sweeping victory that year, defying the normal cyclical patterns that usually deliver setbacks to the presidential party and gaining the most liberal and activist Congress of the entire New Deal era. African Americans helped, responding in key cities to the campaign pledges of white Democrats. Equally noteworthy was the fact that the Democrats had in a few cases slated African American candidates in local and state legislative contests, and they were beginning to win. In Los Angeles, a young Alabama-born lawyer named Augustus Hawkins had taken the black community's State Assembly seat away from the incumbent Republican. In Philadelphia, Rev. Marshall Shephard had pulled another legislative seat into the Democratic column. But the race that attracted real attention was in Chicago, where the Democrats had gone after the only African American in Congress, the very popular Oscar DePriest. The Thompson machine had been driven from city hall three years before, replaced by a Democratic apparatus that quickly shored up its support with the help of relief funds and public works projects supplied by the federal government. Arthur Mitchell, a Mississippi-born lawyer who had tried to climb the ranks of the black Republican machine, now switched parties and upset the popular congressman, becoming the first African American Democrat ever seated in the House of Representatives.[45]

Two years later, in 1936, with the presidential election and congressional races at stake, the national Democratic Party made its first significant public overtures to black voters, organizing black campaign committees, spending money on the black press, and acknowledging African Americans for the first time at a national convention when both Congressman Mitchell and Reverend Shephard addressed the assembly. These tiny gestures became more meaningful when some of the southern white delegates protested. When South Carolina's notorious segregationist Senator "Cotton" Ed Smith stomped out of the convention claiming that the South had been humiliated, the press took note. Black newspapers applauded. Southern conservatives worried. *Time* magazine wrote with some cynicism about Democrats playing "The Black Game" while *Newsweek* caught the historic turn, noting "the new spectacle of national campaigners vying for Negro voters."[46]

African Americans in the northern cities surged behind Roosevelt and other Democrats that year, completing the urban working-class bloc that had first started to form behind Al Smith in 1928. With the number of black registered voters more than doubled in some cities, Roosevelt won majorities in the black belts, ranging from 60 percent in Cleveland to 81 percent in Harlem. Only Chicago held back, giving just 49 percent to the Democrats. Hope on the part of the black press that these votes would be critical to the election process proved otherwise as FDR won a huge plurality in each of the states with significant black populations. Hope that the federal government would respond to African American policy concerns was also frustrated. In 1938, the congressional machinery of the Democratic Party came apart. While urban liberals in Congress paid some attention to black organizations, supporting, even though the president would not, a new effort by the NAACP to pass an anti-lynching law, southern congressional Democrats broke openly with the New Deal. Allying with Republicans to defeat most of what Roosevelt proposed over the next four years, the southern congressmen were reacting to a complex of concerns, but the president's new posture toward African Americans was among the most serious. In the 1938 elections, complaints about the "nigger-loving New Deal" had echoed widely through the South.[47]

In reality, Roosevelt had made only the beginnings of a turn toward African Americans. Historians have traced the evolving relationship with the New Deal administration and are clear on several points. First, African Americans had to do most of the courting, receiving little obvious encouragement from a president who worried about alienating the southern Democratic congressional delegation that had the power to block any of his legislative projects. Second, New Deal programs had contradictory economic effects for African Americans. On the one hand, blacks were able to secure vital economic assistance under programs like the WPA and NYA, which provided not only a job safety net but also new infrastructure development in the form of schools and public housing. On the other hand, programs like the Agricultural Adjustment Act exacerbated near-term poverty, while the Federal Housing Act set the stage for long-term urban segregation. Third, this was the start of a relationship that would bring more measurable policy developments in the 1940s, beginning with Roosevelt's Fair Employment Practices Commission and continuing with Truman's package of civil rights initiatives of the late 1940s. The federal government under Democratic presidents was starting its historic pivot toward racial justice. It would be a long while before the direction was clear, but it was starting.[48]

These moves, subtle as they were in the late 1930s when Roosevelt still refused to endorse any legislation that might anger the segregationists, set up the geometry of party politics that would govern the next thirty years. African Americans, because of their northern votes and because of their northern ties to labor and urban machines, had fought their way into the triangulations of national politics. The Democratic Party faced a conundrum that presidents and presidential candidates would deal with for the next three decades: how to finesse the contradictory relationships involving its oldest and newest constituencies, how to respond to the black voters and civil rights coalitions that were gaining influence in the northern wing, and how to deal with the related risk of losing the white south. From Franklin Roosevelt to Lyndon Johnson, the question would remain constant while the weightings slowly shifted to favor bolder and bolder action.[49]

The Republican Party played a cagey role in this equation, at critical points enticing the Democrats into further commitments to civil rights. As Samuel Lubell puts it in relation to the Eisenhower years, "The unannounced racial strategy of the Republicans was to keep the heat on the Democrats." It was a low-risk game. All through the Roosevelt and Truman years, the GOP competed for black votes, typically offering national party platforms that were more attractive than that of the Democrats and, with the exception of Alf Landon in 1936, offering presidential candidates whose credentials and speeches were potentially attractive to black voters. The campaigns of Wendell Willkie, a New York businessman, in 1940 and Thomas Dewey, New York's governor in 1944 and again in 1948, forced Roosevelt and Truman to pay attention to African American issues and voters. Both Republicans spoke forcefully about their party's historical commitment to civil rights and urged northern black voters to return to their political home.[50]

At other electoral levels, the Republicans also continued the competition. Big city congressional candidates and many Republican senators from the key urban states could be counted on from the mid-1930s onward to take pro–civil rights positions and to campaign in black neighborhoods. Some Republican candidates for governorships and mayoral position were friendly as well, although at the state and local level, the politics of race became much more complicated. But the point is that overall, up until 1964, the Republicans kept the competition for black votes alive. Lubell emphasizes that it was for the GOP largely a win-win strategy: they could win by denying the Democrats black votes in the North, or they could win by forcing the Democrats to alienate their white southern wing.

Northern Civil Rights Movement

It was once well understood that the modern civil rights movement began in the 1940s and that it took shape in the cities of the North. "When, in 1990 perhaps or the year 2000, men come to search for the truly decisive epoch in American race relations," Lerone Bennett Jr. wrote in his 1965 book, *Confrontation: Black and White*, "it seems likely that they will seize on the decade of the forties." The Mississippi-born, Chicago-based contributing editor of *Ebony* magazine understood that the great events that had unfolded after 1954—the federal court decisions that had opened up the battle for school desegregation, the electrifying confrontations in the South and the mediagenic movement that Martin Luther King Jr. had led, the congressional alliance that had, months before his book appeared, passed the historic 1964 Civil Rights Act—all rested upon a foundation that had been built in the Black Metropolises in the 1940s.[51]

Bennett, however, was wrong about the historiography of 1990. By that year, the story of the 1940s civil rights movement had almost been lost as historians focused on the South and ignored what preceded it. But in the last few years, his prediction has started to be realized. No one has yet put it all together, but the story is starting to become clear in the separate city studies that have been published recently by a number of historians. The movement they have excavated was more complicated than what followed in the South. Its methods were less dramatic, its leadership less consistent and charismatic. Indeed, it was a movement with a thousand leaders, many of them known best to their churches, unions, or NAACP chapters. It was a movement that used the picket line and demonstration but also managed to accomplish much with the petition, the conference, and the delegation. It was a movement a later generation criticized as middle-class, although its stalwart institutions were the union, the church, and sometimes the blues club. It was certainly a movement that worked readily with whites, eagerly seeking alliances with Jewish organizations, CIO unions, liberal Catholic and Protestant organizations, and other civic groups, and worked eagerly with the political establishment, maneuvering often behind the scenes for benefits that sometimes would later seem empty or fraudulent. And most confusing, it was a movement that later failed to defend its own reputation against the critics who followed in the Black Power Era. By the late 1960s, the initiatives of the 1940s were being misremembered as timid gestures ascribed to a generation that was more interested in accommodation than conflict, more interested in working with whites than developing resources for black power.[52]

In fact, the critics had it almost backwards. The movement of the 1940s built itself through acts of daring and defiance and depended upon all-black institutions that Robert Self calls "mid-century America's black power institutions." The black press, the Brotherhood of Sleeping Car Porters and some other black-dominated labor organizations, huge NAACP chapters that now involved few if any whites, black churches, ward organizations and political clubs that were exclusively for black voters—these were the key institutions underlying the mobilizations. That the movement depended upon strategic alliances with whites and pursued the goal of integration made the legacy confusing to a later generation that was locked into what Self calls the "integration/separation model for understanding black politics." The 1940s movement was characterized by the "fusion of integration, strategic alliances with whites, and the nurturing of all-black institutions and economic networks." And in that productive fusion lay its ability to move America decisively toward a reconsideration of racial inequality.[53]

The context has also been misunderstood, or perhaps just overemphasized. World War II and the Cold War crisis that followed created new kinds of opportunities for the advocates of civil rights, rearranging governmental priorities and governmental institutions in ways that proved favorable to the cause. The urgent need to keep the peace at home and the international embarrassment of fighting wars in the name of freedom while denying basic rights to millions of American citizens created openings that the civil rights movement effectively exploited. But context is one thing, politics is another. Nothing was going to change without a determined and resourceful political movement. And that is precisely what took shape in the Black Metropolises. Lerone Bennett understood it as the turning point, when America, "as a result of the unrelenting pressure of Negroes of every creed and class . . . began a slow retreat from the bastion of white supremacy."[54]

It began with what historian Thomas Brooks called the "Magnificent Bluff," unfolding in the months just before the United States entered World War II. In September 1940, President Roosevelt signed the Selective Service Act, establishing compulsory military service and setting the nation on a war footing. The law contained vague language about nondiscrimination but was essentially silent about what role African Americans might play in the military or the coming conflict. Meeting soon after with a delegation of three New York–based black leaders—Walter White of the NAACP, T. Arnold Hill of the Urban League, and A. Philip Randolph of the Brotherhood of Sleeping Car Porters—Roosevelt refused demands that he move toward desegregating the military. Moreover, his press secretary released a statement implying that the black leaders concurred with the decision. "The statement fell like a bomb," Walter White later recalled. The NAACP's *Crisis* was appalled "that a President of the United States at a time of National peril should surrender so completely to enemies of democracy."[55]

The shock galvanized something new in the black communities. In the months that followed, key leaders, organizations, and newspapers would put together a campaign of public pressure of a sort that African Americans had never before mounted, that had never before been possible. It daringly flaunted not only public opinion but also some important allies, taking aim straight at the White House and its Democratic resident. It involved threats instead of pleas, indeed the very serious threat of civil disruption in a time of national emergency. It relied on the now-massive publicity apparatus of the black press. And when it worked, it established many of the key instruments for the next generation of civil rights activism.[56]

In January 1941, with the backing of White and Hill and several others, Randolph issued a public call for a "Negro March on Washington." There were very few precedents for massive public demonstrations by African Americans, and the idea of a march in the nation's capital was especially daring, evoking fears of both Bonus Army–style confrontations and massive race riots in that Jim Crow city. Randolph explained the concept to Roi Ottley: "The administration leaders in Washington will never give the Negro justice until they see masses —ten, twenty, fifty thousand Negroes on the White House lawn!" The call had an electrifying effect, winning the support of much of the northern black political apparatus. Key political organizations, both the NAACP and the left-wing National Negro Congress, signed on, as did the unions that were closely tied to the black community.[57]

Equally important, said Ottley, "Press and pulpit played decisive roles in whipping up sentiment." The major newspapers took up the call, making the impending march big news throughout the spring of 1941. The *Chicago Defender* first wondered whether black people would have the courage and commitment to march in significant numbers, declaring that "to get 10,000 Negroes assembled in one spot, under one banner with justice, democracy and work as their slogan would be the miracle of the century." A few months later, the *Defender* was sure that the miracle was happening, claiming that 50,000 were prepared to march. The *Pittsburgh Courier* and *Baltimore Afro-American* were no less enthusiastic, while the *Amsterdam News* produced bold headlines claiming "100,000 in March to Capital."[58]

Whether 100,000 or 50,000 or even 10,000 would have indeed boarded the buses and trains that the March on Washington Movement was supposedly assembling in New York, Philadelphia, Cleveland, Baltimore, Chicago, and other cities is not clear. What is clear is that the black press had made the threat seem to be real enough that Roosevelt and his advisers felt they had to take it seriously. Had the Roosevelt administration not been so closely attuned to New York City, they might not have been so alarmed. New York was headquarters for the March on Washington Movement, and if one assumed that the rest of black America was as fired up as Harlem, then there was reason indeed to pay attention. New York mayor Fiorello La Guardia helped convey the news to Washington and was intimately involved in the subsequent negotiations, first setting up a New York gathering at which Randolph and White met with

Eleanor Roosevelt and then a follow-up meeting with the president himself at the White House. In his autobiography, Walter White recalled that the president turned to him at a key point and asked: "'Walter, how many people will *really* march?' I told him no less than one hundred thousand. The President looked me full in the eye for a long time in an obvious effort to find out if I were bluffing or exaggerating. Eventually, he appeared to believe that I meant what I said. 'What do you want me to do?' he asked." One week later, after more negotiations brokered by La Guardia, the president signed Executive Order 8802, and Randolph and White issued a statement saying that the March on Washington had been postponed.[59]

Executive Order 8802 was an enormous victory and a pivotal development in the struggle for equal rights. Banning employment discrimination in the defense industries and in government offices, the order was not everything that the March on Washington Movement had sought. It did nothing about military segregation. Its enforcement arm, the FEPC, was weak. And most important, it was a temporary measure that would barely outlast the war. But it was momentous in ways that contemporaries could not guess. It set up a key agenda and fired up the morale and energy levels that would drive the civil rights crusades of the next quarter century. Before 1941, African Americans engaged in a variety of important struggles and movements for justice. After 1941, struggles and organizations began to cohere into a momentum-gathering crusade.

The NAACP emerged as one of the key agents of the post-1941 crusade. The organization had struggled through the 1930s, finding it hard to compete with the militancy of the Communists and beset by internal difficulties, some of them relating to the need to forge alliances with organized labor. In the 1940s, the NAACP would come into its own, becoming for the first time a "mass organization." Membership surged upward, from 50,000 at the start of the decade to 400,000 at the end of 1944 and almost half a million the following year. Active chapters now appeared in the South, thanks in part to the amazing abilities of field secretary Ella Baker, who, after thirteen years in New York, was now on the road for the NAACP and finding that organizing was becoming a bit safer in her native South. But the strength of the organization remained in the big cities of the North, where the organization campaigned relentlessly for jobs and justice and where many churches and unions now taught that NAACP membership was second only to voting as a civic responsibility. The Chicago NAACP chapter had had no more than 1,000 members during most of the 1930s. That number rose to 5,000 in 1941 in the wake of the March on Washington victory. By 1945, as Christopher Reed has shown, the organization had changed its tactics, its tone, and its demography. Now led by Oscar Brown, a "live-wire" Mississippi-born lawyer who had once been active in black nationalist movements, the branch had added street protests and picketing to its list of tactics and now drew much of its membership from the black working class, becoming, said Brown, a "people's organization." In 1945, 18,500 black Chicagoans were NAACP members. Chicago, however, was not the organization's largest chapter. That honor went to Detroit, where similar transformations and even tighter ties to key churches and UAW locals had turned the NAACP branch into a massive engine of political activism with 33,000 members.[60]

The black press gave the 1940s civil rights movement its second set of engines. That decade and the one that followed were the golden years for African American publishing, a time of growing circulations and growing influence both inside and outside the black community. Newly equipped with an activist trade organization, the Negro Newspaper Publishers Association, the black press made itself heard in those decades as never before nor since. Black editors had provided key support for the March on Washington threat in 1941, but that had been just the beginning. Defying the censors, the *Courier*, the *Defender*, and a dozen other major newspapers moved the campaign for equal rights to a higher pitch despite massive pressure to get onboard the war effort. The "Double V" campaign that the *Courier*, now the largest black-owned newspaper with a nationwide circulation of 200,000, announced two months after Pearl Harbor energized black communities and brought the newspapers huge increases in circulation and influence. Behind the slogan "Victory at home, victory abroad," the newspapers called for continued protests against job and housing discrimination and loudly denounced the treatment of black soldiers and sailors. Risky, the Double V campaign triggered an angry response from the Roosevelt administration and fierce condemnation from much of the mainstream press. Powerful congressmen and influential newspaper columnists demanded that the African American newspapers be silenced or suppressed. The Justice Department initiated an investigation that nearly resulted in indictments for sedition.[61]

But the gamble paid off. The militancy forced government officials and white media outlets to pay attention. It had an even more singular effect within black communities, creating a climate of expectation and activism. Prior to World War II, the major urban newspapers in the North had styled themselves as champions of the struggle for rights, but as St. Clair Drake and Horace Cayton's survey of the *Chicago Defender* from 1926 to 1937 shows, the newspaper was actually dominated by community news—crime, politics, community activities, and personality profiles. Now racial justice and the call to protest became the central story. Gunnar Myrdal noted the activist role of the press in his 1944 study, saying that the press acted "like a huge sounding board" of black protest. "By expressing the protest, the press also magnifies it."[62]

The power of this sounding board is quickly evident to the reader who compares 1940s editions with those of the previous decade. The wartime *Defender* crackles with excitement, purpose, and a sense of accomplishment. Some of this is focused on the military. Photos of black soldiers and sailors and stories of heroism and combat create a powerful impression that things are changing, while other articles report on the continuing struggle against military Jim Crow. Home-front news moves with the same tension: articles and photos depicting recognition for black leaders, businessmen, and entertainers and others detailing job breakthroughs or new relationships with unions or federal agencies are interwoven with stories of discrimination and protest campaigns. The FEPC, like the military, looms large in this news crusade. Defending it against congressional critics, criticizing its slow progress on key cases, the newspapers monitored the FEPC as closely as a hometown baseball team.[63]

In the FEPC, the 1940s movement found the most critical part of its agenda. Once Executive Order 8802 had been issued and the FEPC had been established, the law and the agency became the focus of intense political activity as black politicians, newspapers, existing organizations like the NAACP, and newer ad hoc organizations campaigned to enforce the new promise of jobs and nondiscrimination. That fight made the difference between a measure that in many places — especially the South — was a symbol but of little consequence for job seekers and one that actually changed labor market conditions. As historian Andrew Kersten has recently shown, by itself the FEPC did little. But in cities where there was an active civil rights movement and cooperative labor leaders and public officials, the FEPC helped open industries and overcome hate strikes. But the relationship should actually be seen as reciprocal. Policy is not only the child of politics but also its parent. The new agency, with its promised powers, invited activism and new forms of organization.[64]

The fact that the FEPC existed only through executive order and lacked the permanence of law contributed to its movement-building potential. Advocates knew that they needed to get a real law through Congress. Indeed, they also needed to defend the existing agency that quickly became the target of congressional conservatives, especially southerners, who managed to tamper with agency funding during the war and kill it altogether in 1946. The campaign to protect the FEPC while it existed and re-establish it once it had been abolished was central to the emerging civil rights movement. That fight dictated the strategy of alliance that bothered and confused later critics. It pushed African

Americans to develop lobbying and brokering capacities, especially in the legislative arenas of state and federal governments.[65]

Prior to 1941, the NAACP and other black organizations had cared more about the courts than Congress, more about working with mayors than legislatures, because apart from a federal law against lynching, it was not clear that legislation was the most efficacious route to social justice. The FEPC convinced activists that laws banning discrimination should be pursued vigorously. The push moved on two fronts. Starting in 1944, FEPC legislation was introduced in every session of Congress, and for a time it seemed that passage would be possible. Led by the National Council for a Permanent FEPC, which had grown out of Randolph's March on Washington organization, the congressional lobbying effort also depended heavily on the CIO, the American Jewish Congress, and B'nai B'rith. In 1944, the Republican Party national platform included a plank endorsing permanent FEPC legislation, and while the Democratic Party platform was weaker, the coalition could count on the votes of most northern congressional Democrats and a good portion of the Republicans. But opposition-maneuvering bottled up the bill the following year and every time it was introduced thereafter. In 1949 and 1950, after African American communities had delivered the votes that had allowed President Truman to win a come-from-behind victory over Thomas Dewey, sponsors were optimistic that the bill would pass. The FEPC bill was introduced as part of a package of civil rights legislation assembled and supported by the president (including anti-lynching and anti–poll tax bills). It was supported by a huge NAACP lobbying effort and "sponsorship of 60 national church, civil, labor, fraternal and minority group organizations." It failed nevertheless, blocked in 1950 by a Senate filibuster by southern conservatives.[66]

Success was easier on the second front. In 1945, the *Nation* reported that "not since the Civil War has there been so much local interest in preventing racial or religious discrimination in employment: forty-nine different bills have been introduced in twenty states this year." New York created the model, passing a comprehensive law and establishing an enforcement commission equipped with greater powers and tougher penalties than the federal agency. Nine other states in the North and West also passed fair employment acts by 1949, along with twenty-eight municipalities. Still more were passed in the 1950s. Indeed, by the time Congress finally okayed the 1964 Civil Rights Act, with its resurrected fair employment practices provisions, most nonsouthern states and virtually all of the major cities had their own laws.[67]

These little FEPCs have been criticized as ineffectual, and many lacked realistic mechanisms for enforcement. They certainly came nowhere close to eradicating the practice of employment discrimination. But as Martha Biondi (and, much earlier, Louis Ruchames) have demonstrated, in New York and presumably other states these laws had very significant impacts. They fired up an entire industry of education, investigation, lobbying, litigation, and protest—all of it aimed at making the law work. NAACP chapters, local race relations committees and metropolitan councils on fair employment, and official enforcement agencies were kept busy handling discrimination complaints, holding hearings, and conducting investigations. High-profile violators became targets for lawsuits and protest demonstrations. White-owned newspapers covered the enforcement process, thus publicizing the cause of civil rights and explaining the law and its prohibitions. The agencies themselves also conducted educational campaigns. The New York State Commission against Discrimination conducted massive drives designed to inform employers, unions, and citizens about the wrongs of racial and religious discrimination. In 1949, it distributed more than 100,000 posters and 300,000 other pieces of literature while also commissioning a *March of Time*–produced newsreel, *An Equal Chance*, that was shown in 354 theaters throughout the state.[68]

These laws and the campaigns to pass them also helped civil rights advocates realign the political and journalistic resources of their states. African Americans had trouble developing electoral power in cities like Detroit, Los Angeles, and Oakland where at-large city council elections or gerrymandered districts minimized the black vote and kept African American politicians out of city government. The fight for state-level fair employment laws opened an alternative basis for electoral organization using legislative districts that were often more favorably mapped than city council districts. In both California and Michigan, fair employment legislation became a potent rallying cry for mobilizing black voters. In west Oakland, C. L. Dellums, head of the sleeping car porters local, and D. G. Gibson, a Texas-born former waiter who made money in Oakland real estate and published a local newspaper, used the campaign for a state law to build the East Bay Democratic Club, which in turn became the core institution for black electoral politics in the Bay Area. In 1948, the organization sent Byron Rumford, an African American pharmacist, to the State Assembly. He pledged to lead the fight for a state fair employment law and repeated that pledge every election until his bill finally passed in 1959.[69]

The campaign was important also for pulling white politicians and daily newspapers into a political relationship with black communities. The state-level fair employment issue—perhaps because it had already for a time been a commitment of the federal government, perhaps because both national parties had declared support—was easier for white politicians to endorse than some of the other demands of the black community. It was also very concise, a no-waffle test of where a politician stood. Surveying candidates at election time, asking them to pledge support on this issue if nothing else, black civic organizations were able to build some ties to legislators who were otherwise standoffish.

Whatever these laws accomplished in the way of labor market changes — and very clearly they did put pressure on employers and gradually helped open up jobs — their political legacy was profound. All the way through the 1940s, the political energy level and palpable sense of progress in the black communities of the North, and increasingly also in the South, had a lot to do with the fight for fair employment.

Northern Ground Wars

The FEPC was not the only agenda of the northern civil rights movement. The other big fight was over urban space. The struggle to break down the walls of urban segregation, to open up commercial and recreational spaces, and especially to gain access to housing and residential space escalated through the 1940s and across the 1950s. It was for the most part an unglamorous, grassroots campaign: incremental, store by store, block by block, a complicated story of political combat with none of the grand victories and not much of the headline-grabbing attention that the southern desegregation campaigns achieved a decade or so later. But out of it came tactics and organizations that would be used in the southern efforts and also measurable changes in the distribution of urban space. Slowly in the course of these struggles, black people in the northern and western cities began to dismantle in-city systems of containment and began to share major portions of their cities, moving into jobs, consumer relations, and housing from which they had been forcefully excluded.

The newly formed Congress of Racial Equality became the most visible of the many organizations that helped interrupt the North's pattern of commercial and recreational segregation, staging sit-ins and other nonviolent demonstrations at parks, swimming pools, skating rinks, movie theaters, stores, and restaurants where African Americans were excluded or mistreated. Some states had civil rights statutes that were left over from the 1870s that prohibited discrimination in places of public accommodation. NAACP chapters in previous decades had sometimes tried, without much success, to have them enforced. Now they brought case after case before judges who often handed down judgments. The *Crisis* instructed chapters how to carry on the campaigns, while black newspapers kept score of the victories. *Ebony* lead its August 1948 issue with a big article headlined "Crusade against Jim Crow" with the subhead "Californian Uses Ironclad Anti-bias Law to War on Restaurants That Bar

Picketers in front of a Seattle grocery store, 1947. Supported by CIO unions, church groups, Jewish organizations, and the Communist Party, black activists forced most stores and restaurants to end "whites only" service policies in that city by the end of the 1940s. In 1949, the same coalition secured a Fair Employment Practices Act for Washington State. (Museum of History and Industry, Seattle, #13693)

Negroes." The article was both a how-to manual demonstrating the tactics developed by the white president of the San Diego NAACP chapter and an assessment of campaigns across the North and West. *Ebony* made it clear that the desegregation efforts had far to go, but the article cheered on the troops with stories of clever campaigns and important victories.[70]

The open-access campaigns did not destroy northern Jim Crow, but as the 1940s rolled into the 1950s, the "whites only" signs were starting to come down. Results varied from city to city, and in most it would not be until the 1960s that African Americans could begin to assume that they might enter most stores and restaurants without incident. But incremental effects were evident much earlier. Thanks to the pressure of the civil rights alliances, the recreational and commercial horizons of black consumers expanded steadily in the war and postwar eras. What is more, this was a struggle that would help shape what followed in the South. The Congress of Racial Equality and the NAACP were trying out tactics—including the sit-in and nonviolent civil disobedience— that would later be taken south. Newspapers, politicians, and judges were also learning important lessons: learning to take seriously laws banning discrimination. So were some transportation companies. Airline and railroad companies that served the South lost a number of lawsuits in the 1940s, filed by angry passengers who used the New York law to challenge Jim Crow seating arrangements designed to comply with southern laws.[71]

The most difficult struggle of the northern civil rights campaign centered on housing. Even as breakouts were being counted on the employment and public access fronts during World War II, the problem of residential containment was growing worse. As wartime migrants poured into the cities, densities in the already overcrowded black belts became unbearable. And the containments mostly held during the war years, shored up by escalating prices and densities in white neighborhoods that were also experiencing in-migration. Federal public housing programs, begun in the 1930s and enlarged during the war, typically reinforced the old demarcations as government agencies shoehorned housing projects for African Americans into existing neighborhoods and excluded blacks from public housing going up in white areas.

But as global war ended, the battle for living space in the big cities heated up. It was fought across multiple fronts. The NAACP and its allies used the courts, winning in 1948 the landmark *Shelley v. Kraemer* ruling that established the unenforceability of restrictive housing covenants. They lobbied the Federal Housing Authority and municipal housing councils to open access to housing projects. Complicated battles raged in local governing institutions as mayors, city councils, and agency heads faced mounting pressures on all sides and usually tried to finesse a limited expansion of black neighborhoods.[72]

The key struggle was on the ground, and its heroes were the thousands of families who put themselves at risk both financially and physically by purchasing property in neighborhoods where they were not wanted and where whites were sure to react in ways that were at least ugly and often very dangerous. All too many books pass quickly over these men and women, treating their actions as an expected or natural response to economic circumstances, as if housing pressures on the one hand and increased incomes on the other would lead anyone to take such steps. Hardly. These were on some fundamental level political acts, integrally tied to a context and a political movement that encouraged the open-housing pioneers and backed them up in various ways.

The evidence is in the newspapers—not in the mainstream daily newspapers, which often handled the tensions around housing through studied silence, but in the African American weeklies. There, the struggle for black living space shows up in detailed coverage of local housing agency meetings and rulings, in articles about lobbying efforts and pending lawsuits, and stories about the ravages of white mobs and the heroic stands made by determined

African American home-owners. Interestingly, there are also laudatory pieces about real estate brokers who engaged in what the white media demonized as "blockbusting." A look at the *Michigan Chronicle* issue of 30 January 1954 demonstrates how the black press helped fuel the housing crusade. A good portion of the advertising that sustained Detroit's major African American–owned newspaper had to do with housing. Several pages of classified ads and display ads bought by real estate companies follow a news section that contains easily a dozen articles referencing housing politics. Included are two big stories about the Detroit Housing Commission; another about the mayor ("Mayor Cobo Denies NAACP Housing Plea"); a large picture and caption congratulating the secretary-manager of the Home Federal Savings and Loan Association, a black-owned institution, for "fostering home ownership among Negroes"; and an equally glowing thank-you piece with large photographs about the Fortune Real Estate company, a white-owned firm that sold houses to African American buyers. Despite a slightly gratuitous comment about the firm's name ("Probably nobody knows better than Pintarich and Friedman why they chose to call the newly merged combine 'Fortune' Realty"), the article lavishly applauds "these forthright young men" as genuine friends of the African American community, noting that they "are probably the only white brokers in Detroit who employ an all-Negro sales force" and that they are also members of the NAACP.[73]

It is easy to misunderstand the housing wars, to see them as exercises in frustration, even defeat. Many of the most public battles ended with white neighborhood associations or white housing rioters celebrating. In Chicago, a sequence of housing riots between 1947 and 1957 kept black families out of many neighborhoods south and west of Bronzeville. Despite national press attention and long, expensive campaigns by the NAACP and the Chicago Commission on Human Relations, by the end of the 1950s it was still impossible for African Americans to purchase or rent housing in most sections of Chicago. In Detroit, whites gave ground in some neighborhoods but set up new lines of "defended neighborhoods" that successfully resisted black advances. In Los Angeles in the early 1950s, street battles raged as African Americans moved into the previously all-white working-class suburb of Compton, settling down only after multiple interventions by the state attorney general's office, the UAW-CIO (which disciplined a segregation leader for "conduct unbecoming to a union member"), and the NAACP. It was a narrow victory, however, for the surrounding suburbs immediately hardened their boundaries to keep African Americans walled into Compton.[74]

Baseball great Willie Mays discovered the difficulties of housing expansion in San Francisco after his team, the Giants, moved west from New York in 1957.

The star centerfielder had been treated like a hero by the local press when the news broke that San Francisco was finally to have a major league team. But when Mays and his wife, Marguerite, tried to buy a home in an upper-income white neighborhood, they learned the limits of that welcome. The first house they tried to buy was taken off the market, then the owner of a second house balked after neighbors and his employer threatened his livelihood "if I sold this house to that baseball player." Only after the team management, the mayor, and the *San Francisco Chronicle* became involved was the deal finally consummated. But the problems were not over. Someone threw a rock through their front window a few days after the family moved into their new home. A few years later they sold it, deciding that New York was a better place to live. "Down in Alabama where we come from," Marguerite Mays told the *Chronicle* in 1957, "you know your place, and that's something, at least. But up here it's all a lot of camouflage. They grin in your face and then deceive you."[75]

Thus, even as the housing struggles gained space, segregation remained. Again and again African American pioneers won access to new neighborhoods only to see the lines of ghetto containment redrawn. Neighborhood segregation remained almost as complete in most cities in 1960 and 1970 as it had been in 1940, and as whites left the city altogether, suburban boundaries promised new forms of spatialized separation and economic inequality.

But the housing wars were not just about integration or even housing. These ground conflicts were a principal arena of political action in northern black communities in the decades after World War II, a major focus for activism that drew upon many segments of those communities, including celebrities (Willie Mays was one of a number of ballplayers and entertainers to have high-profile housing problems), important business sectors (newspapers and realtors), and also tens of thousands of ordinary people who aspired to better housing and realized that the community would have to fight to make it happen.

Turning the Northern Press

With the exception of the major incidents, like the Cicero riots in 1951 and the Willie Mays case in 1957, the mainstream daily newspapers tried to ignore the housing struggles that tore up their cities. Whenever possible, editors buried the kind of news that dominated the black weeklies, claiming that to do otherwise would further "inflame" racial hostilities. This policy of silence was probably another sign that the northern civil rights movement had made an impact. Twenty-five years earlier, most major white-owned newspapers would have loudly sided with the white home-owners who were hysterical about the growth of the black community. In the postwar era, race hysteria was generally left to smaller neighborhood weeklies, like the chain of right-wing newspapers that Floyd McGriff published for Detroit's northwest side neighborhoods. Indeed, to follow the ground wars in the Motor City during the late 1940s and 1950s, one would have to read the weeklies—black and white. The two Detroit dailies—the *Detroit News* and the *Detroit Free Press*—wrote as little as possible about the great urban struggle of their time. As odd as that may seem, that practice represented a meaningful shift in patterns of coverage on racial issues. And it went beyond the daily newspapers. Other northern-based media institutions—magazines, book publishing, and to some extent Hollywood and the radio networks—spent those decades adjusting their ways of depicting African Americans and their response to the subject of racial injustice.[76]

The federal government played a part in this media adjustment. The Office of War Information, charged with building morale on the home front and nervous about racial unrest, pressed media organizations to be careful about racially inflammatory material and gently pushed the concept of "Americans All"— nation before race, "we are all in this together"—during the war. Civil rights advocates pressed further. The NAACP had started monitoring and responding to derogatory material published in major newspapers and other media outlets in 1940. The organization had some earlier experience with what it called "publicity protests" dating back to 1915 when it had organized boycotts to protest showings of *The Birth of a Nation* and had joined in criticism of *Amos 'n' Andy* in the 1930s. But now the effort would be more comprehensive and effective. It involved both public denunciations and a lot of behind-the-scenes pressure, mostly in the form of calm, informative letters from Walter White, Roy Wilkins, and other NAACP officials to editors, corporate executives, and other high-level opinion leaders. When *Harper's* magazine used a joke about Sambo in a 1941 subscription letter, White wrote explaining the hurtful dimensions of the image. The magazine apologized and dropped the promotion. A letter to NBC after a radio performer mentioned the ditty "Ten Little Nigger Boys" brought another quick apology: "The National Broadcasting Company has a standing rule against the use of any terms which are derogatory, condescending, or which in any other fashion may give a legitimate offense to any racial or other group." *Life* magazine also apologized when Wilkins complained in 1941 about its use of the word "pickaninnies." General Manager C. D. Jackson took pains to explain that "*Life* has often published reports on subjects of special interest to the Negro people which show that it is friendly and sympathetic toward them, as toward all other groups in the population," and promised to do more.[77]

Some of the responses were much more defensive, but it seems clear that especially in New York, the NAACP effort had a measurable impact. The New

York office, led by Roy Wilkins, managed to develop ongoing relationships with key media managers of not just the local radio and newspapers but many of the major magazines, wire services, and radio networks headquartered in that media capital. Russell Owen, editor of the Sunday *New York Times,* was on a first-name basis with "Roy" and "Walter" when he wrote defending the newspaper against what does seem to have been a fairly obscure complaint by a NAACP rank and filer. "This thing sort of made me boil a bit," he whined. But it was clear that that newspaper was learning to pay attention to the way it covered African American issues.[78]

The managers of the critically influential Luce enterprises — *Time, Life,* and *Fortune* magazines and *March of Time* newsreels — seem to have also responded. Walter White's letters would usually be answered by high-level managers who indicated that they took the criticism seriously. Frank C. Norris, managing editor of *March of Time,* responded in detail to the criticism that followed a 1942 newsreel sequence on the "Flying Tigers," during which some of the pilots stationed in India sang "an old-fashioned barber shop ballad which did contain the word 'nigger.'" "We had hoped that Americans would be thrilled to hear the singing voice of their most famous fighting pilots," he wrote defending the report, but he did indicate that because of the complaints, "I certainly shall be forewarned in the future."[79]

The Luce empire may deserve to be counted as one of the leaders of the mass-market press reformation. *Time, Fortune,* and *Life* magazines had shown no particular interest in African Americans in the 1930s, but as the new decade got underway, the three magazines seemed to respond to the initiatives coming out of the black community. *Fortune,* well known for its innovative and progressive projects, announced its new commitment early with a pair of pathbreaking articles. The first introduced the young black artist Jacob Lawrence and presented a dozen of his migration series paintings in a beautiful seven-page spread in November 1941. It was followed a few months later with a powerful article on "Negro's War," demonstrating why blacks deserved "a full share in America's greatest undertaking." *Time*'s sympathies were harder to read, although it did offer more articles about racial issues than had appeared in the 1930s. The most important development was in the new look of *Life* magazine.[80]

Life was the nation's premier news outlet, a revolutionary publication that had debuted in 1936 with a circulation of 1 million, hitting 3 million by 1940 and 5 million a few years later. Called by one historian "the closest thing to a national newspaper America had ever had," it reached far beyond its circulation numbers, becoming a favorite fixture for any kind of waiting room and something to be shared among friends. A survey in 1939 indicated an effective readership of more than 20 million; another in 1950 estimated that over half the nation's population saw one or more issues over any three-month period. For a full generation, lasting until television news programs pushed the magazine to the sidelines in the 1960s, *Life* was America's single most popular source of news and public information. And that was only part of its influence. *Life* led a pictorial revolution that changed all of journalism, including the other major news vehicle, daily newspapers. The camera had been around for almost a century and headshot photography had been the newspaper standard for decades, but photos remained a secondary part of journalism until *Life* came along. By the late 1930s, publications of all kinds, including the most conservative big city dailies, were making pictures central. Narratives were shorter and doing less work. Big, attractive full-action pictures and bold captions supported, carried, or interrupted the story. People now "looked at" as well as read the news.[81]

Those pictures had the power to change the way readers understood issues and events and also to change the way they looked at groups of people. Historians have noted the critical influence of photojournalism during the southern civil rights campaigns of the late 1950s, but there is reason to backdate that observation. Changes in the way major print media depicted African Americans are discernible in the early 1940s as some major newspapers and especially *Life* magazine began to publish new kinds of images of black Americans. Media studies have paid little attention to these changes, focusing instead on the ways that the mass-market press continued to ignore and stereotype African Americans long into the postwar period. And that is certainly true. But coverage patterns were changing, perhaps not enough initially to affect most whites, but in ways that would matter to African Americans and probably also to journalists who would extend the media turn.[82]

Prior to the 1940s, news pictures of African Americans rarely appeared in mass-market newspapers or magazines, except for Joe Louis in the sports sections. The images that white Americans did see were in magazine advertisements, where plenty of Aunt Jemimas, Uncle Bens, and other smiling figures maintained an image of good-natured servility. Hollywood films offered a slightly larger range of representations, few of them flattering. Maids, butlers, chauffeurs, singers, dancers, shoeshine men, and convicts were the most common urban context roles. Most filmic images depicted blacks in rural or jungle contexts in a tight range of figures, from African "native" to antebellum slave to contemporary sharecropper or servant. Newsreels were, as historian Thomas Cripps indicates, even worse, typically consisting of "Negro *curiosa* such as 'Harlem Negroes Eating Watermelon,' Elks parades, a freak who had married fifty-six times, chain gangs, colorful mass baptism, Africans dancing, and among the worst, the golfer Joe Kirkwood driving a ball off a prone Negro's pursed lips."[83]

Pictorial representations of African Americans started to change in the early 1940s, and *Life* helped lead the way. In a score of war-era spreads that were mostly feel-good layouts but included also some high-impact reports on racial oppression (most importantly the Detroit race riot report and a photo dramatization of Richard Wright's *Black Boy*), the magazine published pictures of black people that were new and noticeable. Not all of them—the Uncle Ben ads were still there, and a few of the features supported similar or even more demeaning stereotypes, notably a piece on minstrel shows that shared an issue with the 1943 riot. And one can read condescension elsewhere, particularly in the text. It is possible to see, when looking at the pictures, the beginnings of a media strategy that would help to change the fabric of American race relations over the next generation, becoming in time not just *Life*'s project but a pattern for much of the northern-based print media.[84]

There are three noteworthy elements. One is that *Life* printed shocking images of African Americans as victims of bigotry and race hatred. The magazine's bold ten-page spread "Race War in Detroit" included no pictures of white victims, although they were discussed (and lost) in the text. The biggest and most powerful pictures show white mobs attacking well-dressed African Americans who are alone and cornered. Another striking photo shows a white policeman knocked out by white rioters. *Life*'s depiction of the riot hammers home two images that many white readers had been able to avoid until the age of photojournalism: brutal white mobs and sympathetic black victims.[85]

Images of white-against-black violence also appear in other *Life* articles from those years, sometimes even when the focus does not ostensibly demand it. A feature story on Detroit that ran in 1942, a year before the riots, included a prominent shot of the Ku Klux Klan headquarters with a caption reading "The Klan draws its recruits mostly from the 200,000 Southern whites who came to Detroit for jobs in auto plants. It sows dissension in unions and tries to make life miserable for Detroit's Negroes and Jews." A spread about "How Will Negroes Vote?" in the 1944 election featured a photo taken five years earlier of an effigy lynching, the hanged mannequin wearing a sign reading "This Nigger Voted." The "Picture of the Week" in July 1947 shows the bodies of five Georgia inmates who had been shot by guards after refusing an order to get to work. In choosing such images, the magazine was making a powerful and consistent point about racial oppression.[86]

Attire is the second element, and an intriguing one. In almost all of the photos that *Life* published during the 1940s, black people are well dressed. Men usually are shown in a coat and tie or military uniform. Women are also well dressed, usually in ways that suggest respectability and solid incomes. Servants, field hands, and the other stock images of blacks (scrubwomen, construction laborers, idle youths, zoot-suiters) are not readily found in the photo spreads of *Life* magazine in the 1940s, let alone the 1950s. There are a few images of servants or poor families tucked away in stories that were not supposed to be about race ("*Life* Goes Quail Shooting in Tennessee"), but mostly what *Life* offered its readers were images of respectably dressed and dignified-looking men and women.[87]

Many of the pictures focus on highly attractive faces. Some belonged to entertainers, which later critics dismiss as contributing to an unproductive stereotype. But in the 1940s, *Life* would have been aligned with the black press and the brand-new *Ebony* magazine, which likewise lavished attention on entertainers. And there were no Stepin Fetchits among the stars the magazine profiled. Memorable features included a spread on Joe Louis in the army and a large, eye-catching set of photos about Paul Robeson's *Othello*, which opened in 1943, and a similar spread when the musical *Carmen Jones* hit Broadway later that year.

Attractive-looking black soldiers and sailors were another *Life* specialty. A handsome full-page picture of thirteen uniformed officers ("First Negro Ensigns") and a double-page overhead shot of the "Negro Troops Chorus" performing in London's Albert Hall are examples. More intriguing is the way the magazine portrayed black soldiers in its eight-page feature on the building of the Burma Road. Carefully designating the blacks as "Negro engineers" and "bulldozer drivers" and showing them bossing "native laborers," the spread moved between action shots and full-faced portraits of several of the men, all handsome.[88]

The focus on dignified, well-dressed African Americans is especially noticeable when *Life* went south, which is the third important element in its coverage. *Life*'s apparent commitment to supporting the African American campaign for racial justice was mostly focused on the South. This was an old habit of northern media outlets, and it was about to get stronger ("Selmaism," it would later be called). Apart from the Detroit riot coverage, most of *Life*'s coverage of discrimination or segregation involved southern, not northern, places. What is surprising (and probably deliberate) is that when *Life* went south, it mostly stayed away from representations of black poverty and black sharecroppers, focusing instead on the political and social injustices faced by well-dressed and evidently urban African Americans. One of the most memorable Jim Crow stories that the magazine produced during the 1940s was an understated 1947 article entitled "Harvey Jones and the New Car." Harvey Jones of North

Carolina (carefully identified as a navy veteran and "farmer") bought a lottery ticket that happily held the winning number. He promptly tried to claim the prize, a new Cadillac. But when the sponsors found out he was black, they "refunded" his money, redrew the lottery, and gave the car to a white dentist. *Life* tells the story in a few paragraphs and a riveting three-quarter-page picture that shows Jones, calm and dignified, talking without apparent tension to the dentist as they stand in front of the Cadillac. The caption indicates in ironic understatement that the dentist will keep the car since "nobody has asked me to give it back."[89]

Some of *Life*'s southern work takes the well-dressed strategy even further, juxtaposing images of intelligent-looking and upstanding African Americans against overall-wearing, angular-featured whites. A 1944 story on "Voting in the South" opens with the left-side page dominated by the familiar image of a white Alabama politician delivering a stump speech to a crowd of car-leaning, overall-wearing white farmers, while on the facing page three pictures show suit-and-tie-wearing, tall, serious-looking black men being turned away from the polls.[90]

I do not want to make too much of this. *Life* magazine left much to be desired. Its treatment of African Americans was a mere token and sometimes condescending. It ignored northern racial struggles and most of what was happening in the South. It even waffled slightly on whether certain forms of segregation might be tenable in some states. Moreover, it is not clear what *Life*'s new ways of picturing African Americans meant to various readers or whether most even noticed. Still, it was the start of something that would become significant over time. Other publishers and white journalists noticed, and some moved forward along similar lines. Black sociologist Ira De A. Reid was wisely cautious when he surveyed the new approach in a 1944 essay for *Phylon*, writing that mass-market magazines have published "millions of words on the Negro, all of which contained less bilge than we are usually accustomed to read on the subject," but he welcomed the trend, hoping for a "fertile increase in the tribe of sympathetic, intelligent writers, and humane, risk-daring publishers."[91]

The NAACP was also monitoring the trend and understood its importance. In the spring of 1949, as Congress considered the package of civil rights bills that President Truman had called for and pledged to support, the *Crisis* took stock of the nation's newspapers, examining the editorial pages of 300 dailies from all over the country. Author James W. Ivy surveyed editorial positions on the issue of the filibuster, the procedural device that southern senators were using to block the progress of the civil rights bills. Liberals had tried to change the Senate rules that required at least two-thirds of the body to overcome a filibuster and move a bill to a vote. They had failed, and Ivy had been following the newspaper commentary. Finding a "largely consistent division of opinion along strictly geographic lines," Ivy reported that southern newspapers, with some encouraging exceptions, defended the use of the filibuster, while the "majority of northern, as well as many western, editors" called for the changes in Senate rules and an end to filibusters. Ivy was in no mood to celebrate. The four measures (anti-lynching, anti–poll tax, FEPC, and an omnibus civil rights bill) were doomed in the current Congress. So he spent more time high-lighting the northern and western newspapers that had defended the filibuster than those that had sided with the civil rights forces. Some had done so alleg-edly on the grounds of tradition and procedural integrity, others forthrightly opposing the civil rights bills. He was sad to report that even the venerable *Christian Science Monitor* stood behind the southern senators' efforts to block the legislation. Still, the newspaper inventory was a record of what the civil rights movement had accomplished in its struggle to turn the northern press. Northern newspapers would become steadily more sympathetic in the years to come, as long as the issue of civil rights was largely aimed at the South. And Ivy was sure that even southern editors understood the momentum. "There is hardly any doubt that some civil-rights legislation will eventually be passed," he wrote, "and a large number of southern editors are aware of this."[92]

The civil rights movement of the 1940s and early 1950s was no revolution. Its accomplishments were limited and largely unheralded. There were few sen-sational victories and very little that the major media was obliged to cover. Segregation was no less a fact of northern urban life at the end of the period than it had been at the beginning. But the movement's incremental impacts were nevertheless profound and need to be recognized as such. Gradually the movement made changes in the standard of living of many African Americans living in the northern cities. In the twenty years following 1939, the median income for black families living in the North doubled in constant dollars; the distribution of occupations spread well beyond the unskilled and service-class jobs open to blacks before World War II; housing densities were down and housing amenities were improved as ghettos had doubled, tripled, and qua-drupled in size. In Detroit in 1940, almost all African Americans had lived in 56 census tracts. In 1960, the ghetto encompassed 166 census tracts. Scholars who have chalked this up to the trickle-down of postwar economic benefits misunderstand the forces of history. These were improvements that were won through widespread, persistent, and multidimensional political struggle.[93]

Equally important, the movement had broken through critical political bar-riers, winning for the first time in the twentieth century meaningful initiatives from federal and state governments and establishing the alliances with unions, northern white politicians, and media institutions that would be useful in the next phase of struggle. That had been accomplished through an unprecedented mobilization of activism and support within the Black Metropolises, based on the kinds of institutions, "mid-century America's black power institutions," that had been developed there.

"We have known humiliation, we have known abusive language, we have been plunged into the abyss of oppression. And we have decided to rise up only with the weapon of protest. It is one of the greatest glories of America that we have the right of protest." When twenty-seven-year-old Dr. Martin Luther King Jr. addressed these words to the black citizens of Montgomery, Alabama, who had gathered on 23 February 1956 to support the nearly 100 men and women who had just been indicted for participating in the now two-month-old Montgomery bus boycott, it marked a pivotal point in the Montgomery struggle and perhaps in the American struggle against racial apartheid. White Americans outside of Alabama would first meet Martin Luther King that night on their television newscasts and the next morning in the front-page articles that ran in many major dailies. The determined boycott by Alabama women who had decided to no longer ride in the back of the bus would now begin to capture more and more media attention, and the publicity would help the boycotters carry through to victory, 385 days after Rosa Parks had first refused to move.[94]

Many things pivoted on that day: a cause that had been waged most profitably in the North would now be centered in the South; a movement that had been identified with New York–based organizations (the NAACP, the Brotherhood of Sleeping Car Porters) and leaders (A. Philip Randolph, Adam Clayton Powell Jr., Roy Wilkins) would now look to a southerner and southern-originated organizations (the Southern Christian Leadership Conference and the Student Non-violent Coordinating Committee); and it would be a much broader and daring and powerful movement, a movement that ultimately drew hundreds of thousands into acts of protest. Lerone Bennett, from the vantage point of 1965, saw it as a turn from rehearsal to rebellion. The 1940s movement had been a "rehearsal," getting black Americans ready and in position for the great "rebellion" that would visibly and permanently alter the racialized systems of law and thought that had for so long subordinated African Americans.[95]

But "rehearsal" does not quite capture all of the ways that the Southern Diaspora and the building of northern Black Metropolises had laid the foundation for the civil rights struggles of the late 1950s and 1960s. It was not just the civil rights movement itself that was important, it was also the way that geography had enabled African Americans to leverage and realign powerful institutions outside their own community. The breakthroughs of the 1960s were going to depend upon a sympathetic mass media, on the support of key unions, on the northern Democratic Party and most of the Republican congressional delegation, on a federal court system filled with New Deal–appointed judges—and all of these levers in turn rested on the fulcrum of political and cultural institutions that African Americans had created in the great cities of the North.

Re-figuring Conservatism

If numbers were all that mattered, the political legacy of the white diaspora would have been twice as great as that of the African American diaspora. But population does not translate directly into political influence. What counts is the way people and resources are organized and whether there are the right kind of opportunities for political intervention. In the case of African Americans, the organizational fit was extraordinary. Diaspora communities mobilized in ways that enabled them to leverage some of the key historical transformations of the twentieth century. White southern migrants were more dispersed, were less unified, and never came together as the kind of cultural or political force as their black counterparts. Still, at various moments, diaspora whites made an impact on the political life of the places they settled and in some complicated ways helped reshape American history.

This chapter looks at that impact, picking up an issue that historians have studiously ignored. Most accounts of the "hillbilly" and "Okie" migrations have viewed white migrants as victims of history, not its architects. And other historians studying northern and western places usually fail to even note the presence of white southerners, let alone assess their role in political developments. Massive historiographies of labor, urban and suburban politics, and race and ethnicity that fill shelf after shelf in bookstores and libraries are mostly silent on the subject of this sizable segment of the population.

This silence is all the more curious because it is new. Contemporaries, especially during the middle decades of the twentieth century, spoke loudly about the political role of white southerners. What did the white diaspora contribute to American political life? Walter White had an answer. The NAACP executive director thought that southern white migrants inflamed racial hatreds in the North, and he blamed them in particular for the bloody Detroit race riot of 1943. Gunnar Myrdal was inclined to agree on the larger issue. In *American Dilemma*, the Swedish economist observed that the southern white retained his "stronger race prejudice" when moving north and was likely to "communicate it to those he meets," thus helping to increase the level of race prejudice outside the South. Agreeing too was R. J. Thomas, president of the UAW, who joined Walter White in urging an investigation into the activities of the Ku Klux Klan among southern whites in Detroit. Thomas Sancton, the white Louisiana-raised managing editor of the *New Republic*, said much the same thing. In a 1943 article on the Detroit riot, he blamed his fellow migrants and especially the "race-hate preachers and various other kinds of shouters from the South," naming J. Frank Norris in particular. He argued that the South was now exporting its "poisons." What had happened on the streets of Detroit was that "the old subdued, muted, murderous Southern race war was transplanted into a high-speed industrial background."[1]

Contemporaries were saying similar things about the impact of Okies on race relations out west, blaming them for hate strikes and resurgent Klan activities in the early 1940s. And the charges continued across the next two decades, especially when George Wallace headed north to run for president under the banner of segregation and backlash in 1964, 1968, and 1972. All through the second phase of the diaspora, prominent voices claimed that the white migrants were big contributors to the politics of racism.[2]

This is a complicated charge, and one can understand why historians have steered around this issue. But it needs to be examined. Did white southerners indeed lead and reshape northern bigotry politics, or are there other explanations for the claims by black and white liberals and leftists? Were there other political contributions that contemporaries missed or ignored? I will be arguing that contemporary critics were correct up to a point—that the white diaspora did make important contributions to the politics of race but in more complicated ways than contemporaries understood.

Southerners cannot be blamed outright for the numerous bigotry movements. White northerners were well practiced in the ways of white supremacy, and northerners dominated every explosion of violence and hate politics. What southerners supplied were useful symbols and in some cases catalytic leadership, important contributions to be sure. At several different points in the twentieth century, the adaptation of southern-linked symbols substantially changed the dimensions of race politics in the North and West, with implications that extended widely. We will look at the southern re-figuring of northern racial conservatism in three eras, beginning with the 1920s Ku Klux Klan, then continuing through the hate strikes and extremist organizations in the 1930s, 40s, and 50s, and ending with the 1960s, 70s, and 80s when George Wallace's campaigns, tough-guy country music, and the New Christian Right added new dimensions to American conservatism.

I will also make a second argument: bigotry politics was not the only contribution of diaspora whites, and only a portion of the migrant population involved themselves in such projects. Spread across a vast geography, spread across the entire social scale, former southerners were also spread from one end of the political spectrum to the other. In the 1930s, some former southerners were members or leaders of the Black Legion in Michigan and the Ku Klux Klan in California, but others were members and leaders of the Socialist and Communist Parties in those states. Thirty years later, it was no different; from Students for a Democratic Society (SDS) to the Wallace movement, the range of voices was huge.

This can be seen in opinion polls taken in the postwar era, all of which show former southerners sharply divided on issues of race and civil rights. A 1950 survey conducted in Detroit looked at attitudes toward racial integration and found most Detroit whites opposed, with the southern-born sharing the same pro and con distributions as other whites in the city. A follow-up survey in 1956 found southern whites to be somewhat more likely than other whites to oppose school integration, but the authors also pointed out that among the southerners, "there is little unanimity"—39 percent favored complete integration, 12 percent partial integration, 49 percent complete segregation (a third of nonsouthern whites also favored complete segregation). A Los Angeles poll conducted after the 1965 Watts riot found big splits among southern whites on issues of race and integration, with the distributions very similar to other whites. A poll taken among whites in some of the middle-class neighborhoods of Chicago during the violent summer of 1967 provided more detail than the others, probing attitudes regarding the black protest movement as well as integration issues. While in the aggregate, former southerners revealed themselves to be slightly more hostile on both fronts than other whites, the poll also revealed the sharp differences of opinion within the southern group. Of the migrant southerners, 31 percent (and 37 percent of other whites) expressed "full" support for integration, with most of this liberal section also expressing support for civil rights demonstrations and other forms of activism. On the other hand, 29 percent of white former southerners and 28 percent of other whites were militantly opposed to the civil rights movement and resented the integration of schools and sometimes even public facilities. The rest were moderately opposed to the movement and, while ready to accept certain kinds of integration, balked at open housing measures that would change their neighborhoods.[3]

These polls are ambiguous. And that is the main point. We cannot responsibly summarize the political opinions of the southern white migrant population, let alone assume that this was a population wholly committed to racial bigotry and backlash.

Liberal Diaspora

The South had always managed to export a healthy portion of its liberals and radicals. It is thus ironic that the left side of the white diaspora has remained so hidden from contemporary or historical understanding. The writers profiled in chapter 5 belonged to a larger cohort of white expatriates who found in the South's hostility to unions, to Socialism, to interracialism, and to many forms of critical belief and political action reason to contemplate migration. Sprinkled through the biographical dictionaries of labor and the Left are migration stories of women and men like "Aunt" Molly Jackson, H. L. Mitchell, and Claude Williams who risked their lives for a time in the South and then moved west or north. Jackson, an organizer in the Kentucky coal mines and a singer/songwriter who helped lead the Harlan County strike of 1931, settled in New York a few years later and continued to work for the labor movement. Mitchell, a Socialist and founder of the Southern Tenant Farmers Union that tried to organize black and white sharecroppers in Arkansas and Oklahoma in the 1930s, moved his operation to California in the 1940s and concentrated on organizing that state's farmworkers. Williams, a Presbyterian minister associated with the Communist Party, had worked with Mitchell and directed Commonwealth Labor College in Mena, Arkansas, in the 1930s. In the early 1940s, he moved north to help the CIO organize southern whites in the Detroit auto plants. This was a role that drew quite a number of radical white southerners to the midwestern steel cities and auto cities where they were much valued as organizers.[4]

Diaspora white southerners were a minuscule but sometimes visible part of northern and western labor movements. The radical movement liked to highlight its southerners, holding them up as genuine American rural "folk" and using them to counter the impression that radicalism belonged only to big city immigrants. And that fascination with southerners helped diaspora radicals engineer at least one significant change in American labor culture: the development of urban folk music.

Singing southerners were especially valuable to the Left, which was why

Aunt Molly Jackson moved to New York. The Communist Party made her a movement celebrity and kept her busy singing "Harlan County Blues," "I Am a Union Woman," and other hillbilly labor songs at party and union rallies. A few years later, the party stumbled across another singing southerner who would do even more for the movement. Woody Guthrie had followed his fellow Oklahomans to California in 1937 and had achieved a minor reputation as a hillbilly radio singer and "cornpone philosopher" on a Los Angeles station. When he heard that the CIO was planning a campaign to organize the Dust Bowl migrants living in valleys and working in the fields, he began writing songs to aid the cause, songs like "Talking Dust Bowl," "Do Re Mi," and "So Long, It's Been Good to Know You" that emphasized the hardships that his fellow Okies and Arkies faced in California. The *People's World*, the Communist Party's West Coast newspaper, asked him to contribute a daily column and began promoting Guthrie as "the dustbowl refugee, songster and homespun philosopher who has won thousands of friends through his program on KFVD."[5]

In 1940, Woody Guthrie was in New York, scheduled to perform at a "Grapes of Wrath Evening" benefit to raise money for the California farmworkers campaign. With him on the program were Will Geer, Aunt Molly Jackson, Alan and Bess Lomax, and Leadbelly. Biographer Joe Klein describes the event as the birth of modern folk music—the fusion of protest lyrics and hillbilly and blues melodies that would become a powerful resource for the labor movement, the civil rights movement, and various other lefts. Alan Lomax, a Texan who, with his father, John Lomax, had created the Library of Congress Archive of Folk Song, saw the potential that evening. He had discovered the black convict poet Huddie Ledbetter (Leadbelly) in an Arkansas prison; he had encouraged Molly Jackson and several of her relatives to use their musical talents on behalf of the Left; and now he would see to the career of the Okie Troubadour, securing the radio and recording arrangements that made Guthrie famous. With Lomax's support, Guthrie became the central figure in a New York–based community of singer/songwriters who would service the labor movement with material that was supposed to combine the art of authentic rural America with the values of the Left.[6]

This brand-new enterprise was another diaspora product, not unlike the innovations in commercialized branches of southern music that had emerged in New York and Los Angeles. The institutionalization of what would come to be called folk music was brought about by a group of expatriate southerners— Lomax, Guthrie, Jackson, Leadbelly, and also Lee Hays—working with northerners (notably Pete Seeger, Millard Lampell, and Burl Ives) in the unique opportunity structures of Popular Front–era New York.

If the Left offered opportunities for liberal southern whites, so did a more important political organization. Liberal white migrants proved valuable to the Democratic Party in some nonsouthern states, and that encouraged some reverse carpetbagging as ambitious southern white liberals headed north or west looking for political openings. A few became famous. Indeed, at some moments southern expatriates were positioned in history-making ways. One of those occurred on 1 July 1932 at the Democratic National Convention in Chicago, when William Gibbs McAdoo stood and announced that California's delegation, pledged until then to support John Garner of Texas, was switching to Franklin Delano Roosevelt and delivering the final votes needed for nomination.

Georgia-born and Tennessee-raised, McAdoo was a carpetbagger—at least that is what the press had called him in 1922 when he moved to California, hoping to use the state's wide-open Democratic Party machinery to launch his own presidential campaign. McAdoo was Woodrow Wilson's son-in-law, had served as secretary of the treasury, and was widely considered the heir apparent going into the 1920 election. But he had failed to gain the Democratic nomination that year, partly because of opposition in New York, which had been his home for some years. So he had moved to Los Angeles, figuring that he would be able to dominate the weak and divided party in the Golden State and use it as a base for 1924. The plan almost worked. With the state's delegation behind him, McAdoo came close to winning the presidential nomination in 1924. But the convention deadlocked between the expatriate southerner and his New York rival, Al Smith, ultimately turning to the ineffectual John Davis. The years 1928 and 1932 were also presidential disappointments for McAdoo, but his carpetbagging was to be rewarded in other ways. In 1932, Californians sent McAdoo to the U.S. Senate.[7]

He was not the only white southerner involved in California politics that year. Also running for the Senate and securing 26 percent of the votes was "Fighting Bob" Shuler, the fundamentalist Southern Methodist who had moved to Los Angeles from Texas in 1920 and whose radio station had helped elect John C. Porter, a conservative prohibitionist, mayor of that city in 1929. In 1932, in the face of mounting campaigns to end prohibition, Shuler declared for the Senate, running under the banner of the Prohibition Party. Mounting a campaign that fused anti–Wall Street populism with intense Protestant moralism, he came in third but not far behind the Republican candidate. Between them the two southerners, McAdoo and Shuler, had collected 70 percent of California's votes.[8]

California was exceptionally receptive to southern democratic carpetbagging, but political geography helped diaspora southerners win leadership roles in other states as well. The Democratic Party, founded by southerners in the early 1800s and linked to the Confederacy in the 1860s, remained until the New Deal realignment a mostly southern party. The South provided its reliable base, while in northern and western states, party fortunes hinged on complicated rivalries between Protestant and Catholic, rural and urban, progressive and machine, dry and wet factions. Those arrangements sometimes created openings for southern expatriate Democrats who could gain political advantage either by working against the Catholic faction or by offering their Anglo-Saxon names and Protestant credentials to the urban machines. Historian Daniel Sutherland has counted some sixty-one southern migrants who held political office in northern states during the Gilded Age, many of them in New York where Tammany Hall seemed eager to embrace former Confederates.[9]

Political openings for astute southern Democrats continued to appear during the Progressive Era. Newton Baker from West Virginia won election as the Democratic reform mayor of Cleveland in 1912. Still more successful was the Virginian who became first a college professor, then the head of Princeton University, then governor of New Jersey, and in 1912 the president of the United States. Woodrow Wilson benefited enormously from his diaspora geography in his bid for the presidential nomination. As a former southerner, he could count on that region's support, while his New Jersey credentials helped him negotiate the nonsouthern votes needed to win the party nomination. Part of that involved networks of former southerners living in the North. Walter Hines Page and members of the Southern Society of New York provided the funds and publicity resources—including Page's influential monthly magazine, *World's Work*—that made Wilson a credible early contender for the Democratic nomination.[10]

Democratic carpetbagging became less common after the New Deal established strong Democratic Party organizations throughout the country, but southern-born politicians continued to get into office in certain locales. Instead of working the fissures between Catholics and Protestants, some built political careers based in part on the votes of fellow migrants. George Edwards, a former Texan who worked closely with the UAW leadership, held a number of political offices in Detroit and almost became mayor in 1949. New Mexico in the early 1950s had at least three southern-born members of the state senate. Arizona and Oregon also elected southerners in some number. California continued to show a special fondness for southern voices and southern styles of politics. In the 1960s, two of the state's congressmen and at least four members of the state legislature were whites of southern background. Congressman Chet Holifield hailed from Kentucky by way of Arkansas. He had moved to Los Angeles the same year McAdoo did and became involved in Democratic politics during the Depression. Elected to the House of Representatives in 1942, he served his working-class district in the suburbs south of Los Angeles until 1974. Bernie Sisk had grown up in Texas, moved west in the 1937 with the Dust Bowl migration, working and then starting a business in Fresno, and then moved into Democratic politics. In 1954, he won election in his San Joaquin Valley district partly by mobilizing the votes of his fellow "Okies." That was also the year that Jesse Unruh, destined to be the Big Daddy of the legislature from 1962 to 1968, won his first campaign. He built his political base the same way, door-belling through the Ingleside district of Los Angeles, a working-class area where perhaps 20 percent of the population would have thrilled to his southwestern accent and bootstrap stories of a hard childhood in the Texas Panhandle. Tom Carrell, Carlos Bee, and Floyd Wakefield, all of whom served with Unruh in the Assembly in the 1960s, represented districts (Sacramento, San Fernando Valley, South Gate) where former southerners were numerous enough to matter at election time.[11]

The white southern politicians who gained office in northern and western states covered a spectrum of viewpoints. Shuler stood with the Klan in the 1920s and extreme right-wing causes thereafter. Wakefield and Sisk were conservative Democrats. McAdoo was known as a moderate. Baker, a more consistent reformer, served on the board of the Carnegie Foundation during the 1930s and helped design the Myrdal study of American racism. Edwards held the left wing. Unruh was a liberal who took Lyndon Baines Johnson as his model and found his proudest accomplishment in the passage of the 1959 Unruh Civil Rights Act banning employment discrimination in California. There was, in short, no consistent southern perspective or southern interest in the work of the several generations of Democratic carpetbaggers, but their contributions mostly stand in sharp contrast to the other string of political activists identified with the white diaspora.

Spreading the Klan

For much the same reason that southerners found opportunities in the northern Democratic Party or in recording studios that were looking for "authentic" hillbilly singers, some took leadership roles in the Ku Klux Klan and in many of the subsequent movements that were committed to white racial privilege. In the world of white supremacy, no one could claim more authenticity than a white southerner. Only a fraction of migrants participated in these endeavors, but this became the most visible and weighty contribution diaspora whites would make to nonsouthern politics.

The rebirth of the Ku Klux Klan in 1915 was itself in a certain sense a diaspora story. The revival was inspired by the enormous popularity of *The Birth of a Nation*, the 1915 cinematic breakthrough film by an expatriate son of Kentucky, David W. Griffith. A Louisville store clerk turned actor, D. W. Griffith had spent several years with traveling theatrical companies before landing in New York in 1906. Two years later, tired of auditioning for small parts and trying to write plays, he accepted a job with Biograph, one of the little film companies that was just beginning to transform the world of entertainment. He spent six years cranking out one-reel films, ultimately some 400 of them. By 1914 he was in southern California, no longer affiliated with Biograph, making a film that was longer, more expensive, and more technically demanding than anything the New York company had supported. It was based on Thomas Dixon's 1905 novel, *The Clansman*, and when it was released the next year, *The Birth of a Nation* transformed the film industry while setting up the revival of the Invisible Empire.[12]

That autumn in Atlanta, William Joseph Simmons, a former Methodist preacher, conceived of a new fraternal organization that would memorialize the story that Griffith had brought to the screen. The new Ku Klux Klan grew slowly at first and mostly in Georgia and Alabama until 1920, when Simmons acquired the services of an Atlanta advertising agency run by Edward Y. Clarke and Elizabeth Tyler. The pair hired hundreds of recruiters (on commission) and sent them throughout the South and across the Mason-Dixon Line. Estimates of the numbers who joined during the next four years range well above 2 million, with two-thirds of the membership outside the South. Huge Klan organizations were built in Indiana, Ohio, Pennsylvania, Illinois, and Michigan. The West also responded to the Invisible Empire. Oregon elected a Klansman governor in 1922, as did Colorado in 1924, and there were pockets of Klan strength in California and Washington.[13]

Historians have poured over Klan membership lists and have developed some reasonably consistent profiles of the 1920s Klan. It is very clear that diaspora southerners did not dominate the movement in nonsouthern states. Robert Alan Goldberg has the best data, a membership list for the Denver Klavern, which he was able to match with state-of-birth information. This shows that former southerners comprised 15 percent of the initial Denver membership and 9.4 percent of later joiners. Goldberg and others conclude that the 1920s Klan was widely popular among all sorts of white Protestants, drawing upon urban as well as rural and small-town settings, a range of occupations, and the full spectrum of regional birthplaces.[14]

Southerners may have played a larger role in leadership positions than they did within the membership base, especially the early leadership. As the organization expanded beyond its southern foundation, it drew upon the recruiting talents of quite a few southerners, and they in turn found some of their key early support among expatriates from the region. Many of the Kleagles (recruiters) and lecturers hired by Clarke and Tyler to pioneer new territories were southerners. Upstate New York Klan activities were started by two Texans, Rev. Dr. Samuel H. Campbell and Rev. Basil E. Newton, who moved through the area setting up meetings in late 1922; a third organizer from Atlanta, Rev. John H. Moore, followed a few months later. Campbell, one of the national organization's featured lecturers, was also instrumental in setting up Klaverns in Illinois, including Chicago. Oregon was initially organized by southerners. Kleagle Brad Calloway from Houston made the initial foray in Portland in the summer of 1921, while Maj. Luther I. Powell, a native of Louisiana, set up Klaverns in the lumber towns of Medford, Klamath Falls, and Rosemont. Indiana, eventually to be the site of the largest and most politically powerful Klan operation of the 1920s, was also pioneered by a Kleagle arriving from the South, Joe Huffington of Texas.[15]

These groundbreakers sometimes worked their way into new states through contacts with expatriates and relied upon these networks as part of their initial structure of operations. Chapters of the Southern Society and the United Daughters of the Confederacy sometimes helped. So did at least one of the prominent expatriate fundamentalist churches. Bob Shuler's Trinity Methodist congregation in Los Angeles became a key component of the Klan movement in Southern California. *Bob Shuler's Magazine* became the principal media outlet of the Invisible Empire in the region, and more than one scholar has concluded that Shuler "probably did more to encourage the growth of the organization than any other single individual in the state of California."[16]

In Indiana, southern networking became even more important. When Joe Huffington crossed the Ohio River in the fall of 1920 with the title Kleagle and the promise of a $2.50 commission for every new member, he chose Evansville as the place to begin, assuming that river city with its strong ties to Kentucky would provide easy pickings. He was right, and there was a bonus: one of his recruits was a fellow Houston native named D. C. Stephenson who turned out to be the most effective organizer that the Klan of this era would find. A salesman, former typesetter, and former Socialist who had been part of the thriving radical movement in Oklahoma before World War I, Stephenson had served in the army in 1917 and 1918 and then moved to Indiana, looking for opportunities. He now had one. Relocating to Indianapolis, he started a newspaper, the *Fiery Cross*, hired organizers, and watched the membership surge. By July 1923, the Indiana operation had signed up 118,000 members, and Stephenson had secured for himself the title of Grand Dragon and was in charge of recruitment in all the neighboring midwest states. A year later, Indiana alone counted 300,000 Klansmen. Despite a falling-out with Atlanta headquarters and a split in the Indiana organization, the 1924 election season witnessed Stephenson's greatest triumph: first a Klan takeover of the Republican Party, then of the Indiana statehouse. Until he was brought down by a 1925 rape and suicide scandal, Stephenson was the most visible and probably most powerful Klansman in the country.[17]

By facilitating the expansion of the second Klan outside of the South, diaspora southerners like Stephenson were helping to precipitate one of the great political realignments of the twentieth century. But it was not the one they intended. The Klan did not last long as a potent force. It started to fall apart in 1925 amidst charges of theft and other scandals, then succumbed to an anti-Klan "backfire" that continued for decades. Historian David Chalmers uses that term to describe how the third Klan renaissance of the 1950s and 1960s actually helped the civil rights movement that it tried to destroy. The concept works just as well for the 1920s. As the Klan marched north with its frightening program of nativism, anti-Catholicism, and anti-Semitism as well as Negrophobia, it triggered a fierce counterreaction. Catholics organized to beat back the Klan-led attempts to abolish parochial school education and then joined with Jewish organizations and other threatened political groups in laying the foundations for the New Deal Democratic Party, a party that would draw its values and core constituents from the cities and turn against nativism and other forms of narrow intolerance.[18]

This backfire of metropolitanism responded to more than just the Klan. Immigration restriction laws passed in 1920 and 1924, the 18th Amendment and the traumatic imposition of prohibition on defiant urban publics, and a decade of anti-labor campaigns also provided reasons for political mobilization. But the men in white robes with their burning crosses and their legacy of secret terror were an immediate and palpable threat capable of crystallizing opposition that might otherwise have remained dormant. The Klan was the single most potent symbol that the forces of social liberalism and immigrant rights had to work with. Hooded and scary, bigoted beyond what had been the conventional boundaries of northern white Anglo-Saxon bigotry, the Klan in its excesses served ultimately to delegitimize the cause of white Protestant conservatism and empower the countermovement that would reorganize the Democratic Party and set up the New Deal.[19]

William Gibbs McAdoo's plan to become president was one of the first casualties of the reaction against the Klan. At the Democratic nominating convention held in New York City in the summer of 1924, the urban Catholic "wet" faction of the party demanded a strong statement denouncing the Klan and, failing to get it, blocked McAdoo's nomination in a 103-ballot marathon that the southern-born journalist Arthur Krock called "the snarling, cursing, tedious, tenuous, suicidal, homicidal rough-house in New York." It is perhaps interesting that the compromise candidate who in the end secured the 1924 nomination was another diaspora southerner, John W. Davis, a former West Virginia congressman and Wilson administration solicitor general who had headed a prominent Wall Street law firm and worked with New York's Democratic machine since 1921. The follow-up election was a disaster for the party, but not for its urban wing, which now took charge. In 1928, that wing was strong enough to nominate its champion, New York governor Al Smith, who became the first Catholic to lead the party. Although Smith lost badly in November, the Democrats would never again be led by their southern and rural elements. In 1932, the coalition that had been energized by the Klan threat would, with the help of a devastating economic crisis, secure the election of Franklin Roosevelt.[20]

The 1920s Klan had not been dominated by diaspora southerners, but it had depended upon them for early expansion and some of its leadership. With their help, an organization equipped with rituals and symbols designed to memorialize the Confederacy, southern-style chivalry, and white Protestant supremacy had surged across the Mason-Dixon Line and rearranged the politics of race, creating in the short run a new form of racial conservatism and in the long run setting up the alliances for a long era of new liberalism.

Giving Bigotry a Southern Face

The backfire lit against the Klan in the 1920s continued burning in the decades that followed. In the aftermath of the Klan era, organized bigotry would never again enjoy the same kind of power and legitimacy in northern and western states. Make no mistake, white racism and certain forms of nativism would remain as virulent as ever. It would be several decades before there were noticeable changes in the discourses of race. But starting in the 1930s, there would be new obstacles to the exercise of certain forms of racist behavior outside the South. Klan-type organizations openly dedicated to white supremacy or xenophobia would face opposition from much of the press; from mobilized liberal and left-wing groups; from African American, Jewish, and sometimes Catholic and mainstream Protestant organizations; and at times from legal authorities. Racially motivated mob violence would also be positioned differently in the political environment of the mid-twentieth century North. As noted in an earlier chapter, major press coverage of hate strikes and race riots of the 1940s no longer legitimated mob action by racist whites. The press and the forces of urban liberalism had started the turn against bigotry.

Diaspora whites played a complicated role in the northern and western racial politics of the 1930s, 40s, and 50s. Active in many of the racist organizations and violent clashes of the era, they accrued what was probably more blame than they actually deserved. Indeed, the symbol of the southerner as bigot would sometimes obscure the actions of other whites. That symbol also worked to the advantage of the forces of racial liberalism. It makes sense to examine this era of political re-figurings in some detail.

Hate politics in the 1930s took a variety of forms, some of which had nothing to do with white southerners. Father Coughlin's social justice movement, which appealed mostly to Catholics, and the German American Bund are examples. But other organizations, belonging to what historian Leo Ribuffo calls the "Old Christian Right," employed agendas — nativist Protestantism and white supremacy — that were familiar to conservative southern whites. These included the Silver Shirts, a fascist organization based in California; the Black Legion, a Klan spin-off strongest in Ohio, Indiana, and Michigan; the Kansas-based Defenders of the Christian Faith, led by the fiercely anti-Semitic fundamentalist preacher Gerald Winrod; and the projects of Gerald K. Smith, who tried to keep Huey Long's Share the Wealth movement alive after the Kingfish's assassination in 1935 and later found a home in Detroit preaching a mix of anti-Communism, anti-Semitism, and anti-Rooseveltism.[21]

Migrants from the South were said to be part of all of these organizations, especially the Black Legion, a secret society that practiced Negrophobia as well as nativism and bound its members in an oath to uphold the standards of "southern chivalry." Founded in the 1920s and reorganized in 1932, the Black Legion carried on the Klan's crusade against "all aliens, Negroes, Jews and cults and creeds believing in racial equality or owning allegiance to any foreign potentate." Using black robes instead of white ones and equipped with a para-military command structure, the Legion was also more violent, apparently, than the midwestern Klan had been.

Black Legionnaires committed a string of murders as well as arson, kidnappings, floggings, and beatings, most of which took place in Michigan between 1933 and 1936. Many of the victims were suspected Communists, including two men brutally murdered during the 1933 auto industry strikes. At least two of the victims were black, randomly chosen, said one of the killers, because the Legion death squad wanted to know "what it felt like to kill a nigger." The reign of terror finally came to light in May 1936 when Detroit police found the body of Charles Poole, an unemployed auto worker. A Catholic, Poole had been murdered because he allegedly beat and mistreated his young Protestant wife, whose brother-in-law, a Black Legionnaire, had set up the execution. The arrest of thirteen conspirators set off a wave of investigations by federal and local law enforcement agencies. It also woke up the press, which turned the Black Legion and its crimes into one of the big stories of 1936. Newspapers across the country

Detroit detectives show off confiscated robes, masks, and weapons belonging to the Black Legion. Before the Klan-linked organization was broken up in 1936, members had committed a string of murders and assaults in Ohio, Indiana, and Michigan. Newspaper reports claimed that most of the members were former southerners. (Walter P. Reuther Library, Wayne State University)

carried stories about the trial and surrounding investigations. The following year, Warner Brothers released a film about the terror cult starring Humphrey Bogart.[22]

It has never been clear how large the Black Legion membership was, nor are there the kinds of records that might permit a close analysis of the class and regional origins of those who joined. The press liked the number 135,000, almost certainly an exaggeration. Investigators uncovered some high-level connections to politicians, police departments, and Republican Party leaders. The mayor of Highland Park, a suburb of Detroit, was involved, as was the police chief and much of the police department of Pontiac, Michigan. The judge conducting the Pontiac investigation released the names of sixty-four city, county, and state officials. In Toledo, Akron, and Dayton, Ohio, there were also indications of police involvement.[23]

But the organization also attracted men of modest station, and many news reports insisted that white southerners were a significant part of the membership. A *New York Times* reporter described the typical member as an urban-shocked, farm-raised southerner, most likely from Tennessee. The *Detroit News* called the conspiracy something "straight from the heart of the Deep South." The *New York Post* singled out "automobile workers recruited from the South, especially from the benighted and impoverished regions of Kentucky, Tennessee, and Mississippi." Columnist Dorothy Thompson asked, "Who are these men?," then answered that they are from "all walks of life," but many are "Poor folk. Hill billies from the mountains of the South invading Detroit looking for work." The *Nation*'s reporter worked hard to implicate Henry Ford and state officials who served the auto chieftain but also assumed that the organization's rank and file had "emigrated from Klan regions to the north." Most of this was guesswork, but a sociologist studying southern whites in Detroit the following year backed it up. After interviewing both police investigators and a significant number of migrants, Elmer Akers concluded that the Detroit Black Legion units had largely consisted of former southerners. He noted a particular connection between the legion and J. Frank Norris's Temple Baptist Church with its large southern membership. He did not suggest that Norris was a member of the terror cult, but he talked to some Temple people, including an usher, who had been. A church leader also defended the organization, telling Akers that "people didn't understand the Black Legion. It was a much better organization than it was represented to be."[24]

It is possible that these assessments of southern involvement were exaggerated. Few of the men identified in various investigations of the Black Legion were former southerners. Southern whites were clearly involved in the movement, but, as we will see in the other incidents from this era, their visibility may have exceeded their actual representation. Journalists and sociologists had hillbillies on the mind in 1936. The white migration out of the South had recently become news, the funny pages were filled with *Li'l Abner* characters, *Tobacco Road* was one of the most popular plays on the traveling circuit, and it may be that southern migrants were simply more visible and not necessarily more responsible for the Black Legion than they had been for the midwestern Klan activities of the 1920s. In any case, that visibility was self-perpetuating. From now on, southern whites would be prime suspects in incidents involving race hatred and race violence.[25]

Southern whites played a real part in the hate strikes and white-against-black housing riots that occurred in northern and western cities in the 1940s and 1950s. Sociologist Katherine Archibald worked in a shipyard in Oakland, California, during World War II. She witnessed neither riots nor major violent clashes, but in her book *Wartime Shipyard*, she explored the tense racial dynamics of the yard, where about 20 percent of the workers were African American newcomers from the western South and another 20 percent were whites from the same region. The white southerners were in a delicate position, she observed. On the one hand, they were the subject of endless ridicule from California-born workers who delighted in jokes about alleged Okie stupidity and backwardness. On the other hand, Okies often took the lead in whites-only conversations about the "Negro problem." Vicious, uncompromising racism, she pointed out, was widespread, virtually universal among whites of all backgrounds in the shipyard, but the southerners spoke loudly about their hatreds and theories, drawing a sense of authority from their supposed special knowledge about how to handle black people. Talk of lynching was an Okie contribution to the racist discourse: "What you need round here," one former southerner counseled, "is a good old-fashioned lynching. Back in my home state we string a nigger up or shoot him down, every now and then, and that way we keep the rest of them quiet and respectful."[26]

Whether these white supremacists did more than talk is hard to say. There are indications that in some of the most important racial clashes of the 1940s and 1950s, diaspora whites were less active than contemporaries thought. That was the case in the 1943 Detroit race riot. Even before the bullets stopped flying, Detroit's officials and newspapers had opened up a fierce debate about who instigated the deadly conflagration and why. The police department and many conservatives blamed "lawless Negro hoodlums" and "militant" black leaders for the violence, but others, including Democratic mayor Edward J. Jeffries, pointed to southern white migrants and their background of bigotry. A *Detroit News* columnist clarified the charge, claiming that "Southern whites have come here in vast numbers, bringing with them their Jim Crow notions of the Negro." Walter White and Thurgood Marshall of the NAACP flew into Detroit, assembled a press conference, and called for an investigation into Klan activities, joined by R. J. Thomas, president of the UAW. Rev. Claude Williams, the CIO's favorite Presbyterian minister and a white migrant himself from Arkansas, blamed his fellow white southerners for much of the violence and told the same press conference that they were easy "prey of the intolerance groups" and fanatical preachers like J. Frank Norris. Similar assessments came from the city's two African American newspapers.[27]

But it may not be true. Historians Dominic Capeci and Martha Wilkerson have examined the files of the ninety-six white men arrested during the Detroit riots and found only one with a southern birthplace. Most were born in Michigan, half had non-Anglo-Saxon names, and 31 percent were Italian or Polish Americans. In a smaller sample of those charged with felonies, 70 percent were

Catholics. Some southern whites were clearly involved, but if the arrest records mean anything, the gangs that attacked and beat black pedestrians, pulled passengers off streetcars, and shot up black neighborhoods in July 1943 were composed mostly of ethnic whites and Michigan natives. Other recent studies also fail to confirm the story that southern white migrants took a leading role in racial disturbances. Arnold Hirsch looked at the arrest records for five of the housing riots that took place in Chicago between 1947 and 1957 and found few Anglo-Saxon names. Thomas Sugrue examined Detroit housing confrontations of the early 1950s and concluded that the role of southern whites was "greatly exaggerated."[28]

Years earlier, Lewis Killian had also questioned the assumption that white migrants were leading hate strikes and inflaming racial politics. In his 1949 dissertation on southern whites in Chicago, the Georgia-born investigator noted that statements about the activities of the migrants were based on a priori assumptions and had never been closely studied. He argued that southern white migrants were in fact changing behaviors and adopting what he described as northern urban norms. Many of the southerners he spoke with maintained that they had taken a "when in Rome" approach to racial relations, accepting the fact that they would have to share bus seats, workplaces, and some other spaces with African Americans, reconciling to the fact that black people in Chicago had more rights and power than in the South. "There's nothing you can do about the way the niggers are up here," a southern woman who had lived in Chicago for two decades explained. "We're up here in their country and we can't do anything. We have to do what these people up here do, even if we don't like it." Killian stressed that for the most part, attitudes were not changing and that regret and bitterness lurked behind these answers, but he felt that most migrants had learned to operate within the northern pattern of race relations with its "private, informal, and indirect techniques of discrimination."[29]

His second kind of evidence was potentially more convincing. The Near West Side as he studied it in 1947 and 1948 was a changing neighborhood. House by house, street by street, African Americans were moving in and doing so without serious violence. Comparing the peaceful transition of the Near West Side with the terrorism in neighborhoods on the Near North Side, Englewood, and parts of the South Side where Catholics predominated, he challenged the notion that the white migrant was the "instigator of racial conflict" or "an agent for the diffusion of southern patterns of Negro-white relations."[30]

Whether or not Killian was right about changing racial mores of former migrants, one of his points is worth thinking about. The reputation of the southern white bigot was probably bigger than his actual contribution to northern and western hate politics. Why? Perhaps because there was something useful about this figure, the violent racist from Dixie. His presence enabled the productive fiction that there were indeed northern racial norms and that the "race problem" was actually a southern problem. It was not a deliberate fiction. There are no indications that those who fixated on southern whites as the source of racial tension knew that the image was exaggerated, but many of the politicians, civil rights leaders, journalists, and union officials who circulated the charge had reasons for wanting it to be true. It helped maintain the tenuous but critical alliances underpinning the new project of racial liberalism.

Those alliances were at work in Detroit in the days after the 1943 riot when Walter White, R. J. Thomas, Mayor Jeffries, Claude Williams, and other liberals and leftists hoped that the Klan and southern whites would take the blame for the riot. The claim served several purposes. For Jeffries, a centrist Democrat who had been elected with African American and white ethnic working-class votes and who wanted most of all to calm the city, focus on white outsiders helped him avoid stepping on more important toes. That was also the case for Thomas, head of the UAW. The union was a mass of contradictions. Its leftist leadership had made a commitment to racial integration but faced endless resistance from rank-and-file whites, many of whom were first- and second-generation Poles and Italians and from various other European backgrounds. For union leaders who were trying to lead working-class whites into coalitions with the black community, any fiction that hid the enmity between these populations was useful.[31]

African American leaders had different reasons for fixing on the figure of the white southerner. Knowing only too well what horrors white southerners were capable of, it was natural that black migrants would be monitoring their white counterparts. Indeed, one of the earliest known newspaper references to the white diaspora is found in a 1919 edition of the *Independent Clarion*, an African American weekly published in St. Louis. "Southern Whites Going North Too," ran the headline, followed by the subhead "Who is Paying Their Transportation? No Immigration Agent Have been Arrested for Pursuading Them to Leave The South." The article then speculated on the size of the World War I white migration, groused that many were getting prime jobs as "salesmen, managers, agents," and also said that white southerners were finding their way into media organizations, becoming "some of the best writers on newspapers of the north and east."[32]

The monitoring never stopped, and in the black press and also in fiction the white migrant was often depicted as the most dangerous of the racists that African Americans contended with in northern and western settings. Chester Himes implied that in his 1944 novel, *If He Hollers Let Him Go*, about an African American man crushed by a thousand indignities while working in a Los Angeles shipyard. His chief tormentor is a white woman from Arkansas, a fellow worker who falsely accuses him of rape.[33]

Himes was not suggesting that southern whites were the only racists, but one sometimes gets that impression from the way that black journalists flagged southerners as pivotal figures in the evolving patterns of northern racial relations. In a 1944 *Negro Digest* article, Roi Ottley told the story of a "professional Southerner" disrupting a New York nightclub "damning Negroes" and demanding that the proprietor eject Ottley. Instead, two white sailors "jostled the Dixie hot-head toward the door and said bluntly: 'Look, chum, this stuff doesn't go here. This is New York.'" A front-page article in the 1 January 1949 *Michigan Chronicle* used the same device, relating how a "white southern passenger" on a Detroit bus tried "to practice his native Jim-Crowism on a Negro rider" but was thwarted by "roused white passengers" who "informed him that his tactics were unwanted." "The Southerner made a hasty exit from the bus," prompting the *Chronicle* to headline the piece "Next Stop!! All Jim Crow Riders Scram."[34]

In these stories, black journalists were using the figure of the white migrant to advance an extremely optimistic proposition about the direction of northern race relations. The implication was that northern-born whites *were* different, that it was the "professional southerner" who caused the real trouble. Whether this was genuinely believed or just a strategic formulation is not clear, but as with the other allies in the new civil rights coalition, it is evident that African American leaders had found a use for the white migrants.[35]

These evaluations provide a starting point for assessing the impact of the white diaspora on the politics of this era. The bigotry politics that some migrants pursued (and for which others were perhaps disproportionately blamed) seems to have done little to advance the purported cause during the middle decades of the twentieth century. Hate projects repeatedly failed. The Black Legion episode was more notable for fueling a "Brown Scare" backlash against Fascist and xenophobic organizations than for any lasting gains made by the xenophobic Right. And the World War II hate strikes won little for the opponents of African American progress. Instead, it was the cause of civil rights that advanced as the major northern media and the federal government began to rally against extreme forms of racism and move slowly toward formulas of racial justice. That southern whites were so visibly tied to this sequence of events helped the liberals more than the segregationists. An easy target for African Americans and white liberals and labor leaders who wanted to pull complicated constituencies through the civil rights turn, the white diaspora may have, in a very backhanded way, actually helped the delicate project of leveraging the nation toward a more equal framework of race and rights.

Southernizing White Working-Class Conservatism

It would be different in the 1960s, 70s, and 80s. During the decades that followed the civil rights breakthroughs, diaspora whites would contribute meaningfully to the reinvigoration and reformulation of American conservatism. Unlike the earlier episodes, this would be no losing cause. The movements that diaspora whites aided in the last third of the twentieth century would bring not only political victories but also a growing sense of legitimacy and importance for white expatriates from the South. By the mid-1970s, some commentators would claim that America was starting to look and sound and act and vote and worship like the South, that America was in the process of becoming southernized.

John Egerton made that claim in a 1974 book entitled *The Americanization of Dixie: The Southernization of America*. He argued that regional differences were collapsing as the new South adjusted to the end of Jim Crow. At the same time, Egerton noted that southern white commercial, religious, and political forms had taken root in the North and that evangelical religion, stock car racing, barbeque stands, country music, and the kind of politics that George Wallace represented had spread widely beyond the southern homeland.[36]

The "Southernization of America"? Probably not. What Egerton and other journalists were noticing was more limited: symbols of southernization that took hold mostly within the white working class. But the effects were important. Those southern inputs helped shape a new form of conservatism that changed the balance of power in American politics. The emergence of white working-class and lower-middle-class conservatism has been one of the signal political developments of the last forty years, the key to important elections and the legitimizing force behind the revitalization of the conservative movement in America.[37]

Conservatism had endured three difficult decades after 1932, unable to counter the New Deal charge that it belonged to the rich and that it threatened ordinary working Americans. The New Deal had not made all working-class Americans into liberals, but it had hooked so many of the leadership structures of modest-income Americans into the Democratic Party that blue-collar conservatism had few effective voices. Unions, ethnic political organizations, many of the archdioceses of the Catholic Church, and big city party machinery all were part of the New Deal order, the complex of institutions and voter alignments that from the 1930s through the 1960s made the Democratic Party usually dominant in Congress and mostly in control of the presidency while making liberalism the touchstone for domestic policy initiatives even under Republican presidents. White working-class constituents had never voted uniformly Democratic, still less with the liberal wing of the party. There had been defections that had helped Cold War Republicans gain office and defections that had put conservative anti-integration regimes into power in various cities, but these were variations on a central tendency. Right up to 1964, most Americans associated conservatism with wealth and privilege and looked to the northern white working-class to anchor the Democratic Party.[38]

The development of new forms of white working-class conservatism derived most fundamentally from the reconstructions of racial opportunity and politics that had been enabled by the black diaspora. Most scholars agree that the increasing commitment to civil rights by the northern Democratic Party leadership was the key link in the "chain reaction" that broke apart the New Deal order and paved the way for America's right turn. But if the black diaspora was central to these changes, the white diaspora contributed as well, providing not the motive for the surge of white working-class conservatism but ideas, symbols, and leaders that would give it a particular shape. Also important was the fact that two southern-origin institutions—country music and evangelical Protestantism—had by the late 1960s established huge followings among modest-income white Americans in the North and West, and both were becoming explicitly political and explicitly conservative.[39]

When George Wallace stepped off the plane in Milwaukee in March 1964, explaining that he had come to Wisconsin to challenge Lyndon Johnson's claim to the Democratic presidential nomination in that state, few in the press took him seriously. The Alabama governor was just another southern segregationist governor of the sort that northerners, white as well as black, had disparaged for decades. White southern liberals had enough trouble gaining credibility north of the Mason-Dixon Line. Lyndon Johnson, who had inherited the presidency from John F. Kennedy just five months earlier, was about to distinguish himself as the first southern-born nominee of either major party since John Davis in 1924. As a segregationist governor, Wallace was an alien of a still higher order. Famous for his cry "Segregation today, segregation tomorrow, segregation forever," he had been earning headlines as the most colorful and vehement of the governors standing in the way of court-ordered integration. This made him anathema to northern Republicans and Democrats alike. *Time* magazine had recently featured the governor on its cover but had mentioned only briefly his plans to run for president. Why worry? "Wallace sounds like an ordinary Alabama redneck," the cover article emphasized in its lead paragraphs, noting later that he "is in fact a smart, capable lawyer who has in many ways been a first-rate Governor."[40]

Wallace, of course, surprised everyone. It turned out that a lot of Wisconsin residents would vote for a southern segregationist. He shocked the confident Johnson camp by peeling off 34 percent of the Wisconsin primary vote. He followed that with a 30 percent tally in Indiana and 43 percent in Maryland. Johnson was not really in trouble. The president easily won renomination and went on to record a thunderous victory over Republican Barry Goldwater. But Wallace had started something in 1964 that would gather more and more momentum. Over the next eight years, his presidential campaigns would help break the back of the Democratic Party. Wallace was not the underlying reason that the party came apart—that had to do more fundamentally with battles over racial reconstruction and the ravages of an unpopular war in southeast Asia—but the Wallace campaigns helped give a particular shape to the divisions.[41]

Wallace exposed and then helped to institutionalize what journalists were soon calling the northern "backlash." The backlash had been there all along, showing up in city-by-city resistance to housing integration and in local electoral campaigns by politicians who played on white fears of African American advances. But Wallace's campaign crystallized these disparate efforts into a political force of national significance and provided a new demographic and ideological framework. Where it had not been emphasized before, it would now become axiomatic that this was a largely working-class movement acting in defiance of labor leadership. Where working-class conservatism had before seemed to contradict class interests, Wallace supplied an attractive logic of white working-class consciousness.

It was, says historian Dan Carter, a new form of conservatism, new at least to the North and West. The opposition to civil rights was not the new element, nor the fervent anti-Communism. Barry Goldwater also campaigned in 1964 on those planks but had trouble reaching blue-collar voters. Goldwater in particular and Republicans in general seemed unable to transcend their pinstripe suits. They could talk about anti-Communism, law and order, and the right of property owners to resist neighborhood integration, but they lost working-class voters on labor, taxation, and safety-net issues. Wallace, on the other hand, spoke a language of class and reform that had been used by southern Democrats since the turn of the century. Heir to the South's neo-populist tradition, he brought north a syntax that mixed social conservatism with elite bashing and at least a semblance of economic liberalism. Attacking "pointy-headed professors" and "bearded bureaucrats" in the same breath with Communists and Martin Luther King, he declared for the "little people," the "average man on the street," and the "working man" in terms that Republicans could not yet match. His promises crossed the boundaries conventional in northern politics. He sounded like a Republican on welfare, race, and taxes, a Democrat on social security and union rights, and a southerner on the centrality of God-fearing religion. "The genius of George Wallace," Carter writes, "lay in his ability to link traditional conservatism to an earthy language that voiced powerful cultural beliefs and symbols with a much broader appeal."[42]

His segregationist populism found a gap that had opened up between the two major party formations. By the 1960s, the leaders of the northern Democratic Party and most of the labor movement were committed to a civil rights agenda and were not about to carry the backlash banner. Wallace stepped into the vacuum. His statements echoed many of the instincts of that segment of blue-collar whites who felt left behind by the changing agendas of northern liberalism. It was not a perfect marriage, as the electoral tallies made clear. The governor never quite understood his northern following and had to be careful about references to wops, kikes, and the pope. Coming from a right-to-work state, his labor credentials were less than perfect, as trade union liberals pointed out endlessly. And in the end, his support was never as broad as its potential. Homegrown backlash politicians, like Louise Day Hicks of Boston, Sam Yorty in Los Angeles, and Frank Rizzo in Philadelphia, did much better with the same constituencies, and ultimately so did the Republicans, once they understood where the road led. Richard Nixon would triumph with his "Silent Majority" strategy, and ex-Democrat Ronald Reagan would turn conservative populism into the pivotal ideological construction of the late twentieth century. But Wallace had shown the way. It had taken a southerner to rearrange the political language of class and race and show that working-class northerners would respond to the same mix of racism and cultural anti-elitism that had long won the votes of white plainfolks in the South.[43]

Diaspora southerners played an important role in the Wallace campaigns, although as in earlier episodes of bigotry politics, they were only part of the story. It is hard to say very much about the constituency for Wallace's brief northern invasion in 1964. Former southerners were doubtless involved, but the press was more interested in signs that the fiery governor had caught the ear of "ethnic" voters, as he did at Milwaukee's Serbian Memorial Hall where, to the delight of the watching media, a large crowd belted out a rousing chorus of "Dixie" in Polish and Serbian accents. It was also reported that many of his Wisconsin votes came from suburban Republicans using crossover procedures to disrupt the Democratic Party. In the Indiana race, very casual assessments suggest that some Wallace votes came from former southerners, some from angry blue-collar Catholics.[44]

Wallace ran a second time for president in 1968, this time as a third-party candidate under the banner of the American Independent Party. It was a complicated campaign that, like most third-party efforts, fell apart at the end as supporters, sensing the inevitable, had to choose whether to stick with the losing cause or help decide if Richard Nixon or Hubert Humphrey would lead the country. Wallace ended up with 13.3 percent of the nationwide vote and 45 electoral votes, having won five states in the Deep South. Outside of the South, only 8 percent of voters had checked his name, despite polls that a few months earlier had ranged much higher.

How many of the 4,820,543 Wallace voters in nonsouthern states were former migrants is impossible to say. One poll said 10 percent, but it involved a tiny sample that cannot be considered reliable. A number of political analysts, including Samuel Lubell and Kevin Phillips, were sure that former southerners voted disproportionately for Wallace based on the fact that he achieved some of his highest vote totals in communities that were known to have significant southern-born populations. In the Los Angeles area, Wallace piled up his highest percentage in Bell Gardens, long thought of as an Okie suburb. The same was true in northern California, where the blue-collar town of San Pablo, across the bay from San Francisco and home to large numbers of former Oklahomans, Texans, and Arkansans, gave the governor his best totals. Receiving just under 12 percent of the statewide vote in California, he earned 22 percent of San Pablo's presidential ballots. Southerners were an important population element in Akron, Ohio, which gave Wallace 20 percent of its vote, and in Cairo, Illinois, where he won 30 percent. The governor also did well in Ohio's Miami Valley cities and in the white working-class suburbs of Detroit, like Warren and Taylor, where former southerners had settled in some numbers. It makes sense that Wallace would attract support from some who shared his background. Beyond the ideological factors, the governor appealed to former southerners' sense of regional pride. Lubell interviewed a self-described "West Virginia mountain boy" who worked as a car mechanic in Akron and campaigned vigorously for the Alabaman mostly because of regional affinity. The governor campaigned in a style that was familiar: "He speaks flat out like us."[45]

Indeed, migrant support extended beyond voting. Former southerners participated at every level of the campaign apparatus in the nonsouthern states, and sometimes, as had happened with the Klan in the 1920s, Wallace's staff utilized networks of former migrants to start the campaign organizations. The task of launching a third party and gaining access to the ballot in all fifty states was enormously complicated. Many states required tens or even hundreds of thousands of voters to re-register as members of the American Independent Party. Activists willing and able to take on the task of circulating petitions and building the new party were drawn in part from extremist organizations of the Far Right, including the John Birch Society and the Liberty Lobby. Although Robert Welch, the millionaire candy manufacturer who ran the John Birch Society from Belmont, Massachusetts, was himself a diaspora North Carolinian, these organizations were not known to have any particular strength among relocated southerners. But Wallace also drew activists from the networks of the religious right, including churches aligned with Dr. Frederick Schwarz's Christian Anti-Communism Crusade and the radio followers of Rev. Billy James Hargis's, whose Christian Crusade broadcasts were heard on more than 600 stations across the country. And these networks did involve substantial numbers of diaspora southerners.

Still other Wallace campaign activists were brand-new to political action, and if the patterns found in the Detroit area hold up elsewhere, many of these eager novices were of southern background. Sociologist James Canfield studied the Wallace organization in the suburbs surrounding Detroit in 1968, interviewing eighty-one campaign workers, men and women who had circulated petitions to get the American Independent Party on the ballot and had distributed literature and performed other campaign tasks leading up to the election. Forty-one of these campaign workers were former southerners, slightly more than half of the full sample. This was far above the representation of southerners in these communities and far above the southern contribution to the November vote. He found differences in the political background and motivations of the southerners versus the Michigan-born campaign activists. The latter were more experienced and held views that suggest ties to extremist anti-Communist and anti-tax organizations. The southerners were most likely to be former Democrats, and this was often their first activist experience. The Canfield study lends support to the idea that the Wallace campaign, like some earlier versions of bigotry politics, relied substantially on networks of former southerners and might not have been able to develop a credible national presence without them.[46]

But this is not the whole story. While there is evidence that southerners played key roles in his campaigns and voted for him in disproportionate numbers, the great bulk of Wallace's northern votes came from other sources. This is quickly evident in surveys that accompanied the 1968 campaign. In addition to the small University of Michigan sample that indicated that 90 percent of Wallace's northern and western votes came from nonsoutherners, Seymour Martin Lipset and Earl Raab analyzed a collection of local and national surveys and concluded that Wallace enjoyed significant support from a couple of sectors of the population. His support among white-collar class voters was thin, much of it coming from John Birch Society members and other extreme Right elements.

George Wallace enjoyed considerable support in the white suburbs and smaller cities of Michigan. Note the "Vote for Wallace" T-shirt at this 1971 anti-busing demonstration in Pontiac, Michigan. (Walter P. Reuther Library, Wayne State University)

His major base consisted of working-class whites, and within that strata former southerners were outnumbered by northern-born Protestants and Catholics.

Wallace's strength among union members was the big surprise. A Gallup poll taken two months before the election suggested that 25 percent of union members supported the Alabaman, although subsequent efforts by the major unions seem to have ultimately won some of those votes for Hubert Humphrey. Location also mattered. Both pre-election polls and post-election analysis confirmed that Wallace was most popular in white neighborhoods located very near black neighborhoods, so-called barrier zones where residents felt immediately threatened by pressures for housing and school integration. These were the areas where Wallace broke through the religious concerns and attracted Catholic support. In barrier neighborhoods in Newark, Philadelphia, Milwaukee, and parts of New York City, Catholics of Italian, Polish, and Irish ancestry provided most of the Wallace votes. One of the best surveys comes from Gary, Indiana, a steel city where many of the whites were of Polish ancestry and where the rapidly expanding African American population had recently elected Richard Hatcher mayor. One month before the 1968 election, 38 percent of a sample of white working-class Gary residents said they planned to vote for George Wallace.[47]

Wallace's support thus extended far beyond the southern migrant population. By the same token, it is important to understand that most former southerners had nothing to do with the Wallace campaigns. In the University of Michigan sample (again, too small to fully credit), former southerners gave the most votes to Hubert Humphrey, followed by Richard Nixon, while Wallace received only 14 percent. The surveys cited earlier in this chapter also make it clear that former southerners were spread across the political spectrum with only a minority holding the kinds of views expressed by Wallace and his supporters.[48]

But the diaspora had been important, probably critical. A southern politician had galvanized a potent constituency of angry families using a language of militant working-class whiteness while relying on cadres of diaspora migrants to build the movement. He and they had built a bridge that would in the years to come carry many blue-collar northerners away from the Democratic Party and into a pivotal position between the two great parties.

White Working Man's Blues

The Wallace movement was only one of the forces helping to shape new patterns of conservatism among working-class whites in the North and West. Important too was the changing tone and expanded reach of country music. In the 1960s, county music executed a full makeover, turning itself into a politicized entertainment medium with a target audience of lower-middle-income white Americans. It also adopted an explicit message of tough-guy masculinity and love-it-or-leave-it patriotism. All of this was part of an industry survival strategy to counter the challenge of youth market rock and roll, but it had implications that went far beyond the music business.

Rock had hit the music world like an earthquake in the mid-1950s. Country music was present at the birth of the new genre and for a time benefited from it. Many of the breakthrough white artists (Bill Haley, Elvis Presley, Carl Perkins, Buddy Holly, Jerry Lee Lewis)—those who picked up the rhythm and blues sound from the African American artists who invented it and then turned it into something that millions of young white Americans would buy—got their start in country music. And for a time, Nashville profited by cross-marketing their hits. But as the enormous buying power of young rock-obsessed consumers became evident in the late 1950s, the world of country music began to contract. Record companies retooled and dumped recording contracts, performance venues disappeared, and, most tellingly, radio stations reformatted for the youth market. Country music, which had expanded its reach in the 1940s and early 1950s, now faced what every book on country music history calls the "Rock 'n' Roll Crisis."[49]

It met the challenge through a deliberate process of redefinition that had significant consequences for the cultural politics of the 1960s and 1970s. In 1958, industry professionals launched the Country Music Association and began a decade-long effort to reclaim the market by convincing radio station owners that country music was still viable and could bring in audiences and sponsors. The campaign succeeded in increasing the number of full-time country music stations from just 81 in 1961 to 752 in 1972 and stations with a part-country format from 1,377 to 1,784. The sales pitch involved careful efforts to define country music and its audience. There were two sides to the redefinition. On one side, it meant getting rid of the hillbilly and cowboy associations that had long been part of the genre. The Country Music Association would dress up the music and get it out of the hills. On the other side, the message was that this was emphatically not rock and roll: it belonged to the adult market, not the youth market; it appealed to stable families, not wild kids; it had nothing to do with black people or social change; this was a music rooted in heart-of-America traditionalism.[50]

Richard Peterson and Paul Di Maggio have examined the shifting audience for country music during this 1960s transition in their article "From Region to Class, the Changing Locus of Country Music." By the end of the decade, the industry claimed that its audience was no longer principally southern and that two-thirds of record sales occurred in nonsouthern markets. Listener surveys revealed that country music appealed largely to whites in middle-age range, twenty-five to forty-nine, with few younger listeners. And the audience was largely blue-collar families—especially the skilled and semiskilled sectors—with mid-range incomes and modest educations. In the North, former southerners accounted for a vigorous portion of this market, thus approximating the start-up role they played in the Wallace crusades. But the product had spread far beyond that base. Country music had also become popular in ethnic neighborhoods, showing up in all sorts of blue-collar taverns where the records of Johnny Cash, Marty Robbins, and Loretta Lynn now competed with Frank Sinatra for jukebox dimes.

Di Maggio surveyed the country music club scene around Philadelphia in the early 1970s and found that it "does not depend on southern migrants." The sixty clubs that featured country music were mostly located in the suburbs and mostly were "run by Philadelphia-born men of the same ethnic background as the neighborhood," meaning that many were Italian or Irish Americans. So were many of the musicians, 42 percent of whom were natives of the Philadelphia area. Southern whites were active as patrons and comprised 23 percent of his sample of club musicians but in no sense dominated the market. Country music was not the only choice of blue-collar whites — indeed, "easy listening" pop music remained more popular with the same age and occupational strata — but country music had executed a decisive shift and now had found a blue-collar base that included many with no ancestral ties to the South.[51]

This expanded blue-collar appeal had been made possible by some significant changes in the look and sound of 1960s country music. Music historians today have few kind words for what is called the "Nashville Sound" of that era, arguing that industry executives drained much of the country out of country music in their effort to create a smooth pop style that would sell widely. The move was deliberate, almost drastic. Nashville studios threw out their fiddles and steel guitars and brought in pianos and violins. Coats and ties and chiffon dresses replaced the cowboy gear of earlier years, and high-pitched nasal voices gave way to open-throat singing that appealed to those not raised in the South. The rough-edged sounds of honky-tonk-style country music were gone. The model now was a singer like Bobby Bare, Marty Robbins, or Glen Campbell who could take a song up the country music charts and cross over into the bigger market of standard pop.[52]

Song symbolism was also changing. To broaden their markets, Nashville songsmiths needed to adjust the regional and rural imagery that had been so basic to earlier generations of the music. Tennessee waltzes and songs about green mountain homes still found their way into the playlists of the 1960s, but most of the material utilized contemporary themes and unspecific settings, although cities, when referenced, remained dangerous, lonely, and alien places. Unwilling to fully leave the country, songwriters seemed to find in automotive culture a meeting place between rural-origin traditional audiences and the newer urban working-class country music fans. Cars and trucks replaced horses and locomotives as the central icons of the country song. Tying into the car mechanics and stock-car-racing mania that also swept northward during these decades, country song writers elevated long-haul trucking to cult status. The truck driver would become one of the heroes of the 1960s and 1970s country song, perhaps because he brought rural and urban symbolism together in a comfortable compromise. An eighteen-wheel cowboy, master of his own fate, he roamed the wide open spaces in song legend, managing the machinery of modern life without losing independence.[53]

Other elements needed less adjustment. Country music has always been about everyday people and their everyday problems. A largely literary medium, instrumentation and rhythm usually matter less than words and drama. Sometimes jokingly called "three-minute soap operas," country song texts most often fixed upon issues of love, family, morality, and honor — commonplace themes that easily resonated in many white working-class households. They did so within a particular race, class, and gender nexus that likewise needed little adjustment.

Race has always been and remains today an implicit part of country music's marketing and appeal. Since its commercial inception, this had been understood as white people's music, however much it borrowed from black musical traditions. In the 1960s, the racial marking remained very apparent as Nashville positioned itself against the racially integrated imagery and personnel of rock and roll and as George Wallace and other segregationist politicians claimed country music for the backlash cause. Also by tradition, this was common people's music, having long employed symbols keyed to broad audiences of southern whites. Artists presented themselves as "plain folks," down-home and unpretentious, while song texts pressed the message with frequent references to humble origins and dangerous and demanding work settings (especially trucks and coal mines) and occasional swipes at the silver spoon crowd. So too gender, or rather masculinity, was an inescapable theme, arguably *the* central theme of country music. The endless sad songs about broken romances; the loser songs about convicts, ramblers, and fleeing lovers regretting life's wrong turns; even the songs about mama and honky-tonk angels (the usual female personas) in some manner almost always problematized the male and his life choices.[54]

Much of this came together in a pointed way in the late 1960s and served to give the medium a particular political reputation that meshed with the new forces of white working-class conservatism. Usually, country music lends itself to a range of political expression. In the early years of the medium and again after the mid-1970s, some songs and artists supported liberal or even radical views, but rarely in the late 1960s and early 1970s. In those years, country music provided the soundtrack for the revolt of the Silent Majority.[55]

Patriotism was the cardinal issue around which country music's political identity was reorganized. The racial politics of the era were handled for the most part subtextually, although an occasional song like Guy Drake's 1970 hit "Welfare Cadillac Blues" put some of it into words. There was nothing euphemistic about the way the industry responded as the Vietnam War heated up. With almost a singular voice, country music defended American involvement in Vietnam and beyond that an image of an "old-fashioned" patriotic Americanism. Historian Melton McLaurin has tracked the flood of flag-waving songs that climbed the country music charts beginning in 1965, among them Johnny Wright's "Hello, VietNam" and "Keep the Flag Flying," Dave Dudley's "What We're Fighting For," Barry Sandler's "Ballad of the Green Berets,"

Loretta Lynn's "Dear Uncle Sam," Marty Robbins's "Private Wilson White," Bonnie Guitar's "The Tallest Tree," Autry Inmans's "Ballad of Two Brothers," and Nancy Ames's "He Wore a Green Beret." Another stream struck back at antiwar protests and other challenges to rock-ribbed values. When Tom T. Hall recorded "Mama, Tell Them What We're Fighting For," Ernest Tubb answered with "It's for God, Country and You Mom," then followed with two others: "It's America" and "Love It or Leave It." Protesters were also the target in Johnny Sea's "Day of Decision," Bobby Bare's "God Bless America Again," Stonewall Jackson's "The Minutemen Are Turning in their Graves," Bill Anderson's "Where Have All the Heroes Gone?," and Terry Nelson's "Battle Hymn of Lt. Calley." Not until 1970 was there any sort of break in "country music's patriotic front." That year, Johnny Cash asked carefully "What Is Truth?," but even then an actual protest song, "When You Gonna Bring Our Soldiers Home?," by Skeeter Davis, failed to make country station playlists.[56]

With these and other compositions of the late 1960s and early 1970s, country music marked out a politics of patriotism and traditionalism that helped define the emerging force of blue-collar conservatism. Can a popular media actually play such a role? These are just songs, some critics will say, and who knows what they meant to audiences? But they were not just songs. Country music of this era was surrounded by political commentary. DJs, artists, journalists, and music-buying publics recognized that music was a prime battleground for the epic conflicts of the Vietnam era. Politicians did as well. Many of the medium's biggest stars signed up to help Wallace in 1968, performing with the governor as he crisscrossed the country. Nashville's "Music Row was practically a battlefield command post for George Wallace," observed journalist Paul Hemphill, who found also a few Nixon supporters but nary a star who publicly supported Hubert Humphrey. In the years that followed, Republicans moved to take over that command post. Repeatedly (and awkwardly) declaring his fondness for country music, President Nixon courted musicians and Nashville executives, knowing that these entertainers would help secure the new voting blocs that Republicans counted on, working-class whites in the South and working-class whites outside the South.[57]

The artist who perhaps best represented the new face and political significance of country music was a California-born son of the diaspora named Merle Haggard. Born near Bakersfield in 1937, not long after his parents migrated from Oklahoma, Haggard had the kind of "out-of-the-dirt" background that country music publicists dream about. His father died when he was nine, and his hardworking mother, as he later sang in "Mama Tried," did her best. Haggard grew up rough, wild, and beyond the law, paying for it with two years in San Quentin prison. Out of all that came the song material of a lifetime. Released from the "Q" in 1960, Haggard returned to Bakersfield and picked up the guitar that had almost made him a living before his prison venture.[58]

California had its own fertile crescent of country music, and Bakersfield was the center of it. The Okie migration had piled up thousands of country music consumers in that midsized city, and despite the ravages of rock and roll elsewhere, a thriving complex of clubs, a little record label, and a daytime TV show had kept Bakersfield safe for country music through the 1950s. In the early 1960s, the scene turned hot as local boys Wynn Stewart and Buck Owens connected with a string of hit records. The Texas-born Owens then set up a studio and launched his own record label and music publishing company while attracting to Bakersfield a small army of musicians and industry professionals. By the end of the decade, the city would claim five studios, three record labels, two booking agencies, and ten music publishing companies—and journalists were calling it "Nashville West."[59]

Haggard and another young diaspora musician, Glen Campbell, found their footing in that setting. Campbell, who had come to California from Arkansas, signed with Capitol Records in 1962, produced several modest records, and then hit a home run in 1967 with "Gentle on My Mind," using the smooth country pop formula that Nashville had developed. A crossover specialist, his records over the next several years dominated pop as well as country charts, winning him a prime-time network television program and helping country music widen its mainstream appeal.[60]

Haggard took a different road. Unlike the baby-faced Campbell, there was nothing soft or smooth about Merle. He started his career singing about broken hearts, fugitives, and convicts, backed by a whining steel guitar that labeled him a "hard country" traditionalist. Then he began exploring themes of white poverty and pride in compositions that drew on his family's Dust Bowl migrant heritage ("Hungry Eyes" and "I Take a Lot of Pride in What I Am"). By 1968, he was one of the biggest names in the business and ready for a more provocative turn. In a sequence of songs that earned him international attention, he took up the banner of white working-class conservatism. The first, "Workin' Man Blues," plays with class identity. With a quick aside about welfare ("That's one place I won't be"), the song builds a blues anthem around hard work, male responsibilities, and a life of struggle. "I'll keep working," Haggard promises, "long as my two hands are fit to use." Woeful rather than angry, the political intent of the song is muffled, although it was clearly intended for a mobilized audience. As the song ends and the music fades, Haggard tacks on a dedication: "This song is for the workin' man."[61]

Haggard's 1969 composition "Okie from Muskogee" turned up the political volume. In unforgettable lyrics, it celebrates the virtues of flag-waving Muskogee, Oklahoma, where "we don't smoke marijuana" and "the kids still respect the college dean." The tone is light, slightly ironic—"shaggy" hippies and even draft-card burners are rendered as silly rather than threatening figures—but the message is uncompromising. Muskogee becomes the symbol of an America that is in danger: small-town America, homogeneous, virtuous, and brave ("We like livin' right and bein' free"), an America of plain people and simple, old-fashioned ways ("We still wave Old Glory down at the court-house, white lightning is still the biggest thrill of all").[62]

The song "fired his career into another orbit," wrote Georgia-born Paul Hemphill in the *Atlantic Monthly.* Handled like few other songs of that era, "Okie from Muskogee" became not only a hit but also a political conversation piece, played endlessly on radio stations that normally ignored country music and even more endlessly in tavern jukeboxes where patrons raised glasses and sang along. Journalism helped boost its significance, the press hailing the song as the ballad of the Silent Majority, declaring it the anthem of the angry white working class. Haggard kept up the attention with a follow-up song, "The Fightin' Side of Me," that also reached number one on the country music charts. Darker in tone than "Okie," the new song issued a hypermasculine love-it-or-leave-it warning: "When you're running down my country, hoss, your walking on the fightin' side of me." Conservatives loved them both and tried to capitalize on the "Okie from Muskogee" furor. George Wallace called Haggard and asked him to help in his 1970 campaign to regain Alabama's governor's mansion. Merle declined and quickly had a better offer. President Nixon invited him to perform "Okie" at the White House, where he saluted the song, its values, and the hardworking silent majority he said it stood for. The press now called Haggard the "working man's poet" or, as a Dayton newspaperman enthused, "the poet laureate of the hard hats."[63]

All this was great for Merle Haggard's career and also for the evolving formation of white working-class conservatism. With his back-to-back number one songs on the airways and his picture in *Life, Look,* and other magazines, Haggard had given the movement a new set of symbols that moved beyond George Wallace and the image of a racially motivated backlash. Muskogee stood not for segregation but for rock-ribbed patriotic, patriarchal, plain-folk traditionalism —a traditionalism that belonged to whites but did not salute the ugly flag of racism. Attractive to a much broader public than Wallace had mobilized, this version of conservative populism was stamped all over country music by the early 1970s, and both were intertwined with the culture of the blue-collar

North and West as well as the South. White working-class conservatism had moved into another phase, guided by a southern-origin institution of popular culture.[64]

From Silent to Moral Majority

Religion was the third diaspora-linked factor in the refiguring of late-twentieth-century conservatism. The rise of the New Christian Right—the mobilization of evangelical Christians as a defined political force—added another element to the conservative turn made by some modest-income whites. It also helped reshape the agenda of the Republican Party. With the reawakening of politicized Christian conservatism, Republicans grafted moral traditionalism onto the patriotic and racial traditionalism that had been helping them win elections. Opposition to feminism, gay rights, sex education in the schools, and especially abortion offered a new way to appeal to blue-collar and lower-middle-class whites who not long before had been consistent Democrats.[65]

The New Christian Right emerged as a much-publicized force in the 1970s and made its first big impact when Jerry Falwell's Moral Majority and other overtly political organizations were credited with helping Ronald Reagan win the White House in 1980. But long before then, the Baptist and Pentecostal churches that white southerners had built in the North and West had been contributing to the evolving culture of white working-class conservatism. Deeply troubled by the social and cultural transformations of the 1960s, especially changes in youth culture, evangelical institutions had grown rapidly during that decade as they reached out to those worried about the direction of American society. Fired in many cases by the belief that America's difficulties meant that "end times" were near, the evangelicals concentrated on the need for a religious and moral awakening. There were some preachers who talked about political action and lent their energies to the Far Right—notably those affiliated with Billy Hargis's anti-Communist Christian Crusade and Carl McIntire's American Council of Christian Churches—but most evangelicals were not overtly political during that polarizing decade. They were building a base and an agenda. In the 1960s, they were still the sleeper cells of America's right turn.[66]

When they awoke in the mid-1970s, it would be to forge a coalition that defied many of the historic commitments of Protestant evangelicalism. Not only would they be moving directly into the political arena, promoting candidates and key issues, turning churches into electoral organizing bases (something black churches had done but rarely white evangelicals), but they would also be working arm-in-arm with Catholics. Conservative Catholics, animated by the church's explicit denunciation of abortion and the 1973 *Roe v. Wade* Supreme

Court decision and troubled, as were evangelicals, by the proposed Equal Rights Amendment to the Constitution, the advance of homosexual rights, and other moral issues, were also mobilizing. That the two religious forces should come together reversed one of the key antagonisms of the twentieth and earlier American centuries. Fear of Catholics had been part of what had last driven evangelicals into the political arena in the 1920s, when their voices and votes had aided the causes of prohibition, anti-immigration, and the Ku Klux Klan. Now a half century later, the new venture into politics involved an alliance that would have made J. Frank Norris and the old fundamentalist warriors cringe.[67]

Or maybe Norris would have been proud. He certainly would have been able to claim partial credit, for the New Christian Right would not have come together without the infrastructure that he and other diaspora evangelicals had built. A complicated enterprise that had its strongest bases among white evangelicals in the South and Catholics in the North, it also depended upon the lacing together of regional religious institutions that had been accomplished by diaspora white southerners. The key role played by diaspora evangelicals becomes clear in the operations of the two most important organizations leading the Protestant side of the New Christian Right: Christian Voice and the Moral Majority.

Founded in the 1978 and headquartered initially in Pasadena, California, Christian Voice became the major vehicle for political conservatives from the Pentecostal wing of modern evangelicalism. It was especially effective in mobilizing pastors and members of the Assemblies of God, a denomination that through much of its history had stayed aloof from politics. Created initially to support a California ballot proposition that would have prevented public schools from hiring either homosexuals or advocates of homosexuality, Christian Voice pioneered the use of "moral report cards" to rate congressional and presidential candidates and direct-mail campaigning. "This Letter Will Make You Angry! But I am going to tell you the truth about militant gays, liberal educators, cruel atheists and Godless politicians," began a 1979 letter from Rev. Robert G. Grant, the founding president of Christian Voice. Helped also by ties to Rev. Pat Robertson's Christian Broadcasting Network and *700 Club* on cable television, by 1980 Christian Voice had the capacity to distribute voter information guides through thousands of churches and direct-mail appeals to hundreds of thousands of homes, appeals that explicitly supported Ronald Reagan and conservative Republicans.[68]

The Moral Majority worked with conservative Baptists the way Christian Voice worked with Pentecostals. Founded in 1979 by Rev. Jerry Falwell, the Moral Majority traced a direct lineage to J. Frank Norris, G. Beauchamp Vick, and Detroit's Temple Baptist Church. Jerry Falwell proudly acknowledges Norris and Vick as his mentors. Born in 1933 near Lynchburg, Virginia, into a working-class family of no strong religious commitment, Falwell heard the call of faith in his late teens. The Baptist church he attended was affiliated with the Baptist Bible Federation (BBF), the fundamentalist denomination that grew out of the efforts of Norris and Vick. On the advice of his Lynchburg minister, Falwell went off to study at Baptist Bible College, the BBF's seminary located in Springfield, Missouri. He worked closely with Vick, who commuted from Detroit to serve as college president.[69]

The Virginian became Vick's star pupil, setting up a relationship that would last until the Detroit pastor's death in 1975. Falwell, however, would strain those ties at several points. The first came shortly after he graduated in 1956. The young minister returned to Lynchburg, planning to assist at his former church. Then God instructed him to form his own congregation. The decision left him at odds with the BBF and outside the denomination for the next fifteen years. By the time he rejoined the BBF in 1971, his Thomas Road Baptist Church had become a megachurch with a membership of 20,000, an income of $1 million a year, and a new Liberty Baptist College in the works. Falwell had also built a nationwide television and radio following. His *Old Time Gospel Hour* aired weekly on hundreds of television stations across the country, while more hundreds of radio stations carried his daily programs.

Falwell, like most evangelicals (he prefers the label "fundamentalist"), had stayed clear of formal politics as he built his empire. His ministry and Liberty Baptist College were conservative in every way, and the preacher had used his pulpit to rail against the breakdown of morals, the drift away from patriotism, the supposed threats to the family posed by homosexuality and other social changes, and the vile productions of Hollywood and commercial television, and until the late 1960s he had also stood against the civil rights movement and defended the then all-white membership of Thomas Road Baptist Church. Despite all that, he believed, as did his mentor, G. B. Vick, that religion and politics should not mix. But midway through the 1970s, he changed his mind. "Back in the sixties I was criticizing pastors who were taking time out of their pulpit to involve themselves in the Civil Rights Movement or any other political venture. I said you're wasting your time from what you're called to do. Now I find myself doing the same thing," he explained in 1980. "Something had to be done now," he wrote in another context. "The government was encroaching upon the sovereignty of both the Church and the family" with the *Roe* decision, the Equal Rights Amendment, and homosexual rights. "Most Americans were shocked, but kept hoping someone would do something about all this moral chaos."[70]

The organization he launched would try to move Christians "out of the pew and into the precinct," and he would build it using the resources and networks that he and other conservative Baptists had assembled over the years. Key would be the listeners who followed his *Old Time Gospel Hour* and the congregations affiliated with the BBF. The BBF by then counted over 3,000 affiliates, many of them in the North and West, and some were megachurches with thousands of members. BBF congregations became the organizational starting points for the Moral Majority in many parts of the country. While Falwell took to the airwaves and captured the press attention that made the movement a big story in 1979 and 1980, BBF churches were providing the ground troops to start local Moral Majority chapters. Sociologist Robert Liebman examined the local organizations throughout the state of Ohio and found that with few exceptions, they began in churches affiliated with the denomination that Vick had founded.[71]

John Egerton was almost right. As the 1970s progressed, changes in the South did seem to be matched by changes in the North and West. The end of Jim Crow and the development of a two-party political system had made the South behave more like the rest of America. Now the other regions with their reorganized conservative politics were starting to seem a little like the South. Mostly it was the white working-class that showed signs of southernization. That is where the key symbols and institutions had become influential, where southern-origin country music, religious conservatism, and political figures had left their mark. It was not that all working-class white Americans had become Merle Haggard–style or Jerry Falwell–style conservatives; far from it. This had become a politically divided constituency that both Democrats and Republicans mined for votes. But blue-collar culture had changed dramatically since the early 1960s. Conservatives had made huge inroads, and diaspora southerners had helped. The once dramatic differences between the politics and culture of the working-class white South and the politics and culture of the working-class white North had substantially dissolved.

It is important not to overstate these effects. Whites from the South had not remade the North or transformed core institutions. Nor did they southernize northern racial relations, as critics from the 1940s and 1950s often charged. Walter White, Thomas Sancton, Claude Williams, R. J. Thomas, and others in the young civil rights coalition had worried that southern whites would disrupt "northern racial norms." They did not. The "old subdued, muted, murderous . . . race war" that Sancton referenced was not merely southern, and it had not been carried north by white migrants. White southerners moved into regions well practiced in the basics of white supremacy. What they added were symbols and institutions that gave the project new dimensions, at times helping, at other times perhaps hurting, the cause. In the 1920s, a southern-originated organization that celebrated Confederate chivalry and night-riding racial terror caught the imagination of hundreds of thousands of xenophobic white northerners but then became a precipitating force in the realignment of the two major national parties. In the middle decades of the century, the southern contributions to Klan-like organizations and to the wave of hate strikes and housing riots that plagued African Americans in the North and West seemed ironically to limit and marginalize the whole enterprise of white violence and bigotry. In the 1960s, 70s, and 80s, another set of southern inputs pointed the way to forms of racial conservatism that would gain credibility and influence. The contributions changed, and the effects varied radically depending upon the larger configurations of politics and race in each era, but repeatedly the white diaspora had added elements, sometimes very important elements, to the politics of racism and white conservatism.

And that was not all. Thomas Sancton and Claude Williams were testament to the fact that white southerners could contribute to other political projects, including the civil rights movement that had its major base in the communities built by the black diaspora. It is easy to overlook the white liberals and radicals who moved north but a mistake to do so, for they sometimes found themselves in influential positions. The literary liberals, from Erskine Caldwell to Robert Penn Warren to Willie Morris, who did so much to critique the old South and help shape a new one, the radical songsmiths like Woody Guthrie and Aunt Molly Jackson who helped create a musical culture for several generations of radicals, and the diaspora Democrats like William Gibbs McAdoo, George Edwards, and Jesse Unruh—they too were part of the white diaspora.

Great Migrations

"In 1980 I returned to my native ground out of blood and belonging," the writer Willie Morris explained. More than twenty-five years after leaving Mississippi and thirteen years after explaining in *North toward Home* why he could never feel whole or at home in his natal state, Willie Morris was back. His years away had been good. He had spent time in California and in England but mostly in New York, where for nine years he had edited *Harper's* magazine and for another eight wrote stories based on his southern childhood. But eventually he had grown tired of the New York frenzy, and when the University of Mississippi offered him the position of writer in residence, he said yes, ready to make peace with his home state. Things had changed. "The world took a couple of turns," he offered by way of explanation.[1]

Ruby Haynes had returned to Mississippi one year earlier after spending more than thirty years in Chicago. Her world had also taken a couple of turns. Born into poverty and raised on a sequence of cotton plantations in the Mississippi Delta, not far from Yazoo City where Willie Morris would later grow up in modest but not impoverished circumstances, Ruby Haynes and her family were sharecroppers. Married at eighteen and with an eighth grade education that compared well with other black Mississippians, Haynes wanted out of the cotton fields and managed to find a way, first moving to the nearby town of Clarksdale and then in 1946, at age thirty, divorced and with two children, following the chain of relatives that connected black Mississippi with black Chicago. Her life there was complicated. Nicholas Lemann narrates Haynes's story in *The Promised Land*, one of the best-known accounts of the black diaspora, and he emphasizes difficulties and disappointments. She struggled with love (a succession of failed relationships) and near-poverty as she raised eight children while working low-wage jobs. Lemann makes Haynes the central figure in an account that stresses the failures of war on poverty programs in the 1960s and the crisis of the urban underclass. When Ruby Haynes decided to return to Clarksdale in 1979, it was not the triumphant return of Willie Morris. Lemann presents her homecoming as a return of the frustrated or defeated, suggesting that Chicago had proved to be anything but a promised land for Haynes and many other black migrants.[2]

By 1979, the era of the Southern Diaspora was over, its end apparent both in new migration patterns and in the new relationship between the South and other regions. Southerners continued to leave home in the 1970s in numbers that were not much different from the previous decade, and others would follow in the 1980s and 1990s. But out-migration now was accompanied by much higher volumes of in-migration. In the first five years of the 1970s, 2.2 million people left the region and 4.1 million moved there. Between 1975 and 1980, 2.4 million left and 4.2 moved south. The imbalance would become even more pronounced in the 1980s. Long a net exporter of population, the South had become a net importer. And a portion of those immigrants were former southerners now returning home. At least 210,000 black expatriates and 897,000 white expatriates joined the flow of people into the southland in the last five years of the 1970s, 26 percent of the total. Some of the rest were children and grandchildren of the diaspora.[3]

It was a new South in many ways, which is one of the "world turns" that Morris had in mind. No longer the land of cotton, the region now boasted modern new cities and industries. Partly the result of federal investments in the great era of military and civil infrastructure development, partly because of the redirection of private capital away from the old northern manufacturing belt, the South had gone through a dramatic economic restructuring since World War II and now enjoyed significant advantages over the North in the competition for jobs and economic growth. Southern states would see non-agricultural employment increase by 46 percent in the 1970s, including more than a million manufacturing jobs. The Northeast and North Central regions between them lost close to the same number. And that was just the start. In the 1980s, the northern states would suffer through massive deindustrialization while the South continued to gain jobs and people.[4]

It was a new South also in terms of racial rules. Civil rights protests, court decisions, and federal laws were finally having a measurable effect. African Americans no longer contended with state-sanctioned segregation, and the threat of organized white violence was much reduced. Black southerners could point to progress in the desegregation of schools and public accommodations and also in politics in the wake of the 1965 Voting Rights Act. In 1976 there were 1,847 black elected officials in the South, including the mayor of Atlanta (Maynard Jackson) and three congressional representatives (Barbara Jordan, Andrew Young, and Harold Ford).[5]

Clarksdale had changed less than big cities like Atlanta, but Ruby Haynes still was impressed. She returned to a community where African Americans were no longer forced into rigid subservience, where black businessmen and politicians were beginning to take their place alongside white ones, and where many public services (schools, public housing, welfare assistance) that once had been largely for the benefit of whites were now helping blacks. Other things remained much the same. Economic inequality continued to divide the races almost as surely as in the age of Jim Crow, with much of the black population stuck in or near poverty. Various forms of segregation also endured, maintained now through private schools and social networks. Still, it was good enough for Ruby Haynes, who wanted out of the dirty and dangerous housing project that had been her home in Chicago for many years. She found in the new Clarksdale a comfortable and safe place to retire.[6]

But Ruby Haynes and Willie Morris are probably not the best representatives of the return migrants of the post-diaspora period. They were older than most and headed south for reasons that were not particularly common. Only 7 percent of the black former migrants who returned home in the late 1970s were of retirement age, and only 17 percent were aged fifty or older. The pattern was the same among whites: only 18 percent were fifty or older. Many of the returnees were young people who had probably not lived for very long outside the South. The biggest portion (51 percent of blacks, 48 percent of whites) were in the twenty-five to forty-nine age range, prime working years and prime years for thinking about where to raise families. Instead of going home to retire (or semiretire, in the case of Morris), most were probably making the same calculations that Ruby Haynes had made when she moved to Chicago in 1946. That is suggested too in another statistic. Many were not really going home. Of the African American returnees, 39 percent settled in a southern state that was different from their birth state; 50 percent of the whites did as well. These migrants were behaving the way they had when they had initially left home, looking for opportunities, moving where it seemed a better life might be possible.[7]

Homecoming stories like those of Morris and Haynes have had a powerful and misleading impact on the meanings associated with the Southern Diaspora. Ever since demographers caught sight of the reverse migration trends in the 1970s, journalists and many scholars have seen in them the sad end and ultimate irony of southern out-migration. In stories about whites losing jobs in the industrial cities of Ohio and Pennsylvania and heading back to old homes in West Virginia and Kentucky and in stories about blacks leaving the burned-out and boarded-up inner cities for simpler and safer lives in the South, a substantial body of journalism, sociology, and history has updated and re-inscribed the dominant representation of the Southern Diaspora as a troubled experience. In an earlier age of social scientific confidence, this representation had turned mostly on the concept of maladjustment, on the notion that rural whites and blacks from the backward South were not ready for the challenges of the city. The newer version flipped the blame. The cities had failed the migrants. Deindustrialization and the urban crisis had hit at the worst time, destroying the jobs and the dreams of the most recent newcomers to the industrial North, destroying, in effect, the promised land.[8]

There is truth in that construction, but not the whole truth. Former southerners were among the victims of the urban crisis and cycles of deindustrialization, but not the chief victims. Migrants, as they had since 1949, continued to record the same or lower rates of poverty than other portions of the white and black populations. The most common face of white poverty was not someone who had moved north from Appalachia but someone born in Ohio or Pennsylvania or Michigan. Indeed, in the East North Central states, only 7 percent of impoverished white adults in 1979 were former southerners, 6 percent in 1989. Yet writers often made them the center of the story of plant closings and white working-class distress.[9]

So too in black communities, most of the poor were northern-born, and rates of poverty among adults remained slightly lower for southerners than northerners. Former migrants continued on average to earn higher personal incomes and higher family incomes and were more likely to be employed than northern-born African Americans. Former southerners were less likely to hold the professional and clerical jobs that were opening up to well-educated African Americans, but they were more likely to be able to hang on in the shrinking zone of blue-collar employment. Age and experience were part of the reason. Younger workers no longer had access to the industrial jobs that had once been the mainstay of the northern black economy. By 1989, the number of black auto workers and steel workers had fallen almost 50 percent since 1969, from 243,900 to 115,645, and 56 percent of those remaining were southerners. In the deindustrializing economy of the late 1970s and 1980s, there was little good news for African Americans without college degrees, but in general it was not the former migrants who were having the toughest time. Yet that is not the story that gets told. The image of difficult experiences and disappointments continues to shape views of the two southern migrations.[10]

This book has argued that there was more to the diaspora than this, more than stories of difficult experiences, more than powerless people moving long distances in response to conditions they could not control. It takes some effort to put aside such images, but in doing so one discovers other dimensions of the diaspora that are not really about migrant adjustments, good or bad, but are instead about impact, about the ways that the migrants affected the places they settled and became a force in the historical reconstructions of America. Discovered too are some new meanings of the label "Great Migration."

I have constructed this analysis in a particular way, moving across a great swath of twentieth-century history, bringing together subjects that have usually been handled separately, examining side by side the migrations of black southerners and of white southerners. This approach yields a set of observations that are different from what other historians have said about either migration. A short summary follows, emphasizing some of the concepts that guide my analysis.

Whites and blacks left the South for related but somewhat different reasons and found very different opportunities in the North and West. Those differences turned on the central issue of race, and from that flowed other meaningful differences derived from geography, class dynamics, and community formation patterns. It is tempting to outline this logic as a set of maxims: (1) race matters; (2) geography and class matter; and (3) to adequately explore issues of change and influence, we need to pay attention to the institutional matrices that exist at particular times and in particular places.

Race matters. Racial privilege granted white southern migrants significant economic advantages over their black counterparts and also spatial advantages: the choice of where and how and with whom they settled. The whites used that privilege to choose the best housing they could afford in the least dense neighborhoods, often in the outlying as opposed to central urban areas.

Geography matters. The fact that black and white southerners settled in different sorts of places, in different concentrations, would have implications not only for individual migrants and not just for the southern group experiences but also for the North and West and ultimately for the nation as a whole. Black migrants gained capacities that eluded white migrants despite their greater numbers, capacities to influence cultural and political institutions in ways that would dictate profound historical changes. The whites chose dispersion over concentration and opted for places that initially would not be centers of political and cultural power. It was a pattern that worked against the construction of physically defined southern white communities.

Class matters. The different behaviors of middle-class and intellectual segments of the two migrations was an important factor in community formations and subsequent political and cultural impact. The loyalties and activities of elite and middle-class migrants became a key resource for African American communities, while middle-class white expatriates kept their distance from working-class migrants, thus limiting the possibilities for group institution-building and political influence.

Institutions matter. One of the challenges of this study is to explain how mass migrations translate into forces of historical change that affect the broader society. Many are the books that simply assert that the Great Migration of African Americans transformed the cities and forced all of America to confront the problem of race that previously had been regionalized in the South. How this was done is not specified. The reader is left to imagine that relocation itself is an enormously consequential fact capable of overturning racial orders. That is not good enough. I have instead mapped key pathways of influence and change. Migrants became historical actors because they participated in or enabled certain activities, organizations, movements, or cultural formations that had the capacity to exert influence on the larger society. This is where we see the major difference in the impact of the two Southern Diasporas. White migrants, much more numerous than black migrants, were influential in some discrete venues: in the promotion of evangelical churches, in the project of country music, and in the particular brand of racial conservatism and white working-class politics that benefited from southern white symbolism. African American initiatives were more comprehensive and consequential.

This had something to do with the different incentives for cultural and political activism, but it also had to do with the fortuitous institutional matrices of the places where black migrants had settled. Building communities in the big cities of America during an era when those cities monopolized important forms of power gave black migrants unique opportunities for influence. Because of the way the big cities were wired as cultural centers of early- and mid-twentieth-century America, they enabled a far-reaching African American cultural florescence. The presence of key media institutions—publishing houses, major newspapers, magazines, record companies, theater, and film—helped inspire African American publishing, literary production, and musical and artistic innovation and helped spread its significance both throughout black America and across the boundaries of race. The slow but meaningful changes in major media acknowledgment of black musicians, writers, and sports figures and the rise of first a few, then more and more African American cultural celebrities depended upon the unique institutional configuration of the big cities.

The political institutions of the northern metropolises worked the same way. The particular arrangement of parties, unions, and municipal and federal governments during the "long New Deal" gave black voters and activists some extraordinary opportunities to leverage governmental power. Working with allies that were available only in those places, finding balance-of-power openings that appeared as urban regimes reorganized and as the northern Democratic Party tried to consolidate its hold on federal power, using tactics that were safe and effective only in those settings, black political activists managed to loosen some of the seams of power in a governmental system that until then rarely responded to the demands of socially despised minorities.

The final point is that migration matters. Migrating African Americans had done something extraordinary. In leaving the South, they had put themselves in a position to begin to change the rules of race not only where they settled but ultimately throughout the nation. Despite modest numbers, despite the overwhelming hostility of the host population, despite the never-ending obstacles that limited economic and social opportunities, despite their apparent lack of resources, a few million black Americans had left their homes and moved north and had found there the leverage to initiate one of the great historical turns in American history.

The white diaspora also contributed to the reorganization of American racial systems, often in ways that were interactive with black initiatives. Keenly aware of each other and also joined through some of the media and academic fixations of the era, white migrants and black migrants were frequently positioned as political antagonists. That was what was going on as some white southerners participated in or led various sequences of white supremacist politics. In more subtle ways, that opposition also showed up in the two major institutions (country music and conservative evangelical Protestantism) that the white diaspora brought north. Both helped shape new discourses of working-class whiteness and social conservatism that seemed to be responding in part to changes introduced by African Americans. But the interactions could also be collaborative, as with the liberal and leftist white southerners who aided the cause of racial reconstruction. In any case, the diasporas were never fully separate. The two Great Migrations were also one.

Regional reconstruction was the other important legacy of the Southern Diaspora, and again the effects were interactive. Over time, both groups of migrants southernized aspects of the regions they settled, introducing tastes, practices, and institutions—including food, music, religion, accents, and political styles—that moderated the differences between the South and other parts of the United States. At the same time, both white and black expatriates played a part in changing the region they had left. While the Black Metropolises of the North served as staging grounds for the southern struggle against Jim Crow and the broad racial and political reconstructions that followed, some of the projects of white migrants also circled back to affect the South. The liberal writers and academics achieved just such an effect as they wrote their novels, poems, histories, and journalism critiquing the South of old. In subtle ways, diaspora country music and the diaspora Baptist and Pentecostal movements also helped change the home region. As those enterprises reached out to nonsoutherners, achieving the exciting patterns of growth that made them important on a national (and international) level, they desouthernized some symbols and practices to accommodate the new audiences, and those changes flowed back into the South. There was, in short, a circuitry to the Great Migrations and their institutional matrices that made them agents of regional convergence. John Egerton did not quite understand the wiring, but he had a nice way of labeling the dual effects. The Southern Diaspora contributed to the "Southernization of America" and at the same time to the "Americanization of Dixie."

Appendix A: Tables

Additional tables and charts can be found on the companion Web site: ‹http://faculty.washington.edu/gregoryj/diaspora›.

TABLE A.1. Leaving the South: Calculating Migration Volumes by Decade

		Southern-Born Persons Living outside the South	Start of Decade	End of Decade	Estimated Decade Mortality	Minimum Return Migration	Estimated Migration from South by Decade
1900–1910	Blacks	335,200	456,953	69,810	12,819	204,382
	Whites	1,117,600	1,474,320	213,103	146,721	716,545
1910–20	Blacks	456,953	785,996	91,055	17,056	437,154
	Whites	1,474,320	1,914,321	250,162	202,904	893,067
1920–30	Blacks	785,996	1,326,213	136,699	30,912	810,614
	Whites	1,914,321	2,718,480	266,559	274,647	1,472,886
1930–40	Blacks	1,326,213	1,516,743	254,164	49,734	391,641
	Whites	2,718,480	3,166,463	332,839	333,048	986,350
1940–50	Blacks	1,516,743	2,572,154	275,136	116,682	1,447,229
	Whites	3,166,463	4,847,209	380,312	575,697	2,636,755
	Hispanics	45,938	102,066	2,623	7,848	66,599
1950–60	Blacks	2,572,154	3,175,751	363,851	138,389[a]	1,105,836
	Whites	4,847,209	6,446,444	462,813	1,106,548[a]	3,168,596
	Hispanics	102,066	193,463	4,460	NA	95,857
1960–70	Blacks	3,175,751	3,342,546	439,546	206,566	812,907
	Whites	6,446,444	6,972,520	579,456	1,409,264	2,514,796
	Hispanics	193,463	490,411	8,515	52,872	358,335
1970–80	Blacks	3,342,546	4,080,492	483,812	330,860	1,552,618
	Whites	6,972,520	7,366,854	694,740	1,570,883	2,659,958
	Hispanics	490,411	510,866	29,746	95,658	145,859
1980–90	Blacks	4,080,492	3,640,458	614,362	429,144	603,471
	Whites	7,366,854	7,326,943	803,990	1,417,833	2,181,912
	Hispanics	510,866	574,761	31,360	72,116	167,371
1990–2000	Blacks	3,640,458	2,961,684	760,250	434,440	515,916
	Whites	7,326,943	7,289,695	948,284	1,442,348	2,353,384
	Hispanics	574,761	716,531	43,809	123,340	308,919

Estimated number of blacks who left the South, 1900–2000	7,881,768
Estimated number of whites who left the South, 1900–2000	19,584,249
Estimated number of Hispanics who left the South, 1900–2000	1,142,940
Estimate total[b] southern out-migrants, 1900–2000	28,608,955

Note: See appendix B for methods.

[a]Hispanics included in racial categories.

[b]Does not include Native Americans, Asians, and "other races."

TABLE A.2. Return Migration at Selected Intervals by Southern-Born Persons Living in North and West

- Whites consistently returned at much higher rates than African Americans. In most intervals, whites were three times as likely to return.
- Throughout the postwar period, there was rapid turnover in the white migrant population. In the late 1950s, for every ten whites leaving the South, five returned. After 1965, the turnover exceeded 75%.
- Black return rates were also very high in 1949 and soared again after 1975. In the past two decades, more southern-born African Americans have returned to the South than have left it.

		Returnees	1 Year Return Rate	New Migrants from South	Ratio: Returnees/ Migrants
1949–50	Blacks	43,143	1.7%	39,879	1.08
	Whites	228,800	4.7	258,538	.88

			5 Year Return Rate		
1935–40	Blacks	25,673	1.8	127,015	.20
	Whites	176,682	6.4	595,981	.30
1955–60[a]	Blacks	78,010	2.7	361,168	.22
	Whites	647,786	10.6	1,194,039	.54
1965–70	Blacks	114,296	3.7	336,578	.34
	Whites	781,687	11.6	999,363	.78
1975–80	Blacks	210,800	5.2	278,600	.76
	Whites	897,400	12.2	915,600	.98
1985–90	Blacks	229,113	6.3	241,892	.95
	Whites	733,902	10.4	984,267	.75
1995–2000	Blacks	232,985	7.7	176,642	1.32
	Whites	772,076	10.8	907,550	.85

Sources: 1940 IPUMS, 1950 IPUMS, 1970 State Form 2 IPUMS, 1980 Rural Urban IPUMS, 1990 5% IPUMS, 2000 1% IPUMS; U.S. Bureau of the Census, *U.S. Census of Population: 1960. Subject Reports: Lifetime and Recent Migration* (1961), table 3, pp. 9–15.

[a]1955–60 includes Hispanics in both racial categories and "other races" in the black category.

TABLE A.3. Where Southerners Lived in 1970: States

- Southerners made a large combined impact in California, Illinois, Indiana, Michigan, and Ohio, where both blacks and whites settled in significant numbers.
- The Northeast attracted more black southerners than whites, especially New York and New Jersey.
- White southerners spread widely throughout the Midwest and West.

	Black Southern-Born	White Southern-Born	Hispanic Southern-Born	Total[a] Southern-Born	% of State Population
Northeast					
Connecticut	59,881	71,994	800	132,675	4.2
Maine	1,708	20,324	100	22,132	2.1
Massachusetts	49,589	107,441	1,201	158,231	2.7
New Hampshire	700	17,325	300	18,325	2.3
New Jersey	231,285	195,659	5,003	431,947	6.0
New York	567,152	270,842	12,712	850,706	4.6
Pennsylvania	254,708	341,340	5,505	601,553	5.0
Rhode Island	4,702	26,727	800	32,229	3.6
Vermont	100	7,214	100	7,414	1.8
North Central					
Illinois	452,008	458,002	45,141	955,151	8.3
Indiana	119,244	478,701	17,917	615,862	11.6
Iowa	7,506	51,658	2,304	61,968	2.2
Kansas	33,151	195,068	8,520	241,940	10.5
Michigan	358,168	445,248	27,130	833,250	9.3
Minnesota	8,007	47,558	2,404	58,169	1.6
Missouri	126,076	303,641	7,113	438,332	9.2
Nebraska	11,115	44,961	2,102	58,578	3.7
North Dakota	1,100	11,321	100	12,521	2.0
Ohio	321,719	1,061,425	22,126	1,409,481	12.8
South Dakota	1,000	14,128	100	15,328	2.0
Wisconsin	46,564	56,284	7,808	111,357	2.5
West					
Alaska	6,706	43,068	901	50,775	16.4
Arizona	19,833	193,340	16,625	232,099	13.1
California	571,337	1,686,022	213,482	2,497,277	12.4
Colorado	27,630	184,874	13,015	226,420	10.1
Hawaii	3,308	37,250	1,401	45,760	6.1
Idaho	1,100	34,649	4,109	40,658	5.7
Montana	1,002	22,826	500	24,328	3.3
Nevada	8,308	52,461	1,901	62,771	12.8
New Mexico	8,310	166,950	15,223	191,784	18.6

	Black Southern-Born	White Southern-Born	Hispanic Southern-Born	Total[a] Southern-Born	% of State Population
Oregon	9,910	126,163	3,008	140,084	6.7
Utah	2,601	28,225	700	31,726	3.1
Washington	27,321	180,641	13,107	224,374	6.5
Wyoming	1,900	23,138	1,002	26,040	7.5
Total non-South	3,342,546	6,972,520	490,411	10,877,963	

Source: 1970 State Form 1 IPUMS.

[a]Other nonwhite racial groups are included in the totals but not shown separately.

TABLE A.4. Comparing Family Incomes: Median Family Incomes for Black and White Southerners and Nonsoutherners Living outside the South, 1939–1989

- Both black migrants and white migrants earned family incomes comparable to other residents of each race.
- The median black family earned roughly two-thirds of the income of the median southern-born white family, and that ratio remained constant through five decades.

	Southern-Born Blacks	Other Blacks	Southern-Born Whites	Other Whites
In Actual Dollars				
1939[a]	$839	$844	$1,360	$1,500
1949	2,050	2,050	3,050	3,150
1959	3,850	3,750	5,550	5,650
1969	6,350	6,050	9,150	9,250
1979	11,215	11,010	17,625	18,005
1989	20,688	21,224	30,000	30,728
In Constant 2000 Dollars				
1939[a]	11,150	11,150	15,746	17,344
1949	14,832	14,832	22,068	22,791
1959	22,782	22,190	32,843	33,434
1969	29,795	28,387	42,933	43,402
1979	26,598	26,114	41,802	42,812
1989	27,774	28,724	41,743	42,952

Sources: 1940 IPUMS, 1950 IPUMS, 1960 IPUMS, 1970 State Form 1 IPUMS, 1980 Metro 1% IPUMS, 1990 1% Metro IPUMS.

[a]Wage and salary income only. Households headed by those who indicated self-employment were excluded.

TABLE A.5. Wages of Blackness and Whiteness: Comparing Average Personal Earnings of Working-Age (25–54) Southerners Living in Metropolitan Areas of Great Lakes States, 1939–1969, Controlling for Education

- In 1939, black southern-born men and women earned not much more than 50% of what comparably educated white southern migrants earned.
- From 1949 to 1969, black southern-born men earned 60–80% of the incomes of white southern-born men. The disparity was at its worst at higher education levels.
- Black women earned 70–80% of white southern women's wages at most educational levels in 1949 and 1959. In 1969, they caught up.

	Males: Southern-Born			Females: Southern-Born		
	Black	White	Ratio: B/W	Black	White	Ratio: B/W
1939[a]						
0–8 grade	$765	$1,208	63%	$426	$722	59%
9–12 grade	794	1,660	48	453	824	55
College[b]	1,083	2,587	42	746	1,353	55
All	784	1,525	51	452	848	53
N	1,455	1,900		549	452	
1949						
0–8 grade	2,364	3,022	78	1,283	1,647	78
9–12 grade	2,686	3,398	79	1,373	1,914	72
College[b]	2,726	4,332	63	2,246	2,322	97
All	2,488	3,329	75	1,394	1,871	75
N	856	853		361	293	
1959						
0–8 grade	3,912	4,979	79	1,807	2,485	73
9–12 grade	4,196	5,765	73	2,154	2,870	75
College[b]	4,914	8,219	60	3,303	4,033	82
All	4,106	5,771	71	2,145	2,888	74
N	2,967	4,171		1,634	1,615	
1969						
0–8 grade	7,022	8,678	81	3,507	3,995	88
9–12 grade	7,617	9,630	79	4,167	4,531	92
College[b]	9,567	14,418	66	6,733	5,955	113
All	7,705	10,215	75	4,499	4,631	97
N	2,505	3,835		1,795	1,790	

Sources: 1940 IPUMS, 1950 IPUMS, 1960 IPUMS, 1970 State Form 1 IPUMS.

Note: The Great Lakes states are Illinois, Indiana, Michigan, Ohio, and Wisconsin.

[a]Wage and salary income only.

[b]One or more years of college.

TABLE A.6. Southern White Residence and Home-Ownership Patterns, 1960, 1970

- Few southern whites lived in dense central city neighborhoods in the Great Lakes states, and even fewer in the Pacific states.
- Suburbs and small towns were the usual choice, even for the most recent migrants from the South.
- High rates of home-ownership were evident by 1960, reaching 63% in the Great Lakes states in 1970.
- Recent migrants shared the residential distributions of their predecessors, more than two-thirds settling in suburban or rural/small cities.

	1960		1970		
	Southern-Born Whites	Other U.S.-Born Whites	Southern-Born Whites	Other U.S.-Born Whites	Recent Migrants[a]
Great Lakes States[b]					
% in core city: multifamily housing	13[c]	9[c]	9	8	12
% in core city: house or duplex	24[c]	25[c]	22	20	16
% in suburbs	35	32	47	42	50
% in rural/small cities	29	33	23	31	22
% total[c]	101	99	101	101	100
N	8,522	86,111	10,022	93,590	1,003
% home-ownership	56	71	63	71	31
Pacific States[d]					
% in core city: multifamily housing	8[c]	11[c]	9	12	17
% in core city: house or duplex	19[c]	26[c]	19	23	14
% in suburbs	50	44	56	51	51
% in rural/small cities	23	18	16	14	17
% total[c]	100	99	100	100	99
N	7,785	47,266	8,795	55,415	654
% home-ownership	56	62	57	60	19

Sources: 1960 IPUMS, 1970 State Form 1 IPUMS.

[a]Migrants who had left the South between 1965 and 1970.
[b]Illinois, Indiana, Michigan, Ohio, and Wisconsin.
[c]Proportional allocation of some missing values of central city housing types was necessary in the 1960 sample.
[d]Alaska, California, Hawaii, Oregon, and Washington.

TABLE A.7. Occupations of Former Southerners and Others in the Civilian Labor Force outside the South, 1920

- In 1920, 70% of southern black men worked in unskilled or service jobs, compared to only 22% of southern white males.
- Southern black women were twice as likely to be in the labor force as southern white migrant women.
- 62% of employed southern black women worked in domestic service, compared to only 13% of southern white females.

	Southern-Born Blacks	Other Blacks	Southern-Born Whites	Other U.S.-Born Whites	Foreign-Born Whites	All Hispanics
Males						
% professionals/managers	3	4	14	14	12	4
% clerical/sales	3	4	11	14	6	5
% skilled/foremen	9	8	20	20	23	10
% semiskilled	15	17	16	15	22	17
% laborers	48	35	12	11	20	30
% service	20	23	3	2	5	4
% farmers/family	1	4	17	19	9	12
% farm laborers	2	5	7	6	3	17
% Total	101	100	100	101	100	99
N	3,428	2,304	7,351	152,948	60,492	1,561
Females						
% professionals/managers	3	5	17	18	9	8
% clerical/sales	2	3	27	36	14	16
% skilled/forewomen	1	0	2	2	3	2
% semiskilled	14	14	20	23	34	37
% laborers	3	1	3	2	3	4
% service: nondomestic	16	18	14	7	11	5
% service: domestic	62	58	13	10	23	18
% farm sector	1	1	4	2	3	9
% Total	102	100	100	100	100	99
N	1,517	972	1,357	44,004	10,780	221
% in labor force	47	41	19	25	19	17

Source: 1920 IPUMS.

TABLE A.8. Occupations of Former Southerners and Others in the Civilian Labor Force outside the South, 1950

- By 1950, southern-born blacks were finding more factory and other blue-collar jobs, but service and unskilled labor accounted for half of all jobs.
- Southern-born whites were anchored in secure blue-collar jobs and well represented in white-collar sectors.

	Southern-Born Blacks	Other Blacks	Southern-Born Whites	Other U.S.-Born Whites	Foreign-Born Whites	All Hispanics
Males						
% professionals/managers	5	7	17	20	20	8
% clerical/sales	6	12	11	15	9	8
% skilled/foremen	11	13	23	21	24	13
% semiskilled	28	25	25	21	20	24
% laborers	29	21	9	7	10	19
% service[a]	20	21	5	5	11	10
% farmers/family	1	1	6	10	5	4
% farm laborers	2	2	5	3	2	15
% Total	102	102	101	102	101	101
N	10,835	5,090	18,353	293,760	9,601	5,773
Females						
% professionals/managers	5	10	17	18	16	6
% clerical/sales	7	16	33	42	20	26
% skilled/forewomen	1	2	1	2	2	1
% semiskilled	25	23	23	20	32	43
% laborers	2	2	1	1	1	1
% service: nondomestic	21	21	18	11	19	13
% service: domestic	39	28	5	4	10	6
% farm sector	0	0	3	3	1	4
% Total	100	102	101	101	101	100
N	5,492	2,834	5,582	103,209	3,005	1,975
% in labor force	42	41	29	31	26	30

Source: 1950 IPUMS.

[a]Police, fire, and protective services included in skilled category.

TABLE A.9. Occupations of Former Southerners and Others in the Labor Force outside the South, 1970

- By 1970, domestic service and unskilled labor were becoming less important for black workers. Southern-born men and women were overrepresented among factory workers and also getting skilled blue-collar positions.
- Southern-born whites remained overrepresented in the blue-collar sector but had incomes that matched other whites.

	Southern-Born Blacks	Other Blacks	Southern-Born Whites	Other U.S.-Born Whites	Foreign-Born Whites	All Hispanics
Males						
% professionals/managers	8	11	22	25	25	11
% clerical/sales	9	15	11	15	12	11
% skilled/foremen	16	14	22	21	25	18
% semiskilled	31	27	22	18	18	28
% laborers	14	13	6	7	6	11
% service[a]	16	17	7	7	11	13
% farm sector	1	1	3	5	2	7
% military	4	3	8	2	1	3
% Total	99	101	101	100	100	102
N	12,165	12,977	26,745	331,492	22,902	16,097
Females						
% professionals/managers	11	13	17	19	15	9
% clerical/sales	23	36	40	47	36	32
% skilled/forewomen	2	1	2	2	2	2
% semiskilled	21	16	17	13	23	31
% laborers	2	1	1	1	1	1
% service: commercial	27	23	20	16	17	17
% service: domestic	14	9	3	3	5	3
% farm sector	1	1	1	1	0	4
% Total	101	100	101	102	99	99
N	11,707	12,186	20,264	261,221	17,450	11,958
% in labor force	49	44	40	41	32	37

Source: 1970 State Form 1 IPUMS.

[a]Police, fire, and protective services included in skilled category.

	Southern-Born Blacks	Other Blacks	Southern-Born Whites	Other U.S.-Born Whites	Foreign-Born Whites	All Hispanics
Mid-Atlantic States						
Median family income	$6,050	$6,050	$9,950	$9,750	$7,250	$6,150
% white collar	19	29	51	44	38	29
% skilled/semiskilled	47	41	34	40	43	45
% laborers/service	33	30	13	14	19	25
% farmers/farm laborers	1	1	2	2	1	1
% Total	100	101	100	100	101	100
N	3,566	5,148	2,501	84,655	9,209	4,273
Great Lakes States						
Median family income	$7,050	$6,150	$9,450	$9,650	$7,850	$8,550
% white collar	15	22	25	37	34	21
% skilled/semiskilled	56	47	59	44	48	55
% laborers/service	29	30	14	14	16	22
% farmers/farm laborers	0	1	2	5	2	3
% Total	100	100	100	100	100	101
N	4,749	4,373	9,310	93,846	5,117	2,236
Pacific States						
Median family income	$6,200	$5,450	$9,050	$9,450	$7,750	$7,300
% white collar	22	29	38	46	47	19
% skilled/semiskilled	42	36	44	36	35	47
% laborers/service	34	33	15	15	15	23
% farmers/farm laborers	2	2	4	4	3	11
% Total	100	100	101	101	100	100
N	2,153	1,409	7,602	53,604	3,987	6,172

Source: 1970 State Form 1 IPUMS.

TABLE A.11. Comparing Economic Outcomes for Migrants from Different Subregions of the South, 1969

- Black migrants from the nominally southern states of Florida, Maryland, Delaware, and Washington, D.C., often achieved higher incomes, but their numbers were small.
- White migrants born in South Atlantic and Gulf states achieved higher median incomes than those from Kentucky, Tennessee, West Virginia, or the western South, but the difference was not large.

	Kentucky, Tennessee, West Virginia	Virginia, Carolinas, Georgia	Alabama, Mississippi	Texas, Arkansas, Oklahoma, Louisiana	Florida, Maryland, Delaware, Washington, D.C.
Black Migrants					
Living outside South					
Median family income	$6,750	$6,150	$6,450	$6,350	$6,650
% below poverty line	23	23	26	25	18
% male white-collar	19	18	15	20	24
N	1,506	5,597	4,407	3,820	755
Living in Great Lakes States					
Median family income	$6,750	$7,100	$6,850	$7,050	$7,450
% below poverty line	23	22	25	23	12
N	1,064	1,156	2,898	1,067	117
White Migrants					
Living outside South					
Median family income	$8,950	$9,450	$9,650	$8,950	$9,950
% below poverty	13	10	10	12	9
% male white-collar	27	42	35	35	53
N	10,069	3,469	1,711	11,988	2,107
Living in Great Lakes States					
Median family income	$9,050	$10,050	$10,050	$10,050	$10,550
% below poverty line	12	10	8	9	9
% male white-collar	20	25	16	25	45
N	6,847	1,074	630	1,462	377

Source: 1970 State Form 1 IPUMS.

TABLE A.12. White Male Opportunities, 1969: Comparing Poorly Educated Southern Migrants, Recent Southern Migrants, and Other White Males (Age 25–54) Living in Great Lakes States

- Even southern white males with poor educational backgrounds and those who had arrived within the past five years did reasonably well in the postwar economy.
- Their incomes trailed better-educated northern-born white males by 20%, but they found secure blue-collar jobs, and two-thirds owned their homes.
- White males of eastern European background and migrants from the Northern Plains states did even better.

	Southern-Born White Males			Other U.S.-Born White Males		
	0–8 Years School	9+ Years School	Recent Migrants[a]	9+ Years School	Migrants from Northern Plains States[b]	Of Italian and Eastern European Fathers
Median personal income	$8,050	$9,250	$8,050	$10,050	$10,450	$10,050
Median family income	10,150	11,500	10,050	12,350	13,150	13,150
% poverty	7	3	6	3	2	3
% home-ownership	66	68	37	84	69	82
% white-collar	7	36	36	47	58	44
% skilled/semiskilled	77	56	54	44	34	50
% unskilled/service	14	9	11	6	6	9
% farm sector	1	1	0	3	2	1
N	1,693	3,658	579	42,178	1,400	5,302

Source: 1970 State Form 1 IPUMS.

[a]Recent migrants left South 1965–70.
[b]Iowa, Kansas, Minnesota, Nebraska, and the Dakotas.

TABLE A.13. Industrial Concentrations of White Southerners in Selected States, 1970

- In the Great Lakes states, southern whites built job concentrations in the region's core industries—steel, auto, and electrical—while holding 19% of the jobs in the region's tire plants. They were also overrepresented in trucking and lumber, especially in Indiana and Ohio.
- In California, southern whites had large concentrations in the aircraft and construction industries and still larger enclaves in oil (19%) and lumber (15%).
- Everywhere, they were heavily overrepresented among military personnel.

Number and Percentage of Southern-Born Whites
(Male and Female) by Industry

Industry	California	Illinois	Indiana	Michigan	Ohio
Steel	25,900	14,300	24,700	16,800	43,700
	(12%)	(7%)	(17%)	(11%)	(16%)
Construction	61,000	12,600	15,400	11,400	29,600
	(14%)	(5%)	(14%)	(7%)	(13%)
Auto	7,700	5,600	16,600	49,700	28,100
	(7%)	(6%)	(16%)	(10%)	(14%)
Electrical	22,600	13,100	14,100	3,700	22,000
	(10%)	(7%)	(12%)	(8%)	(15%)
Food service	31,300	6,700	7,800	7,400	20,500
	(11%)	(5%)	(11%)	(6%)	(14%)
Tires	1,500	700	3,800	1,500	12,900
	(10%)	(6%)	(24%)	(11%)	(18%)
Trucking	13,300	4,800	5,900	4,000	11,100
	(11%)	(5%)	(17%)	(9%)	(15%)
Aircraft	21,700	500	1,900	500	5,900
	(11%)	(5%)	(11%)	(7%)	(15%)
Lumber	7,500	1,100	3,700	800	1,500
	(15%)	(8%)	(23%)	(5%)	(12%)
Oil	9,600	2,300	1,100	700	1,900
	(19%)	(9%)	(15%)	(7%)	(16%)
Military personnel	59,800	9,100	1,400	2,600	4,000
	(17%)	(18%)	(15%)	(15%)	(18%)
All other sectors	656,100	159,400	154,500	140,800	335,700
	(10%)	(4%)	(10%)	(6%)	(11%)
Total white southerners in labor force	858,200	221,100	246,700	237,300	512,900
	(11%)	(5%)	(12%)	(7%)	(12%)

Source: 1970 State Form 2 IPUMS.

Note: Numbers are population estimates obtained by multiplying IPUMS 1% sample by 100.

TABLE A.14. Southern Whites, Southern Blacks, and Other Groups in Three Industries, Great Lakes States, 1970

- Southern-born whites were the largest population group in the steel mills and tire plants in the Midwest, outnumbering both African Americans and eastern Europeans (first- and second-generation). They were the second largest group after African Americans in the auto industry.
- More than other whites, their jobs remained on the shop floor. But large numbers of the men found skilled or foremen positions.
- Southern whites earned less in these industries on average than eastern Europeans but matched other whites and earned quite a bit more than blacks or Latinos.

	Southern-Born Whites	Southern-Born Blacks	Other Blacks	Eastern Europeans[a]	Other Whites
Steel Industry					
# males	86,200	48,100	29,600	62,400	456,100
Median personal income	$8,450	$7,450	$7,050	$9,100	$8,750
% professional/technical/ managerial	5	1	2	10	14
% skilled/foremen	34	24	21	40	32
# females	14,700	3,800	3,800	11,400	92,900
Median personal income	$5,050	$4,050	$4,300	$5,550	$5,050
Auto Industry					
# males	85,900	69,100	70,600	48,900	519,800
Median personal income	$9,050	$8,050	$7,050	$10,050	$9,050
% professional/technical/ managerial	5	2	3	13	14
% skilled/foremen	24	15	15	32	27
# females	15,100	7,800	11,100	9,900	110,000
Median personal income	$6,050	$4,100	$4,050	$6,550	$5,250
Tire Industry					
# males	13,700	5,300	2,300	3,800	63,000
Median personal income	$9,550	$8,050	$6,050	$9,100	$8,850
% professional/technical/ managerial	7	0	0	16	22
% skilled/foremen	16	6	9	10	18
# females	5,200	700	800	2,600	21,500
Median personal income	$4,750	$5,450	$4,050	$6,350	$4,650

Source: 1970 State Form 2 IPUMS.

Note: Numbers are ¹⁄₁₀₀ of population estimates.

[a]Eastern European–born or children of eastern European–born.

TABLE A.15. Home-ownership Rates among Black Households in Metropolitan Areas outside the South, 1920–1970

- Southerners were less likely to own houses than other blacks in the early years of the diaspora, but 63% of home-owners were southern-born.
- In the postwar era, southerners were more likely to own their homes than nonsoutherners.

	Black Male Heads of Household			Black Female Heads of Household		
	Southern-Born	Other U.S.-Born	Foreign-Born	Southern-Born	Other U.S.-Born	Foreign-Born
1920 home-owners	26,300	12,700	2,000	5,600	3,800	500
% of group	17	22	14	17	21	14
N	1,580	582	141	340	182	37
1940 home-owners	51,500	24,300	3,700	13,600	8,400	900
% of group	15	22	15	11	19	12
N	3,513	1,096	251	1,212	433	77
1960 home-owners	333,900	152,200	1,700	75,400	38,800	400
% of group	38	34	15	22	20	9
N	8,878	4,462	117	3,422	1,925	44
1970 home-owners	451,200	314,400	23,400	124,200	97,000	6,000
% of group	48	39	29	25	21	16
N	9,425	8,145	803	4,995	4,694	378

Sources: 1920 IPUMS, 1940 IPUMS, 1960 IPUMS, 1970 State Form 2 IPUMS.

TABLE A.16. Best Jobs and Nonelite Jobs Held by African Americans in Metropolitan Areas outside the South, 1920

- Northern- and western-born men and women were overrepresented in many of the best jobs, especially clerical and sales, in 1920.
- Even though they were underrepresented, southerners held the majority of the best jobs.

	Southern-Born Male	Other U.S.-Born Male	Southern-Born Female	Other U.S.-Born Female	Foreign-Born Both Sexes	Total
Best Jobs						
Proprietors, managers	3,800	2,800	1,200	600	500	8,900
Educators	600	200	900	1,100	100	2,900
Clergy	1,800	500	100		300	2,700
Musicians, entertainers	800	900	300	500		2,500
Other professionals	2,300	1,200	800	800	500	5,600
Sales	1,500	2,000	700	600	300	5,100
Clerical	6,700	6,100	1,400	2,400	1,400	18,000
Police, fire	700	500				1,200
Craftsmen, foremen	25,400	11,300	500	200	3,100	40,500
Total best jobs	43,600	25,500	5,900	6,200	6,200	87,400
Best jobs as % of all jobs	15	18	4	10	14	13
Nonelite Jobs						
Factory, delivery, drivers	41,300	21,700	20,600	8,100	10,000	101,700
Unskilled laborers	144,400	48,700	3,400	700	6,800	204,000
Barbers, beauticians	2,300	2,300	2,300	1,400	300	8,600
Porters	19,500	10,900	100		3,600	34,100
Other nondomestic service	33,400	16,400	18,700	11,600	7,100	87,200
Domestic service	5,100	3,100	85,100	33,500	8,500	135,300
Total in labor force	289,600	126,600	136,100	61,500	42,500	658,300

Source: 1920 IPUMS.

Note: Population estimates are used here to give some sense of the changing numbers of people involved in these occupations. But IPUMS sample values are very small for some occupations, and these smaller estimates may not be reliable. Sample *N*s are ¹⁄₁₀₀ of shown estimates. Labor force totals include some uncategorized workers.

TABLE A.17. Best Jobs and Nonelite Jobs Held by African Americans in Metropolitan Areas outside the South, 1940

• Northern- and western-born men and women still had job advantages in 1940.

	Southern-Born Male	Other U.S.-Born Male	Southern-Born Female	Other U.S.-Born Female	Foreign-Born Both Sexes	Total
Best Jobs						
Proprietors, managers	11,320	3,631	3,320	1,681	2,223	22,175
Educators	1,492	1,111	2,490	4,333		9,426
Clergy	2,882	281		101	273	3,537
Musicians, entertainers	2,897	2,696	583	606	303	7,085
Other professionals	6,641	4,229	3,422	3,397	1,515	19,204
Sales	7,823	4,954	2,577	2,249	1,907	19,510
Clerical	11,855	10,869	4,427	7,604	2,815	37,570
Police, fire	842	606				1,448
Craftsmen, foremen	42,508	19,395	1,774	1,401	3,550	68,628
Total best jobs	88,260	47,772	18,593	21,372	12,586	188,583
Best jobs as % of all jobs	17	25	7	19	29	17
Nonelite Jobs						
Factory, delivery, drivers	86,518	31,322	42,326	16,069	8,143	184,378
Unskilled laborers	212,324	60,725	2,626	1,268	7,455	284,398
Barbers, beauticians	3,523	997	4,765	2,007	202	11,494
Porters	40,117	13,683	101	202	2,783	56,886
Other nondomestic service	63,296	30,402	33,014	15,487	5,925	148,124
Domestic service	15,816	6,772	173,184	54,996	7,022	257,790
Total in labor force	509,854	191,673	274,609	111,401	44,116	1,131,653

Source: 1940 IPUMS.

Note: Population estimates are used here to give some sense of the changing numbers of people involved in these occupations. But IPUMS sample values are very small for some occupations, and these smaller estimates may not be reliable. Sample *N*s are 1/100 of shown estimates. Labor force totals include some uncategorized workers.

TABLE A.18. Best Jobs Held by African Americans in Metropolitan Areas outside the South, 1950

- Northern- and western-born continued to have greater access to most white-collar jobs in 1950.
- Southerners achieved equal representation among proprietors/managers/officials, clergy, and craftsmen/foremen.

Best Jobs	Southern-Born Male	Other U.S.-Born Male	Southern-Born Female	Other U.S.-Born Female	Foreign-Born Both Sexes	Total
Proprietors, managers, officials	25,914	10,843	6,570	2,460	1,171	46,958
Educators	1,865	1,311	4,511	5,011		12,698
Clergy	3,570	1,037	575	432		5,614
Musicians, entertainers	2,705	2,335	584	1,868		7,492
Other professionals, technical	8,763	7,588	10,231	10,497		37,079
Real estate, insurance	6,618	3,817	1,823	2,364	786	15,408
Other sales	10,114	8,532	7,948	5,337	309	32,240
Clerical	40,998	33,122	25,096	28,793	544	128,553
Police, fire	1,609	2,228				3,837
Craftsmen, foremen	89,594	43,009	3,432	3,306	457	139,798
Total best jobs	191,750	113,822	60,770	60,068	3,267	429,677
Best jobs as % of all jobs	23	33	13	29	28	23
Total in labor force	835,553	348,046	474,281	207,217	11,875	1,876,972

Source: 1950 IPUMS.

Note: Population estimates are used here to give some sense of the changing numbers of people involved in these occupations. But IPUMS sample values are very small for some occupations, and these smaller estimates may not be reliable. Sample Ns are ⅟₁₀₀ of shown estimates.

TABLE A.19. Best Jobs Held by African Americans in Metropolitan Areas outside the South, 1960

• Northern- and western-born continued to have greater access to most white-collar jobs in 1960.
• Southerners maintained equal representation among proprietors/managers/officials, clergy, and craftsmen/foremen.

Best Jobs	Southern-Born Male	Other U.S.-Born Male	Southern-Born Female	Other U.S.-Born Female	Foreign-Born Both Sexes	Total
Proprietors, managers, officials	20,100	11,300	6,900	4,500	400	43,200
Educators	3,800	3,900	10,700	10,900		29,300
Clergy	3,600	1,000	600	300		5,500
Musicians, entertainers	900	2,400	800	1,000		5,100
Other professionals, technical	14,700	18,900	20,900	21,600	900	77,000
Real estate, insurance	7,000	5,600	3,500	5,800	100	22,000
Other sales	9,100	12,100	9,100	10,500	100	40,900
Clerical	63,400	62,200	53,700	81,400	2,000	262,700
Police, fire	3,100	6,000	100	300		9,500
Craftsmen, foremen	117,800	61,500	7,200	4,600	1,300	192,400
Total best jobs	243,500	184,900	113,500	140,900	4,800	681,600
Best jobs as % of all jobs	27	41	19	43	24	30
Total in labor force	904,100	452,600	601,900	324,900	19,800	2,303,300

Source: 1960 IPUMS.

Note: Population estimates are used here to give some sense of the changing numbers of people involved in these occupations. But IPUMS sample values are very small for some occupations, and these smaller estimates may not be reliable. Sample *N*s are 1/100 of shown estimates.

TABLE A.20. Best Jobs Held by African Americans in Metropolitan Areas outside the South, 1970

• Northern- and western-born continued to have greater access to most white-collar jobs in 1970.
• Southerners were slightly overrepresented among proprietors/managers/officials, clergy, and craftsmen/foremen.

Best Jobs	Southern-Born Male	Other U.S.-Born Male	Southern-Born Female	Other U.S.-Born Female	Foreign-Born Both Sexes	Total
Proprietors, managers, officials	28,200	27,900	8,500	11,500	2,600	78,700
Educators	10,200	11,900	29,200	25,900	2,500	79,700
Clergy	2,300	1,700	200	100	100	4,400
Musicians, entertainers	2,500	3,200	600	1,700	100	8,100
Other professionals, technical	39,300	59,900	50,600	66,400	15,900	232,100
Real estate, insurance	7,900	13,000	11,300	25,900	3,600	61,700
Other sales	13,200	29,800	17,900	30,800	4,400	96,100
Clerical	74,100	106,500	162,900	272,300	31,100	646,900
Police, fire	6,200	10,900	300	400	400	18,200
Craftsmen, foremen	153,200	149,600	12,900	12,500	16,000	344,200
Total best jobs	337,100	414,400	294,400	447,500	76,700	1,570,100
Best jobs as % of all jobs	37	44	42	57	51	45
Total in labor force	902,700	947,100	696,800	786,100	150,300	3,483,000

Source: 1970 State Form 1 IPUMS.

Note: Population estimates are used here to give some sense of the changing numbers of people involved in these occupations. But IPUMS sample values are very small for some occupations, and these smaller estimates may not be reliable. Sample *N*s are ¹⁄₁₀₀ of shown estimates.

TABLE A.21. Personal Earnings for Southern-Born and Other Working-Age (25–54) Black Adults in Metropolitan Areas outside the South, 1939–1969

- Northern-born black men and women earned more than southern-born men and women at all educational levels in 1939.
- From 1949 to 1969, southern-born men earned higher incomes than northern-born men at the lower educational levels and comparable incomes at higher educational levels.
- Southern-born women continued to earn less than northern-born women, but the gap closed in 1969.

	Black Males 25–54 in Labor Force			Black Females 25–54 in Labor Force		
	Southern-Born	Other U.S.-Born	Ratio: Southern-Born/ Other-Born	Southern-Born	Other U.S.-Born	Ratio: Southern-Born/ Other-Born
1939						
0–8 grade	$776	$802	97%	$441	$524	84%
9–11 grade	799	1,002	80	542	612	89
High school graduate	922	1,046	88	475	580	82
College[a]	1,012	1,388	73	745	1,190	62
All	798	921	87	479	644	74
N	3,472	1,118		1,829	608	
1949						
0–8 grade	2,275	2,085	109	1,288	1,338	96
9–11 grade	2,538	2,382	107	1,334	1,469	91
High school graduate	2,568	2,513	102	1,558	1,748	89
College[a]	2,759	2,825	98	2,095	2,052	102
All	2,390	2,355	101	1,404	1,590	88
N	1,963	657		1,010	329	
1959						
0–8 grade	3,776	3,430	110	1,859	2,013	92
9–11 grade	4,085	3,929	104	2,010	2,137	94
High school graduate	4,149	4,311	96	2,426	2,686	90
College[a]	4,960	4,969	100	3,231	3,469	93
All	4,019	4,049	99	2,172	2,501	87
N	7,085	4,029		4,414	2,754	

	Black Males 25–54 in Labor Force			Black Females 25–54 in Labor Force		
	Southern-Born	Other U.S.-Born	Ratio: Southern-Born/ Other-Born	Southern-Born	Other U.S.-Born	Ratio: Southern-Born/ Other-Born
1969						
0–8 grade	6,503	5,983	109	3,474	3,473	100
9–11 grade	6,882	6,413	107	3,712	3,827	97
High school graduate	7,394	7,119	104	4,469	4,678	96
College[a]	9,420	9,362	101	6,243	6,468	97
All	7,308	7,074	103	4,390	4,614	95
N	6,487	5,927		4,719	4,658	

Sources: 1940 IPUMS, 1950 IPUMS, 1960 IPUMS, 1970 State Form 1 IPUMS.

[a]College graduates and nongraduates.

TABLE A.22. Financial Benefits of Migration, 1949: Comparing Average Income at Prime Earning Age (35–49) for Southerners Who Left and Those Who Stayed behind by Race, Sex, Education

	Migrants	Remained in South	% Gain/ (Loss)	Migrants in Metropolitan Non-South	Living in Metropolitan South	% Gain/ (Loss)
Mean 1949 Income for Southern-Born Black Males						
All	$2,375	$1,415	68	$2,409	$1,776	36
0–8 grade	2,253	1,318	71	2,288	1,699	35
9–12 grade	2,604	1,858	40	2,623	1,913	37
Some college	2,940	2,351	25	2,957	2,505	18
N	1,109	2,325		1,036	987	
Mean 1949 Income for Southern-Born White Males						
All	3,449	2,850	21	3,629	3,495	4
0–8 grade	2,825	2,156	31	2,950	2,716	9
9–12 grade	3,597	3,248	11	3,702	3,632	2
Some college	5,026	4,705	7	5,214	5,077	3
N	1,870	8,681		1,149	3,142	
Mean 1949 Income for Southern-Born Black Females						
All	1,273	761	67	1,290	941	37
0–8 grade	1,167	640	82	1,183	782	51
9–12 grade	1,379	884	56	1,390	1,045	33
Some college	1,737	1,950	(11)	1,738	2,138	(19)
N	713	1,726		673	762	
Mean 1949 Income for Southern-Born White Females						
All	1,534	1,531	0	1,463	1,509	(3)
0–8 grade	1,236	1,104	12	1,259	1,033	22
9–12 grade	1,602	1,565	2	1,544	1,686	(8)
Some college	2,028	2,213	(8)	1,961	2,297	(15)
N	877	3,703		1,268	2,362	

Source: 1950 IPUMS.

TABLE A.23. Financial Benefits of Migration, 1969: Comparing Average Income of Prime Earning Age (35–49) Southerners Who Left and Those Who Stayed behind by Education

	Migrants	Remained in South	% Gain/ (Loss)	Migrants in Metropolitan Non-South	Living in Metropolitan South	% Gain/ (Loss)
Mean 1969 Income for Southern-Born Black Males						
All	$7,548	$5,036	50	$7,618	$5,590	36
0–8 grade	6,681	4,111	63	6,765	4,698	44
9–12 grade	7,376	5,389	37	7,423	5,634	32
Some college	10,206	8,238	24	10,290	8,306	24
N	3,584	5,967		3,326	3,098	
Mean 1969 Income for Southern-Born White Males						
All	10,950	9,575	14	11,427	10,989	4
0–8 grade	8,370	6,446	30	8,863	7,396	20
9–12 grade	9,926	8,860	12	10,196	9,618	6
Some college	15,127	14,154	7	15,714	15,186	3
N	7,762	29,768		5,601	13,871	
Mean 1969 Income for Southern-Born Black Females						
All	4,342	3,066	42	4,341	3,355	29
0–8 grade	3,512	2,032	73	3,494	2,155	62
9–12 grade	4,063	2,932	39	4,057	3,147	29
Some college	6,499	6,024	8	6,497	6,201	5
N	2,563	5,119		2,386	2,744	
Mean 1969 Income for Southern-Born White Females						
All	4,756	4,316	10	4,938	4,759	4
0–8 grade	3,778	3,168	19	4,012	3,424	17
9–12 grade	4,518	4,120	10	4,690	4,462	5
Some college	6,265	5,883	6	6,473	6,223	4
N	3,893	16,312		2,866	7,681	

Source: 1970 State Form 1 IPUMS.

TABLE A.24. Residential Patterns for Southerners Living Outside the South 1940, 1970

	1940		1970	
	Blacks	Whites	Blacks	Whites
Rural/small cities[a]	143,979	1,339,881	239,600	2,814,800
Small/medium metropolitan areas	370,426	877,513	1,003,700	2,478,300
Major Metropolitan Areas				
New York–Newark	326,894	179,765	600,800	215,100
Philadelphia	176,636	98,377	201,800	147,300
Chicago-Gary	203,865	110,162	417,800	279,800
Cleveland	54,525	29,502	107,900	118,100
Detroit	102,158	117,162	267,800	252,400
St. Louis	80,323	67,554	107,600	114,000
Los Angeles–Long Beach	47,735	280,427	313,800	567,200
San Francisco–Oakland	10,909	72,333	136,700	172,300
Total major metropolitan areas	1,003,045	955,282	2,154,200	1,866,200
% in central cities[b]	81	55	58	37
% in suburbs[b]	19	45	42	63
Total outside South	1,517,450	3,172,076	3,397,500	7,159,300

Sources: 1940 IPUMS, 1970 Neighborhood IPUMS, 1970 State Form 1 IPUMS, 1970 Metro Form 2 IPUMS.

[a]Less than 50,000 population.

[b]Based on all metropolitan areas with 1 million or more persons.

Appendix B: Note on Methods

My calculations of migration volumes in chapter 1 and economic performance in chapter 3 rely principally on census data that have been compiled in machine-readable form by the Integrated Public Use Microdata Series (‹http://www.ipums.umn.edu/›). These are large samples of individual households (generally 1 percent of all cases) taken from each census except 1930. Since they are samples, they are subject to some degree of error. I have not calculated confidence intervals, but I do show sample size in almost all tables. In most cases, these are comfortably large. In a few of the tables (notably A.16–A.20), some of the cell categories are too small to be considered reliable.

The decadal censuses are the most accurate and comprehensive source we have for evaluating mass migrations, but they are far from perfect. Two kinds of accuracy problems have been noted. One involves missed households. Undercounting of poor people in cities and of transients has always been a problem. And some experts think that the undercounting of minority populations reaches as high as 10 percent in particular decades. The other problem involves omissions and inaccuracies in the responses of those who do participate. These have tended to increase in the second half of the century. Prior to 1960, less than 1 percent of respondents failed to answer the place-of-birth question. That rose to 2.7 percent in 1960 and 4.6 percent and 4.9 percent in the following decades. These issues, while worthy of concern, should not undercut confidence in the broad patterns that I follow in this book. I have used rounded numbers rather than precise counts in most references so as not to suggest that these data are absolutely accurate. For more on these issues, see Larry Long,

Migration and Residential Mobility in the United States (New York, 1988), appendix A, and also the IPUMS users guide (‹http://www.ipums.umn.edu/›).

The estimates of migration volumes (figure 1.2 and table A.1) required a number of procedures and assumptions that need to be explained in some detail.

Race and ethnic categories: Note first that there is no separate designation of southern-born American Indians, Asians, or other races. The categories "southern-born blacks" and "southern-born whites" exclude individuals identified as Hispanic. The Hispanic designation is complicated. Since 1970, the census has asked respondents whether or not they identify themselves as Hispanic. For earlier decades, we have to make do with a different set of questions. I have coded as Hispanic any person who meets any of the following criteria: Spanish surname, Spanish "mother tongue," born in Latin America, father or mother born in Latin America. Parental place of birth and "mother tongue" are not available in the 1940 and 1950 samples, resulting in an undercount of Hispanics in those years.

New migrant formula: The new migration during a decade can be calculated if we know the population of expatriate southerners at the beginning of the decade, the population at the end of the decade, the number of deaths during the decade, and the number who returned home during the decade. This is a modified version of the Census Forward Survival Rate procedure.[1]

Formula (1) can be written:

$$P^{ED} = P^{SD} + D + R + N$$

Where: P^{ED} = End-of-decade population of expatriates
P^{SD} = Start-of-decade population of expatriates
D = Deaths
R = Return migrants
N = New migrants

The sources for the two population counts (P^{S} and P^{E}) are the IPUMS samples of the United States Census. Deaths (D) are estimated using mortality tables for the starting year of each decade. These provide average mortality rates in a given year on the basis of sex, race, and age. Separate mortality rates for Hispanics were not available. To be conservative, I used white rates in those calculations.[2]

Return migrants: Estimating return migration (R) is the most controversial aspect of the procedure. In all but one census since 1940, respondents have been asked to identify where they lived exactly five years earlier. This is a problematic but still useful guide to mobility. It is problematic because not everyone answers the question, and some who do may not answer accurately given the difficulty of remembering domiciles five years earlier. Another problem is that any two-way moves that have taken place within the five-year interval remain uncounted. The result is an undercounted snapshot of population movement. How much of an undercount? In the 1950 census, respondents were asked to identify where they had lived just one year earlier. The recorded mobility rate was more accurate and also much higher than those derived from the five-year question. Table A.2 displays the data on return migration derived from each of the decadal censuses. Notice that the five-year rates are low in comparison to the one-year rate derived from the 1950 questionnaire, when 1.7 percent of all black expatriates and 4.7 percent of all white expatriates said that they had returned to the South in the previous twelve months. That year, 1949, was admittedly exceptional. A postwar recession encouraged some of the southerners who had moved north or west during World War II to head home. Still, it is hard to believe that the rust-belt-era return migrations did not come close to the 1949 rate, despite what the five-year interval numbers show.

The fact that the five-year interval data yield undercounts of actual return migration rates is nevertheless useful. It gives us minimum estimates that we can work with to fill in the intervals for which census data is not available. For some decades (1930s, 1950s, 1960s, 1990s), I have assumed that rates for both five-year intervals will be equal. For the early 1970s, I averaged the rates of the preceding and following half decades and did the same for the 1980–85 interval. The 1940s posed special problems since the only data come from the final year and since migration trends rode a roller coaster during the decade. Seeking a minimal estimate, I took the 1949–50 count and tripled it, applying that total to the 1945–50 interval while assuming zero return migration for the war years 1940–45. All of these estimates appear in table A.1 as "minimum return migration."

I am reasonably confident in these interpolation strategies for the years following 1935, but the first-wave era poses a problem of a different order. There are simply no mobility data from the earlier censuses. I have resorted therefore to a policy of minimal estimates based on the 1935–40 rates. That interval recorded the very lowest rates of return migration of any of the census counts, and there is every reason to believe that the decades before 1935 would have known rates considerably higher. In fact, it would probably have been safe to take the next highest set of rates (1955–60) and apply them to much of the earlier era. The first-wave migration volume estimates would then become larger than in figure 1.2.

Data: IPUMS provided most of the data for both expatriate population counts and return rates. I used the following samples: 1900 general, 1910 general, 1920 preliminary general, 1930 preliminary 1/500, 1940 general, 1950 general, 1960 general, 1970 State Form 1 (for distributions outside the South), 1970 State Form 2 (for return migrants), 1980 State 5 percent, 1990 State 5 percent, 2000 1 percent census.[3]

The 1960 IPUMS posed a problem. The Census Bureau collected data on region-to-region mobility and published it in the official reports but did not include it in the IPUMS samples, using instead a less specific mobility variable that recorded five-year migration across state lines without identifying which states. What I have done is taken the volumes and rates of return migration from the published tables and the age-sex profiles from the IPUMS mobility variable. Unfortunately, these 1955–60 tables do not distinguish Hispanics. Consequently, the volume of 1950s return migration and new migration attributed to whites is inflated slightly, while the volume of new Latino migration is undercounted. The difference is not huge (probably 10,000–20,000).[4]

The 1970 census changed the wording in the "place of birth" question that yields the critical information about state of birth, and demographers think that there was a significant underreporting that year of persons identified as living outside their state of birth. That error probably shows up in figures 1.1 and 1.2, which record the number of southern-born living outside the South and estimate the decade-by-decade migration volumes. It is likely that the volumes shown for the 1960s are an undercount and the volumes for the 1970s something of an overcount.

Calculations: The following steps were used to account for death rates and return migration rates and calculate the likely number of new migrants who left the South each decade. First, an iterative formula was applied to each age-sex cohort (ten-year intervals after age five), subtracting the estimated dead and departed one year at a time.

Formula (2):

$$P^{SY} \times (1 - DR) \times (1 - RR) = P^{EY}$$

Where: P^{SY} = expatriate population of age-sex cohort at start of year
P^{EY} = expatriate population of age-sex cohort at end of year
DR = annual death rate for age-sex cohort
RR = annualized return rate for age-sex cohort

After ten years, P^{EY} reflects the loss of expatriate population due to death and return migration. The total number of new migrants is then calculated by subtracting P^{EY} from the number of southern-born counted in the next decadal census.

Notes

INTRODUCTION

1. The details of this story are from James Richardson, *Willie Brown: A Biography* (Berkeley, 1996), 105–16.

2. Ibid., 144; *California Political Almanac, 1995–1996* (Santa Barbara, Calif., 1996), 219.

3. Richardson, *Willie Brown*, 105–7, tells Unruh's story. See also James R. Mills, *A Disorderly House: The Brown-Unruh Years in Sacramento* (Berkeley, 1987), 75–78.

4. Quoted in Richardson, *Willie Brown*, 41.

5. See table A.1 in appendix A.

6. Aretha Franklin and David Ritz, *Aretha: From These Roots* (New York, 1999); Merle Haggard with Peggy Russell, *Sing Me Back Home: My Story* (New York, 1981).

7. Nick Salvatore, *Singing in a Strange Land: C. L. Franklin, the Black Church, and the Transformation of America* (Boston, 2005); C. L. Franklin, *Give Me This Mountain: Life History and Selected Sermons*, ed. Jeff Todd Titon (Urbana, Ill., 1989); Marshall Frady, *Billy Graham: A Parable of American Righteousness* (Boston, 1979).

8. Willie Morris, *North toward Home* (Boston, 1967), 387; Albert Murray, *South to a Very Old Place* (New York, 1971).

9. Joe William Trotter Jr. surveys the historiography of the black migration in the introduction to *The Great Migration in Historical Perspective: New Dimensions of Race, Class, and Gender* (Bloomington, 1991), 1–21. Stewart E. Tolnay surveys the sociological literature in "The African American 'Great Migration' and Beyond," *Annual Review of Sociology* 29 (2003): 209–33. Key studies include James R. Grossman, *Land of Hope: Chicago, Black Southerners, and the Great Migration* (Chicago, 1989); Nicholas Lemann, *The Promised Land: The Great Black Migration and How It Changed America* (New York, 1991); Kimberley L. Phillips, *AlabamaNorth: African-American Migrants, Community, and Working-Class Activism in Cleveland, 1915–45* (Urbana, Ill., 1999);

Carole Marks, *Farewell—We're Good and Gone: The Great Black Migration* (Bloomington, 1989); Peter Gottlieb, *Making Their Own Way: Southern Blacks' Migration to Pittsburgh, 1916–30* (Urbana, Ill., 1987); and Daniel M. Johnson and Rex R. Campbell, *Black Migration in America: A Social Demographic History* (Durham, 1981), 32–42.

Studies focused on white southerners include Chad Berry, *Southern Migrants, Northern Exiles* (Urbana, Ill., 2000); Phillip J. Obermiller, Thomas E. Wagner, and E. Bruce Tucker, eds., *Appalachian Odyssey: Historical Perspectives on the Great Migration* (Westport, 2000); James N. Gregory, *American Exodus: The Dust Bowl Migration and Okie Culture in California* (New York, 1989); William W. Philliber, *Appalachian Migrants in Urban America: Cultural Conflict or Ethnic Group Formation?* (New York, 1981); Walter Stein, *California and the Dust Bowl Migration* (Westport, 1973); and Marsha L. Weisiger, *Land of Plenty: Oklahomans in the Cotton Fields of Arizona, 1933–1942* (Norman, 1995).

Jack Temple Kirby pointed the way toward an integrated analysis in "The Southern Exodus, 1910–1960: A Primer for Historians," *Journal of Southern History* 49 (November 1983): 585–600. Jacqueline Jones devotes two substantial chapters to the subject in *The Dispossessed: America's Underclasses from the Civil War to the Present* (New York, 1992), 205–68. J. Trent Alexander wrote an important dissertation comparing white and black southern migrant experiences in Cincinnati and Indianapolis: "Great Migrations: Race and Community in the Southern Exodus, 1917–1970" (Ph.D. diss., Carnegie Mellon University, 2001). Sociologists have sometimes compared the two migrant groups and their reasons for leaving; see Neil Fligstein, *Going North: Migration of Blacks and Whites from the South, 1900–1950* (New York, 1981); Sam Joseph Dennis, *African-American Exodus and White Migration, 1950–1970: A Comparative Analysis of Population Movements and Their Relations to Labor and Race Relations* (New York, 1989); and Rashida Qureshi, "Dependency and Internal Migration: A Comparative Study of Outmigration from the Appalachian South and the Core South" (Ph.D. diss., Kansas State University, 1996).

10. John Shelton Reed, *One South: An Ethnic Approach to Regional Culture* (Baton Rouge, 1982), 4.

11. Thirty years have passed since the publication of George W. Pierson's cultural analysis, *The Moving American* (New York, 1973). A few historians have kept their eyes on the subject, notably Walter Nugent, *Into the West: The Story of Its People* (New York, 1999); and Donna Gabaccia, "Two Great Migrations: American and Italian Southerners in Comparative Perspective," in *The American South and the Italian Mezzogiorno: Essays in Comparative History*, ed. Enrico Dal Lago and Rick Halpern (New York, 2002), 215–32.

12. Several theoretical schools are evaluated in Stephen Castles and Mark J. Miller, *The Age of Migration: International Population Movements in the Modern World*, 3rd ed. (New York, 2003), 21–30; see also Qureshi, "Dependency and Internal Migration," 3–15. Dennis outlines migration systems theory (also called exodus theory) in *African-American Exodus and White Migration*, 54–63, and it is elaborated in Marks, *Farewell—We're Good and Gone* and Townsand Price-Spratlen, "African American Community Development and Migration Streams: Patterns of Change in 20th Century Metropolitan Migration" (Ph.D. diss., University of Washington, 1993).

13. Robert Ezra Park surveyed this literature in "Human Migration and the Marginal Man," *American Journal of Sociology* 33, no. 6 (1928): 881–93. The writings of Frederick Jackson Turner and Theodore Roosevelt reflect this understanding of migration as a fundamental force of history.

CHAPTER ONE

1. On definitions, see Robin Cohen, *Global Diasporas: An Introduction* (Seattle, 1997).

2. Diasporas take different forms. Sociologist Robin Cohen lists them as victim diasporas (refugees or captive migrants); imperial diasporas (both colonial and nation spreading projects); labor diasporas (of workers seeking jobs); trade diasporas (featuring entrepreneurial or professional networks); and postcolonial diasporas (a grab bag for all sorts of mass population movements that do not fit the other definitions). See also Stephen Castles and Mark J. Miller, *The Age of Migration: International Population Movements in the Modern World*, 3rd ed. (New York, 2003).

3. Calculated from United States Census Office, *Twelfth Census of the United States, Taken in the Year 1900*, vol. 1 (Washington, D.C., 1902), table 26, 690–93. For nineteenth-century white migration patterns, see Jason Carl Digman, "Which Way to the Promised Land? Changing Patterns in Southern Migration, 1865–1920" (Ph.D. diss., University of Illinois–Chicago, 2001); David Hacket Fischer and James C. Kelley, *Bound Away: Virginia and the Westward Movement* (Charlottesville, 2000); Phillip J. Schwartz, *Migrants Against Slavery: Virginians and the Nation* (Charlottesville, 2001); and Daniel E. Sutherland, "Southern Fraternal Organizations in the North," *Journal of Southern History*, 53, no. 4 (1987): 587–612, and also *The Confederate Carpetbaggers* (Baton Rouge, 1988).

4. Calculated from United States Census Office, *Twelfth Census of the United States*, vol. 1, table 29, 702–5. On nineteenth-century black migration, see Carter G. Woodson, *A Century of Negro Migration* (Washington, D.C., 1918); Daniel M. Johnson and Rex R. Campbell, *Black Migration in America: A Social Demographic History* (Durham, 1981); Digman, "Which Way to the Promised Land?"; Nell Irvin Painter, *Exodusters: Black Migration to Kansas after Reconstruction* (Topeka, 1986); William Cohen, *At Freedom's Edge: Black Mobility and the Southern White Quest for Racial Control, 1861–1915* (Baton Rouge, 1991); and Steven Hahn, *A Nation under Our Feet: Black Political Struggles in the Rural South from Slavery to the Great Migration* (Cambridge, Mass., 2003), 330–63.

5. Steven Ruggles, Matthew Sobek, Trent Alexander, Catherine A. Fitch, Ronald Goeken, Patricia Kelly Hall, Miriam King, and Chad Ronnander, *Integrated Public Use Microdata Series: Version 3.0* (machine-readable database) (Minneapolis, 2004). Integrated Public Use Microdata Series are large samples (generally 1 percent of all households) taken from each manuscript census except that of 1890. Information about IPUMS is available at ‹http://www.ipums.umn.edu/›. Since they are samples, they are subject to some degree of error, but because of the huge size of the samples, the error is modest. A second issue is the accuracy of the underlying census, which was subject to enumeration errors (particularly affecting poor and mobile populations) and also inaccurate responses. Still, compared with every other kind of historical source, the

U.S. Census has been reliable and reasonably accurate. Recent migration studies that have employed IPUMS include J. Trent Alexander, "Great Migrations: Race and Community in the Southern Exodus, 1917–1970" (Ph.D. diss., Carnegie Mellon University, 2001); Digman, "Which Way to the Promised Land?," and various articles by Stewart Tolnay, which will be cited below. This is also the place to acknowledge the critical contributions of Larry Long, who has presided over the study of internal migration since the early 1970s. His book *Migration and Residential Mobility in the United States* (New York, 1988) is a key resource for migration studies.

6. For less complete estimates, see Johnson and Campbell, *Black Migration in America*, 32–42; and Jack Temple Kirby, "The Southern Exodus, 1910–1960: A Primer for Historians," *Journal of Southern History* 49 (November 1983). In my earlier work, I too neglected to account for mortality and return migration. See James N. Gregory, "The Southern Diaspora and the Urban Dispossessed: Demonstrating the Census Public Use Microdata Samples," *Journal of American History* 82, no. 1 (1995): 112.

7. Nicholas Lemann, *The Promised Land: The Great Black Migration and How It Changed America* (New York, 1991), 6. Confusion over the size of the two migrations results from a failure by some scholars to distinguish between rates and volumes. Blacks left the South at higher rates relative to population, but white volumes were greater. Other problems derive from improper interpretation of "net migration" statistics (out-migration minus in-migration), which are not useful for calculating volumes. On that point, see Digman, "Which Way to the Promised Land?," 50–60.

8. There have been a number of important studies of return migration in the very last stages of the diaspora: Anne S. Lee, "Return Migration in the United States," *International Migration Review* 8 (1974): 283–300; and Larry H. Long and Kristin A. Hansen, "Trends in Return Migration to the South," *Demography* 12 (1975): 601–14, and "Selectivity of Black Return Migration to the South," *Rural Sociology* 42 (Fall 1977): 317–31.

9. For more on return migration, see J. Trent Alexander, " 'They're Never Here More Than a Year': Return Migration in the Southern White Exodus, 1940–1970," *Journal of Social History* (forthcoming).

10. Robert M. Adelman, Chris Morett, and Stewart E. Tolnay, "Homeward Bound: The Return Migration of Southern Born Black Women, 1940–1990," *Sociological Spectrum* 20 (2000): 433–63; Gretchen Lemke-Santangelo, *Abiding Courage: African American Migrant Women and the East Bay Community* (Chapel Hill, 1996), 148–51.

11. Stewart E. Tolnay, *The Bottom Rung: African American Family Life on Southern Farms* (Urbana, Ill., 1999), 145; Reynold Farley and Walter R. Allen, *The Color Line and the Quality of Life in America* (New York, 1987), 134; Johnson and Campbell, *Black Migration in America*; George A. Davis and O. Fred Donaldson, *Blacks in the United States: A Geographic Perspective* (Boston, 1975), 29–51.

12. U.S. Bureau of the Census, *Historical Statistics of the United States, Colonial Times to 1970*, Part 1 (Washington, D.C., 1975), table A, 177–94, 22; 1970 State Form 2 IPUMS sample.

13. Net migration flows and impacts on states are shown in Everett S. Lee, Ann Ratner Miller, Carol P. Brainerd, and Richard A. Easterlin, *Methodological Considerations*

and Reference Tables, vol. 1 of *Population Redistribution and Economic Growth: United States, 1870–1950* (Philadelphia, 1957), 65–95.

14. For a sampling of migration literature, see Caroline B. Brettell and James F. Hollifield, eds., *Migration Theory: Talking across Disciplines* (New York, 2000); R. Paul Shaw, *Migration Theory and Fact: A Review and Bibliography of Current Literature* (Philadelphia, 1975); and Clifford J. Jansen, ed., *Readings in the Sociology of Migration* (Oxford, 1970).

15. Classic internal migration studies include Hope T. Eldridge and Dorothy Swaine Thomas, *Demographic Analyses and Interrelations*, vol. 3 of *Population Redistribution and Economic Growth: United States, 1870–1950* (Philadelphia, 1964); Donald J. Bogue, Henry S. Shryock Jr., and Siegfried A. Hoermann, *Streams of Migration between Subregions*, vol. 1 of *Subregional Migration in the United States, 1935–1940* (Oxford, Ohio, 1957). More recently, see Bernard L. Weinstein, Harold T. Gross, and John Rees, *Regional Growth and Decline in the United States*, 2d ed. (New York, 1985).

16. James R. Grossman, *Land of Hope: Chicago, Black Southerners, and the Great Migration* (Chicago, 1989), 13–19, draws a useful distinction between the observable "causes" that invite migration and the "motivations" of migrants, which are much more complicated.

17. Elliott Robert Barkan, *And Still They Come: Immigrants and American Society 1920 to the 1990s* (Wheeling, Ill., 1996), 197, 199; Roger Daniels, *Coming to America: A History of Immigration and Ethnicity in American Life* (New York, 1990).

18. Calculated from E. S. Lee et al., *Methodological Considerations and Reference Tables*, 685, 732, 753, tables M-3, 4.6, Y-1. See also Mark Perlman, *Patterns of Regional Economic Decline and Growth* (Washington, D.C., 1982), table A-2, 37–39, for a second measure of state-level economic output in 1929. His tables give the nine northern states 56 percent of the nation's economic output in 1929.

19. Calculated from E. S. Lee et al., *Methodological Considerations and Reference Tables*, 609–21, table L-4. On southern economic conditions, see Jack Temple Kirby, *Rural Worlds Lost: The American South 1920–1960* (Baton Rouge, 1987); Gavin Wright, *Old South, New South: Revolutions in the Southern Economy since the Civil War* (New York, 1986); James C. Cobb, *Industrialization and Southern Society 1877–1984* (Lexington, Ky., 1984); Pete Daniel, *Standing at the Crossroads: Southern Life in the Twentieth Century* (New York, 1986), 72–87; and Gilbert C. Fite, *Cotton Fields No More: Southern Agriculture 1865–1980* (Lexington, Ky., 1984), 66–119. On the region's key industries, see Daniel Letwin, *The Challenge of Interracial Unionism: Alabama Coal Miners, 1878–1921* (Chapel Hill, 1998); Henry M. McKiven Jr., *Iron and Steel: Class, Race and Community in Birmingham, Alabama, 1875–1920* (Chapel Hill, 1995); Bryant Simon, *A Fabric of Defeat: The Politics of South Carolina Millhands, 1910–1948* (Chapel Hill, 1999); Jacquelyn Dowd Hall, James Leloudis, Robert Korstad, Mary Murphy, Lu Ann Jones, and Christopher B. Daly, *Like a Family: The Making of a Southern Cotton Mill World* (Chapel Hill, 1987).

20. Charles S. Johnson, "How Much Is the Migration a Flight from Persecution?" *Opportunity* 1 (September 1923): 272–74, reprinted in *Up South: Stories, Studies, and Letters of This Century's Black Migrations*, ed. Malaika Adero (New York, 1993), 44. On

the association between out-migration and lynching, see Stewart E. Tolnay and E. M. Beck, *A Festival of Violence: An Analysis of Southern Lynchings, 1882–1930* (Urbana, Ill., 1995); Florette Henri, *Black Migration: Movement North 1900–1920* (Garden City, N.Y., 1975), 51–59; and Grossman, *Land of Hope*, 13–37. Key studies of the African American experience in the South up to the time of the Great Migration include Leon Litwack, *Trouble in Mind: Black Southerners in the Age of Jim Crow* (New York, 1998); Neil R. McMillen, *Dark Journey: Black Mississippians in the Age of Jim Crow* (Urbana, Ill., 1989); Hahn, *A Nation under Our Feet*; and Tera Hunter, *To 'Joy My Freedom: Southern Black Women's Lives and Labors after the Civil War* (Cambridge, Mass., 1997).

21. Labor force changes are from Doug McAdam, *Political Process and the Development of Black Insurgency, 1930–1970* (Chicago, 1985), 74. Grossman, *Land of Hope*, 66–97, is excellent on recruiting patterns among African Americans. Carole Marks, *Farewell—We're Good and Gone: The Great Black Migration* (Bloomington, 1989), also emphasizes "lines of communication." For whites, see Chad Berry, *Southern Migrants, Northern Exiles* (Urbana, Ill., 2000), 121–28; and James N. Gregory, *American Exodus: The Dust Bowl Migration and Okie Culture in California* (New York, 1989), 6–9.

22. A sample of the debate: Neil Fligstein, *Going North: Migration of Blacks and Whites from the South, 1900–1950* (New York, 1981), develops a statistical argument that agricultural reorganization rather than northern opportunities was the major cause. William Vickery, *The Economics of the Negro Migration, 1900–1920* (New York, 1977), makes the case for northern job opportunities. G. Wright, *Old South, New South*, 200–207, develops an argument about the reconstruction of national labor markets that draws upon an earlier study by Flora Gill, "Economics and the Black Exodus" (Ph.D. diss., Stanford University, 1974). Sam Joseph Dennis, *African-American Exodus and White Migration, 1950–1970: A Comparative Analysis of Population Movements and Their Relations to Labor and Race Relations* (New York, 1989), presents a model that includes both economic opportunities and racial oppression as migration factors. Adding a layer of dependency theory is Rashida Qureshi, "Dependency and Internal Migration: A Comparative Study of Outmigration from the Appalachian South and the Core South" (Ph.D. diss., Kansas State University, 1996). Townsand Price-Spratlen, "African American Community Development and Migration Streams: Patterns of Change in 20th-Century Metropolitan Migration" (Ph.D. diss., University of Washington, 1993), models the social and political attractions of the cities.

23. Elisabeth Rauh Bethel, *Promiseland: A Century of Life in a Negro Community* (Philadelphia, 1981), esp. 185–88; Jacqueline Jones, *The Dispossessed: America's Underclasses from the Civil War to the Present* (New York, 1992), 125–66, shows the mobility of black and white southern workers in this period.

24. Bethel, *Promiseland*, 186–87.

25. Audie Moffitt interview by author, 5 June 1981, Long Beach, in author's possession. On the economic and population mobility in this area see Gregory, *American Exodus*, 7–19; William H. Metzler, "Population Trends and Adjustments in Arkansas," *Arkansas Agricultural Experiment State Bulletin*, No. 388 (May 1940); and Sheila Goldring Manes, "Depression Pioneers: The Conclusion of an American Odyssey, Oklahoma to California, 1930–1950, a Reinterpretation" (Ph.D. diss., University of California, Los Angeles, 1982).

26. The migrants' superior educational background is demonstrated in Stewart E. Tolnay, "Educational Selection in the Migration of Southern Blacks, 1880–1990," *Social Forces* 77 (December 1998): 487–514; and Digman, "Which Way to the Promised Land?" 99–103. Selectivity theories are surveyed in Shaw, *Migration Theory and Fact* (Philadelphia, 1975), and Wen Lang Li, *Models of Migration* (Taipei, 1994).

27. Using the census survival and return migration formulas explained above, women accounted for 47 percent of white migrants and 48 percent of black migrants in the 1910–20 period. In the 1920s, white male migrants still outnumbered white female migrants (737,368 to 715,518), but black females now accounted for 53.8% of black migrants (435,937 black females to 374,677 black males). New York and Philadelphia attracted a higher percentage of black females than midwestern cities, including Chicago. Black women may have had particular reasons to leave relating to the climate of racial and sexual violence. See Darlene Clark Hine and Kathleen Thompson, *A Shining Thread of Hope: The History of Black Women in America* (New York, 1998), 213–19; Darlene Clark Hine, "Black Migration to the Urban Midwest: The Gender Dimension, 1915–1945," in *The Great Migration in Historical Perspective: New Dimensions of Race, Class, and Gender*, ed. Joe William Trotter Jr. (Bloomington, 1991); and Beverly A. Bunch-Lyons, *Contested Terrain: African-American Women Migrate from the South to Cincinnati, Ohio, 1900–1950* (New York, 2002), 23–42.

28. See chap. 3 and table A.7 for data on the occupational distributions of migrants.

29. J. T. Kirby, *Rural Worlds Lost*, 10–13.

30. W. J. Cash, *The Mind of the South* (New York, 1941), 328; C. Horace Hamilton, "Educational Selection of Net Migration from the South," *Social Forces* 36 (1959): 33–42.

31. Wolfe's biographer, David Herbert Donald, recalls the influence the book had on him: "Later, as an adolescent, I really read *Look Homeward, Angel* and was certain that Thomas Wolfe had told my life story." *Look Homeward: A Life of Thomas Wolfe* (Boston, 1987), xi. Sutherland, *Confederate Carpetbaggers*, explores the intellectual exodus of an earlier generation.

32. Stressing nonagricultural migration are Marks, *Farewell—We're Good and Gone*, 32–48; J. Trent Alexander, "The Great Migration in Comparative Perspective," *Social Science History* 22, no. 3 (1998): 349–76; and G. Wright, *Old South, New South*, 203–6. Emphasizing rural backgrounds are Grossman, *Land of Hope*, 183, and J. Jones, *The Dispossessed*, 210. See also Tolnay, "Educational Selection in the Migration of Southern Blacks," and *Bottom Rung*, 146–47.

33. Carter Goodwin Woodson, *The Negro Professional Man and the Community* (Washington, D.C., 1934), esp. 29–42, 192, 287. Later studies confirmed the tendency of better-educated blacks to migrate: C. Horace Hamilton, "The Negro Leaves the South," *Demography* 1 (1959): 273–95; Daniel C. Thompson, *A Black Elite: A Profile of Graduates of UNCF Colleges* (Westport, 1986), 74–75.

34. Erdmann Doane Beynon, "The Southern White Laborer Migrates to Michigan," *American Sociological Review* 3 (June 1938): 337; Elmer Akers, "Southern Whites in Detroit" (unpublished ms., n.d. [1937?]), 47, available through University Microfilms.

35. Charles Denby, *Indignant Heart: A Black Worker's Journal* (Boston, 1978; orig. 1952), 37–38.

36. Fite, *Cotton Fields No More*, 121; G. Wright, *Old South, New South*, 220–23.

37. Gregory, *American Exodus*, 19–34; Walter Stein, *California and the Dust Bowl Migration* (Westport, 1973), 3–27; Marsha L. Weisiger, *Land of Plenty: Oklahomans in the Cotton Fields of Arizona, 1933–1942* (Norman, 1995).

38. Gregory, *American Exodus*, 6–10. On interregional migration streams during the 1930s and other decades, see Eldridge and Thomas, *Demographic Analyses and Interrelations*, 121–25.

39. Black migration during the 1930s has been studied much less than other eras. See Townsand Price-Spratlen, "Livin' for the City: African American Ethnogenesis and Depression Era Migration," *Demography* 36 (November 1999): 553–68; Johnson and Campbell, *Black Migration in America*, 95–100; J. Jones, *The Dispossessed*, 217–24; and Kimberley L. Phillips, *AlabamaNorth: African-American Migrants, Community, and Working-Class Activism in Cleveland, 1915–45* (Urbana, Ill., 1999).

40. 1940 IPUMS sample. See also Noel P. Gist, C. T. Philbald, and C. S. Gregory, *Selective Factors in Migration and Occupation* (Columbia, Mo., 1944); Tolnay, *Bottom Rung*, 129–41; Long, *Migration and Residential Mobility*, 177; and Johnson and Campbell, *Black Migration in America*, 95–96. That urban-to-urban migration was the dominant pattern of the decade was demonstrated in Donald J. Bogue, Henry S. Shryock Jr., and Siegfried A. Hoermann, *Streams of Migration between Subregions*, vol. 1 of *Subregional Migration in the United States, 1935–1940* (Oxford, Ohio, 1957), 46–63. The authors do note a tendency of respondents to designate a city as their 1935 place of residence even though they may have lived in nearby rural areas. Other respondents failed to identify their earlier places of residence.

41. Depression-era conditions are examined in St. Clair Drake and Horace R. Cayton, *Black Metropolis: A Study of Negro Life in a Northern City* (New York, 1962; orig. 1945); Cheryl Lynn Greenberg, *"Or Does It Explode?" Black Harlem in the Great Depression* (New York, 1991); and K. L. Phillips, *AlabamaNorth*, 190–225. Transients were theoretically eligible for WPA work, but most states found ways to discriminate against newcomers. See Joan M. Crouse, *The Homeless Transient in the Great Depression: New York State, 1929–1941* (Albany, 1986), 210.

42. "James Boggs," in *Untold Tales, Unsung Heroes: An Oral History of Detroit's African American Community, 1918–1967*, ed. Elaine Latzman Moon (Detroit, 1994), 150.

43. Lily Tomlin interview with author, 5 October 2000, in author's possession; Jeff Sorensen, *Lily Tomlin: Woman of a Thousand Faces* (New York, 1989), 11–13. On the Paducah-Detroit connection, see Akers, "Southern Whites in Detroit." On southern white migration during the 1930s, see Beynon, "Southern White Laborer," 47; and Berry, *Southern Migrants, Northern Exiles*, 31–56.

44. Long, *Migration and Residential Mobility*, 51, 308 (tables 2.6, B.4); George W. Pierson, *The Moving American* (New York, 1973), 22; Paul J. Schwind, *Migration and Regional Development in the United States 1950–1960* (Chicago, 1971); Weinstein, Gross, and Rees, *Regional Growth and Decline in the United States*.

45. Fite, *Cotton Fields No More*, table A-1, 233. J. T. Kirby, *Rural Worlds Lost*, 276, estimates that the farm population shrank by 8 million between 1920 and 1960 and notes that this was a more dramatic and "chronologically compressed" rural depopulation

than that experienced by any other region of the United States. On western develop-ment and population shifts, see Gerald D. Nash, *The American West Transformed: The Impact of World War II* (Bloomington, 1985); and Walter Nugent, *Into the West: The Story of Its People* (New York, 1999), 255–311.

46. Donald Holley, *The Second Great Emancipation: The Mechanical Cotton Picker, Black Migration and How They Shaped the Modern South* (Fayetteville, Ark., 2000), 119–63; Lemann, *Promised Land*, 3–58; J. T. Kirby, *Rural Worlds Lost*, 135–54. Dennis, *African-American Exodus and White Migration*, emphasizes the political and psycho-logical dimensions of black migration in this era.

47. Bobby Seale, *Seize the Time: The Story of the Black Panther Party and Huey P. Newton* (New York, 1970); Quintard Taylor, *In Search of the Racial Frontier: African Americans in the American West, 1528–1990* (New York, 1998), 251–77; Shirley Ann Wilson Moore, *To Place Our Deeds: The African American Community in Richmond, California, 1910–1963* (Berkeley, 2000); Marilynn S. Johnson, *The Second Gold Rush: Oakland and the East Bay in World War II* (Berkeley, 1993); Albert S. Broussard, *Black San Francisco: The Struggle for Racial Equality in the West, 1900–1954* (Lawrence, Kans., 1993), 133–79; Lemke-Santangelo, *Abiding Courage*; Lawrence Brooks de Graaf, *Negro Migration to Los Angeles, 1930 to 1950* (San Francisco, 1974).

48. David Montejano, *Anglos and Mexicans in the Making of Texas, 1836–1986* (Aus-tin, 1987); Neil Foley, *The White Scourge: Mexicans, Blacks and Poor Whites in Texas Cotton Culture* (Berkeley, 1997). On the changing geography of Mexican Americans, see Dennis Nodin Valdes, *Barrios Nortenos: St. Paul and Midwestern Mexican Com-munities in the Twentieth Century* (Austin, 2000), and *Al Norte: Agricultural Workers in the Great Lakes Region, 1917–1970* (Austin, 1992); Zaragosa Vargas, *Proletarians of the North: A History of Mexican Industrial Workers in Detroit and Midwest, 1917–1933* (Berkeley, 1993); and Erasmo Gamboa, *Mexican Labor and World War II: Braceros in the Pacific Northwest 1942–1947* (Seattle, 1990).

49. Hispanic midwest calculations are from 1970 State Form 1 IPUMS sample. See also table A.3 in appendix A. Marc Simon Rodriguez argues that Texas Mexicans en-abled the Chicano civil rights movement in Wisconsin in "Obreros Unidos: Migration, Migrant Farm Worker Activism, and the Chicano Movement in Wisconsin and Texas, 1950–1980" (Ph.D. diss., Northwestern University, 2000).

50. 1970 State Form 1 IPUMS. On Indian Territory, see Murray R. Wickett, *Contested Territory: Whites, Native Americans, and African Americans in Oklahoma 1865–1907* (Baton Rouge, 2000). See the essays in J. Anthony Paredes, ed., *Indians of the South-eastern United States in the Late 20th Century* (Tuscaloosa, Ala., 1992).

51. Charles Roberts, "A Choctaw Odyssey: The Life of Lesa Phillip Roberts," *Ameri-can Indian Quarterly* 14, no. 3 (1990): 259–76. For other Indian migration stories, see Wilma Mankiller and Michael Wallis, *Mankiller: A Chief and Her People* (New York, 1993); and Joyce Maresca's interview in Bill AuCoin, *Redneck* (Matteson, Ill., 1977), 139–43. On policy, see Donald L. Fixico, *Termination and Relocation: Federal Indian Policy, 1945–1960* (Albuquerque, 1986).

52. James S. Brown and George A. Hillery Jr., "The Great Migration, 1940–1960," in *The Southern Appalachian Region*, ed. Thomas R. Ford (Lexington, Ky., 1962), 54–78;

Clyde B. McCoy and James S. Brown, "Appalachian Migration to Midwestern Cities," in *The Invisible Minority: Urban Appalachians*, ed. William W. Philliber and Clyde B. McCoy (Lexington, Ky., 1981); J. T. Kirby, *Rural Worlds Lost*, 80–111; Paul Salstrom, *Appalachia's Path to Dependency: Rethinking a Region's Economic History 1730–1940* (Lexington, Ky., 1994). See also the essays in Phillip J. Obermiller, Thomas E. Wagner, and E. Bruce Tucker, eds., *Appalachian Odyssey: Historical Perspectives on the Great Migration* (Westport, 2000); and Allen Batteau, ed., *Appalachia and America: Autonomy and Regional Dependence* (Lexington, Ky., 1983).

53. Helen Lefkowitz Horowitz, conversations with the author. Jews were also moving into the South. See Leonard Reissman, "The New Orleans Jewish Community," in *Jews in the South*, ed. Leonard Dinnerstein and Mary Dale Palsson (Baton Rouge, 1973), 292–93.

54. 1960, 1970 State Form 1 IPUMS samples. These include both graduates and nongraduates of all kinds of colleges. On education selectivity, see C. Horace Hamilton, "Continuity and Change in Southern Migration," in *The South in Continuity and Change*, ed. John C. McKinney and Edgar T. Thompson (Durham, 1965), 69–75; and Long, *Migration and Residential Mobility*, 173–75.

55. 1970 State Form 2 IPUMS sample. On military migration influences, see Weinstein, Gross, and Rees, *Regional Growth and Decline in the United States*, 19–21.

56. Henry Louis Gates Jr., "King of Cats," in *Thirteen Ways of Looking at a Black Man* (New York, 1997), 21–46. The joint influence of a military and writing career also led Carl Rowen to move north.

57. C. H. Hamilton, "Continuity and Change in Southern Migration," 53; Weinstein, Gross, and Rees, *Regional Growth and Decline in the United States*, 9, table 1.3; Long, *Migration and Residential Mobility*, 70–82, table 3.1.

58. Calculated from U.S. Bureau of the Census, *Current Population Reports. Geographical Mobility: March 1975 to March 1980* (Washington, D.C., 1981), 1, table A and table B; U.S. Bureau of the Census, *Current Population Survey*, Internet release data 12 July 2000, table 2-1, ‹www.census.gov/population/socdem/migration/tab-a-2.txt›.

59. Bruce J. Schulman, *From Cotton Belt to Sunbelt: Federal Policy, Economic Development, and the Transformation of the South, 1938–1980* (New York, 1991); Robert J. Newman, *Growth in the American South: Changing Regional Employment and Wage Patterns in the 1960s and 1970s* (New York, 1984); Cobb, *Industrialization and Southern Society*, 99–135; G. Wright, *Old South, New South*, 255; Jeremy Rifkin and Randy Barber, *The North Will Rise Again: Pensions, Politics and Power in the 1980s* (Boston, 1978); Stephen D. Cummings, *The Dixification of America: The American Odyssey into the Conservative Economic Trap* (Westport, 1998), 107–18.

60. David R. Goldfield, *Black, White, and Southern: Race Relations and Southern Culture 1940 to the Present* (Baton Rouge, 1990), 199–278; Steven F. Lawson, *Running for Freedom: Civil Rights and Black Politics in America since 1941* (Philadelphia, 1991), 146–221; Manning Marable, *Race, Reform, and Rebellion: The Second Reconstruction in Black America, 1945–1990*, 2d ed. (Jackson, Miss., 1990).

61. In the late 1980s and 1990s, return rates among whites slowed somewhat while black rates increased (table A.2). On return migration, see Stewart E. Tolnay, "The Af-

rican American 'Great Migration' and Beyond," *Annual Review of Sociology* 29 (2003): 209–33; Long and Hansen, "Trends in Return Migration to the South," 601–14; J. Boyce, "Reverse Migration," *Time*, 27 September 1976, 5; C. Wallis, "Southward Ho for Jobs," *Time*, 11 May 1981, 3; Kenneth R. Weiss, "80-Year Tide of Migration by Blacks Out of the South Has Turned Around," *New York Times*, 11 June 1989, 1:29; and "South toward Home: Facing Long Odds—and Painful History—Blacks Are at Last Moving Back to the Old Confederacy," *Newsweek*, 14 July 1997, 36. Carol Stack, *Call to Home: African Americans Reclaim the Rural South* (New York, 1996).

CHAPTER TWO

1. George W. Pierson, *The Moving American* (New York, 1973), 3.

2. Social history and media theory have been slow to come together. While cultural critics have developed elaborate notions of how information and entertainment systems transform public and personal life, these arguments often seem too abstract to most social historians. Key theoretical statements include Frederick Jameson, *Postmodernism, or the Cultural Logic of Late Capitalism* (Durham, 1992); and Mark C. Taylor and Esa Saamen, eds., *Imagologies: MediaPhilosophy* (London, 1994). For important uses of media theory by U.S. historians, see Philip Joseph Deloria, *Playing Indian* (New Haven, 1998); George Lipsitz, *Time Passages: Collective Memory and Popular Culture* (Minneapolis, 1990); Henry Yu, *Thinking Orientals: Migration, Contact, and Exoticism in Modern America* (New York, 2001); and Susan A. Glenn, *Female Spectacle: The Theatrical Roots of Modern Feminism* (Cambridge, Mass., 2000).

3. The following assessment of press coverage relies on the hundreds of articles compiled in the Tuskegee Institute News Clippings File (Microfilming Corporation of America, 1976) covering the years 1916–18, series 1, reels 5, 6, 8. On the new capacities of newspapers, see Sidney Kobre, *Development of American Journalism* (Dubuque, 1969), 513–26; and Michael Schudeson, *Discovering the News: A Social History of American Newspapers* (New York, 1978), esp. 88–120.

4. *Montgomery Advertiser*, 20 August 1916 (also 9 August, 5 November, 12 December 1916); *Jacksonville Times Union*, undated; *Galveston News*, 13 August 1917; *Atlanta Constitution*, 24 November 1916, 7 January 1917 (also 10 May, 15 August 1917) (all clippings from reels 5 and 6, Tuskegee Institute News Clippings File). See also James R. Grossman, *Land of Hope: Chicago, Black Southerners, and the Great Migration* (Chicago, 1989), 46–50; and Florette Henri, *Black Migration: Movement North 1900–1920* (Garden City, N.Y.), 72–73.

5. Henry Lewis Suggs, ed., *The Black Press in the South, 1865–1979* (Westport, 1983), ix, and *P. B. Young Newspaperman: Race, Politics, and Journalism in the New South 1910–1962* (Charlottesville, 1988), 33–36; Frederick G. Detweiler, *The Negro Press in the United States* (Chicago, 1922).

6. "J. H. Butler Charged with Deporting Labor," *Savannah Tribune*, 19 August 1916, and in the same issue "2,000 Laborers Disappointed," reel 5; "Should Negroes Leave the South," *Norfolk Journal and Guide*, 21 October 1916, also 23 and 25 March, 14 April 1917, reel 6, Tuskegee Institute News Clippings File. Estimated circulation figures are

from N. W. Ayer and Sons, *American Newspaper Annual and Directory for 1916* (Philadelphia, 1916).

7. Examples of exodus headlines in black southern newspapers: "The Negro Exodus," *Star of Zion*, 19 July 1916 or 1917; and "Just Reasons for the Exodus," *Dallas Express*, 11 August 1917; in white newspapers: *Montgomery Advertiser*, 12 December 1916; *Birmingham Herald*, 21 March 1917; the quote is from *Atlanta Independent*, 26 May 1917; another example of leverage plea: "Facts of Labor Migration," *Norfolk Journal and Guide*, 24 March 1917 (all in reels 5 and 6, Tuskegee Institute News Clippings File). See also William Cohen, "The Great Migration as a Lever for Social Change," in *Black Exodus: The Great Migration from the American South*, ed. Alferdteen Harrison (Jackson, Miss., 1991), 73.

8. *Columbus State Journal*, 22 August 1917, in reel 6, Tuskegee Institute News Clippings File.

9. "100,000 Negroes Sent from South: Evidence of Plan to Colonize G.O.P. Voters in North," *New York World*, 29 October 1916; "An Alarming Migration of Negro Labor: Half a Million Black Workers Have Come North in a Year," *New York Tribune*, 22 October 1916 (both in reel 5, Tuskegee Institute News Clippings File).

10. These articles are all from the Tuskegee Institute News Clippings File, reels 5 and 6. For a survey of anxious headlines in the Chicago papers, see Chicago Commission on Race Relations, *The Negro in Chicago: A Study of Race Relations and a Race Riot* (Chicago, 1922), 529–30.

11. Chicago Commission, *Negro in Chicago*, 524; the index to the *New York Times* suggests similar patterns. See also Noel P. Gist, "The Negro in the Daily Press," *Social Forces* 10, no. 3 (1932): 405–11; and George E. Simpson, *The Negro in the Philadelphia Press* (Philadelphia, 1936).

12. *Los Angeles Times*, 29 July 1919, 1:1; *New York Times*, 29 July 1919, 1:1; Associated Press report as published in *Los Angeles Times*, 30 July 1919, 1:3. See also Tuskegee Institute News Clippings File, reel 10. Some dailies took a more sympathetic stance toward blacks. Monroe N. Work, ed., *The Negro Yearbook, 1921–1922* (Tuskegee, 1922), 81–82, cites the following newspapers: *Hartford Post, Hartford Courant, Indianapolis News, Newark News, New York Mail, New York Post, Pittsburgh Leader, New York Globe*, and *Boston Globe*.

13. A careful twentieth-century history of the black press is much needed. Important sources include Henry Lewis Suggs's two anthologies, *The Black Press in the South, 1865–1979* and *The Black Press in the Middle West, 1865–1985* (Westport, 1996); Roland E. Wolseley, *The Black Press, U.S.A.* (Ames, Iowa, 1971); Andrew Buni, *Robert L. Vann of the* Pittsburgh Courier: *Politics and Black Journalism* (Pittsburgh, 1974); Henry G. LaBrie III, *A Survey of Black Newspapers in America* (Kennebunkport, 1979); Roi Ottley, *Lonely Warrior: The Life and Times of Robert S. Abbott* (Chicago, 1955); and Armistead S. Pride and Clint C. Wilson II, *A History of the Black Press* (Washington, D.C., 1997).

14. Arna Bontemps and Jack Conroy, *Anyplace but Here* (New York, 1966; orig. 1945), 105–6; Ottley, *Lonely Warrior*.

15. The circulation estimates are assessed in Grossman, *Land of Hope*, 79, which is also one of the best sources on the *Chicago Defender*'s role in the migration. See

also Ottley, *Lonely Warrior*; Detweiler, *Negro Press*, 7–31; Juliet E. K. Walker, "The Promised Land: The Chicago *Defender* and the Black Press in Illinois, 1862–1970," in Henry Lewis Suggs, ed., *The Black Press in the Middle West, 1865–1985* (Westport, 1996), 24–25.

16. The *Chicago Defender* coverage seems to begin with the 12 August 1916 issue. "Farewell, Dixie Land" is from the 7 October issue. Examples of similar coverage in other newspapers include *New York News*, 11 September 1916; and *St. Louis Argus*, 23 March 1917; and see "Negro Press on Migration North" in *New York Age*, 15 March 1917 (all except the *Chicago Defender* in Tuskegee Institute News Clippings File, reel 6). See also E. D. Walround, "The Negro Comes North," *New Republic*, 18 July 1923, 200–201.

17. *Chicago Defender*, 19 August 1916. This cartoon is reprinted in Grossman, *Land of Hope*, 84.

18. Grossman, *Land of Hope*, 87.

19. The ad for "The Evil Women Do" is from the 14 October 1916 issue.

20. Migrant quote is from Grossman, *Land of Hope*, 87 (misspelling in original). See also Buni, *Robert L. Vann*; Charles Alexander Simmons, "A Comparative Look at Four Black Newspapers and Their Editorial Philosophies during the Eras of the Northern Migration and World War I, World War II, and the Civil Rights Movement" (Ed. D. diss., Oklahoma State University, 1995); Henri, *Black Migration*, 79; and Walker, "Promised Land," 27.

21. *New York Amsterdam News*, 11 September 1916. Also "Our Guests," *Chicago Defender*, 21 April 1917; "Labor from the Southland Is Facing New Conditions," *New York Age*, 5 April 1917 (all in Tuskegee Institute News Clippings File, reel 6); Grossman, *Land of Hope*, 143–45.

22. The label "Great Migration" was in widespread use by the 1940s. It was featured in Gunnar Myrdal, *An American Dilemma: The Negro Problem and Modern Democracy* (New York, 1944), 191, and in St. Clair Drake and Horace R. Cayton, *Black Metropolis: A Study of Negro Life in a Northern City* (New York, 1962; orig. 1945), 58. See also Bontemps and Conroy, *Anyplace but Here*, 177.

23. Charles Scruggs, *Sweet Home: Invisible Cities in the Afro-American Novel* (Baltimore, 1993), 16, notes that some early novels by black authors featured urban settings but doesn't consider it a major theme in black literature until the Great Migration. The shifting literary geography of black people in mass circulation periodicals can be followed in issues of *The Readers Guide to Periodical Literature*.

24. Rollin Lynde Hartt, *The Independent*, 2 April 1921, 334–35+.

25. The *Survey*'s special issue on "Harlem: The Negro Mecca" (1 March 1925) reached a readership of less than 30,000, and the book that followed it, Alain Locke's seminal anthology, *The New Negro*, sold modestly as well. Dorothy Jones, "The Survey," in *American Mass-Market Magazines*, ed. Alan Nourie and Barbara Nourie (New York, 1990), 486. On Harlemania, see David Levering Lewis, *When Harlem Was in Vogue* (New York, 1989); Steven Watson, *The Harlem Renaissance: Hub of African-American Culture, 1920–1930* (New York, 1995), 103–9; and Nathan Irvin Huggins, *Harlem Renaissance* (New York, 1971), 13–18.

26. Chester Theodore Crowell, "World's Largest Negro City," *Saturday Evening Post*,

8 August 1925, 8–9, 93; Rudolph Fisher, "Caucasian Storms Harlem," *American Mercury*, August 1927, 393–98; Eric D. Walroud, "Imperator Africanus: Marcus Garvey, Menace or Promise?" *Independent*, 3 January 1925, 8–11; Konrad Bercovici, "Black Blocks of Manhattan," *Harper's*, October 1924, 613–23.

27. James Weldon Johnson, *Black Manhattan* (New York, 1968; orig. 1930), 1.

28. Thomas Cripps, *Slow Fade to Black: The Negro in American Film, 1900–1942* (New York, 1977); Donald Bogle, *Toms, Coons, Mulattos, Mammies, and Bucks: An Interpretative History of Blacks in American Films*, rev. ed. (New York, 1992), 101–16.

29. Cripps, *Slow Fade to Black*; Nagueyalti Warren, "From Uncle Tom to Cliff Huxtable, Aunt Jemima to Aunt Nell: Images of Blacks in Film and the Television Industry," in *Images of Blacks in American Culture*, ed. Jessie Carney Smith (New York, 1988), 59.

30. Melvyn Patrick Ely, *The Adventures of Amos 'n' Andy: A Social History of an American Phenomenon* (New York, 1991), 54–57.

31. Ely, *Adventures of Amos 'n' Andy*, 11–25.

32. In addition to Ely, see J. Fred MacDonald, *Don't Touch That Dial! Radio Programming in American Life, 1920–1960* (Chicago, 1979), esp. 27–30, 98–103; Joseph Boskin, *Sambo: The Rise and Demise of an American Jester* (New York, 1986); Arthur Frank Werheim, *Radio Comedy* (1979); and William Barlow, "Commercial and Noncommercial Radio," in *Split Image: African Americans in the Mass Media*, ed. Jannette L. Dates and William Barlow (Washington, D.C., 1990), 176–84.

33. Ely, *Adventures of Amos 'n' Andy*, 160–91; Arnold Shankman, "Black Pride and Protest: The Amos 'N' Andy Crusade," *Journal of Popular Culture* 12 (Fall 1979): 238–47; Buni, *Robert L. Vann*, 227–30.

34. Ely, *Adventures of Amos 'n' Andy*, esp. 64–96.

35. Indeed, one of the few newspapers to note the early white migration was an African American publication, the *St. Louis Independent Clarion*, 18 October 1919, which headlined "Southern Whites Going North Too" and noted that their labor contractors were not being arrested. Thanks to Jason Carl Digman for bringing this to my attention. See Digman, "Which Way to the Promised Land? Changing Patterns in Southern Migration, 1865–1920" (Ph.D. diss., University of Illinois–Chicago, 2001), 45.

36. A pair 1920s articles noted the increase of white southerners in rural areas of California: Max Stern, "Cotton Goes West," *Nation* 123 (14 July 1926); and D. J. Whitney, "White Labor Harvested Raisins," *Pacific Rural Press* (22 October 1921), 416.

37. On migration anxiety and policy, see Eric Beecroft and Seymour Janow, "Toward a National Policy of Migration," *Social Forces* 17 (May 1938): 475–92; Joan M. Crouse, *The Homeless Transient in the Great Depression: New York State, 1929–1941* (Albany, 1986); Walter Stein, *California and the Dust Bowl Migration* (Westport, 1973); and James N. Gregory, *American Exodus: The Dust Bowl Migration and Okie Culture in California* (New York, 1989), 78–113.

38. George B. Tindall, *The Emergence of the New South, 1913–1945* (Baton Rouge, 1967), 184–218; Jack Temple Kirby, *Media-Made Dixie: The South in the American Imagination* (Baton Rouge, 1978), 39–66.

39. Jerry Tompkins, ed., *D-Days at Dayton: Reflections on the Scopes Trial* (Baton Rouge, 1965), 36.

40. Erskine Caldwell, *Tobacco Road* (New York, 1931). The sequel, *God's Little Acre* (New York, 1934), was equally popular. See also Shields McIlwaine, *The Southern Poor-White from Lubberland to Tobacco Road* (Norman, Okla., 1939), 163–241; and Sylvia Jenkins Cook, *From Tobacco Road to Route 66: The Southern Poor White in Fiction* (Chapel Hill, 1976), and *Erskine Caldwell and the Fiction of Poverty* (Baton Rouge, 1991).

41. Mildred Rutherford Mell, "Poor Whites of the South," *Social Forces* 17 (December 1938): 153; McIlwaine, *Southern Poor-White*, 242; Erskine Caldwell, *Call It Experience* (London, 1960), 106–7; Cook, *From Tobacco Road to Route 66*.

42. Henry D. Shapiro, *Appalachia on Our Mind: The Southern Mountains and Mountaineers in the American Consciousness, 1870–1920* (Chapel Hill, 1978), 119; Anthony Harkins, *Hillbilly: A Cultural History of an American Icon* (New York, 2004).

43. J. W. Williamson, *Hillbillyland: What the Movies Did to the Mountains and What the Mountains Did to the Movies* (Chapel Hill, 1995); Harkins, *Hillbilly*, 47–70; Eric Peter Verschuure, "Stumble, Bumble, Mumble: TV's Image of the South," *Journal of Popular Culture* 16 (Winter 1982): 92–96.

44. Archie Green, "Hillbilly Music: Source and Symbol," *Journal of American Folklore* 78 (July–September 1965): 204–28; Harkins, *Hillbilly*, 71–101; Bill C. Malone, *Country Music U.S.A.: A Fifty-Year History* (Austin, 1985).

45. Harkins, *Hillbilly*, 103–40; Williamson, *Hillbillyland*, 40–43.

46. Paul S. Taylor, "Again the Covered Wagon," *Survey Graphic* (July 1935), 348–51+; Walter Davenport, "California, Here We Come," *Collier's*, 10 August 1935, 10–11+; Gregory, *American Exodus*, 78–88. Charles J. Shindo explores the subsequent circulation of these images in *Dust Bowl Migrants in the American Imagination* (Lawrence, Kans., 1997).

47. Louis Adamic, "The Hill-Billies Come to Detroit," *Nation*, 13 February 1935, 177–78; Chad Berry, *Southern Migrants, Northern Exiles* (Urbana, Ill., 2000), 113–14.

48. My thinking about the role of social science discourse has been influenced by several recent books: Yu, *Thinking Orientals*; Daryl Michael Scott, *Contempt and Pity: Social Policy and the Image of the Damaged Black Psyche 1880–1996* (Chapel Hill, 1997); and Ellen Herman, *The Romance of American Psychology: Political Culture in the Age of Experts* (Berkeley, 1995).

49. Daniel O. Price and Melanie M. Sikes, *Rural-Urban Migration Research in the United States* (Washington, D.C., 1974); Varden Fuller, *Rural Worker Adjustment to Urban Life: An Assessment of the Research* (Ann Arbor, 1970); Clifford J. Jansen, "Migration: A Sociological Problem," in *Readings in the Sociology of Migration*, ed. Clifford J. Jansen (New York, 1970).

50. Fred H. Mathews, *Quest for an American Sociology: Robert E. Park and the Chicago School* (Montreal, 1977).

51. Eli Zaretsky notes the importance of *The Polish Peasant in Europe and America* for the sociology of migration as well as immigration in his introduction to the University of Illinois Press edition (Urbana, Ill., 1984), 1–53. "Human Migration and the Marginal Man," in Robert Ezra Park, *Race and Culture*, 350. See also Stow Persons, *Ethnic Studies at Chicago 1905–45* (Chicago, 1987); Martin Bulmer, *The Chicago School of Sociology: Institutionalization, Diversity, and the Rise of Sociological Research* (Chicago,

1984); Vernon J. Williams Jr., *Rethinking Race: Franz Boaz and His Contemporaries* (Lexington, Ky., 1996), 86–101, and *From a Caste to a Minority: Changing Attitudes of American Sociologists toward Afro-Americans, 1896–1945* (Westport, 1989). Robert E. L. Faris, *Chicago Sociology, 1920–1932* (San Francisco, 1967), includes a complete list of dissertations and masters theses.

52. Grace G. Leybourne, "Urban Adjustments of Migrants from the Southern Appalachian Plateaus," *Social Forces* 16, no. 2 (1937): 238–46. Two other studies also supported by the WPA were underway in Michigan: Elmer Akers, "Southern Whites in Detroit" (unpublished ms., n.d. [1937?]), available through University Microfilms; and Erdmann Doane Beynon, "The Southern White Laborer Migrates to Michigan," *American Sociological Review* 3 (June 1938): 333–43.

53. *Harper's*, October 1941, 460–67; *Newsweek*, 6 March 1944, 70; *New York Times Magazine*, 21 May 1944, 14+. The subject shift shows up in *The Readers Guide to Periodical Literature*. Whereas during World War I, articles indexed under the heading "Negro Migration" far outnumbered all stories indexed under the general term "Migration," in the 1940s the heading "Negro Migration" falls into disuse.

54. *Life*, 17 August 1942, 15–23.

55. On West Coast press hostility, see Carey McWilliams, "Jim Crow Goes West," *Negro Digest*, August 1945; Shirley Ann Wilson Moore, *To Place Our Deeds: The African American Community in Richmond, California, 1910–1963* (Berkeley, 2000); and Albert S. Broussard, *Black San Francisco: The Struggle for Racial Equality in the West, 1900–1954* (Lawrence, Kans., 1993), 167–71. Marilynn S. Johnson, *The Second Gold Rush: Oakland and the East Bay in World War II* (Berkeley, 1993), 151–84, shows that the reaction against black newcomers was linked to hostility toward white southerners.

56. Dominic J. Capeci Jr. and Martha Wilkerson, *Layered Violence: The Detroit Rioters of 1943* (Jackson, Miss., 1991); Alfred McClung Lee and Norman D. Humphrey, *Race Riot* (New York, 1968; orig. 1944); Richard W. Thomas, *Life for Us Is What We Make It: Building Black Community in Detroit, 1915–1945* (Bloomington, 1992), 161–73.

57. "Troops Rout Mobs in Detroit Riot," *Los Angeles Times*, 22 June 1943, 1:1; "Army Rules Detroit," *Chicago Tribune*, 22 June 1943, 1:1; "23 Dead in Detroit Rioting; Federal Troops Enter City on the Orders of Roosevelt," *New York Times*, 22 June 1943, 1:1; "U.S. Troops Quell Detroit Race Riot: Death Toll 23," *Seattle Post-Intelligencer*, 22 June 1943, 1:1. None of this restraint applied to the *Detroit News* and *Detroit Free Press*, both of which provided detailed accounts of the fighting.

58. The white mob photos are even more dominant in the mass circulation magazines. See "Race War in Detroit," *Life*, 5 July 1943, 93–102; and Walter Davenport, "Race Riots Coming," *Collier's*, 18 September 1943, 22. Carl Sandburg discusses the impact of the camera in "Golgotha to Detroit," *Negro Digest*, September 1943, 69–70.

59. *New York Times*, 22 June 1943, 1:8; *Los Angeles Times*, 23 June 1943, 1:10, 2:4. The social-psychological gaze was very evident in the Detroit reports and investigations that followed the riot. These are described in Capeci and Wilkerson, *Layered Violence*.

60. "Troops Restore Calm in Detroit," *Chicago Tribune*, 23 June 1943. The blaming of southern whites was an even stronger media theme in Detroit. See Capeci and Wilkerson, *Layered Violence*, esp. 23–24. However, they find that just one of the ninety-six whites arrested in the riot was southern-born (61).

61. *Chicago Tribune*, 23 June 1943, 1:2, 12; 24 June 1943, 1:1, 2. The *Detroit News* and various public officials in that city also blamed both groups of southerners and focused on the issue of migration as a destabilizing force. See Lee and Humphrey, *Race Riot*, esp. 91–92; Capeci and Wilkerson, *Layered Violence*; Berry, *Southern Migrants, Northern Exiles*, 142.

62. Harriette Arnow, *The Dollmaker* (New York, 1954). Joyce Carol Oates wrote an afterward for the 1972 edition, which went through at least seven printings in the early 1970s. The book became, like country music, a template for both investigators and former migrants. See Jim Hammitte interview by Mary Thompson, 3 December 1974, Samford University Library, 3. Both interviewer and interviewee have read *The Dollmaker*.

63. *The Dollmaker* also became an influential television drama with feminist overtones staring Jane Fonda in 1984. On the publishing history and critical assessment, see Wilton Eckley, *Harriette Arnow* (New York, 1974); and Haeja K. Chung, ed., *Harriette Simpson Arnow: Critical Essays on Her Work* (East Lansing, 1995).

64. "Corn Is Green, Beverly Hillbillies," *Newsweek*, 3 December 1962, 70; Richard Warren Lewis, "Golden Hillbillies," *Saturday Evening Post*, 2 February 1963, 30+; Harkins, *Hillbilly*, 186–202; Horace Newcomb, "Appalachia on Television: Region as Symbol in American Popular Culture," *Appalachia Journal* 7 (Fall–Winter 1979–80): 155–64; Williamson, *Hillbillyland*, 56.

65. "Detroit City" by Danny Dill and Mel Tillis, copyright 1963 by Cedarwood Publishing Co. Inc., as quoted in Dorothy Horstman, *Sing Your Heart Out, Country Boy* (Nashville, 1996), 10.

66. Cecilia Tichi, *High Lonesome: The American Culture of Country Music* (Chapel Hill, 1994), explores the centrality of home.

67. "City Lights" by Bill Anderson, copyright 1958 by TNT Music, as quoted in Horstman, *Sing Your Heart Out*, 225. On anti-urbanism, see A. Green, "Hillbilly Music"; Ivan M. Tribe, "The Hillbilly versus the City: Urban Images in Country Music," *John Edwards Memorial Foundation Quarterly* 10 (1974): 41–51; and D. K. Wilgus, "Country-Western Music and the Urban Hillbilly," *Journal of American Folklore* 83 (April–June 1970): 157–79.

68. An early example of reading values and attitudes from the music is Charles Todd and Robert Sonkin, "Ballads of the Okies," *New York Times Magazine*, 17 November 1940, 6–7, 18, and similar references are found throughout journalism and sociology right up through the late 1970s, for example, Anthony O. Edmonds, "Myths and Migrants: Images of Rural and Urban Life in Country Music," *Indiana Social Studies Quarterly* 28 (Winter 1975–76): 71; Atleia Clarkson and W. Lynwood Montell, "Letters to a Bluegrass DJ: Social Documents of Southern White Migrants in Southeastern Michigan 1964–1974," *Southern Folklore Quarterly* 39 (1975): 219–32. The most elaborate attempt to read experience through songs is Patricia Averill's massive dissertation, "Can the Circle Be Unbroken: A Study of the Modernization of Rural Born Southern Whites since World War I Using Country Music" (Ph.D. diss., University of Pennsylvania, 1975).

69. For a related discussion of authenticity, see Joli Jensen, *The Nashville Sound: Authenticity, Commercialization, and Country Music* (Nashville, 1998).

70. Migration novels are the subject of several excellent literary studies: Farah Jasmine Griffin, *"Who Set You Flowin'?": The African-American Migration Narrative* (New York, 1995); Lawrence R. Rodgers, *Canaan Bound: The African-American Great Migration Novel* (Urbana, Ill., 1997); Scruggs, *Sweet Home*.

71. Wright's links to the University of Chicago sociologists are discussed in the works in note 70 immediately above and in more detail in Carla Cappetti, *Writing Chicago: Modernism, Ethnography, and the Novel* (New York, 1993); and Michel Fabre, *The Unfinished Quest of Richard Wright* (New York, 1973). D. Scott, *Contempt and Pity*, 99–102, emphasizes Wright's return influence on social science.

72. *Chicago Tribune* series, March 1957; "Anglo-Saxon Migration," *Time*, 18 March 1957, 73–74; "Chicago's Segregation Tragedy," *Look*, 30 September 1958, 76–81; Albert N. Votaw, "The Hillbillies Invade Chicago," *Harper's*, February 1958, 64–67. All this seems to have been prompted by a report issued by the Chicago Commission on Human Relations, "The Uptown Community Area and the Southern White In-Migrant — A Human Relations Story" (mimeographed, n.p., May 1957, in Regenstein Library, University of Chicago).

73. Votaw, "Hillbillies Invade Chicago," 64, 67; "Anglo-Saxon Migration," *Time*, 73. Chad Berry discusses what he calls the "mountain pathology school" in *Southern Migrants, Northern Exiles*, 172.

74. See chap. 8 for examples and assessments of the bigot image.

75. Horace Mann Bond, "A Negro Looks at His South," *Harper's*, June 1931, 98, as quoted in Patricia Sullivan, *Days of Hope: Race and Democracy in the New Deal Era* (Chapel Hill, 1996), 12; Chana Kai Lee, *For Freedom's Sake: The Life of Fannie Lou Hamer* (Urbana, Ill., 1999). The image of the northern-born African American was also reversing, propelled by the northern civil rights struggles that focused on the containments and limitations of urban life outside the South. Two powerful and widely read memoirs published in the mid-1960s carried the new imagery, both of them taking direct aim at the North as Promised Land story. The *Autobiography of Malcolm X* (1964) told one story of a Native Son born not in the South but in the northern ghetto. Claude Brown's *Manchild in the Promised Land* (1965) told another. The narratives replayed Richard Wright while dropping the migrant pathology. Malcolm X and Claude Brown described themselves as young Bigger Thomases whose problems had nothing to do with southern origins or rural-urban transitions. Each manchild blamed the Promised Land. The problem now was the northern ghetto.

CHAPTER THREE

1. Robert Coles, *The South Goes North* (Boston, 1972), 325–37.

2. Parts of this analysis appeared in James N. Gregory, "The Southern Diaspora and the Urban Dispossessed: Demonstrating the Census Public Use Microdata Samples," *Journal of American History* 82, no. 1 (1995): 111–34.

3. Emphasizing economic difficulties are Jacqueline Jones, *The Dispossessed: America's Underclasses from the Civil War to the Present* (New York, 1992), 233–68; Jon C. Teaford, *Cities of the Heartland: The Rise and Fall of the Industrial Midwest* (Bloomington,

1993), 232–33; William W. Philliber, *Appalachian Migrants in Urban America: Cultural Conflict or Ethnic Group Formation?* (New York, 1981); and Dan M. McKee and Phillip J. Obermiller, *From Mountain to Metropolis: Urban Appalachians in Ohio* (Cincinnati, 1978).

4. Although they have been ignored by historians, there were studies that undercut the story of economic difficulties: Gene B. Petersen, Laure M. Sharp, and Thomas F. Drury, *Southern Newcomers to Northern Cities: Work and Social Adjustment in Cleveland* (New York, 1977); Lloyd A. Bacon, "Poverty among Interregional Rural to Urban Migrants," *Rural Sociology* 36 (June 1971): 125–40; David L. Featherman and Robert M. Hauser, *Opportunity and Change* (New York, 1978), 411–18.

5. Calculations from 1940 IPUMS, 1950 IPUMS. See also James N. Gregory, *American Exodus: The Dust Bowl Migration and Okie Culture in California* (New York, 1989), esp. 172–90, 239–53; and Dan Morgan, *Rising in the West: The True Story of an "Okie" Family from the Great Depression through the Reagan Years* (New York, 1992); Marsha L. Weisiger, *Land of Plenty: Oklahomans in the Cotton Fields of Arizona, 1933–1942* (Norman, 1995); and Bill Ganzel, *Dust Bowl Descent* (Lincoln, Neb., 1984). On 1950s definitions of poverty, see Donald J. Bogue, *The Population of the United States* (New York, 1959), 655–57.

6. There will be more on the hillbilly ghettos in chap. 5.

7. On 1930s dispersion, see Elmer Akers, "Southern Whites in Detroit" (unpublished ms., n.d. [1937?]), 13, available through University Microfilms; Gregory, *American Exodus*, 42–45; Los Angeles County Coordinating Councils, *Juvenile Delinquency and Poor Housing in the Los Angeles Metropolitan Area* (Los Angeles, 1937); Charles B. Spaulding, "The Development of Organization and Disorganization in the Social Life of a Rapidly Growing Working-Class Suburb within a Metropolitan District" (Ph.D. diss., University of Southern California, 1939). Postwar suburbanization is examined in Philliber, *Appalachian Migrants in Urban America*, 20–25; J. Jones, *The Dispossessed*, 24–25; and Harry K. Schwarzweller, James S. Brown, and Joseph J. Mangalam, *Mountain Families in Transition* (University Park, Pa., 1971). On the different settlement options for black and white migrants, see Stewart E. Tolnay, Kyle D. Crowder, and R. M. Adelman, "Race, Regional Origins, and Residence in Northern Cities at the Beginning of the Great Migration," *American Sociological Review* 67 (2002): 456–75.

8. More detailed tables showing occupational and income comparisons for the Great Lakes region, the Pacific Coast states, and the Mid-Atlantic states can be found on "The Southern Diaspora" companion Web site: ‹http://faculty.washington.edu/gregoryj/diaspora›.

9. Trent Alexander, "'Continued Interest in the Appalachian Migrant Is Not Warranted': Appalachian Migrants in the Larger Southern White Exodus" (paper delivered at Social Science History Association annual meeting, Chicago, Ill., November 2004).

10. On the era of blue-collar opportunity and its race and gender segmentations, see David M. Gordon, Richard Edwards, and Michael Reich, *Segmented Work, Divided Workers: The Historical Transformation of Labor in the United States* (Cambridge, 1982), 202–15; David Halle, *America's Working Man: Work, Home, and Politics among Blue-*

Collar Property Owners (Chicago, 1984); Mike Davis, *Prisoners of the American Dream: Politics and Economy in the History of the U.S. Working Class* (London, 1986); and Kim Moody, *An Injury to All: The Decline of American Unionism* (London 1988).

11. On the racial effects of deindustrialization, see J. Jones, *The Dispossessed*, 233–65; William Julius Wilson, *When Work Disappears: The World of the New Urban Poor* (New York, 1996); and Thomas J. Sugrue, *The Origins of the Urban Crisis: Race and Inequality in Postwar Detroit* (Princeton, 1996).

12. Lewis M. Killian, "Southern White Laborers in Chicago's West Side" (Ph.D. diss., University of Chicago, 1949), 220–27, and also his book, *White Southerners* (New York, 1970), 108–9. Chad Berry explores stereotypes in *Southern Migrants, Northern Exiles* (Urbana, Ill., 2000), esp. 172–80. See also Gregory, *American Exodus*, 100–113; Alan Clive, *State of War: Michigan in World War II* (Ann Arbor, 1979), 179–81; Akers, "Southern Whites in Detroit," 13–15; and Rosemary Deyling, "Hillbillies in Steelville: A Study of Participation in Community Life" (MA thesis, University of Chicago, 1949), 41–52.

13. Killian, "Southern White Laborers," 220–27; Akers, "Southern Whites in Detroit," 21–39; Chicago Commission on Human Relations, "The Uptown Community Area and the Southern White In-Migrant—A Human Relations Study" (mimeographed, n.p., May 1957, in Regenstein Library, University of Chicago), 13–14; Edwin S. Harwood, "Work and Community among Urban Newcomers: A Study of the Social and Economic Adaptation of Southern Migrants in Chicago" (Ph.D. diss., University of Chicago, 1966), 18–29.

14. John Leslie Thompson, "Industrialization in the Miami Valley: A Case Study of Interregional Labor Migration" (Ph.D. diss., University of Wisconsin, 1955), 132–35, 148; Berry, *Southern Migrants, Northern Exiles*, 118. See also the data in Petersen, Sharp, and Drury, *Southern Newcomers to Northern Cities*, 66–78; the profiles in Carl E. Feather, *Mountain People in a Flat Land: A Popular History of Appalachian Migration to Northeast Ohio, 1940–1965* (Athens, Ohio, 1998); and essays by Harry K. Schwarzweller, John D. Photiadis, and William W. Philliber in *The Invisible Minority: Urban Appalachians*, ed. William W. Philliber and Clyde B. McCoy (Lexington, Ky., 1981).

15. *New York Times*, 6 March 1940. For expressions of union anxiety, see Louis Adamic, "The Hill-Billies Come to Detroit," *Nation*, 13 February 1935, 177–78; Akers, "Southern Whites in Detroit," 58–59; Katherine Archibald, *Wartime Shipyard: A Study in Social Disunity* (Berkeley, 1947), 47–50; Gregory, *American Exodus*, 154–64.

16. The Building Trades Council statement is in *Bakersfield Californian*, 18 June 1938. See table A.13 for construction industry employment.

17. J. L. Thompson, "Industrialization in the Miami Valley," 19, 132–35, 148. See also Varden Fuller, *Rural Worker Adjustment to Urban Life: An Assessment of the Research* (Ann Arbor, 1970), 68.

18. Chad Berry, "Social Highways: Southern White Migration to the Midwest, 1910–1990" (Ph.D. diss., Indiana University, 1995), 244. The interview does not appear in Berry's book. Akers, "Southern Whites in Detroit," 21–39, interviewed auto industry managers and examined employment barriers in detail. Peter Friedlander discusses tensions in *The Emergence of a UAW Local, 1936–1939: A Study of Class and Culture* (Pittsburgh, 1975).

19. Killian, *White Southerners*, 109. Charles Denby testifies to the discriminatory hiring in *Indignant Heart: A Black Worker's Journal* (Boston, 1978; orig. 1952), 87–88.

20. J. Jones, *The Dispossessed*, 237; also Jacqueline Jones, *American Work: Four Centuries of Black and White Labor* (New York, 1998), 339–68; and Lizabeth Cohen, *Making a New Deal: Industrial Workers in Chicago, 1919–1939* (New York, 1990).

21. On the theory of employment networks and comparative examples, see John Bodnar, Michael Weber, and Roger Simon, "Migration, Kinship, and Urban Adjustment: Blacks and Poles in Pittsburgh, 1900–1930," *Journal of American History* 66 (December 1979); John Bodnar, *Workers' World: Kinship, Community, and Protest in an Industrial Society, 1900–1940* (Baltimore, 1982), 168–76; and Ivan H. Light, *Ethnic Enterprise in American Business and Welfare among Chinese, Japanese, and Blacks* (Berkeley, 1972).

22. Nancy Lynn Quam-Wickham, "Petroleocrats and Proletarians: Work, Class, and Politics in the California Oil Industry, 1917–1925" (Ph.D. diss., University of California, Berkeley, 1994), 70, reports that in the early years of the California industry, southerners were not heavily represented.

23. James Richard Wilburn, "Social and Economic Aspects of the Aircraft Industry in Metropolitan Los Angeles during World War II" (Ph.D. diss., University of California, Los Angeles, 1971), 90–96; John McCann, *Blood in the Water: A History of District Lodge 751 of the International Association of Machinists and Aerospace Workers* (Seattle, 1989), 47–49.

24. Daniel Nelson, *American Rubber Workers and Organized Labor, 1900–1940* (Princeton, 1988). See also his *Farm and Factory: Workers in the Midwest 1880–1990* (Bloomington, 1995), 97, 182–83; and Gregory Pappas, *The Magic City: Unemployment in a Working-Class Community* (Ithaca, 1989), 3–15.

25. Phillip J. Obermiller and Michael E. Maloney, "Looking for Appalachians in Pittsburgh: Seeking Deliverance, Finding the Deer Hunter," in *From Mountain to Metropolis: Appalachian Migrants in American Cities*, ed. Kathryn M. Borman and Phillip J. Obermiller (Westport, 1994), 13–24.

26. Attempts to calculate the income effects of race have typically ignored region and migration, either comparing all blacks with all whites, as in Dorothy K. Newman et al., *Protest, Politics, and Prosperity: Black Americans and White Institutions, 1940–75* (New York, 1978), 249–83; or white foreign-born with black migrants, as in Stanley Lieberson, *A Piece of the Pie: Blacks and White Immigrants since 1880* (Berkeley, 1980), and John Bodnar, Roger Simon, and Michael P. Weber, *Lives of Their Own: Blacks, Italians, and Poles in Pittsburgh, 1900–1960* (Urbana, Ill., 1982). Two earlier studies have explored the direct comparison of black and white migrants, although not over time: Larry H. Long and Lynne R. Heltman, "Migration and Income Differences between Black and White Men in the North," *American Journal of Sociology* 80 (May 1975): 1391–409, which uses the 1970 census; and Featherman and Hauser, *Opportunity and Change* (New York, 1978), 422–23, who used the large Occupational Changes in a Generation surveys of 1961 and 1972 to calculate the dollar effects of race.

27. There is a huge literature on racialized opportunity systems. Among the key theoretical and comprehensive works: Daniel R. Fusfeld and Timothy Bates, *The Political Economy of the Urban Ghetto* (Carbondale, Ill., 1984); William Julius Wilson, *The*

Declining Significance of Race: Blacks and Changing American Institutions (Chicago, 1978); Michael Reich, *Racial Inequality: A Political-Economic Analysis* (Princeton, 1981); Douglas S. Massey and Nancy A. Denton, *American Apartheid: Segregation and the Making of the Underclass* (Cambridge, 1993); Stephan Thernstrom and Abigail Thernstrom, *America in Black and White: One Nation, Indivisible* (New York, 1997).

28. J. Jones, *American Work*, 301–36; William H. Harris, *The Harder We Run: Black Workers since the Civil War* (New York, 1982), 38–50; Bodnar, Simon, and Weber, *Lives of Their Own*, 58–62; Philip S. Foner, *Organized Labor and the Black Worker 1619–1973* (New York, 1974), 64–128.

29. Occupational distributions were little changed by 1930. See tables in *Southern Diaspora* companion Web site: ‹http://faculty.washington.edu/gregoryj/diaspora›. Joe William Trotter Jr., *Black Milwaukee: The Making of an Industrial Proletariat, 1915–45* (Urbana, Ill., 1985); Bodnar, Simon, and Weber, *Lives of Their Own*, 238–43; J. Jones, *American Work*, 301–68; Thomas Klug, "Employers' Strategies in the Detroit Labor Market, 1900–1929," in *On the Line: Essays in the History of Auto Work*, ed. Nelson Lichtenstein and Stephen Meyer (Urbana, Ill., 1989), 42–74; Kenneth L. Kusmer, *A Ghetto Takes Shape: Black Cleveland, 1870–1930* (Urbana, Ill., 1976), 66–90.

30. The reserve labor force concept was introduced by Sterling D. Spero and Abram L. Harris, *The Black Worker: The Negro and the Labor Movement* (New York, 1931), then refined by St. Clair Drake and Horace R. Cayton, *Black Metropolis: A Study of Negro Life in a Northern City* (New York, 1962; orig. 1945), 214–62; Trotter, *Black Milwaukee*; and Peter Gottlieb, *Making Their Own Way: Southern Blacks' Migration to Pittsburgh, 1916–30* (Urbana, Ill., 1987), 89–115. Depression-era occupational conditions are detailed in Kimberley L. Phillips, *AlabamaNorth: African-American Migrants, Community, and Working-Class Activism in Cleveland, 1915–45* (Urbana, Ill., 1999); and Cheryl Lynn Greenberg, *"Or Does It Explode?" Black Harlem in the Great Depression* (New York, 1991).

31. J. Jones, *American Work*, 336–68.

32. Calculated from 1950, 1960, and 1970 State Form 1 IPUMS. These calculations combine data for southern-born and northern-born, males and females, displayed in tables A.7, A.8, and A.9 in appendix A.

33. Drake and Cayton, *Black Metropolis*, 481; Francis A. J. Ianni, *Black Mafia: Ethnic Succession in Organized Crime* (New York, 1974), 107–23; Nathan Thompson, *Kings: The True Story of Chicago's Policy Kings and Numbers Racketeers* (Chicago, 2003).

34. Stephen P. Erie, "Public Policy and Black Economic Polarization," *Policy Analysis* 6 (1980): 305–17; Thernstrom and Thernstrom, *America in Black and White*, 184–89.

35. For a detailed portrait of labor markets in two cities, see Sugrue, *Origins of the Urban Crisis*, 91–123; and Robert Self, *American Babylon: Race and Power in Postwar Oakland* (Princeton, 2003).

36. There is considerable debate about the significance of these labor market changes. W. J. Wilson, *Declining Significance of Race*, and Thernstrom and Thernstrom, *America in Black and White*, see this as an era of "remarkable change" that erased the major effects of racism. I join most other scholars in regarding the changes as amelioration but by no means an elimination of the color line. Two of the more forceful arguments

along these lines are J. Jones, *American Work*, 337–68; and Massey and Denton, *American Apartheid*.

37. For a historical overview of housing struggles, see Stephen Grant Meyer, *As Long as They Don't Move Next Door: Segregation and Racial Conflict in American Neighborhoods* (Lanham, Md., 2000); Richard W. Thomas, *Life for Us Is What We Make It: Building Black Community in Detroit, 1915–1945* (Bloomington, 1992), 89–102; Dominic J. Capeci Jr., *Race Relations in Wartime Detroit: The Sojourner Truth Housing Controversy of 1942* (Philadelphia, 1984), 3–27; David M. Katzman, *Before the Ghetto: Black Detroit in the Nineteenth Century* (Urbana, Ill., 1973); and David Allen Levine, *Internal Combustion: The Races in Detroit, 1915–1926* (Westport, 1976).

38. In Chicago, fifty-eight homes were bombed between 1917 and 1921. See Drake and Cayton, *Black Metropolis*, 178. On the Sweet incident, see Kevin Boyle, *Arc of Justice: A Sage of Race, Civil Rights, and Murder in the Jazz Age* (New York, 2004). Key studies of ghettoization include Robert C. Weaver, *Negro Ghetto* (New York, 1967; orig. 1948); Otis Dudley Duncan and Beverly Duncan, *The Negro Population of Chicago: A Study of Residential Succession* (Chicago, 1957); Allan H. Spear, *Black Chicago: The Making of a Negro Ghetto 1890–1920* (Chicago, 1967); Gilbert Osofsky, *Harlem, The Making of a Ghetto: Negro New York, 1890–1930*, 2d ed. (Chicago, 1996); Kusmer, *A Ghetto Takes Shape*; and Massey and Denton, *American Apartheid*.

39. On rent differences, see Osofsky, *Harlem*, 137; and Thomas, *Life for Us Is What We Make It*, 92–94. On the multiple ways that ghetto containment doubled the effects of discrimination, see Fusfeld and Bates, *Political Economy of the Urban Ghetto*, 136–70; and Massey and Denton, *American Apartheid*.

40. Paul Kantor with Stephen David, *The Dependent City: The Changing Political Economy of Urban America* (Glenview, Ill., 1988), 164–295; John H. Mollenkopf, *The Contested City* (Princeton, 1983), 47–96. Home-ownership figures are from D. Newman et al., *Protest, Politics, and Prosperity*, 163.

41. Roi Ottley, *"New World A-Coming": Inside Black America* (Boston, 1943), 158.

42. Arnold R. Hirsch, *Making the Second Ghetto: Race and Housing in Chicago, 1940–1960* (Cambridge, 1983); Sugrue, *Origins of the Urban Crisis*, 181–207; Konrad E. Taeuber and A. F. Taeuber, *Negroes in Cities: Residential Segregation and Neighborhood Change* (Chicago, 1965). For a later phase of ghetto morphology, see W. J. Wilson, *When Work Disappears*, esp. 3–50.

43. U.S. Bureau of the Census, *The Social and Economic Status of the Black Population in the United States, 1790–1978: An Historical View* (Washington, D.C., 1978), table 102, p. 141. Home-ownership rates from 1940 IPUMS; 1970 State Form 2 IPUMS sample. These rates apply to all blacks, not just southern-born.

44. W. E. B. Du Bois, *The Philadelphia Negro: A Social Study* (Philadelphia, 1899), 67; E. Franklin Frazier, *The Negro Family in the United States* (Chicago, 1939); Drake and Cayton, *Black Metropolis*, 584–657; Daniel P. Moynihan, *The Negro Family: The Case for National Action* (Washington, D.C., 1965); Edward C. Banfield, *The Unheavenly City: The Nature and Future of Our Urban Crisis* (Boston, 1970), 71.

45. Larry H. Long, "Poverty Status and Receipt of Welfare among Migrants and Nonmigrants in Large Cities," *American Sociological Review* 39 (February 1974): 54;

also Long and Heltman, "Migration and Income Differences," 1391–409; and Stanley Lieberson and Christy A. Wilkinson, "A Comparison between Northern and Southern Blacks Residing in the North," *Demography* 13 (May 1976): 199–224. Recently Stewart Tolnay has extended this analysis to black family structure and finds that southern migrants were more likely than northern-born to maintain "traditional" family patterns. See "The Great Migration and Changes in the Northern Black Family, 1940 to 1990," *Social Forces* 75 (June 1997): 1213–38; and Tolnay and Kyle D. Crowder, "Regional Origin and Family Stability in Northern Cities: The Role of Context," *American Sociological Review* 64 (February 1999): 97–112.

46. Nicholas Lemann, *The Promised Land: The Great Black Migration and How It Changed America* (New York, 1991). See also the critique of Lemann in David Whitman, "The Great Sharecropper Success Story," *Public Interest* 101 (Summer 1991): 3–19, and his reply in the next issue. J. Jones, *The Dispossessed*, 205–65.

47. Using longitudinal data for African Americans living in Pittsburgh in 1900, Bodnar, Simon, and Weber compared southern- and northern-born experiences in *Lives of Their Own*, 140–42. Stewart E. Tolnay, "The Great Migration Gets Underway: A Comparison of Black Southern Migrants and Nonmigrants in the North, 1920," *Social Science Quarterly* 82 (2001): 235–52; Kyle D. Crowder, Stewart E. Tolnay, and Robert M. Adelman, "Intermetropolitan Migration and Locational Improvement for African American Males, 1970–1990," *Social Science Research* 30 (2001): 449–72; Thomas N. Maloney, "Migration and Economic Opportunity in the 1910s: New Evidence on African-American Occupational Mobility in the North," *Explorations in Economic History* 38 (2001): 147–65; J. Trent Alexander, "Great Migrations: Race and Community in the Southern Exodus, 1917–1970" (Ph.D. diss., Carnegie Mellon University, 2001).

48. For more detailed examinations of housing and job acquisition in particular cities, see James R. Grossman, *Land of Hope: Chicago, Black Southerners, and the Great Migration* (Chicago, 1989), 181–245; Gottlieb, *Making Their Own Way*, 89–210; Kusmer, *A Ghetto Takes Shape*, 190–205; Quintard Taylor, *In Search of the Racial Frontier: African Americans in the American West, 1528–1990* (New York, 1998), 222–36; Trotter, *Black Milwaukee*; and Raymond A. Mohl and Neil Betten, *Steel City: Urban and Ethnic Patterns in Gary, Indiana, 1906–1950* (New York, 1986), 48–90.

49. The most detailed look at female job acquisition is Victoria W. Wolcott, *Remaking Respectability: African American Women in Interwar Detroit* (Chapel Hill, 2001), 80–91. See also Beverly A. Bunch-Lyons, *Contested Terrain: African-American Women Migrate from the South to Cincinnati, Ohio, 1900–1950* (New York, 2002), 43–59.

50. Calculated from Joseph J. Boris, ed., *Who's Who in Colored America*, vol. 1 (New York, 1927). Home-buying by southerners is described in Chicago Commission on Race Relations, *The Negro in Chicago: A Study of Race Relations and a Race Riot* (Chicago, 1922), 217–19; and Drake and Cayton, *Black Metropolis*, 551.

51. On the differences in family composition, see Stewart E. Tolnay, "Migration Experience and Family Patterns in the 'Promised Land,' " *Journal of Family History* 23 (1998): 68–89; and "The Great Migration and Changes in the Northern Black Family," 1213–38.

52. Table A.21 shows the earnings by education for black males and females in non-

South metropolitan areas. For southern-born white males, the 1949 averages were $3,718 for high school graduates and $2,954 for those who were grammar-schooled (1950 IPUMS).

53. Long, "Poverty Status and Receipt of Welfare among Migrants and Nonmigrants in Large Cities," 54; Stewart E. Tolnay reviews these arguments in "The African American 'Great Migration' and Beyond," *Annual Review of Sociology* 29 (2003): 209–31.

54. The possibility that southerners were "doubly selected" has also been raised: ambitious southerners moving north and those who have trouble returning home. But an examination of those returning in the late 1960s does not support the argument. See Larry H. Long and Kristin A. Hansen, "Selectivity of Black Return Migration to the South," *Rural Sociology* 42 (Fall 1977): 317–31; Lieberson and Wilkinson, "A Comparison between Northern and Southern Blacks Residing in the North," 199–224; and Featherman and Hauser, *Opportunity and Change*, 422.

55. These comparisons leave out non-wage benefits like health care and pension plans, which were more likely to accompany jobs in the North than in the South.

56. Featherman and Hauser, *Opportunity and Change*, 417, 421–22. Just what is included in these calculations is not clear. Background factors are controlled, but it is not clear whether the demographers also assume that the same kinds of jobs are available in both regions. Nor is the sample N for southern migrants available.

57. Important archival collections are the Pittsburgh Oral History Project, Historical and Museum Commission, Harrisburg; the People of Indianapolis History Project, Indiana University Oral History Research Center; the Walter P. Reuther Library Oral History Collections, Wayne State University; and the Dust Bowl Migration Digital Archive, California State College Bakersfield Library, ‹http://www.lib.csub.edu/special/dustbowl.html›.

58. James P. Comer, *Maggie's American Dream: The Life and Times of a Black Family* (New York, 1989), 227.

59. E. Marvin Goodwin, *Black Migration in American from 1915 to 1960: An Uneasy Exodus* (Lewiston, N.Y., 1990), 38–39.

60. Timuel D. Black Jr., *The Bridges of Memory: Chicago's First Wave of Black Migration* (Evanston, Ill., 2003); Feather, *Mountain People in a Flat Land*; Dona L. Irvin, *The Unsung Heart of Black America: A Middle-Class Church at Midcentury* (Columbia, Mo., 1992). Other published oral histories: Elaine Latzman Moon, ed., *Untold Tales, Unsung Heroes: An Oral History of Detroit's African American Community, 1918–1967* (Detroit, 1994); A. O. Faulkner, M. A. Helser, W. Holbrook, and S. Geismar, eds., *When I Was Comin' Up: An Oral History of Aged Blacks* (Hamden, Conn., 1982).

61. Joy Bennett Kinnon, "Factory Worker Gives $700,000 to Charity," *Ebony*, October 1996, 62; Morgan, *Rising in the West*; Whitman, "The Great Sharecropper Success Story," 3–19.

CHAPTER FOUR

1. Joe William Trotter Jr. first attacked the ghetto paradigm in *Black Milwaukee: The Making of an Industrial Proletariat, 1915–45* (Urbana, Ill., 1985). Richard W. Thomas,

Life for Us Is What We Make It: Building Black Community in Detroit, 1915–1945 (Bloomington, 1992), xi–xiv; Albert S. Broussard, *Black San Francisco: The Struggle for Racial Equality in the West, 1900–1954* (Lawrence, Kans., 1993); Quintard Taylor, *The Forging of a Black Community: Seattle's Central District from 1870 through the Civil Rights Era* (Seattle, 1994); Kimberley L. Phillips, *AlabamaNorth: African-American Migrants, Community, and Working-Class Activism in Cleveland, 1915–45* (Urbana, Ill., 1999); Lillian Serece Williams, *Strangers in the Land of Paradise: The Creation of an African American Community, Buffalo, New York 1900–1940* (Bloomington, 1999); Shirley Ann Wilson Moore, *To Place Our Deeds: The African American Community in Richmond, California, 1910–1963* (Berkeley, 2000); Josh Sides, *L.A. City Limits: African American Los Angeles from the Great Depression to the Present* (Berkeley, 2003). Two exemplary southern studies have also advanced the discussion of community building: Earl Lewis, *In Their Own Interests: Race, Class, and Power in Twentieth-Century Norfolk, Virginia* (Berkeley, 1991); and Elsa Barkley Brown, "Uncle Ned's Children: Negotiating Community and Freedom in Postemancipation Richmond, Virginia" (Ph.D. diss., Kent State University, 1994).

2. St. Clair Drake and Horace R. Cayton, *Black Metropolis: A Study of Negro Life in a Northern City* (New York, 1962; orig. 1945), 12. Richard Wright quote is from xvii. For a discussion of the project, which began in 1936, see Richard S. Hobbs, *Cayton Legacy: An African American Family* (Pullman, Wash., 2002), 103–26.

3. Roi Ottley, *"New World A-Coming": Inside Black America* (Boston, 1943), quotes from 1–2. To get a sense of the enthusiastic reception, see Dexter Teed, "New World A-Coming," *Negro Digest*, May 1944, 81–83. On the other hand, Wallace Van Jackson slammed the book in a review for the new Atlanta-based journal of race and culture, *Phylon* 5 (1944): 93–94. Jackson criticized Ottley for ignoring the South and the vast majority of black Americans. A radio series, *New World A-Coming*, followed in 1944, broadcast on WMCA (New York). See Barbara Dianne Savage, *Broadcasting Freedom: Radio, War, and the Politics of Race 1938–1948* (Chapel Hill, 1999), 246–77.

4. Historians of the next generation worked to correct Ottley's romanticized portrait of Harlem. See Gilbert Osofsky, *Harlem, The Making of a Ghetto: Negro New York, 1890–1930*, 2d ed. (Chicago, 1996); and Nathan Irvin Huggins, *Harlem Renaissance* (New York, 1971). But some of Ottley's interest in political vitality has reemerged in the most recent historiography: Cheryl Lynn Greenberg, *"Or Does It Explode?" Black Harlem in the Great Depression* (New York, 1991); Martha Biondi, *To Stand and Fight: The Struggle for Civil Rights in Postwar New York* (Cambridge, 2002).

5. Adam Green, *Selling the Race: Culture, Community, and Black Chicago, 1940–1955* (Chicago, forthcoming 2005); Suzanne E. Smith, *Dancing in the Street: Motown and the Cultural Politics of Detroit* (Cambridge, Mass., 1999). Also Bill V. Mullen, *Popular Fronts: Chicago and African-American Cultural Politics, 1935–1946* (Urbana, Ill., 1999); Carole Marks and Diana Edkins, *The Power of Pride: Stylemakers and Rulebreakers of the Harlem Renaissance* (New York, 1999).

6. On suburban settlers, see Andrew Wiese, *Places of Their Own: African American Suburbanization in the Twentieth Century* (Chicago, 2004); on non-urban settlement in the West, see Quintard Taylor, *In Search of the Racial Frontier: African Americans in*

the *American West, 1528–1990* (New York, 1998), esp. 134–91; and Geta LeSeur, *Not All Okies Are White: The Lives of Black Cotton Pickers in Arizona* (Columbia, Mo., 2000).

7. W. E. B. Du Bois, "Hosts of Black Labor," *Nation*, 9 May 1923, 540. See also Louise Venable Kennedy, *The Negro Peasant Turns Cityward: Effects of Recent Migrations to Northern Centers* (New York, 1930), 221–28.

8. Richard R. Wright Jr., *The Negro in Pennsylvania: A Study in Economic History* (New York, 1969; orig. 1912); W. E. B. Du Bois, "The Black Vote of Philadelphia," and John T. Emlen, "The Movement for the Betterment of the Negro in Philadelphia," both reprinted in *Black Politics in Philadelphia*, ed. Miriam Ershkowitz and Joseph Zikmund II (New York, 1973); Clara A. Hardin, *The Negroes of Philadelphia: The Cultural Adjustment of a Minority Group* (Bryn Mawr, Pa., 1945); Allen B. Ballard, *One More Day's Journey: The Story of a Family and a People* (New York, 1984).

9. Sadie T. Mossell, "The Standard of Living Among One Hundred Negro Migrant Families in Philadelphia," *Annals of the American Academy* 98 (November 1921): 177. A. Ballard, *One More Day's Journey*, 191–216, emphasizes tensions. See also Charles Pete T. Banner-Haley, *To Do Good and To Do Well: Middle-Class Blacks and the Depression, Philadelphia, 1929–1941* (New York, 1993), 45–62.

10. Robert Gregg, *Sparks from the Anvil of Oppression: Philadelphia's African Methodists and Southern Migrants, 1890–1940* (Philadelphia, 1993), 194, 208, argues that the tensions were not serious. On immigrant community factionalism, see Donna Gabaccia, "Two Great Migrations: American and Italian Southerners in Comparative Perspective," in *The American South and the Italian Mezzogiorno: Essays in Comparative History*, ed. Enrico Dal Lago and Rick Halpern (New York, 2002), 226; John Bodnar, *The Transplanted: A History of Immigrants in Urban America* (Bloomington, 1985), 117–30; and Victor R. Greene, *American Immigrant Leaders 1800–1910: Marginality and Identity* (Baltimore, 1987).

11. On Pittsburgh, see Peter Gottlieb, *Making Their Own Way: Southern Blacks' Migration to Pittsburgh, 1916–30* (Urbana, Ill., 1987); and John Bodnar, Roger Simon, and Michael P. Weber, *Lives of Their Own: Blacks, Italians, and Poles in Pittsburgh, 1900–1960* (Urbana, Ill., 1982). On Cincinnati, see Joe William Trotter Jr., *River Jordan: African American Urban Life in the Ohio Valley* (Lexington, Ky., 1998); Henry Louis Taylor Jr., ed., *Race and the City: Work, Community, and Protest in Cincinnati, 1820–1970* (Urbana, Ill., 1993); J. Trent Alexander, "Great Migrations: Race and Community in the Southern Exodus, 1917–1970" (Ph.D. diss., Carnegie Mellon University, 2001); and Wendell P. Dabney, *Cincinnati's Colored Citizens* (New York, 1970; orig. 1926).

12. Osofsky, *Harlem*; James Weldon Johnson, *Black Manhattan* (New York, 1968; orig. 1930). On Brooklyn, see Harold X. Connolly, *A Ghetto Grows in Brooklyn* (New York, 1977); and Clarence Taylor, *The Black Churches of Brooklyn* (New York, 1994).

13. Ira De A. Reid, *The Negro Immigrant: His Background, Characteristics and Social Adjustment, 1899–1937* (New York, 1939), 107–8; Edward R. Lewinson, *Black Politics in New York City* (New York, 1974), 161–74; Ottley, *"New World A-Coming,"* 68–81; Osofsky, *Harlem*, 129–35.

14. Chester Wilkins interview by William Tuttle Jr., 25 June 1969, Chicago, as quoted

in James R. Grossman, *Land of Hope: Chicago, Black Southerners, and the Great Migration* (Chicago, 1989), 139. Grossman discusses the evolving relationships between old settlers and newcomers with more subtlety than we have time for here. On the bombings: Chicago Commission on Race Relations, *The Negro in Chicago: A Study of Race Relations and a Race Riot* (Chicago, 1922), 122–33; Drake and Cayton, *Black Metropolis*, 61–64.

15. Allan H. Spear, *Black Chicago: The Making of a Negro Ghetto 1890–1920* (Chicago, 1967), 51–90; Grossman, *Land of Hope*, 123–60. Similar leadership transformations in Cleveland and Detroit are explored in Kenneth L. Kusmer, *A Ghetto Takes Shape: Black Cleveland, 1870–1930* (Urbana, Ill., 1976). Thomas, *Life for Us Is What We Make It*.

16. Charles S. Johnson, *The Negro War Worker in San Francisco* (n.p., 1944), 91–93, recorded some resentment among old settlers. Q. Taylor examines the "community ethos" in Seattle in *Forging of a Black Community*, 135–56. Broussard, *Black San Francisco*, 170–73; S. Moore, *To Place Our Deeds*.

17. If the talent list included men and women who completed their educations in the North, it would be much larger and more impressive. The disproportionate number of lawyers and other professionals working outside the South as of the 1930 census is tabulated in Carter Goodwin Woodson, *The Negro Professional Man and the Community* (Washington, D.C., 1934), esp. 29–42, 192, 287. There are dozens of individual stories in Richard Bardolph, *The Negro Vanguard* (Westport, 1959).

18. On southern leaders in Philadelphia, see *Who's Who in Colored America*, vol. 1 (New York, 1927); "Slave to Banker," *Ebony*, November 1945, 43–47; A. Ballard, *One More Day's Journey*, 202–3; Gregg, *Sparks from the Anvil*, 207–8.

19. K. L. Phillips, *AlabamaNorth*, 161–89. World War II created similar dynamics in some of the West Coast cities that until then had only tiny black populations. Gretchen Lemke-Santangelo describes the effect in Oakland: "Southern Migrant Culture Simply Swallowed the Tiny Prewar East Bay Black Population," in *Abiding Courage: African American Migrant Women and the East Bay Community* (Chapel Hill, 1996), 135. On Cleveland: Kusmer, *A Ghetto Takes Shape*; Russell H. Davis, *Black Americans in Cleveland from George Peak to Carl B. Stokes 1796–1969* (Washington, D.C., 1972). On Detroit: Thomas, *Life for Us Is What We Make It*; David Allen Levine, *Internal Combustion: The Races in Detroit, 1915–1926* (Westport, 1976); Victoria W. Wolcott, *Remaking Respectability: African American Women in Interwar Detroit* (Chapel Hill, 2001).

20. Ottley's childhood memories are from Teed, "New World A-Coming," 82. Southernization is described in Grossman, *Land of Hope*, 154–60; and A. Ballard, *One More Day's Journey*, 202–3.

21. Grossman, *Land of Hope*, 150. Wolcott, *Remaking Respectability*, 53–92, has an extended discussion of socialization efforts and the status of North and South. On accents, see Lawrence W. Levine, *Black Culture and Black Consciousness: Afro-American Folk Thought from Slavery to Freedom* (New York, 1975), 149; and Bridget LeAnn Anderson, "An Acoustic Study of Southeastern Michigan Appalachian and African American Southern Migrant Vowel Systems" (Ph.D. diss., University of Michigan, 2003). On class and region, see Drake and Cayton, *Black Metropolis*, 551.

22. Weekly notices about the activities of Detroit Memphis can be found in the 1954 editions of *Michigan Chronicle*.

23. The term "cultural apparatus" originated with C. Wright Mills and was rescued by Michael Denning, *The Cultural Front: The Laboring of American Culture in the Twentieth Century* (New York, 1996). In describing a black cultural apparatus, I am changing its meaning. They used the term to suggest a single hegemonic network of institutions. On class relations: Adam Green, "Selling the Race: Cultural Production and Notions of Community in Black Chicago, 1940–1955" (Ph.D. diss., Yale University, 1998), 140–46. Anthropologist Steven Gregory makes a similar argument in *Black Corona: Race and the Politics of Place in an Urban Community* (Princeton, 1998), 37–40. They are correcting notions that have been standard for fifty years, put forth most importantly by Drake and Cayton in *Black Metropolis* and E. Franklin Frazier, *The Black Bourgeoisie* (New York, 1962). On consumer power: Robert E. Weems Jr., *Desegregating the Dollar: African American Consumerism in the Twentieth Century* (New York, 1998).

24. Ottley, *"New World A-Coming,"* 270.

25. Catherine R. Squires, "Rethinking the Black Public Sphere: An Alternative Vocabulary for Multiple Public Spheres," *Communication Theory* 12 (November 2002): 446–68. There is a great deal of debate about the terms of public sphere theory and no settled meaning for the concepts of "counterpublic" and "black public sphere" (versus black public spheres). There are other arguments about periodization, some claiming that a black counterpublic emerges in the 1930s. For useful arguments, see the essays by Houston Baker, Michael Dawson, Elsa Barkley Brown, and Thomas Holt in *The Black Public Sphere*, ed. Black Public Sphere Collective (Chicago, 1995). Nikhil Pal Singh, *Black Is a Country: Race and the Unfinished Struggle for Democracy* (Cambridge, Mass., 2004); Michael Warner, "Publics and Counterpublics," *Public Culture* 14, no. 1 (2002): 49–90. On turn-of-the-century information systems, see Jacqueline M. Moore, *Leading the Race: The Transformation of the Black Elite in the Nation's Capital, 1880–1920* (Charlottesville, Va., 1999); and August Meier, *Negro Thought in America 1880–1915* (Ann Arbor, 1968).

26. Roi Ottley, *Lonely Warrior: The Life and Times of Robert S. Abbott* (Chicago, 1955); Juliet E. K. Walker, "The Promised Land: The Chicago *Defender* and the Black Press in Illinois, 1862–1970," in *The Black Press in the Middle West, 1865–1985*, ed. Henry Lewis Suggs (Westport, 1996), 9–50; Mullen, *Popular Fronts*, 44–74; Grossman, *Land of Hope*, 66–97.

27. Lawrence W. Hogan, *A Black National News Service: The Associated Negro Press and Claude Barnett, 1919–1945* (Rutherford, N.J., 1984); Green, "Selling the Race," 122–95; Armistead S. Pride and Clint C. Wilson II, *A History of the Black Press* (Washington, D.C., 1997), 164–67; Roland E. Wolseley, *The Black Press, U.S.A.* (Ames, Iowa, 1971), 61–65; John H. Johnson with Lerone Bennett Jr., *Succeeding against the Odds* (New York, 1989), 113–71.

28. For a valuable assessment of the New York and other black periodicals, see Abby Arthur Johnson and Ronald Maberry Johnson, *Propaganda and Aesthetics: The Literary Politics of Afro-American Magazines in the Twentieth Century* (Amherst, 1979); Wolseley, *Black Press*, 44–49; and Beth Tompkins Bates, *Pullman Porters and the Rise of Protest Politics in Black America 1925–1945* (Chapel Hill, 2001), 35–39.

29. W. E. B. Du Bois, "Editing 'The Crisis,'" *Crisis*, March 1951, 147–51. See also in

that issue: Roy Wilkins, "The Crisis, 1934–49," 154–57, and George S. Schuyler, "Forty Years of 'The Crisis,'" 159–60. There is a good discussion of the *Crisis* and some of the newspapers in William G. Jordan, *Black Newspapers and America's War for Democracy, 1914–1920* (Chapel Hill, 2001). For an example of the echo effect that the *Crisis* had in the black press, see the *Baltimore Afro-American*, 30 October 1927, where there are three articles referring to the *Crisis*.

30. Andrew Buni, *Robert L. Vann of the* Pittsburgh Courier: *Politics and Black Journalism* (Pittsburgh, 1974); Vishnu V. Oak, *The Negro Newspaper* (Westport, 1948), esp. 69–71; Pride and Wilson, *History of the Black Press*, 137–40.

31. On the key role of Howard: Jonathan Scott Holloway, *Confronting the Veil: Abram Harris Jr., E. Franklin Frazier, and Ralph Bunche, 191–1941* (Chapel Hill, 2002). On Washington: Carl Abbott, *Political Terrain: Washington, D.C., from Tidewater Town to Global Metropolis* (Chapel Hill, 1999), 73–77; Willard B. Gatewood, *Aristocrats of Color: The Black Elite, 1890–1920* (Bloomington, 1990); J. Moore, *Leading the Race.* The *Norfolk Journal and Guide* and the *Atlanta World* were two other large circulation southern-based newspapers. The *World*, founded in 1928, became a daily in 1931 and remained so until 1969. It also established a syndicate of newspapers in other cities of the South. Alton Hornsby Jr., "Georgia," in *The Black Press in the South, 1865–1979*, ed. Henry Lewis Suggs (Westport, 1983), 127–39.

32. Key studies of African American urban formations in southern cities include: E. Lewis, *In Their Own Interests*; George C. Wright, *Life behind a Veil: Blacks in Louisville, Kentucky, 1865–1930* (Baton Rouge, 1985); Lewis A. Randolph and Gayle T. Tate, *Rights for a Season: The Politics of Race, Class, and Gender in Richmond, Virginia* (Knoxville, 2003); and David Andrew Harmon, *Beneath the Image of the Civil Rights Movement and Race Relations: Atlanta, Georgia, 1946–1981* (New York, 1996). Joe Trotter compares northern and southern urban formations in the final chapter of *Black Milwaukee*, 226–41. For an earlier era, see Howard N. Rabinowitz, *Race Relations in the Urban South, 1865–1890* (Urbana, Ill., 1980).

33. Haywood Farrar, *The "Baltimore Afro-American," 1892–1950* (Westport, 1998); Ralph J. Bunche, *The Political Status of the Negro in the Age of FDR*, ed. Dewey W. Grantham (Chicago, 1973), 473, 554; Harold A. McDougall, *Black Baltimore: A New Theory of Community* (Philadelphia, 1993).

34. Oak, *Negro Newspaper*, 152–65.

35. All of the articles mentioned in this paragraph are from the 24 October 1925 *Baltimore Afro-American*.

36. Ibid., 1917 and 1925 issues.

37. For an overview, see William M. Banks, *Black Intellectuals: Race and Responsibility in American Life* (New York, 1996); Harold Cruse, *The Crisis of the Negro Intellectual: A Historical Analysis of the Failure of Black Leadership* (New York, 1984; orig. 1967). For turn-of-the-century intellectual formations, see Kevin K. Gaines, *Uplifting the Race: Black Leadership, Politics, and Culture in the Twentieth Century* (Chapel Hill, 1996); and Hazel V. Carby, *Reconstructing Womanhood: The Emergence of the Afro-American Woman Novelist* (New York, 1987).

38. On Harlem: Huggins, *Harlem Renaissance*; David Levering Lewis, *When Harlem*

Was in Vogue (New York, 1989); James De Jongh, *Vicious Modernism: Black Harlem and the Literary Imagination* (New York, 1990). On Chicago: Mullin, *Popular Fronts*; Green, "Selling the Race." Q. Taylor, *In Search of the Racial Frontier*, 245, describes the Los Angeles literary renaissance.

39. George Hutchinson, *The Harlem Renaissance in Black and White* (Cambridge, 1995), 6; Ann Douglas, *Terrible Honesty: Mongrel Manhattan in the 1920s* (New York, 1995); D. Lewis, *When Harlem Was in Vogue*; Marks and Edkins, *Power of Pride*; Steven Watson, *The Harlem Renaissance: Hub of African-American Culture, 1920–1930* (New York, 1995).

40. Banks, *Black Intellectuals*, 93–100. The sociologist Horace R. Cayton Jr. twice accepted southern teaching posts only to flee back to Chicago at the end of each term. See *Long Old Road: An Autobiography* (Seattle, 1964), 189–206, 233–35. L. D. Reddick discussed the complications in "Why I Left the North," *Negro Digest*, September 1949, 3–9.

41. Richard Robbins, *Sidelines Activist: Charles S. Johnson and the Struggle for Civil Rights* (Jackson, Miss., 1996). See also Robbins's essay "Charles S. Johnson," in *Black Sociologists: Historical and Contemporary Perspectives*, ed. James E. Blackwell and Morris Janowitz (Chicago, 1974), 56–84.

42. Holloway, *Confronting the Veil*, 136–46; Anthony M. Platt, *E. Franklin Frazier Reconsidered* (New Brunswick, 1991); G. Franklin Edwards, "E. Franklin Frazier," in *Black Sociologists*, ed. Blackwell and Janowitz, 85–117.

43. John White, "John Hope Franklin: Southern History in Black and White," in *Reading Southern History: Essays on Interpreters and Interpretations*, ed. Glenn Feldman (Tuscaloosa, 2001), 151–66; August Meier and Elliott Rudwick, *Black History and the Historical Profession, 1915–1980* (Urbana, Ill., 1986).

44. Bardolph, *Negro Vanguard*, 225–39; Doug McAdam, *Political Process and the Development of Black Insurgency, 1930–1970* (Chicago, 1985), 100–102; Douglas L. Smith, *The New Deal in the Urban South* (Baton Rouge, 1988), 240–43; Adam Fairclough, *Better Day Coming: Blacks and Equality, 1890–2000* (New York, 2001), 176–78; Raymond Wolters, *The New Negro on Campus: Black College Rebellions of the 1920s* (Princeton, 1975).

45. Langston Hughes, *The Big Sea* (New York, 1940), 228, quoted and perhaps made famous by Cruse, *Crisis of the Negro Intellectual*, 33. For an example of how the black press supported the literati, see the *Baltimore Afro-American* issue of 30 October 1927. On the front page is an article about an essay just published by W. E. B. Du Bois in the *Crisis*. On page 8 is "Book Chats," a regular column by Mary Ovington White, in this case reviewing a book translated from the French called *Primitive Negro Sculpture*, followed by an article, "Wellesley Hears Countee Cullen." On page 10 is a longer article, "Cullen Takes Second Prize in the Crisis Poetry Award," and on page 13 is a report about the recent meeting of the Association for the Study of Negro Life and History where the history of Haiti and Garveyite ideas about race superiority were debated. The 30 October issue was not typical, but similar notices are easy to find in this and other newspapers.

46. Important statements on the role of African American music include L. Levine,

Black Culture and Black Consciousness; Samuel A. Floyd Jr., *The Power of Black Music: Interpreting Its History from Africa to the United States* (New York, 1995); and Mark Anthony Neal, *What the Music Said: Black Popular Music and Black Public Culture* (New York, 1999). On Afro-Americanization, see Cornell West, *Race Matters* (New York, 1994), 121; and Henry Louis Gates Jr. and Cornel West, *The African-American Century: How Black Americans Have Shaped Our Country* (New York, 200), xv.

47. Leroy Ostransky, *Jazz City: The Impact of Our Cities on the Development of Jazz* (Englewood Cliffs, N.J., 1978).

48. On the early blues and jazz history, see William Barlow, *"Looking Up at Down": The Emergence of Blues Culture* (Philadelphia, 1989); Ted Gioia, *The History of Jazz* (New York, 1997); and Lawrence Cohn, ed., *Nothing but the Blues: The Music and the Musicians* (New York, 1993).

49. William Barlow, "Cashing In," in *Split Image: African Americans in the Mass Media*, ed. Jannette L. Dates and William Barlow (Washington, D.C., 1990), 29–30.

50. Willie (the Lion) Smith, *Music on My Mind: The Memoirs of an American Pianist* (New York, 1964), 112.

51. J. W. Johnson, *Black Manhattan*, 74–125; Thomas L. Riis, *Just before Jazz: Black Musical Theater in New York, 1890 to 1915* (Washington, D.C., 1989).

52. Jervis Anderson, *This Was Harlem: 1900–1950* (New York, 1982); Gioia, *History of Jazz*, 93–134.

53. U.S. Bureau of the Census, *Negroes in the United States 1920–1932* (Washington, D.C., 1935), table 12; Woodson, *Negro Professional Man and the Community*, 264–65, 335–40; Gunnar Myrdal, *An American Dilemma: The Negro Problem and Modern Democracy* (New York, 1944), 329–30. There are all sorts of accuracy and definitional issues behind these census numbers, and the caveats discussed in appendix B apply.

54. Bureau of the Census, *Negroes in the United States 1920–1932*, table 12; William Howland Kenney, *Chicago Jazz: A Cultural History 1904–1930* (New York, 1993); Green, "Selling the Race," 47–122.

55. Paul De Barros, *Jackson Street after Hours: The Roots of Jazz in Seattle* (Seattle, 1993); Clora Bryant et al., eds., *Central Avenue Sounds: Jazz in Los Angeles* (Berkeley, 1998); Ross Russell, *Jazz Style in Kansas City and the Southwest* (New York, 1997).

56. Charley Gerard, *Jazz in Black and White: Race, Culture, and Identity in the Jazz Community* (Westport, 1998); Lewis A. Erenberg, *Swingin' the Dream: Big Band Jazz and the Rebirth of American Culture* (Chicago, 1998); Jeffrey Melnick, *A Right to Sing the Blues: African Americans, Jews, and American Popular Song* (Cambridge, 1999); Burton W. Peretti, *The Creation of Jazz: Music, Race, and Culture in Urban America* (Urbana, Ill., 1992).

57. Barlow, *"Looking Up at Down,"* gives an excellent sense of the musical geography of the era. For a southern city comparison, see Steve Goodson, *Highbrows, Hillbillies and Hellfire: Public Entertainment in Atlanta 1880–1930* (Athens, Ga., 2002), 162–83.

58. "Stage Folk" participated in the information network of the *Chicago Defender*. See Walker, "Promised Land," 24.

59. Chris Albertson, *Bessie* (New York, 1972).

60. See the huge ads that Columbia ran in the *Baltimore Afro-American* in the sum-

mer of 1927. Daphne Duval Harrison, *Black Pearls: Blues Queens of the 1920s* (New Brunswick, 1988).

61. Hazel V. Carby, "It Jus Be's Dat Way Sometime: The Sexual Politics of Women's Blues," *Radical America* 20 (June–July 1986): 8–22; Angela Davis, *Blues Legacies and Black Feminism* (New York, 1998); Wolcott, *Remaking Respectability*, 36–38; Deborah Gray White, *Too Heavy a Load: Black Women in Defense of Themselves 1894–1994* (New York, 1999), 126–29.

62. Myrdal, *An American Dilemma*, 329. The latest argument that black celebrity can turn into a biologized trap focuses on sports: John Hoberman, *Darwin's Athletes: How Sport Has Damaged Black America and Preserved the Myth of Race* (New York, 1997). See also the essays in Dates and Barlow, eds., *Split Image*.

63. *Chicago Defender* (St. Louis edition), 6 January 1945, 6. Or see the headlines on 30 September 1944, 7: "Philly Awaits Arrival of Lena Horne's Show," "Writer Returns to Paris and Spot American Musicians Made," "Satchmo Plays Spotlight Air Show October 6," "N.C. Drummer Is Hit in Europe." Some early *Ebony* cover stories: "Two Decades with the Duke" (January 1946); "How Joe Louis Spent $2,000,000" (May 1946); "World's Greatest Musician" (December 1952).

64. Paul Denis, "The Negro in Show Business," *Negro Digest*, February 1943, 34, 36.

65. Ottley, *"New World A-Coming,"* 186–89.

66. Henry Lewis Suggs, "Conclusion: An Interpretative History of the Black Press in the Middle West, 1865–1985," in *The Black Press in the Middle West, 1865–1985*, ed. Henry Lewis Suggs (Westport, 1996), 352; Jerome Holtzman, ed., *No Cheering in the Press Box* (New York, 1974); Douglas A. Noverr and Lawrence E. Ziewacz, *The Games They Played: Sports in American History, 1865–1980* (Chicago, 1983), 67–96.

67. Robert Peterson, *Only the Ball Was White* (Englewood Cliffs, N.J., 1970); Mark Ribowsky, *A Complete History of the Negro Leagues 1884 to 1955* (New York, 1995).

68. Robert Peterson, *Only the Ball Was White*, 83–84. Foster was the darling of the *Defender* sports page as early as 1916.

69. Ribowsky, *Complete History of the Negro Leagues*, 100; Robert Peterson, *Only the Ball Was White*, 93. There are now excellent team histories, including Richard Bak, *Turkey Stearnes and the Detroit Stars: The Negro Leagues in Detroit, 1919–1933* (Detroit, 1994); James Bankes, *The Pittsburgh Crawfords: The Lives and Times of Black Baseball's Most Exciting Team* (Dubuque, 1991); Janet Bruce, *The Kansas City Monarchs: Champions of Black Baseball* (Lawrence, Kans., 1985); and Donn Rogosin, *Invisible Men: Life in Baseball's Negro Leagues* (New York, 1983).

70. Peterson, *Only the Ball Was White*, 101.

71. For a compilation of their articles, see Jim Reisler, ed., *Black Writers/Black Baseball: An Anthology of Articles from Black Sportswriters Who Covered the Negro Leagues* (Jefferson, N.C., 1994).

72. Some examples: "Negro Stars on the Playing-Fields of America," *Literary Digest*, 2 March 1935, 32; "Josh the Basher," *Time*, 19 July 1943, 75+; "Home-run Josh," *Newsweek*, 27 August 1945, 72+; Hy Turkin, "Brown Superman," *Ebony*, January 1946. *Ebony* made a point of identifying the author as a white sportswriter for the *New York Daily News*.

73. G. Edward White explores the *Courier*'s promotion of the East-West All-Star game in *Creating the National Pastime: Baseball Transforms Itself, 1903–1953* (Princeton, 1996), 139–43. Larry Lester, *Black Baseball's National Showcase: The East-West All-Star Game, 1933–1953* (Lincoln, Neb., 2001).

74. *Defender*, 2 August 1941, reprinted in Reisler, *Black Writers/Black Baseball*; "New Day A-Coming," *Newsweek*, 27 August 1945, 72+.

75. Quoted in Chris Mean, *Champion — Joe Louis: Black Hero in White America* (New York, 1985), 134.

76. Ibid., 50–51. The Runyon quote is from page x. L. Levine, *Black Culture and Black Consciousness*; Ottley, *"New World A-Coming,"* 186–202.

77. Mean, *Champion — Joe Louis*, 1–7; Joe Louis with Edna and Art Rust Jr., *Joe Louis: My Life* (New York, 1981).

78. Mean, *Champion — Joe Louis*, 37–43.

79. Richard Wright, "The Shame of Chicago," *Ebony*, December 1951, 24–32.

80. "Return of the Native Son," *Ebony*, December 1951, 98.

81. Ted Poston and Roi Ottley, "New York vs. Chicago," *Ebony*, December 1952, 17.

82. Ibid., 24, 27.

83. Ibid., 19.

CHAPTER FIVE

1. Lily Tomlin interview with author, 5 October 2000, in author's possession; Jeff Sorensen, *Lily Tomlin: Woman of a Thousand Faces* (New York, 1989).

2. Nick Salvatore, *Singing in a Strange Land: C. L. Franklin, the Black Church, and the Transformation of America* (Boston, 2005); C. L. Franklin, *Give Me This Mountain: Life History and Selected Sermons*, ed. Jeff Todd Titon (Urbana, Ill., 1989); "Chronicle Selects Detroit's Spiritual Leaders for 1953," *Michigan Chronicle*, 2 January 1954, 20.

3. Aretha Franklin and David Ritz, *Aretha: From These Roots* (New York, 1999), 50. The prominence of the Franklin family is evident in the pages of the *Michigan Chronicle*. For an early family photo: "Final Rites Held for Mrs. Louise Bryant," 6 February 1954, 22; "Congressman Powell Speaks at New Bethel," 10 April 1954, 25.

4. This survey has often been misused by scholars who think it shows that Detroit residents were more likely to single out southern whites as "undesirable" than African Americans. Actually, 80 out of 525 residents said negative things about the whites. In another question, 288 residents expressed unfavorable feelings about blacks. Arthur Kornhauser, *Detroit as the People See It: A Survey of Attitudes in an Industrial City* (Detroit, 1953), 46–47, 90–93.

5. Jim Hammitte oral history interview by Mary Thompson, 3 December 1974, Samford University Library, 2. For more on southern whites in Detroit, see Alan Clive, *State of War: Michigan in World War II* (Ann Arbor, 1979), 170–84.

6. For more detailed discussions of prejudice and response, see James N. Gregory, *American Exodus: The Dust Bowl Migration and Okie Culture in California* (New York, 1989), 114–34; Chad Berry, *Southern Migrants, Northern Exiles* (Urbana, Ill., 2000), 182–200; Lewis M. Killian, *White Southerners* (New York, 1970), and "Southern White

Laborers in Chicago's West Side" (Ph.D. diss., University of Chicago, 1949), 123–46; and Clyde B. McCoy and Virginia McCoy Watkins, "Stereotypes of Appalachian Migrants," in *The Invisible Minority: Urban Appalachians*, ed. William W. Philliber and Clyde B. McCoy (Lexington, Ky., 1981), 20–34.

7. For a thought-provoking contemporary analysis of the situational uses of "hillbilly," see John Hartigan Jr., *Racial Situations: Class Predicaments of Whiteness in Detroit* (Princeton, 1999), esp. 88–102.

8. Killian, "Southern White Laborers," 127. See also Joyce Maresca's interview in Bill AuCoin, *Redneck* (Matteson, Ill., 1977), 139–43.

9. Bruce Ray Berryhill, "The Relationship between Regional and Social Dialects and Linguistic Adaptation" (MA thesis, California State University, Fresno, 1976). Another linguist has recently argued that in Detroit, the vowel patterns of black and white former southerners have converged while both remain distinct from white Detroit speech. See Bridget LeAnn Anderson, "An Acoustic Study of Southeastern Michigan Appalachian and African American Southern Migrant Vowel Systems" (Ph.D. diss., University of Michigan, 2003).

10. David Lyon, "Campfires Dotted the Still Night," *Bakersfield Californian*, 27 May 1979; Gregory, *American Exodus*, 118–36.

11. Killian, "Southern White Laborers," 141–42.

12. Ibid., 81, 141, 266–77; see also Erdmann Doane Beynon, "The Southern White Laborer Migrates to Michigan," *American Sociological Review* 3 (June 1938): 338–39.

13. Daniel E. Sutherland, *The Confederate Carpetbaggers* (Baton Rouge, 1988), 134.

14. United Daughters of the Confederacy, *Minutes of the Thirty-ninth Annual Convention of the Daughters of the Confederacy Incorporated Held in Memphis Tennessee, November 15–19, 1932*, 333, 312.

15. Ibid., 333, 312; Karen L. Cox, *Dixie's Daughters: The United Daughters of the Confederacy and the Preservation of Confederate Culture* (Gainesville, Fla., 2003).

16. United Daughters of the Confederacy, *Minutes of the Fiftieth Annual Convention of the Daughters of the Confederacy Incorporated Held at Columbus Ohio, November 18–21 1943*, 213. On the *Gone with the Wind* years in the South, see Grace Elizabeth Hale, *Making Whiteness: The Culture of Segregation in the South, 1890–1940* (New York, 1998), 251–84.

17. United Daughters of the Confederacy, *Minutes of the Forty-seventh Annual Convention Held at Montgomery Alabama, Nov. 19–22, 1940*, 243. UDC units survive today in some nonsouthern states (‹http://www.hqudc.org›). For the Jefferson Davis Memorial Highway, see the Federal Highway Administration memo at ‹http://www.fhwa.dot.gov/infrastructure/jdavis.htm›. Thomas Sancton describes Southern Society activities as of 1943 in "Bloody Shirt Once More," *New Republic*, 11 January 1943, 50. Daniel E. Sutherland, "Southern Fraternal Organizations in the North," *Journal of Southern History* 53, no. 4 (1987): 608, tracks its decline.

18. The community is the subject of one famous book: Todd Gitlin and Nanci Hollander, *Uptown: Poor Whites in Chicago* (New York, 1970), and is discussed at length in Killian, *White Southerners*. The big public discovery may have begun with a Chicago Commission on Human Relations report, "The Uptown Community Area and the

Southern White In-Migrant—A Human Relations Study" (mimeographed, n.p., May 1957, in Regenstein Library, University of Chicago), then jumped to newspaper and magazine pieces: Albert N. Votaw, "The Hillbillies Invade Chicago," *Harper's*, February 1958, 64–67; Hal Bruno, "The Hillbilly Ghetto," *Reporter*, 4 June 1962; Donald Janson, "Displaced Southerners Find Chicago an Impersonal Haven," *New York Times*, 31 August 1963. Uptown has also been the subject of a number of important dissertations, most recently Roger Stephen Guy, "Diversity to Unity: Uptown's Southern Migrants, 1950–1970" (Ph.D. diss., University of Wisconsin–Milwaukee, 1996). Others include Edwin S. Harwood, "Work and Community among Urban Newcomers: A Study of the Social and Economic Adaptation of Southern Migrants in Chicago" (Ph.D. diss., University of Chicago, 1966); and Don Edward Merten, "Up Here and Down Home: Appalachian Migrants in Northtown" (Ph.D. diss., University of Chicago, 1974).

19. Harwood, "Work and Community among Urban Newcomers," shows the transient nature of the community.

20. Killian, "Southern White Laborers," 248–56, 304.

21. Campbell quoted in Guy, "Diversity to Unity," 181; Phillip J. Obermiller and Thomas E. Wagner, "'Hands-Across-the-Ohio': The Urban Initiatives of the Council of the Southern Mountains, 1954–1971," in *Appalachian Odyssey: Historical Perspectives on the Great Migration*, ed. Phillip J. Obermiller, Thomas E. Wagner, and E. Bruce Tucker (Westport, 2000), 121–40; Gitlin and Hollander's book *Uptown* grew out of a social service project by former SDS members. I want to thank Jeri L. Reed for sharing his observations about Uptown.

22. There are other regions that might qualify as southernized geographies, including Ashtabula County in northeast Ohio and a large swath of New Mexico and Arizona. See Carl E. Feather, *Mountain People in a Flat Land: A Popular History of Appalachian Migration to Northeast Ohio, 1940–1965* (Athens, Ohio, 1998).

23. Oliver Carlson, "Up from the Dust," *U.S.A.* (August 1952), 101; Gregory, *American Exodus*, 70–77.

24. Key studies of southern whites in this subregion include William W. Philliber, *Appalachian Migrants in Urban America: Cultural Conflict or Ethnic Group Formation?* (New York, 1981); Clyde B. McCoy and James S. Brown, "Appalachian Migration to Midwestern Cities," in *The Invisible Minority*, ed. Philliber and McCoy, 35–78; Dan M. McKee and Phillip J. Obermiller, *From Mountain to Metropolis: Urban Appalachians in Ohio* (Cincinnati, 1978); Gary L. Fowler, "Up Here and Down Home: Appalachians in Cities," in *Perspectives on Urban Appalachians*, ed. Steven Weiland and Phillip Obermiller (Cincinnati, 1978), 197–209; and Harry K. Schwarzweller, James S. Brown, and Joseph J. Mangalam, *Mountain Families in Transition* (University Park, Pa., 1971). See also J. Trent Alexander, "Great Migrations: Race and Community in the Southern Exodus, 1917–1970" (Ph.D. diss., Carnegie Mellon University, 2001). Alexander emphasizes the differences in white migrant community formation patterns between Cincinnati and Indianapolis and links them to patterns of African American political development.

25. Jack Temple Kirby, *Rural Worlds Lost: The American South 1920–1960* (Baton Rouge, 1987), 327–30; John Leslie Thompson, "Industrialization in the Miami Valley:

A Case Study of Interregional Labor Migration" (Ph.D. diss., University of Wisconsin, 1955); Berry, *Southern Migrants, Northern Exiles*, 21, 119–20.

26. Tomlin interview; Harwood, "Work and Community among Urban Newcomers," 89–93. His data come from a National Opinion Research Center survey with a subsample of 269 southern whites. The pattern of residential dispersion was noted in two studies from the 1930s: Beynon, "Southern White Laborer," 340–42; and Elmer Akers, "Southern Whites in Detroit" (unpublished ms., n.d. [1937?]) available through University Microfilms.

27. These calculations involved combining the two 1970 IPUMS Neighborhood Samples to increase the size of each neighborhood sample. For the six major metropolitan areas, the samples included 6,402 southern-born white household heads living in 2,126 neighborhoods. Internal tests on these data suggest that larger and more reliable samples would show that southern white neighborhood densities were smaller than indicated here. Preferred neighborhoods can be identified by locating Southern Baptist and Assemblies of God churches. In Detroit, the 1958–60 *Directory of Churches and Other Religious Organizations of the Detroit Metropolitan Area* and its 1969 follow-up edition show continued migration toward the blue-collar suburbs mentioned in the text. See also Judy Stamp Humphrey, *Segregation and Integration: A Geography of People in Metropolitan Detroit* (Detroit, 1972), 17; and Robert Sinclair and Bryan Thompson, *Metropolitan Detroit: An Anatomy of Social Change* (Cambridge, 1977), 35–40. For favored neighborhoods in other cities, see Feather, *Mountain People in a Flat Land*, 13; John D. Photiadis, *Selected Social and Sociopsychological Characteristics of West Virginians in Their Own State and in Ohio* (Morgantown, W.V., 1975); Gregory, *American Exodus*; and Becky M. Nicolaides, *My Blue Heaven: Life and Politics in the Working-Class Suburbs of Los Angeles, 1920–1965* (Chicago, 2002), 43.

28. Hammitte interview, 4.

29. Ibid., 7. For more stories of going home, see Feather, *Mountain People in a Flat Land*; Berry, *Southern Migrants, Northern Exiles*; and Clive, *State of War*, 181–84.

30. Tomlin interview and e-mail message to author, 7 October 2000.

31. Beynon, "Southern White Laborer," 334; Stuart M. Jamieson, "A Settlement of Rural Migrant Families in the Sacramento Valley, California," *Rural Sociology* (March 1942): 49–61; Killian, "Southern White Laborers," quotes are from 143–45.

32. See the essays in Philliber, *Appalachian Migrants in Urban American*; Photiadis, *Selected Social and Sociopsychological Characteristics of West Virginians*; and the essays in Philliber and McCoy, eds., *The Invisible Minority*; and Obermiller, Wagner, and Tucker, eds., *Appalachian Odyssey*. Helping to shape the 1970s ethnicity discussion were Killian, *White Southerners*; and John Shelton Reed, *The Enduring South: Subcultural Persistence in Mass Society* (Chapel Hill, 1972).

33. Gregory, *American Exodus*, 139–41.

34. Tomlin interview.

35. John F. Rooney Jr., *A Geography of American Sport: From Cabin Creek to Anaheim* (Reading, Mass., 1974), 26–36, plots the origins of major leaguers for each decade. The one-third estimate is derived roughly from his map schematics. Wendell Smith, "A Strange Tribe," *Pittsburgh Courier*, 11 May 1938, reprinted in Jim Reisler, ed., *Black*

Writers/Black Baseball: An Anthology of Articles from Black Sportswriters Who Covered the Negro Leagues (Jefferson, N.C., 1994), 36–38.

36. Charles C. Alexander, *Ty Cobb* (New York, 1984), 107, 112.

37. John E. DiMeglio, "Baseball," in *Encyclopedia of Southern Culture*, ed. Charles R. Wilson and William Ferris (Chapel Hill, 1989), 1210–11.

38. Ibid.; Enos Slaughter with Kevin Reid, *Country Hardball: The Autobiography of Enos "Country" Slaughter* (Greensboro, N.C., 1991). BaseballLibrary.com is a helpful resource for identifying southern players and biographical literature about them.

39. "Dizzy, Daffy, and the Dangerous Dramatics," *Literary Digest*, 20 October 1934, 36; "1935 Baseball Drama: Ruth vs. the Deans," *Literary Digest*, 20 April 1935, 36; Curt Smith, *America's Dizzy Dean* (St. Louis, 1978).

40. J. R. Stockton, "Me and Paul," *Saturday Evening Post*, 16 March 1935, 12. Also by Stockton in the *Saturday Evening Post*: "Me and My Public: 'What Happened to Dizzy,'" 12 September 1936, 8–9; "Born for the Gashouse," 24 April 1937, 34. C. Smith, *America's Dizzy Dean*, 119–23.

41. *New York Times* article quoted in Jimmy Powers, *Baseball Personalities* (New York, 1949), 201.

42. Dan Burley, "Major League 'Dozens' Playing," *Amsterdam News*, 25 June 1947, reprinted in Reisler, *Black Writers/Black Baseball*, 139–42; Tom Meany, "Jackie's One of the Gang Now," *Negro Digest*, November 1949, 11–17; Walter Winchell, "Snub to a Southerner," *Negro Digest*, July 1949, 80; Robert Peterson, *Only the Ball Was White* (Englewood Cliffs, N.J., 1970), 198–99.

43. The WSB description is quoted in Charles Wolfe, "The Triumph of the Hills: Country Radio, 1920–1950," in *Country: The Music and the Musicians*, ed. Country Music Foundation (New York, 1994), 43.

44. Bill C. Malone, *Country Music U.S.A.: A Fifty-Year History* (Austin, 1985), 39; Archie Green, "Hillbilly Music: Source and Symbol," *Journal of American Folklore* 78 (July–September 1965): 204–28; Richard A. Peterson, *Creating Country Music: Fabricating Authenticity* (Chicago, 1997), 12–32; Douglas B. Green, *Country Roots: The Origins of Country Music* (New York, 1976).

45. A. Green, "Hillbilly Music," 213; Richard A. Peterson, *Creating Country Music*, 55–80.

46. Dorothy Horstman, *Sing Your Heart Out, Country Boy* (Nashville, 1996), xi; Curtis W. Ellison, *Country Music Culture: From Hard Times to Heaven* (Jackson, Miss., 1995), xix.

47. Bill C. Malone, *Don't Get above Your Raisin': Country Music and the Southern Working Class* (Urbana, Ill., 2002), 15, and *Southern Music American Music* (Lexington, Ky., 1979); Richard A. Peterson and Russell Davis Jr., "The Fertile Crescent of Country Music," *Journal of Country Music* (Spring 1975): 19–27; Melton A. McLaurin, "Songs of the South: The Changing Image of the South in Country Music," in *You Wrote My Life: Lyrical Themes in Country Music*, ed. Melton A. McLaurin and Richard A. Peterson (Philadelphia, 1992), 15–34.

48. The details of this story are from Loretta Lynn with George Vecsey, *Loretta Lynn: Coal Miner's Daughter* (Chicago, 1976).

49. Ibid., 64.

50. On the West Coast country music scene, see Gerald W. Haslam, *Workin' Man Blues: Country Music in California* (Berkeley, 1999); and Gregory, *American Exodus*, 222–45.

51. On the changing institutional geography, see Ronnie Pugh, "Country across the Country," in *Country*, ed. Country Music Foundation; and Malone, *Country Music U.S.A.*

52. Haslam, *Workin' Man Blues.*

53. Malone, *Country Music U.S.A.*, 43–63.

54. The primacy of the south is vigorously challenged by Haslam in *Workin' Man Blues*. Patricia Averill also develops an argument about the creative effects of the southern migrant population in "Can the Circle Be Unbroken: A Study of the Modernization of Rural Born Southern Whites since World War I Using Country Music" (Ph.D. diss., University of Pennsylvania, 1975), 209–32.

55. Richard A. Peterson, *Creating Country Music*, 81–84.

56. Gene Autry with Mickey Herskowitz, *Back in the Saddle Again* (New York, 1978), 14; the Vallee reference quote is from Gene Autry, "Three Pals," *Country Song Roundup*, January 1950, 15, as quoted in Douglas B. Green, "Singing Cowboy: An American Dream," *Journal of Country Music* 7 (May 1978): 17.

57. Green, "Singing Cowboy," 22.

58. See for example *The Billboard Encyclopedia of Music 1946–1947*, 8th annual ed. (Cincinnati, 1946–47), Section 6, "American Folk Music."

59. *Billboard*, March 1943, 25, quoted in Peter La Chapelle, " 'Gonna Start Livin' Like White Folks': Dust Bowl Migrants, Country Music, and the Construction of Whiteness in Southern California," 10 (paper delivered at the Organization of American Historians meeting, Washington, D.C., 13 April 2002); *Detroit News*, 9 October 1943, as cited in Clive, *State of War*, 265 n. 12.

60. Killian, "Southern White Laborers," 303.

61. Haslam, *Workin' Man Blues*, 20, 68; Gregory, *American Exodus*, 222–48; La Chapelle, " 'Gonna Start Livin' Like White Folks.' "

62. The issue of the expatriate white southern writer receives some attention in Sutherland, "Southern Fraternal Organizations in the North," 587–612, and in his *Confederate Carpetbaggers*. See also Ruth A. Banes, "Southerners Up North: Autobiographical Indications of Southern Ethnicity," in *Perspectives on the American South*, vol. 3, ed. James C. Cobb and Charles R. Wilson (New York, 1985), 1–16.

63. This list is far from complete. Others who might be added include Upton Sinclair and Ken Kesey, both of whom grew up outside the South but held strongly to a southern identity. It becomes clear how important the expatriates were to the development of twentieth-century southern letters when you sift through the biographies in the following anthologies and overviews of southern literature: Robert Bain, Joseph M. Flora, and Louis D. Rubin Jr., eds., *Southern Writers: A Biographical Dictionary* (Baton Rouge, 1979); Louis D. Rubin et al., eds., *The History of Southern Literature* (Baton Rouge, 1985); J. A. Bryant Jr., *Twentieth-Century Southern Literature* (Lexington, Ky., 1997); and Richard H. King, *A Southern Renaissance: The Cultural Awakening of the American South, 1930–1955* (New York, 1980).

64. David Herbert Donald's *Look Homeward: A Life of Thomas Wolfe* (Boston, 1987) is the work of one expatriate narrating the life and vision of an earlier expatriate.

65. On the southern Renaissance: Daniel Joseph Singal, *The War Within: From Victorian to Modernist Thought in the South, 1919–1945* (Chapel Hill, 1982); Rubin et al., *History of Southern Literature*; Bryant, *Twentieth-Century Southern Literature*; R. King, *Southern Renaissance.*

66. John Milton Cooper Jr., *Walter Hines Page: The Southerner as American 1855–1918* (Chapel Hill, 1977), 206; Fred Hobson, "The Rise of the Critical Temper," in *History of Southern Literature*, ed. Rubin et al., 252–57.

67. Erskine Caldwell, *Call It Experience* (London, 1960), 34–35; Evelyn Scott, *Background in Tennessee* (Knoxville, 1980; orig. 1937); D. A. Callard, *Pretty Good for a Woman: The Enigmas of Evelyn Scott* (London, 1985).

68. Charles Fountain, *Sportswriter: The Life and Times of Grantland Rice* (New York, 1993), 109–20; William A. Harper, *How You Played the Game: The Life of Grantland Rice* (Columbia, Mo., 1999), 169–79.

69. Carl Rollyson, *Lillian Hellman: Her Legend and Her Legacy* (New York, 1988); Jacob H. Adler, "Modern Southern Drama," in *History of Southern Literature*, ed. Rubin et al., 436–39.

70. Carson McCullers, "Brooklyn Is My Neighborhood," *Vogue* (1941), quoted in *Fifty Southern Writers after 1900: A Bio-Bibliographical Source Book*, ed. Joseph M. Flora and Robert Bain (Westport, 1987), 302; Warren to Owsley quoted in Joseph Blotner, *Robert Penn Warren: A Biography* (New York, 1997), 256.

71. Lewis M. Killian, *Black and White: Reflections of a White Southern Sociologist* (New York, 1994), 171; the homesickness in his case was real. Twenty years later he returned to Florida.

72. United Daughters of the Confederacy, *Minutes of the Forty-seventh Annual Convention, 1940*, 154–201; Sutherland, *Confederate Carpetbaggers*, 257–59. For comments on literary southerners drawing together, see Killian, *White Southerners*, 113–16; and Willie Morris, *North toward Home* (Boston, 1967).

73. See 1943 *New Republic* articles: 4, 11, 18 January, 8 February, 26 April, 5 July, 20 December.

74. Thomas Sancton, "The Race Riots," *New Republic*, 5 July 1943, 12, and "A Southern View of the Race Question," *Negro Quarterly* (January 1943): 197–206; Patricia Sullivan, *Days of Hope: Race and Democracy in the New Deal Era* (Chapel Hill, 1996), 166–67; John Egerton, *Speak Now against the Day: The Generation before the Civil Rights Movement in the South* (Chapel Hill, 1994); Morton Sosna, *In Search of the Silent South: Southern Liberals and the Race Issue* (New York, 1977).

75. Thomas Sancton, "North and South," *Negro Digest*, February 1943, 17, and "Go North, Black Man!" 5 July 1943, 37–39.

76. Harold Preece, "The Living South," *Chicago Defender* (St. Louis edition), 15 June 1944, 13, and 19 August 1944, 13; Arna Bontemps, "White Southern Friends of the Negro," *Negro Digest*, August 1950, 91–93. Erskine Caldwell was also actively promoting civil rights. His novel *Place Called Estherville* was praised and excerpted by *Negro Digest*, December 1949. Another enlightened southern white migrant is profiled in "Homes for the Homeless," *Negro Digest*, November 1949, 45–48.

77. On Buck's life and influence, see Peter Conn, *Pearl S. Buck: A Cultural Biography* (Cambridge, 1996). The much-quoted Marco Polo reference appears in Conn's preface but originates with James Thompson, "Why Doesn't Pearl Buck Get Respect?" *Philadelphia Inquirer*, 24 July 1992.

78. Pearl S. Buck with Eslanda Goode Robeson, *American Argument* (New York, 1949), 4. Significantly, this was the one part of the 206-page book that *Negro Digest* chose to excerpt: "American Argument," May 1949, 82–86.

79. In 1955, he also published *Band of Angels*, his first novel to deal with racial issues. Blotner, *Robert Penn Warren*, 301–4; Singal, *War Within*, 339–71.

80. Robert Penn Warren, "Divided South Searches Its Soul," *Life*, 9 July 1956, 111–14. A longer version was published the same year as *Segregation: The Inner Conflict in the South* (New York, 1956).

81. Ellison letter to Nathan A. Scott Jr., 17 July 1989, quoted in Blotner, *Robert Penn Warren*, 302, 307.

82. Morris, *North toward Home*, 319–20. Authors mentioned can be found in *Harper's* issues beginning March 1964, including the April 1965 special supplement, "The South Today 100 Years after Appomattox"; Albert Murray's "Stonewall Jackson's Waterloo" appears in the February 1969 issue. See also Willie Morris, *New York Days* (Boston, 1993); and Larry L. King, "Playing Cowboy: That Widespread Breed, the Expatriate," *Atlantic*, March 1975, 40–45.

83. Morris, *North toward Home*, 386–87.

84. Emerson eagerly promoted Morris's book when it appeared, publishing a long excerpt in the *Saturday Evening Post*. See Morris, *New York Days*, 71–78.

85. Sandra L. Ballard, "Harriette Simpson Arnow's Life as a Writer," in *Harriette Simpson Arnow: Critical Essays on Her Work*, ed. Haeja K. Chung (East Lansing, 1995), 15–32; Wilton Eckley, *Harriette Arnow* (New York, 1974).

86. Farah Jasmine Griffin, *"Who Set You Flowin'?": The African-American Migration Narrative* (New York, 1995), 3; Lawrence R. Rodgers, *Canaan Bound: The African-American Great Migration Novel* (Urbana, Ill., 1997).

CHAPTER SIX

1. Lily Tomlin interview with author, 5 October 2000, in author's possession; Aretha Franklin and David Ritz, *Aretha: From These Roots* (New York, 1999), 11–21.

2. The call for attention to religion is articulated smartly by John T. McGreevy, *Parish Boundaries: The Catholic Encounter with Race in the Twentieth-Century Urban North* (Chicago, 1996), 3–5; and Robert Wuthnow, "Understanding Religion and Politics," *Daedalus* (Summer 1991): 1–20.

3. On pluralism, see Robert Wuthnow, *The Restructuring of American Religion: Society and Faith since World War II* (Princeton, 1988); Charles H. Lippy, *Pluralism Comes of Age: American Religious Culture in the Twentieth Century* (London, 2000); Barry A. Kosmin and Seymour P. Lachman, *One Nation under God: Religion in Contemporary American Society* (New York, 1993); and George M. Marsden, *Religion and American Culture* (San Diego, 1990). The issue of southernization is most fully developed in

Mark A. Shibley, *Resurgent Evangelicalism in the United States: Mapping Cultural Change since 1970* (Columbia, S.C., 1996).

4. C. L. Franklin, *Give Me This Mountain: Life History and Selected Sermons*, ed. Jeff Todd Titon (Urbana, Ill., 1989). Titon, a musicologist, analyzes the style of the sermons, 212–16. There is a description of a 1968 sermon in Charles Fager, *Uncertain Resurrection* (Grand Rapids, 1969), 102–3. See also the new biography by Nick Salvatore, *Singing in a Strange Land: C. L. Franklin, the Black Church, and the Transformation of America* (Boston, 2005).

5. Jesse Jackson, foreword to *Give Me This Mountain*, by C. L. Franklin, vii. The Franklin quote is from page 28. Franklin's stature in black Detroit can be seen in the community's major newspaper, the *Michigan Chronicle*: "Chronicle Selects Detroit's Spiritual Leaders for 1953," 2 January 1954, 20. For a picture of twelve-year-old Aretha and her family, see "Final Rites Held for Mrs. Louis Bryant," *Michigan Chronicle*, 6 February 1954, 22. See also Suzanne E. Smith, *Dancing in the Street: Motown and the Cultural Politics of Detroit* (Cambridge, Mass., 1999), 40–44.

6. Elmer Akers, "Southern Whites in Detroit" (unpublished ms., n.d. [1937?]), 57, available through University Microfilms; Douglas James Curlew, "'They Ceased Not to Preach': Fundamentalism, Culture, and the Revivalist Imperative at the Temple Baptist Church of Detroit" (Ph.D. diss., University of Michigan, 2001). Curlew could not validate membership claims but does find attendance records that show an average Sunday attendance at more than 4,000 in the late 1940s. Other sources include J. Frank Norris, ed., *Inside History of First Baptist Church, Fort Worth, and Temple Baptist Church, Detroit: Life Story of Dr. J. Frank Norris* (New York, 1988; orig. 1938); Barry Hankins, *God's Rascal: J. Frank Norris and the Beginnings of Southern Fundamentalism* (Lexington, Ky., 1996), 54; and C. Allyn Russell, *Voices of American Fundamentalism* (Philadelphia, 1976), 20–46. The *Baptist Tribune* contains several useful articles on Temple Baptist.

7. Akers, "Southern Whites in Detroit," 57; C. Russell, *Voices of American Fundamentalism*, 29–39. Two of Norris's sermons can be heard at ‹www.baptistfire.com›.

8. "Congressman Powell Speaks at New Bethel," *Michigan Chronicle*, 10 April 1954, 21.

9. The recorded sermon, released as Chess LP-36, is reprinted in Franklin, *Give Me This Mountain*, 80–88.

10. Jesse Jackson, foreword to *Give Me This Mountain*, by C. L. Franklin, vii.

11. Quoted in Hankins, *God's Rascal*, 54.

12. *Fundamentalist*, 29 September 1934, as quoted in Curlew, "'They Ceased Not to Preach,'" 237.

13. "The Triple Major Operation in Detroit" sermon, 13 January 1935, in Norris, *Inside History of First Baptist Church*, 156.

14. Edward L. Queen II, *In the South the Baptists Are the Center of Gravity: Southern Baptists and Social Change, 1930–1980* (Brooklyn, 1991); Paul Harvey, *Freedom's Coming: Religious Culture and the Shaping of the South from the Civil War through the Civil Rights Era* (Chapel Hill, 2005), and *Redeeming the South: Religious Cultures and Racial Identities among Southern Baptists, 1865–1925* (Chapel Hill, 1997); Samuel S. Hill Jr.,

Southern Churches in Crisis (Boston, 1968); Charles Reagan Wilson, ed., *Religion in the South* (Jackson, Miss., 1985).

15. The changing geography of American religion can be followed in Edwin S. Gaustad and Philip L. Barlow, eds., *New Historical Atlas of Religion in America* (New York, 2001); Kosmin and Lachman, *One Nation under God*, 49–113; and Wilbur Zelinsky, "An Approach to the Religious Geography of the United States: Patterns of Church Membership in 1952," *Annals of the Association of American Geographers* 51 (June 1961): 139–93.

16. The researcher is quoted in Richard W. Thomas, *Life for Us Is What We Make It: Building Black Community in Detroit, 1915–1945* (Bloomington, 1992), 178–79. On proliferating churches, see Wallace Best, "The South and the City: Black Southern Migrants, Storefront Churches, and the Rise of a Religious Diaspora," in *Repositioning North American Migration History: New Directions in Modern Continental Migration, Citizenship, and Community*, ed. Marc S. Rodriguez (Rochester, 2004), 302–27; Gilbert Osofsky, *Harlem, The Making of a Ghetto: Negro New York, 1890–1930*, 2d ed. (Chicago, 1996), 144; St. Clair Drake and Horace R. Cayton, *Black Metropolis: A Study of Negro Life in a Northern City* (New York, 1962; orig. 1945), 412–14; and Kimberley L. Phillips, *AlabamaNorth: African-American Migrants, Community, and Working-Class Activism in Cleveland, 1915–45* (Urbana, Ill., 1999), 172.

17. For anxiety about over-churching, see Benjamin Elijah Mays and Joseph William Nicholson, *The Negro's Church* (New York, 1933), 198–229.

18. This is discussed in more detail in James N. Gregory, *American Exodus: The Dust Bowl Migration and Okie Culture in California* (New York, 1989), 191–221. For a Detroit study, see Ted T. Jitodai, "Migrant Status and Church Attendance," *Social Forces* 43, no. 2 (1964): 241–48. Henry J. Pratt, *The Liberalization of American Protestantism: A Case Study in Complex Organizations* (Detroit, 1972), 73–78; Hankins, *God's Rascal*, 98; Paul A. Carter, *Decline and Revival of the Social Gospel: Social and Political Liberalism in American Protestant Churches, 1920–1940* (Ithaca, 1956).

19. Ruth and Wofford Clark interview by author, 8 June 1981, La Mirada, Calif., in author's possession. Key works on the trajectory of the Southern Baptist Convention include Ellen M. Rosenberg, *The Southern Baptists: A Subculture in Transition* (Knoxville, 1989); Harvey, *Redeeming the South*; Barry Hankins, *Uneasy in Babylon: Southern Baptist Conservatives and American Culture* (Tuscaloosa, 2002); Queen, *In the South the Baptists Are the Center of Gravity*; James J. Thompson Jr., *Tried as by Fire: Southern Baptists and the Religious Controversies of the 1920s* (Macon, 1982); John Lee Eighmy, *Churches in Cultural Captivity: A History of the Social Attitudes of Southern Baptists* (Knoxville, 1972).

20. The key studies of religious transformation: Milton C. Sernett, *Bound for the Promised Land: African American Religion and the Great Migration* (Durham, 1997); Wallace Best, *Passionately Human, No Less Divine: Religion and Culture in Black Chicago, 1915–1952* (Princeton, 2005). On black Baptists in the South: Evelyn Brooks Higginbotham, *Righteous Discontent: The Women's Movement in the Black Baptist Church, 1880–1920* (Harvard, 1993); James Melvin Washington, *Frustrated Fellowship: The Black Baptist Quest for Social Power* (Macon, 1986); Harvey, *Redeeming the South*.

21. Drake and Cayton, *Black Metropolis*, 674; Best, "The South and the City," 310; Michael W. Harris, *The Rise of Gospel Blues: The Music of Thomas Andrew Dorsey in the Urban Church* (New York, 1992), 117–24.

22. Sernett, *Bound for the Promised Land*, 186.

23. George Edmund Haynes, *Negro Newcomers in Detroit* (New York, 1969; orig. 1918), 33; Mays and Nicholson, *Negro's Church*, 312; Thomas, *Life for Us Is What We Make It*, 175–80.

24. Nick Salvatore was kind enough to share this information about the early history of New Bethel in advance of his book *Singing in a Strange Land*, 112–21.

25. Gregory, *American Exodus*, 192–99; Nancy Tatom Ammerman, *Baptist Battles: Social Change and Religious Conflict in the Southern Baptist Convention* (New Brunswick, 1990), 50–51.

26. Curlew, "'They Ceased Not to Preach,'" 251–83. Other examples of the southernization of Northern Baptist congregations include First Baptist Church of Hammond, Indiana, and First Baptist in Ashtabula, Ohio. See Jerry Falwell with Ed Dobson and Ed Hindson, eds., *The Fundamentalist Phenomenon: The Resurgence of Conservative Christianity* (Garden City, N.Y., 1981), 141; and Carl E. Feather, *Mountain People in a Flat Land: A Popular History of Appalachian Migration to Northeast Ohio, 1940–1965* (Athens, Ohio, 1998), 8.

27. Curlew, "They Ceased Not to Preach," 251–52.

28. Ibid.; G. B. Vick, "The How—Methods of Enlisting Members," in Norris, *Inside History of First Baptist Church*, 273–78; Mike Randall, "G. Beauchamp Vick Founder and Leaders of the BBFI," *Baptist Bible Tribune*, 15 January 2000; Hankins, *God's Rascal*, 90–117.

29. Ammerman, *Baptist Battles*; Tom J. Netters, "Southern Baptists: Regional to National Transition," *Baptist History and Heritage* 16 (1981): 13–23; G. Thomas Halbrooks, "Growing Pains: The Impact of Expansion on Southern Baptists since 1942," *Baptist History and Heritage* 17 (July 1982): 50–51.

30. Floyd Looney, *History of California Southern Baptists* (Fresno, 1954), 13–19; Orville Sanders, *The Fruit Hangs Ripe* (N. Hollywood, 1951), 6; Elmer L. Gray, *Heirs of Promise: A Chronicle of California Southern Baptists, 1940–1978* (Fresno, 1978), 16–27. Growth numbers calculated from Douglas W. Johnson, Paul R. Picard, and Bernard Quinn, eds., *Churches and Church Membership in the United States: 1971* (Washington, D.C., 1974), table 2; and Martin B. Bradley et al., eds., *Churches and Church Membership in the United States: 1990* (Atlanta, 1992), table 3, 12–36. Missouri is considered part of the Southern Baptist home region in these calculations.

31. Calculated from 1963 Northern California Church Study dataset in State Data Center, Berkeley, Calif. In this carefully designed survey of church membership in San Francisco, San Mateo, and Marin Counties, 2,233 white Protestants participated; 231 said they had been raised in either the South or Southwest. San Francisco has long had lower rates of church membership and attendance than most cities, and that may have created opportunities for southerners that might not have existed elsewhere.

32. The classic account of unorthodox religious movements is Arthur H. Fauset, *Black Gods of the Metropolis: Negro Religious Cults in the Urban North* (Philadelphia,

1971; orig. 1944). More recent studies have seen these not as aberrant but as innovative: Gayraud S. Wilmore, *Black Religion and Black Radicalism: An Interpretation of the Religious History of Afro-American People* (Maryknoll, N.Y., 1983), 152–60; Sernett, *Bound for the Promised Land*, 180–209; Best, "The South and the City."

33. Clarence Taylor, *The Black Churches of Brooklyn* (New York, 1994); Sernett, *Bound for the Promised Land.*

34. Important works on the history of Pentecostalism include Harvey Cox, *Fire from Heaven: The Rise of Pentecostal Spirituality and the Reshaping of Religion in the Twenty-first Century* (Reading, Mass., 1995); Margaret M. Poloma, *The Assemblies of God at the Crossroads: Charisma and Institutional Dilemmas* (Knoxville, 1989); Robert Mapes Anderson, *Vision of the Disinherited: The Making of American Pentecostalism* (New York, 1979); David Edwin Harrell Jr., *All Things Are Possible: The Healing and Charismatic Revivals in Modern America* (Bloomington, 1975); Vincent Synan, *The Holiness-Pentecostal Movement in the United States* (Grand Rapids, 1971).

35. Mason quoted in C. Eric Lincoln and Lawrence H. Mamiya, *The Black Church in African American Experience* (Durham, 1990), 81; David M. Tucker, *Black Pastors and Leaders: Memphis, 1819–1972* (Memphis, 1975), 87–99; Cheryl J. Sanders, *Saints in Exile: The Holiness-Pentecostal Experience in African American Religion and Culture* (New York, 1996).

36. Women also were kept from the pulpits of the Church of God in Christ, which became the largest black Pentecostal denomination. Miles Mark Fischer, "Organized Religion and the Cults," January 1937, 9–10; Drake and Cayton, *Black Metropolis,* 632–45; Fauset, *Black Gods of the Metropolis*; Sernett, *Bound for the Promised Land*, 195; Wilmore, *Black Religion and Black Radicalism*, 156; H. Cox, *Fire from Heaven*, 123–28; Joseph R. Washington Jr., *Black Sects and Cults* (New York, 1972), 80–81. Arthur E. Paris, *Black Pentecostalism: Southern Religion in an Urban World* (Amherst, 1982), is a study of a small New England–based denomination. Frances Kostarelos does the same for a Chicago church in *Feeling the Spirit: Faith and Hope in an Evangelical Black Storefront Church* (Columbia, S.C., 1995).

37. Edith L. Blumhofer, *Aimee Semple McPherson: Everybody's Sister* (Grand Rapids, 1993); Gregory H. Singleton, *Religion in the City of Angeles: American Protestant Culture and Urbanization, Los Angeles, 1850–1930* (Ann Arbor, 1979). Poloma, *Assemblies of God at the Crossroads*, 101–21, analyzes Pentecostalism's irregular openness to female prophets and preachers.

38. On Pentecostal expansion in the Midwest in 1940s, see Brewster Campbell and James Pooler, "Hallelujah in Boomtown," *Collier's*, 1 April 1944, 18. On the broader expansion: Harrell, *All Things Are Possible*; H. Cox, *Fire from Heaven*; Margaret Poloma, *The Charismatic Movement: Is There a New Pentecost?* (Boston, 1982); Edith L. Blumhofer, Russell P. Spittler, and Grant A. Wacker, eds., *Pentecostal Currents in American Protestantism* (Urbana, Ill., 1999).

39. Drake and Cayton, *Black Metropolis,* passim; Fauset, *Black Gods of the Metropolis*; Gunnar Myrdal, *An American Dilemma: The Negro Problem and Modern Democracy* (New York, 1944), 858–78; E. Franklin Frazier, *The Negro in the United States* (New York, 1949), 334–66, and *The Negro Church in America* (New York, 1966; orig. 1963).

40. Important reevaluations of the historic and contemporary role of black religion include Clarence Taylor, *Black Religious Intellectuals: The Fight for Equality from Jim Crow to the Twenty-first Century* (New York, 2002); Fredrick C. Harris, *Something Within: Religion in African-American Political Activism* (New York, 1999); Lincoln and Mamiya, *Black Church in African American Experience*, 122–23; and Wilmore, *Black Religion and Black Radicalism*. Arguing against the recent trend is Adolph L. Reed Jr., *The Jesse Jackson Phenomenon* (New Haven, 1986).

41. Higginbotham, *Righteous Discontent*, 173; Sernett, *Bound for the Promised Land*, 249. Also Mays and Nicholson, *Negro's Church*, 119–23.

42. Lillian B. Horace, *"Crowned with Glory and Hope": The Life of Rev. Lacey Kirk Williams* (Hicksville, N.Y., 1978); James R. Grossman, *Land of Hope: Chicago, Black Southerners, and the Great Migration* (Chicago, 1989), 156–60; Allan H. Spear, *Black Chicago: The Making of a Negro Ghetto 1890–1920* (Chicago, 1967), 177–78; Sernett, *Bound for the Promised Land*, 119, 156–57.

43. Robert Gregg, *Sparks from the Anvil of Oppression: Philadelphia's African Methodists and Southern Migrants, 1890–1940* (Philadelphia, 1993), 63–64. On Detroit, see Thomas, *Life for Us Is What We Make It*, 175–80; Victoria W. Wolcott, *Remaking Respectability: African American Women in Interwar Detroit* (Chapel Hill, 2001); and Horace A. White, "Who Owns the Negro Church?" *Christian Century*, 9 February 1938, 176.

44. Wolcott, *Remaking Respectability*, esp. 156–64; Higginbotham, *Righteous Discontent*, 171–229.

45. Wilmore, *Black Religion and Black Radicalism*, 142.

46. Gregg, *Sparks from the Anvil*, 46–50; Wilmore, *Black Religion and Black Radicalism*, 161–66.

47. Robert Weisbrot, *Father Divine* (Boston, 1983), 145.

48. Beth Tompkins Bates, *Pullman Porters and the Rise of Protest Politics in Black America 1925–1945* (Chapel Hill, 2001), 64, 102–3; August Meier and Elliott Rudwick, *Black Detroit and the Rise of the UAW* (New York, 1979), 70–71; Randall K. Burkett, "The Baptist Church in the Years of Crisis: J. C. Austin and the Pilgrim Baptist Church, 1926–1950," in *African-American Christianity: Essays in History*, ed. Paul E. Johnson (Berkeley, 1994), 134–58.

49. Harold F. Gosnell, *The Negro Politicians: The Rise of Negro Politics in Chicago* (Chicago, 1967; orig. 1935), 94.

50. Meier and Rudwick, *Black Detroit and the Rise of the UAW*, 113–16.

51. James F. Findlay Jr., *Church People in the Struggle: The National Council of Churches and the Black Freedom Movement, 1950–1970* (New York, 1993), 17. A more critical take on the National Council of Churches is found in Pratt, *Liberalization of American Protestantism*.

52. "Protestants Condemn Segregation," *Crisis*, January 1949, 8; Quintard Taylor, *The Forging of a Black Community: Seattle's Central District from 1870 through the Civil Rights Era* (Seattle, 1994), 168–71. Cooperation between liberal Catholics and black ministers is described in McGreevy, *Parish Boundaries*, 140–54.

53. "Congressman Powell Speaks at New Bethel," 21; C. L. Franklin, *Give Me This*

Mountain, 31–32. Church leadership in Memphis where Franklin preached before coming north is described in Tucker, *Black Pastors and Leaders*, 101–11.

54. Gregory, *American Exodus*, 209–15.

55. On recent issues of civic engagement, see the essays in Michael Cromartie, ed., *A Public Faith: Evangelicals and Civic Engagement* (Lanham, Md., 2003).

56. James Bright Wilson, "Religious Leaders, Institutions and Organizations among Certain Agricultural Workers in the Central Valley of California" (Ph.D. diss., University of Southern California, 1944), 197, 262. For similar observations, see Walter Goldschmidt's descriptions of churches in *As You Sow: Three Studies in the Social Consequences of Agribusiness* (Montclair, N.J., 1978; orig. 1947).

57. Gregory, *American Exodus*, 191–221.

58. Becky M. Nicolaides, *My Blue Heaven: Life and Politics in the Working-Class Suburbs of Los Angeles, 1920–1965* (Chicago, 2002), 112.

59. Joel A. Carpenter, *Revive Us Again: The Reawakening of American Fundamentalism* (New York, 1997). For an effective overview of evangelical movements and politics, see William Martin, *With God on Our Side: The Rise of the Religious Right in America* (New York, 1996); Leo P. Ribuffo, *The Old Christian Right: The Protestant Far Right from the Great Depression to the Cold War* (Philadelphia, 1983), treats only the neofascist elements of this group.

60. C. Russell, *Voices of American Fundamentalism*, 79–106.

61. Ibid., 47–78.

62. Ibid., 107–61, 156–59; Jerry Falwell with Ed Dobson and Ed Hindson, eds., *The Fundamentalist Phenomenon: The Resurgence of Conservative Christianity* (Garden City, N.Y., 1981), 92–102, 126–28.

63. Mark Sumner Still, "'Fighting Bob' Shuler": Fundamentalist and Reformer" (Ph.D. diss., Claremont Graduate School, 1988), 141; Edward Drewry Jervey, *The History of Methodism in Southern California and Arizona* (Nashville, 1960), 36–37.

64. Still, "'Fighting Bob' Shuler," 170–98; Kevin Starr, *Material Dreams: Southern California through the 1920s* (New York, 1990), 136–42.

65. Thomas Sitton, *John Randolph Haynes: California Progressive* (Stanford, 1992), 220.

66. Still, "'Fighting Bob' Shuler," 424–56.

67. Carpenter, *Revive Us Again*, evaluates the transformation in detail. Overviews of the twentieth-century movement include George M. Marsden, *Understanding Fundamentalism and Evangelicalism* (Grand Rapids, 1991); G. Hart, *That Old-Time Religion in Modern America: Evangelical Protestantism in the Twentieth Century* (Chicago, 2002); and W. Martin, *With God on Our Side*.

68. Carpenter, *Revive Us Again*, 167. "Puff YFC" is from Martin E. Marty, *Modern American Religion*, vol. 3, *Under God, Indivisible, 1941–1960* (Chicago, 1996), 151.

69. Marshall Frady, *Billy Graham: A Parable of American Righteousness* (Boston, 1979).

70. *Life*, 21 November 1949, 97–100; Carpenter, *Revive Us Again*, 223–26; Frady, *Billy Graham*.

71. W. Martin, *With God on Our Side*, 33.

72. On the conservative implications of the evangelical movement, see James Davison Hunter, *American Evangelicalism: Conservative Religion and the Quandary of Modernity* (New Brunswick, 1983); Albert J. Menendez, *Evangelicals at the Ballot Box* (Amherst, N.Y., 1996); and Kenneth D. Wald, *Religion and Politics in the United States*, 2d ed. (Washington, D.C., 1992). On progressive evangelicals, see David Striklin, *A Genealogy of Dissent: Southern Baptist Protest in the Twentieth Century* (Lexington, Ky., 1999); and Falwell, *Fundamentalist Phenomenon*, 165–67. The magazine *Sojourner* is today a principal voice of left-wing evangelicalism.

73. Hankins, *God's Rascal*, 167–69.

74. Curlew, " 'They Ceased Not to Preach,' " 299; Falwell, *Fundamentalist Phenomenon*, dedicates the volume "In memory of G. B. Vick (1901–1975)." On Falwell's training in the Baptist Bible Fellowship, see Susan Friend Harding, *The Book of Jerry Falwell: Fundamental Language and Politics* (Princeton, 2000).

75. Vick to Constantine Fika, 4 May 1949, in J. Frank Norris Papers, quoted in Curlew, " 'They Ceased Not to Preach,' " 328. Curlew interviewed dozens of Temple veterans and sensitively explores the racial issues. See also "Deacons at Michigan Church Vote to End a Ban on Blacks," *New York Times*, 23 September 1986; "White Church Lifts Its Policy of Banning Blacks," *Jet*, 13 October 1986, 24.

76. Curlew, " 'They Ceased Not to Preach.' " The role in neighborhood resistance is documented in Detroit Urban League files and discussed in Thomas J. Sugrue, *The Origins of the Urban Crisis: Race and Inequality in Postwar Detroit* (Princeton, 1996), 214.

77. Quoted in McGreevy, *Parish Boundaries*, 138, 212; Harvie M. Conn uses the term "evangelical absenteeism" in *The American City and the Evangelical Church: A Historical Overview* (Grand Rapids, 1994), 142. Some church integration in Oakland was claimed by 1969 in Home Mission Board of Southern Baptist Convention, *A Descriptive Study of Southern Baptists in the Greater San Francisco Bay Area* (Atlanta, 1969), 33. On church segregation struggles in southern states, see also Mark Newman, *Getting Right with God: Southern Baptists and Desegregation 1945–1995* (Tuscaloosa, 2001).

78. First Baptist churches can be identified in Home Mission Board, *Southern Baptists in the Greater San Francisco Bay Area*, 30–32. For an example of a Detroit congregationalist church that did not flee, see Barbara Brown Zikmund, "Home Church: Congregating," *Christian Century*, 18 January 1995, 38–39.

79. Bennett Berger, *Working-Class Suburb* (Berkeley, 1960), studies Milpitas, a white-flight suburb in the Bay Area where many of the residents were former southerners and where Baptist churches helped set the tone for community life.

80. Nicolaides, *My Blue Heaven*. For more on evangelical conservatism in southern California, see Lisa McGirr, *Suburban Warriors: The Origins of the New American Right* (Princeton, 2000). Argue quoted in Edward Gilbreath, "Catching Up with the Dream: Evangelicals and Race 30 Years after the Death of Martin Luther King, Jr.," *Christianity Today*, 2 March 1998, 20–30.

81. International Missions Board, Southern Baptist Convention, ‹http://www.imb.org/core/fastfacts.asp›, accessed 26 October 2003; Brian H. Smith, *Religious Politics in Latin America, Pentecostal vs. Catholic* (Notre Dame, Ind., 1998); David Martin,

Tongues of Fire: The Explosion of Protestantism in Latin America (Cambridge, Mass., 1993).

82. Information on the changing social base of these organizations comes from author interviews with several ministers and staff members of the Northern District headquarters of the Assemblies of God and at Bethel College, both located in Santa Cruz, California; Rev. Bob Friesen phone interview by author, 16 November 1986; and Rev. Buren Higdon interview with author, 5 June 1979, Oakland. Higdon was the head of the East Bay Regional Council of the Southern Baptist Convention. See also Gregory, *American Exodus*, 215–21. Shibley, *Resurgent Evangelicalism*, 35, 134, discusses the "Americanization" of these movements.

CHAPTER SEVEN

1. Influential accounts of the battle for rights include Adam Fairclough, *Better Day Coming: Blacks and Equality, 1890–2000* (New York, 2001); Philip A. Klinkner with Rogers M. Smith, *The Unsteady March: The Rise and Decline of Racial Equality in America* (Chicago, 1999); John Hope Franklin and Alfred A. Moss Jr., *From Slavery to Freedom: A History of African Americans* (New York, 1994); Lerone Bennett Jr., *The Shaping of Black America: The Struggles and Triumphs of African Americans, 1619 to the 1990s* (New York, 1993); Steven F. Lawson, *Running for Freedom: Civil Rights and Black Politics in America since 1941* (Philadelphia, 1991); Jack M. Bloom, *Class, Race, and the Civil Rights Movement* (Bloomington, 1987); Aldon D. Morris, *The Origins of the Civil Rights Movement: Black Communities Organizing for Change* (New York, 1984); Mary Frances Berry and John W. Blassingame, *Long Memory: The Black Experience in America* (New York, 1982); Harvard Sitkoff, *The Struggle for Black Equality 1954–1980* (New York, 1981); and Thomas R. Brooks, *Walls Come Tumbling Down: A History of the Civil Rights Movement 1940–1970* (Englewood Cliffs, N.J., 1974). Only Brooks and Lawson pay much attention to geography and the political importance of the northern cities.

2. Some new works point in the right direction: Jeanne Theoharis and Komozi Woodard, eds., *Freedom North: Black Freedom Struggles Outside the South, 1940–1980* (New York, 2003); Robert Self, *American Babylon: Race and Power in Postwar Oakland* (Princeton, 2003); and Martha Biondi, *To Stand and Fight: The Struggle for Civil Rights in Postwar New York* (Cambridge, 2002).

3. Ralph J. Bunche, *The Political Status of the Negro in the Age of FDR*, ed. Dewey W. Grantham (Chicago, 1973); James Q. Wilson, "The Negro in American Politics: The Present," in John P. Davis, ed., *The American Negro Reference Book* (Englewood Cliffs, N.J., 1966), 431–57; James Q. Wilson, *Negro Politics: The Search for Leadership* (New York, 1960); Ira Katznelson, *Black Men, White Cities: Race, Politics, and Migration in the United States, 1900–1930, and Britain, 1948–68* (New York, 1973); Manning Marable, *Black American Politics: From the Washington Marches to Jesse Jackson* (London, 1985). Two recent books show the effects of this strict definition of politics. *The Unsteady March* by political scientists Philip Klinkner and Rogers Smith and *Cold War Civil Rights: Race and the Image of American Democracy* (Princeton, 2000) by legal historian

Mary L. Dudziak minimize the importance of African American political mobilizations while arguing that foreign policy considerations drove the nation through its civil rights turn.

4. Alan B. Anderson and George W. Pickering, *Confronting the Color Line: The Broken Promise of the Civil Rights Movement in Chicago* (Athens, Ga., 1986). Political scientists focus more on the limitations of black politics than on the capacities and successes. Examples include Paul Frymer, *Uneasy Alliances: Race and Party Competition in America* (Princeton, 1999); Rickey Hill, "The Study of Black Politics: Notes on Rethinking the Paradigm," and most other essays in Hanes Walton Jr., ed., *Black Politics and Black Political Behavior: A Linkage Analysis* (Westport, 1994). A great deal of recent literature on the crisis of the ghettos erases black politics while concentrating on federal policy failures. Examples are Nicholas Lemann, *The Promised Land: The Great Black Migration and How It Changed America* (New York, 1991); and Douglas S. Massey and Nancy A. Denton, *American Apartheid: Segregation and the Making of the Underclass* (Cambridge, 1993).

5. Recent works that stress black political ingenuity and accomplishments include Robin D. G. Kelley, *Race Rebels: Culture, Politics, and the Black Working Class* (New York, 1994); Charles M. Payne, *I've Got the Light of Freedom: The Organizing Tradition and the Mississippi Freedom Struggle* (Berkeley, 1995); Glenda Elizabeth Gilmore, *Gender and Jim Crow: Women and the Politics of White Supremacy in North Carolina, 1896–1920* (Chapel Hill, 1996); Steven Hahn, *A Nation under Our Feet: Black Political Struggles in the Rural South from Slavery to the Great Migration* (Cambridge, Mass., 2003); Shirley Ann Wilson Moore, *To Place Our Deeds: The African American Community in Richmond, California, 1910–1963* (Berkeley, 2000); William J. Grimshaw, *Bitter Fruit: Black Politics and the Chicago Machine, 1931–1991* (Chicago, 1992); and Vincent Harding, Robin D. G. Kelley, and Earl Lewis, "We Changed the World: 1945–1970," in *To Make Our World Anew: A History of African Americans*, ed. Robin D. G. Kelley and Earl Lewis (New York, 2000).

6. Brooks, *Walls Come Tumbling Down*, 17. On the effects of competitive balance of power arrangement, see Henry Lee Moon, *Balance of Power: The Negro Vote* (Westport, 1977; orig. 1948); Richard A. Keiser, *Subordination or Empowerment? African-American Leadership and the Struggle for Urban Political Power* (New York, 1997); and Lawson, *Running for Freedom*, 31–40.

7. On protest tactics, see the essays in August Meier and Elliot Rudwick, eds., *Along the Color Line: Explorations in the Black Experience* (Urbana, Ill., 1976), and Edward S. Greenberg, Neal Milner, and David J. Olson, eds., *Black Politics: The Inevitability of Conflict* (New York, 1971).

8. Paul Kantor with Stephen David, *The Dependent City: The Changing Political Economy of Urban America* (Glenview, Ill., 1988); John J. Gunther, *Federal-City Relations in the United States: The Role of Mayors in Federal Aid to Cities* (Newark, 1990); Jon C. Teaford, *The Twentieth-Century American City: Problem, Promise, and Reality* (Baltimore, 1986).

9. Harold F. Gosnell, *The Negro Politicians: The Rise of Negro Politics in Chicago* (Chicago, 1967; orig. 1935), 114. Bunche, *Political Status of the Negro*, 576, discusses the

critical role of churches. Of the 1,247 black lawyers and judges enumerated in the 1930 census, 65 percent lived in the North. U.S. Bureau of the Census, *Negroes in the United States 1920–1932* (Washington, D.C., 1935), 9, 293.

10. Allan H. Spear, *Black Chicago: The Making of a Negro Ghetto 1890–1920* (Chicago, 1967), 191. For an excellent overview and analysis, see Grimshaw, *Bitter Fruit*.

11. On white immigrant political participation, see Stephen P. Erie, *Rainbow's End: Irish Americans and the Dilemmas of Urban Machine Politics, 1840–1985* (Berkeley, 1988), 67–106; John M. Allswang, *A House for All Peoples* (Lexington, Ky., 1971); and Quintard Taylor, *The Forging of a Black Community: Seattle's Central District from 1870 through the Civil Rights Era* (Seattle, 1994), 87–105, 119–34.

12. Gosnell, *Negro Politicians*, 18; James R. Grossman, *Land of Hope: Chicago, Black Southerners, and the Great Migration* (Chicago, 1989), 175–76.

13. Calculated from Gosnell, *Negro Politicians*, 16–17. The argument that the black "submachine" yielded little real influence and the community was "shortchanged" is developed in J. Q. Wilson, *Negro Politics*, and Katznelson, *Black Men, White Cities*. Gosnell saw the matter differently in 1935, as does Grimshaw, *Bitter Fruit*.

14. Kenneth L. Kusmer, *A Ghetto Takes Shape: Black Cleveland, 1870–1930* (Urbana, Ill., 1976), 271–73; Bunche, *Political Status of the Negro*, 579–84. Gary, Indiana, might be counted as similarly promising in the 1920s; see Raymond A. Mohl and Neil Betten, *Steel City: Urban and Ethnic Patterns in Gary, Indiana, 1906–1950* (New York, 1986), 84–87, although they emphasize that this was a "clientage" system that offered blacks little real power.

15. W. E. B. Du Bois, "The Black Vote of Philadelphia," in *Black Politics in Philadelphia*, ed. Miriam Ershkowitz and Joseph Zikmund II (New York, 1973), 31–39; Bunche, *Political Status of the Negro*, 594–99.

16. Richard W. Thomas, *Life for Us Is What We Make It: Building Black Community in Detroit, 1915–1945* (Bloomington, 1992), 252–70; Bunche, *Political Status of the Negro*, 585–91. Edward H. Litchfield, "A Case Study of Negro Political Behavior in Detroit," *Public Opinion Quarterly* (June 1941): 267–74, found much lower voting rates among blacks than whites. See also Gunnar Myrdal, *An American Dilemma: The Negro Problem and Modern Democracy* (New York, 1944), 493.

17. On the breakup of machines and the cycles of competitive politics, see Erie, *Rainbow's End*, 107–39.

18. Dorothy Thompson, *New York Herald Tribune*, 11 August 1936, as quoted in H. Moon, *Balance of Power*, 40; Bunche, *Political Status of the Negro*, 576–78; *Chicago Defender* (St. Louis edition), 15 July 1944, 12. For a systematic critique of this stereotype of black voters, see Hanes Walton Jr., *Invisible Politics: Black Political Behavior* (Albany, 1985).

19. Edwin R. Lewinson, *Black Politics in New York City* (New York, 1974), 44–69; Gilbert Osofsky, *Harlem, The Making of a Ghetto: Negro New York, 1890–1930*, 2d ed. (Chicago, 1996), 159–78.

20. Katznelson, *Black Men, White Cities*, 72.

21. Roi Ottley, *"New World A-Coming": Inside Black America* (Boston, 1943), 242–53; Mark Naison, *Communists in Harlem during the Depression Years* (New York, 1983);

Harold Cruse, *The Crisis of the Negro Intellectual: A Historical Analysis of the Failure of Black Leadership* (New York, 1984; orig. 1967).

22. Ira De A. Reid, *The Negro Immigrant: His Backgrond, Characteristics and Social Adjustment, 1899–1937* (New York, 1939), 146–70; Robert A. Hill and Barbara Bair, eds., *Marcus Garvey: Life and Lessons: A Centennial Companion to The Marcus Garvey and Universal Negro Improvement Association Papers* (Berkeley, 1987); Tony Martin, *Race First: The Ideological and Organizational Struggles of Marcus Garvey and the Universal Negro Improvement Association* (Westport, 1976). For the longer term political relations between West Indians and other African Americans, see John C. Walter, *The Harlem Fox: J. Raymond Jones and Tammany, 1920–1970* (Albany, 1989).

23. On "clientage politics," see Martin Kilson, "Political Change in the Negro Ghetto, 1900–1940," in *Key Issues in the Afro-American Experience*, ed. Nathan I. Huggins, Martin Kilson, and Daniel M. Fox (New York, 1971), 2:167–92.

24. The classic attack against alliance politics is Stokley Carmichael and Charles V. Hamilton, *Black Power: Politics of Liberation in America* (New York, 1967). See also Chuck Stone, *Black Political Power in America* (Indianapolis, 1968). The theory that alliance building is key to ethnic political effectiveness is explained in Lawrence H. Fuchs, *American Kaleidoscope: Race, Ethnicity, and the Civic Culture* (Hanover, N.H., 1990); and Rufus P. Browning, Dale Rogers Marshall, and David H. Tabb, eds., *Racial Politics in American Cities*, 2d ed. (New York, 1997), 24–28.

25. August Meier, *Negro Thought in America 1880–1915* (Ann Arbor, 1968), 110–18; Louis R. Harlan, *Booker T. Washington: The Wizard of Tuskegee, 1901–1915* (New York, 1983); James D. Anderson, *The Education of Blacks in the South, 1860–1935* (Chapel Hill, 1988). On the ideas of the Tuskegee group, see Kevin K. Gaines, *Uplifting the Race: Black Leadership, Politics, and Culture in the Twentieth Century* (Chapel Hill, 1996).

26. Jesse Thomas Moore Jr., *A Search for Equality: The National Urban League, 1910–1961* (University Park, Pa., 1981); Nancy J. Weiss, *The National Urban League 1910–1940* (New York, 1974). For a discussion of Urban League influence brokering in the New Deal Era, see Arvarh E. Strikland, *History of the Chicago Urban League* (Urbana, Ill., 1966), 104–36. On Rosenwald: John H. Stanfield, *Philanthropy and Jim Crow in American Social Science* (Westport, 1985), 97–118.

27. Studies of the NAACP include Charles Flint Kellogg, *NAACP: A History of the National Association for the Advancement of Colored People 1909–1920* (Baltimore, 1967); Mark Tushnet, *The NAACP's Legal Strategy against Segregated Education, 1925–1950* (Chapel Hill, 1992); Adam Fairclough, *Race and Democracy: The Civil Rights Struggle in Louisiana, 1915–1972* (Athens, Ga., 1995); Barbara Joyce Ross, *J. E. Springarn and the Rise of the NAACP, 1911–1939* (Boston, 1972); Stephen Grant Meyer, *As Long as They Don't Move Next Door: Segregation and Racial Conflict in American Neighborhoods* (Lanham, Md., 2000).

28. The best account of the NAACP in a single city is Christopher Robert Reed, *The Chicago NAACP and the Rise of Black Professional Leadership, 1910–1966* (Bloomington, 1997). See also Kusmer, *A Ghetto Takes Shape*, 258–65; Thomas, *Life for Us Is What We Make It*, 229–57; Joe William Trotter Jr., *Black Milwaukee: The Making of an Industrial Proletariat, 1915–45* (Urbana, Ill., 1985), 115–39; Albert S. Broussard, *Black San Fran-*

cisco: The Struggle for Racial Equality in the West, 1900–1954 (Lawrence, Kans., 1993); and Q. Taylor, *Forging of a Black Community*, 79–105.

29. C. Reed, *Chicago NAACP and the Rise of Black Professional Leadership*, 53–58.

30. Meier and Rudwick, *Along the Color Line*, 94–127.

31. "Protestants Condemn Segregation," *Crisis*, January 1949, 9; James F. Findlay Jr., *Church People in the Struggle: The National Council of Churches and the Black Freedom Movement, 1950–1970* (New York, 1993), 18–19; Stanfield, *Philanthropy and Jim Crow*.

32. Horace R. Cayton and George S. Mitchell, *Black Workers and the New Unions* (Chapel Hill, 1939); William H. Harris, *The Harder We Run: Black Workers since the Civil War* (New York, 1982), 95–122; Joe William Trotter Jr., *Coal, Class, and Color: Blacks in Southern West Virginia, 1915–32* (Urbana, Ill., 1990); Daniel Letwin, *The Challenge of Interracial Unionism: Alabama Coal Miners, 1878–1921* (Chapel Hill, 1998); Rick Halpern, *Down on the Killing Floor: Black and White Workers in Chicago's Packinghouses, 1904–54* (Urbana, Ill., 1997).

33. Dan T. Carter, *Scottsboro: A Tragedy of the American South* (Baton Rouge, 1969). The Communist Party moved south in the early 1930s trying to organize black sharecroppers and white miners and textile workers. See Robin D. G. Kelley, *Hammer and Hoe: Alabama Communists during the Great Depression* (Chapel Hill, 1990); Nell Irvin Painter, *The Narrative of Hosea Hudson, His Life as a Negro Communist in the South* (Cambridge, 1979).

34. Judith Stepan-Norris and Maurice Zeitlin, *Left Out: Reds and America's Industrial Unions* (New York, 2003), 212–65; Roger Horowitz, *"Negro and White, United and Fight!" A Social History of Industrial Unionism in Meatpacking, 1930–90* (Urbana, Ill., 1997); Michael K. Honey, *Southern Labor and Black Civil Rights: Organizing Memphis Workers* (Urbana, Ill., 1993).

35. Nikhil Pal Singh, *Black Is a Country: Race and the Unfinished Struggle for Democracy* (Cambridge, Mass., 2004); Michael Denning, *The Cultural Front: The Laboring of American Culture in the Twentieth Century* (New York, 1996); Bill V. Mullen, *Popular Fronts: Chicago and African-American Cultural Politics, 1935–1946* (Urbana, Ill., 1999); William J. Maxwell, *New Negro, Old Left: African-American Writing and Communism between the Wars* (New York, 1999); Kelley, *Race Rebels*, 103–22. Gerald Horne has written extensively about African Americans and the Communist Party, including *Communist Front? The Civil Rights Congress, 1946–1956* (Cranbury, N.J., 1988).

36. Cheryl Lynn Greenberg, *"Or Does It Explode?" Black Harlem in the Great Depression* (New York, 1991), and her article "The Politics of Disorder: Re-examining Harlem's Riots of 1935 and 1943," *Journal of Urban History* 18 (August 1992); Meier and Rudwick, *Along the Color Line*, 307–404; Wilson Record, *Race and Radicalism: The NAACP and the Communist Party in Conflict* (Ithaca, 1964); Kimberley L. Phillips, *AlabamaNorth: African-American Migrants, Community, and Working-Class Activism in Cleveland, 1915–45* (Urbana, Ill., 1999), 190–225.

37. Joe William Trotter Jr., *Black Milwaukee: The Making of an Industrial Proletariat, 1915–45* (Urbana, Ill., 1985); Eric Arnesen, *Brotherhoods of Color: Black Railroad Workers and the Struggle for Equality* (Cambridge, 2001); Beth Tompkins Bates, *Pullman Porters and the Rise of Protest Politics in Black America 1925–1945* (Chapel Hill, 2001).

Bruce Nelson, *Divided We Stand: American Workers and the Struggle for Black Equality* (Princeton, 2001), stresses the pragmatic and limited response of CIO unions and their white members. See also Robert Korstad and Nelson Lichtenstein, "Opportunities Found and Lost: Labor, Radicals, and the Early Civil Rights Movement," *Journal of American History* 75, no. 3 (1988).

38. On the relationship between the NAACP and the new unions, see Raymond Wolters, *Negroes and the Great Depression: The Problem of Economic Recovery* (Westport, 1970), 169–213.

39. Lizabeth Cohen, *Making a New Deal: Industrial Workers in Chicago, 1919–1939* (New York, 1990), 333–49; Halpern, *Down on the Killing Floor*; R. Horowitz, *"Negro and White, United and Fight!"*

40. On Detroit: August Meier and Elliott Rudwick, *Black Detroit and the Rise of the UAW* (New York, 1979); and Beth T. Bates, "'Double V for Victory' Mobilizes Black Detroit, 1941–1946," in *Freedom North*, ed. Theoharis and Woodard, 17–40. On the lasting alliance with the UAW, see Kevin Boyle, *The UAW and the Heyday of American Liberalism 1945–1968* (Ithaca, 1995); and Wilbur C. Rich, *Coleman Young and Detroit Politics: From Social Activist to Power Broker* (Detroit, 1989).

41. On the changing form of the state, see Kenneth Finegold and Theda Skocpol, *State and Party in America's New Deal* (Madison, 1995). Nancy J. Weiss, *Farewell to the Party of Lincoln: Black Politics in the Age of FDR* (Princeton, 1983), 228–29, shows the soaring voter participation.

42. E. Franklin Frazier, "The American Negro's New Leaders," *Current History* 28 (April 1928): 56–59, and *The Negro in the United States* (New York, 1949), 546–49; Robert J. Norrell, *Reaping the Whirl-Wind: The Civil Rights Movement in Tuskegee* (New York, 1985), 19–43; Douglas L. Smith, *The New Deal in the Urban South* (Baton Rouge, 1988), 232–59; Patricia Sullivan, *Days of Hope: Race and Democracy in the New Deal Era* (Chapel Hill, 1996).

43. Walter White, *A Man Called White: The Autobiography of Walter White* (Bloomington, 1948), 99–116, 168–70; Harvard Sitkoff, *A New Deal for Blacks: The Emergence of Civil Rights as a National Issue* (New York, 1978), 58–83; N. Weiss, *Farewell to the Party of Lincoln*, 120–35; J. Joseph Hutmacher, *Senator Robert F. Wagner and the Rise of Urban Liberalism* (New York, 1971), 171–74, 218.

44. John B. Kirby, *Black Americans in the Roosevelt Era: Liberalism and Race* (Knoxville, 1980), 18–35.

45. Sitkoff, *New Deal for Blacks*, 84–89; Grimshaw, *Bitter Fruit*, 72–79.

46. "Black Game," *Time*, 17 August 1936, 10; "Colored Vote Race," *Newsweek*, 12 September 1936, 18; N. Weiss, *Farewell to the Party of Lincoln*, 180. Also at the 1936 convention, Roosevelt forced a change in the two-thirds rule that had long given the white South a veto over nominees.

47. N. Weiss, *Farewell to the Party of Lincoln*, 180–208; Sitkoff, *New Deal for Blacks*, 114.

48. Kevin J. McMahon, *Reconsidering Roosevelt on Race: How the Presidency Paved the Road to Brown* (Chicago, 2003); Sitkoff, *New Deal for Blacks*; J. B. Kirby, *Black Americans in the Roosevelt Era*; N. Weiss, *Farewell to the Party of Lincoln*.

49. This electoral geometry was first analyzed by Henry Lee Moon in his 1948 book *Balance of Power*. Related arguments include Samuel Lubell, *The Future of American Politics* (New York, 1951), 81–99; and John Frederick Martin, *Civil Rights and the Crisis of Liberalism: The Democratic Party 1945–1976* (Boulder, 1979).

50. Samuel Lubell, *The Hidden Crisis in American Politics* (New York, 1970), 155.

51. Lerone Bennett Jr., *Confrontation: Black and White* (Chicago, 1965), 169.

52. Self, *American Babylon*; Biondi, *To Stand and Fight*; Shirley Ann Wilson Moore, *To Place Our Deeds: The African American Community in Richmond, California, 1910–1963* (Berkeley, 2000); Quintard Taylor, *Forging of a Black Community* and *In Search of the Racial Frontier: African Americans in the American West, 1528–1990* (New York, 1998), 278–310; Thomas, *Life for Us Is What We Make It*; Heather Ann Thompson, *Whose Detroit?: Politics, Labor, and Race in a Modern American City* (Ithaca, 2001); Mathew Countryman, "Civil Rights and Black Power in Philadelphia, 1945–1971" (Ph. D. diss., Duke, 1999); Broussard, *Black San Francisco*; Gretchen Lemke-Santangelo, *Abiding Courage: African American Migrant Women and the East Bay Community* (Chapel Hill, 1996).

53. Self, *American Babylon*, 106–7. "Labor-based civil rights movement" is the term Robert Korstad and Nelson Lichtenstein use in their influential article "Opportunities Found and Lost," 786–811.

54. Bennett, *Confrontation*, 183. Books that overemphasize context include Klinkner and Smith, *Unsteady March*.

55. White, *A Man Called White*, 187; *Crisis*, November 1940, 350; Herbert Garfinkel, *When Negroes March: The March on Washington Movement in the Organizational Politics for FEPC* (New York, 1969; orig. 1959), 34–36.

56. Brooks, *Walls Come Tumbling Down*; Garfinkel, *When Negroes March*.

57. Ottley, *"New World A-Coming,"* 291.

58. Ibid.; *Chicago Defender*, 8 February 1941, as quoted in Garfinkel, *When Negroes March*, 39. See 39–59 for the other headlines and discussion of press support.

59. White, *A Man Called White*, 187, 192; Garfinkel, *When Negroes March*, 60–61; Brooks, *Walls Come Tumbling Down*, 9–32.

60. "400,000 Now in NAACP Ranks," *Chicago Defender* (St. Louis edition), 13 January 1945, 3; C. Reed, *Chicago NAACP and the Rise of Black Professional Leadership*, 117; Thomas, *Life for Us Is What We Make It*, 246–48; Thomas J. Sugrue, *Origins of the Urban Crisis: Race and Inequality in Postwar Detroit* (Princeton, 1996), 170–77. On the expansion of the NAACP in the South, see Fairclough, *Better Day Coming*, 182–85. In 1948, the membership was 300,000 as reported in *Crisis*, August–September 1949, 246.

61. Ottley, *"New World A-Coming,"* 268–88; Patrick S. Washburn, *A Question of Sedition: The Federal Government's Investigation of the Black Press during World War II* (New York, 1986); Lee Finkle, *Forum for Protest* (Cranbury, N.J., 1975); Robert Hill, ed., *The FBI's RACON: Racial Conditions in the United States during World War II* (Boston, 1995).

62. St. Clair Drake and Horace R. Cayton, *Black Metropolis: A Study of Negro Life in a Northern City* (New York, 1962; orig. 1945), 402; Myrdal, *American Dilemma*, 911.

63. Observations from 1944 issues of *Chicago Defender* (St. Louis edition). Mullen argues in *Popular Fronts* that the change in *Defender* editorial position dated from 1940 when John H. Sengstacke assumed control and reflected his links to the popular front community of black Chicago (44–47).

64. Andrew Edmund Kersten, *Race, Jobs, and the War: The FEPC in the Midwest, 1941–46* (Urbana, Ill., 2000). On the FEPC in the South, see Merl E. Reed, *Seedtime for the Modern Civil Rights Movement: The President's Committee on Fair Employment Practice, 1941–1946* (Baton Rouge, 1991); and Fairclough, *Better Day Coming*, 185–88.

65. The *Chicago Defender* (St. Louis edition) closely monitored FEPC legislation with banner stories like "Dem Platform Skips FEP, Poll Tax Pledges," 22 July 1944, 1.

66. Louis Ruchames, *Race, Jobs, and Politics: The Story of FEPC* (New York, 1953), 209; Garfinkel, *When Negroes March*, 148–70.

67. Will Maslow, "Fair Employment State by State," *Nation*, 14 April 1945, 410; "16 States Consider 'Little FEPC' Bills," *Chicago Defender* (St. Louis edition), 20 January 1945, 6; Ruchames, *Race, Jobs, and Politics*, 165.

68. Biondi, *To Stand and Fight*, 18–32; Ruchames, *Race, Jobs, and Politics*, 168. See also Trotter, *Black Milwaukee*, 165–75; Garfinkel, *When Negroes March*, 170–74.

69. Self, *American Babylon*, 79–82. Sugrue, *Origins of the Urban Crisis*, 170–77, details the campaign in Michigan that led to the 1955 law.

70. The Congress of Racial Equality's campaign received extensive coverage in the *Chicago Defender* (St. Louis edition) in stories like "Fight to Crack White City Jim Crow Rink," 16 September 1944, 11; "Crusade against Jim Crow: California Uses Iron-clad Anti-bias Law to War on Restaurants That Bar Negroes," *Ebony*, August 1948, 3–18; and "Pickets Break Job Bias in Biggest Cleveland Bank," *Ebony*, December 1951, 15–22. The *Crisis* covered campaigns in its regular feature "Along the N.A.A.C.P. Battlefront."

71. Biondi, *To Stand and Fight*, 79–97; August Meier and Elliott Rudwick, *CORE: A Study in the Civil Rights Movement 1942–1968* (New York, 1973).

72. Meyer surveys a century of housing struggles in *As Long as They Don't Move Next Door*. For detailed accounts of Detroit, Chicago, and Oakland, see Sugrue, *Origins of the Urban Crisis*; Arnold R. Hirsch, *Making the Second Ghetto: Race and Housing in Chicago, 1940–1960* (Cambridge, 1983); and Self, *American Babylon*. For a look at housing struggles in a city where home-ownership was not the norm, see Roberta Gold, "City of Tenants: New York Housing Struggles and the Challenge to Postwar America" (Ph.D. diss., University of Washington, 1994). In suburban contexts: Andrew Wiese, *Places of Their Own: African American Suburbanization in the Twentieth Century* (Chicago, 2004), 125–42.

73. "Fortune Real Estate Builds on 40 Yrs. Firm Foundation" and other articles, *Michigan Chronicle*, 30 January 1954.

74. Walter White, "This Is Cicero," *Crisis*, August–September 1951, 434–40; Hirsch, *Making the Second Ghetto*; Meyer, *As Long as They Don't Move Next Door*, 117–29.

75. The quotes are from the *San Francisco Chronicle*, 14–15 November 1957. Meyer, *As Long as They Don't Move Next Door*, 130–33, has the fullest description of these events.

76. On McGriff and the role of the white neighborhood weeklies, see Sugrue, *Origins of the Urban Crisis*, 82, 223. The assessment of the *Detroit News* or the *Detroit Free Press* is based on the spring of 1954 and the contrasting coverage in the *Michigan Chronicle*. Indexers for the *San Francisco Chronicle* identified only fifteen articles on the subject of "race problems — residential restrictions" during the decade 1940–1949 and twenty-one articles during the 1950s, including the Mayses' stories, with many of the rest referring to problems in cities other than the Bay Area. Calculated from *San Francisco Newspapers Index: 1904–1959* and *San Francisco Chronicle Index 1950–1980* (Commercial Microfilm Service, 1986). Hirsch, *Making the Second Ghetto*, 51–63, discusses the press silence in Chicago but does not see it as a useful change.

77. Unsigned copy of NBC letter, 11 February 1941; *Harper's* Dear Subscriber letter (undated); C. D. Jackson to Roy Wilkins, 27 November 1941, all in Papers of the NAACP, part 15, Segregation and discrimination, complaints and responses, 1940–1955, series B, microfilm reel 11 (Fredericktown, Md., 1991). On the Office of War Information and the broader subject of media transformation, see Barbara Dianne Savage, *Broadcasting Freedom: Radio, War, and the Politics of Race 1938–1948* (Chapel Hill, 1999); Gerd Horten, *Radio Goes to War: The Cultural Politics of Propaganda during World War II* (Berkeley, 2002); and Clayton R. Koppes and Gregory D. Black, *Hollywood Goes to War: How Politics, Profits and Propaganda Shaped World War II Movies* (Berkeley, 1990).

78. Russell Owen to Roy Wilkins, 24 April 1940, in Papers of the NAACP, part 15, series B, reel 11. Thomas Cripps describes the NAACP effect on Hollywood in *Slow Fade to Black: The Negro in American Film, 1900–1942* (New York, 1977), 375–89.

79. Frank Norris to Walter White, 25 May 1942, in Papers of NAACP, part 15, series B, reel 11.

80. "And the Migrants Kept Coming: Negro Artist Paints the Story of the Great American Minority," *Fortune*, November 1941, 102–9; "Negro's War," *Fortune*, June 1942, 76–80; "White Man's War?" *Time*, 2 March 1942, 13; "Second Front in Harlem: Elder Michawx and His Choir," *Time*, 21 December 1942, 74. Walter White defended *Time* when the *Baltimore Afro-American* called it a "race-hating magazine" and promptly received a thank you from James Parton of *Time*. See White to Carl Murphy, 22 August 1941, and Parton to White, 9 September 1940, both in Papers of the NAACP, part 15, series B, reel 11.

81. Vicki Goldberg, *The Power of Photography: How Photographs Changed Our Lives* (New York, 1991); Alice G. Marquis, *Hope and Ashes: The Birth of Modern Times 1929–1939* (New York, 1986), 137; Simon Michael Bessie, *Jazz Journalism: The Story of Tabloid Newspapers* (New York, 1938).

82. V. Goldberg, *Power of Photography*, 200–12; David J. Garrow, *Protest at Selma: Martin Luther King Jr. and the Voting Rights Act of 1965* (New Haven, 1978), 150–53; Henry Hampton, "The T.V. Camera as Double-Edged Sword," *New York Times*, 15 January 1989. The standard view of press patterns was much influenced by the Kerner Commission *Report of the National Advisory Commission on Civil Disorders* (New York, 1968), which blasted the press for ignoring black communities and their problems. Carolyn Martindale, *The White Press and Black America* (New York, 1986), discusses the numerous studies and follow-up reports that seemed to confirm the commission's

charges. Most of those studies, including her own, were methodologically awkward (counting inches of news coverage and looking for certain kinds of stories) and inclined to dismiss other things as tokens.

83. Cripps, *Slow Fade to Black*, 297.

84. "Minstrel Shows," *Life*, 5 July 1943. The magazine's interest in racial justice got off to an awkward start in the late 1930s with such features as "50 Million Watermelons Go to Market," 9 August 1937, and "Negroes: The U.S. Also Has a Minority Problem," 3 October 1938. See the discussion in Nicholas Natanson, *The Black Image in the New Deal: The Politics of FSA Photography* (Knoxville, 1992), 1819. My assessment of *Life*'s racial look in the 1940s differs from that of Mary Alice Sentman, who used a counting strategy to test the magazine's coverage patterns: "Black and White: Disparity in Coverage by *Life* Magazine from 1937 to 1972," *Journalism Quarterly* 60 (Autumn 1983): 501–8. See also Guido Stempel III, "Visibility of Blacks in News and News-Picture Magazines," *Journalism Quarterly* 48 (Summer 1971): 337–39; and Paul Lester and Ron Smith, "African-American Photo Coverage in *Life, Newsweek*, and *Time*, 1937–1988," *Journalism Quarterly* 67 (Spring 1990).

85. "Race War in Detroit," *Life*, 5 July 1943, 93–102. There is a sharp contrast between *Life*'s sympathetic coverage of blacks in the Detroit conflict and its hostile portrayal of Mexican Americans just two weeks earlier in "Zoot Suit Riots," 21 June 1943, 30–31.

86. The following articles appear in *Life*: "Detroit Is Dynamite," 17 August 1942, 15–23; "Voting in the South," 15 May 1944, 33–35; "How Will Negroes Vote?" 16 October 1944, 89–95; 21 July 1947, 29. See also "White Man Turns Negro," 9 June 1947, 131–39; and "Race Riot in St. Louis," 4 July 1949, 30–31.

87. The following articles appear in *Life*: 24 January 1944, 94–98; "Capitol Cleanup," 6 September 1943, 89–92; "Outlaw's Bridge," 20 March 1944, 47. *Life* did run unflattering stories about a pair of black evangelists: "Prophet Jones," 27 November 1944, 57–63; and "Daddy Grace," 1 October 1945, 51–56.

88. Coverage of entertainers in *Life* in 1943: 13 September, 34–45; 11 October, 117; 22 November, 87–90; 6 December, 116–17; 20 December, 111–17. Coverage of the military: 8 November 1943, 36–37; 14 August 1944, 65–73; 24 August 1944, 44.

89. *Life*, 28 July 1947, 36. To see the power of *Life*'s pictorial storytelling, compare the same story in *Newsweek*, 28 July 1947, 24. On Selmaism: Martindale, *White Press and Black America*, 65.

90. *Life*, 15 May 1944. Other shabby southern whites: "Oklahoma Politics," *Life*, 13 July 1942, 21–13; "The Home Folks," 13 September 1943, 119–; "Hillbilly Singer Elected Governor," 13 March 1944, 32–33; "Life Visits the Hatfields and McCoys," 22 May 1944, 108–16; "Holiness Faith Healers," 3 July 1944, 59–62. Well-dressed southern blacks: "Heaven Bound," 17 May 1943, 26–29; "First Negro Votes in Texas Primary," 17 August 1944, 25; "How Will Negroes Vote?" 16 October 1944, 93–94; "One Negro's University," 29 September 1947, 69–70.

91. Editorial, *Life*, 24 April 1944, 32, stresses the need to deal with voting rights and economic discrimination but says social issues will have to be worked out. *Life*'s major competitors (*Collier's, Look*, and the *Saturday Evening Post*) spent less coverage on race relations and were more likely to picture African Americans in undermining ways in

the early 1940s but improved by the end of the decade. Likewise, *Time* and *Newsweek* provided increasing coverage of riots and segregation challenges. Ira De A. Reid, "The Literature of Race and Culture," *Phylon* 5 (1944): 384–85. See also Abby Arthur Johnson and Ronald Maberry Johnson, *Propaganda and Aesthetics: The Literary Politics of Afro-American Magazines in the Twentieth Century* (Amherst, 1979), 125–26.

92. James W. Ivy, "Editors Speak on the Senate Filibuster," *Crisis*, June 1949, 170–73, 189–90.

93. See chap. 3 and the noted tables in appendix A for the income and occupational data. On housing, see the maps in Sugrue, *Origins of the Urban Crisis*, 183–87. Detroit's black population had increased by a factor of 2.2; its physical size had tripled. A prime statement of the trickle-down thesis is Stephan Thernstrom and Abigail Thernstrom, *America in Black and White: One Nation, Indivisible* (New York, 1997), 69–96. They refer to the improvements of the 1940s as a "Remarkable Change."

94. David J. Garrow, *Bearing the Cross: Martin Luther King, Jr., and the Southern Christian Leadership Conference* (New York, 1986), 65–66.

95. Bennett, *Confrontation*, 256.

CHAPTER EIGHT

1. White and Rev. Claude Williams are quoted in "Troops Restore Calm in Detroit: Death Toll 28," *Chicago Tribune*, 23 June 1943, 2. Gunnar Myrdal, *An American Dilemma: The Negro Problem and Modern Democracy* (New York, 1944), 79; Thomas Sancton, "The Race Riots," *New Republic*, 5 July 1943, 9–12. The other quotes are from Dominic J. Capeci Jr. and Martha Wilkerson, *Layered Violence: The Detroit Rioters of 1943* (Jackson, Miss., 1991), 22–31, and Chad Berry, *Southern Migrants, Northern Exiles* (Urbana, Ill., 2000), 142.

2. On claims that Okies were responsible for hate strikes in the West, see Lawrence Brooks de Graaf, *Negro Migration to Los Angeles, 1930 to 1950* (San Francisco, 1974), 202–3; and Harry Kitano and Roger Daniels, *American Racism: Exploration of the Nature of Prejudice* (Englewood Cliffs, N.J., 1970), 72.

3. Of course, one always wonders how truthful white respondents are in such surveys, but it is unlikely that southern-born whites were less honest than other whites. The Detroit surveys: Arthur Kornhauser, *Detroit as the People See It: A Survey of Attitudes in an Industrial City* (Detroit, 1953), 89; *Detroit Area Study, A Social Profile of Detroit/1956* (Ann Arbor, 1957), 55–58. Los Angeles: Richard T. Morriss and Vincent Jeffries, "The White Reaction Study," in *The Los Angeles Riots: A Socio-Psychological Study*, ed. Nathan Cohen (New York, 1970). The Chicago survey: Donald J. Bogue and Richard McKinlay, *Militancy for and against Civil Rights and Integration in Chicago: Summer 1967*, Report 1 of University of Chicago Community and Family Study Center (1 August 1967), 14–17. Two national surveys also show former southerners mirroring other whites: Paul B. Sheatsley, "White Attitudes toward the Negro," *Daedalus* 95 (Winter 1966): 277, and Richard F. Hamilton, *Class and Politics in the United States* (New York, 1972), 474 n. 20. The only contrary data I have found showing southern

migrants to be more racist than northern whites is Angus Campbell, *White Attitudes toward Black People* (Ann Arbor, 1971), 44–45.

4. Williams later returned south and played a major role in CIO and civil rights activities. His story is told in Robert H. Craig, *Religion and Radical Politics: An Alternative Christian Tradition in the United States* (Philadelphia, 1992), 144–71. Other biographies can be found in Mari Jo Buhle, Paul Buhle, and Dan Georgakas, eds., *Encyclopedia of the American Left* (Urbana, Ill., 1992); and Gary M. Fink, ed., *Biographical Dictionary of American Labor Leaders* (Westport, 1974). Another expatriate labor organizer was South Carolinian Lane Kirkland, who eventually became head of the AFL-CIO.

5. Lynn Weiner, "Aunt Molly Jackson," in *Encyclopedia of Southern Culture*, ed. Charles R. Wilson and William Ferris (Chapel Hill, 1989), 1578–79; *People's World* quotation from Joe Klein, *Woody Guthrie: A Life* (New York, 1980), 125; Charles J. Shindo, *Dust Bowl Migrants in the American Imagination* (Lawrence, Kans., 1997), 167–210.

6. Klein, *Woody Guthrie*, esp. 142; Robbie Lieberman, *"My Song Is My Weapon": People's Songs, American Communism, and the Politics of Culture, 1930–1950* (Urbana, Ill., 1989).

7. Royce Delmatier, "The Rebirth of the Democratic Party," in *The Rumble of California Politics 1848–1970*, ed. Royce Delmatier, Clarence F. McIntosh, and Earl G. Waters (New York, 1970), 230–71; Jordan A. Schwarz, *The New Dealers: Power Politics in the Age of Roosevelt* (New York, 1993), 3–31; William Gibbs McAdoo, *Crowded Years* (Boston, 1931).

8. Mark Sumner Still, "'Fighting Bob' Shuler: Fundamentalist and Reformer" (Ph.D. diss., Claremont Graduate School, 1988), 362–86.

9. California's experience started in 1849 when it selected Peter Burnett as its first governor and William M. Gwin as one of its initial senators. Both were from Tennessee. Walton Bean and James J. Rawls, *California: An Interpretative History*, 4th ed. (New York, 1983), 100–107; Daniel E. Sutherland, *The Confederate Carpetbaggers* (Baton Rouge, 1988), 99–107. On the Democratic party internal alignments, see David Burner, *The Politics of Provincialism: The Democratic Party in Transition 1918–1932* (Cambridge, 1986); and Douglas B. Craig, *After Wilson: The Struggle for the Democratic Party 1920–1934* (Chapel Hill, 1992).

10. John Milton Cooper Jr., *Walter Hines Page: The Southerner as American 1855–1918* (Chapel Hill, 1977), 235–41.

11. Serving in Congress with Holifield and Sisk in 1970 were nine other representatives and two senators who were whites of southern birth serving nonsouthern states. Like Lee Hamilton of Indiana and Brock Adams of Washington, many had left the South as children and seem to have made no use of their southern backgrounds. Four of the group were Republicans, including Hugh Scott, the Virginia-born senator from Pennsylvania; and Frank Horton, a Texan who represented Rochester, New York, in the House. On Edwards, see Heather Ann Thompson, *Whose Detroit? Politics, Labor, and Race in a Modern American City* (Ithaca, 2001), 14, 21; Henry Lee Moon, *Balance of Power: The Negro Vote* (Westport, 1977; orig. 1948), 151. On Holifield and Sisk: Michael

Barone, Grant Ujifusa, and Douglass Mathews, *The Almanac of American Politics, 1972* (New York, 1972), 71–73. James R. Mills, *A Disorderly House: The Brown-Unruh Years in Sacramento* (Berkeley, 1987), profiles Unruh, Carrell, and Bee. Bee was born in Sacramento. His ancestors were Confederate generals and Texas politicians. On Wakefield, see Becky M. Nicolaides, *My Blue Heaven: Life and Politics in the Working-Class Suburbs of Los Angeles, 1920–1965* (Chicago, 2002), 273–76.

12. Robert M. Henderson, *D. W. Griffith: The Years at Biograph* (New York, 1970).

13. Kenneth T. Jackson, *The Ku Klux Klan in the City 1915–1930* (New York, 1967), 15; David M. Chalmers, *Hooded Americanism: A History of the Ku Klux Klan* (New York, 1981); Nancy MacLean, *Behind the Mask of Chivalry: The Making of the Second Ku Klux Klan* (New York, 1994).

14. Robert Alan Goldberg, *Hooded Empire: The Ku Klux Klan in Colorado* (Urbana, Ill., 1981), 40; Leonard J. Moore, *Citizen Klansmen: The Ku Klux Klan in Indiana, 1921–1928* (Chapel Hill, 1991), 53–57. Earlier studies, without doing the careful examination of membership lists, were inclined to exaggerate the role of southerners. See Norman F. Weaver, "The Knights of the Ku Klux Klan in Wisconsin, Indiana, Ohio, and Michigan" (Ph.D. diss., University of Wisconsin, 1954), 177, 285.

15. Shawn Lay, *Hooded Knights on the Niagara: The Ku Klux Klan in Buffalo, New York* (New York, 1995), 47; David A. Horowitz, ed., *Inside the Klavern: The Secret History of a Ku Klux Klan of the 1920s* (Carbondale, Ill., 1999), 5; K. T. Jackson, *Ku Klux Klan in the City*, 196–97; L. Moore, *Citizen Klansmen*, 13–15.

16. Robert Lee Salley, "Activities of the Knights of the Ku Klux Klan in Southern California: 1921–1925" (MA thesis, University of Southern California, 1963), 113, as quoted in Still, "'Fighting Bob' Shuler," 191. Also K. T. Jackson, *Ku Klux Klan in the City*, 191.

17. L. Moore, *Citizen Klansmen*; K. T. Jackson, *Ku Klux Klan in the City*, 144–60.

18. Lynn Dumenil, *The Modern Temper: American Culture and Society in the 1920s* (New York, 1995), 250–63; and further developed in Dumenil, "The Tribal Twenties," *Journal of Ethnic History* 11 (Fall 1991): 21–49.

19. David Chalmers, *Backfire: How the Ku Klux Klan Helped the Civil Rights Movement* (Lanham, Md., 2003). He makes the point briefly about the second Klan in his earlier book, *Hooded Americanism*.

20. Arthur Krock, "The Damn Fool Democrats," *American Mercury*, March 1925, 257, as quoted in Burner, *Politics of Provincialism*, 115. Burner provides the richest account of the 1924 convention and party reorganization. See also Alan J. Lichtman, *Prejudice and Old Politics: The Presidential Elections of 1928* (Chapel Hill, 1979).

21. Leo P. Ribuffo, *The Old Christian Right: The Protestant Far Right from the Great Depression to the Cold War* (Philadelphia, 1983); Philip Jenkins, *Hoods and Shirts: The Extreme Right in Pennsylvania, 1925–1950* (Chapel Hill, 1997).

22. This account is based on Kenneth R. Dvorak, "Terror in Detroit: The Rise and Fall of Michigan's Black Legion" (Ph.D. diss., Bowling Green State University, 2000), quotes are from 110–11, 158. See also State of Michigan, Circuit Court for the County of Oakland, *Report of Black Legion Activities in Oakland County, George B. Hartwick, Circuit Judge* (September 1930), 13; and Ribuffo, *Old Christian Right*.

23. Press coverage can be sampled in clipping files that comprise part 3 of the FBI Freedom of Information file on the Black Legion, available online at ‹http://foia.fbi. gov/foiaindex/blackleg.htm›.

24. *New York Times* and *Detroit News* quotes are from Dvorak, "Terror in Detroit," 25, 31. The other newspaper quotes are from clippings in part 3, FBI Freedom of Information file on the Black Legion: "The Black Legion Happened Here," *New York Post,* 28 May 1936; Dorothy Thompson, "Black Legion Blame Put on Public," *Washington Star,* 28 May 1936; Paul W. Ward, "Who's Behind the Black Legion," *Nation,* 3 June 1936, 695. Elmer Akers, "Southern Whites in Detroit" (unpublished ms., n.d. [1937?]), 35, 66, available through University Microfilms.

25. Dvorak, "Terror in Detroit," 18, concludes that the notion that membership consisted largely of southern whites "may be erroneous."

26. Katherine Archibald, *Wartime Shipyard: A Study in Social Disunity* (Berkeley, 1947), 75; "Race Hate Goes West," *Negro Digest,* August 1947, 82–84 (reprint from *Newsweek,* 19 May 1947); James N. Gregory, *American Exodus: The Dust Bowl Migration and Okie Culture in California* (New York, 1989), 164–71. In Michigan: Alan Clive, *State of War: Michigan in World War II* (Ann Arbor, 1979), 138–43.

27. White and Rev. Claude Williams are quoted in "Troops Restore Calm in Detroit: Death Toll 28," 2. The other quotes are from Capeci and Wilkerson, *Layered Violence,* 22–31; Berry, *Southern Migrants, Northern Exiles,* 142. Liberal white journalists followed up. Earl Brown, "The Truth about the Detroit Riots," *Harper's,* November 1943, 489, looked into a variety of factors but stressed the idea that southern racial tensions had moved north. Vastly exaggerating the number of migrants, Brown claimed that "Detroit to a considerable extent is a city of transplanted Southerners."

28. Capeci and Wilkerson, *Layered Violence,* 61–63; Thomas J. Sugrue, *The Origins of the Urban Crisis: Race and Inequality in Postwar Detroit* (Princeton, 1996), 212; Arnold Hirsch, "Race and Housing: Violence and Communal Protest in Chicago, 1940–1960," in *The Ethnic Frontier: Essays in the History of Groups Survival in Chicago and the Midwest,* ed. Melvin G. Holli and Peter d'A. Jones (Grand Rapids, 1977), 331–415.

29. Lewis M. Killian, "The Adjustment of Southern White Migrants to Northern Urban Norms," *Social Forces* 32 (October 1953): 68, and "Southern White Laborers in Chicago's West Side" (Ph.D. diss., University of Chicago, 1949), 326–55.

30. Killian, "Southern White Laborers," 328.

31. On the delicate maneuvers of the UAW leadership, see August Meier and Elliot Rudwick, *Black Detroit and the Rise of the UAW* (New York, 1979); and H. Thompson, *Whose Detroit?* Jeffries soon stopped caring about blacks or liberal voters. In 1945 he was reelected after a campaign that was anti-black and anti-labor.

32. Spelling and grammar in the original. *St. Louis Independent Clarion,* 18 October 1919, in Tuskegee Institute News Clippings File (Microfilming Corporation of America, 1976), series 1, reel 9. Thanks to Jason Digman for sharing this item.

33. Chester B. Himes, *If He Hollers Let Him Go: A Novel* (New York, 1986; orig. 1944); Himes also accused southern white sailors of helping to lead the Zoot Suit riots in Los Angeles: "Zoot Riots Are Race Riots," *Crisis* (July 1943), 200–201, 222.

34. Dexter Teed, "New World A-Coming," *Negro Digest,* May 1944, 81–83; *Michigan*

Chronicle, 1 January 1949, 1. See also G. James Fleming, "Paradise Invites You to Stay Out," *Negro Digest*, July 1947, 25–27; and Louis E. Martin, "Detroit Still Dynamite," *Crisis*, January 1944, 25. It is also likely that the frequent stories in the black press about Ku Klux Klan activities carried an implied reference to southern whites: "Ku Kluxers Join Fight on Chicago's West Chesterfield Housing Project," *Chicago Defender* (St. Louis edition), 9 September 1944, 5.

35. Charles Denby, a radical black worker living in Detroit, had a very different view of southern white and northern white racial norms. In his 1952 autobiography, *Indignant Heart: A Black Worker's Journal* (Boston, 1978; orig. 1952), 105–6, 118, 144, he repeatedly asserts that it was easier to get along with the southerners. "A Southerner, if he changes will sit back and talk to you about anything and he won't say, nigger, any more. They really change, they treat us better" (144).

36. John Egerton, *The Americanization of Dixie: The Southernization of America* (New York, 1974).

37. I explored this in a slightly different way in James N. Gregory, "Southernizing the American Working Class: Post-War Episodes of Regional and Class Transformation," *Labor History* 39, no. 2 (1998): 135–54.

38. David Plotke, *Building a Democratic Political Order: Reshaping American Liberalism in the 1930s and 1940s* (New York, 1996). Other useful guides to voting and party patterns include R. Hamilton, *Class and Politics in the United States*; and Michael Barone, *Our Country: The Shaping of America from Roosevelt to Reagan* (New York, 1990).

39. Thomas Byrne Edsall with Mary D. Edsall, *Chain Reaction: The Impact of Race, Rights, and Taxes on American Politics* (New York, 1992); Stanley B. Greenberg, *Middle Class Dreams: The Politics and Power of the New American Majority* (New Haven, 1996). On blue-collar social life and politics: Arthur B. Shostak, *Blue-Collar Life* (New York, 1969); Patricia Cayo Sexton and Brendan Sexton, *Blue Collars and Hard-Hats* (New York, 1971); Irving Howe, ed., *The World of the Blue-Collar Worker* (New York, 1972); Joseph A. Ryan, ed., *White Ethnics: Life in Working-Class America* (Englewood Cliffs, N.J., 1973).

40. "Where the Stars Fall," *Time*, 27 September 1963, 17–21.

41. Dan T. Carter, *The Politics of Rage: George Wallace, the Origins of the New Conservatism, and the Transformation of American Politics* (New York, 1995), 204; Stephan Lesher, *George Wallace: American Populist* (Reading, Mass., 1994), 274–77.

42. Carter, *Politics of Rage*, 12. See also Seymour Martin Lipset and Earl Raab, *The Politics of Unreason: Right Wing Extremism in America, 1790–1970* (New York, 1970), 340–50, 407; Lewis Chester, Godfrey Hodgson, and Bruce Page, *An American Melodrama: The Presidential Campaign of 1968*, 261–94; and Michael Kazin, *The Populist Persuasion: An American History* (New York, 1995), 221–244.

43. Examples of local backlash campaigns: J. Anthony Lukas, *Common Ground* (New York, 1985), 115–38; John C. Bollens and Grant B. Geyer, *Yorty: Politics of a Constant Candidate* (Pacific Palisades, 1973); Jonathan Rieder, *Canarsie: The Jews and Italians of Brooklyn against Liberalism* (Cambridge, Mass., 1985); Ronald P. Formisano, *Boston against Busing: Race, Class, and Ethnicity in the 1960s and 1970s* (Chapel Hill,

1991); Kenneth D. Durr, *Behind the Backlash: White Working-Class Politics in Baltimore, 1940–1980* (Chapel Hill, 2003). On Nixon's strategy: Kevin Phillips, *The Emerging Republican Majority* (New Rochelle, 1969); Samuel Lubell, *The Hidden Crisis in American Politics* (New York, 1970).

44. Carter, *Politics of Rage*, 208–12; Lesher, *George Wallace*, 284–96; Phillip Crass, *The Wallace Factor* (New York, 1975), 66–72.

45. Lubell, *Hidden Crisis*, 75, 84; Jody Carlson, *George C. Wallace and the Politics of the Powerless: The Wallace Campaigns for the Presidency, 1964–1976* (New Brunswick, 1981), 88. On San Pablo, see Lillian B. Rubin, *Busing and Backlash: White against White in a California School District* (Berkeley, 1972), 147–54, and also Rubin's *Worlds of Pain: Life in the Working-Class Family* (New York, 1976).

46. James Lewis Canfield, *A Case of Third Party Activism: The George Wallace Campaign Worker and the American Independent Party* (Lanham, Md., 1984), 32–35. Carter, *Politics of Rage*, 297, 343, discusses the Far Right networks, as do Lipset and Raab in *Politics of Unreason*, 338–77.

47. The argument for a blue-collar base is developed in Lipset and Raab, *Politics of Unreason*, 358–97 (survey 363–65), and echoed by Crass, *Wallace Factor*, esp. 66, 128, 148. Border neighborhoods are explained in Lubell, *Hidden Crisis*, 91.

48. Canfield, *Case of Third Party Activism*, 32–35; R. Hamilton, *Class and Politics in the United States*, 474 n. 20.

49. "Howling Hillbilly Success," *Life*, April 4, 1956, 64; Bill C. Malone, *Country Music U.S.A.: A Fifty-Year History* (Austin, 1985); Country Music Foundation, ed., *Country: The Music and the Musicians* (New York, 1994), 296.

50. For radio station numbers, see George O. Carney, "Country Music and the Radio: A Historical Geographic Assessment," *Rocky Mountain Social Science Journal* 11 (January 1974): 25 (table 1), and also his essays in Carney, ed., *The Sounds of People and Places: A Geography of American Folk and Popular Music* (Lanham, Md., 1994). On the Country Music Association, see Bill Ivey, "The Bottom Line: Business Practices That Shaped Country Music," in *Country*, ed. Country Music Foundation, 296–307.

51. Richard A. Peterson and Paul Di Maggio, "From Region to Class, the Changing Locus of Country Music: A Test of the Massification Hypothesis," *Social Forces* 53 (March 1975): 497–506. Other important sources on the diffusion of country music include Bill C. Malone's two books *Country Music U.S.A.* and *Southern Music American Music* (Lexington, Ky., 1979); D. K. Wilgus, "Country-Western Music and the Urban Hillbilly," *Journal of American Folklore* 83 (April–June 1970): 157–79; and Archie Green, "Hillbilly Music: Source and Symbol," *Journal of American Folklore* 78 (July–September 1965): 204–22. For an example of its place in tavern life, see E. E. LeMasters, *Blue-Collar Aristocrats: Life-Styles at a Working-Class Tavern* (Madison, 1975), 143–44.

52. The battles over the Nashville Sound are still playing out among both artists and analysts. Among recent examples of the later: Barbara Ching, *Wrong's What I Do Best: Hard Country Music and Contemporary Culture* (New York, 2001).

53. Robert Shelton, "Meet a New Folk Hero, the Truck River," *New York Times*, 4 December 1966; Malone, *Country Music U.S.A.*, 296–97. The fad got a big boost from

the 1963 hit "Six Days on the Road" by Dave Dudley. On anti-urbanism, see Ivan M. Tribe, "The Hillbilly versus the City: Urban Images in Country Music," *John Edwards Memorial Foundation Quarterly* 10 (1974): 41–51; and Anthony O. Edmonds, "Myths and Migrants: Images of Rural and Urban Life in Country Music," *Indiana Social Studies Quarterly* 28 (Winter 1975–76): 67–72.

54. A good place to start an examination of country music's social themes is Patricia Averill's encyclopedic dissertation, "Can the Circle Be Unbroken: A Study of the Modernization of Rural Born Southern Whites since World War I Using Country Music" (Ph.D. diss., University of Pennsylvania, 1975); Cecilia Tichi, *High Lonesome: The American Culture of Country Music* (Chapel Hill, 1994); and Alex Freedman, "The Sociology of Country Music," *Southern Humanities Review* 3 (February 1969): 358–62.

55. The best assessment of the changing patterns of country music politics is Bill C. Malone, *Don't Get above Your Raisin': Country Music and the Southern Working Class* (Urbana, Ill., 2002), 210–52. See also Jens Lund, "Fundamentalism, Racism, and Political Reaction in Country Music," and Paul Di Maggio, Richard A. Peterson, and Jack Esco Jr., "Country Music: Ballad of the Silent Majority," in *The Sounds of Social Change*, ed. R. Serge Denisoff and Richard A. Peterson (New York, 1972), 79–91. See also Averill's compilation of political references in "Can the Circle Be Unbroken," 665–83, 1197–206.

56. Melton McLaurin, "Country Music and the Vietnam War," in *Perspectives on the American South*, vol. 3, ed. James C. Cobb and Charles R. Wilson (New York, 1985), 145–61. Other titles are from Averill, "Can the Circle Be Unbroken," appendix B, 1184–206. Most appeared on Billboard Top Ten lists or in *Country Song Roundup*. See also Malone, *Don't Get above Your Raisin'*, 210–52, and *Country Music U.S.A.*, 311–20. The unanimity of political perspective was not accidental. When Glen Campbell recorded "The Universal Soldier" in 1965, the response was so hostile that he felt compelled to apologize.

57. Paul Hemphill, *The Nashville Sound: Bright Lights and Country Music* (New York, 1970), 90, 162; Malone, *Don't Get above Your Raisin'*, 238.

58. Merle Haggard with Peggy Russell, *Sing Me Back Home: My Story* (New York, 1981); Paul Hemphill, "Merle Haggard," *Atlantic Monthly*, September 1971, 98–103.

59. Gerald W. Haslam, *Workin' Man Blues: Country Music in California* (Berkeley, 1999); Hemphill, *Nashville Sound*, 205–21.

60. Haslam, *Workin' Man Blues*, 186–87.

61. "Workin' Man Blues" by Merle Haggard, copyright 1969, Tree Publishing.

62. "Okie from Muskogee" by Merle Haggard, copyright 1969, Tree Publishing.

63. Hemphill, "Merle Haggard"; Kristine McKenna, "Living the Legend He Sings About," *Los Angeles Times Calendar*, 23 November 1980, 66. Merle Haggard's politics have changed decisively since his 1970 Love It or Leave days. He opposed the Iraq war.

64. A. G. Aronowitz, "New Country Twang Hits Town," *Life*, 31 May 1968, 12; C. S. Wren, "Merle Haggard," *Look*, 13 July 1971, 36–38.

65. William Martin, *With God on Our Side: The Rise of the Religious Right in America* (New York, 1996); Robert C. Liebman and Robert Wuthnow, eds., *The New Christian*

Right (New York, 1983); Albert J. Menendez, *Evangelicals at the Ballot Box* (Amherst, N.Y., 1996); Perry Deane Young, *God's Bullies: Native Reflections on Preachers and Politics* (New York, 1982).

66. Richard V. Pierard, *The Unequal Yoke: Evangelical Christianity and Political Conservatism* (Philadelphia, 1970), surveys and criticizes the 1960s trends from a left-evangelical perspective. W. Martin, *With God on Our Side*, 74–143; Robert Wuthnow, *The Restructuring of American Religion: Society and Faith since World War II* (Princeton, 1988), 181–207.

67. Menendez, *Evangelicals at the Ballot Box*, 104–24, 258–90, shows how potent evangelical anti-Catholicism was in the 1960 presidential election and evaluates the later alliance. In 1979, Jerry Falwell and many other evangelical conservatives also embraced Israel. On details of the 1970s mobilization, see Ruth Murray Brown, *For a "Christian America": A History of the Religious Right* (Amherst, N.Y., 2002), 29–137.

68. The organization began as Citizens United, founded in California in 1976. The quote is from "Preachers in Politics," *U.S. News and World Report*, 24 September 1979, 37; Tom Morganthau, "The Religion Lobby," *Newsweek*, 16 July 1979, 37; "Evangelical Group Disagrees with 276 in Congress," *New York Times*, 2 November 1980, sec. 1, pt. 1, 34; "A Tide of Born-Again Politics," *Newsweek*, 15 September 1980, 28; Mathew C. Moen, *The Christian Right and Congress* (Tuscalocsa, Ala., 1989), 75–77; Kenneth D. Wald, *Religion and Politics in the United States*, 2d ed. (Washington, D.C., 1992), 232–37, 242. California was also the source of other Christian Right enterprises, including Concerned Women for America and American Coalition for Tradition Values, founded by diaspora southerners Tim and Beverly LaHaye, and Focus on the Family, guided by Louisiana-born Christian psychologist James Dobson. See Brown, *For a "Christian America,"* 167–78.

69. W. Martin, *With God on Our Side*, 55–73; Susan Friend Harding, *The Book of Jerry Falwell: Fundamental Language and Politics* (Princeton, 2000), esp. 85–104, probes the Falwell biography; Dinesh D'Souza, *Falwell before the Millennium: A Critical Biography* (Chicago, 1984).

70. Jerry Falwell with Ed Dobson and Ed Hindson, eds., *The Fundamentalist Phenomenon: The Resurgence of Conservative Christianity* (Garden City, N.Y., 1981), 144, 188.

71. Robert C. Liebman, "Mobilizing the Moral Majority," in *New Christian Right*, ed. Liebman and Wuthnow, 50–73; Wald, *Religion and Politics*, 241–43; Wuthnow, *Restructuring of American Religion*, 197–200. Temple Baptist's relationship to the Moral Majority is discussed in Douglas James Curlew, "'They Ceased Not to Preach': Fundamentalism, Culture, and the Revivalist Imperative at the Temple Baptist Church of Detroit" (Ph.D. diss., University of Michigan, 2001), 378–79. As in many other BBF churches, the move into politics was controversial.

CHAPTER NINE

1. Willie Morris, *New York Days* (Boston, 1993); Peter Applebome, "Willie Morris, 64, Writer on the Southern Experience," *New York Times*, 3 August 1999, A13.

2. Nicholas Lemann, *The Promised Land: The Great Black Migration and How It Changed America* (New York, 1991).

3. Net migration figures are from Bernard L. Weinstein, Harold T. Gross, and John Rees, *Regional Growth and Decline in the United States*, 2d ed. (New York, 1985), 9; southern-born return figures are from table A.2 in appendix A in this volume.

4. Calculated from Weinstein, Gross, and Rees, *Regional Growth and Decline in the United States*, tables 1-5, 1-6, pp. 11–20. See also Bruce J. Schulman, *From Cotton Belt to Sunbelt: Federal Policy, Economic Development, and the Transformation of the South, 1938–1980* (New York, 1991); James C. Cobb, *Industrialization and Southern Society 1877–1984* (Lexington, Ky., 1984); and Robert J. Newman, *Growth in the American South: Changing Regional Employment and Wage Patterns in the 1960s and 1970s* (New York, 1984).

5. Steven F. Lawson, *Running for Freedom: Civil Rights and Black Politics in America since 1941* (Philadelphia, 1991), 157, 187; David R. Goldfield, *Black, White, and Southern: Race Relations and Southern Culture, 1940 to the Present* (Baton Rouge, 1990).

6. Lemann, *Promised Land*, 309–39.

7. Calculated from 1980 5 percent State IPUMS. See also Stewart E. Tolnay, "The African American 'Great Migration' and Beyond," *Annual Review of Sociology* 29 (2003): 209–33; and Larry H. Long and Kristin A. Hansen, "Trends in Return Migration to the South," *Demography* 12 (1975): 601–14, and "Selectivity of Black Return Migration to the South," *Rural Sociology* 42 (Fall 1977): 317–31.

8. Examples of the journalism include "It's Good to Be Home Again," *Ebony*, August 1971, 66–71; "Why More Blacks Are Moving South," *U.S. News and World Report*, 26 February 1973, 53–55; "Okies of the 1970s," *US News*, 24 March 1975, 16–20; J. Boyce, "Reverse Migration," *Time*, 27 September 1976, 5; "Flight from Inner Cities Goes On," *US News*, 11 September 1978, 49; C. Wallis, "Southward Ho for Jobs," *Time*, 11 May 1981, 3; Kenneth R. Weiss, "80-Year Tide of Migration by Blacks Out of the South Has Turned Around," *New York Times*, 11 June 1989, 1:29; and "South toward Home: Facing Long Odds—and Painful History—Blacks Are at Last Moving Back to the Old Confederacy," *Newsweek*, 14 July 1997, 36. Books include Jacqueline Jones, *The Dispossessed: America's Underclasses from the Civil War to the Present* (New York, 1992), 263–65; Lemann, *Promised Land*; and Carol Stack, *Call to Home: African Americans Reclaim the Rural South* (New York, 1996).

9. Calculated from 1980 5 percent State IPUMS and the 1990 1 percent unweighted IPUMS.

10. Ibid.

APPENDIX B

1. The Census Forward Survival Rate method is explained in Everett S. Lee, Ann Ratner Miller, Carol P. Brainerd, and Richard A. Easterlin, *Methodological Considerations and Reference Tables*, vol. 1 of *Population Redistribution and Economic Growth: United States, 1870–1950* (Philadelphia, 1957), 15–56. The three-volume work is an essential resource for migration studies.

2. Since migrants undoubtedly had health patterns that differed somewhat from national norms, none of the mortality rates are completely accurate. 1900–1980 mortality rates are from Donald J. Bogue, *The Population of the United States: Historical Trends and Future Projections* (New York, 1985), 208–9, table 5-4; 1990 rates are from the Berkeley Mortality Database: ‹www.demog.Berkeley.edu/wilmoth/mortality/States/decennial/mort.rate/b.mx.5x3› and ‹www.demog.Berkeley.edu/wilmoth/mortality/States/decennial/mort.rate/w.mx.5x3›, accessed 22 January 2004.

3. When the 1930 IPUMS is officially released, it will contain weighting values not available in the preliminary sample. This will change the numbers slightly, but the difference should be minor.

4. U.S. Bureau of the Census, *U.S. 1960 Census of Population: 1960. Subject Reports: Lifetime and Recent Migration* (Washington, D.C., 1961), table 3, 9–15.

Index

Baer, Max, 146
Baker, Ella, 122, 264
Baker, George, 28, 122
Baker, Newton, 289, 290
Baker, Ray Stannard, 185
Bakersfield, 91, 162–63, 313–14
Bakker, Jim and Tammy Faye, 213
Baldwin, James, 75
Baltimore, 22, 128–31, 144
Baltimore Afro-American, 129–31, 145, 146, 263, 389 (n. 45), 415 (n. 80)
Baptist Bible Fellowship (BBF), 225, 231, 318, 319
Baptist church: in Detroit, 153–54, 166, 198–204, 207–9, 216, 217, 219, 220–22, 231–32, 297, 317, 400 (n. 6); and black migrants, 153–54, 197–202, 205–8; in Chicago, 161, 215–16; in California, 162, 222, 223, 233, 406 (n. 79); and white migrants, 166, 197–206, 208–9; in South, 204; Northern Baptist churches, 204, 205–6, 208, 210, 233, 248, 402 (n. 26); Southern Baptist Convention, 206, 208, 209, 234; and church-building, 207–9; southernization of Northern Baptist congregations, 208, 402 (n. 26); membership statistics for, 209; and fundamentalists, 223–26; in Boston, 224; in New York City, 224; and Moral Majority, 317–18
Barber, Red, 184
Bare, Bobby, 73, 311, 313
Barnett, Claude, 126–27
Barrett, Beverly, 157
Barrow, Joe Louis. *See* Louis, Joe
Barrow, Lillie and Munroe, 148
Barthé, Richmond, 131
Baseball, 143–46, 169–73, 193, 272–73
Basie, Count, 136, 141
Bee, Carlos, 290, 419 (n. 11)
Bell, Cool Papa, 145
Bennett, Lerone, Jr., 260–61, 262, 281
Benswanger, William, 146
Berry, Chad, 91, 111

Berryhill, Bruce, 156
Beverly Hillbillies, 63, 73
Beynon, Erdman, 166–67
Bilbo, Theodore, 189
Billington, Dallas, 225
Binga, Jesse, 121
The Birth of a Nation, 128, 274, 290–91
Black, Julian, 148
Black, Timuel D., Jr., 111
Blackburn, Jack, 148
Black Legion, 77, 285, 295–97, 301
Black Metropolis: as story of Southern Diaspora, 54–59; as concept, 114; social sciences on, 114–16; social class in, 115; statistics on black migration to northern urban areas, 117; black "old settlers" versus newcomers in, 117–22; boomtown dynamics of, 117–24; and community-building patterns, 117–24; professionals in, 121–22, 240–41; southernization of, 122–24; cultural institutions in, 124–31; and newspapers and magazines, 124–31; and intelligentsia, 131–35, 195; and jazz, 135–42, 193; and sports, 142–49; *Ebony* articles on, 149–52; churches and religious movements in, 205, 210–21, 230; political influence of blacks in, 240–47; and civil rights movement, 260–81. *See also* Harlem; Politics and civil rights for blacks; *and specific cities*
Black Metropolis (Drake and Cayton), 114–16, 214–15
Black migrants: in nineteenth century, 12–13; statistics on, 14–16, 39–40, 330, 331, 362 (n. 7); return of, to South, 16–17, 23, 29, 40, 322–24, 330, 331, 368 (n. 61); percentage of, among all southern-born adults, 17, 18; demographic effects of, 17–18; population of, in specific states and regions, 18–19, 20, 332–33; and first phase of Southern Diaspora, 23–25, 27, 78; in Chicago, 25, 26, 27; women as, 26, 365

(n. 27), 382–83 (n. 52); occupational
and social backgrounds of, 28; as professionals and intelligentsia, 28, 54,
105–6, 121–22, 131–35, 195, 240–41,
253, 336–38, 345–46, 386 (n. 17), 409
(n. 9); during Depression, 30–31;
education of, 30–31, 36–37; unemployment of, 31; and second phase of
Southern Diaspora, 33–34, 37–38, 65–
66, 78; college students as, 36–37; in
military, 37–38; media coverage of,
45–55, 72, 75–79; and Harlem, 54–55,
119; social sciences on, 67, 82, 103–4,
111; as maladjusted migrants, 72; as
dangerous, 75–78; income of, 83, 84,
95–97, 102, 103, 106–9, 110, 333–34,
339–40, 343, 350–53; poverty of, 84,
103, 324, 340; employment discrimination against, 92–93, 97–100; and
unions, 93, 98, 99; employment of,
95–100, 104–5, 336–39, 343, 345–49;
educational level and income of,
96–97, 106–9, 334, 352–53, 382–83
(n. 52); in ghettos, 100–103, 114, 116,
152; residential patterns of, 100–103,
344, 354; home-ownership of, 103,
104, 344; and crime, 103–4; religion
of, 153–54, 197–202, 205–8, 209–12,
214–21, 230, 235; as members of Congress, 241; in suburbs, 354; family
patterns of, 382 (n. 45). *See also* Blacks
(northern-born); Black women; Politics and civil rights for blacks

Black Panther Party, 34

Blacks (northern-born): and farming,
24, 29, 30, 33–34; income of, 84, 85,
106–7, 333, 339, 343, 350–53; poverty
of, 84, 103, 324; and unions, 93, 98,
99; employment of, 94, 104–5, 106,
336–39, 343, 345–49; education of, 99;
and crime, 103–4; as professionals,
106, 336–38, 345–46; and Republican
Party, 239–40

Black women: as migrants, 26, 365
(n. 27); income of, 96–97, 106, 107,

109, 334, 343, 350–53, 382–83 (n. 52);
employment of, 98, 100, 105, 343,
345–49; as blues singers, 140; and
churches, 205, 217; as professionals,
336–38, 345–46

Blotner, Joseph, 191

Boggs, James, 31

Bond, Horace Mann, 77

Bontemps, Arna, 131, 133, 135, 192

Boxing, 142–43, 146–49, 276

Braddock, Jimmy, 147

Branham, William, 213

Briggs, Cyril, 247

Brinkley, David, 184

Britt, Elton, 179

Brooks, Cleanth, 191

Brooks, Gwendolyn, 131

Brooks, Thomas, 239, 262

Brotherhood of Sleeping Car Porters,
218–19, 261, 262, 281

Brown, Claude, 376 (n. 75)

Brown, Edmund G. "Pat," 1

Brown, John Mason, 184

Brown, Sterling, 131, 133

Brown, Tom, 136

Brown, Willie, 1–3

Buck, Pearl, 189–90, 194

Building industry. *See* Construction
industry

Bunche, Ralph, 129, 132, 238, 257

Burgess, Ernest, 67

Bush, George W., xi–xii

Butler, Eliza, 207

Cable, George Washington, 185

Caldwell, Erskine, 61–62, 184, 185–86,
195, 320, 398 (n. 76)

California: southern politicians in, 1–3,
289–90; black migrants in, 19; white
migrants to, 19, 25–26, 30, 84–86;
Hispanic migration to, 19, 34, 35; cotton production in, 27, 30, 85, 162; during Depression, 30; Dust Bowl migration to, 30, 64, 287; Native American
migrants to, 36; lifestyle migrants to,

39; Okies in, 64, 65, 77, 78, 85, 90, 91, 156–57, 162, 167, 298; residential patterns of white migrants in, 85–86; construction trades in, 91; oil industry in, 93, 379 (n. 22); steel industry in, 94; United Daughters of the Confederacy in, 158–59; San Joaquin Valley of, 160, 161–62; churches in, 162, 209, 213, 222–23, 225–26, 233; "Okie music" in, 183; fair employment law in, 268; Democratic Party in, 288–89; Ku Klux Klan in, 291; Wallace supporters in, 306; country music in, 314; employment of white migrants in, 342; Christian Right in, 424 (n. 68). *See also* Bakersfield; Los Angeles; San Francisco

Calloway, Brad, 292

Camp, Wofford B., 27

Campbell, Glen, 179, 311, 314, 423 (n. 56)

Campbell, Raleigh, 161

Campbell, Rev. Dr. Samuel H., 292

Canfield, James, 307

Capeci, Dominic, 298–99

Capote, Truman, 184

Carey, Archibald James, 122, 219

Carlson, Oliver, 162

Carnera, Primo, 143, 146

Carpenter, Joel, 223, 228

Carrell, Tom, 290

Carson, Fiddlin' John, 174

Carter, Art, 145

Carter, Dan, 304, 305

Carter, Jimmy, 230

Carter family, 180

Cash, Johnny, 313

Cash, Wilbur, 28

Catholic church: anti-Catholicism of evangelicals, 203–4, 225, 231; and black migrants, 210; and charismatic movement, 213; in suburbs, 223; and segregation, 232, 233; in Latin America, 234; and Irish immigrants in nineteenth century, 235; and Ku Klux Klan, 293; and Detroit race riots, 298–99; and conservatism, 316–17

Cayton, Horace R., 114–16, 132, 133, 207, 214, 219, 265

Chalmers, David, 293

Chapman, Ben, 172

Charleston, Oscar, 145

Chauncey, Herbert, 122

Chicago: black migrants in, 25, 26, 27, 54, 111, 114–15, 116, 117, 120–21, 133; unemployment in, 31; race riots and violence against blacks in, 48–49, 69–70, 71, 120, 285, 295; Promised Land image of, 51–53; South Side (Bronzeville) of, 54, 114–15, 137–38, 150, 151, 214–15; radio stations in, 56, 174, 178, 179, 181; white migrants in, 76, 81, 82, 85, 110–11, 157–58, 160–61, 164, 167, 299; problems of migrants in, 81–82; Uptown community of, 85, 86, 160–61, 393–94 (n. 18); steel industry in, 94; gambling in, 99, 215; residential patterns and segregation in, 115, 120, 160, 164, 238, 272, 354; nineteenth-century black leaders in, 120–21; newspapers and magazines owned by blacks in, 126–27; black intelligentsia in, 131, 132; Urban League in, 133; entertainment zone in, 137–38; baseball in, 144; Wright on, 149–50; Ottley on, 151; Near West Side of, 160, 161, 299; and hillbilly music, 174, 178, 179, 181, 182; churches in, 205, 207, 212, 214–16, 219; Olivet Baptist Church in, 215–16; civil rights for blacks in, 238; political influence of blacks in, 240, 241–42, 244, 245, 253, 258, 259; NAACP in, 251, 264–65; unions in, 252; housing riots in, 272, 299; Ku Klux Klan in, 292

Chicago Defender: on black migration, 50–54, 122, 123; circulation of, 51, 126, 128, 130; on *Amos 'n' Andy*, 58; sales of, 125; on music, 138, 141; on baseball, 144, 145, 146; "Living South" column

Daughters of the Confederacy. *See* United
Daughters of the Confederacy
Davis, Ben, 257
Davis, Frank Marshall, 132
Davis, John W., 294
Davis, Russell, 175
Davis, Skeeter, 313
Dawson, Matel, Jr., 112
Dawson, William, 28, 122
Dean, Dizzy, 145, 171–72
Dearden, Archbishop John, 232
Defense Migration story, 78
Dellums, C. L., 268
Democratic Party: Mississippi Free-
dom Democratic Party, 77; national
conventions of, 77, 258, 294–95; and
blacks, 218, 245–47, 252, 253, 255–60,
268; and civil rights for blacks, 219,
267, 303, 305; and Tammany Hall, 245,
246, 289; in California, 288–89; and
southern-born whites, 288–90; and
New Deal, 293; and working class,
302–3; and white South in 1936, 412
(n. 46)
Demography of Southern Diaspora,
12–19
Denby, Charles, 29, 421 (n. 35)
Denis, Paul, 142
Depression (1930s), 28–32, 60–61, 98, 218
DePriest, Oscar, 121, 241, 242, 258
Desegregation. *See* Integration
Detroit: during Depression, 29, 31; auto
industry in, 29, 31, 33, 112, 286; black
population of, 31, 116, 122–23, 153–55,
417 (n. 93); white migrants to, 31–32,
65, 85, 153–55, 160, 163, 164–66; race
riots in, 69–71, 77, 277, 284, 298–300,
374 (n. 60), 375 (n. 61), 420 (n. 27); in
music, 73, 74; gambling in, 99; statistics on population of, 122, 155; clubs
and musicians in, 138, 182; baseball
in, 144, 169; residential patterns and
segregation in, 153, 160, 163, 164, 272,
280, 354; New Bethel Baptist Church

in, 153–54, 198–202, 207–8, 220–21;
Cass Corridor in, 160, 163; suburbs of,
165; Temple Baptist Church in, 166,
198–204, 208–9, 222, 231–32, 297,
317, 400 (n. 6); and hillbilly music,
182; radio station in, 182; civil rights
for blacks in, 202, 274; statistics on
churches in, 205; Nation of Islam in,
210; churches' civic role in, 216; Second Baptist Church in, 216, 217, 219;
Urban League in, 217; NAACP in, 217,
250; political influence of blacks in,
240, 243; segregation in, 272; Wallace
supporters in, 306; racial attitudes
and norms in, 392 (n. 4), 421 (n. 35);
speech patterns in, 393 (n. 9)
Detroit Free Press, 274, 374 (n. 57)
Detroit News, 274, 297, 298, 374 (n. 57),
375 (n. 61)
Dewey, Thomas, 260, 267
Diaspora: definition of, 11–12; types of,
361 (n. 2). *See also* Southern Diaspora
Dickinson, Luren, 201
Dies, Martin, 189
Diggs, Charles, Sr. and Jr., 154
Di Maggio, Paul, 310
DiMeglio, John, 170
Disciples of Christ, 210
Divine, Father, 210, 218
Dixon, Thomas, 185, 291
Dobson, James, 424 (n. 68)
Dodd, William C., 184
The Dollmaker (Arnow), 72–73, 81, 195,
375 (n. 62)
Donald, David Herbert, 184
Dorsey, Thomas, 141
Douglass, Aaron, 131
Drake, St. Clair, 114–16, 132, 207, 214,
219, 265
Du Bois, W. E. B., 103, 117, 128, 131, 133,
135, 249, 251, 253, 257–58
Dunham, Katherine, 131
Durr, Virginia, 188
Dust Bowl migration, 30, 64, 111, 287

Horne, Mother Rosa, 212
Hornsby, Rogers, 170
Horstman, Dorothy, 175
Housing. *See* Residential patterns
Howard University, 129, 134, 243
Huffington, Joe, 292
Hughes, Langston, 131, 135, 253
Humbard, Rex, 213
Humphrey, Hubert, 306, 309
Hurston, Zora Neale, 131, 133
Hutchinson, George, 132
Hydrology, 19

Ickes, Harold, 251, 252, 257
Illinois: southern-born population of, 19; Hispanic migration to, 35; residential patterns in, 85, 335; construction trades in, 91; United Daughters of the Confederacy in, 158–59; Ku Klux Klan in, 291, 292; Wallace supporters in, 306; employment of white migrants in, 342. *See also* Chicago
Immigration, 21–22, 24, 35, 66–67, 235, 242, 293
Income: in North, 22; in South, 22, 109–10, 352–53; of white migrants, 82–89, 95, 96, 109–10, 339–40, 343, 352–53; of black migrants, 83, 84, 95–97, 102, 103, 106–9, 110, 339–40, 343, 350–53; and state of origin of migrants, 88, 340; by educational level, 88–89, 96–97, 106–8, 109, 110, 334, 341, 352–53, 382–83 (n. 52); of black women, 96–97, 106, 107, 109, 334, 343, 350–53, 382–83 (n. 52); of white women, 96–97, 334, 343, 352–53; of foreign-born whites, 339; by industry, 343
Independent, 54, 55
Independent Clarion, 300
Indiana: Hispanics in, 35; residential patterns in, 85, 335; employment of white migrants in, 91, 94, 342; Ku Klux Klan in, 291, 292–93; Wallace supporters in, 308–9

Industries: and deindustrialization, 324; employment by, 342–43; income by, 343. *See also* Manufacturing; *and specific industries*
Integrated Public Use Microdata Series (IPUMS), 13, 82, 86, 104, 163–64, 355, 357–58, 361–62 (n. 5)
Integration: of baseball, 172–73; of education, 190–91; political activism for, 269–73; of housing, 271–73; white migrants' attitudes toward, 285–86; in South, 322–23. *See also* Politics and civil rights for blacks
Intelligentsia, 28, 37, 38, 54, 131–35, 183–95, 239–41, 253, 286, 320, 321. *See also* Professionals
Internal migration. *See* Migration; Southern Diaspora
International Association of Machinists, 93
International League against War and Fascism, 218
Irvin, Dona L., 111
Ives, Burl, 287
Ivy, James W., 279–80

Jackson, "Aunt" Molly, 286, 287, 320
Jackson, C. D., 274
Jackson, Jesse, 199, 202, 215
Jackson, Joseph H., 122
Jackson, Mahalia, 141, 154
Jackson, Maynard, 323
Jackson, "Shoeless" Joe, 170
Jacksonville Times Union, 45, 46
James, C. L. R., 253
Jamieson, Stuart, 167
Jazz, 135–42, 193
Jeffries, Edward, 298, 300, 420 (n. 31)
Jews, 36, 204, 224, 225, 239, 249, 251, 261, 267, 293, 295
Jobs. *See* Employment
John Birch Society, 307
Johnson, Albert, 208
Johnson, Charles S., 23, 127, 131–35
Johnson, J. Rosamond, 137

240, 258; Watts riot in, 285; southern politicians in, 289–90; Wallace supporters in, 306

Los Angeles Times, 49, 70, 71

Louis, Joe, 143, 146–49, 276

Lubell, Samuel, 260, 306

Lusky, Louis, 192

Lynching and anti-lynching campaigns, 23, 46, 128, 239, 252, 255, 259, 280, 298

Lynn, Doolittle, 176–77

Lynn, Loretta, 175–78, 312–13

Machen, J. Gresham, 224–25

Maddox, Rose, 179

Magazines. *See* Newspaper and magazine coverage; *and specific magazines*

Malcolm X, 376 (n. 75)

Malone, Bill, 175

Maloney, Thomas, 104

Manufacturing, 22, 24, 26–27, 31, 322. *See also* Industries; *and specific industries*

Marable, Manning, 238

Marginal man theory, 67

Marshall, Thurgood, 298

Martin, Sallie, 141

Mason, Charles Harrison, 211

Massee, J. C., 224

Mass migration, 11. *See also* Migration; Southern Diaspora

Mays, Marguerite, 273

Mays, Willie, 272–73

McAdoo, William Gibbs, 288, 290, 293–94, 320

McCarthy, Clem, 147

McCoy, Clyde, 167

McCullers, Carson, 184, 185, 186

McGill, Ralph, 188

McGreevy, John T., 232

McIntire, Carl, 225, 227, 316

McIntyre, Cardinal Francis, 233

McKay, Claude, 131

McLaurin, Melton, 312

McPherson, Aimee Semple, 213, 225

McWilliams, Carey, 188

Mead, Christopher, 147

Mencken, Henry Louis, 61, 185

Messenger, 127, 246

Methodist church, 204, 206, 209, 210, 223, 225–26, 248

Metropolitan areas. *See* Black Metropolis; *and specific cities*

Miami Valley of Ohio, 90–92, 160, 161–63

Michigan: southern-born population of, 19; during Depression, 29; Hispanics in, 35; Black Legion in, 77, 285, 295, 296; residential patterns of white migrants in, 85, 335; construction trades in, 91; fair employment law in, 268; Ku Klux Klan in, 291; employment of white migrants in, 342

Michigan Chronicle, 272, 301

Migration: and convergence of regional forms, 7; equilibrium theory of, 7, 19, 21; scholarship on, 9–10; definition of mass migration, 11; in nineteenth century, 12–13; internal migration linked with immigration, 66–67. *See also* Black migrants; Return to South; Southern Diaspora; White migrants

Migration systems theory, 9

Military service, 37–38, 262, 265, 266, 278, 342

Mills, C. Wright, 184, 387 (n. 23)

Mississippi Freedom Democratic Party, 77

Mitchell, Arthur, 122, 258

Mitchell, H. L., 286

Mitchell, Margaret, 159

Mitchell, Thomas, 184

Moffitt, Audie and Walter, 25–26, 30

"Monkey trial," 61, 203, 228, 252

Montana, Patsy, 179

Moore, Fred, 50

Moore, Rev. John H., 292

Moore, Terry, 172–73

Moral Majority, 198, 316–19

Moretti, Robert, 3

Morris, Willie, 5, 184, 185, 191–92, 194–95, 320, 321, 323, 399 (n. 84)

263–81 passim; of Defense Migration story, 78; of black literati, 135, 389
(n. 45); of sports, 143–47, 169, 170–71;
of Youth for Christ, 228; of Scottsboro
Boys, 252; right-wing newspapers,
273–74; *Life* magazine photographs
of blacks, 276–79; of Black Legion,
295–97. *See also specific newspapers
and magazines*

Newsweek, 258, 417 (n. 91)

Newton, Rev. Basil E., 292

New York Age, 50, 127, 247

New York Amsterdam News, 50, 53

New York City: unemployment in, 31;
gambling in, 99; black community
in, 117, 119–20; residential patterns
in, 119, 354; foreign-born blacks in,
119–20; intelligentsia in, 131, 132, 192;
entertainment zone in, 137; baseball
in, 144; Poston on, 151; white migrants
in, 158; Southern Society in, 158, 159,
187, 289; and hillbilly music, 178; radio
stations in, 178; churches in, 205, 212,
224; Kingdom and Peace Missions in,
210, 218; political influence of blacks
in, 240, 245–47; Tammany Hall in,
245, 246, 289; NAACP in, 251; unions
in, 252. *See also* Harlem

New York newspapers, 47, 297

New York State, 158–59, 267–68, 292

New York Times, 49, 71, 172, 275, 297

Nicolaides, Becky, 223, 233

Nixon, Richard, 226, 305, 306, 309, 313,
315

Norfolk Journal and Guide, 46, 388 (n. 31)

Norris, Frank C., 275

Norris, J. Frank, 200–204, 208–9, 214,
222–27, 231, 284, 297, 298, 317–18

Northern Baptist Convention (NBC),
206

Northern-born. *See* Blacks (northern-
born); Whites (northern-born)

Oates, Joyce Carol, 375 (n. 62)

Obermiller, Phillip, 167

Occupations. *See* Employment

Ohio: and presidential election of 2004,
xi–xii; southern-born population of,
19; Hispanics in, 35; residential patterns of white migrants in, 85, 335;
employment of white migrants in,
90–92, 94, 342; United Daughters of
the Confederacy in, 158–59; Miami
Valley of, 160, 161–63; Ku Klux Klan
in, 291; Black Legion in, 296; Wallace
supporters in, 306

Oil industry, 93, 379 (n. 22)

"Okie music," 183

"Okies," 64, 65, 77, 78, 85, 90, 91, 156–57,
162, 167, 298

Oklahoma, 18, 29–30, 35–36, 91

Oliver, King, 138

Olivet Baptist Church (Chicago), 215–16

Opera, 141

Opportunity, 54, 127, 133

Oregon, 289, 291, 292

Ottley, Roi, 115–16, 123, 125, 135, 142–43,
151, 152, 263, 301, 384 (nn. 3–4)

Owen, Chandler, 127, 246

Owen, Russell, 275

Owens, Buck, 177, 179, 314

Owsley, Frank, 187

Page, Walter Hines, 185, 289

Paige, Satchel, 145, 146

Park, Robert, 67, 133, 134

Parks, Gordon, 132

Parks, Rosa, 281

Pearson, George, 32

Peer, Ralph, 64, 174

Pennsylvania, 94, 158, 291. *See also* Philadelphia; Pittsburgh

Pentecostal church, 161, 162, 210–13,
222–23, 227, 228, 234, 317, 403
(nn. 36–37)

Perkins, Carl, 309

Peterson, Richard, 175, 310

Petry, Ann, 75

Philadelphia: unemployment in, 31;
black community in, 103, 117–19, 122;

churches in, 118, 212, 216; clubs and musicians in, 138, 310–11; baseball in, 144; political influence of blacks in, 240, 243, 258; residential patterns in, 354

Philadelphia newspapers, 47, 48, 122

Philanthropy, 248, 251–52

Philliber, William, 167

Phillips, Kevin, 306

Phillips, Kimberley, 122

Photiadis, John D., 167

Photojournalism, 276–79

Pierson, George W., 43

Pittsburgh, 119, 128, 240, 243, 250

Pittsburgh Courier, 50, 58, 115, 128, 144–46, 169, 263

Politics and civil rights for blacks: media coverage of, 77, 263, 265–66, 268, 273–81; black elected officials, 103, 241, 243, 258, 268, 323; and black churches, 198, 202, 215, 219–21; in Detroit, 202, 243–44; introduction to, 237–38; in Chicago, 238, 241–42, 244, 245, 258, 259; northern civil rights movement, 238, 260–81, 376 (n. 75); and voting, 239, 242, 244–45, 277, 279, 323; and alliances, 239, 247–55, 261–62; and protest and street tactics, 239, 253–54, 265, 270; and sectionalism, 239–40; political tools for, 239–41; and migration of professionals and intelligentsia, 240–41; and balances of power, 241–47; in Cleveland, 242–43, 244, 259; in Pittsburgh, 243; in Philadelphia, 243, 258; in Harlem, 245–47; clientage politics, 247, 248; and New Deal realignments, 255–60; and fair employment laws, 259, 264, 266–69; March on Washington (1941), 263–64; and segregation, 269–73; and Montgomery bus boycott, 281; in South, 322–23

Politics of white migrants: and liberalism, 188–91, 285, 286–90, 320; and bigotry, 283–86, 294–302; and Ku Klux Klan, 290–94; and working-class conservatism, 302–9, 316–20; and Moral Majority, 316–19

Poole, Charles, 295

Porter, John C., 226, 288

Porter, Katherine Anne, 184, 191

Poston, Ted, 122, 151, 152

Potter, David, 184

Poverty, 82–85, 103, 324, 340

Powell, Adam Clayton, Jr., 154, 198, 202, 215, 221, 281

Powell, Luther I., 292

Preece, Harold, 189

Presbyterian church, 204, 223, 224–25, 248

Presley, Elvis, 309

Press coverage. *See* Newspaper and magazine coverage

Price, Daniel O., 66

Professionals: black migrants as, 28, 105–6, 121–22, 336–38, 345–46, 386 (n. 17), 409 (n. 9); in Black Metropolis, 121–22, 240–41; white migrants as, 168–69, 336–38; and civil rights for blacks, 240–41. *See also* Intelligentsia

Promised Land story of Southern Diaspora, 49–54

Protestantism. *See* Religion; *and specific denominations*

Pulitzer, Joseph, 45

Pullman, George, 219

Raab, Earl, 307

Race. *See* Black migrants; Hispanics; Native Americans; Race riots; White migrants

Race riots: in Chicago, 48–49, 69–70, 71, 120, 285; media coverage of, 48–49, 69–71, 77; in Detroit, 69–71, 77, 277, 284, 298–300, 374 (n. 60), 375 (n. 61), 420 (n. 27); in Harlem, 254; housing riots, 272, 299; Watts riot, 285

Racism: and southern whites, 77, 92–93; in employment, 92–93; and evangelical preachers, 231; bigotry politics of white migrants, 283–86, 294–302. *See also* Ku Klux Klan

Radio: *Amos 'n' Andy* on, 56–59, 75, 123; hillbilly characters on, 63; discrimination against blacks on, 142; boxing on, 143, 147; and hillbilly music, 173–75, 178, 179, 181–83; preachers on, 199, 200–201, 208, 212, 226, 318; and NAACP, 274–75

Rainey, Ma, 140

Randolph, Asa Philip, 28, 122, 127, 218–19, 246, 252, 262–64, 281

Rankin, John, 189

Rawls, Lou, 154

Reagan, Ronald, 305, 316, 317

Rector, John, 174

Reed, Christopher, 251, 264–65

Reed, John Shelton, 7

Reese, Pee Wee, 173

Region, 7–8

Reid, Ira De A., 120, 132, 279

Religion: of black migrants, 153–54, 197–202, 205–8, 209–12, 214–21, 230, 235; and Pentecostalism, 161, 162, 210–13, 222, 223, 227, 228, 234, 317, 403 (nn. 36–37); of white migrants, 197–206, 208–9, 210, 213, 221–35; and evangelicalism, 198, 199, 213, 222–35, 316–19; and civil rights for blacks, 198, 202, 215, 219–21; and conservatism of white migrants, 198, 316–20; radio ministries, 199, 200–201, 212, 226, 318; and Christian modernism, 203, 206, 231; and fundamentalism, 203–4, 206, 208, 223–27; diversity of northern Protestantism, 204; regional nature of, before Southern Diaspora, 204; statistics on, 205, 209, 212; women and church membership, 205, 217; "shouting" in black churches, 206–7; innovations in, from Southern Diaspora, 209–13; and charismatic movement, 213, 234; television ministries, 213, 317, 318, 319; gateway role of churches, 214, 221–22; civic role and political activ-

ism of churches, 214–21, 226, 230–34; coalitions of black and white ministers, 220; in suburbs, 227, 232–34; and Youth for Christ, 227–28, 231; and revivalist preachers, 228–30; segregation and white evangelicals, 230–34; and missions in foreign countries, 234; and Moral Majority, 316–19. *See also specific denominations*

Republican Party: and blacks, 121, 126, 239–41, 243, 245–48, 256, 258, 260; and black churches, 217; and fundamentalists, 223; and FEPC legislation, 267; and Black Legion, 296; and Moral Majority, 316–19

Republic of New Africa, 202

Residential patterns: and suburbs, 85–86, 101, 165, 335, 354; of white migrants, 85–86, 159–64, 335, 354; segregation in, 100–102, 271–73; and ghettos, 100–103, 114, 116, 152; of black migrants, 100–103, 119, 120, 344, 354; and New Deal programs, 101; and home-ownership, 101, 103, 104, 335, 344; and public housing projects, 101, 271

Return to South, 16–17, 23, 29, 40, 321–24, 330, 331, 368 (n. 61)

Rhodes, Eugene Washington, 122

Ribuffo, Leo, 295

Rice, Grantland, 184, 186

Rickey, Branch, 172

Riley, William Bell, 224, 228–29

Riots. *See* Race riots

Ritter, Tex, 179, 181

Rizzo, Frank, 305

Robbins, Marty, 311, 313

Roberts, Lesa Phillip, 36

Roberts, Oral, 213, 228

Robertson, Pat, 213, 317

Robeson, Eslanda, 190, 194

Robeson, Paul, 141, 190, 278

Robinson, Bishop Ida, 212

Robinson, Jackie, 145–46, 172–73, 193

Rodgers, Jimmie, 180, 181

lems in census information, 82, 355; methodology in, 82, 355–58; on Black Metropolis, 114–16; black social scientists, 132, 133–34; white social scientists, 184; on black and southern white churches, 214

South: definition of, 7–8; cities in, 22, 32; income in, 22, 109–10, 352–53; economy of, 22–23, 24, 29–30, 39, 322; violence against blacks in, 23; during Depression, 29–30; statistics on in-migration during 1970s–1990s, 38, 322; in 1970s and 1980s, 39, 322–23; white-owned newspapers in, 45–46; black-owned newspapers in, 46–47; cultural criticism of, 61–62; poverty in, 103; NAACP in, 128, 220, 264; black colleges in, 132–34; jazz and blues in, 139–40; Protestantism in, 204; *Life* magazine coverage of, 278–79; civil rights for blacks in, 322–23. *See also* Farming; Return to South; Southern Diaspora

Southern Baptist Convention (SBC), 206, 208, 209, 234

Southern Christian Leadership Conference, 202, 281

Southern Diaspora: statistics on, 4, 13–18, 330, 331, 362 (n. 7); definition of, 11; dates of, 12; demography of, 12–19; and World War II, 13, 14, 21, 32, 98; and World War I, 13, 21, 23–24, 37; first phase of, 14–16, 23–28, 78; second phase of, 14–16, 32–38, 65–66, 78; by states and regions, 18–19, 20, 332–33; and hydrology, 19; and labor market analysis, 19, 21–22, 24; and immigration restriction, 21–22, 24; gender of migrants in, 26, 365 (n. 27); occupational and social backgrounds of migrants, 26–28; and Depression, 28–32; post-diaspora period, 38–40, 322–24; exodus image for, 45–51, 53–54; media coverage of, 45–54, 78–79; as Promised Land story, 49–54; so-

cial scientists on, 65–72; and urban "adjustment," 66–68, 72–74; third dimension of, in interaction of black and white migrants, 193–94; conclusions on, 324–28. *See also* Black Metropolis; Black migrants; Politics and civil rights for blacks; White migrants

Southernization, 122–24, 159–63, 198, 234–35, 302, 319, 327–28

Southern Renaissance, 184–85

Southern Society of New York, 158, 159, 187, 289, 292

Southern Tenant Farmers Union, 286

Speaker, Tris, 170

Spear, Alan, 241

Sports, 142–49, 169–73, 193, 272–73, 276

Squires, Catherine, 125–26

Stanky, Eddie, 173

Steel industry, 91–92, 94, 128, 324, 342, 343

Steinbeck, John, 84, 162, 195

Stephenson, C. D., 292–93

Stereotypes of white migrants, 89–93, 155–56, 167, 187

Stewart, Wynn, 314

St. Louis, 117, 138, 144, 240, 354

St. Louis newspapers, 48, 171, 372 (n. 35)

Stockton, J. Roy, 171

Straton, John Roach, 224

Stribling, T. S., 61

Strong, Nat C., 144

Student Non-Violent Coordinating Committee, 202, 281

Students for a Democratic Society (SDS), 285

Styron, William, 184, 185, 191, 192

Suburbs, 85–86, 101, 165, 227, 232–34, 335, 354

Suggs, Henry Lewis, 46, 143

Sugrue, Thomas, 299

Sullivan, Leon Howard, 122

Sun Belt, 13, 21, 38–40, 192

Sunday, Billy, 229

Survey, 54, 371 (n. 25)

Survey Graphic, 64

Swaggart, Jimmy, 213
Sweet, Ossian, 101, 122

Tate, Allen, 191
Taylor, Clarence, 210
Taylor, Paul, 64
Tejanos. *See* Hispanics
Television, 63, 73, 77–78, 213, 317, 318, 319
Temple Baptist Church (Detroit), 166,
 198–204, 208–9, 222, 231–32, 297, 317,
 400 (n. 6)
Thomas, R. J., 71, 284, 298, 300, 319
Thomas, Richard, 114
Thomas, William I., 67
Thompson, Dorothy, 244, 297
Thompson, John, 90
Thompson, William Hale, 241, 258
Thorman, Wallace, 131
Time, 76, 258, 275, 303–4, 415 (n. 80), 417
 (n. 91)
Tindall, George, 61
Tire industry, 94, 342, 343
Tobacco Road (Caldwell), 61–62, 297
Tolnay, Stewart, 104, 382 (n. 45)
Tomlin, Guy and Lillie Mae, 31–32, 153,
 163, 166, 205, 208–9
Tomlin, Lily, 32, 153, 154, 163, 166, 169,
 197, 199–200, 205, 208–9
Toomer, Jean, 131
Townsend, James S., 27
Travis, Merle, 179
Trotter, Joe, 254
Trotter, William Monroe, 249
Truman, Harry, 260, 267, 279
Tucker, Bruce, 167
Tucker, Sophie, 136
Tuskegee Institute, 47, 133
Tyler, Elizabeth, 291, 292

Unions: and white migrants, 91–92, 94–
 95, 300; and blacks, 93, 98, 99, 218–19,
 254–55, 300; and black churches,
 218–19, 221; and black politics and
 civil rights, 247, 252, 254–55, 261,
 267, 272; and Communist Party, 252,

253; and coal miners, 286; and white
 southern liberals, 286; and Wal-
 lace supporters, 308. *See also specific
 unions*
United Auto Workers (UAW), 71, 92, 221,
 265, 272, 284, 289, 298, 300
United Colored Democracy, 246
United Daughters of the Confederacy
 (UDC), 158–59, 187, 292
United Mine Workers, 252, 254
United Negro Improvement Association
 (UNIA), 120, 127, 217, 246–47
University of Chicago, 66, 68, 133, 134,
 157
University of Michigan, 68, 166, 307, 309
University of Minnesota, 13, 68
Unruh, Jesse, 1–3, 290, 320
Urban "adjustment," 66–68, 72–74,
 81–82
Urban areas. *See* Black Metropolis; *and
 specific cities*
Urban League, 54, 118, 127, 133, 217,
 248–49, 251

Vann, Robert, 50, 128
Vick, G. Beauchamp, 208, 225, 231–32,
 317–18, 319
Vietnam War, 312–13
Violence against blacks. *See* Ku Klux
 Klan; Lynching and anti-lynching
 campaigns; Race riots
Voorhis, Jerry, 226
Votaw, Albert, 76
Voting, 239, 242, 244–45, 277, 279, 323.
 See also Politics and civil rights for
 blacks

Wages. *See* Income
Wagner, Robert F., 252, 257
Wakefield, Floyd, 290
Wakely, Jimmie, 179
Walker, George, 137
Walker, Margaret, 132
Wallace, George, 284, 285, 302, 303–9,
 312, 313, 315